THE LAW OF COMPANY INSOLVENCY

MICHAEL FORDE

The Law of Company Insolvency

WITH A FOREWORD BY

The Honourable Mr Justice Hugh O'Flaherty
of the Supreme Court

THE ROUND HALL PRESS

This book was typeset by
Gilbert Gough Typesetting and
output by Typeset Origination Services Ltd for
THE ROUND HALL PRESS LTD
Kill Lane, Blackrock, Co. Dublin.

A catalogue record for this book
is available from the British Library.

ISBN 1-85800-013-0

Printed in Ireland by
Colour Books Ltd, Dublin

For Richard and Laura

Foreword

In the foreword that he contributed to Dr Forde's *Commercial Law in Ireland*, my late, much-lamented colleague Niall McCarthy in his usual elegant manner referred to Dr Forde's prodigious industry when he wrote:

> Since 1985 he has contributed authoritative works on Company Law, Constitutional Law and Extradition Law. His work on Bankruptcy is about to be published and here is his book on Commercial Law, whilst one on Company Insolvency is in an advanced stage of gestation. Indeed, adopting the obstetrical metaphor, his works will cover the law affecting companies from conception through to birth, childhood, middle age and old age to demise—from solution to dissolution.

I know that Niall McCarthy would have taken a vicarious pride on the coming to fruition of yet another work by Michael and I have no doubt that he would have been the first choice to provide this foreword.

However, Michael has asked me mainly because, I suspect, of my provincial origins—or, more accurately, because of the Province from which I hail. Others, as practitioners and judges, have ploughed this field with straighter furrows and neater tilths—and more often than I—but this is all the more reason why I, and my likes, should be grateful for this book. Here is a definitive treatise on company receiverships, examinations and winding-up/liquidations, together with various security and equivalent interests arising in insolvency. It is written with Dr Forde's usual direct style, replete with citation of authorities from many jurisdictions and he is ever mindful of the European dimensions which, as I have said before, should now form an essential part of every practitioner's baggage.

In the year that an Irish team conquered Mount Everest—and by the difficult route—it is appropriate to point out that Michael Forde writes legal textbooks for much the same reason that people climb mountains—because the subjects are there to be conquered.

I think he has conquered this complicated subject of company insolvency and reduced it to a certain order but it would be a great misrepresentation to say that what he embarked upon was an easy subject.

Aoibhínn beatha an scríbhneora!

Hugh O'Flaherty,
The Supreme Court, Dublin.

30 June 1993

Preface

This book seeks to provide the reader with a comprehensive picture of the law of company insolvency. Much of it—the parts on liquidations and on examinations—concerns complicated statutotory frameworks for dealing with companies which are making substantial losses or are otherwise unable to pay their debts. Most of the remainder—the parts on receivers and on priorities—deals with the mainly judicially-created common law and equitable principles that bear on the position of secured creditors and related matters. Company Insolvency is far too large and distinct a topic to incorporate in a general book on Company Law, although there are considerable overlaps between both subjects.

A series of evening lectures I gave some six years ago in UCD on Insolvency Law probably got this project up and going. It was abandoned for several years until enactment of the two Companies Acts of 1990 marked a significant change in the regulatory regime for insolvent companies and their management. Practice in the courts, often in relation to insolvency issues, has given me some insight into how the regime actually functions.

While the 1990 Acts may have been what caused me to write this book, I derived enormous assistance from some superb Australian books on the general area, most notably perhaps Judge McPherson's, *Law of Company Insolvency* (3rd ed., 1987); Professor O'Donovan's, *Company Receivers and Managers* (2nd ed., 1981) and Professor Sykes, *The Law of Securities* (4th ed., 1986). Those three books undoubtedly are the definitive words on those topics and set an example of thoughtful organisation and clarity of exposition that I have sought, hopefully with some success, to emulate. I have tried to note the law as at 1st June 1993.

Marie Armah-Kwantreng once again proved to be a magnificently efficient and accurate typist and this work would still be a half-completed manuscript but for her speed and enthusiasm. Michael Adams and Bart Daly of The Round Hall Press again have been most supportive publishers and have always been unstinting in their assistance. Gilbert Gough did a remarkably quick job on the galleys and page proofs and Terri McDonnell showed great ingenuity in the marketing domain.

I am most grateful to the Honourable Mr Justice Hugh O'Flaherty of the Supreme Court for once again writing an extravangantly flattering foreword.

Finally an expression of special gratitude to Catherine, Patrick and Peter whose good humour and tolerance enabled me to persist with an endeavour which at times it was very tempting to leave aside.

M.F.
Mountain View Road
Dublin 6.

Midsummer's Day, 1993

Contents

PART III: WINDING UP/LIQUIDATIONS

Table of Statutes

Table of Cases

1

Introductory

Insolvency law concerns mainly collective procedures, whereby a company's assets are administered for the benefit of all of its creditors, depending on what securities they may have and statutory priorities, if any, they possess. However, the conventional receivership does not fit that model and the various procedures whereby single unsecured creditors may obtain satisfaction impinge on many aspects of insolvency.

HISTORICAL CONTEXT

In the beginning most commercial societies developed legal collection remedies for individual creditors,[1] in part to reduce violence and other externality-producing behaviour accompanying self help. For centuries this was done through the writ of *fieri facias*, under which the sheriff was empowered to seize the debtor's assets and sell them, paying the judgment creditor from the proceeds of that sale. There was a comparable ancient procedure for obtaining satisfaction from the debtor's land, the writ of *elegit*,[2] but in the middle of the last century it was replaced by the statutory procedure of registering a judgment mortgage.[3] In 1634 legislation was enacted against fraudulent conveyances and other devices to defeat creditors;[4] its central provisions still remain in force. With the increasing commercialisation of society, procedures were adopted whereby individual creditors could attach debts owed to their debtor or attach and obtain a charge over stocks and shares registered in his name.

The first Irish Bankruptcy Act was passed in 1772,[5] the stated purpose of which was to 'prevent frauds committed by bankrupts'. What was so novel about this Act is that it inaugurated group collection procedures. These offered the possibility of achieving economies of scale in creditors' efforts to realise the value of their debtors' assets; these procedures also facilitated the reduction of many costs caused by the disorderly scramble of individual creditors to be first to collect, regardless of any adverse impact on other creditors or on the

1. See generally, T. Kerr Anderson, *The Law of Execution* (1889) and infra pp. 8 et seq.
2. See generally, J. Williams, *The Law of Real Property* (23rd ed., 1920) pp 288-289 and Anderson, supra n. 1, pp. 363-411.
3. See generally, J.C.W. Wylie, *Irish Land Law* (2nd ed., 1986) pp. 705-712 and infra p. 9-10.
4. 10 Car. I sess. II, c.3.   5.   11 & 12 Geo. II c.8.

overall value to be realised on the debtor's assets. Rules about voidable preferences also reduced some substantial costs of uncoordinated action. Although the 1772 Act had been introduced as a temporary measure, it was continued in force by subsequent legislation, subject to various amendments. Eventually in 1836 it was replaced by the Bankruptcy law of that year,[6] which was in turn replaced by an Act of 1857.[7] The present legal regime for personal bankrupts is based in the Bankruptcy Act, 1988.[8]

Deed of settlement companies   As is explained elsewhere,[9] the immediate predecessor of today's registered company was the deed of settlement company, which was a hybrid of a partnership and a trust. For all practical purposes, this form of business organisation is now almost extinct, although a variant of it seems to be flourishing in Australia under the description of the 'trading trust'.[10] There was no special legislative regime for deed of settlement companies and no special rules governed their insolvency. The same principles applied as apply to partners; each member of the company had unlimited liability for the firm's debts and if he was unable to satisfy the firm's creditors, he faced bankruptcy under the 1772 Act or its successor. However, the courts always drew some distinction between the members' separate estates.[11] Provision was made in the Irish Bankrupt and Insolvent Act, 1857, ss.151-177 for winding up insolvent 'joint stock companies' which had a head office in Ireland, other than registered companies.[12]

Winding Up Act of 1845   There were no winding up provisions in the Joint Stock Companies Act, 1844,[13] the measure which first enabled companies to be incorporated by registration. All that the 1844 Act said in connection with insolvency was s.66, which provided that a judgment against the company could be enforced against the company's assets but also against the property of its members. It took another ten years before limited liability was allowed for registered companies.[14]

In the year following the passing of the first Companies Act, the Winding Up (Ireland) Act, 1845,[15] was enacted which contained the mechanism for winding up Irish-registered companies on the grounds of insolvency. In much the same way as insolvent individuals, under the 1845 Act companies could be made bankrupt if they had engaged in certain conduct equivalent to the

6.   6 Will. IV c. XIV.
7.   20 & 21 Vic. c. 60, as amended by 35 & 36 Vic. c.57.
8.   See generally, M. Forde, *Bankruptcy Law in Ireland* (1990).
9.   *Company Law* (2nd ed.) pp. 7-9.
10. See articles cited ibid n.26.
11. E.g. *Hayden v Carroll* (1796) 3 Ridg Parl Rep 545.
12. Cf. Companies Act 1963, Part X (winding up unregistered companies).
13. 7 & 8 Vic. c. 110.
14. Limited Liability Act 1855, 18 & 19 Vic. c.133.
15. 8 & 9 Vic. c. 98.

established 'acts of bankruptcy'[16]—for instance, the company filing a declaration that it could no longer pay its debts,[17] disobedience of a court order to pay a debt etc.[18] Thereafter, a *fiat* in bankruptcy might issue and the normal bankruptcy procedure would follow. According to s.10, 'the law and practice in bankruptcy now in force in Ireland shall extend, so far as may be applicable, . . . to commissions in bankruptcy issued by virtue of this Act and to all proceedings under such commissions, save and except as may be otherwise directed by this Act.'[19] Provision was made for examining persons who had dealings with the company, and they could be ordered to deliver up books and papers in their possession which related to those dealings. There was a procedure whereby the Bankruptcy Court might direct the creditors' assignees to apply to Chancery for such orders and directions as might be necessary for the final winding up and settling the affairs of the company and for compelling a just contribution from all the members towards the full payment of the company's debts. Accounts would then be taken and inquiries made to see how much money must be raised from the shareholders, either by calls or contributions. They then were personally liable to pay those sums. If they could not do so, they faced personal bankruptcy and the Court would make the necessary adjustments to the amounts required from the other shareholders.

Only creditors could initiate winding up proceedings under this Act. Three years later another Act was passed to enable the members to petition the Chancery Court to wind up their company, either by reason of its insolvency or for several other stipulated reasons, including that it was 'just and equitable' to do so.[20] However, inadequacies in the 1845 and 1848 winding up procedures were soon afterwards highlighted in the complications caused during the winding up of the Royal British Bank,[21] which gave rise to a spate of litigation, often exaccerbated by the rivalry between the Bankruptcy and the Chancery Courts. That particular debacle was ultimately resolved by a special Act of Parliament being passed in 1857,[22] enabling the shareholders and creditors to reach a compromise.

Companies Acts of 1856 and 1862 In the next year after limited liability was inaugurated, the modern approach to winding up proceedings was adopted, in the Joint Stock Companies Act, 1856.[23] This was then incorporated, with some alterations, in the consolidating measure that stood for nearly half a century, the Companies Act, 1862.[24] There were five grounds for which, on hearing a petition, the court could wind up a company.[25] Additionally, a company could

16. S.1.   17. S.3.   18. S.5.
19. For a fuller account, see McPherson, *The Law of Company Liquidation* (3rd ed., 1987), pp. 14-17.
20. Joint Stock Companies Winding Up Act 1848, 8 & 9 Vic. c. 45.
21. E.g. *Re Royal British Bank, ex p. Marcus* (1856) 26 LJ Bk 1 and *Ex p. Shore* (1857) 26 LJ Bk 17.
22. 20 & 21 Vic. c. 78.
23. 19 & 20 Vic. c. 47; see too 20 & 21 Vic. c. 14 and c. 78.
24. 25 & 26 Vic. c. 89.   25. S.79.

wind itself up by its members passing a special resolution to that effect.[26] A liquidator took charge of the company and he would dispose of its assets and make calls on the shareholders, whose liability usually would be limited.

As regards insolvent companies, the principal change was that their creditors could no longer go directly against the shareholders, even if they had unlimited liability. As described by Lord Cairns in *Webb v Whiffin*,

> by the Act of 1862 that state of things is entirely swept away. A capital is created, sometimes limited, sometimes without a limit; but that capital is to be made good in the shape of a common fund, and that common fund it is which is to be the source of the payment of every creditor of the company. And although it is quite true that members and ex members of the company are placed by the Act under liability, that liability is a liability, not to make payments to creditors, but it is a liability to contribute to and make good what should be the proper amount of the common fund. Then, having got into the common fund every sum which ought to be contributed to it by every person whomsoever, the Legislature takes possession of that common fund and proceeds to distribute it amongst the creditors of the company.[27]

Liquidations since 1862 Developments in the law of liquidations since 1862 can be dealt with briefly. Reference first should be made to the seminal *Salomon & Co.*[28] case decided in 1896, which highlighted the extent to which shareholders enjoy limited liability under the Companies Acts; once the bare formalities for registration were completed and the issued shares were fully paid up, in principle the members are no longer answerable for the company's unpaid debts due to those who had dealings with the company. Whether this principle equally applies to all tort creditors of the company has never been authoritatively resolved.[29] *Salomon & Co.* also drew attention to the role of the floating charge in corporate financing,[30] which in 1900 led to the system of registering company charges in the registry of companies.[31] An 1890 Act,[32] dealing with procedures in company liquidations, did not apply to Ireland.

Several reforms adopted in Britain in the inter-war years were incorporated in the Companies Act, 1963, for instance the creditors voluntary liquidation and the concept of fraudulent trading. In 1982 the 'Cork Committee' Report[33] was published in Britain, which contained a thorough review of the law and practice there regarding insolvency. Many of the reforms proposed in it were enacted here in the Companies Act, 1990, for instance the restrictions on directors of

26. S.129.
27. (1872) LR 5 HL 711, at p. 734
28. [1897] AC 22; see *Company Law*, pp. 51-52.
29. See post p. 272.
30. See *Company Law*, pp. 494 et seq.
31. Companies Act 1900, s.14.
32. Companies (Winding Up) Act 1890.
33. Insolvency Law and Practice (Cmnd. 8558).

insolvent companies,[34] the restrictions on a variety of transactions with 'connected persons'[35] and the concept of reckless trading.[36] The present statutory regime governing liquidations of registered companies is contained in Part VI of the 1963 Act (ss.206-313), as amended by Part VI of the 1990 Act (ss. 206-313).

Receivers   A receiver is a person appointed to get in some of a debtor's assets and realise them, usually for the benefit of a secured creditor. The commonest kind of company receiver is the receiver and manager appointed by a secured creditor under an express power to do so in a debenture given by the company. A typical receivership can best be understood as a deliberately slowed-down liquidation procedure. Receivers cum-managers are given an adequate flexible period of time in which to operate the debtor's business while looking for the best buyer or buyers. The more time receivers have, the better the price they might get for particular assets of the debtor. Even more important, they might find a person willing to buy all or most of the business as a going concern and at a price reflecting the true going-concern value, rather than at a distress price caused by forcing a quick sale in an illiquid or otherwise imperfect market for particular kinds of capital goods and businesses. Whenever the going-concern value of an insolvent debtor's business exceeds its piecemeal liquidation value, and the receivership preserves that excess value, there is a net gain for creditors. But this efficient procedure creates a new valuation problem, for the receiver or the supervising court must decide whether going-concern value does in fact exceed liquidation value.

The evolution of the law on company receivers has been almost entirely one of judicial development—the elaboration and application of contract law and equitable principles to the power often given in debentures to appoint receivers. An excellent account and analysis of the role of receivers is contained in Rigby LJ's judgment in *Gaskell v Golsong*[37] given near the end of the last century. Part VII of the 1963 Act (ss.314-323) lays down some procedures that receivers must follow and places certain restrictions on their extensive freedom of action, within the terms of the debenture. Some additional requirements were imposed by Part VIII of the 1990 Act (ss.170-179).

Reorganisation   Undoubtedly the most recent major development in the law of company insolvency is the adoption, in 1990, of a reorganisation law which closely resembles Chapter 11 of the United States Bankruptcy Code.[38] A mechanism for reorganising insolvent individuals' affairs was first incorporated in ss.343-356 of the Bankruptcy (Ireland) Act, 1857.[39] A mechanism

---

34. See *Company Law*, pp. 113-114 and post pp. 167-169
35. See id. pp. 108, 134, 162.   36. See post pp. 261-267
37. [1896] 1 QB 669 (dissent), approved [1897] AC 575.
38. 11 U.S. Code ss. 1101-1174 (1988).
39. See generally, J.H. Robb, *The Law and Practice of Bankruptcy and Arrangements in Ireland* (1907), ch. 18.

for structured company reorganisations was adopted in the Joint Stock Companies Act, 1870;[40] this was the predecessor of ss.201-203 of the Companies Act, 1963, which applies to solvent as well as to insolvent companies.[41] There was also the Railways Companies Act, 1867,[42] which was designed to assist railway enterprises overcome their financial difficulties. The scheme for court protection and examination of insolvent companies, adopted in the Companies (Amendment) Act, 1990, (often referred to as the 'Goodman Act') owes much to how U.S. courts developed their equitable jurisdiction in the latter part of the last century.[43]

The U.S. receivership evolved to the point where all or many of the creditors of the insolvent business debtor could themselves act as the buyers of the business—which would be kept as a going concern, if that made sense—using not cash as the means of payment, but their own creditor claims, such as notes, bonds, debentures, or the like, usually valued at face value plus accrued interest. The creditors could, in effect, initiate a transformation of their debt holdings into stock, or into some mixture of new debt and stock, and at the same time exercise their contractual rights of priority among themselves and against the residual claimants (the old shareholders) in a way that was just as definitive as a real liquidation sale to an outside buyer. This procedure made economic sense whenever there were no or few potential outside buyers with accurate and timely information about the state of affairs and the future prospects of the business, and when the process of searching for and informing outside buyers would itself be very expensive. However, this U.S.-style equity receivership never took root in Ireland, presumably because the very small scale and simple structures of Irish business organisation never demanded a very sophisticated restructuring technique. What perhaps triggered the imaginative use of the old remedies of receivership and foreclosure in the U.S. was the collapse of numerous major railway companies near the end of the last century, owning enormous assets and with enormous and elaborate liabilities.

Under the Chapter 11 procedure, now transplanted in the 'Goodman Act',[44] the ritual of the self-sale was dropped. All companies in reorganisation would presumptively be subjects of a reorganisation plan that would primarily involve a reshuffling of the paper claims against the business assets. Furthermore, such restructuring of debt might be accomplished by majority votes within the classes of debtors, so that a good plan might be forced on otherwise obstreperous creditors. These refinements simply increased the need for careful judicial supervision of the valuation process.

---

40. 33 & 34 Vic. c. 104.
41. See generally *Company Law*, pp. 389
42. 30 & 31 Vic. c. 127.
43. See generally Note, 'Failed Markets and Failed Solutions: The Unwitting Formulation of the Corporate Reorganisation Technique', 90 *Columbia L Rev* 783 (1990).
44. See Part II of this book.

ENFORCEMENT OF JUDGMENTS

Where a company refuses or neglects to pay any of its secured creditors, that creditor may be entitled, under the debenture, to appoint a receiver over the charged property. If the creditor does not have security, one option is to seek a liquidation of the company under s.213(e) of the 1963 Act. But if there is any substantial dispute about his claim, usually that route cannot be followed. If the company possesses easily identifiable assets, it often is far more advantageous simply to enforce the creditor's claim against those assets; this process of immediate debt collection is much quicker and cheaper than the complex collective procedures. The main modes of enforcing judgments and claims call for some comment, especially because an important issue in the collective procedures and in receiverships is the relation between them and each single unsecured creditor's mode of enforcing judgments.

Pre-judgment remedies—the *Mareva* **injunction** Unlike the position in the United States and in parts of Continental Europe, Irish and United Kingdom law provides comparatively little assistance to creditors until they have first obtained a judgment against their debtors. Generally, the fact that the creditor is confident of winning his claim, when it is heard, does not entitle him to attach or otherwise hold or restrict the use of his debtor's property. Until at least a judgment is obtained against him, the debtor is free to carry on his business in the normal way. An exception to this principle, however, is what is popularly referred to as the *Mareva* injunction.[45] Before 1975 the law was that 'you cannot get an injunction to restrain a man who is alleged to be a debtor from parting with his property'.[46] In that year, the English Court of Appeal in the *Mareva* case[47] gave a plaintiff an interlocutory injunction restraining the defendant from removing its property outside of the jurisdiction, on the grounds that there would be no assets left against which the plaintiff could enforce its judgment if it should succeed. Since then this equitable jurisdiction has been extended to instances which do not at all involve removing assets abroad, beyond the jurisdiction of the courts. Moreover, it is no longer essential to show that the plaintiff's case is almost certain to succeed when it is heard.

The purpose underlying these injunctions is to prevent a defendant from dissipating his assets, to the detriment of the plaintiff if his action succeeds.[48] The following broad guidelines laid down by Lord Denning are followed here:

> 1. The plaintiff should make a full and frank disclosure of all matters in his knowledge which are material for the judge to know.
> 2. The plaintiff should give particulars of his claim against the defendant,

---

45. See generally, R. Keane, *Equity and the Law of Trusts in the Republic of Ireland* (1988) pp. 234-241.
46. *Lister & Co. v Stubbs* (1890) 45 Ch D 1, p. 13.
47. *Mareva Compania Navicra S.A. v International Bulk Carriers S.A.* [1975] 2 Ll LR 509.
48. *Polly Peck Int'l plc v Nadir* [1992] 4 All ER 769.

stating the grounds of his claim and the amount thereof and fairly stating the points made against it by the defendant.

3. The plaintiff should give some grounds for believing that the defendant has assets within the jurisdiction. . . . The existence of a bank account is enough, whether it is in overdraft or not.

4. The plaintiff should give some grounds for believing that there is a risk of the assets being removed.

5. The plaintiff must give an undertaking in damages in case he fails.[49]

It is entirely a matter of judicial discretion whether pre-judgment relief of this nature should be given. On several occasions it has been emphasised that an injunction given imposes a personal obligation on individuals and does not create any form of security interest over the property which is affected by the injunction.

Execution   By execution in this context is meant the enforcement of a judgment.[50] Some methods of execution are based on the common law, most notably the *fieri facias* procedure whereby the under-sheriff or county registrar can seize a debtor's goods and chattels. Other execution methods are provided for by statute, such as the system for registering judgment mortgages against the debtor's lands. These and the other execution methods are supplemented by the rules of court, which stipulate the precise steps to be followed in levying execution. According to Order 42, rule 3 of the Rules of the Superior Courts,

A judgment for the recovery by or payment to any person of money may be enforced by execution order or by any other mode authorised by these rules or by law.

An 'execution order' is defined in those Rules as 'includ[ing] orders of *fieri facias*, sequestration and attachment' against the debtor. The 'other modes' set out in those Rules are committal to prison, charging orders and stop orders, attachment of debts and appointment of a receiver by way of equitable execution. These remedies are available in the Circuit Court[51] as much as in the High Court, except that the Circuit Court will never enforce money judgments by way of committal of or attachment against the debtor's person[52] and it does not have jurisdiction to order sequestration of a debtor's assets. The only form of execution that can be channelled through the District Court is imprisonment for refusal to pay a judgment.[53]

Many of the enforcement mechanisms described here applied originally to judgments of the High Court and of the Supreme Court, or their predecessors,

---

49.   *Third Chandris Shipping Corp. v Ultra Marine S.A.* [1979] QB 645, at pp. 668-669.
50.   See generally, T. Kerr Anderson, *The Law of Execution* (1989).
51.   Circuit Court Rules Ord. 33.
52.   Id. Ord. 33 r.4 and Ord. 36, r.3.
53.   See generally, *Bankruptcy Law*, p. 9.

the 'Superior Courts' of Ireland.[54] However, there are various statutory provisions placing judgments of the Circuit Court and decrees of the District Court on the same footing, for the purpose of the enforcement method in question, as those of the Superior Courts, for instance with regard to imprisonment of debtors, judgment mortgages, execution by the Sheriff and charging orders over stocks and shares. In 1937 the procedure for registering judgments in the Central Office of the High Court was extended to Circuit Court judgments[55] and in 1981 that procedure was extended to District Court decrees.[56]

Judgment mortgage   Where the judgment debtor owns land, the judgment can be enforced against his land by means of a judgment mortgage.[57] If the judgment is registered against the land in the appropriate registry, it almost operates as if the debtor had mortgaged that land to the judgment creditor. If payment is not duly made, the creditor can proceed to enforce sale of that land, reimbursing himself from the proceeds. As described by Madden,[58] which is the leading authoritative work on the subject, '[j]udgments are converted into statutory mortgages by the registration of an affidavit of ownership by the judgment creditor.'[59] At common law, execution could not be levied against land or any interest in land, with the anomalous exception of leasehold interests. Consequently, for most interests in land to be exigible, there must be legislation which provides for such process. The present procedure is contained in the Judgment Mortgage (Ireland) Act, 1850,[60] as amended in 1858.[61] It replaced a similar procedure in s.22 of the Debtors (Ireland) Act, 1840;[62] and methods of enforcement against land provided for in ss.19 and 21 of the 1840 Act, those of *elegit* and statutory receivership, where abolished in 1850. Thenceforth, the only means of enforcing judgments against land was the judgment mortgage. It applies to judgments of the Supreme Court, of the High Court, of the Circuit Court[63] and, since 1981, decrees of the District Court.[64]

The interests in land which can become the subject of a judgment mortgage are where the debtor

> is seised or possessed at law or in equity of any lands, tenements or hereditaments of any nature or tenure or has any disposing power over such [property] which he may without the assent of any other person exercise for his own benefit.[65]

Thus, an extensive range of legal and equitable interests in land are covered so

---

54. Cf. Supreme Court of Judicature (Ireland) Act 1887.
55. Circuit Court (Registration of Judgments) Act, 1937.
56. Courts Act 1981, s.25.
57. See generally, J.C.W. Wylie, *Irish Land Law* (2nd ed., 1986) pp. 705-712.
58. D.H. Madden, *Registration of Deeds, Conveyances and Judgment Mortgages* (2nd ed., 1901).
59. Id. at p. 117.   60. 13 & 14 Vic. c. 29.
61. 21 & 22 Vic. c. 105.   62. 3 & 4 Vic. c. 107.
63. Supra n.55.   64. Supra n.56.   65. 1850 Act s.6.

long as they are in existence when the judgment is registered. Leasehold interests,[66] tenancies at will,[67] lands subject to an order for sale[68] and even another judgment mortgage[69] are all exigible in this manner. So also is a next of kin's share in property;[70] a specific devise under a will where the devisee was let into possession by the executors but no assent was executed in his favour;[71] the interest of a sole proving executor of a will.[72] Among the matters remaining to be resolved is whether judgment mortgages can be registered against the interest of an unpaid or partly paid vendor of land, under an agreement for sale, and also against the purchaser's interest under an agreement for the sale of land where all or part of the purchase price has not been paid. Interests of an individual joint tenant and of a tenant in common in land are exigible, although their co-tenants owe nothing to the judgment debtor. The effect of registering a judgment mortgage against property held under a joint tenancy is to convert the holding into a tenancy in common.[73]

In order to register an effective judgment mortgage, the procedure laid down must be followed with precision. In particular, all the requisite details must be set down in the affidavit[74] which will be registered either in the Registry of Deeds or the Land Registry.

The legal effects of registration of a judgment are defined in s.7 of the 1850 Act as

> operat[ing] to transfer and to vest in the creditor registering such affidavit all the lands, tenements and hereditaments mentioned therein, for all the estate and interest of which the debtor . . . shall at the time of such registration be seised or possessed at law or in equity, or might at such time create by virtue of any disposing power which he might then without the assent of any other person exercise for his own benefit. . . .

Thus, the beneficial title in the debtor's interest is transferred to the registering judgment creditor, for whom that interest in the land is thereby mortgaged. But that mortgage is subject to all equities subsisting at the time the affidavit is registered. On several occasions it has been stressed that the judgment mortgage is only 'a process of execution and is not a charge created for valuable consideration.'[75]

Seizure by the sheriff   The procedure known as *fieri facias* is a method, under

66.   *Tevlin v Gilsenan* [1902] 1 IR 514.
67.   *Devlin v Kelly*, 20 ILTR 76 (1886).
68.   *Re Scanlon's Trustee's Estates* [1897] 1 IR 462.
69.   *Rossborough v McNeill* (1889) 23 LR Ir 409.
70.   Supra n.66.
71.   *Kavanagh v Best* [1971] NI 89.
72.   *Munster & Leinster Bank v Fanning* [1932] IR 671.
73.   *M'Ilroy v Edgar* (1881) 7 LR Ir 521.
74.   Cf. *Allied Irish Banks v Griffin* [1992] ILRM 590.
75.   *Tempany v Hynes* [1976] IR 101, at p. 110.

common law, whereby the sheriff of the county could seize the debtor's goods and chattels and have them sold, paying the proceeds to the judgment creditor, less the expenses of the execution. As described in Dixon & Gilliland,[76] which is the authoritative work on the subject,

> The writ of *fieri facias* is that writ of execution by which a suitor usually puts into effect a judgment recovered either for debt, damages or costs. . . . By this writ the sheriff is commanded that of the goods and chattels of the party against whom judgment is recovered, being in his bailiwick, he cause to be made the sum recovered, with interest . . . immediately after the execution of the writ, to be paid to the party by whom judgment has been recovered.[77]

Today, execution by way of this procedure is carried out in Dublin and Cork by under-sheriffs and in other counties by county registrars.[78] Money and certain securities can be taken, as well as personal property. The procedure applies with regard to judgments of the Supreme Court, of the High Court, of the Circuit Court and decrees of the District Court. Unpaid taxes can also be collected in this way by Revenue sheriffs without the need for judgment being given against the tax-payer.

Fieri facias   Before filing the praecipe or requisition, which must be filed before a *fi. fa.* is issued, the creditor is not obliged to make any formal demand for payment of what is due.[79] There is no need to leave a reasonable time for payment to be made before having the order issued.[80] Save in exceptional circumstances, the application for an order must be on notice. The procedure to be followed is laid down in Order 42, rules 8-35 of the Rules of the Superior Courts and in Order 33 of the Circuit Court Rules.

Not every form of personal property can be the subject of execution in this manner.[81] At common law, the sheriff could execute only against tangible goods and chattels, severable fixtures to land, leases and growing crops. In 1840, in recognition of the greater commercialisation of society, the Legislature also rendered exigible any 'money or bank notes . . . and any cheques, bills of exchange, promissory notes, bonds, specialities, or other securities for money belonging to' the debtor.[82] Money for these purposes does not include book debts owing to the judgment debtor.[83] And it has been held that cheques which were issued but not delivered to him are not his property and, accordingly, are

76. G.Y. Dixon & W.L. Gilliland, *The Law Relating to Sheriffs in Ireland* (1888).
77. Id. at p. 23.
78. Courts Officers Act 1926, s.38 and Enforcement of Court Orders Act 1936, Part I.
79. *Kelly v O'Beirne* (1867) 1 Ir Eq. 540 and *Land Credit Co. of Ireland v Lord Fermoy* (1870) 5 Ch App 323.
80. *Smith v Smith* (1874) LR 9 Exch 121.
81. *Dixon & Gilliland*, supra n. 76, ch. 4.
82. Debtors (Ireland) Act 1840, s.20.
83. These can be got at through attachment; infra pp. 14-16.

not exigible.[84] Securities for money, which are exigible, include fully paid up life insurance policies[85] but not a beneficiary's interest in an insurance policy.[86] The basis for this distinction is that the 1840 Act empowers the sheriff to hold securities for money and to sue but, since it contains no express authority to keep up payments, for instance insurance premiums, policies which have not matured are not rendered exigible. The precise scope of the term 'securities for money' remains somewhat unclear. It would seem that Government securities and stocks and shares in registered companies and in public bodies are not encompassed by the term.

Equitable interests in land and equitable interests in personal property other than goods and chattels, such as property comprised in a debenture, cannot be taken by way of *fi. fa.*[87] Some partial legal interests in goods are exigible, like a pawnbroker's interest in redeemable pledges[88] and goods owned jointly by the judgment debtor with another,[89] but not goods which are being held by virtue of a lien for work done.[90] After 1877 even some equitable interests in goods were deemed exigible.[91] The sheriff cannot take property belonging to third parties, such as property acquired under hire purchase and property otherwise subject to retention of title. As Lord Chelmsford observed,

> the right of a judgment creditor under an execution is to take the precise interest, and no more, which the debtor possesses in the property seized, and consequently that such property must be sold by the Sheriff with all the charges and encumbrances, legal and equitable, to which it was subject in the hands of the debtor. In other words, what the debtor has power to give is the exact measure of that which the execution creditor has the right to take.[92]

Formerly any goods and chattels owned by the debtor which were in his possession when the *fi. fa.* was issued were exigible. Because of the obvious injustice that this rule caused to purchasers of goods from the debtor and who were not aware of impending execution, s.26(1) of the Sale of Goods Act, 1893, stipulates that delivery to the sheriff of the order shall not prejudice subsequent buyers of goods in good faith and for valuable consideration, unless they had notice of the *fi. fa.'s* existence. Those types of personal property which were made exigible by the 1840 Act are never bound until they are actually seized.

---

84. *Courtoy v Vincent* (1852) 15 Beav 486.
85. *Beamish v Stephenson* (1886) 18 LR Ir 319.
86. *Re Sergeant's Trusts* (1879) 18 LR Ir 66.
87. *Re Opera* [1891] 3 Ch 260.
88. *Re Rollason* (1887) 34 ChD 495.
89. E.g. partnership assets.
90. *Legg v Evans* (1840) 6 M & W 36.
91. *Stevens v Hince* (1914) 110 LT 835, at p. 937.
92. *Wickham v New Brunswick & New Caledonian Rly. Co.* (1865) LR 1 PC 64, at pp. 431-432.

Where a dispute arises with regard to what goods can be taken in execution there exists a procedure known as interpleader for resolving the matter.[93]

A return will be made stating the outcome of the under-sheriff's or county registrar's attempts at execution.[94] If no goods have been taken, the return will state *'nulla bona'*. A sale of any goods seized will then be arranged for the best price obtainable in the circumstances.[95] Where goods have been seized but not sold, the creditor can get an order known as *venditioni exponas* directing sale of the goods.[96] After deducting fees, expenses and poundage, the balance of the proceeds of sale will be paid over to the judgment creditor, up to the amount of his debt.

Revenue sheriff Part XXXIII (ss.476-498) of the Income Tax Act, 1967, deals with various modes by which the Revenue Commissioners collect income and other taxes which have become payable. One of these is recovery by the sheriff or county registrar seizing the taxpayer's 'goods, animals and other chattels' and selling them. Section 485 of this Act empowers the Collector General to certify that a certain sum is owing by the taxpayer and naming the person on whom that sum is levyable. The sheriff can then seize his chattels and is given all the rights and powers of a sheriff levying execution under a *fi. fa.* The Revenue believe they are empowered to confer sheriff's powers under this section on somebody other than him or the county registrar.[97]

Charging and attachment of stocks and shares When the scope of *fi. fa.* was extended in 1840, not all forms of choses in action were brought within its reach. However, ss.23 and 24 of the Debtors (Ireland) Act, 1840,[1] created an alternative method of execution against certain stocks and shares. These are 'any Government stock, funds, or annuities, or any stock or shares of or in any public company in Ireland (whether incorporated or not . . .).' The mode of execution is a charging order, which is a declaration by the court that the securities in question stand charged for the benefit of the judgment creditor. An argument could be made that charging orders under s.23 of the 1840 Act are not executions in the strict sense and that statutory provisions regarding 'execution' do not apply to them; although that contention has been rejected in England in respect of charging orders on land.[2]

The precise scope of the term 'Government stock, funds or annuities' has never been judicially determined. It can hardly be doubted that such securities issued by or for some foreign governmental entity cannot be charged under this

---

93. See generally, M. Crababe, *Interpleader and Attachment of Debts* (1881).
94. Dixon & Gilliland, supra n.76, ch.16.
95. Id. ch. 9.
96. Id. ch. 11.
97. They have done so for some counties outside of Cork and Dublin.
1. 3 & 4 Vic. c. 105. See generally, T. Kerr Atkinson, *The Law of Execution* (1889) pp. 475-488.
2. *Re Overseas Aviation Engineering (G.B) Ltd* [1963] 1 Ch 24.

procedure. But it could be doubted whether securities issued by local government bodies and the like are 'governmental' for this purpose. As for the term
'public companies', it should be remembered that the modern system of
incorporating companies by registration was not established when this charging
order procedure was created. The courts have interpreted this term liberally, as
including all kinds of entities which could be called companies and which have
an element of compulsory publicity, such as the duty to maintain registers of
members and to file annual returns with the companies' office. Thus the shares
of private registered companies, as well as in p.l.c.s and other statutory corporations, can be charged under these procedures. But the company must be
registered in Ireland or be established by Irish legislation; it is unlikely that the
shares of a company which is registered under Part XI of the Companies Act,
1963, can be so charged. Debentures are not stocks or shares for these purposes.[3]

Charging orders apply to judgments of the Superior Courts and also of the
Circuit Court and decrees of the District Court. When a charging order is made,
the securities affected 'stand charged' with the payment of the judgment sum
and the interest thereon. And it is provided that this order 'shall entitle the
judgment creditor to all such remedies as he would have been entitled to if such
charge had been made in his favour by the judgment debtor.'[4] The full import
of this provision has not been determined; if it is given its literal meaning, then
a charging order will be treated as a consensual charge and, accordingly, as
more than a method of executing judgments.

Even where such an order is not made, ss.132 and 133 of the Common Law
Procedure Amendment Act (Ireland), 1853,[5] authorise the court to attach and
to order the transfer to the sheriff of certain securities belonging to the judgment
debtor. These securities are the same as those which can be the subject of a
charging order. As well as being a judgment creditor, the applicant for orders
under this execution procedure must be in a position to issue execution and there
must be in existence a *fi. fa.* which is levyable.[6]

Attachment of debts   Attachment of debts, which is also referred to as
garnishment of debts, enables the judgment creditor to get money which is
owing to the debtor to be paid instead to himself.[7] A credit balance in the
debtor's bank account, as well as other sums due to him, can be attached for the
benefit of the judgment creditor. This remedy is both a powerful and a harsh
one, because it can greatly diminish the debtor's cash flow and it can put third
parties on notice of the judgment awarded against the debtor. Attachment
originated in the Common Law Procedure Act, 1856,[8] and the present procedure
is set out in Order 45 of the Rules of the Superior Courts and in Order 37 of the

3.   *Sellar v Bright* [1904] 2 KB 446.
4.   S.23 of the 1840 Act.
5.   16 & 17 Vic. c. 113.
6.   *Donohue v Mullarkey* (1886) 18 LR Ir 125.
7.   See generally, T. Kerr Anderson, *The Law of Execution* (1889) pp. 448-474.
8.   19 & 20 Vic. c. 105.

Circuit Court Rules. Special provision was made in 1988 to enable the Revenue Commissioners to attach tax-payers' funds.

Garnishee order The procedure for attaching debts due to one's debtors is usually referred to as obtaining a garnishee order. Before attachment of debts will be directed, there must be a judgment or order of the Superior Courts, or of the Circuit Court or the District Court, requiring the debtor to pay money and that money must not have been paid. In that event, the judgment creditor can then proceed to have attached funds which are payable by others to the defaulting debtor. The order will be made against 'all debts owing or accruing from' the third person, known as the garnishee, to the judgment debtor. For the garnishee's debt to be 'owing and accruing', payment by the garnishee must not be subject to any conditions or contingencies other than the effluxion of time. According to Brett MR, an 'accruing debt' for these purposes means as follows:

> Now can it mean any debt which may at any future time arise between the judgment debtor and the person sought to be made a garnishee, there being no contract at that time between the judgment debtor and such person, or anything which can make any relation of any kind, legal or equitable, between them? To state the proposition is to show its absurdity. Then can it be this, that it may be a debt which there is some probability may in future arise? Who can say where there is nothing out of which a debt can be said in law to arise, that it is probable that a debt may arise, as for instance a probability that the parties will make a contract. If it is not a debt it will not do. It must be something which the law recognises as a debt.[9]

Instances of liabilities which have been held incapable of garnishment include a portion of the surplus due to a shareholder in the winding up of a company[10] and money in a savings bank account belonging to the judgment debtor.[11] In *O'Leary v Buttimer*,[12] it was held that payments to be made under a building contract upon the issue of an architect's certificate can be attached in anticipation of the certificate being given. A contrary view was taken by the English courts.[13] It has been held that a joint bank account cannot be garnished by the creditors of one depositor.[14] It furthermore has been held that, where a husband opened a bank account in his wife's name and all the payments into it were made by him, that account could not be attached by the wife's own

---

9. *Webb v Stanton* (1883) 11 QBD 518, at p. 523.
10. *Spence v Coleman* [1901] 2 KB 199.
11. *Bagley v Winsome* [1952] 2 QB 236 and *Re Australia & New Zealand Savings Bank* (1972) VR 690.
12. [1953-4] Ir Jur Rep 15.
13. *Dunlop & Ranken Ltd v Hendall Steel Structures Ltd* [1957] 3 All ER 344.
14. *Hirschorn v Evans* [1938] 2 KB 801.

creditors;[15] there was a resulting trust in the husband's favour, the presumption of advancement having been rebutted.

Even where the debt is capable of being attached, the courts have a discretion whether to direct this mode of execution. Garnishment will not be allowed where it would result in the judgment creditor obtaining an unfair advantage over all the other creditors[16] or where the result would be most unfair to the judgment debtor[17] or, indeed, to other persons who have claims to the money it is being sought to attach.[18]

The procedure for obtaining an attaching order is two-stage, the first of which is an *ex parte* application for an order *nisi*. This order directs the garnishee to show cause why the funds in question should not be attached and, in the meantime, attaches that debt to the amount specified. Until this order is duly served, the intended garnishee is free to deal with the debt in whatever way the judgment debtor requires. Once the order *nisi* is served on the garnishee, it binds the debt specified to the amount stated in the order. But it would seem that the 'binding' is far from having an absolute effect and that service of the order *nisi* does not operate to transfer or assign the debt to the judgment creditor, either absolutely or by way of security.[19] The garnishee is forbidden to pay the debt either to the judgment debtor or to someone else at the latter's directions; the money or an equivalent sum must instead be paid to the judgment creditor. While the judgment creditor's rights regarding the debt attached *nisi* have occasionally been called a charge, the better view and the logic underlying the cases is not to regard them as a charge or a lien.[20] The precise impact of service of an order *nisi* on funds held by a company, and which are the subject of a floating charge, has generated considerable controversy.[21]

Like an executing creditor, an attaching creditor can only attach such property in the debt as the debtor possesses. According to Andrews J in *O'Connor v Ireland*,

> The garnishee order only binds the attached debt in so far as the judgment debtor is entitled to deal with it, and does not affect the claims of creditors in whose favour he has charged it, even though they may not have given notice of their claims, and . . . no charge affecting the debt when the garnishee order is made is displaced by that order.[22]

15. *Harrods Ltd v Tester* [1937] 2 All ER 236; cf. *Plunkett v Barclays Bank Ltd* [1936] 2 KB 107.
16. *Pritchard v Westminster Bank Ltd* [1969] 1 All ER 999 and *G. Lee & Sons (Bldrs) Ltd v Olink* [1972] 1 All ER 359.
17. *Martin v Nadel* [1906] 2 KB 26.
18. *Roberts v Death* (1881) 8 QBD 319.
19. *Norton v Yates* [1906] 1 KB 112.
20. Ibid. and *Robson v Smith* [1895] 2 Ch 118.
21. See post pp. 183-184.
22. [1897] 2 IR 150, at p. 155.

Revenue attachments Section 73 of the Finance Act, 1988, as amended,[23] establishes a method whereby the Revenue can attach funds owing to a taxpayer without going through the above procedure. Under this, where a person has not paid a tax which has been assessed or is otherwise due by him, the Revenue can require persons who owe money to that taxpayer or who have financial assets belonging to him to pay directly to the Collector General a sum equivalent to these outstanding taxes.[24]

Receiver by way of equitable execution There are several circumstances where the courts will appoint a receiver over all or part of another's property, such as to enforce the rights of creditors with a security interest in the property or to preserve property pending litigation.[25] In an appropriate case, the courts will also appoint a receiver over a judgment debtor's property in order to enforce a judgment rendered against him by taking his property and paying the proceeds of sale over to the creditor.[26] Indeed, in a suitable case, a receiver can be appointed even before judgment has been given so as to prevent property from being dissipated.[27] This method of execution was devised by the Chancery Courts in an era when the common law methods were most inadequate and before the statutory reforms of 1840. The present procedure is provided for in Order 45, rule 9 of the Rules of the Superior Courts and in Order 38 of the Circuit Court Rules.

It is not every species of property that can be made the subject of this form of execution, and over the last hundred years the courts have taken an even more restrictive view of what property is exigible in this manner. The turning point was *Re Shephard*,[28] where it was held that the remedy was not available over assets against which execution could be levied by way of any of the other methods for enforcing judgments. According to Fry LJ,

> The idea that a receivership order is a form of execution is in my opinion erroneous. A receiver was appointed by the Court of Chancery in aid of a judgment at law when the plaintiff shewed that he had sued out the proper writ of execution, and was met by certain difficulties arising from the nature of the property which prevented his obtaining possession at law, and in these circumstances only did the Court of Chancery interfere in aid of a legal judgment for a legal debt. Relief by the appointment of a receiver went on the ground that execution could not be had, and therefore it was not execution. Moreover, the appointment of a receiver was an act

23. Finance Act 1992, s.241.
24. See generally, N. Judge, *Irish Income Tax* (1986) par. 2.710.
25. See post pp. 21-22.
26. See generally, T. Kerr Anderson, *The Law of Execution* (1889) pp. 489-510 and H. Picarda, *The Law Relating to Receivers, Managers and Administers* (2nd ed., 1990), p. 293
27. *Anglo Italian Bank v Davies* (1878) 9 ChD 275.
28. (1889) 43 ChD 131.

requiring. the exercise of judicial power on the part of the court; the circumstances to which I have referred had to be proved before the court would make the order. All these considerations tend to shew that the appointment of a receiver was not execution, but was equitable relief granted under circumstances which made it right that legal difficulties should be removed out of the creditor's way. It has often been spoken of by judges as 'equitable execution', but I am afraid that this concise expression has led to the erroneous idea that the appointment of a receiver is a form of execution which can be obtained without shewing to the court the existence of the circumstances creating the equity on which alone the jurisdiction arises.[29]

Another restriction imposed around the same time was that this remedy could not be used against an asset which was not exigible either at common law or in equity before the Judicature Acts, such as the debtor's future earnings[30] or future profits of his business,[31] or an amount to be paid when a contract to execute work is performed.[32] As specialist works on receivers show, there is a long catalogue of cases dealing with what types of assets can be taken under this procedure.[33] There are no leading reported modern Irish cases which define where the line should be drawn for these purposes.

Appointment of a receiver by way of equitable execution over specified property does not give the judgment creditor who secured that appointment any mortgage, charge or lien over the property.[34] And when the receiver takes possession of the property, it is not held for the creditor but for the court, which will direct what shall be done with it, such as by selling it and paying the proceeds over to the creditor. As Bowen J observed, regarding the appointment of a receiver over a fund, '[i]t does not amount to the creation of an equitable interest in the nature of a charge on the fund. It falls short of that. It is a mere direction to the receiver to receive money, and to pay it over to the creditors when he does receive it. There is nothing to create an interest in the fund. . . .'[35]

29. Id. at p. 138.
30. *Holmes v Millage* [1893] 1 QB 551.
31. *Manchester & Liverpool District Banking Co. v Parkinson* (1880) 22 QBD 173.
32. *Re Johnson* [1898] 2 IR 551. Cf. *McCreery v Bennett* [1904] 2 IR 69.
33. See Picarda, supra n.26.
34. *Re Lough Neagh Ship Co. ex. p. Thompson* [1896] 1 IR 29.
35. *Re Potts* [1893] 1 QB 648, at p. 662.

PART I

·Receiver

A receiver is someone who is duly appointed in order to take control of all or part of another's assets for the benefit of the latter's creditor or creditors.[1] Depending on the circumstances, a receiver may be appointed either by the High Court or by the creditor; the vast majority of company receivers today are appointed directly by secured creditors under a power of appointment contained in a debenture. A receiver's functions also will differ depending on the terms of appointment; those functions can vary from merely receiving income accruing to the debtor and handing that money over the creditor, to managing and disposing of the debtor's entire assets and giving the proceeds up to the creditor in discharge of the indebtedness. Usually a company receiver's primary function is to sell the business assets with a view to paying off the secured creditor from the proceeds of sale and, in order to obtain the best price reasonably possible, to manage the company's business pending the sale.

Many receivers go about their task in such a single minded manner that at times they are criticised for destroying potentially viable businesses, in their enthusiasm to get the job done quickly. There is a view that if receivers can be more imaginative and patient, viable businesses can be salvaged and, in the end, their appointing creditor would be financially better off. However, there are no special legal rules which require the receiver to act in that manner. His primary responsibility is to whoever appointed him, who usually will be anxious to recover what money is owing as soon as possible. In a leading case on the liability of receivers for negligence, it was observed that

> *While in practice receiverships are sometimes used to achieve a moratorium and rehabilitation of the company's business, that is legitimate only where it is an incident of the receiver's proper role. The receiver is there to enforce the security and only for that purpose to trade. He is not a white knight. . . .[2]*

Before dealing with the appointment, status, powers and duties of company receivers, it is instructive to consider the different legal types of receiverships.

1. See generally, J. O'Donovan, *Company Receivers and Managers* (1981) (hereinafter referred to as O'Donovan), Picarda, *The Law of Receivers, Managers and Administrators* (2nd ed., 1980) (hereinafter referred to as Picarda), G. Lightman & G. Moss, *The Law of Receivers of Companies* (1986) and R. Walton ed., *Kerr on Receivers* (16th ed, 1983).
2. *First City Corporation Ltd v Downside Nominees Ltd* [1990] 3 NZLR 265, at p. 275.

2

Different Forms of Receivers

Although the predominant form of company receivership today is the receiver and manager appointed by the creditor under powers given in a security instrument, there are other kinds of receiverships.

RECEIVERS IN EQUITY

The principles of equity, as administered by the courts, lay down where, for example, injunctions will be awarded, orders of specific performance granted, contracts rescinded etc. One of the traditional remedies which was obtainable in the Chancery Court was the appointment by the court of a receiver.[1] Because in the past the common law and statute provided inadequate protection for persons who wished to safeguard their equitable interests in property, Chancery developed the practice of appointing a receiver to that end. On several occasions, for example, receivers were appointed over all or part of the assets of canal and railway companies in order to safeguard security provided to lenders.[2] It was not until end of the last century that the courts began to authorise receivers, in an appropriate case, to manage the business of the debtor, as opposed to merely receive its income so that the money can be paid over to the secured creditor.

Under the Supreme Court of Judicature (Ireland) Act, 1877,[3] the Common Law and the Chancery Courts were in effect merged and the new High Court of Justice was empowered to administer both law and equity. Section 28(8) of that Act summed up the pre-1877 practice regarding receivers by stating that a receiver can be appointed by interlocutory order where it is 'just and convenient' to do so. Indeed a receiver will be appointed by the court at any stage of proceedings where it is 'just and convenient' to do so. This term does not mean that the court's discretion should be applied arbitrarily; it signifies where it is practical and the interests of doing justice require that appointment.

While there is no fixed category of cases in which receivers will be appointed by the court, the following are the principal situations:[4]

 i. Where a security becomes enforceable;

1. See generally R. Keane, *Equity and the Law of Trusts in the Republic of Ireland* (1988) ch. 22 and R.P. Meagher et al., *Equity Doctrines and Remedies* (2nd ed., 1984) ch. 28.
2. E.g. *Hopkins v Worcester & Birmingham Canal Proprietors* (1868) LR 6 Eq 437.
3. 40 & 41 Vic. c. 57.
4. See generally, O'Donovan ch. 16 and Picarda ch. 20.

ii. Where a security is in jeopardy;

iii. Where other assets of the debtor are in jeopardy;

iv. To preserve partnership property when a dispute arises among the partners;

v. To preserve the estate of deceased persons which is at risk, for instance because of the executor's misconduct.

Mention has already been made of the receiver by way of equitable execution.[5] In very exceptional circumstances the court will appoint a receiver on the application of unsecured creditors even before they obtain a judgment.[6] Order 50 of the Rules of the Superior Courts lays down certain procedures in respect of appointing receivers.

The classic receiver in equity has been described as

A person who receives rents or other income, paying ascertained out-goings, but who does not . . . manage the property in the sense of buying or selling or anything of that kind. We were most familiar with the distinction in the case of a partnership. If a receiver was appointed of partnership assets, the trade stopped immediately. He collected all debts, sold the stock in trade and other assets and then . . . the debts of the concern were liquidated and the balance divided. If it was desired to continue the trade at all it was necessary to appoint a manager, or a receiver and manager as it was generally called. He could buy and sell and carry on the trade.[7]

STATUTORY RECEIVERSHIPS

Several statutory provisions authorise the appointment of a receiver over another's property. In 1840, when the writ of *elegit* was abolished, it was replaced by the judgment mortgage and also by a system of court-appointed receivers under s.21 of the Debtors (Ireland) Act, 1840.[8] When the judgment mortgage procedures were recast in 1850,[9] this statutory receiver was discontinued. In the Winding Up (Ireland) Act, 1845,[10] a Chancery Master was empowered to appoint a receiver to recover from shareholders the sums due by them to the creditors of their insolvent company.[11] This power also lapsed when the modern winding up machinery was adopted in 1856.[12] Another such measure, which is no longer of any great practical relevance, is s.4 of the

5.   Ante pp. 17-18.
6.   E.g. *National Australia Bank Ltd v Bond Brewing Holdings Ltd*, 64 ALJLR 239 (1990) and case note in 107 *Cam LJ* 551 (1991).
7.   *Re Manchester & Milford Rly. Co.* (1880) 14 Ch D 645 at p. 653.
8.   3 & 4 Vic. c. 105.
9.   Judgment Mortgage (Ireland) Act 1850, 13 & 14 Vic. c. 29.
10. 8 & 9 Vic. c. 98.   11. S.19.
12. 19 & 20 Vic. c. 47.

Railway Companies Act, 1867.[13] This stipulates that a railway company's rolling stock shall not be taken in execution. But it goes on to provide that a railway company's judgment creditor can apply to the court to have a receiver and manager appointed over the undertaking, whose function would be to continue operating the business and to pay any surplus left, over the operating costs, to the judgment-creditor. This receiver might be described as a receiver of the company's net income. There are special provisions in the Merchant Shipping Acts regarding receivers of wrecks,[14] in the Lunacy (Ireland) Acts concerning receivers of lunatics[15] and in the now defunct Charitable Loan Societies Acts.[16]

The Conveyancing Act, 1881,[17] gives all morgagees by deed of land the power to appoint a receiver over the income of the mortgaged property whenever the amount owing has fallen due and, under the mortgage, the mortgagee is entitled to exercise a power of sale. This provision is of particular significance because, under it, it is not necessary to apply to or petition the court in order to have a receiver appointed; the mortgagee, in the circumstances, can simply designate someone a receiver of the income. This power was first conferred by Lord Cranworth's Act, 1860,[18] and gave legislative form to a clause which had almost become universal in real property mortgages. It was extended somewhat in the 1881 Act. According to s.19(1)(iii) of the latter Act, a mortgagee by deed

> shall, by virtue of the Act, have . . . power . . . to appoint a receiver of the income of the mortgaged property, or any part thereof.[19]

Of course, this power is of little practical consequence where the mortgage deed itself authorises the mortgagee to appoint a receiver—either of the income or of the entire mortgaged property.

CONTRACTUAL RECEIVERSHIPS

Parties to a contract may agree that one of them shall be entitled to appoint a receiver, or receiver and manager, over all or some of the other party's assets. This principle is subject to limited exceptions, for instance, public policy will not allow a receiver to be appointed over another's future salary.[20] There are several advantages in contractual, or out-of-court, receiverships. These avoid the costs of a debenture holder's action in court, to enforce his security, and also dispense with the need for sureties, which the court usually will insist on

13. 30 & 31 Vic. c. 127.
14. Merchant Shipping Act 1894, s.567.
15. See generally, L. Harris, *Law and Practice in Lunacy* (1930) pp. 44-45.
16. Cf. *O'Reilly v Connor* [1904] 2 IR 601.
17. 44 & 45 Vic. c. 41.
18. 23 & 24 Vic. c. 145.
19. See generally, O'Donovan ch. 15 and Picarda ch. 18.
20. *Picton v Cullen* [1900] 2 IR 612 and *McCreery v Bennett* [1904] 2 IR 69.

when it makes the appointment. Most importantly, the debenture-holder can act and have his receiver *in situ* much more quickly and, for practical purposes, many of the receiver's functions, powers and responsibilities can be stipulated by the creditor in his debenture.

The commonest type of company receiver is the receiver and manager appointed by a holder of a floating charge under express authority in the debenture or charge to do so. One of the terms on which the company borrows money or otherwise obtains credit may be that the debenture-holder, in the specified circumstances, can appoint a receiver and manager over all or part of the company's assets. On being appointed, that person can then manage the business and can sell off the charged assets in order to reimburse the secured creditor. A typical stipulation in these terms would provide as follows:

Power to appoint a receiver

At any time after the principal moneys hereby secured become payable (or after the security constituted by the trust deed below mentioned becomes enforceable) the registered holder of this debenture may from time to time, with the consent in writing of the holders of the majority in value of the outstanding debentures of the same series, appoint by writing any person or persons (approved by the trustees of the said trust deed) to be a receiver or receivers of the property charged by the debentures (and not comprised in such trust deed), and may with the like consent apply to the court to remove any such receiver, and every such appointment or removal shall be as effective as if all the holders of debentures of the same series had concurred therein, and a receiver so appointed shall have power (1) to take possession of, collect and get in the property charged by the debentures, and for that purpose to take all proceedings in the name of the company or otherwise as may seem expedient;
(2) to carry on or concur in carrying on the business of the company, and for that purpose to raise money on the premises charged in priority to the debentures or otherwise;
(3) to sell or concur in selling all or any of the property charged by the debentures after giving to the company at least seven days' notice of his intention to sell, and to carry any such sale into effect by conveying in the name and on behalf of the company or otherwise;
(4) to make any arrangement or compromise which he or they shall think expedient in the interest of the debenture holders.
A receiver so appointed shall be deemed to be the agent of the company and the company shall be solely responsible for his acts or defaults and for his remuneration.[21]

Because the ordinary company receiver's appointment and authority are based on contract, much of the law on company receivers is contract law.

---

21.   From sample debenture in Palmer's *Company Law* (23rd ed., 1982).

Principles of equity also play a significant role, because the mortgagor—mortgagee relationship has traditionally been the domain of equity. Most of the law has been developed on a case by case basis by the judiciary; there is comparatively little legislative provision directly relating to receivers. A fundamental principle in the law here is that of freedom of contract; in general, the creditor and debtor are free to make whatever arrangements they wish about the security and the authority of any receiver who may be appointed. For instance, it is common to stipulate that the receiver shall be deemed to be the agent of the company, even though he was appointed by the debenture-holder and is really acting on its behalf. Because the company has agreed that he is its agent, then liability for his wrongdoing will often be attributed to the company, his deemed principal, and not to the secured creditor whose interests he is advancing. Part VII of the Companies Act, 1963, as amended by Part VIII of the 1990 Act, contains some restrictions on the parties' freedom of contract.

3

Appointment of Receiver, Status and Remuneration

A receiver may be appointed by the court in the various circumstances provided for by statute and, also, where traditionally the Chancery Court would designate receivership as the appropriate remedy.[1] A receiver can be appointed by the secured creditor, without any resort to the court, in the circumstances where the debenture or other security agreement provides for such appointment.

GROUNDS FOR APPOINTMENT

It depends on the very terms of the relevant security instrument whether, in the circumstances, a secured creditor can appoint a receiver. These circumstances vary somewhat from one debenture to another but they usually include most of the following events:

> Whenever the principal sum falling due under the agreement becomes payable;

> Whenever the company fails to pay any instalment, or the principal sum or the interest, due under the agreement;

> Whenever the company contravenes any of several covenants contained in the security instrument;

> Whenever the company ceases or threatens to cease carrying on its business;

> Whenever a resolution is passed, a petition is presented or an order is made to wind up the company;

> Whenever the company acts in such a way as endangers or jeopardises the security created by the debenture;

> Whenever any prior debenture becomes enforceable against the company.

The major banks' and other financial institutions' security instruments will designate several other circumstances as 'crystallising events', entitling them to appoint a receiver, for instance:

1.   See generally O'Donovan ch. 16 and Picarda ch. 20.

Whenever the company is unable to pay its debts;

Whenever it appears from the balance sheet that the company's liabilities are in excess of its assets, including its uncalled capital;

Whenever the company, without the debenture-holder's consent, creates any mortgage or charge ranking in priority to or *pari passu* with the security created by the debenture;

Whenever the company reduces its capital.

In deciding whether to appoint a receiver under any of these or equivalent clauses, it is a matter of construction of the relevant clause to ascertain whether it covers the company's present circumstances. If the decision to appoint a receiver is contested, the debenture-holder will have to show that its decision was justified by the facts in the light of whatever clause is being relied upon.

The courts will not readily imply a ground for appointment that is not spelt out in the debenture. For instance, on the application of a secured creditor, a court will normally appoint a receiver where the security is in jeopardy.[2] But in *Cryne v Barclays Bank*,[3] it was held that a debenture-holder himself cannot appoint a receiver on those grounds unless a power to do so is expressly stated in the debenture.

Unable to pay debts   The question of whether a company is unable to pay its debts arises in several contexts in insolvency law, for instance, in determining whether an examiner should be appointed under the Companies Amendment Act, 1990,[4] in deciding whether a company should be wound up under s.213(e) of the 1963 Act,[5] and in contesting allegedly preferential payments made and floating charges given shortly before the company was wound up.[6] The principles laid down in the cases concerning these matters are applicable to the question whether a receiver can be appointed on the grounds of the company's insolvency, where the debenture grants such a power. In *Byblos Bank S.A.L. v Al-Khudhanry*,[7] it was observed that it is 'trite law that [i]f a debt presently payable is not paid because of lack of means, that will normally suffice to prove that the company is unable to pay its debts. That will be so even if, on an assessment of all the assets and liabilities of the company, there is a surplus of assets over liabilities.'[8] Where the debenture does not require account to be taken of prospective and contingent liabilities, it has not yet been established whether account must be taken of them in deciding whether a company is insolvent, when appointing a receiver on that ground. In the *Byblos Bank* case, express provision had been made to include those liabilities in determining the company's solvency.

2.   E.g. *Re New York Taxicab Co.* [1913] 1 Ch 1.
3.   [1987] BCLC 584.   4. See post p. 81.
5.   See post pp. 149-152   6. See post pp. 238 and 248.
7.   [1987] BCLC 232.   8. Id. at p. 247.

Money repayable 'on demand'   Where a receiver may be appointed if money is not repaid by the company 'on demand', must the creditor allow the company a reasonable time to get in that money and, if so, what length of time is reasonable? There is some Canadian authority to the effect that the courts should be somewhat generous to debtors in determining how much time in those circumstances is reasonable for getting in and paying over the money.[9] But the English courts have adopted a more restrictive view of the matter, holding that the debtor is only entitled to such time as normally would be needed to effect the payment and that the debtor is not entitled to any extra time for going out and raising the funds before they can be paid. Thus in *Bank of Baroda v Panessar*,[10] where money was payable on demand, the creditor sought payment and very shortly afterwards, as the money had not been paid, appointed a receiver. At the time the debtor did not possess the funds and needed some time in order to raise them. It was held that what is a reasonable time in these circumstances is determined by the 'mechanics of payment', as opposed to 'time to raise the money if it is not there to be paid.'[11] In these situations the relevant question is whether there was sufficient time to pay the money if the company had it at hand. A similar approach is adopted in New Zealand, where the position has been summarised as follows:

> the only proper justification for allowing any time for payment after the actual demand is made is the practical commercial consideration that the borrower is not expected to have large cash sums immediately at hand. However, he is expected to pay from resources which are presently accessible to him but have to be converted into immediate cash or utilised within the same time to obtain financial cover. It is the time reasonably required to achieve that, always bearing in mind that it is a demand liability which must be met. And further time to negotiate a loan with a third party is not comprehended within that reasonable time. The test is objective and produces the certainty which commercial parties require in order to be clear from the outset as to their rights and obligations. To allow the elasticity and subjectivity inherent in the Canadian approach appears with respect to be contrary to commercial reality in this country and to lead to undesirable uncertainty to borrower and lender alike.[12]

Abusing power to appoint   As is explained below, in order for an appointment of a receiver to be valid, the formalities for appointing which are set out in the security instrument must be followed scrupulously. A matter that has not been much canvassed in the courts is whether this power of appointment can be 'abused' by a creditor, in the sense of being used for a completely extraneous purpose, such as to force the company into liquidation in the hope of gaining

9.   See Picarda at pp. 66-70. See too *Banbury Foods Pty. Ltd v National Bank of Australia*, 153 CLR 491 (1984).
10.   [1987] 2 WLR 208.   11.   Id. at p. 217.
12.   *A.N.Z. Banking Group (NZ) Ltd v Gibson* [1986] NZLR 556, at p. 565.

some collateral advantage from that situation. It was held by Hoffman J in *Re Potters Oils Ltd*[13] that a debenture holder 'is under no duty to refrain from exercising his rights merely because to exercise them may cause loss to the company or its unsecured creditors. He owes a duty of care to the company but this duty is qualified by being subordinated to the protection of his own interests.'[14] It was alleged there that it would have been far more advantageous for the company and its creditors generally if a receiver had not been appointed and, instead, the company was put into liquidation. Even if this were so, it was held that the debenture-holder was still entitled to protect his own interests by putting in a receiver.[15] It is conceivable that an appointment which falls within one or more of the designated grounds, but which clearly was made in order to obtain some unfair advantage from the company, would be deemed to be unlawful abuse of the debenture-holder's powers.[16]

FORMALITIES AND VALIDITY

There is no prescribed form for appointing an out-of-court receiver and manager. As has been observed above, any formalities for appointment set out in the security instrument must be scrupulously followed; if they are deviated from to any appreciable extent, the appointment will be a nullity and the so-called receiver will be a trespasser on the company's property. Moreover, the appointment will be invalid if the charging instrument itself was defective, for instance, if it was not duly registered under s.99 of the 1963 Act,[17] if it was a fraudulent conveyance under the Act of 1634[18] or it was a fraudulent preference under s.289 of the 1963 Act.[19] Also, other charges may have priority over the present charge and there is always the possibility that the charge was not properly executed by the company.

The debenture may set out numerous formalities to be followed for appointment. It may require the creditor to make a formal demand for payment of the amount owing. It is an open question whether such a requirement would be implied into the instrument; most likely it would not. Generally, it is not necessary for a demand for payment to state the actual amount which is owing. As Walton J observed in the *Bank of Baroda* case,[20] regarding an all-moneys debenture, 'I cannot see any reason why the creditor should not do precisely what he is, by the terms of his security, entitled to do; that is to say, to demand repayment of all moneys secured by the debenture.'[21] The judge went on to observe that if 'the debtor is in a position to pay off the sum demanded and wishes to know the exact and precise sum, he can communicate with the creditor and ask the creditor what sum he is expecting to be paid.'[22] It was also held in

13. [1986] 1 WLR 201.   14. Id. at p. 206.
15. Cf. *Shamji v Johnson Matthey & Co.* [1991] BCLC 36.
16. Cf. *British American Nickel Corp. v O'Brien Ltd* [1927] AC 369.
17. See *Company Law* pp. 512 et seq.
18. See post p. 230.   19. See post pp. 236-246.
20. [1987] 2 WLR 208.   21. Id. at p. 216.
22. Ibid.

that case that a demand for payment is not invalid merely because it was sent to the company's only place of business and not to its registered office. Where, under the debenture, money is payable on demand, the debtor must be afforded 'a reasonable opportunity of implementing whatever reasonable mechanics of payment he may need to employ to discharge the debt.'[23] Where the secured liability is one which arises on foot of a guarantee, it is a sufficient demand if the creditor demands to be paid the sum which is due under the guarantee.[24] The debenture may very well require that the appointment of a receiver be made in writing or even by deed.[25] In the case of a series of debentures, the prior consent of a certain number of debenture-holders may be required.[26]

A purported appointment is not effective until it is communicated to the intended receiver and is accepted. As Goff J put it in *Cripps (Pharmaceuticals) Ltd v Wickenden*, 'an appointment under hand takes effect when the document of appointment is handed to the receiver by a person having authority to do that in and circumstances from which it may fairly be said that he is appointing a receiver, and the receiver accepts the proffered appointment.'[27] Generally, acceptance of the appointment may be tacit and be inferred from the conduct of the designated appointee. The appointment takes effect from the time of acceptance; the date recited on the instrument of appointment is not invariably the day on which the receivership commences. Often an instrument of appointment will be typed up and dated some days before the appointment is actually accepted.

A liquidator who is subsequently appointed almost invariably will consider the propriety of the receiver's appointment and may very well mount a challenge in the courts to its validity. Occasionally even the company itself, at the instigation of its directors[28] or of some judgment or execution creditor,[29] may challenge the receiver's appointment. Where the appointment was invalid because the charge in question transpired to be ineffective, s.316(3) of the 1963 Act gives the court a discretion to relieve the receiver from personal liability resulting from the invalid appointment. But in that event, the person who made the purported appointment is rendered liable for any loss or damage resulting from the error.

QUALIFICATIONS

Several countries' laws lay down minimum qualifications for acting as a company receiver.[30] This is not the case in Ireland, although in practice most

23. Id. at p. 217.
24. *D.F.C. Financial Services Ltd v Samuel* [1990] 3 NZLR 156.
25. E.g. *Windsor Refrigerator Co. Ltd v Branch Nominees Ltd* [1961] 1 Ch 375.
26. E.g. *Re 'Slogger' Automatic Feeder Co. Ltd* [1915] 1 Ch 478.
27. [1973] 1 WLR 944, at p. 953.
28. E.g. *Newhart Developments Ltd v Co-Operative Commercial Bank Ltd* [1978] QB 814.
29. Eg. *Kasofsky v Kreegers* [1937] 4 All ER 374
30. E.g. in Britain; Insolvency Act 1986, s.388—he must be a licensed insolvency practitioner.

receivers are qualified accountants. But anybody can be appointed as a company receiver unless they are disqualified from so acting by the Companies Acts. Corporate bodies are so disqualified;[31] it is a criminal offence for any such body to act as a company receiver. Undischarged bankrupts are disqualified.[32] In 1990 the grounds for disqualification were significantly extended to persons who were already closely connected with the company's management.[33] These are any person who, within the 12 months prior to the appointment, was an 'officer', employee or auditor of the company or of one of its closely associated companies; these persons include any parent, spouse, brother, sister or child of such person. Who is a company officer for this purpose is not defined, except to include the auditor. A person who was previously appointed as receiver, under a debenture, is not an officer of the company.[34] If any of the above persons are disqualified in respect of the company's subsidiary or holding company, or another subsidiary of its holding company, they cannot be receivers to the company. A creditor of the company or a mortgagee of its property is not disqualified from acting as its receiver.

Any receiver who becomes disqualified by virtue of this section is required, within 14 days of such time, to vacate the office and notify in writing the company, the registrar of companies and the appointing debenture-holder or court, as the case may be, of that fact.[35] Disqualified persons acting as receivers can be fined up to £5,000 if convicted on indictment.

AGENT OF COMPANY OR OF CREDITORS?

Company receivers are in a somewhat anomalous situation, which gives rise to certain peculiar legal results in that, even though they are appointed by the debenture-holder in order to serve his ends, usually they are designated by the charging instrument as the agent of the company rather than of their appointer.[36] In the absence of such designation, almost invariably they will be deemed to be agents for their appointing debenture-holder.[37] Where they are agents for the company, they still have some agency relationship with the debenture-holder as well.

By designating a receiver as the company's agent, the company and not the debenture-holder is primarily responsible for the receiver's remuneration and indemnity, and for his torts and other wrongs. Also the receiver can make contracts that bind the company, such as disposing of its property. It is for these and other reasons that, even throughout the last century, when a mortgagee sought to enter into possession of the charged property, usually he would enter as the mortgagor's agent. As Rigby LJ explained in *Gaskell v Golsong*,

31. 1963 Act s.314. Cf. *Portman Bldg. Soc. v Gallwey* [1955] 1 WLR 96.
32. Id. s.315(1)(a).
33. 1990 Act s.170, amending 1963 Act s.315.
34. This follows from *Re B. Johnson & Co. (Builders) Ltd* [1955] Ch 634.
35. 1963 Act s.315(2).
36. See generally, Milman, 'Receivers as Agents', 44 *Mod L Rev* 658 (1981).
37. *Re Vimbos Ltd* [1900] 1 Ch 470.

> The mortgagee, as agent of the mortgagor, appointed a person to receive the income, with directions to keep down the interest of the mortgage, and to account for the surplus to the mortgagor as his principal. These directions were supposed to emanate, not from the mortgagee, but from the mortgagor; and the receiver therefore, in the relation between himself and the mortgagor, stood in the position of a person appointed by an instrument to which the mortgagee was no party. . . . By degrees the forms of appointment of receivers became more complicated, and their powers of management more extensive; but the doctrine . . . was consistently adhered to and it remained true throughout that the receiver's appointment, and all directions and powers given and conferred upon him, were supposed to emanate from the mortgagor, and the mortgagee, though he might be the actual appointor, and might have stipulated for all the powers conferred upon the receiver, was in no other position, so far as responsibility was concerned, than if he had been altogether a stranger to the appointment.[38]

Because the practice of designating receivers as the mortgagor's agent became so common, it was incorporated into statutes governing the law of property; first in Lord Cranworth's Act of 1860[39] and then in s.24(2) of the Conveyancing Act, 1881.[40]

This state of affairs leads to several peculiar consequences. Thus, the debenture-holder cannot seek to restrain third parties who are interfering with the receiver's activities.[41] A *Mareva* injunction binding on the company also binds the receiver.[42] And the receiver is obliged to furnish detailed accounts to the company.[43] It has been suggested, however, that even where the receiver is strictly the company's agent circumstances can arise where he has a right of indemnity against the debenture-holder, for instance, where he is carrying out the latter's instructions.[44]

The deemed agency of the company comes to an end once the company is put into liquidation. From then on it depends on all the circumstances of the case who the receiver's principal is. In *American Express International Banking Corp. v Hurley*[45] which concerned claims regarding a receiver's negligence, the position was summarised in these terms:

> A receiver appointed under the common form of charge . . . acts as the agent of the mortgagor. . . . If the mortgagor is put into liquidation then the agency terminates. . . . If the receiver continues to act he does not

---

38. [1896] 1 QB 669, at pp. 692-693.   39. 23 & 24 Vic. c. 145.
40. 44 & 45 Vic. c. 41.   41. *Bose v Harris* (1942) S.J. 376.
42. *Cretanor Maritime Co. Ltd v Irish Marine Management Ltd* [1979] 1 WLR 966.
43. *Smiths Ltd v Middleton* [1970] 3 All ER 842.
44. *R.A. Price Securities Ltd v Henderson* [1989] 2 NZLR 257, at p. 262.
45. [1986] BCLC 52.

automatically become the agent of the mortgagee . . . but he may become so if the mortgagee treats him as such.[46]

On account of the constant communication between the bank and the receiver in that case, in which the receiver frequently sought bank approval for steps he proposed taking, it was held that he had thereby become the bank's agent. Accordingly, the bank were liable for his negligence in the manner in which he sold the company's assets but, in turn, were entitled to be indemnified by him under the usual agent's implied indemnity.

REMUNERATION

Before accepting the appointment, in addition to ensuring that the debenture holder can validly appoint him, the intended receiver usually will want to know how much he will get paid and who will be responsible for the payment.

Responsibility for payment　Ordinarily, the charging instrument or the terms of appointment will stipulate who will pay the receiver's remuneration and, generally, that obligation will be imposed on the debtor company and not on the appointing creditor. If there is no express reference to remuneration, whoever is the receiver's principal must pay that remuneration.[47] For this reason, among others, receivers usually are designated as the agent of the company. In the absence of an expressed designation of agency, it will depend on the entire circumstances who the receiver is acting for. Thus, in one instance where the debenture was silent as regards agency, but which incorporated provisions of the Conveyancing Act, 1881, and gave the receiver powers in addition to those given in that Act, it was held that the receiver was the debenture-holder's agent and the latter, therefore, was responsible for his remuneration.[48]

Quantum　As for the rate or amount of remuneration, usually it will be expressly provided for in the charging instrument or in the terms of appointment; it would be most exceptional for receivers to embark on their task without having first agreed their rate of payment. At times, instead of stipulating a particular rate or amount, the instrument will provide that the amount of remuneration shall be determined by agreement between the debenture-holder and the receiver. It will depend on the terms in the debenture or in the agreement whether the remuneration shall include costs incurred by the receiver. Debenture-holders do not have an unfettered discretion in fixing the remuneration, in that their 'power to agree the receiver's remuneration, like other powers of the mortgagee, has . . . to be exercised in good faith and with regard to the qualified duty of care to the company. . . .'[49]

46. Id. at p. 57.　　　　　　　　47. *Re Vimbos Ltd* [1900] 1 Ch 470.
48. *Deyes v Wood* [1911] 1 KB 806.
49. *Re Potters Oils Ltd* [1986] 1 WLR 201, at p. 206.

Where the debenture is entirely silent on the matter of remuneration, the courts will usually imply a term that the receiver is entitled to a reasonable remuneration, the entire circumstances of the receivership determining what that amount is. Alternatively, the receiver could claim reasonable remuneration for services rendered under the restitutionary principle of *quantum meruit.*

Variation   Section 318 of the 1963 Act gives the court power to intervene in fixing the remuneration, on the application of either the company, any creditor or the liquidator. Even where the debenture states what the remuneration shall be, any of these parties may apply to the court to fix or vary the remuneration and the amount fixed by the court can even apply in respect of services which have already been rendered. Indeed in 'special circumstances' the court can require a receiver to account for remuneration which has already been paid and which exceeds the amount fixed in the court's order. It was held in *Re Potter's Oils Ltd*[50] that, while the court's discretion in an application under s.318 was 'entirely unfettered', nevertheless, because intervention involves interfering with contractual rights for the benefit of the unsecured creditors, the court should only intervene where the remuneration 'can clearly be seen to be excessive'.[51] It is not certain if a receiver, whose remuneration has already been agreed, can apply to the court to have that remuneration increased because of special unforeseen circumstances which arose.

Forfeiture   If the company's assets do not realise a sufficient sum then the receiver may very well go unremunerated, unless his terms of appointment addressed that very exigency. If the receiver's appointment is defective, then he may also not be entitled to remuneration, although it is possible that he has some claim to payment on the basis of *quantum meruit.* Where he acts beyond the scope of his authority, he is not entitled to be paid for those actions. And if he has misconducted himself, for instance by acting dishonestly or recklessly or otherwise in breach of his duties, he may be disallowed from receiving any payment or part of what would be owing to him. For instance, in *R.A. Price Securities Ltd v Henderson,*[52] it was held that the receiver had acted recklessly in continuing the company's business when he should have promptly sold part of its assets. His claim for payment of remuneration was rejected and he was ordered to pay damages. The extent of any forfeiture of remuneration depends on the nature of the wrongdoing.

INDEMNITY

Before accepting the appointment, a receiver usually will require to be indemnified against all costs, expenses and possible liabilities that may be incurred

---

50. [1986] 1 WLR 201.   51. Id. at p. 207.
52. [1989] 2 NZLR 257.

in the course of the receivership. Usually, it is the appointing debenture-holder who will be required to provide that indemnity. Without being so indemnified, a receiver may suffer loss where the assets subject to the charge are not enough to cover the secured debt and the expenses of receivership. In the absence of an express indemnity, the court may imply an indemnity from the receiver's agency; the principal (usually the company) may be deemed to have agreed to indemnify the receiver. This implied indemnity may extend even to liabilities incurred under an honest error of judgment. Where the company is insolvent an implied indemnity may be worthless because, even assuming there are unencumbered assets, the indemnity does not enjoy any statutory priority but ranks as an ordinary unsecured debt of the company. The indemnity can be enforced against the company's assets where the receiver was deceived by the company into committing a breach of duty, such as by false information concerning preferred debts.[53]

A question which has not yet been decided is whether a receiver and manager, designated as the company's agent, is its 'officer' for the purpose of s.200 of the 1963 Act.[54] For if a receiver is an officer in this context, an express indemnity cannot include 'negligence, default, breach of duty or breach of trust'.[55]

Where a receiver misconducts himself, he may very well also forfeit his entitlement to be indemnified, for instance, by acting negligently, unlawfully or otherwise in breach of duty. Thus, in *R.A. Price Securities Ltd v Henderson*,[56] where the receiver was negligent and had run up large legal costs while unnecessarily running the company's business, the court refused to indemnify him against those costs. If the receiver simply exceeds his powers and his actions are then ratified by the company, he does not loose his indemnity.

In the exceptional instance of the receiver being the debenture-holder's agent, the implied indemnity will be against the latter.[57] That agency can easily arise when the company has been put into liquidation. Indeed in the *R.A. Price Securities Ltd* case,[58] one judge ventured that other circumstances can arise where the receiver, although strictly the company's agent, may be entitled to be indemnified by the debenture holder.[59]

RESIGNATION

A receiver may be in breach of contract and become liable in damages by resigning from the office without the consent of the appointing debenture-holder. But it is most unlikely that a court would order specific performance of

53. *Westminster City Council v Treby* [1936] 2 All ER 31.
54. See *Company Law* pp. 170-172.
55. Cf. *Harris v S.* (1976) 2 ACLR 51 at p. 55
56. [1989] 2 NZLR 257.
57. E.g. *American Express Int'l Banking Corp. v Hurley* [1986] BCLC 52.
58. [1989] 2 NZLR 297.
59. Id. at p. 262.

the agreement to act as receiver. Section 322C of the 1963 Act requires receivers to give at least one month's notice of their intention to resign to the company or its liquidator and to the holders of any fixed charge or floating charge over all or part of the company's property. A receiver who becomes disqualified under s.315(1) of the 1963 Act must thereupon vacate his office and notify the company, the registrar of companies and others of the fact within 14 days.

REMOVAL

Frequently, the instrument of appointment will provide that the debenture-holder may remove the receiver in specified circumstances, such as where the charged assets have been disposed of and the debt has been discharged, and also for misconduct or where differences of opinion arise between them. Even in the absence of any such provision, there is an inherent power in the court to remove a receiver for serious misconduct or for flagrant breach of duty where the very security may be in danger. Moreover, s.322A of the 1963 Act provides that the court may remove a receiver 'on cause shown'.[60] The liquidator of a company can apply to the court for an order that a receiver shall cease to act either entirely or in respect of part of the company's assets.[61]

60. Cf. similar provision on removing liquidators from office; see post pp. 189-190.
61. 1963 Act s.322.

4

Effects of Receivership

The Companies Acts do not spell out in any detail the various legal consequences of a company receiver being appointed. Those consequences to a large extent depend on the scope of the security. It may be limited to certain assets or, while formulated in comprehensive terms, certain categories of assets may be expressly excluded. What property is caught by the charge and, therefore, comes within the receivership is a matter of interpretation.[1] For instance, where a colliery company's business was undoubtedly intended to form part of the security, it was held that a receiver and manager could be appointed even though the business was not expressly referred to in the debenture.[2] Frequently, the debenture will give a fixed charge over a range of designated assets and then an all- embracing floating charge over the entire assets and undertaking. Where a floating charge crystallises,[3] as by a receiver being appointed, it becomes a fixed charge. The effects of appointing a receiver over a company's assets on the various parties involved in the company and on its assets are as follows.

MEMBERS

The appointment of a receiver has no significant legal effect on the company's members or shareholders. They can still attend and vote at meetings of the company and they remain entitled to get copies of the annual accounts and of all proposed special and equivalent resolutions. And if they can find purchasers, they can dispose of their shares, subject of course to any restrictions in the company's articles of association.

DIRECTORS

Where a receiver is appointed under a floating charge over all or most of the company's assets, a statement of affairs verified by at least one of the company's directors and an officer or employee of the company must be given to the receiver within 14 days of his appointment.[4] Apart from that, a receivership has no significant legal effect on the company's directors other than that they

1. E.g. *Donohoe v Agricultural Credit Corp.* [1986] IR 165.
2. *County of Gloucester Bank v Rudry Merthyr etc. Colliery Co.* [1895] 1 Ch 629.
3. See *Company Law*, pp. 508 et seq.
4. 1963 Act s.319(1)(b).

no longer have any right to get in, control and deal with the charged assets. But where, as frequently is the case, the debenture empowers the receiver to manage the company's undertaking or business, the directors no longer have any direct say in running that business until the receivership comes to a conclusion. As an Australian judge put it,

> Receivership and management may well dominate exclusively a company's affairs in its dealings and relations with the outside world. But it does not permeate a company's internal domestic structure. That structure continues to exist notwithstanding that the directors no longer have authority to exercise their ordinary business-management functions. A valid receivership and management will ordinarily supersede, but not destroy, the company's own organs through which it conducts its affairs. The capacity of those organs to function bears a direct inverse relationship to the validity and scope of the receivership and management.[5]

A striking illustration of the fact that the directors are far from being entirely *functus officio* while the company is in receivership is *Newhart Developments Ltd v Co-operative Commercial Bank Ltd*,[6] which held that the directors remain free to act in the company's interests so long as they do not impinge on the debenture-holder's security. The plaintiff company and a subsidiary of its bankers engaged in a joint venture to develop property, which eventually ran into difficulties, causing the bank to withdraw its financial support for the project. The company had given the bank a charge over its assets and the bank appointed a receiver-manager of its property. Subsequently, the directors formed the view that the bank had acted wrongly when it withdrew support for the joint venture and they, accordingly, proposed to bring suit against the bank for breach of the funding contract. Predictably, the receiver sought to enjoin them from commencing this action, contending that once receivership starts only the receiver can institute proceedings on the company's behalf. The directors were prepared to indemnify the company against its costs incurred in the action. It was held that the receivership was not a bar against the company proceeding with its claim, at the directors' instigation. According to Shaw LJ,

> One has got to see what the function of the receiver is. It is not, of course, to wind up the company. It is perhaps interesting to note in passing that when a liquidator is appointed, certainly in a winding up by the court, the powers of the directors immediately cease by statutory provision. There is no such provision in relation to the appointment of a receiver, whose duty it is to protect the interests of the mortgagee or debenture-holders, as the case may be. In so far as it is requisite and necessary for him, in the course of his dealing with the assets of the company, bringing them in and realising them, and so on, to bring actions as well, he is empowered

5. *Hawkesbury Development Co. v Landmark Finance Pty Ltd* (1970) WN (NSW) 199, at p. 209.
6. [1978] QB 814.

to do so by the debenture trust deed in the name of the company. That makes it possible for him to institute such proceedings without exposing himself to the risk of a liability for costs if those proceedings should fail. But the provision in the debenture trust deed giving him that power is an enabling provision which invests him with the capacity to bring an action in the name of the company. It does not divest the directors of the company of their power, as the governing body of the company, of instituting proceedings in a situation where so doing does not in any way impinge prejudicially upon the position of the debenture-holders by threatening or imperilling the assets which are subject to the charge.[7]

In comparable Australian and New Zealand cases[8] the directors were permitted to contest the effectiveness of the security under which a receiver had been appointed and thus, the appointment itself. But in *Tudor Grange Holdings Ltd v Citibank N.A.*,[9] the directors were not allowed to sue in the company's name because the company did not have a full indemnity from them against costs that might be incurred. Provided a full indemnity is given, presumably directors may even challenge the actions of a validly appointed receiver for excess of authority or misfeasance. But since they may not have access to the company's books, records and financial statements, the directors can be in an invidious position.

In the *Newhart Developments Ltd* case Shaw LJ went on to explain the division of powers between receivers-managers and company directors as follows:

> What . . . the directors cannot do, and to this extent their powers are inhibited, is to dispose of the assets within the debenture charge without the assent or concurrence of the receiver, for it is his function to deal with the assets in the first place so as to provide for the means of paying off the debenture-holders' claims. [And the directors cannot take] any action which would interfere with the proper discharge of the receiver's function in gathering in the assets of the company. . . .

> [Usually t]here is in the debenture deed itself a provision to the effect that the receiver may carry on the business of the company or concur in carrying on its business, which itself demonstrates that there is not a total extinction of the function of the directors. It is only within the scope of its assets which are covered by the debenture, and only in so far as it is necessary to apply those assets in the best possible way in the interests of the debenture-holders, that the receiver has a real function. If in the exercise of his discretion he chooses to ignore some asset such as a right of action, or decides that it would be unprofitable from the point of view of the debenture holders to pursue it, there is nothing in any authority

7. Id. at p. 819.
8. E.g. *Paramount Acceptance Co. v Souster* [1981] 2 NZLR 38.
9. [1992] Ch 53.

which has been cited to us which suggests that it is not then open to the directors of the company to pursue that right of action if they think it would be in the interests of the company. Indeed, in my view, it would be incumbent on them to do so, because notwithstanding that the debenture holders have got the right to be satisfied out of the assets subject to the charge, other creditors are entitled to expect that those concerned with the management of the company should exercise their best efforts to ensure that, when the time comes, they too will find themselves in the position that there is a fund available to pay them, if not in full, at least something of what they are owed.

The receiver is entitled to ignore the claims of anybody outside the debenture holders. Not so the company; not so therefore the directors of the company. If there is an asset which appears to be of value, although the directors cannot deal with it in the sense of disposing of it, they are under a duty to exploit it so to bring it to a realisation which may be fruitful for all concerned.[10]

CONTRACTS

The effects of receivership on contracts with the company depends on whether the contract in question was made before or after the receivership commenced;[11] assuming, of course, that the contract concerns matters within the receiver-manager's general area of responsibility. Contracts outside that area of responsibility are in no way affected by the receivership.

Pre-receivership contracts Except where specific provision to the contrary is made, appointment of a receiver has no significant legal effect on contracts which the company has already made. Assuming that these contracts fall within the receiver's general area of responsibility, they may still be enforced by the company and against the company. Thus, generally, the receivership does not put an end to employment contracts with the company[12] or to leases it has.[13] A landlord can still sue for arrears of rent and institute ejectment proceedings. And subject to the Hire Purchase Acts, the owner of chattels which have been hired by the company remains entitled to enforce his contractual remedies, for instance, repossess the goods for non-payment of instalments.[14] There is no legislative equivalent to s.49 of the Bankruptcy Act, 1988, which avoids forfeiture provisions in leases and in hire purchase agreements.[15] Subject to

---

10. [1978] QB at pp. 821 and 820-821.
11. See generally Blanchard, 'The Contracts of a Company in Receivership', 13 *NZUL Rev* 237 (1987).
12. *Griffith v Secretary of State for Social Services* [1974] QB 468; see post pp. 383-384
13. See post p. 56.
14. *Re Morrison Jones & Taylor Ltd* [1914] 1 Ch 50.
15. See *Bankruptcy Law*, p. 81.

certain qualifications, pre-receivership rights of set-off remain effective,[16] as are contractual liens given before the receiver was appointed.

Pre-receivership contracts may not be enforced directly against the receiver. Thus in *Ardmore Studios (Ireland) Ltd v Lynch*,[17] which centred on a trade dispute, one question which arose was whether the receiver and manager of the plaintiff company was bound by a collective agreement the company had entered into some time previously with trade unions. McLoughlin J held that the receiver was not so bound because, although he was indeed the agent of the company, the company was never the receiver's agent for the purpose of imposing liability on him. Similarly, the receiver is not personally liable under contracts of employment and tenancy agreements which the company made before the receivership commenced.

Unlike liquidators, there is no statutory mechanism to which receivers can resort in order to reduce a company's exposure under onerous contracts.[18] As is explained below,[19] however, because receivers cannot be made personally liable for breach of any contract that the company has entered into, to some extent receivers can frustrate performance by the company of its contracts and, in a sense, disclaim those contracts. This state of affairs often makes it easier for receivers to achieve what are termed 'hive downs'.

Post-receivership contracts With regard to contracts made after the receivership has commenced and where, as usually is the case, under the debenture the receiver was designated an agent of the company, both the company and also the receiver personally are liable on the contract, although there are exceptions and qualifications to the receiver's own liability. The reason why the company and not the appointing debenture-holder is liable on these contracts is explained by Rigby LJ in *Gaskell v Golsong*.[20] There the plaintiff sought, unsuccessfully, to have the debenture-holder made liable for contracts made by a receiver who had been designated as the company's agent. It was held that the fact that those debenture- holders had de facto control, via the receiver, of the company's business did not render them the principals of the business; they were and remained mere creditors of the business. Moreover, the court must give effect to any contractual designation of agency, with the result that 'a receiver and manager appointed by a mortgagee under an agreement that he shall be the agent of the mortgagor is in the same position as if appointed by the mortgagor himself, and as if every direction given to him emanated from the mortgagor himself.'[21]

Being a mere agent of the company, at common law the receiver is not personally liable on contracts made in the course of the receivership. However, s.316(2) of the 1963 Act provides for personal liability in these circumstances:

16. See post p. 335-339.
17. [1965] IR 1.   18. See post p. 224-229.
19. Infra p. 54.   20. [1896] 1 QB 669.
21. Id. at p. 697; see too *Cully v Parsons* [1983] 2 Ch 512.

[he] shall be personally liable on any contract entered into by him in the performance of his functions (whether such contract is entered into by him in the name of such company or in his own name as receiver or otherwise). . . .

This personal liability is subject to two qualifications. The contract in question can stipulate that the receiver shall not be liable on it. It has not been decided if a provision to that effect can be implied into the contract or whether it must always be expressed.[22] Furthermore, every receiver is entitled to be indemnified out of the company's assets in respect of any liability arising from the contract.[23]

LITIGATION

In the case of claims which the company has brought or could bring, generally those would be assets of the company which, under the debenture, have vested in the extensively secured creditor. Accordingly, bringing or the further conduct of those claims usually is exclusively a matter for the receiver. Unless there is clear authority in the debenture to do so, the receiver cannot bring a claim, on behalf of the company, in his own name. But he may sue in the company's name, without its consent. For instance, in *M. Wheeler & Co. v Warren*,[24] it was held that the receiver could sue, in the company's name, for rescission of a contract for the sale of a premises which was being constructed and for forfeiture of the deposit or, alternatively, for specific performance. Usually, defendants can get security for costs in claims of this nature. In the case of claims against the company, generally it will be for the receiver to defend or seek to compromise them.

Where the litigation may adversely affect the charged assets, the company cannot proceed with the case without the receiver's consent, unless some arrangement is made to prevent the action having that adverse effect. It will be remembered that in the *Newhart Developments Ltd* case[25] the company's directors undertook to indemnify the company's costs in bringing a claim against a bank, which had appointed the receiver, thereby enabling them to sue in the company's name. By contrast, in the *Tudor Grange* case,[26] a similar claim was struck out because *inter alia*, a full indemnity against costs had not been given.

COMPANY PROPERTY

Once appointed, the receiver has the exclusive right to control and dispose of the charged property; the company no longer has any say in what should be done with those assets. Almost invariably, the receiver will seek to sell that property and pay the proceeds of sale to the debenture-holder. The terms of the charge determine what property falls within the receiver's control.[27] But certain

22. Cf. 1963 Act s.37(2); see *Company Law*, p. 426.
23. Infra p. 53.   24. [1928] 1 Ch 840
25. [1978] QB 814; supra pp. 38-40   26. [1992] Ch 53; supra p. 39.
27. E.g. *Donohoe v Agricultural Credit Corp.* [1986] IR 165.

property described in the charge may not indeed belong to the company and, accordingly, the receiver will have no rights in respect of it. Whether the asset in question does belong to the company depends on the law governing the acquisition of rights to property, for instance, the Sale of Goods Acts and the Bills of Exchange Acts. For instance, in *Re Blyth Shipbuilding etc. Co.*,[28] a shipyard company gave a debenture over its entire undertaking. When a receiver was appointed over its assets, the question arose of who owned a ship which was being built in its yard—the company or the customer for whom the ship was being built. It was held that, under the shipbuilding contract there, the customer owned the partly completed ship and also certain materials lying around the yard which were ready to be incorporated into the hull. Similarly, the debenture-holder's charge will not affect property held under a valid retention of title clause,[29] property which is subject to a hire purchase or credit sale agreement,[30] or some other form of bailment, property held in trust and property which is subject to some prior charge.[31]

In the case of a floating charge where the charged property may be the entire undertaking or, instead, a category or categories of assets, it will include assets of the category described and which the company acquired following crystallisation of the charge.[32] Appointment of a receiver crystallises the incomplete assignment effected by the floating charge and the secured creditor thenceforth has a full equitable interest in the charged assets. The company's authority, while the charge floated, to deal with its assets in the ordinary course of its business is immediately revoked. Crystallisation of a floating charge does not vest the charged property in the receiver but a receiver can call in that property by bringing an action in the company's name and can dispose of the property in the company's name.[33]

CREDITORS' REMEDIES

Frequently a receiver appointed under a floating charge will be confronted by other creditors seeking to enforce their own security rights over the company's property or seeking to execute judgments against property which is caught by the charge, for instance, by way of *fieri facias*, registering a judgment mortgage, garnishment and equitable execution. If any of these forms of execution were completed before the charge crystallised then the judgment creditor is entitled to retain the fruits of the execution. But uncompleted execution cannot be continued following crystallisation.[34]

---

28. [1926] 1 Ch 494.
29. See post pp. 314-320.
30. See post p. 311-313.
31. See chs. 22 and 24.
32. See post p. 351 and see generally, Milman, 'The Floating Charge and After-Acquired Assets', [1979] *Conv* 138.
33. *M. Wheeler & Co. v Warren* [1928] Ch 840 and *Industrial Development Authority v Moran* [1978] IR 159.
34. See generally, Calnan, 'Priorites Between Execution Creditors and Floating Charges', 10 *NZL Rev* 111 (1982).

Repossession   Where property in the company's possession is being held under a valid retention of title clause, the supplier of those goods may be able to repossess them or may be entitled to the proceeds of any sub-sales of those goods. The extent of any such right of repossession depends on the terms of the retention of title clause in question and on the clause not really being a charge which should have been registered under s.99 of the Companies Act.[35]

Enforcing charge   Certain parts of the company's property may have been charged as well to persons other than the debenture-holder who appointed the receiver. Who then is entitled to that property—those chargees or the debenture-holder—depends on which charge takes priority over the other.[36] In the case of land, there are elaborate rules regarding priorities between mortgagees.[37] The same general principles apply to priorities between charges of chattels and of choses in action.[38] Briefly, as between two legal interests, the earliest prevails, i.e. legal mortgages rank in accordance with the time they were given. Legal mortgages prevail over equitable mortgages and charges, even if the latter are prior in time, except where the legal mortgagee had notice of the previous equitable security.

Execution   As soon as the order of *fi. fa.* is made, the sheriff is entitled to seize the goods. He may seize them even from third parties claiming an interest in them under a subsequent disposition of the debtor,[39] unless they obtained legal title to the goods in good faith and for valuable consideration before the seizure.[40] It would appear that where, on behalf of some other debtor, the sheriff seizes goods before the debenture-holder's floating charge crystallises, the execution creditor obtains priority over the receiver in respect of those goods.[41] But if the charge crystallises between seizure and sale, the charge-holder obtains priority.[42] There is no authority squarely on the question of who gets priority where the charge crystallises after the sheriff has sold the goods but before the proceeds from the sale are handed over to the execution creditor; the outcome depends on whether this form of execution is completed when the sale occurs[43] or when the money is handed over. Where the sheriff seizes goods but, in order to prevent their sale, the company pays the sheriff all or part of the debt, and a floating charge then crystallises, clearly those goods are captured by the charge; but the money paid over to the sheriff is not caught by it.[44] If automatic crystallisation is accepted by the courts in this country, a question that will then

---

35. See *Company Law*, pp. 512 et seq.   36. See post p. 352.
37. See generally J.C.W. Wylie, *Irish Land Law* (2nd ed., 1986) pp. 689 et seq.
38. See generally, M. Forde, *Commercial Law in Ireland* (1990) pp. 200 et seq.
39. *Giles v Grover* (1832) 9 Bing. 128.
40. Sale of Goods Act 1893, s.26(1).
41. Following *Evans v Rival Granite Quarries Ltd* [1910] 2 KB 979.
42. *Re Opera Ltd* [1891] 3 Ch 260.
43. Cf. *Robson v Smith* [1895] 2 Ch 118.
44. *Robinson v Burnells' Vienna Bakery Ltd* [1910] 2 KB 624.

arise is the effect of a clause in a debenture stipulating that crystallisation shall occur as soon as any step is taken to execute a judgment.

Attachment If the process of attaching debts, or garnishment, is completed before the floating charge crystallises, the money which is attached must be paid over to the judgment creditor and not to the receiver; once garnishment is completed, the attached fund becomes the judgment creditor's property in equity.[45] But the time of completion is not when the order *nisi* is made[46] nor when that order is made absolute.[47] The making of a garnishee order absolute does not transfer the property in the garnished debt, which remains the judgment debtor's own property, and rights arising from the attachment of the debt are subject to any rights and equities affecting the garnished debt. Thus, although the order absolute is a form of security it does not override a secured priority acquired before payment to a garnishor. However, where, with knowledge that the floating charge exists, the garnishee pays the debt to the garnishor pursuant to an order absolute, he cannot then be required to pay it over again to the debenture-holder. As an Australian judge explained,

> if prior to the crystallising of a floating charge a judgment creditor receives payment from a garnishee, then the mere existence of the floating charge is not sufficient to give the mortgagee a right to the debt. The debt must be a security under the charge by its crystallisation before payment to the judgment creditor.[48]

Registering judgment mortgages The effect of a judgment mortgage on priorities is described by Professor Wylie as follows:

> So far as unregistered land is concerned, the general rule is that the judgment mortgage registered in the Registry of Deeds takes effect subject to all equities affecting the land at the date of registration, so that a prior unregistered deed still has priority. However, it has been held . . . that 'a subsequent registered deed carries a judgment mortgage on its back', i.e. a subsequent registered deed made for value secures priority for the judgment mortgage over prior unregistered deeds, though only where an issue of priority arises as between the prior unregistered deeds and the subsequent registered one. So far as subsequent mortgages or charges are concerned, the judgment mortgage has, in general, the same priority accorded to it as other registered instruments.[49]

With respect to registered land, s.71(4) of the Registration of Title Act, 1964, provides that the charge on the interest of the judgment debtor is subject to

45. *Evans v Rival Granite Quarries Ltd* [1910] 2 KB 979.
46. *Norton v Yates* [1906] 1 KB 112.
47. *Cairney v Back* [1906] 2 KB 746.
48. *M. G. Charley Pty. Ltd v F.H. Wells Pty Ltd* (1963) 80 WN (NSW) 754.
49. *Irish Land Law* (2nd ed., 1986) par. 13.181.

existing registered burdens and burdens affecting the interest without registration, and 'all unregistered rights subject to which the judgment debtor held that interest at the time of registration of the affidavit.'[50]

Receivers   The effect of having a receiver by way of equitable execution appointed over property which is subject to a floating charge is a matter of some conflicting authority in England. In one instance it was held that such an order creates a specific charge over the property in question[51] but, six years later, it was concluded that this is not the case and that such an order is not equivalent to seizure of the property in execution; it is 'simply an uncompleted process to obtain payment of money'.[52] In *Re Lough Neagh Ship Co., ex p. Thompson*,[53] where the judgment creditor obtained an order appointing himself as receiver of the beneficial interest in a ship, it was held that the receivership order did not make the judgment creditor a secured creditor of the company. In order to attain that status, the creditor must go and take steps to enforce payment of the money owed. According to Porter MR,

> The [receivership] order is nothing more than a declaration that the plaintiff is creditor for the amount named on it, and that he is entitled to be paid that amount out of the property . . . over which he is, by the court, appointed receiver, and that he is entitled to proceed to receive this amount out of that property. If he had acted on the order and got possession, he could not have been deprived of the fruits of his equitable execution.[54]

Once a floating charge crystallises, the charged property cannot any longer be appropriated by a receivership order.

Winding up   The appointment of a receiver over a company's assets ordinarily does not prevent any unpaid creditor of the company from petitioning to have it wound up. However, the High Court has some discretion in this matter and special circumstances may warrant the court refusing to wind up the company.[55]

---

50. See id. par. 13.182.
51. *Lavasseur v Mason & Barry* [1891] 2 QB 73.
52. *Crowshaw v Lindhurst Ship Co.* [1897] 2 Ch 154, at p. 160.
53. [1896] 1 IR 29.
54. Id. at p. 35.
55. E.g. *Re Bula Ltd* [1990] 1 IR 440; see post p. 160.

5

Receivers' Powers and Duties

Receivers appointed by mortgagees in accordance with the Conveyancing Act, 1881, are empowered to 'demand and recover all the income of the property ... by action, distress or otherwise. ...'[1] Where a receiver is appointed by a creditor under provisions in a debenture, almost always the instrument will set out what powers are being entrusted to him. Most debentures taken by banks and the other financial institutions contain substantially similar lists of powers. Usually, one power will be to manage the business of the company; absent such a stipulation, the receiver has no authority whatsoever to get involved in running the business. It would seem that a receiver who is the company's agent does not have power to act in a way that would be *ultra vires*, if the company had so acted, but there is no reported authority on the effect of s.8(1) of the Companies Act, 1963, in those circumstances. It might be helpful if the powers most frequently given to receivers were enumerated in the Companies Acts, somewhat like the model articles of association in Table A, thereby avoiding many minor drafting variations.

Where a receiver's authority to adopt a certain course of action is challenged, it is for him to demonstrate that he has been duly empowered to do so. It is not enough to point to a letter of appointment and invoke the maxim *omnia rite esse acta praesumuntur*. For instance, where a receiver sought recovery of goods from an execution creditor and his appointment was questioned, it was held that he had to prove that he was properly appointed. There was 'no presumption which will discharge him from proving that, if the appointment is made, the steps necessary to make a valid appointment have been taken.'[2]

If questions arise about the propriety of any proposed course of action, an application under s.316 of the 1963 Act may be made to the High Court for appropriate directions or for the court to make a declaration of the rights in question. This application can concern 'any particular matter arising in connection with the performance of his functions.' Applications under s.316 can be made by the receiver, by any officer or member of the company, by any creditor, by the liquidator or by any contributory and also by at least half of the company's full-time employees. If in the circumstances a receiver feels that the debenture does not give him sufficient power to cope with some pressing exigency, the creditor can always apply to the court for a court-appointed receiver clothed with the powers he needs.

1. S.24(3).   2. *Kasofsky v Kreegers* [1937] 4 All ER 374, at p. 378.

Receivers' duties and liabilities derive from three principal sources, viz. the terms of their appointment, the very nature of the position they hold and the Companies Acts. Where, as usually is the case, the receiver is designated the company's agent, in principal his duties are owed primarily to the company. However, under the terms of his appointment, generally it will be clear that he has obligations to the debenture-holder as well—principally, to get in the charged assets and realise them with a view to paying the secured creditor's debt.

In *Downside Nominees Ltd v First City Corp.,*[3] a case where a receiver was held to have been reckless in the manner in which he ran the company's business rather than selling it off reasonably promptly, the Privy Council endorsed the classic exposition of a receiver's duties:

> The primary duty of the receiver is to the debenture holders and not to the company. He is receiver and manager of the property of the company for the debenture holders, not manager of the company. The company is entitled to any surplus of assets remaining after the debenture debt has been discharged, and is entitled to proper accounts. But the whole purpose of the receiver and manager's appointment would obviously be stultified if the company could claim that a receiver and manager owes it any duty comparable to the duty owed to a company by its own directors or managers.
>
> In determining whether a receiver and manager for the debenture holders of a company has broken any duty owed by him to the company, regard must be had to the fact that he is a receiver and manager—that is to say, a receiver, with ancillary powers of management—for the debenture holders, and not simply a person appointed to manage the company's affairs for the benefit of the company. . . . The duties of a receiver and manager for debenture holders are widely different from those of a manager of the company. He is under no obligation to carry on the company's business at the expense of the debenture holders. Therefore he commits no breach of duty to the company by refusing to do so, even though his continuance of the business may be detrimental from the company's point of view. Again, his power of sale is, in effect, that of a mortgagee, and he therefore commits no breach of duty to the company by a *bona fide* sale, even though he might have obtained a higher price and even though, from the point of view of the company, as distinct from the debenture holders, the terms might be regarded as disadvantageous.
>
> In a word, in the absence of fraud or *mala fides* . . . the company cannot complain of any act or omission of the receiver and manager, provided that he does nothing that he is not empowered to do, and omits nothing that he is enjoined to do by the terms of his appointment. If the company conceives that it has any claim against the receiver and manager for breach of some duty owed by him to the company, the issue is not whether the

3.   [1993] 2 WLR 86.

> receiver and manager has done or omitted to do anything that it would be wrongful in a manager of a company to do or omit, but whether he has exceeded or abused or wrongfully omitted to use the special powers and discretions vested in him pursuant to the contract of loan constituted by the debenture for the special purpose of enabling the assets comprised in the debenture holders' security to be preserved and realised.'[4]

While often the secured creditor's interests will coincide with those of the unsecured creditors and also of the shareholders, for instance, getting the best possible price for the assets, occasions arise where those interests conflict. In such cases, usually the debenture or terms of appointment will make it clear that the secured creditor's interests will prevail.

Receivers must act strictly within the terms of their appointment and not exceed the powers which have been conferred on them. Throughout, they must act bona fide and serve the purposes for which they were appointed. They will not be held liable in damages for simple acts of negligence. But they must not act recklessly and unnecessarily injure the interests of other creditors, the company and persons who have guaranteed payment of the secured debt. Where money has been paid to a receiver and manager which amounts to a fraudulent preference, it has been held that he does not have to refund that money provided he acted in good faith.[5] Moreover, he cannot be compelled to disgorge moneys he paid into a receivership account before he received a notice of a claim against the company in respect of that money.[6]

TAKING POSSESSION OF CHARGED PROPERTY AND PROTECT IT

Receivers are almost always authorised to take possession of the charged property and to take appropriate measures to protect it. Such powers include the right to bring actions in order to acquire or protect those assets and, to that end, defend actions. Lawrence J observed that the power to take possession

> implies a power to do all things necessary or proper for the purposes of getting in the property and in particular a power for the purpose of collecting debts and other moneys . . . in the hands of third parties to take all proper legal proceedings. . . . It is true that in many debentures there is found express authority to bring proceedings in the company's name, but . . . there is no real necessity for the insertion of such a provision, which . . . is clearly implied. If such authority were implied, the power conferred on the receiver for the greater security of the debenture-holder of getting in the property . . . would be illusory.[7]

---

4. Id. at pp. 98-99, approving Jenkins CJ in *In re B. Johnson & Co. (Builders) Ltd* [1955] Ch 634, at pp. 662-3.
5. *Re Morant & Co.* [1924] 1 Ch 79.
6. *D. Owen & Co. v Cronk* [1895] 1 QB 265.
7. *M. Wheeler & Co. v Warren* [1928] Ch 840, at p. 845.

The court may very well require a receiver to give security for costs before he can proceed with a claim, which usually he would bring in the company's name.

Although taking out insurance is a particular method of protecting property, it would seem that the receiver's implied power to insure under this heading is somewhat restricted. Accordingly, debentures usually confer an extensive express power to insure. The same applies to carrying out repairs on the charged property.

In *Re Emmadart Ltd*,[8] where the company was insolvent, the receiver sought to have the company wound up in order to obtain the benefit of an exemption from rates which existed for companies that are being liquidated. It was held that, although the directors, as such, normally cannot present a petition to wind up the company,[9] in those circumstances a petition would be entertained at the receiver's initiative. Although the debenture there did not expressly refer to preserving and protecting the assets, that power was incidental to having possession of the assets. Since the company was unable to pay its debts and 'a winding up order will have the effect of protecting the assets under the control of the receiver from depletion by a levy of rates in respect of vacant property, ... the receiver has the requisite authority by virtue of his appointment to present a petition in the name of the company, and the court has jurisdiction to make a winding up order on that petition.'[10]

RECOVERING PROPERTY IMPROPERLY TRANSFERRED

Where any property of the company was disposed of in such a way as defrauded the company, its creditors or members, s.178 of the Companies Act, 1990, authorises a receiver to bring proceedings in order to recover that property or its worth. The transfer in question may be by way of conveyance, mortgage, security, loan or by any other means; that transfer may be indirect as well as direct. Where the court is satisfied that a transfer of this nature occurred and it is 'just and equitable' to do so, it may order recovery of the property from whoever presently has that property or the proceeds of its sale or the product of those proceeds. But regard must be had to the rights of any bona fide purchaser for value. A 'fraudulent preference' under the terms of s.286 of the 1963 Act is not an improper transfer of property for these present purposes. This power to recover property is the only power that company receivers possess under the companies legislation.

COMPROMISE CLAIMS

Often when a receivership commences there will be litigation outstanding involving the company, and further litigation may very well arise during the course of the receivership. Accordingly, it is usually stipulated that the receiver shall have the power to make any arrangement with parties in dispute with the

8.   [1979] Ch 540.
9.   *Re Galway & Salthill Tramway Co.* [1918] 1 IR 62.
10. [1979] Ch at p. 547.

company and to compromise claims that concern the company. In *Robinson Printing Co. v Chic Ltd*[11] where the receiver was the debenture-holders' agent, it was held that his express authority to make arrangements in the debenture-holders' interests included a power to pledge the company's assets in priority to their charge, if he thought doing so would facilitate the company continuing doing business.

MANAGING THE BUSINESS

Company receivers appointed in pursuance of a floating charge are usually expressly authorised to carry on the business pending realisation of the assets; these receivers are referred to as receivers and managers. Whether they actually exercise these powers depends on commercial considerations. Among the matters which would suggest that the receiver should trade on, at least for a short term, is to enable work in progress to be completed; to realise a higher price; to be in a better position to evaluate the company's business before deciding to trade on a more prolonged basis. Continued trading may also prevent set-offs arising against book debts. A receiver's primary function is not to salvage all or part of the business. However, if he concludes that the company could trade out of insolvency, he may decide to take that course, in the expectation that the company can then repay the entire debt or come to some settlement with the secured creditor. Even if the company's prospects are not that bright, the receiver may conclude that a better price can be obtained if the company's business is sold off as a going concern rather than in a break up.

Making the choice   Where powers of management are given, then, unless the debenture or the terms of appointment require otherwise, it is the receiver's responsibility to decide if the business should be carried on for some while. If he is instructed to do that by the debenture-holders, they then become his principals and are responsible for all his actions when running the business. Ordinarily, neither the debenture-holders' consent nor the company's consent is required before the receiver may continue trading. It may very well be in the general interests of the company's employees or in the wider public interest that the receiver continues trading but those considerations are not legally any of his concern. On the other hand, he has a statutory obligation to the preferred creditors—the Revenue and employees—to ensure that their priority position is not undermined.[12] Accordingly, if there exists a substantial fund of money or quantity of readily realisable assets, he should first be confident that those are not lost in the course of trading. The conventional wisdom, and hence the critique of many receivers, is when in doubt they proceed forthwith to sell off the assets rather than engaging in speculative trading.

Formerly, the view was that, no matter how rosy the company's future, a receiver was never obliged to continue trading. In a leading case in 1955 the

11. [1905] 2 Ch 123.
12. Companies Act 1963, s.98; see post pp. 364-365.

Master of the Rolls rejected the proposition that a receiver 'owes some duty to the company to carry on the business of the company and to preserve the goodwill.'[13] In *Kernohan Estates Ltd v Boyd*[14] the defendant, who was the receiver and manager of a company, failed in his attempts to sell the undertaking as a going concern. He then decided that, rather than continue running the business, the most economical thing was to close it down and dismiss all but the maintenance staff. It was contended that he had no right to do this and that, as manager, he had an obligation to preserve the business' goodwill. Lowry J refused to enjoin the shutdown on the grounds that, if the defendant was a mere receiver, then provided that he acted in good faith he would be entitled to close the business, because the power of sale over all or any of the 'assets of the company endows a receiver and manager with the *prima facie* ability to destroy the goodwill in whole or in part.'[15] Lowry J added that 'the appointment of a receiver to be a manager as well gives him additional powers and is very often considered to be beneficial to the debenture-holder. It would be curious if the widening of his powers were to place the receiver or his debenture-holder in greater difficulty in realising the security.'[16]

Since then, however, it has been established that receivers owe some duty of care to the company and to subordinate secured creditors, especially when they are disposing of assets, and in 1990 that duty was incorporated into s.316A of the Companies Act, 1963.[17] It is very likely that receivers' general duty of care will be extended by the courts to decisions about continuing the business; that if in all the circumstances it was abundantly clear that trading on would enhance the value of the company, the receiver should continue to trade. Before any duty of this nature could arise, the company should have sufficient funds to finance the business, the business could not be sold as a going concern if the company ceased trading, there is a real prospect of selling the company as a going concern in the near future and ceasing trading would result in realising the assets for their break up value.

Circumstances can just as easily arise where it is foolhardy for a receiver to continue trading. An excellent example is *R.A. Price Securities Ltd v Henderson*,[18] where a creditor, who was owed $NZ 210,000, appointed a receiver and manager over a small petrol filling station. The receiver decided to continue running the business, during which time he incurred debts of $NZ 68,000, together with legal costs of $NZ 8,000. Then the landlord took possession of the premises, rendering further trading impossible. By this stage the company was insolvent and the receiver was not able to recover any significant part of the secured debt. It was held that he had acted negligently; that he was unduly preoccupied with preserving the goodwill and paid insufficient heed to his main task, being to recover the secured sum.

---

13. *Re B. Johnson & Co. (Builders) Ltd* [1955] 1 Ch 634, at p. 645.
14. [1967] NI 27.
15. Id at p. 29   16. Ibid.
17. Inserted by 1990 Act s.172.   18. [1989] 2 NZLR 257.

Manager's powers   The management powers clause frequently incorporates power to do various other things incidental to management, like to perform existing contracts and to enter into fresh contracts, to employ and to dismiss workers, to delegate, to borrow etc.; although it is not essential that these powers be given expressly. A receiver-manager has implied power to adopt any agreements entered into by the company prior to the appointment.

Although there is no authority squarely on the point, it would seem that the power to borrow for running the business is implicit in the management powers; such a power is often mentioned in the management powers clause. Indeed, the power to borrow for carrying on the business and for other purposes is frequently the subject of an entirely separate clause. Where there is an implied or express power to borrow, a power to charge the company's assets to secure the borrowing will also exist.

Treatment of business contracts   Assuming the receiver decides to carry on the business for some time, he must then decide what to do about the many contracts the company has made and contracts which must be entered into in the course of the business. This question has been dealt with in the outline above when considering the impact of receiverships generally on contracts.[19] Regarding contracts entered into after the receivership commenced, s.316(2) of the Companies Act, 1963, makes the receiver personally liable on them, except where liability is excluded by the very terms of the contract. Accordingly, a receiver exposes himself to potentially heavy liabilities if he decides to trade on, which is one reason why many do not follow that course of conduct. However, the receiver is entitled to be indemnified out of the company's assets in respect of that liability,[20] and often there will be sufficient assets to meet that indemnity, which must be satisfied before any other debts can be paid out of the assets. Also, the receiver may have obtained the added protection of an indemnity from the debenture-holder.

With regard to contracts already made by the company before the receivership commenced, often the receiver has a choice. Because those contracts are assets of the company, when the floating charge crystallised the benefit of those contracts became assigned to the debenture-holder. The receiver therefore may decide to enforce them and ordinarily it is no defence for the other contracting party that the company is now in receivership. By enforcing pre-receivership contracts, the receiver does not make himself personally liable on them. For instance, if a receiver causes the company to supply goods under a contract for sale, made before he was appointed, he does not become personally liable if the goods transpired to be unmerchantable or unfit for their purpose, or did not comply with any of the other terms implied under the Sale of Goods Acts.

A receiver will not be permitted to enforce a contract concluded with the company if at the same time he is not prepared to cause the company to honour its side of the bargain. He cannot obtain the benefit of the contract while at the

19.   Supra pp. 40-42.
20.   Companies Act 1963, s.316(2).

same time denying the other party any rights which he may have under the contract. For instance, if the company agreed to buy land but the conveyance has not yet been executed, the receiver will not be allowed to claim specific performance or damages for breach of the contract unless he causes the company to tender the outstanding price.

Unlike in liquidations and in companies under the protection of the court,[21] there is no statutory mechanism whereby a receiver can disclaim or repudiate onerous contracts. By onerous contracts here is meant contractual obligations which would cost the company more to perform than the amount of damages it would have to pay for the breach of the contracts. However, because pre-receivership contracts do not bind receivers, they can simply prevent the company from performing its contractual obligations and thereby in effect disclaim the contract. When the company does not fulfil these obligations, the other party has a right of action against it for damages. But that claim ranks after the debenture, so that generally the receiver is not concerned with the claim. In sum, therefore, unless the company stands to make a profit from the contract, the receiver will not cause the company to perform its side of the bargain. For instance, in *Macleod v Alexander Sutherland Ltd*,[22] the company sold land and undertook in the contract to perform specified building and construction work on it. That work was never carried out and the company was placed in receivership. It was held that the company, through the receiver, could not be compelled to perform that work. The court's reasoning was that, '[s]ince ex hypothesi the responsibility for whatever is done [under] the contract must in fact be done by the receiver, it [is] out of the question to pronounce a decree ostensibly against the company, which would in effect result in the receiver either incurring personal liability or in his bearing the responsibility for contempt of court.'[23]

A receiver who is the company's agent cannot, for that very reason, be held liable to the other contracting party for inducing breach of contract in these circumstances.[24] But a receiver who is the debenture-holder's agent may very well incur liability under that head, although such interference may possibly be protected by the defence of justification.

An exception to the principle which permits non-performance is where the other party would be entitled to an order of specific performance of the contract, had the company not gone into receivership. The advent of the receiver will not be permitted to alter that position, subject to the discretion of the court which obtains in all applications for equitable relief. Thus, where the company agreed to sell land, the fact that a debenture which encompasses that land has crystallised does not provide a defence to an action for specific performance. By virtue of that crystallisation, the contract of sale was assigned in equity to

---

21. See post pp. 100-101 and pp. 224-229..
22. (1977) SLT (notes) 44, considered in detail in *Freevale Ltd v Metrostore Holdings Ltd* [1984] 2 WLR 496.
23. Ibid.
24. *Lathia v Secretary of State for Social Services* [1974] QB 468; see further post p. 69.

the debenture-holder, but subject to the prior equitable interest of the purchaser. In *Freevale Ltd v Metrostore Holdings Ltd*,[25] the company agreed to sell land but shortly afterwards a receiver was appointed over all its assets. The purchaser was given an order of specific performance against the company, which the receiver had to comply with. Unlike in the *Macleod* case, there could be no question of the receiver having to incur any personal liability in order to comply with the court's directions.

When equitable relief is being sought against a company which is in receivership, the first question is whether the contract is one which can be the subject of an order for specific performance. It is only where the subject matter of a contract for sale is unique that the contract will be specifically enforced, for instance, contracts to sell land, intellectual property or rights in shares which give a controlling interest in a company. That is not the end of the matter, however. The court must then ask whether the receivership has introduced some novel element which affects its equitable jurisdiction. That the company and thereby its creditors generally will suffer loss in consequence of such an order is not relevant. But the court will not order the receiver to lay out funds which results in the debenture-holders being deprived of their priority. Nor will the court order the receiver to incur a personal liability which it is reasonable for him to want to avoid.

Employment contracts Employment contracts will not be specifically enforced, although in recent years in exceptional cases employers have been enjoined from dismissing their employees in breach of contract.[26] Accordingly, receivers are not bound by pre-receivership employment contracts, i.e. the contracts under which the company's workforce are employed at the time a receiver was appointed. That appointment ordinarily does not constitute a repudiation by the company of employment contracts,[27] thereby in effect bringing them to an end, subject to the employees' right to damages for being dismissed without obtaining the prescribed notices of dismissal. Depending on the circumstances of the case, the appointment of a receiver and manager may operate as a dismissal of a managing director who, under his contract, exercises wide powers of management. The appointment of a receiver and manager by the court on the other hand, operates to discharge all the employment contracts.

Where an employee is dismissed, either on account of the receiver's appointment or by the action of the receiver, he may possibly have a good claim under the Unfair Dismissal Act, 1977, notably for 'unfair redundancy'. Any unpaid wages up to £2,500, holiday pay, sick pay, pension contributions or payments, compensation for accidents, compensation for unfair dismissal and redundancy payments due to the employee from the company are preferential debts, for which he can hold the receiver responsible. These preferential debts and also

25. [1984] Ch 199.
26. See generally, M. Forde, *Employment Law* (1992), pp. 173-174.
27. See post pp. 383-384.

the Transfer of Undertakings Directive and the Insolvency Fund are considered in some detail later in this book.

If, instead of dismissing an employee, the receiver decides to retain his services, the receiver is not personally responsible for the remuneration and for other incidents of the employment relationship. It would be otherwise if the employee was discharged and was then hired by the receiver under a new contract. In *Nicoll v Cutts*,[28] the managing director of a company, of which he was a minority shareholder as well, sued a receiver, who had been appointed over the company's assets, for remuneration. The receiver was appointed in March and dismissed the plaintiff in May, just before selling the company as a going concern. Because the receiver never entered into an employment contract with the plaintiff, he was not liable for the plaintiff's unpaid remuneration. It was also held that the plaintiff's unpaid salary for those three months could not be regarded as costs and expense of the receivership.

Leases   In principle, the appointment of a receiver over a company's assets does not affect the rights and obligations of the lessor; it does not prevent the lessor from suing for unpaid rent or for breach of one of the other covenants, or from instituting ejectment proceedings. Similarly, the company, through the receiver, retains its rights under the lease, including the statutory right to the renewal of a business lease. It is very common, however, for leases to stipulate that they may be forfeited on a receiver being appointed over the property. However, the receiver may cause the company to apply for relief from forfeiture on equitable grounds[29] and at the same time may apply to have the lease assigned to a suitable purchaser.

A receiver is not liable to the lessor of land or of goods for rent falling due before his appointment. Nor is he liable for rent accruing after that time, not even if he entered the premises and made some use of the land or goods.[30] Thus, in *Ratford v Northavon D.C.*,[31] a rating case, where a receiver and manager occupied property the company had leased, in order to carry on the business, it was held that the company remained the true occupier because the receiver entered the property as its agent. Accordingly, the receiver could not be held liable for rates. Before a receiver can be held liable for rent or rates it must be shown that he no longer is in possession as the company's agent; the very nature or quality of his possession must have changed. That can be the case where, under the debenture, he is not the company's agent or where he makes it clear to the landlord that he is in occupation in his own right. But merely managing the company's assets, including either premises or goods held on lease, and paying the outgoings is quite consistent with the company remaining in legal possession.

A remedy that landlords could avail of is to distrain for unpaid rent, i.e. seize

28.   [1985] BCLC 322.
29.   *Gough's Garages Ltd v Pugsley* [1930] 1 KB 615.
30.   *Hand v Blow* [1901] 2 Ch 721.
31.   [1987] QB 357.

goods on the premises whether or not they belong to the tenant. Even though the floating charge has crystallised, the landlord may still distrain for unpaid rent. So it was held by the High Court of Australia in *Purcell v Public Curator*.[32] According to Higgins J there, the landlord's entitlement to distrain is a common law right, and the landlord 'stands, . . . aloof from the other creditors, in a position similar to that of a mortgagee who holds specific security.'[33] Landlords need not obtain the court's permission to levy distress, except where the receiver is court-appointed. The distraint must not be excessive and only a reasonable quantity of goods may be taken. There is a possibility that distress would be held to be unconstitutional.

Of course, if outstanding rent has not been paid, the lessor can resort to the usual procedures for termination of the lease and regaining possession. Accordingly, the receiver may be forced to decide whether it is in the debenture-holder's interests to pay over the sum demanded or be dispossessed.

'HIVE DOWN'

If all or some substantial part of the business which is in receivership appears to be viable, especially if that business is no longer encumbered by the company's debts, the receiver will give serious consideration to what has been termed a 'hive down'. By this is meant that all or part of the business assets are transferred to a 'clean' new company which is controlled by the receiver. Eventually, the shares in that new company will be sold in the expectation that a far better price would be obtained than in a more straightforward sale of the company's assets. The purchasers of those shares may be complete third parties or may be the company's former executives and employees under a management buy out.

The many attractions of a hive down include the following. Where the receiver wants to continue trading, if he transfers the asset into a new company which he controls and the actual trading is done by that company, he cannot then be held personally liable on contracts entered into in the course of the business. For those contracts are binding on the hived down company and not on the receiver. All the profitable assets of the debtor company along with the debtor's tax losses can be transferred into the new company, thereby rendering that company a very attractive purchase. Moreover, that company will not have any debts of its own and will not have taken over the debtor company's debts and liabilities. Suppliers of gas, electricity and telephone services are entitled to cut off supplies to the debtor or to the receiver unless all arrears due to them have been paid.[34] Since, however, the new company does not owe any money to those suppliers, they must treat its application for supplies in the same way as that of any other new applicant.[35] They cannot penalise the new company

---

32. 31 CLR 220 (1922).   33. Id. at p. 230.
34. Cf. *W. & L. Crowe Ltd v Electricity Supply Board* (Costello J, 9 May 1984).
35. Ibid.

merely because the transferor of its assets was indebted to them. Even if the debtor company is forced into liquidation, the hived down company can continue trading.

The principal reported example of a hive down and of the limits to which this technique can be used is *Airline Airspares Ltd v Handley Page Ltd*.[36] An aircraft manufacturing company was put into receivership and its only really valuable asset was a design for one type of aircraft. The receiver decided to hive off that design into a clean subsidiary. However, the company had a contract with the plaintiff, whereby the plaintiff was given the exclusive right to sell all aircraft of that design or was to be paid a commission for every such aircraft which the company sold. If the design was sold off to the subsidiary, these rights could no longer be exercised by the plaintiff. It therefore sought an injunction against the company and the receiver, restraining the proposed hive off. On the grounds that ordinarily a receiver cannot be forced to cause the company to perform a pre-receivership contract, it was held that the receiver could not be prevented from carrying out his proposals here.

The extent to which receivers in this way can in effect disregard contracts binding the company was stated as follows:

> the receiver, within limit[s] . . . is in a better position than the company, qua current contracts. . . . [O]therwise almost any unsecured creditor would be able to improve his position and prevent the receiver from carrying out, or at any rate carrying out as sensibly and as equitably as possible, the purpose for which he was appointed. . . .
>
> It would not be equitable for the receiver to prefer [one contractor] to other unsecured creditors, and it is in the best interests of all such creditors that he should be able to sell that part of [the company's] business which will constitute a viable unit in the way which will secure the highest price. If, in so doing, he does decline to take over [one] contract, he may, of course, render the [company] liable in damages and may also, to some extent, at any rate, damage their reputation as a trustworthy company which can be expected to honour its contracts. This, however, . . . he is entitled to do, so long as the realisation of the net assets of the company . . . to the best advantage is not impaired.[37]

As has been explained above, performance may be ordered of pre-receivership contracts which ordinarily can be the subject of an order for specific performance. In the *Airlines Airspares Ltd* case, it was accepted by the parties that the contract there did not fall into this category. Additionally, a receiver may be prevented from in effect repudiating contracts where the breach of contract would seriously damage the company's goodwill, although the exact scope of this principle is unclear. In a case decided in 1912, concerning a receiver appointed by the court on the application of debenture holders, it was said that

36. [1970] 1 Ch 193.
37. Id. at pp. 199 and 198.

'[t]he goodwill of the company is . . . part of that which is charged to them, and the receiver and manager has . . . to do his best to preserve the whole of the property that is put in his care. It is not his duty to do what would ultimately sacrifice the value of the undertaking and to consider it a sufficient justification that by so doing he would obtain somewhat more money from the sale of the specific assets of the company.'[38] However, this may be overstating the obligations of a receiver directly appointed by debenture-holders. In the *Airlines Airspares Ltd* case, it was said that a receiver should not abandon a contract 'where declining to adopt the contract of the company would so seriously impair the goodwill of the company that realisation [of its assets] would be adversely affected. . . .'[39] It depends on the facts of each case whether such a state of affairs exists. It was held that these circumstances did not obtain in that case because the only goodwill of real value in the company was the very aircraft design which it was proposed to transfer to the company's subsidiary. It has been held in Australia[40] that a receiver will not be permitted to in effect avoid a pre-receivership contract where damages may be an inadequate remedy; in those circumstances, the court may grant the other party an order of specific performance or injunctive relief.

Where the entire business is hived down, the company's employees are thereby treated as having been dismissed.[41] Where the hive down is partial, in the sense that only some of the business is transferred to a company, it depends on all the circumstances whether particular employees' contracts have been repudiated.[42] However, under the European Communities (Safeguarding of Employees Rights on Transfer of Undertakings) Regulations, 1980, the transferor company's rights and obligations regarding employees may be transferred to the hived down company.[43]

SELLING THE CHARGED PROPERTY

The essential object of a receivership is to realise the charged property so that the debenture-holder can be paid off; the relevant instrument almost invariably will contain a power to sell or to concur in a sale.

Duty of good faith Receivers' duties generally are dealt with separately below, but it is convenient to consider here the duties that arise in connection with the power of sale. It has long been accepted that a mortgagee is not the trustee of the power of sale for the mortgagor.[44] Nonetheless, that power must be exercised in good faith. Ordinarily, the receiver or his agent should never

38. *Re Newdigate Colliery Ltd* [1912] 1 Ch 468, at p. 475.
39. [1970] 1 Ch at p. 190.
40. *Re Diesels & Components Pty. Ltd* (1985) 9 ACLR 825.
41. *Pambankien v Brentford Nylons Ltd* [1988] ICR 665.
42. Ibid.
43. See post pp. 385-387.
44. See generally, E. Tayler ed., Fisher & Lightwood's *Law of Mortgage* (10th ed., 1988) pp. 388 et seq.

purchase any of the company's assets, regardless of whether a fair price would be paid because the potential conflict of interest provides very strong incentives for unfair advantage taking.[45]

There is no blanket prohibition against a sale to a company in which the receiver has some interest. It was said in *Tse Kwong Lam v Wong Chit Sen* that

> there is no hard and fast rule that a mortgagee may not sell to a company in which he is interested. [Nevertheless, t]he mortgagee and the company seeking to uphold the transaction must show that the sale was in good faith and that the mortgagee took reasonable precautions to obtain the best price reasonably obtainable at the time. . . . [For instance, the mortgagee] ought to show that he protected the interests of the borrower by taking expert advice as to the method of the sale, as to the steps which ought reasonably be taken to make the sale a success and as to the amount of the reserve.[46]

In that case, when the company defaulted, the mortgagee arranged to sell the security, which was valuable leasehold property. A company in which the mortgagee had extensive interests bought the property at a public auction but at which there were no other bidders. The mortgagee was a successful property speculator and the purchasing company was owned entirely by his family, who were its only directors. When arranging for the sale, the mortgagee never consulted estate agents about the mode of the sale or the reserve price, and the auction was not widely publicised. In those circumstances, it was held that the mortgagee had acted improperly. The fact that the sale is by way of public auction does not establish the validity of the transaction.

Duty of care   Good faith and potential conflict of interests aside, the receiver must exercise due care when selling the charged property, i.e. must take such steps as are necessary to obtain the best price. Whether this duty arose in tort or was entirely an equitable obligation is debateable; in 1993 the Privy Council concluded that the main duties of receivers are founded in equity rather than arising from the law of negligence.[47] With regard to security, however, a resolution of this issue of principle is not so fundamental because, in 1990, the receiver's duty of care when selling was given statutory formulation. Section 316A(i) of the 1963 Act[48] provides that

> A receiver, in selling property of a company, shall exercise all reasonable care to obtain the best price reasonably obtainable for the property as at the time of sale.

There have been no cases yet decided on this section and it remains to be seen

---

45. Cf. *Holder v Holder* [1968] Ch 353.
46. [1983] 1 WLR 1349, at p. 1355 and p. 1357.
47. *Downside Nominees Ltd v First City Corp. Ltd* [1993] 2 WLR 86.
48. Inserted by 1990 Act s.172.

whether it imposes a standard of care that is more demanding than that reflected in the pre-1990 case law and, also, to whom is their statutory duty owed.

Even before s.316A(i) was enacted, it was acknowledged that equity imposed a duty of care on receivers. According to Ó Dálaigh CJ in *Holohan v Friends Provident & Century Life Office*,

> it is the duty of a mortgagee when realising the mortgaged property by sale to behave in conducting such realisation as a reasonable man would behave in the realisation of his own property, so that the mortgagor may receive credit for the full value of the property sold. . . . The reasonable man sets himself a higher standard than to act in good faith. There is no room for doubting the bona fides of the reasonable man. He will, while rightly looking to his own interest, also bear in mind the interest of the mortgagor. Whether or not the property to be sold is value for the amount of the mortgagee's debt, the mortgagor has a very real interest in the best price being obtained. If there should be a surplus it is for his benefit; equally he benefits by the best price being obtained: his indebtedness is thereby reduced as much as possible. Mortgagor and mortgagee are not in like case in this respect. A mortgagee who is not fully paid off because the best price is not obtained still has a right to sue the mortgagor for the balance, while the mortgagor must abide the disadvantage of a poor price being realised. Moreover, there is the interest of second and other mortgagees to be safeguarded.[49]

Formerly, the receiver's duty of care could be excluded by the parties to the security agreement.[50] It remains to be seen whether the new statutory duty under s.316A(i) is one which can be waived.

Standard of care It will depend on the circumstances of each case whether the receiver in fact exercised due care. Thus in *W.P. McCarter & Co. v Roughan*[51] where the receiver agreed to sell a small shirt factory in Buncrana, he did not seek any estate agent's valuation before agreeing to sell, and the property was not advertised but instead it was sold to the plaintiff on the introduction of the Industrial Development Authority, whose prime concern is ensuring continuance of employment in the area. Subsequent estimates of the property's value indicated that the agreed price was far too low. McWilliam J concluded that in the circumstances the receiver had acted unreasonably. However, because the company was so tardy in pursuing its claim, McWilliam J declined to set the agreement aside and left the company to its remedy in damages. A similar instance is *American Express International Ltd v Hurley*,[52] where a receiver was appointed over the assets of a company which had been

---

49. [1966] IR 1, at pp. 20-21; see too, *Cuckmere Brick Co. v Mutual Finance Ltd* [1971] 1 Ch 949 and the *Downview Nominees* case, supra n. 47.
50. *Bishop v Bonham* [1988] BCLC 656.
51. McWilliam J, 11 February 1985.
52. [1986] BCLC 52.

engaged in supplying sound and lighting equipment to pop concerts. When the floating charge was granted, its assets were valued at £193,000. Three years later, a receiver was appointed and he continued the business for some while until the company was liquidated. He then sold the equipment for £34,500. He was held to have been negligent because he failed to get expert advice about the sale or to advertise the equipment in specialist publications.[53]

It has been observed on many occasions that the mortgagee has a completely free hand in choosing the actual time of the sale: that '[i]t matters not that the moment may be unpropitious and that by waiting a higher price could be obtained. He has the right to realise his security by turning it into money when he likes.'[54] Section 316A(i) of the 1963 Act would seem to endorse this view; or at least the statutory duty of care does not extend to choosing the time to sell the property. But the view that the common law duty of care is never concerned with the time of sale was rejected by the Court of Appeal in *Standard Chartered Bank v Walker*[55] and by Carroll J in *McGowan v Gannon*.[56] It has been said that, while there are *dicta* 'to the effect that the mortgagee can choose his own time for the sale, . . . [this does not] mean that he can sell at the worst possible time. It is at least arguable that, in choosing the time, he must exercise a reasonable degree of care.'[57] The position as stated in *Re Charnley Davies Ltd (No. 2)*[58] is that, 'it is not an absolute duty to obtain the best price that circumstances permit, but only to take reasonable care to do so; and . . . that means the best price that circumstances as he reasonably perceives them to be permit'[59] A receiver-manager who cannot dispose of the assets may in the circumstances be entitled to shut down the entire business. Several of the cases where receivers were held liable for recklessly carrying on the company's business and incurring large losses[60] are the other side of the coin of not selling off the assets in time.

Duty to whom   As for who is owed the receiver's duty of care, the 1993 Privy Council decision[61] rejecting a duty arising in the law of tort puts a question mark over the cases decided in recent years where it was accepted that receivers, like almost all other professionals, are subject to the law of negligence. Whether that analysis would be followed entirely in Ireland is debatable, especially since receivers are now deemed to be 'officers' of the company for certain purposes and, more importantly, when s.316(A)(i) of the 1963 Act now imposes a statutory duty of care. The position in the case law, prior to the 1993 decision, can be summarised as follows.

Where he is the company's agent, that duty is owed to the company. There

53.   See too, *Re Charnley Davies Ltd (No. 2)* [1990] BCLC 760.
54.   *Cuckmere Brick Co. v Mutual Finance Ltd* [1971] 1 Ch at p. 965.
55.   [1982] 1 WLR 410.
56.   [1983] ILRM 516.   57.   Supra n.17, at p. 415.
58.   [1990] BCLC 760.   59.   Id. at p. 775.
60.   E.g. *R.A. Price Securities Ltd v Henderson* [1989] 2 NZLR 257.
61.   *Downview Nominees Ltd v First City Corp. Ltd* [1993] 2 WLR 86.

is no authority squarely on whether a duty is owed to the debenture-holder when the receiver is acting as the company's agent. However, in *American Express Banking Corp. v Hurley*,[62] once the company went into liquidation, the deemed agency for the company ceased and the receiver became the bank's agent. Because he had been negligent in selling off the company's assets, his principal, the bank, was held liable. But the bank, in turn, was held to be entitled to reimbursal from the receiver of the damages, on foot of the normal indemnity implied into a contract of agency. Accordingly, unless the terms of his appointment provide otherwise, for all practical purposes the receiver owes a duty of care to the secured creditor when he is acting as its agent.

It was well established that the receiver also owes a duty of care to whoever guaranteed the secured loan. According to Lord Denning MR in *Standard Chartered Bank v Walker*:

> The receiver is the agent of the company [and] owes [it] a duty to use reasonable care to obtain the best possible price which the circumstances of the case permit. . . . [H]e also owes a duty [of care] to the guarantor because the guarantor is liable only to the same extent as the company. The more the overdraft is reduced the better for the guarantor . . . [The guarantor] is well within the test of 'proximity'.[63]

These views were endorsed in *McGowan v Gannon*.[64] However, Carroll J there went on to hold that, although the receiver is obliged to inform the company, its principal, about the details of the proposed sale, there is no corresponding obligation to tell the guarantor:

> the guarantor is [not] entitled to any information regarding the sale of the company's assets. . . . [A] receiver is [not] a trustee for a guarantor. There is no contractual relationship between a guarantor and a receiver. Therefore . . . there is no basis on which a guarantor can require the information. . . . [C]reditors . . . are in no better position than a guarantor and are not entitled to the information either.[65]

It has been held in England, where a restrictive stance has been taken to the general question of liability for pure financial loss,[66] that a mortgagee selling the charged property owes no duty of care to other persons holding a beneficial interest in that property.[67] In that case, the property being sold belonged to a husband, whose wife had a beneficial interest in it. By contrast, in New Zealand it has been held that, in an appropriate case, there can be a duty of care to second mortgagees of the charged property. This was because both second mortgagees and the debenture-holder 'both have direct interests in the property subject to the prior charge and the proximity between receiver and manager on the one hand and mortgagor or second mortgagee on the other could scarcely be

62. [1986] BCLC 52.   63. [1982] 1 WLR at pp. 1415-1416.
64. [1983] ILRM 516.   65. Id. at p. 518.
66. *Murphy v Brentwood D.C.* [1991] 1 AC 398.
67. *Parker-Tweedale v Dunbar Bank* (C App 14 December 1989).

closer.'[68] It is an open question whether the reasoning adopted in that case would be applied by the Irish courts to a receiver's sale where the requisite degree of 'proximity' existed.

Conveyancing points Where the debenture creates a legal mortgage, the debenture-holder is capable of conveying the legal estate. But since a floating charge creates merely an equitable interest in the property, a receiver appointed on the crystallisation of such a charge will usually be unable to convey a legal estate in the property without the company's consent, which is evidenced by affixing its seal. Accordingly, the relevant instrument usually grants the receiver a power of attorney to convey the legal estate in the company's name. In *Industrial Development Authority v Moran*,[69] a company issued a debenture to the bank creating a fixed charge on some lands and also a floating charge, and authorised the appointment of a receiver-manager in the event of default. Eventually the company was placed in receivership and it sought to convey part of the charged lands to the purchaser. Although it was provided in the company's articles of association that the company's seal can only be used by the authority of the directors, the seal was affixed to the conveyance on the directions of the receiver and without the directors' approval. The Supreme Court held that, in the light of the provision in the company's articles, the seal had been irregularly affixed and to that extent the conveyance was ineffective. This was because '[w]hen a receiver is appointed over the assets of a company, the articles of association continue in force and bind him. A receiver, as receiver, has no authority to use the seal of the company.'[70]

However, one of the conditions on the debenture there was that the receiver was to be the company's attorney with authority to execute, seal and deliver any instrument.[71] The Supreme Court rejected the contention that a company has no power to act by attorney to execute deeds within the State. And since the company's articles gave the directors broad management powers, similar to those arising from article 80 of Table A, the company's directors had authority to grant a receiver the power by attorney to execute and seal deeds for the company. Accordingly, it was not necessary to have the shareholders' approval before that power could be given. By virtue of s.46 of the Conveyancing Act, 1881, a person with a power of attorney is entitled to execute any instrument with his own name, signature and seal whenever the donor of the power is required to use a seal. In the *I.D.A.* case, the conveyance's testimonium stated that the deed is 'signed, sealed and delivered' by the receiver in the presence of his solicitor, across from which was placed the company's seal and the receiver's signature. It was held by the Supreme Court that, by the receiver executing the deed in this way, it was effectual to transfer the land to the purchasers.

68. *First City Corp. v Downside Nominees Ltd* [1990] 3 NZLR 265, at p. 277.
69. [1978] IR 159.   70. Id. at p. 163.
71. Cf. 1963 Act s.40, *Sowman v David Samuel Trust Ltd* [1978] 1 WLR 22, and *Phoenix Properties Ltd v Wimpole St. Nominees Ltd* (C App 1 December 1989).

Kenny J in the *I.D.A.* case drew attention to a clause that is often contained in debentures, according to which the receiver is empowered 'to carry any such sale into effect by deed in the name and on behalf of the company.' According to Kenny J,

> When a receiver is selling under such a clause, the more usual and better practice is for him to execute the deed of transfer by writing the name of the company and underneath this to write words that indicate that the name of the company has been written by the receiver as attorney of the company under the power of attorney given by the debenture. In addition, he should execute the deed in his own name. In that way he has the best of both worlds. The writing of the name of the company by the authority of the company given when it executed the debenture brings the case within the words of the debenture itself, and execution by the attorney personally gives the advantage of s.46 of the Conveyancing Act, 1881.[72]

DISTRIBUTION

Almost invariably the debenture will stipulate that the receiver must pay any profits from the business and the proceeds of sale of the company's assets to the debenture-holder but, once that full indebtedness is paid off, the residue must be paid over to the company. Section 98 of the 1963 Act imposes a statutory duty of distribution to the company's preferential creditors (mostly taxes and employees' remuneration).[73] This duty applies where the company is not being wound up and where the receiver was appointed under a floating charge over all or part of the company's property. In those circumstances, the various

> preferential payments [must] be paid in priority to all other debts, . . . out of any assets coming into the hands of the receiver . . . in priority to any claim for principal or interest in respect of the debentures.[74]

A preferential creditor who is not paid in accordance with this provision is entitled to damages against the receiver for the loss thereby suffered.[75]

The purpose of s.98 has been described as to 'give priority to debts and other liabilities which would have been preferential in a winding up by reference to the period ending on the appointment of a receiver, or the taking of possession by the debenture holder, notwithstanding that[, as a result, those] cease to be assets of the company capable of being dealt with by the company for the purposes of its business.'[76] But if a liquidator has been appointed before a receiver arrives on the scene, s.98 then has no application; it applies only where the company 'is not at the time in the course of being wound up'.[77]

---

72. [1978] IR at p. 166.
73. See post pp. 364-365.
74. S.98(1).
75. *Inland Revenue Cmrs. v Goldblatt* [1972] Ch. 498.
76. *Re Christonette International Ltd* [1982] 1 WLR 1245, at p. 1250.
77. Id. at p. 1252.

ACCOUNTING

Usually the debenture will state that the receiver shall provide full accounts to the debenture-holder at periodic intervals. But a receiver who is designated an agent of the company is obliged, by virtue of that agency, also to account to the company. This duty is fortified where the terms of the appointment require the receiver to pay over to the company any surplus on a sale of assets and mere adherence to the statutory provisions on accounting is not sufficient compliance. In *Smiths Ltd v Middleton's*[78] it was held that this duty to account arises once the receivership has come to an end.

Depending on the circumstances, there may even be a duty to provide accounts to the company during the currency of the receivership. The scope of this qualified duty was spelt out by Hoffman J in *Gomba Holdings Ltd v Homan*[79] as follows:

> any right which the company may have to be supplied with information must be qualified by the receiver's primary duty to the debenture-holder. If the receiver considers that disclosure of the information would be contrary to the interests of the debenture-holder in realising the security, . . . he must be entitled to withhold it and probably owes a duty to the debenture-holder to do so. The company may be able to challenge the receiver's decision on the grounds of bad faith or possibly that it was a decision which no reasonable receiver could have made, but otherwise . . . . the receiver is the best judge of the commercial consequences of disclosing information about his activities. . . .
>
> During the receivership, the company's right to information beyond the statutory accounts must . . . depend upon demonstrating a 'need to know' for the purposes of enabling the board to exercise its residual rights or perform its duties.[80]

TAXATION

Unlike in liquidations, the beginning of a receivership does not bring an end to or otherwise affect the then accounting period. Therefore, any capital gain made on the disposal of assets before the end of the accounting period can be set-off against losses incurred in that period. Nor does a receivership affect the group position of a company in a group for corporation tax purposes. The company remains liable for corporation tax on profits earned during the receivership. It was held in *Re Wayte (Holdings) Ltd*[81] that a receiver cannot be personally liable to pay any such tax—in that instance, tax due on interest earned on money which the receiver kept on deposit.

Where a capital gain is made on the disposal of an asset, s.8(5) of the Capital Gains Tax Act, 1975, attributes the gain to the company rather than to the debenture-holder. The effect of the *Re Wayte* case on capital gains was reversed

78. [1979] 3 All ER 842.   79. [1986] 1 WLR 1301.
80. Id at pp. 1307-1308.   81. [1986] IR 448.

by s.56 of the Finance Act, 1983, which renders the receiver an 'accountable person' for the purpose of capital gains made during his tenure and makes him personally liable to pay the 'referable' gains tax due on any gain that was made.

For the purposes of value added tax (V.A.T.), under s.78 of the Finance Act, 1983, goods and property disposed of by a receiver are deemed to have been supplied by a taxable person in his business. Therefore receivers are personally liable for V.A.T. and should register separately. It has been held that receivers are personally liable for certain custom duties which became payable during their tenure.[82] But a receiver and manager who is the company's agent is not normally liable for rates on the company's premises.[83]

ADMINISTRATIVE MATTERS

Receivers' duties under the Companies Acts concern primarily administrative matters. Mention has already been made of the requirement for a receiver of the 'whole or substantially the whole' of a company's property, who was appointed under a floating charge, forthwith to notify the company of the appointment and, within seven days, to publish a notice in the *Iris Oifigiúil*.[84] On receipt of the company's verified statement of affairs, the receiver must send copies of it and of any comments to be made on it to the registrar of companies and to the debenture-holders.[85] This statement must show, as at the time of the receiver's appointment, particulars of the company's assets, debts and liabilities, the names and addresses of its creditors, the securities held by creditors and the dates when those securities were given, and any such further or other information as may be prescribed.[86] Where no such statement has been furnished within two months of the appointment, s.320A of the 1963 Act requires the receiver, within 30 days, to prepare a statement of affairs and to send copies as aforesaid. At six monthly intervals the receiver must send abstracts, in the prescribed form, to the registrar of companies, dealing with the assets which the receiver got possession of, their estimated value, the proceeds of the sale of any assets and the receipts and payments for the six months period.[87]

Where a receiver has been appointed over a company's property, a statement to that effect must be inserted on every invoice, order for goods or business letter issued by or on behalf of the company or of the receiver.[88]

Where it appears to the receiver that any officer or member of the company was guilty of an offence in relation to it, the matter must be reported to the Director of Public Prosecutions.[89]

It will depend on the circumstances of each case whether the company has

---

82. *Spain v Revenue Cmrs.* [1980] ILRM 21.
83. *Ratford v Northavon D.C.* [1987] QB 357.
84. 1963 Act ss.107 and 319(1).
85. Id s.319(1)(c).   86. Id ss 319 and 320.
87. Id. s.321.   88. Id. s.317.
89. 1990 Act s.170, applying 1963 Act s.299(2)-(5) to receivers.

established a 'need to know' facts and whether disclosure would jeopardise the receivership. In the *Gomba Holdings Ltd* case, the sole director of a company, which was in receivership, claimed that he had made an agreement with an undisclosed party which would enable the company to pay off its entire indebtedness. In order to conclude the negotiations on that agreement, the company sought information about all disposals of assets made or proposed by the receiver. It was held that, in the circumstances, the company had not demonstrated a need to know information over and above that contained in the regular statutory accounts.

FIDUCIARY DUTIES

Being agents who are entrusted with the care of other peoples' property, receivers may be fiduciaries and, consequently, owe fiduciary duties. However, eminent Australian commentators on the principles of equity have described the privately-appointed receiver as 'perhaps, the only genuinely non-fiduciary agency'[90] on account of the common stipulation that the receiver shall be the company's agent. Whether or not receivers are technically classified as fiduciaries, they are subject to some of the main constraints which the law places on fiduciaries.[91] The complete scope of these duties has never been defined but they include not taking unfair advantage, such as profiting from their position, and avoiding all undue conflicts of interest and acting throughout in good faith.

LIABILITY OF RECEIVER

As with all professionals doing a job, receivers run the risk of being held liable in damages for errors they make or other wrong doing. They may be protected from the financial consequences of liability by an indemnity they have got; now that they are officers of the company for certain purposes, any indemnity they have from the company may very well be void under s.200 of the 1963 Act.[92] Formerly, a receiver was not an officer of the company for the purpose of a misfeasance suit under s.298 of the 1963 Act[93] but s.142 of the 1990 Act now brings him within the misfeasance rule. Accordingly, where the company has been liquidated or where it has been left as a mere shell without any formal winding up,[94] proceedings can be brought under s.298 in respect of the receiver's wrongdoing.[95] Another way of penalising errant receivers is to disallow them all or part of their remuneration, costs and expenses.

Contract   The extent to which receivers can be held personally liable in contract has been considered above when discussing s.316(2) of the 1963 Act.[96]

90. R. Meagher et al., *Equity Doctrines and Remedies* (2nd ed., 1984) at p. 669.
91. *Tse Kwong Lam v Wong Chit Sen* [1983] 1 WLR 1349. See generally, P. Finn, *Fiduciary Obligations* (1977).
92. See *Company Law*, pp. 170-71.
93. *Re B. Johnson & Co. (Builders) Ltd* [1955] Ch 643.
94. 1990 Act s.251.   95. See post pp. 253-258   96. See supra p. 53.

Tort There are various circumstances in which a receiver can incur extra-contractual liability for damages. Thus, a receiver who was invalidly appointed but who takes possession of the charged assets is liable to the company in trespass. In such a case the court is given a discretion to relieve the receiver from personal liability, either in whole or in part.[97] A receiver who sold goods which were the subject of retention of title would be liable in conversion to the owner of those goods. If the receiver can be regarded an 'officer' of the company for the purposes of s.391 of the 1963 Act, then he might be excused from liability, either entirely or in part, under that section if he acted honestly and reasonably and ought fairly to be excused.[98]

A receiver who caused the company not to honour its contracts is protected from tort liability for inducing breach of contract if he was the company's agent, unless he acts *mala fides* or beyond the scope of his authority. In *Lathia v Dronsfield Bros. Ltd*,[99] the company had contracted to supply equipment to the plaintiff but, at the receiver's instigation, refused to supply it. The court struck out a claim brought against him for damages for inducing breach of contract because there was no basis for concluding he had acted *mala fides* or exceeded his authority.

Negligence In carrying out their tasks, in particular when managing the business and selling the charged property, receivers must exercise reasonable care and skill. But in *Downside Nominees Ltd v First City Corp.*,[1] the Privy Council overruled numerous recent cases (most on receivers' duties when selling the charged assets) and held that, generally, receivers cannot be held liable in the law of negligence for exclusively economic loss. According to Lord Templeman, '[t]he decisions of a receiver and manager whether to continue the business or close down the business and sell assets chosen by him cannot be impeached if those decisions are taken in good faith while protecting the interests of the debenture holders in recoving the monies due under the debenture, even though the decisions of the receiver and manager may be disadvantageous for the company.'[2] It can be debated whether this analysis would be followed in Ireland, where for certain purposes receivers are deemed to be officers of the company and where their potentially most controversial decision, selling off the assets, is subject to a new statutory duty of care. Also, Irish courts have not taken as restrictive a view of negligently inflicted economic loss as the English courts have. Leaving aside s.316(A)(i) of the 1963 Act, the present position may be as follows. Because, for all practical purposes, receivers are linked to the company through the debenture, their duties to the company, and perhaps to guarantors of the secured debt, are governed exclusively by that contract and equitable principles. But their duty to others may

97. 1963 Act s.316(3).   98. See *Company Law*, pp. 173-174.
99. [1987] BCLC 321.
1. [1993] 2 WLR 86. See generally, Berg, 'Duties of Mortgagee and a Receiver' [1993] *J. Bus. L.* 213.
2. Id. at p. 96.

be governed by the same principles that bind all professionals, *viz.* a duty of care in tort where the requisite proximity exists and there are no special policy grounds for not imposing liability. This state of affairs would not significantly disadvantage the company and its guarantors because they are protected by the new statutory duty to obtain the best price when selling the assets and the standards imposed by equity are demanding. The following summarises the case law prior to the recent Privy Council decision.

Standard of care   To an extent, the actual standard of care will depend on the nature of the company in question and on the receiver's own training, experience and qualifications. Many of the reported cases on the duty of care concern the circumstances in which the company's assets were sold and have been considered separately above. The position under the general law is now buttressed by s.316A(i) of the 1963 Act (inserted in 1990), which requires a receiver, when selling the company's property, to 'exercise all reasonable care to obtain the best price reasonably obtainable for the property as at the time of sale.' There have been no recent reported cases in Britain or Ireland on the standard of care outside of that context. In *First City Corp. v Downside Nominees Ltd*,[3] over $NZ 2,500,000 damages were awarded against a receiver who recklessly carried on the company's business for over twelve months, made large losses and adversely affected the value of the plaintiff's second charge on the company's assets.[4] It depends on the evidence in any particular case whether the receiver did act recklessly—whether in all the circumstances he acted in a manner which no reasonably prudent receiver would have done.

Where lack of care is not sufficient to give rise to a right of action in damages, it may be grounds for disallowing all or part of the receiver's remuneration, costs and expenses. That happened in *R.A. Price Securities Ltd v Henderson*[5] where the receiver, who had only to recover a comparatively small sum from the secured assets, became preoccupied with running the company's business, in the course of which he incurred large liabilities and then was not able to recover a penny for the debenture holder. His claim for remuneration and to be reimbursed the large legal costs he had incurred was rejected, and in addition he was ordered to pay damages, being the sum he should have recovered for the debenture-holder if he had acted properly.

Duty to whom   Where the receiver did act recklessly, to whom is his duty of care owed? In *Downside Nominees Ltd v First City Corp. Ltd*,[6] the Privy Council rejected the view that a receiver owes a duty of care in tort to the company and to any subsequent chargees of the company's assets. According to Lord Templeman,

3.   [1990] 3 NZLR 265.
4.   The Privy Council, on appeal, agreed with the result in this decision, although it rejected the conceptual approach to receivers' liability: [1993] 2 WLR 86.
5.   [1989] 2 NZLR 257.   6. [1993] 2 WLR 86.

the general duty of a receiver and manager appointed by a debenture holder [in equity] leaves no room for the imposition of a general duty to use reasonable care in dealing with the assets of the company. The duties imposed by equity . . . would be quite unnecessary if there existed a general duty in negligence to take reasonable care in dealing with the assets of the mortgagor company.[7]

As for duties to other third parties, this depends on the general principles governing when can liability exist for negligently inflicted exclusively economic loss, an issue which has given rise to a vast case law in recent years.[8] The approach adopted by the Supreme Court to this question[8] is closer to that followed in New Zealand[10] than that adopted in Britain in recent years.[11] In the *Downview Nominees* case,[12] where a receiver was ordered to pay large damages, the New Zealand Court of Appeal summed up the law in these terms:

> The legal duties resting on a receiver and manager appointed as agent of the company in receivership are not owed exclusively to the holder of the debenture under which the receiver was appointed. Inevitably there are other interests involved. The receiver has some obligations to the company as its agent. He cannot be oblivious to the interests of the other secured and unsecured creditors who are directly affected by the commercial decisions he makes in the receivership. While the due performance of the duties to the debenture holder of enforcing the security and for that purpose of exercising powers of sale and of management pending sale must prevail, there may be room in the particular circumstances for the existence of a concomitant duty of care to others applying ordinary negligence principles. As to when a duty of care in tort arises no hard and fast rules may be laid down and there must be a step by step application to the facts of particular cases. There are two broad fields of inquiry. First, the degree of proximity or relationship between the alleged wrongdoer and the person who has suffered damage (which is not a simple question of foreseeability of harm as between the parties and involves the degree of analogy with cases in which duties are already established); and, second whether there are other policy considerations tending to negate or restrict the duty in that class of case. [It depends on the facts of each case whether the requisite proximity exists.] As to the second field of inquiry there were no policy reasons which overall ought to have negated such a duty of care. The recognition of a duty of care in this class of case served two important social objectives. First, to compensate deserving plaintiffs where a receiver had traded with property in which they had a security interest; and

7. Id. at p. 98.
8. See generally, McMahon & Binchy, supra n.24.
9. *Ward v McMaster* [1988] IR 337.
10. E.g. *Hamlin v Bruce Stirling Ltd* [1993] 1 NZLR 374.
11. *Murphy v Brentwood D.C.* [1991] 1 AC 398.
12. [1990] 3 NZLR 265.

second, to promote professional competence, the sanction of a negligence suit providing an incentive for professionals undertaking receiverships to conform their conduct to a standard of reasonable care. Furthermore, the framework of the duty of care in this class of case was defined and limited, there being no risk that receivers would be exposed to liability in an indeterminate amount for an indeterminate time to an indeterminate class.[13]

The proposition stated in several cases, that receivers do not owe a duty of care to the general creditors, to contributories, to officers of the company and members[14] remains true in most if not all cases.

Breach of statutory duty   In certain circumstances a receiver would be liable for breach of statutory duty as the possessor or the occupier of the company's property, even where he is the company's agent. For instance, in *Meigh v Wickenden*[15] a receiver and manager was successfully prosecuted for an offence under the old Factories Act. The previous case law in that context had given a very extensive interpretation to the word occupier. Because the receiver there was 'complete master of the affairs of the company' and had 'absolute and complete power to manage the property of which he took possession, including the factory',[16] then as between him and the company he was the person occupying the factory.

---

13. Headnote.
14. *American Express Int'l Banking Corp. v Hurley* [1986] BCLC 52.
15. [1942].
16. Id. at p. 168.

6

Overlap with Liquidation

Often, some time after a receiver was appointed, the company goes into liquidation. Occasionally, the liquidation occurs first and then a secured creditor may want to appoint a receiver. The extent to which the activities or powers of receivers affects liquidators depends on the extent of the security. Where the security is the entire undertaking, under an extensive fixed charge and a floating charge, there is always some risk of clashes between a receiver and a liquidator.

APPOINTMENT OF RECEIVER

Where the debenture empowers the appointment of a receiver, that power is not affected by the winding up. Once the circumstances for exercising that power exist, the secured creditor can go ahead and appoint his receiver. And if he had appointed a receiver before the liquidation commenced, the advent of winding up does not affect that appointment. All of this follows from the fact that the debenture-holder has rights outside the winding up; he has a proprietary interest in all or part of the company's assets which cannot be affected by the liquidation.

Where the secured creditor is not empowered to appoint a receiver, he must apply to the court to do so under its general equitable jurisdiction. If the court decides to designate an official receiver, usually it will appoint the same person as the liquidator, especially if he is an official liquidator.[1] The justification for this practice is to avoid the expense of having two persons, both empowered to perform somewhat similar tasks. This is only a practice arising from prudence and in an appropriate case will be departed from. But where the secured creditor possesses a power of appointment, he is entirely free to select his receiver and has no obligation to choose the liquidator.[2]

When the company has been wound up by the court and a receiver then appointed by the debenture-holder, the former practice was for him to apply to the court for its permission to take possession of the charged assets. Without such leave, it was believed that the receiver would be risking liability for contempt of court by encroaching on the domain of an officer of the court. It has been held in Australia, however, that leave is not necessary except where there is a distinct risk of a dispute arising between the receiver and the liquidator.[3]

1. *Re Joshua Stubbs Ltd* [1891] 1 Ch 475.   2. Ibid.
3. *Re Landmark Corp.* (1988) 88 WN (Pf. 1) (NSW) 195.

The fact that a company is in receivership does not prevent a person from petitioning to have it wound up. Even if all of the company's assets are caught by the debenture, the court may still order a liquidation.[4] Such an order may be made even if the petitioning creditor cannot demonstrate a tangible advantage he will get from the winding up.[5] Where, however, the petitioner is the very party who appointed a receiver over all the assets, his motives may be questioned. In *Re Bula Ltd*,[6] where a petition of that nature was made for a collateral purpose, the Supreme Court declined to wind up the company and characterised the application as an abuse of process.

EFFECTS OF LIQUIDATION

A liquidation will terminate the receiver's usual agency but he still retains extensive powers and also has continuing obligations. However, s.322B of the 1963 Act authorises the liquidator to apply to the court to have the receivership terminated or restricted.

Agency   Usually, receivers are designated as agents of the company. Once a resolution to wind up is passed[7] or a winding up order is made,[8] that agency is terminated. The receiver no longer has power to act on behalf of the company or bind it in any way. In particular, the express power to manage the company's business comes to an end; any further trading by the company may only be carried out by the liquidator.

Any contract the receiver thereafter purports to make for the company becomes binding on him personally and not on the company. For instance in *Thomas v Todd*,[9] some days after the company resolved to wind itself up, the receiver and manager of the company hired the plaintiff. It was held that the contract had been made with the receiver himself.

Once the company's agency comes to an end, a receiver does not automatically become the debenture-holder's agent instead. However, the court will readily infer from post-liquidation dealings between these two parties that the receiver has become the agent of the secured creditor.[10] For instance, in *American Express Corp. v Hurley*,[11] where the defendant had guaranteed the company's debts and was alleging that the receiver acted negligently, it was held that in the circumstances there the bank had constituted the receiver its agent.

Powers   The onset of liquidation does not deprive the receiver of all of his powers, even though his authority as agent of the company ends. He cannot any longer call in uncalled capital of the company.[12] Nor can he incur debts on behalf

4.   *Re Chic Ltd* [1905] 2 Ch 345.
5.   Ibid.   6.   [1990] 1 IR 440.
7.   *Thomas v Todd* [1926] 2 KB 511.   8.   *Gosling v Gaskell* [1879] 2 KB 575.
9.   [1926] 2 KB 511.   10. *Re Wood* [1941] Ch 112.
11. [1986] BCLC 52.   12. *Re Henry Pond, Son & Hutchins* (1889) 42 Ch D 402.

of the company which can be proved in the liquidation against the uncharged assets. Once a receiver is appointed, however, all the charged assets belong in equity to the secured creditor. Accordingly, the receiver remains entitled to take possession of those assets.

Litigation He can take proceedings, even in the company's name, to get in those assets comprised in the debenture and protect them. Thus in *Gough's Garages Ltd v Pugsley*,[13] the receiver had brought proceedings, on behalf of the company, against its landlord to get a new lease under the Landlord and Tenant legislation. When the company was then wound up, it was claimed that those proceedings could not be continued. That view was flatly rejected, on the grounds that 'to deprive the debenture-holders of a right under . . . the debenture . . . to realise a valuable right of the company because the company has gone into liquidation, is to nullify one of the valuable rights given to the receiver by the debenture.'[14] The same principle applies to proceedings which the company itself had commenced.[15] Therefore, a receiver can be made personally liable for costs incurred after the liquidation, although subject to whatever right of indemnity he has.

Running the business Although liquidation puts an end to the receiver's trading power, on behalf of the company, this does not prevent him carrying on business with the charged assets on his own behalf or for the debenture holder. What the receiver cannot do is trade in a manner which involves the company itself incurring fresh liabilities.

Selling assets Notwithstanding the liquidation, a receiver retains his power to dispose of the charged assets, without reference to the liquidator. Often by agreement the liquidator will sell those assets for the receiver, or directly for the secured creditor. In such cases, the liquidator is entitled to deduct from the proceeds of sale the costs he incurred in arranging for the disposal. But should the receiver so choose, he can go ahead and dispose of the charged property. In *Sowman v David Samuel Trust Ltd*,[16] it was held that the receiver could even use the company's name in effecting that disposal. Where the debenture expressly or by implication granted a power to sell in the company's name, 'such powers are given by the disposition of the company's property which it made (in equity) by the debenture itself. That disposition is binding on the company and those claiming through it, as well in liquidation as before liquidation. . . .'[17] The only exception to this principle is where the debenture itself is invalid or ineffective, for instance, as a fraudulent preference or for non-registration. Because the secured creditor has a beneficial interest in the charged assets, a sale by the receiver of them is not a disposition rendered invalid by s.218 of the 1963 Act.

---

13. [1930] 1 KB 615. 14. Id. at p. 621.
15. *Bacal Contracting Ltd v Modern Engineering (Bristol) Ltd* [1980] 2 All ER 655.
16. [1978] 1 WLR 22. 17. Id. at p. 30.

PART II

Examination

The system of temporary protection, investigation and administration of companies' affairs by court-appointed examiners was introduced by the Companies (Amendment) Act, 1990. This procedure was part of the more extensive reform of Company Law which had been before the Oireachtas for several years.[1] But the crisis is Iraq in August 1990 and the impact of those events on the Goodman group of companies caused the Oireachtas to be reconvened and the measure to be enacted within a few days.[2] On the evening on which the Bill was signed and became law, the President of the High Court appointed an examiner over many companies of the Goodman group. Rules for proceedings under the 1990 Act are contained in R.S.C. Order 75A.[3]

What the protection and examination procedure seeks to achieve is to save all or part of the undertaking and to prevent the company from being wound up. This Act is not quite as novel as it may appear at first sight because it extends to companies, within the Companies Acts, 1963-1990, the kind of protection from creditors which individuals enjoy under Part IV of the Bankruptcy Act, 1988,[4] and its predecessor, ss.345-353 of the Bankruptcy (Ireland) Act, 1857.[5] The 1990 Act also resembles the court administration procedure which has existed in Britain since 1986[6] and Chapter 11 of the United States Bankruptcy Act, 1987,[7] which are aimed at rescuing ailing companies by encouraging a compromise between the claims of the creditors and of the company's owners. Under the 1990 Act, an examiner is appointed by the High Court to look into the company's affairs, to see if there is any real prospect of rescuing the business. Among the effects of such an appointment are to freeze all new litigation involving the company and to prevent creditors, secured as well as unsecured, from levying execution against its assets. If there is a prospect of the company's survival, the examiner reports back to the court and he then seeks to negotiate a compromise between the creditors, the

1. Companies (No. 2) Bill, 1987, Part IX.
2. See Dáil Debates 28 Aug. 1990, Vol. 401, no. 8.
3. SI No. 147 of 1991.   4. See generally, *Bankruptcy Law*, ch. 3.
5. See generally, J.H. Robb, *The Law and Practice of Bankruptcy and Arrangements in Ireland* (1907) ch. 18.
6. Insolvency Act 1986, ss.8-27; see generally E. Bailey et al., *Corporate Insolvency—Law and Practice* (1992) ch. 4.
7. 11 U.S. Code ss.1101-1174 (1988). See generally M. Bienenstock, *Bankruptcy Reorganisation* (1987).

shareholders and the company. When this is voted on by all the parties, the arrangement is brought before the court, which will sanction it if it secures a reasonable degree of support and is 'fair and equitable' to the parties and is not 'unfairly prejudicial' to any creditor or shareholder.

7

Obtaining Court Protection

Once a petition in the prescribed form and containing the prescribed information is presented in the Central Office of the High Court, the company in question enjoys the protection of the court against its creditors, in that they cannot enforce a wide range of remedies against the company or its property.[1] Obtaining that protection is not conditional on the petition being opened before a judge of the High Court. However, under Order 75A, on the same day as the petition is presented in the Central Office, the petitioner is required to make an *ex parte* application to the court for directions as to what steps should then be taken.[2] Under the comparable British legislation, the court must make a decision on the petition before the company can acquire protection from its creditors, but in cases of extreme urgency the courts there will make an 'administration order' on an undertaking to present the petition.[3]

THE PETITION

A petition for protection may be presented by any of the following:[4] by any creditor of the company, including any contingent or prospective creditor; by one or more members of the company, provided that they own more than one-tenth of the voting shares in the company; by the company itself and by the company's directors. Where the application is being made by the directors, it would seem that there must have been agreement among a majority of them to make the application; probably unanimity among them is not required, but a minority of them cannot make an application (unless they own 10% of the voting shares and apply as members). In Britain, where a winding up petition can be presented by 'the directors', it was held that this term means all of them.[5] However, since the directors can only act as a body, or board, and ordinarily the board acts by majority rule, the better view would seem to be that a majority of them at a duly convened board meeting can resolve to have an examiner appointed.[6]

1. See infra pp. 92-95.
2. Rule 4(4).
3. *Re Shearing & Loader Ltd* [1991] BCLC 764.
4. S.3(1) and Rules 3 and 4.
5. *Re Instrumentation Electrical Services Ltd* [1988] BCLC 550.
6. *Re Equitycorp International plc* [1989] 1 WLR 1010.

In an application by the company itself, it would seem that there must have been approval by the majority of the company's members with votes; in other words, a decision of the directors is not sufficient to authorise an application in the name of the company.[7] However, since an application can be made by the directors as such, the court may take the view that an application made in the name of the company and sanctioned by the directors is a good application unless there is evidence that the company's members are opposed to the application. In the case of an application by a contingent or prospective creditor, they are required first to provide security for costs.[8]

Full disclosure   When presenting a petition under this Act, the utmost good faith is required; the *ex parte* application to have an examiner appointed has been described as an *uberrima fides* procedure.[9] Not alone must the petition be factually correct but it ought to give an overall accurate account of the circumstances which give rise to the application. The lack of good faith on the petitioner's part could easily jeopardise ultimate sanction for a scheme of arrangement which might otherwise have secured the court's approval. One of the reasons why proposals, which had been approved by several classes of creditors, were rejected in *Re Wogans (Drogheda) Ltd (No. 2)*[10] was because the company's initial petition very significantly understated its liabilities; two of its directors knew that large sums were owing to the Revenue but those were not disclosed in the balance sheet in the petition. Costello J castigated the petition as an abuse of process by the company and its directors and recommended that, in future, once a discrepancy of that nature is discovered, the examiner should immediately bring the matter to the court's attention. There, as soon as he learned of the discrepancy, the examiner immediately notified the Revenue and shortly afterwards the main secured creditor, and then set out the true position in his s. 15 or '21 day' report to the court. Neither the Revenue nor any of the creditors ever suggested to the examiner that an application should be made to the court there and then or later to consider the implications of what he had found.

    When the examiner in that case later sought approval for his remuneration, costs and expenses, there was conflicting evidence about a brief meeting he had with one of the directors on the morning the petition was presented. The director said he mentioned to the proposed examiner that there had been 'some under the counter payments', although he did not elaborate on what they were or their amount. The examiner said that he had no recollection of that remark but, if it had been made, he thought it was about a tax problem which had later been resolved by a firm of consultants the company had hired. Costello J preferred the version of the director and held that the mere mention by the director of 'under the counter payments' should have alerted the intended examiner, that

7.   Cf. *Re Galway & Salthill Tramway Co.* [1918] 1 IR 62.
8.   S.3(5).
9.   *Re Selukwe Ltd* (Costello J, 20 December 1991).
10.   Costello J, 7 May 1992.

he then (before even being appointed) should have investigated this matter and should have alerted the company's solicitor that the petition (which he had not seen) might contain inaccuracies.

Grounds for protection　The petition must be supported by evidence that the applicant has 'good reason for requiring' an examiner to be appointed.[12] Examples of such reasons may include, to prevent a receiver being appointed over the company's assets, to block some other mode of execution being effected or to have litigation stayed. It depends on all the circumstances what kind of evidence the court requires for this purpose. Evidence should also be provided that the company is 'likely to be unable to pay its debts',[13] i.e. that the company either is, or probably is, insolvent. Indeed, in particular instances insolvency alone may be sufficient 'good reason' for having an examiner appointed. By being unable to pay its debts is meant[14] that either the company cannot meet its debts as they fall due; or the company's liabilities exceed its assets, both contingent and prospective; or that a form of execution issued against the company was returned unsatisfied in whole or in part; or, finally, a written demand has been left with the company for more than three weeks to pay a debt exceeding £1,000 but the company has not paid, secured or compounded that sum. In other words, the circumstances would warrant it being wound up by the court on the grounds of insolvency.[15] A new indicia of likely insolvency is added by the 1990 Act, that the company has sought from its creditors a significant extension of time to pay its debts.[16]

Costs　There is no indication in the 1990 Act as to who should bear the costs of a petition which has been granted. In *Re Brooke Marine Ltd*[17] it was held that the costs of the petition for an administration under the 1986 British Act could be regarded as costs of the administration itself and thereby be paid out of the company's assets. According to Harman J, 'the petitions having achieved their purpose of having administrators appointed who have achieved their purposes of a better realisation of most of the assets and a continuation of part of the business, it must be seen that the petitions have been wholly successful and in the interest of all persons interested in the companies, creditors, whether preferential or unsecured and, so far as it is relevant, members, although their interest is tenuous in the extreme and it is right . . . to direct that the costs of the administration petitions should be taxed on the standard basis and raised and paid by the administrators as costs of the administration out of the assets of the company.'[18] In an instance where the examination was not successful,[19] the examiner having recommended a winding up at the '21 day report' stage, Murphy J declined to award the petitioner his costs or direct that they should be a cost of the liquidation.

12.　S.3(3)(b).　　　　　　　13.　S.2(1)(a).　　14.　S.2(3).
15.　See post pp. 149-152　　16.　S.2(4).　　　　17.　[1988] BCLC 546.
18.　Id. at p. 548.
19.　*Re Merrytime (Ireland) Ltd*, Murphy J, 29 June 1992 (*ex tempore*).

Consequent formalities   Regardless of the outcome of the application, once a petition for protection is presented, the registrar of companies must be notified of that fact within the next three days.[20] Where an examiner is appointed, he is required to fulfil the following formalities. Within three days of his appointment, he must deliver to the registrar of companies a certified copy of the court's order.[21] Within the same period, he must cause to be published in two daily newspapers, circulating where the company's registered office or principal place of business is located, a notice of his appointment and the date that happened;[22] where a date was fixed by the court for considering his report, that date also must be stated. Within 21 days of his appointment, he must cause a similar notice to be placed in the *Iris Oifigiúil*.[23] Failure to meet any of these requirements does not invalidate the appointment, although deliberate omission to give the requisite notices may be grounds for the court vacating the protection. Within seven days of the court's order, the directors must make out a sworn statement of affairs of the company and give it to the examiner.[24]

PROCEEDINGS IN CAMERA

Section 31 of the 1990 Act authorises the court to hear any or all of the proceedings under this Act *in camera*. It may do so where it considers that excluding the public from the hearing is required in the interests of the company or of its creditors and that it is in the 'interests of justice' to do so. The interests of justice formula here provides scanty guidelines for individual cases. At least one proceeding in the Goodman International Ltd examination was heard *in camera*. However, in *Re R. Ltd*,[25] which was a case under the 'oppression' provisions of s.205 of the Companies Act, 1963, the Supreme Court ruled that courts should be very slow to direct that proceedings be heard otherwise than in public. The Constitution requires that all trials be held in public, save where there is statutory provision to the contrary. Any provision of that nature, like s.31 of the 1990 Act, giving the court a discretion to exclude the public should be applied only where a very clear case of likely serious prejudice to one of the parties is made out. According to Walsh J, the party seeking an *in camera* hearing 'must be able to satisfy the court that not only would the disclosure of information be seriously prejudicial to the legitimate interests of the company [or the creditors], but it must also be shown that a public hearing of the whole or of that part of the proceedings which it is sought to have heard other than in a public court would fall short of the doing of justice.'[26]

GROUP ENTERPRISES

In *Re Bray Travel Ltd*,[27] which concerned the winding up of an insolvent travel agency which had several subsidiary and closely-related companies, the Supreme Court ordered that they all should be liquidated together. Express

---

20. S.12(1).   21. S.12(3).   22. S.12(2).
23. S.12(3).   24. S.14.   25. [1989] IR 126.
26. Id. at p. 137.   27. Supreme Court, 13 July 1981.

power is now given to the court to make a protection order over several related companies.[28] In deciding whether to make an order applying to such companies, the criterion is whether that order is 'likely to facilitate the survival of the company, or of the related company, or both, and the whole or any part of its or their undertaking, as a going concern.'[29] In other words, is a consolidated protection and examination likely to salvage one or more of the companies?

Companies are deemed to be related for these purposes where one is the other's holding or subsidiary company; where a company and its related companies own half of the equity share capital in the other company; where the members of each company own more than half of the equity in the other, whether directly or indirectly; where a company and its related companies exercise or control half of the voting power in general meetings of the other company; where the business of both companies has been carried on in such a way as that their separate businesses are readily identifiable; where there is another company with which both companies are related in accordance with the criteria here.

Where a group of companies is put under protection, it was held by a New Zealand court[30] that circumstances can warrant an order being made that the examiner's costs should be pooled. That is to say, while ordinarily he should deal with each company in the group or network on an individual basis, and charge his costs accordingly to each company, there may be some companies with either no or no unencumbered assets but in respect of which he has incurred expenses which cannot be recovered from that company. In such a case, the court directed that some other company or companies he is examining shall bear all or part of those costs. However, the 1990 Act does not contain a provision identical to the one which was the basis for this decision.[31]

COMPANIES BEYOND THE SCOPE OF PROTECTION

Not every company can be the subject of court protection and administration under the 1990 Act. If the company clearly is solvent an order will not be made appointing an examiner over its affairs. With regard to insolvent entities, it is only companies within the general scope of the Companies Acts that can obtain protection. These are companies which are registered under the Companies Act, 1963, or the earlier companies legislation—the Companies (Consolidation) Act, 1908, the Companies Act, 1862, and the Joint Stock Companies Act.[32] Accordingly, the 1990 Act would seem to have no application to companies which are registered outside the State, even where they have a place of business in the State and are registered under Part XI of the 1963 Act.[33] Provision is made in s.36 of the 1990 Act for the Irish courts to recognise and give effect to orders

---

28. S.4.   29. S.4(2).
30. *McDonald v Australian Guarantee Corp. (N.Z.)* [1990] 1 NZLR 227.
31. Corporation (Investigations and Management) Act 1989,s.59.
32. 1963 Act s.2(1).
33. See post p. 134.

of recognised foreign courts in comparable proceedings, so that the affairs in Ireland of foreign registered companies may in that way be made subject to court protection and reorganisation schemes. The 1990 Act does not apply to industrial and provident societies, friendly societies, statutory corporations and any type of business entity other than a company registered in the State. It would seem, however, that protection can be extended to those entities where they are 'related' to a company within court protection, because those bodies can be wound up by the High Court, as can certain foreign-registered companies.[34]

34.   See post p. 134.

8

Appointment of Examiner, Status and Remuneration

Before an examiner will be appointed, the applicant must be qualified to present the petition, the petition and accompanying matters must meet the prescribed requirements, a winding up of the company must not have commenced, the company must not have been in receivership for more than three days continuous before the petition was presented and it must appear to the court that the company is 'likely to be unable to pay its debts'.

INTERIM EXAMINER

At times the court will appoint an interim examiner pending the hearing of the petition and any objections that may be raised.[1] It can be helpful that someone is appointed albeit on a temporary basis because some weeks might elapse before the petition is heard. When that hearing takes place the interim appointee may be able to provide the court with a reliable objective assessment of the company's general prospects; he may even have come to the early conclusion that there is no reasonable prospect of survival, thereby rendering further examination unnecessary. However, some judges are reluctant to make interim appointments unless very convincing reasons exist.

APPOINTMENT

Although the court has a discretion to refuse an application to appoint an examiner where the above requirements are met, that power of refusal will be strictly regulated in accordance with relatively well defined principles. However, if protection 'would be likely to facilitate the survival of the company, and the whole or any part of its undertaking, as a going concern',[2] the Act creates a form of presumption in favour of appointing an examiner. In England it was held that the word 'likely' in a similar context means 'a real prospect that . . . the stated purpose may be achieved';[3] not a more onerous requirement, that there must be at least a 50% probability of bringing about the company's survival. A similar approach was endorsed by the Supreme Court in *Re Atlantic*

---

1. S.3(8).   2. S.2(2).
3. *Re S.C.L. Building Services Ltd* [1990] BCLC 98, *Re Primlaks (U.K.) Ltd* [1989] BCLC 734 and *Re Harris Simon Construction Ltd* [1989] 1 WLR 368.

Magnetics Ltd;[4] in that instance, a receiver had already been appointed and it was contended that there was no real prospect of an examination under the 1990 Act proving to be a success. Because the application to appoint an examiner is the first step in a process, which could lead to the company's financial position being carefully scrutinised by the court when a scheme of arrangement has been drawn up, within a relatively short space of time, it would not be appropriate to require a petitioner to prove that the company probably could survive. That probability is something which the court would have to look at in due course during the examination.

If, however, there is a very high likelihood of any reasonable proposals an examiner might make being rejected by the overwhelming mass of the creditors, the court might decline to make the appointment. In an English case,[5] where the proposed mode of salvaging the company was to 'hive down' the company's business into a 'clean' subsidiary, in much the same way as is done by receivers, the petition was rejected on the grounds that this procedure did not envisage the survival of the company and part of its undertaking as a going concern. Several other aspects of that case led the judge to conclude that none of the statutory purposes of an administration could have been achieved there.

Qualifications   Only persons qualified to be liquidators of the company are eligible, under s.28, to become its examiner.

Selection   Ordinarily, the person designated by the petitioner will be appointed as the examiner. Unless a very good explanation is given why he should not be appointed, the court will not appoint the person preferred by other interested parties, even if they are the principal creditors or the main unsecured creditor.[6]

Ancillary orders   Where an examiner is appointed, the court may make such other directions as it thinks fit.[7] Directions may concern, for example, the operation of the company's bank account, the conduct and management of its business, the appointment of a committee of inspection and the conditions under which certain powers may be exercised by the examiner. Even where it adjourns the hearing, the court may make such interim orders as it thinks fit in the circumstances; one such order may be restricting the directors' powers.[8]

A striking innovation in the 1990 Act is that it gives the Circuit Court some jurisdiction in Company Law matters, which it lost entirely in 1936.[9] Where the total liabilities of the company which has been given protection do not appear to exceed £250,000 the entire matter may be remitted to the Circuit Court—in the Circuit where the company either has its registered office or its principal place of business. In such a case, the Circuit Court can exercise all the powers which the 1990 Act confers on the High Court. But if the Circuit Court

4.   Supreme Court, 5 Dec. 1991.
5.   *Re Rowbotham Baxter Ltd* [1990] BCLC 397.
6.   *Re Wogans Drogheda Ltd* (Blayney J, 13 January 1992) ex tempore.
7.   S.3(7).   8.   S.3(8).   9.   Courts Act 1936, s.18.

finds that the company's total liabilities exceed £250,000 it can order that the matter be sent back to the High Court.

STATUS OF THE EXAMINER

Like court-appointed receivers and official liquidators,[10] the examiner is an officer of the court. His primary duties are to the court, to which he can apply for directions on a wide range of matters. Being under the discipline and control of the court, he is required at all times to act in an honest, impartial and high-minded fashion and is directly responsible to the court for the due performance of his duties.

REMUNERATION AND EXPENSES

Where a scheme of arrangement is approved by the court, ordinarily that scheme will make adequate provision for paying the examiner's remuneration and expenses and also any liabilities certified under s.10 of the 1990 Act as necessary to ensure the company's survival at the time. Where, however, no scheme is approved or one is approved but the company nevertheless goes into liquidation, the question arises of the priority ranking of what is owing to the examiner and to creditors with his certificates. This became quite a controversial matter in early 1992 at the end of the United Meat Packers Ltd examination,[11] when thousands of farmers held what they descried as 'examiner's cheques' for cattle they had supplied to that company shortly after it went into examination. In the event, the matter seems to have been resolved by agreement between the then examiner and the receiver who replaced him; there was no ruling on the main questions of principle.

The position is governed by s.29 of the 1990 Act. What is being claimed by the examiner and by certified creditors must first be sanctioned by the court, which may want to satisfy itself that the debts were reasonably incurred and there was no extravagance or waste. For this purpose, examiners are required to make optimum use of the company's own staff and facilities.[12] The sums so approved must be paid either from the company's revenue or from its assets, when realised, including investments—unless the court orders otherwise. If the company is forced into receivership or liquidation, s.29(3) provides that those sums

> shall be paid in full and shall be paid before any other claim, secured or unsecured, . . . in any receivership or winding up of the company. . . .

Three main questions appear to arise from this provision.

What are the 'assets' of the company out of which, when realised, those sums must be paid? For instance, is property which has been mortgaged to a creditor an asset in this context? A strong argument could be made, especially in view of the Constitution's guarantee of private property, that the only company asset

---

10. See post p. 192.   11. April 1992.   12. S.29(4).

is the equity of redemption. Against that, use of the term 'asset', as contrasted with the term 'property', may have significance.

If there are insufficient unencumbered assets, must the sums approved be paid from the proceeds of sale of assets which were the subject of a floating charge and even of a fixed charge? All that s.29(3) says is that there is a priority over 'secured' claims. This may include claims that are secured by an outright mortgage. In *Re Atlantic Magnetics Ltd*,[13] the Supreme Court ruled that certified liabilities have priority over assets which are subject to a fixed charge, a view accepted by Blayney J some nine months earlier in another case.[14] It was held that the phrase 'before any other claim, secured or unsecured,' was unambiguous and must be given its literal meaning. It could be argued that property which is subject to a fixed charge is not an 'asset' of the company, on the grounds that, in insolvency, the word 'asset' traditionally has meant property which is unencumbered or is only subject to a floating charge.[15] Against that, the clear legislative intention appears to include specific security here.

What liabilities are not 'claims' in a receivership or liquidation and, accordingly, not affected by s.29(3)'s priority? Presumably that word means any debts or claims which could be proved in a liquidation.[16] If this is so then a liquidator's remuneration and expenses would rank before the examiner's expenses etc. and certified liabilities. There is some practical logic in this approach in that it may be necessary to appoint a liquidator in order to realise the assets, in order that claims can get paid. Of course, in an official liquidation the court has an extensive discretion over what should be paid to the liquidator.[17] On the other hand, it would seem that where charged assets are realised by a receiver, appointed by secured creditors, his remuneration and expenses are a claim against the company, which rank after what is due to the examiner. Nevertheless, the court might grant the receiver an allowance to cover the expenses necessarily incurred in realising the assets in order that any payments can be made.[18]

In *Re Wogans (Drogheda) Ltd (No. 3)*,[19] Costello J refused to sanction any of the examiner's remuneration, costs and expenses for a variety of reasons. As was explained above, the company had been defrauding the Revenue for several years and the directors did not put into its petition the true amount of its tax liability. At the s.29 hearing, the Revenue alleged that the examiner had been in league with the directors but, in the event, were unable to provide any evidence which might support that charge. There was evidence, which was

13. Supreme Court, 5 December 1991.
14. *Re Acorn Automation Ltd* (Blayney J, 11 February 1991) ex tempore.
15. *Re Christonette International Ltd* [1982] 1 WLR 1245. Cf. *McDonald v Australian Guarantee Corp. (N.Z.) Ltd* [1990] 1 NZLR 227 and *Re ACL Insurance Ltd* [1991] 1 NZLR 211.
16. See ch. 19.   17. See post p. 191.
18. *Re Berkeley Applegate (Consultants) Ltd* [1989] Ch 32. Cf. *Re Ararimu Holdings* [1989] 3 NZLR 487.
19. Costello J, 9 February 1993.

contradicted, that one of the directors had mentioned to the intended examiner that there had been 'some under the counter payments'. Costello J accepted this evidence and ruled that the intended examiner should have understood by that remark that the company had a substantial undisclosed Revenue liability, that it was likely that this debt was not revealed in the petition, and that he should have looked into the matter there and then and have alerted the company's solicitor. The examiner was also castigated on other grounds, the principal ones being as follows.

At the outset, an application to appoint him as interim examiner was refused by Murphy J but that judge suggested that there was no reason why the intended examiner should not provide the company with necessary assistance until its petition was heard, some three weeks later. Assistance was provided for this period and the examiner was paid a small sum by the company. Costello J held that he should have disclosed this payment to the court when the petition was heard and that, if it had been disclosed, it was 'highly probable' that he would never have been appointed to the office; that 'none of the [objecting] creditors' had been aware of his connection with the company. However, the main objecting creditor, a bank, had been informed by the intended examiner, almost immediately after the interim application, of what he was doing for the company and he had at least one meeting with the bank, about the proposed examination, but the bank made no mention of this matter at all in court when objecting to his appointment. Proposed examiners rarely if ever are represented in court when the petition for their appointment is being heard.

When drawing up his proposals, the examiner decided not to include in them provisions regarding guarantees the two directors had given the bank and he informed the bank and the directors of this decision. A meeting had taken place with the directors, prior to an informal creditors' meeting, at the conclusion of which there was a brief discussion between the examiner's counsel and the directors' solicitor about the possible effect of examinations on guarantees and that solicitor was told to get his own counsel's opinion on the matter. The conclusions Costello J drew from this evidence was that

> The examiner . . . had formed an opinion as the legal consequences of the confirmation of his proposals on the Wogan's guarantees (i.e. that they would be discharged by it); that he brought counsel to a meeting with the directors to convey this opinion to them; and that the purpose of doing so had been to influence a decision on their part favourable to acceptance of the proposals he was formulating. [Moreover] in his oral evidence [in] the confirmation proceedings the examiner made no mention of [this] meeting and stated that his attitude to the guarantees was that they were matters with which he was not concerned and that he did not consider that they should form part of the scheme of arrangement.[20]

20. The author of this book was the counsel, who advised and represented the examiner throughout his examination. Professional etiquette prevents any comment here on these findings of fact, which are strongly disputed.

Another criticism concerned certain tax conditions the examiner included in his scheme, which the Revenue objected to. Costello J held that an application should have been made to the court at an earlier stage for approval of those conditions. At the same time, however, the examiner was criticised for having brought one court application, to ascertain whether the bank had a fixed or floating charge on the company's debtors, without having first obtained the consent of the court. In fact the High Court upheld the examiner's view in that application but was overruled by the Supreme Court,[21] which nevertheless directed that the examiner's costs should be paid out the examination. Costello J refused to give him even those costs.

Another criticism still was of a provision in the proposed scheme, that the money being put up by the investor, who would finance the scheme, was to be paid into a trust account in the examiner's name and a specified sum of that would be in respect of the examiner's remuneration and costs. It is common in schemes drawn up under Chapter 11 in the United States to provide for paying the costs and expenses of the process in this manner. Section 29 of the 1990 Act provides that an examiner's remuneration and expenses 'shall be paid' from the company's revenue or assets, unless the court orders otherwise. Costello J said that '[t]he the examiner did not request the court to make such an order and advanced no reason why such an order should be made.' However, the money being held in the bank account would belong to the company, in the name of the examiner as trustee. The remuneration envisaged, therefore, was to be paid from the company's assets, as augmented by the investor. The whole purpose of the examiner's court application under s.29 was to seek the court's approval for payment of that sum. In the light of the stipulation about how the remuneration etc. was intended to be paid, there was no question of seeking payment 'otherwise' than from the company's assets. Other criticisms still of the examiner and his scheme were made by the learned judge.

RESIGNATION AND REMOVAL

Section 13(1) of the 1990 Act provides that an examiner may resign. Presumably like official liquidators, a resignation does not become effective until it is accepted by the court. Where an examiner has resigned, either the committee of creditors, the company or any 'interested party' can apply to have a replacement appointed by the court.[22]

Section 13(1) also provides that an examiner may be removed from office by the court 'on cause shown'. In exercising this power, presumably the court will be guided by the same general considerations as when asked to remove a liquidator.[23]

---

21. Compare *Re New Bull & Trading Ltd* [1993] BCLC 251.
22. S.13(2).
23. See post pp. 189-190.

9

Effects of Protection

Once the originating petition has been presented, the company comes under the court's protection for the prescribed period. The immediate objective and consequence of protection is to provide the company or companies in question with extensive immunity against its creditors and against claims being made against it. By virtue of the 1990 Act, the company becomes legally insulated from a wide range of adverse actions against it.

MEMBERS

Unless the court gives directions otherwise, protection has no immediate effect on the company's members or shareholders. They can continue participating in general meetings and may transfer their shares as if nothing had happened. However, once a company comes into court protection, no order may be made against it for relief under s.205 of the 1963 Act against 'oppression'.[1]

DIRECTORS

The same principle applies to the company's directors; subject to the court's directions otherwise, during the protection they can continue to manage the company's business and its affairs. However, from the outset the court may restrict the exercise of any of their powers; as is explained below, the court may order that all or any of the directors' powers be exercisable only by the examiner.[2] Moreover, the examiner is authorised to convene, set the agenda for and to attend board meetings and meetings of the company's members.[3] Within seven days of an examiner's appointment the directors must give him a sworn statement of affairs.[4]

CONTRACTS

Similarly, the advent of protection ordinarily does not affect subsisting contracts with the company, except that goods held under retention of title, a hire purchase agreement, a conditional sale or some other form of bailment cannot be repossessed.[5] As is explained below, the company may apply to the court either to affirm or repudiate contracts, other than payment obligations.[6]

1. S.5(1)(g).
4. S.14.
2. S.3(g).
5. S.5(2)(e).
3. S.7(2) and (3).
6. S.20; see post pp. 100-101.

LITIGATION

Protection insulates the company from fresh litigation unless the court directs otherwise. No proceedings against the company or 'in relation to' it may be commenced without the leave of the court and subject to such terms as the court fixes.[7] However, the court readily grants leave to bring proceedings, when sought, although usually putting a stay on any steps following delivery of the statement of claim. As for proceedings already in being relating to the company, the examiner is authorised to apply to the court to have them stayed or for any other order regarding the action.[8] What criteria should guide the court in granting leave or imposing a stay in such cases are not stated. It has been held in New Zealand that the criteria followed in similar applications when a company is in liquidation are not always apposite to companies in protection.[9]

COMPANY PROPERTY

Unless the court gave directions to the contrary, protection does not affect the title to the company's property. There is no express provision whereby title in the property vests in the examiner, although he may be authorised by the court to engage in transactions with that property,[10] even property which is subject to a charge or is held under a hire purchase agreement. But once the company comes under protection, its property cannot be affected by creditor's remedies in any of the ways described below.

CREDITORS' PROPERTY

Where property belonging to a creditor is in the company's possession, he may not be able to recover it while the company is under protection. It was observed that the 1990 Act 'does not . . . extinguish any entitlement whether of proprietary or contractual rights. It merely restricts to a substantial extent the enforcement of that entitlement while the [protection] remains in force.'[11] Where, during the course of the protection, the company makes use of another's property in one way or another, the value of that use becomes an expense of the entire process which, eventually, must be defrayed from the company's own assets. *Re Atlantic Computer Systems plc*[12] concerned complicated leasing arrangements between what were known as 'funders', the company in question and lessees from the company. It was held that 'if the chattels belonging to a funder and made available to the company under hire purchase agreements or leases are used in the course of the business of the company or realised . . ., then the funder is entitled to receive as an expense . . . the payment provided for by that hire

7.   S.5(3).   8. Ibid.
9.   *Wilson v Aurora Group Ltd* [1990] 1 NZLR 61. Cf. *Re Atlantic Computer Systems plc* [1992] 2 WLR 367.
10. S.11; see post pp. 100, 101.
11. *Re Atlantic Computer Systems plc* [1990] Ch 508 BCLC 729 at p. 741.
12. [1992] Ch 508.

purchase agreement or lease. The same may well apply to other forms of property made available [to the company] under other types of arrangement. . . .'[13] The court there went on to consider exactly what sums should be paid to the funders as expenses.

CREDITORS' REMEDIES

Remedies which the law affords creditors against their debtors' property are drastically curtailed where the debtor is a company and a petition for its protection has been presented. A creditor who resorts to any of these remedies, while the company enjoys the court's protection, commits contempt of court.[14] If he does so deliberately and conscious of the legal implications, he risks a substantial fine and even imprisonment.[15] These restrictions on creditors' remedies can be waived by the examiner but there is no provision, comparable to that in the British legislation, whereby the court may also give leave to realise a security or resort to any of the other remedies.[16]

Repossession Goods held under retention of title, a hire purchase or a credit sale agreement or some other form of bailment which can last at least three months, do not belong to the company until they have been paid for.[17] However, once protection commences, no steps may be taken to repossess such goods if they are in the company's possession, except with the examiner's consent.[18]

Determining when are goods in the company's possession can be a complicated matter; the law has not worked out a completely logical and exhaustive definition of what is possession and the meaning of this word tends to vary with the context in which it is used. In *Re Atlantic Computer Systems plc*,[19] it was held that equipment leased to the company and then sub-leased by it to end-users was not in the company's possession while those users had it. Accordingly, the statutory provisions were no obstacle to that equipment being repossessed from those users, in accordance with the terms of the leasing agreement.

Enforcing charge Unless the examiner consents, no charge over all or part of the company's property can be enforced, in the sense of taking action to realise all or part of the security.[20] Charges so affected include those over the company's assets or income. The term charge here is not defined, which leaves open the question whether a charge here applies to non-possessory securities, like pledges or liens.

The term used in the British legislation in this context is 'security', rather

---

13. [1990] BCLC 729.
14. *Bristol Airport plc v Powdrill* [1990] 1 Ch 744.
15. See generally, C.J. Miller, *Contempt of Court* (1989) pp. 388-391.
16. Cf. *Atlantic Computer* case, supra n.9.
17. See post ch. 21.   18. S.5(2)(e).
19. [1992] 2 WLR 367.   20. S.5(2)(d).

than charge, which has been held to include a possessory lien,[21] and also a landlord's right of re-entry under a lease.[22] It was held in *Bristol Airport plc v Powdrill*[23] that a right of detention enjoyed by airport authorities under statute, over aircraft standing in their airports, was a security under the comparable British legislation. Accordingly, any attempt by an authority to exercise that right was prohibited by the Act; in this instance, the attempt was held to be a contempt of court, although there was no suggestion of the authority there knowingly seeking to flout the Act. Even if the authority's right there could not strictly be characterised as a lien, it was some other form of security within the contemplation of that definition. Since the 1990 Act does not contain any definition of what is a charge, this case throws no light on the position under that Act. However, the fact that the 1990 Act does not expressly apply to liens and other possessory securities would strongly suggest that it was not intended to apply to them, especially since the draftsman expressly brings retention of title and similar arrangements within that Act.

Execution, attachment, sequestration and distress The traditional creditors' remedies of execution by the sheriff (or *fieri facias*), sequestration and distress cannot be 'put into force' against the company's property without the examiner's consent.[24] The term 'put in force' in this context has a precise connotation. In the case of *fi. fa.*, execution is put in force only when the sheriff has seized the goods.[25] For all modes of execution, the test is whether proceedings have reached such a stage as the creditor has obtained a charge over the property.[26] However, it would seem to follow from the previously mentioned restriction that, even when a charge has been so obtained, it cannot be realised—unless the two subsections are mutually exclusive.

Set-off Except with the examiner's consent, there cannot be any set-off between the bank accounts of a company which has court protection.[27] Bank accounts here include accounts with the Agricultural Credit Corporation, the Post Office Savings Bank, any certified trustee savings bank, a building society, an industrial and provident society, a friendly society, a unit trust or collective investment scheme, as well as licensed banks. But protection does not affect any set-off which may arise otherwise than between accounts with any of these bodies.

Judgment mortgage There is no express reference in the 1990 Act to registering a judgment mortgage against the company's land. Such a measure

---

21. *Re Sabre International Products Ltd* [1991] BCLC 470.
22. *Exchange Travel Agency Ltd v Triton Property Trust plc* [1991] 396.
23. [1990] BCLC 585.
24. S.5(2)(e).
25. *Re London & Devon Biscuits Co.* (1871) 12 Eg 190.
26. *Crowshaw v Lindhurst Ship Co.* [1897] 2 Ch 154.
27. S.5(2)(h).   28. S.5(2)(d).

hardly constitutes 'action to realise' the security,[28] which is prohibited without the examiner's consent.

Receiver A receiver may not be appointed over the property or undertaking of a company which enjoys court protection.[29] But where a receiver has already been appointed for more than three continuous days, the court cannot then grant the company protection.[30] As for a receiver who, within three days of the petition for protection being presented, has been appointed to all or any part of the company's properties, the court may make such order as it deems fit regarding what he may or should do.[31] In particular, the court may direct that he shall cease to act; that he may act only in respect of certain assets; that he deliver all books and papers and other records regarding the company to the examiner; that he gives the examiner all particulars of his dealings with the company's property or undertakings. In deciding whether to restrict the receiver's activities, the court will have regard to whether that is 'likely to facilitate the survival of the company, and the whole or any part of its undertaking, as a going concern.'[32]

Winding up Court protection cannot be obtained where the company has resolved to wind itself up or it has been wound up by the court.[33] But once protection commences, no such resolution can be passed nor proceedings for a winding-up be commenced.[34] Where a winding-up petition has been presented, it was held in England that the court may restrain the advertising of that petition pending the outcome of the examination.[35] Under the 1990 Act, in such cases both petitions should be heard at the one time, except where a provisional liquidator has already been appointed.[36] If there is a provisional liquidator, the court may make such orders as it deems fit regarding what he should or should not do, in particular, that he shall be the examiner as well, that he shall cease to act, that he shall deliver papers concerning the company to the examiner and provide particulars regarding his dealings with the company's property. Any direction that he shall cease to act shall be in order to facilitate the company's survival as a going concern.

Sureties, indemnors and the like So long as the company is under the court's protection, persons who have guaranteed or given indemnities for obligations to be performed by the company are protected against proceedings concerning the company's liabilities and also against modes of enforcing execution against their property in connection with those obligations.[37] The category of persons who are so protected is defined as those who 'under any enactment, rule of law or otherwise [are] liable to pay all or any part of the debts of the company.'[38]

29. S.5(2)(b).   30. S.3(6).   31. S.6(1).
32. S.6(3).   33. S.2(1).   34. S.5(2)(a).
35. Cf. *Re A Company (No. 001992 of 1988)* [1988] BCLC 9.
36. S.6(5); cf. *Re West Tech plc* [1988] BCLC 600.
37. S.5(2)(f).   38. Ibid.

EXTRATERRITORIAL IMPACT OF PROTECTION

Many Irish companies have a significant business presence in foreign countries, especially within the European Community. That presence may take the shape of having a foreign branch or subsidiary or having foreign associated companies, or it may be no more than doing business in a foreign country. Two principal questions arise with regard to extraterritoriality: the effects abroad, so far as Irish law is concerned, of court protection and examination under the 1990 Act and the effects in Ireland of comparable foreign proceedings.

The 1990 Act applies in principle to Irish registered companies and not to companies which are registered abroad. An argument could be made that some foreign companies which are 'related' to a company being protected, in the terms of s.4 of the Act, can be brought within the protection. This is where that company is one which could be wound up under the Companies Acts; for the term related company is defined to include 'any body which is liable to be wound up under the Companies Acts.'[39] Granted, in exceptional cases there is a jurisdiction to wind up foreign registered companies.[40] But the reference here most likely is to other forms of indigenous legal entities which can be wound up, like industrial and provident societies and building societies.[41] The occasional reference elsewhere in the 1990 Act to events outside the State suggests that the 'liable to be wound up' clause was not intended to embrace foreign companies.

Special statutory provisions aside, the circumstances in which an Irish court would give effect to the orders of a foreign court in proceedings similar to protection under the 1990 Act call for complex analysis of the conflict of laws, property law and jurisdictional questions. Some of these matters were explored in *Felixstowe Dock & Rly. Co. v United States Lines Inc.*,[42] which concerned an application made in England to give effect to stays on proceedings ordered by a U.S. bankruptcy court in a Chapter 11 case. The Brussels Convention on Jurisdiction and the Enforcement of Judgments of 1968,[43] as amended, does not apply to reorganisation proceedings; excluded from its scope are *inter alia* 'judicial arrangements, compositions and analogous proceedings'.[44]

However, s.36 of the 1990 Act facilitates giving effect to orders made in foreign schemes of arrangement and comparable proceedings; this resembles s.142 of the Bankruptcy Act, 1988.[45] Under s.36, the Minister may recognise the courts of such foreign countries as he chooses for these purposes. If an order is then made by a court which has been so recognised, in the course of reorganising or restructuring a company, the High Court may enforce that order as if it had been made here by the High Court. It would seem that, in principle,

---

39. S.4(6).   40. See post pp. 134-135.
41. Compare *Re International Bulk Commodities Ltd* [1992] BCLC 1074.
42. [1989] 1 AB 360.
43. Given effect by Jurisdiction of Courts and Enforcement of Judgments (European Communities) Act 1988.
44. Art. 1(2).   45. See *Bankruptcy Law*, pp. 186-190.

orders of that nature which could not be made in protection proceedings under the 1990 Act can be enforced if made by a recognised foreign court. However, the High Court has a general discretion under this jurisdiction and there are several reasons why it may not enforce an order which it has no original jurisdiction to make.

10

Examiner's Powers and Duties

Examiners' principal functions are two-fold, viz. to investigate the affairs of the company and report thereon to the court[1] and, secondly, to seek to put together some scheme or compromise, which will result in the company's survival, and report thereon to the court.[2] In order to facilitate carrying out these tasks, the 1990 Act gives the examiner a wide range of powers.

CREDITORS' COMMITTEE

An examiner may decide to appoint a creditors' committee to help him perform his functions and must appoint such a committee when directed to do so by the court.[3] This committee should not exceed five members and must contain representatives of the three largest unsecured creditors, unless the court directs otherwise.

DIRECTORS' AND SHAREHOLDERS' MEETINGS

An examiner is entitled to reasonable notice of all meetings of the company's directors and of its shareholders, including a description of the business to be transacted.[4] He, moreover, may convene any such meeting, set the agenda, preside at it, be heard at it, give reports and propose motions.[5]

POWERS OF AUDITORS

Company auditors have an extensive range of powers for obtaining information regarding a company's financial affairs and persons connected with the company are obliged to assist the auditors in their investigations.[6] All of these rights and powers are conferred on a company's examiner.[7]

LIQUIDATORS' POWERS

Where the court orders that the examiner may exercise all or part of the directors' powers, it may also confer on him all or part of the powers which can be exercised by a liquidator.[8] Examples include disclaiming onerous property and contracts[9] and bringing misfeasance claims.[10]

---

1. S.15(1).   2. S.18(1) and (2).   3. S.21.
4. S.7(2) and (3).   5. Ibid.   6. See *Company Law*, pp. 264-265.
7. S.7(1).   8. S.9(4).   9. See post pp. 224-229.

PRODUCTION OF DOCUMENTS AND EVIDENCE

Specific provision is made in s.8 of the 1990 Act to enable the examiner to get documents and evidence concerning the company's affairs. Breach of these requirements can be certified by the examiner and, on the court considering the matter and any witness, can be punished in the same way as a contempt of court. Obligations of this nature are imposed on all officers and agents of the company, and on present and past auditors, bankers and solicitors of the company. Regarding former officers and agents, as thus defined, they must produce to the examiner all books and documents concerning the company in their custody or over which they have power. They must attend before the examiner when required to do so, must give him all reasonable assistance in connection with his functions and they may be examined on oath by the examiner, either orally or on written interrogatories. These same obligations apply to any other person who is in possession of any information concerning the company's affairs or who may have such information. Any information covered by legal professional privilege previously does not have to be disclosed as required here.[11] Provision is made for obtaining details of transactions where any director of the company, including a 'shadow director' or 'connected person', either has or had a bank account, either in his own name or jointly and either in the State or abroad.

In the comparable British legislation, the administrator's power to interrogate on oath is within the same framework as a liquidator's authority to examine persons on oath before the court—the equivalent of s.245 of the 1963 Act.[12] That is not the case under the 1990 Act but, since the court can confer liquidators' powers on the examiner, he can thereby use the s.245 inquisition procedure. Guidelines have been laid down on the circumstances in which persons should not be required to cooperate entirely with liquidators under s.245.[13] Presumably those also apply where the examiner carries on his interrogation entirely outside of that section.

CERTIFYING LIABILITIES

When a company obtains court protection, its suppliers, bankers and others may be reluctant to continue dealing with it and extend it credit unless their position is duly safeguarded. If they cease dealing with the company, its business may very well collapse rapidly and there may no longer be any viable trading arrangements to be salvaged through a scheme with the creditors. Section 10 of the 1990 Act goes a long way to meet this situation. Where the examiner is of the view that, unless particular transactions are entered into, the company's survival as a going concern would be seriously prejudiced, he may certify liabilities the company undertakes in respect of those transactions. This applies only to liabilities incurred during the period when he is the examiner and the certification must be made at the time those liabilities were incurred or were to

10. See post pp. 253-258.
11. S.8(5B)   12. See post pp.199-206.
13. E.g. *Cloverbay Ltd v Bank of Credit & Commerce International* [1991] Ch 90.

be incurred. The effect of any such certification is to treat those liabilities as an expense of the examination which, under s.29 of the Act, must be paid in full before any other claim against the company may be paid.[14] Those who extend credit to the company and whose entitlements are duly certified are thereby guaranteed payment, provided of course the company has sufficient assets to meet those claims.

EXERCISING DIRECTORS' POWERS

When an examiner is being appointed, the court may direct that the directors' powers shall be restricted.[15] Additionally, s.9 of the 1990 Act authorises the examiner to apply to the court to take over all or any of the directors' functions and powers, for instance, to borrow money, to manage all or part of the company's business and to bring and defend actions involving the company. Before it can make an order of this nature, the court must have regard to the following matters, although what weight or significance is given to them is not indicated, other than that they must show that it is 'just and equitable' to confer the powers being sought on the examiner. Those matters are whether the conduct of the company's affairs are calculated to prejudice the interests of either the company, its employees or its creditors as a whole, or whether the interests of those parties would otherwise be safeguarded. Use of the term 'interests' here and not just rights enables the court to consider a wide range of matters. Other matters which the court should take into account include whether a transfer of power to the examiner is expedient for preserving the company's assets, whether the company or its directors support a transfer of powers and 'any other matter in relation to the company the court thinks relevant'. When due account is to be taken of all of these, the question then is whether it is just and equitable to order a divesting of the directors' powers. Conditions may be imposed on any such order and ancillary orders may be made by the court.

REPUDIATING CONTRACTS

Generally, company receivers and managers can carry out their functions in disregard of contracts binding the company,[16] other than contracts which can be the subject of an order for specific performance. Where their authority covers the company's entire assets and undertaking, receivers and managers can in effect repudiate contracts, but that action does not relieve the company of the liability to pay damages for breach of the contract. In *Astor Chemicals Ltd v Synthetic Technology Ltd*,[17] it was held that examiners do not have a similar ability to rid the company of its contractual duties, because examiners have a completely different function from that of receivers. A receiver's job is to realise the company's assets for the benefit of one creditor; an examiner's objective, when he has been given directors' powers, is to manage the company's affairs for the benefit of all interested parties.

14. See ante pp. 87-88.   15. S.3(8).
16. See ante pp. 53-55.   17. [1990] BCLC 1.

However, s.20 of the 1990 Act gives the company, not the examiner as such, power to repudiate certain contracts, which resembles the power of disclaimer enjoyed by liquidators.[18] Where the examiner is not a party to the company's application, he must be notified of the fact and may appear and be heard on the matter. It is only contracts the performance of which do not involve paying money which can be repudiated; an obligation to pay money cannot be ended in this manner. This power is exerciseable only when proposals for a scheme of arrangement 'are to be formulated'; the Act does not indicate how far advanced those proposals must be. Where the power is exercised, the other contracting party then stands as an unsecured creditor for the damages which ensue from this breach of contract. Where, in order to facilitate acceptance of proposals for a compromise, it is necessary to quantify the damages which would result from repudiating a contract, the court may hear the matter and determine how much the amount of those damages shall be.

AGREEING CLAIMS

If he is empowered to do so by the court, either directly[19] or by virtue of obtaining the powers of a liquidator, the examiner can ascertain and agree claims against the company.

DISPOSING OF CHARGED PROPERTY

Not alone are secured creditors prevented from enforcing their security while a company is under protection, but s.11 of the 1990 Act enables the examiner to dispose of or deal with their security in accordance with the conditions laid down there. Charged property for these purposes includes property which is subject to a floating charge, to a hire purchase or a conditional sale agreement, to retention of title and also any property which is held under a bailment capable of subsisting for more than three months. The criterion of when an examiner is to be permitted by the court to dispose of or to otherwise deal with charged property in this sense is whether doing so 'would be likely to facilitate the survival of the whole or any part of the company as a going concern'; the court must be satisfied that this is indeed the case. When considering such applications, 'the court has to make a balancing exercise between the prejudice that would be felt if the order is made by the secured creditor, against the prejudice that would be felt by those interested in the promotion of' this criterion.[20]

However, the examiner cannot thereby interfere with the secured creditors' priority or substantially diminish the value of their security. Where that property is sold, the net proceeds of disposal must be applied towards discharging the sum secured.[21] By the sum secured here is meant not alone the capital sum and outstanding interest but any cost which the security-holder is entitled to add in accordance with the general law and the security instrument. If that sum falls

18. See post pp. 224-229.   19. S.7(7).
20. *Re A.R.V. Aviation Ltd* [1989] BCLC 664, at p. 666.
21. S.11(3).

below what would have been realised in a free sale in an open market, the difference between the two prices must be applied by the examiner in discharging the secured debt. If the property is replaced by other property, for instance in a floating charge, any replacement property is subject to the same order of priority.

RECOVERING PROPERTY FRAUDULENTLY DISPOSED OF

Where the company's property has been fraudulently disposed of, the examiner can take steps to have it or its worth recovered. Section 139 of the Companies Act, 1990, applies where property of the company has been disposed of in a manner which perpetrated a fraud on the company, its creditors or its members; s.139 applies to any type of property and to any mode of disposition. The examiner may apply to the court and, if he shows that a fraudulent disposal has taken place, the court may order that the property be delivered up to him or that a sum be paid to him in respect of the property. An order to that effect will be made if it is 'just and equitable' to do so but the court is required to take account of the interests of any bona fide purchaser for value of the property.

PREVENTING 'DETRIMENT' TO THE COMPANY, A CREDITOR OR MEMBER

Section 7(5) of the 1990 Act gives the examiner an extensive power to take appropriate action to protect the company, any creditor or member from suffering detriment. The full text reads:

> Where an examiner becomes aware of any actual or proposed act, omission, course of conduct, decision or contract, by or on behalf of the company to which he has been appointed, its officers, employees, members or creditors or by any other person in relation to the income, assets or liabilities of that company which, in his opinion, is or is likely to be to the detriment of that company, or any interested party, he shall, subject to the rights of parties acquiring an interest in good faith and for value in such income, assets or liabilities, have full power to take whatever steps are necessary to halt, prevent or rectify the effects of such act, omission, course of conduct, decision or contract.

What exactly the examiner is permitted to do under this provision will require judicial elaboration.

APPLICATION FOR DIRECTIONS

Where matters arise during the examination which require clarification by the court, a wide range of persons concerned can apply to have the question ruled on. Under s.7(6) the examiner can apply to have 'any question arising in the course of his office' determined by the court. Any member, contributory, director or creditor of the company can apply in relation to any of the powers the 1990 Act gives the court. And under s.13(7) the company itself or any 'interested party' can apply for a determination of any question regarding the performance or otherwise by the examiner of his functions.

FIRST REPORT ON THE EXAMINATION

The examiner's principal function is 'to conduct an examination of the affairs of the company'.[22] It is to enable him to assess the company's financial and trading position, and the true value of its assets and liabilities, that he is given the same powers as are possessed by auditors and additional powers to compel production of certain documents and information. Within 21 days of being appointed, the examiner must present to the court a report on his findings;[23] a longer period may be allowed by the court.[24] At the same time a copy of this report must be given to the company and, on request, copies must be made available to any member or creditor of the company.[25] If the court so directs, there may be omitted, from copies of the report given to members and creditors, information 'which would be likely to prejudice the survival of the company, or the whole or any part of its undertaking.'[26]

Contents of the report   Those matters which must be contained in the report are set out in s.16 of the 1990 Act:

(a) the names and permanent addresses of the officers of the company and, in so far as the examiner can establish, any person in accordance with whose directions or instructions the directors of the company are accustomed to act,

(b) the names of any other bodies corporate of which the directors of the company are also directors,

(c) a statement as to the affairs of the company, showing, insofar as is reasonably possible to do so, particulars of the company's assets, debts and liabilities (including contingent and prospective liabilities) as at the latest practicable date, the names and addresses of its creditors, the securities held by them respectively and the dates when the securities were respectively given,

(d) whether in the opinion of the examiner any deficiency between the assets and the liabilities of the company has been satisfactorily accounted for or, if not, whether there is evidence of a substantial disappearance of property that is not adequately accounted for,

(e) a statement of opinion by the examiner as to whether the company, and the whole or any part of its undertaking, would be capable of survival as a going concern and a statement of the conditions which he feels are essential to ensure such survival, whether as regards the internal management and controls of the company or otherwise,

22. S.15(1).   23. Ibid.   24. Ibid.   25. S.15(3) and (4).

(f)   his opinion as to whether the formulation, acceptance and confirmation of proposals for a compromise or scheme of arrangement would facilitate such survival,

(g)   whether, in his opinion, an attempt to continue the whole or any part of the undertaking of the company would be likely to be more advantageous to the members as a whole and the creditors as a whole, than a winding-up of the company,

(h)   recommendations as to the course he thinks should be taken in relation to the company including, if warranted, draft proposals for a com- promise or scheme of arrangement,

(i)   his opinion as to whether the facts disclosed would warrant further enquires [regarding fraudulent or reckless trading or trading for any other fraudulent purpose],

(j)   such other matters as the examiner thinks relevant or the court directs, and

(k)   his opinion as to whether his work would be assisted by a direction of the court extending the role or membership of any creditors' committee [which was appointed].

Hearing on the report   What happens next depends on whether the examiner discovered serious wrong doing and his evaluation of the company's prospects of being rescued from insolvency. If his conclusions are adverse in this sense, the court will direct a prompt hearing into the matters arising from his report.[27] By adverse here is meant where he concludes that there has been a substantial disappearance of company property that has not been adequately accounted for or that there had been other serious irregularities in the company's affairs.[28] Adverse conclusions here also include where the examiner takes the view that neither all nor any part of the company's undertaking would be capable of surviving as a going concern, or that no compromise or scheme which might be adopted would facilitate the survival of the undertaking or any part of it, or that winding up the company would be more advantageous to its members as a whole and its creditors as a whole than attempting to continue the whole or part of its business.[29] At this hearing, the examiner, the company, any member and any creditor are entitled to appear and to be heard.[30] So also is any person who is referred to in the report in connection with property disappearing or serious irregularities.[31]

What the outcome of that hearing should be is entirely at the court's discretion; it may 'make such order or orders as it deems fit'. Section 17(4) of the Act lists a whole range of orders which can be made, without prejudice to the court's general discretion. These are:

26. S.15(4) and (5).   27. S.17(1).   28. Ibid.
29. Ibid.   30. S.17(2).   31. Ibid.

(a) the discharge from the protection of the court of the whole or any part of the assets of the company,

(b) the imposition of such terms and conditions as it sees fit for the continuance of the protection of the court,

(c) the winding-up of the company,

(d) the sale of the whole or any part of the undertaking of the company on such terms and conditions,, including terms and conditions relating to the distribution of the proceeds of such sale, as the court sees fit, and, if necessary for that purpose, the appointment of a receiver,

(e) the formulation by the examiner of proposals for a compromise or scheme of arrangement,

(f) the summoning of the meetings mentioned in this Act for the purpose of considering proposals for a compromise or scheme of arrangement,

(g) the calling, holding and conduct of a meeting of the board of directors, or a general meeting of the company, to consider such matters as the court shall direct.

NEGOTIATING PROPOSALS FOR A RESCUE PACKAGE

If the examiner's conclusions from his report are favourable or if he is otherwise so directed by the court, having put in his report, he must formulate proposals for rescuing the company. By favourable conclusions here is meant that the examiner takes the view that each of the following three conditions obtain:[32] that all or part of the company's undertaking is capable of surviving as a going concern; that adopting a compromise or scheme would facilitate such survival; that it is more advantageous to all the members and creditors as a whole to carry on and seek to salvage the company rather than wind it up there and then. It is only in the most hopeless circumstances that this last condition would not obtain.

Just six weeks are allowed, from when the examiner was appointed, for the parties to consider his proposals and to report back to the court on the parties' reaction to the proposals.[33] An extension of time may be obtained.[34] In drawing up proposals, the creditors must be divided into different classes, but the 1990 Act provides no criteria for determining the class composition. Most likely the same approach would be adopted as for schemes of arrangement under s.201 of the Companies Act, 1963,[35] for differentiating between the groups of creditors. Usually, there would be at least three classes of creditors—secured,

32. S.18(1).   33. S.18(2).
34. S.18(3)   35. See *Company Law*, pp. 391 and 393.

preferred and unsecured creditors. The class composition of the shareholders would be determined by the criteria in the case law for ascertaining members' class rights.[36]

Contents of proposals   Among the matters to be dealt with in those proposals are the following:[37]

> Each class of members and of creditors must be specified;
> Those classes whose interests will be 'impaired' and those classes whose interest will not be impaired must be specified;
> Whatever changes should be made in the management and direction of the company, where the examiner considers such changes would facilitate its survival as a going concern;
> Whatever changes should be made in the company's memorandum and articles which the examiner considers would facilitate its survival;
> Provisions for implementing the proposals;
> A full account of each class meeting and a copy of the proposals put to that meeting.

The only requirement regarding the proposals' intrinsic merits is equality within classes, i.e. except where the class members agree otherwise, all members of the same class must be treated equally.[38]

Where the proposed scheme involves persons investing money in the company, in one instance Costello J ruled that a copy of the contract, under which the money is to be put in, should be incorporated into the scheme itself.[39] This appears to be the practice in the United States. However, in a previous instance Costello J approved a scheme where a contract of this nature was not a part of the proposals.[40] Indeed schemes have been approved at times where intending investors were not contractually and unconditionally bound to put in money.[41]

A statement of affairs, as of the date of the proposals, must be attached to them.[42] There must also be attached to them an estimate of how each class of creditor and member would fare in the event of a liquidation.[43] Additional matters must be included where the court so directs and the examiner may include such other matters as he deems appropriate.

Convening meetings   The examiner must then convene meetings of such classes of members and of creditors as he deems appropriate to consider these proposals.[44] There is no need to call meetings of creditors whose interests will not be directly affected by the proposals. In *Re British & Commonwealth*

36. Id. pp. 373-375.   37. S.22(1).
38. S.22(1)(d).
39. *Re Wogans (Drogheda) Ltd (No. 2)* (7 May 1992).
40. *Re Selukwe Ltd* (20 December 1991).
41. E.g. *Re Animedia Teo* (Costello J, August 1992).
42. S.22(2).   43. S.22(3).   44. S.23(1).

Holdings plc (No. 3),[45] it was held that there was no need to admit to a creditors' meeting the trustee for subordinated creditors there. This was because, under the loan agreement, the only way the subordinated creditors' rights could be enforced was by the trustee petitioning to wind up the company and then they would rank behind all the other creditors. Accordingly, until a winding up commenced, their trustee had no right at all to oppose the proposals.

There is no express requirement to include with the notices of these meetings copies of the actual proposals and of the statement of affairs and estimate of the creditors' position in a liquidation. But the notices must be accompanied by a statement setting out the general effects of the compromise or scheme being put forward;[46] there must be set out, in particular, its effect on any 'material interest' of the company's directors, whether those interests are as directors of the company or as its creditors or otherwise. Where the proposals affect debenture-holders whose affairs are in the hands of trustees, the notices must explain the proposals' effects on those trustees and on any 'material interest' they may have.[47]

The examiner presides at these meetings. Care should be taken that the interested parties are in their proper classes. Difficulties can arise where, for instance, a major shareholder is also a very substantial creditor and where a major secured creditor is also a large unsecured creditor. Diplomatic and social skills, as well as financial and commercial expertise, may be needed to convince the several groups to accept the proposals, either as they stand or as modified. Any person present may put forward modified proposals but none of them can be accepted without the examiner's consent to them.[48]

Acceptance of proposals Having duly considered them, the various classes must then vote on the proposals. Votes can be cast either in person or by proxy.[49] Even the Revenue and other State and local authorities, which generally are not permitted by law to compromise obligations due to them, are authorised to vote for and accept proposals they otherwise could not accept.[50] This is one of the main differences between rescue schemes under the 1990 Act and schemes under s.201 of the Companies Act, 1963; under the latter the Revenue take the view that they are not free to accept bonds, securities and other forms of property in lieu of tax which is due and payable.[51] If proposals are agreed and some classes of creditors and members accept them, they are then put before the court to be confirmed and made binding on all classes. If agreement cannot be reached on the proposals, the matter goes back to the court, which may direct that the company be wound up.[52]

There is acceptance by each class of shareholder if a bare majority of the

45. [1992] BCLC 322.   46. S.23(8).
47. S.23(6); cf. *Re Dorman Long & Co.* [1934] Ch 635.
48. S.23(2).
49. S.23(3); see Rules 10-14.   50. S.23(5).
51. Cf. *Re Pye (Ireland) Ltd* (Costello J, 11 March 1985).
52. S.24(11)(b).

votes cast by the class are in favour of the proposals.[53] There is acceptance by each class of creditors when both a majority in number of the class *and* at the same time a majority in value of them vote in favour to the proposals.[54]

FIDUCIARY DUTIES

Being an officer of the court, the examiner is a fiduciary agent and, like official liquidators,[55] is subject to the usual fiduciary duties—to use the powers arising under the 1990 Act for their proper purposes, not to profit from or take unfair advantage from his office and to avoid all undue conflicts of interest. As has been said regarding company liquidators, '[t]here is between [them] on the one side and the shareholders or creditors of the company on the other a fiduciary relationship which prevents the liquidators making a profit out of their trust [and] prohibit[s] any arrangement by which a liquidator may receive extra remuneration than that allowed by the Acts. . . .'[56] The usual procedure for obtaining redress against liquidators is the misfeasance claim under s.298 of the Companies Act, 1963, which in 1990 was extended to apply to company receivers and examiners.[57]

LIABILITY OF EXAMINER

Contract   Except where the contract provides otherwise, examiners are personally liable on any contract they enter into in the performance of their functions—whether the contract be in their own name, in the name of the company or otherwise.[58] This is one of the occupational risks of examiners. It is a question of fact whether any particular contract excludes their personal liability. However, an examiner is entitled to an indemnity out of the company's assets in respect of contracts properly entered into by him[59] and that indemnity must be paid, along with remuneration and expenses, before any other debt can be paid.[60]

Tort and misfeasance   The question of the liability of an examiner in tort has not yet been considered by the courts. The 1990 Act does not give him any immunity from tort liability. In dealing with allegations of negligence, presumably an examiner will be held to the standards of the normal prudent professional person in that position. Presumably, his duty of care is owed to all those who have the requisite 'proximity', subject to any special policy reasons for not imposing liability in damages.[61]

53. S.23(3).   54. S.23(4).
55. See post pp. 218-219.
56. *Re R. Gertzenstein Ltd* [1937] 1 Ch 115, at pp. 116-117.
57. 1963 Act s.142.
58. S.13(6).   59. Ibid.
60. See ante pp. 87-88.
61. See generally B. McMahon & W. Binchy, *Irish Law of Torts* (2nd ed. 1990) ch. 10.

11

The Proposed Rescue Package

The last stage in the process is the proposals being set down for consideration by the court. From the time of his appointment, the examiner has 42 days (six weeks) within which to have the proposals considered and voted on and report to the court on the outcome of those deliberations.[1] But the court may permit him a longer time to make his report. Four months from the date of the petition being presented is the very maximum period within which a report can be made to the court[2] but, once a report is in by that time, the court may extend the protection period to enable it to decide on the proposals and the court may take so long as it needs for this purpose.[3] There is no statutory deadline although, given the very nature of the issues to be decided, ordinarily the court would give them prompt attention.

On the same day as the court gets the examiner's report, a copy must be given to the company and copies must also be given to any member or creditor who requests it in writing.[4] However, the court may direct that extracts should be omitted from any copy given to shareholders and creditors, where inclusion of that information is likely to prejudice the company's survival or the survival of all or part of its undertaking.[5]

CONTENTS OF REPORT

What the examiner's report must contain is set out in s.19 of the 1990 Act:

(a) the proposals placed before the required meetings,

(b) any modification of those proposals adopted at any of those meetings,

(c) the outcome of each of the required meetings,

(d) the recommendation of the committee of creditors, if any,

(e) a statement of the assets and liabilities (including contingent and prospective liabilities) of the company as at the date of his report,

(f) a list of the creditors of the company, the amount owing to each such creditor, the nature and value of any security held by any such creditor, and the priority (i.e. preferential) status of any such creditor

1. S.18(2).   2. S.18(3).   3. S.18(4).
4. S.18(5).   5. S.18(6).

under s.285 of the Companies Act, 1963, or any other statutory provision or rule of law,

(g) a list of the officers of the company,

(h) his recommendations,

(i) such other matters as the examiner deems appropriate or the court directs.

THE HEARING

The stage is then set for the high point of the examination. At this hearing, the company and the examiner may appear and be heard;[6] so also may any creditor or member whose interests are impaired. A creditor's interests are impaired[7] if, under the proposals, he is to obtain less than the full amount which was due to him when the protection commenced. A shareholder's interests are impaired[8] if, under the proposals, either the nominal value of his shares is reduced; a fixed dividend to which he is entitled is reduced; his proportionate interest in the entire share capital is diminished; he is otherwise to be deprived of all or part of his rights as a shareholder, like voting rights; or he is to lose his entire shareholding. Proposals can be made and confirmed which do not involve impairing any party's interests in the company. In deciding whether to accept the proposals, with or without modification, the following separate hurdles must crossed. To use the parlance of American corporate reorganisation law, these are the standards against which any 'cram down' of the dissenting creditors and members are to be judged.

Class acceptance   First, from the classes whose interests would be impaired in the manner just described, the proposals must have secured acceptance by at least one class of creditors and one class of members.[9] If only creditors' rights are impaired, it suffices if one class of them accepted the proposals. A majority in value *and* in number is required for acceptance by any class of creditors.[10]

Material irregularity   One ground of objection which may be raised at the hearing is that there was a 'material irregularity' at or in relation to any of the meetings at which the proposals were considered.[11] What deviations from proper procedure would amount to a material irregularity in this context depends on all the circumstances of the case.

Improper means and improper purpose   Two other grounds of objection are that acceptance of the proposals was obtained by improper means or that the proposals were made for an improper purpose.[12] Again, what methods and

---

6.   S.24(2).   7. S.22(5).   8. S.22(6).
9.   S.24(4)(a).   10. S.23(4).   11. S.25(1)(a).
12.   S.25(1)(b) and (c).

what objectives would be regarded as improper for these purposes will depend on the circumstances of the case. It remains to be seen whether objectives other than tax-avoidance would be deemed to be improper in this context; in the light of the court's general discretion under the Act, the answer would seem to be yes.

Tax avoidance Where the sole or primary purpose of the scheme is to avoid paying tax, it cannot be confirmed by the court.[13] This gives statutory form to several Australian cases where schemes of arrangement, designed primarily to make substantial gains from the tax losses of insolvent companies, were rejected by the courts there.[14] But the mere fact that the proposals, when implemented, will or may give rise to a fiscal windfall should not thereby defeat them.

Not unfairly prejudicial The position of individual creditors and share-holders within the various classes will be considered. A party may object on the grounds that the proposals would 'unfairly prejudice' his interests and, if that complaint is sustained, the court cannot give its sanction to the scheme.[15] By unfair prejudice here presumably is meant that, while a party's class in general may be getting fair and equitable treatment, his special individual circumstances may render that treatment exceptionally harsh. For instance, that person may stand to incur some unique tax penalty with which fellow class members are not confronted.[16] If this is indeed the case, the only way in which the proposals can be salvaged is for the court to permit departure from the equality within the class principle in respect of that person.

Fair and equitable to each class As has been observed, within each class the members must be treated equally, save where the class members agree or the court directs otherwise. When it comes to comparing each class, whose interest are impaired, with other classes also being impaired, the burden which the different classes will bear must be 'fair and equitable' in relation to each other.[17] In other words, some classes must not be expected to bear far too great a reduction in their rights while others will be sacrificing very little. It depends on all the circumstances whether any particular class is being treated unfairly and inequitably for these purposes. No doubt this is a question which will spawn an abundance of case law in due course.

It was contended in support of several schemes proposed under the 1990 Act that, what fair and equitable in this context means is, when the proposals for an accepting class and for a dissenting class are compared, the acceptors must not be making a relatively light sacrifice compared with the heavy sacrifice which the objectors are being asked to make. The test is the comparative burden being

13. S.24(4)(b).
14. E.g. *Re Data Home Pty. Ltd* [1972] 2 NS WLR 23.
15. Ss.25(1)(d) and 24(4)(c)92).
16. Cf. *Re Hellenic & General Trust Ltd* [1976] 1 WLR 123.
17. S.24(4)(c)(i).

imposed on the classes—a comparison of the proposed 'impairments' of parties' rights and interests. The general criterion used in the United States Bankruptcy Code, Chapter 11, is that 'the plan does not discriminate unfairly, and is fair and equitable, with respect to each class of claims or interests that is impaired . . . under the plan'.[18] Some assistance may be obtained from cases dealing with schemes of arrangement among shareholders, under s.201 of the Companies Act, 1963,[19] and its predecessors. The cases are referred to and the principles are summarised in *Re Dorman Long & Co.*,[20] in *Re John Power & Sons Ltd*[21] and *Carruth v Imperial Chemical Industries.*[22] But these cases deal with a slightly different issue. The focus is entirely on whether the terms are fair for one particular class, regardless of how other classes may fare, because the contention in these cases is that the majority vote of the class, i.e. that in voting for the proposals, a significant portion of the class were motivated more by entirely extraneous considerations than the interests of the class as such. The issue here is not so much whether the terms are fair *vis-à-vis* the class which accepted the proposals; it is whether they are fair and reasonable to be forced on the dissenting class.

That the proposals are unfair and inequitable to a class of members or of

18.   11 U.S.C. s.1129. The position of secured creditors under the U.S. Chapter 11 procedure has been summarised as follows: If a class of secured creditors is impaired and does not accept the plan, the plan must be fair and equitable to that class in order to be confirmed [by the court]. In order for the plan to be fair and equitable with respect to a dissenting class of secured claims, the plan must at a minimun satisfy one of three separate requirements. First, the plan may provide for the holders of claims in the class to retain the share that secures their claims to the extent of the allowed amount of their claims. (If the class has not elected application of section 1111(b)(2), then the allowed amount is the value of the collateral; if an election is made then the allowed amount is the amount of the debt). Additionally, the plan must provide for the class to receive deferred cash payments totalling at least the allowed amount of their claims (the 'principal amount' test) and the payments must have a present value, as of the effective date of the plan, generally equal to the value of the collateral (the 'present value' test). Second, the plan may propose to sell collateral free and clear of the charge held by members of the dissenting class as long as the class has a chance to bid in their claims and the charge attached to the proceeds. The plan must also propose to treat the charge on proceeds under one of the other two prescribed methods. Third, the plan may propose that each member of the dissenting class realise the 'indubitable equivalent' of his allowed secured claim. The legislative history states that abondonment of the collateral to the class would satisfy this standard, as would a replacement charge on similar collateral. But present cash payments to the class less than the amount of the allowed secured claims would not satisfy the standard. Nor are unsecured notes or equity securities sufficient to constitute the 'indubitable equivalent' of secured claims. Klee, 'All You Ever Wanted to Know about Cram Down Under the New Bankruptcy Code', 53 *American Bankruptcy LJ* 133 (1979) pp. 154-155.

19.   See *Company Law*, pp. 393-394.

20.   [1934] 1 Ch 635, at pp. 655-656.

21.   [1934] IR 412, at pp. 424-425.

22.   [1937] AC 707, at pp. 749-751 and 769-771.

creditors is not enumerated as one of the grounds of objection which can be raised at the confirmation hearing.[23] It is possible, however, that the basis for complaint on these grounds can also be used to demonstrate that the proposals 'unfairly prejudice' the objector.[24] In any event, unless the court is satisfied that the proposals are fair and equitable to the affected classes confirmation will not be forthcoming.

Other considerations The court may take account of circumstances other than those set out above in deciding whether to confirm or reject proposals for a scheme of arrangement. Section 24(3) states that the 'court may, as it thinks proper', confirm or refuse its confirmation or modify the proposals, subject to ss.24 and 25 of the Act. The very first case in which a set of proposals were presented to the High Court, *Re Coombe Importers Ltd*[25] is a good example of other considerations causing the court to reject the scheme. The company was heavily insolvent and, if liquidated, it was unlikely that the Revenue's preferential debt would be discharged. Under the proposals made by the examiner and accepted by the overwhelming value and number of the creditors, other than the Revenue, creditors were to be paid 15 pence in the pound; the Revenue's preferential debt would be paid at 21 pence in the pound and their pre-preferential debt at 80 pence in the pound but that would be in equal instalments over a five years period. At the time the examiner was negotiating with several investors to put funds into the company, which would finance the proposed settlement and provide working capital for the business, but no binding agreement had been reached to make this investment. Hamilton P rejected the proposals as being not fair and equitable to the Revenue for several reasons, namely; the company's principal shareholders and directors had been involved in a company in the very same trade some years earlier, which was liquidated with a very large deficiency; the company's accounts had never been audited; there was some evidence which suggested that not all payments made to the company had been retained by the company. Additionally, because there was not yet a contract with a known individual to finance the proposals, the requirement of s.2(1)(e) that the proposals shall 'provide for [their] implementation' had not been met. But in another instance where no legally binding agreement existed, Costello J extended the protection for some time so that an agreement could be signed up.[26]

Some weeks after the *Coombe* case Hamilton P was presented with the proposed scheme in *Re Goodman International Ltd*[27] and that company's many related and connected companies. The principal creditors here were banks—the two major Irish banks and also leading British, French and German banks—who were owed hundreds of millions of pounds. Evidence had earlier been given in court by some of these banks which suggested that they had been

23. S.25.   24. S.25(1)(d).
25. Hamilton P, 28 Nov 1990.
26. *Re Animedia Teo* (Costello J, August 1992).
27. Hamilton P, 28 January 1991.

deceived or at least misled into extending very large credit facilities to the Goodman group. In the event, the proposals secured very substantial support from the banks and other creditors and were approved by the court. One of the terms was that the creditors would not seek to commence civil proceedings against Mr Goodman, the managing director and principal shareholder in those companies. Even though the 1990 Act does not expressly authorise a composite across-the-group scheme, Hamilton P held that the very 'purposes of the Act . . . would be nullified if the examiner were not entitled to take into account the position with regard to each and every one of the related companies and to formulate a scheme . . . which would deal with the overall picture.'[28]

Inaccuracies in originating affidavit   Mention has already been made of the *uberrimae fidei* nature of petitions, verified by affidavit, when seeking the appointment of an examiner.[29] If there are major discrepancies between the facts the petitioner deposed to and the true position, as subsequently ascertained, this can be grounds for rejecting the scheme.[30] That the petitioner may no longer be involved in the company, once reorganised, will not necessarily prevent proposals being rejected on those grounds.[31]

Preferential debts   There are categories of preferential creditors who are entitled to be paid in a liquidation or in a receivership before a penny can be distributed to the general unsecured creditors, most importantly, the Revenue Commissioners.[32] Unlike the comparable legislation in the U.S.A., the 1990 Act does not say how the preferential debts are to be treated in a reorganisation.[33] Under the U.S. Chapter 11, each priority tax claim must be paid in full but payments can be deferred by way of instalments over a period not exceeding six years;[34] also, those payments must have a present value equal to the amount of the tax claim. Additionally, in any reorganisation under Chapter 11, every class of creditor, and not just the U.S. Revenue, must receive as much as they would have obtained if the company had been liquidated.[35]

All that the 1990 Act says about debts to the Revenue is that the tax authorities are empowered to make binding compromises of claims for tax[36] and that, in considering any proposed scheme, the court must reject it if its primary purpose was tax avoidance.[37] Beyond that, the Act is silent. The inference, therefore, would seem to be that there will be no rule of thumb for all companies; each set of proposals will be dealt with on their own merits. The circumstances of a particular case may call for the entire preferential debt being paid off, perhaps in instalments. But the failure to enact an across-the-board

---

28. Id. at p. 16.
29. *Re Selukwe Ltd* (Costello J, 20 December 1991).
30. E.g. *Re Wogans (Drogheda) Ltd* (Costello J, 7 May 1992).
31. Ibid.   32. See post pp. 360-364.
33. Nor does the British Insolvency Act 1986.
34. S.1129(a)(9)(C).   35. S.1129(a)(7).
36. S.23(5).   37. S.24(4)(b).

rule to this effect suggests that there can be cases where the Revenue will be compelled to forego part of their preferential debts, perhaps even part of a pre-preferential amount as well. Indeed, it could be argued that the omission from the Act of a rule for these debts indicates an intention that the normal principle applicable to unsecured creditors should apply, i.e. equality between the creditors.

In *Re Gallaghers Boxty House Ltd*,[38] the proposals first put by the examiner and which were approved by several classes of creditors included payment of the preferential debts in full over a period of six years and also that the Revenue would waive corporation tax which might be levied on the 'write down' under s.24(1) of the Finance Act, 1970. These were vigorously opposed by the Revenue. They were then modified during the course of the hearing on the report; the waiver of any tax due under s.24(1) was taken out and, instead, the Revenue were to be treated in much the same way as the general unsecured creditors. The Dáil Debates[39] on the 1990 Act strongly suggest that the Oireachtas' intention was that schemes of arrangement should be approved even though the full amount of the preferential debts will not be repaid. Denham J approved the amended proposals because, in all the circumstances of the case, she found them fair, reasonable and equitable as between all classes of creditors and the members.

Secured creditors So far, the courts have not ruled on perhaps the most important issue of principle under the 1990 Act, the extent to which secured creditors can be impaired. An express power to that effect is not contained in the 1990 Act but neither does this Act expressly deny such a power. Although s.11 of the Act authorises the examiner to deal with charged property, that provision does not provide any strong indication as to the legislative intention behind the powers of the court to sanction schemes. Assuming the Act purports to enable secured creditors' rights to be impaired in this manner, would that power be consistent with the Constitution's guarantee of private property? Arguments could be made for and against this proposition; the answer is not demonstrably clear and certain. The outcome may depend on whether the security was obtained before or after the Act was enacted on 19 August 1990. In 1935 the United States Supreme Court[40] struck down a law, enacted to protect farmers who were in serious financial difficulties, which drastically impaired the rights of existing secured creditors. Brandeis J there observed that the Fifth Amendment (i.e. private property) guarantee commands that

> however great the nation's need, private property shall not be thus taken even for a wholly public use without just compensation. If the public interest requires, and permits, the taking of property of individual mortgagees in order to relieve the necessities of individual mortgagors, resort

38. Denham J, 5 November 1991, ex tempore.
39. Esp. Special Committee, 24 May 1990, D. 31, no. 17, cds. 1029-1034.
40. *Louisville Joint Stock Land Bank v Radford*, 195 US 555 (1935).

must be had to proceedings by eminent domain (i.e. expropriation); so that, through taxation, the burden of the relief afforded in the public interest may be borne by the public.[41]

However, the U.S. cases decided since then permit some degree of impairment of secured creditors' rights in the interest of their insolvent debtor.[42]

The present version of the U.S. Chapter 11 contains detailed rules on this topic; before the 1978 reforms, the principal criterion of fairness was whether those creditors were faring better than they would in a liquidation.[43] For many years the principle was that 'if the creditor, in lieu of the return of the property, receives cash in the appraised value of that property, the creditor receives the "value of the debt" and the creditor is adequately protected . . . and the plan can be confirmed without [his] consent. . . .'[44] Where the amount of debt far exceeds the present value of the security, the post-1978 position has been summarised as follows: '[t]here can be a cash payment cram down [of that claim], and the discounted value of these payments must equal at least the value of the collateral.'[45] It remains to be seen whether the value of the security (liquidation or going concern value?) will be the benchmark of what is just and equitable for secured creditors under the 1990 Act.

Perhaps the inference to be drawn from the fact that the 1990 Act does not lay down how the court is to deal with secured creditors is that their proprietary interests cannot be substantially diminished in a reorganisation.[46] The absence of express protection for secured creditors suggests that some impairment of secured creditors' rights may be permitted. This may apply especially to floating charges which, by legislation, have been ranked after preferential debts.[47] If it is permissible to place the floating charge behind certain revenue and employee debts, surely some impairment of a fixed charge for the purpose of a reorganisation is allowed?

Guarantees   Often the scheme will make express provision concerning debts of the company which have been secured by guarantees—usually personal guarantees given by directors and major shareholders. In one instance, Murphy J approved proposals that those guarantees should lapse if the company paid the sums falling due under the scheme.[48] But in another instance Costello J

41. Id. at p. 589.
42. See generally, Rogers, 'The Impairment of Secured Creditors' Rights in Reorganisations: A Study in the Relationship Between the First Amendment and the Bankruptcy Clause', 96 *Harvard L Rev* 973 (1983).
43. Id. and Blum & Kaplan, 'The Absolute Priority Doctrine in Corporate Reorganisations', 41 *U. Chicago L Rev* 651 (1974).
44. *Re Pine Gate Associates Ltd*, 2 BR Ct. Dec. (CRR) 1478 (1976).
45. *Re Griffiths*, 27 BR 873 (1983). See generally, Kaplan, 'Nonrecourse Unsecured Creditors Under the New Chapter 11', 53 *American Bankruptcy LJ* 269 (1979).
46. The British Insolvency Act 1986, is also silent in this regard.
47. 1963 Act. s.285(7)(b).
48. *Re Presswell Ltd*, 7 November 1991, *ex tempore*.

refused to sanction a scheme incorporating similar terms.[49] Instead, he directed that not alone should the guarantees of a creditor which had opposed the proposals in court remain in force but that, if the guarantors discharged their obligations to that creditor, they should not have the normal right of indemnity. There were similar terms in this scheme for another creditor, who did not oppose the proposals at the hearing; the stipulation that its guarantees should be modified was not altered in any way.

In *Re Wogans (Drogheda) Ltd. (No. 2)*[50] the examiner decided not to include in his scheme a provision about how the directors' personal guarantees should be treated, leaving it entirely to them and the bank to agree on what should be done, or to apply to the court as they saw fit. The scheme of arrangement was rejected there, principally because the initial petition had contained deliberate misstatements and also certain tax issues which arose. But Costello J there explained that in schemes involving creditors with guarantees, some provision should normally be made to deal with the guarantors' right of indemnity against the company in the event of them making payments under their guarantees. If the sums involved are very substantial, the absence of such a provision could seriously jeopardise the company's financial future when the guarantors stand in the shoes of the principal creditor, whom they have paid off. Where, however, the guarantors are the company's owners and directors, whose mismanagement brought on its financial difficulties and who supported the petition for an examination, it is likely that their usual implied right of indemnity no longer exists. Of course any express indemnity would not be so affected.

If the proposals do not deal with the position of those who have guaranteed the company's debts, it is an open question whether or not approval of a scheme operates to discharge the guarantee. The very terms of a guarantee may provide a clear answer to this question. Where the guarantee does not address the matter, some light may be thrown on the subject by cases on court-approved compositions[51] and on the Official Assignee and liquidators disclaiming leases in which the performance of covenants have been guaranteed.[52] If the guarantee refers to liability in respect of money which 'remains due and owing', it would seem that the guarantee would be discharged if the scheme releases the principal debtor.[53] In Britain and Northern Ireland, disclaimer of a lease operates to discharge guarantees for the performance of obligations under the lease on the grounds that, if there was no discharge, the whole point of disclaimer would be defeated by the guarantor claiming his indemnity. A similar logic would seem to apply in examinations; if the guarantee is not discharged, the guarantor can often in effect upset the entire settlement by enforcing his right of indemnity.

49. *Re Selukwe Ltd*, 20 December 1991.
50. Costello J, 7 May 1992.
51. E.g. *Re London Chartered Bank of Australia* [1893] 3 Ch 540 and *Re Southern World Airlines Ltd* [1993] 1 NZLR 597.
52. E.g. *Stacey v. Hill* [1901] 1 KB 660; compare *Re Farm Machinery Ltd* [1984] ILRM 273.
53. Cf. *Perrott v Newton King Ltd* [1933] NZLR 1131.

Although Costello J in the *Wogans* case criticised the examiner for not making express provision for the guarantees, he declined to indicate what the actual legal position is with guarantors, because it was 'not relevant'. The Irish Banks Standing Committee has sought legislation to ensure that guarantees remain in force in this context.

Tax adjustments Two years after the U.S. Congress passed the present version of Chapter 11, it enacted a special tax measure to deal with the various tax consequences of reorganisations.[54] No comparable provisions are contained in the Finance Acts of 1991 or 1992. However, there are a number of tax difficulties which could jeopardise otherwise viable schemes of arrangement. One concerns what may be called the tax payable on any 'write down', under s.24(1) of the Finance Act, 1970. This brings into the tax net any debts which have been 'released', in whole or in part, where a tax deduction had previously been allowed for those debts. The precise scope of this section has not been the subject of authoritative interpretation, nor has the question of whether approval of proposals under the 1990 Act constitutes a release for that purpose. Another matter is the appropriate treatment of value added tax claims refunds, where the amount to be paid to the creditor-supplier is being substantially reduced under a proposed scheme. Another still is the question of undisclosed or hidden tax liabilities, especially where the scheme involves an outside investor committing large sums to the company. Ordinarily he will be reluctant to do that, no matter how promising the company's prospects are, unless he can be assured that he will not some day be confronted by substantial hidden liabilities.

In *Re Wogans (Drogheda) Ltd (No. 2)*[55] the proposed scheme envisaged the ownership of the company passing into entirely new hands, a company in the same general line of business, which would invest approximately £500,000 in the company under protection, much of that money going to pay off the creditors under the examiner's proposals. Since there were no measures comparable to those in the U.S. Bankruptcy Tax Act, 1980, the examiner's revised proposals included provisions to deal with the problems referred to above. The 'write down' would not be taxed, in exchange for which the company would not carry forward any of its losses; VAT consequences of the settlement would be treated in the same way as in a receivership or in a liquidation; and the company would not become liable for any outstanding taxes the existence of which was not known at the time the scheme was approved. However, Costello J declined to make orders along those lines, observing that schemes ought to function within the ordinary tax regime, and rejected the proposals. Later, when dealing with the examiner's application to approve his expenses, Costello J said that the examiner should have brought a separate application before the court for a ruling on this aspect of his proposals—although at the same time he criticised

---

54. Bankruptcy Tax Act 1980, 94 Stat. 3389. See generally, Phelan, 'Kick 'Em While They're Down—A Taxation and Bankruptcy Critique of the Technical and Policy Aspects of the Bankruptcy Tax Act of 1980', 33 Sw. LJ 833 (1981).
55. Costello J, 7 May 1992.

the examiner for having brought a separate application for directions on whether the secured creditor had a fixed or floating charge over the company's debtors.

EFFECTS OF CONFIRMATION

Court confirmation of the proposals operates to bind the various parties affected by them. According to s.24(6) of the 1990 Act, regarding the creditors, on confirmation:

> the proposals shall . . . be binding on all the creditors or the class or classes of creditor, as the case may be, affected by the proposals in respect of any claim or claims against the company.

Unlike the position with bankruptcy schemes of arrangement,[56] it is not stipulated that the confirmed scheme binds only those creditors who had notice of the confirmation hearing. All creditors of the affected class, without qualification, are bound by the scheme. If a creditor who was completely unaware of the proposed scheme can show that the examiner knew of his existence but failed to take reasonable steps to appraise him of the situation, he may possibly have a right of action against the examiner for damages.[57] Confirmation may also release third parties who are liable for any obligations of the company, like guarantors.[58]

The precise time the confirmation takes effect is fixed by the court, which must be within 21 days of the confirmation date.[59] What protection as the company enjoys against creditors' actions and others also ceases on that day, although the court may direct that protection shall come to an end some time earlier. When confirming proposals for a scheme or compromise, the court can make such orders as it deems fit for implementing its decision.[60] A copy of the confirmation order must be given to the register of companies by the examiner or by such other person as the court directs.[61] Within 14 days of its being made, notice of the order must be published in the *Iris Oifigiúil*.[62]

CONTESTING THE CONFIRMATION

The mere fact that a creditor has not been informed of the examination and thereby was prevented from participating in the class decisions is not grounds for setting aside the confirmation. However, if any creditor or member can show that the confirmation was procured by fraud, they can apply to the court within 180 days of the decision to have it revoked. If the court is satisfied that there indeed was fraud, s.27 of the Act empowers it to revoke its confirmation on such terms as it deems fit; but it is required to have regard for the interests of any bona fide purchaser for value of property who relied on the confirmation.

56. Bankruptcy Act 1988, s.92(1)(b).
57. Cf. *Pulsford v Devenish* [1903] 2 Ch. 625; liquidator held liable in comparable circumstances.
58. Supra p. 117.   59. S.24(9).   60. S.24(8).
61. S.24(10).   62. S.30.

Even if there was no fraud or if the 180 days period has expired, a confirmation may always be challenged by an application to have the company wound up on just and equitable grounds.[63] For instance, if the proposals envisaged a certain course of action being taken in respect of the company but, without any suggestion of fraud, that action was not taken, the circumstances may very well warrant the company being wound up on those grounds.

FRAUD

When liquidators or receivers go into a company, occasionally they discover that those involved in managing the company have been committing frauds, either on particular creditors or on the creditors generally, or otherwise. Where they come across evidence of criminal offences committed by an officer of the company, they are required to make a report on the matter to the Director of Public Prosecutions and to provide him with reasonable assistance should he decide to initiate prosecutions.[64] However, prosecutions in such circumstances rarely if ever occur, for a variety of reasons, including the archaic nature of the criminal law regarding fraud and the seriously deficient rules of evidence. At times liquidators bring claims against officers of the company for 'fraudulent trading', but liability under this head is notoriously difficult to establish.[65] Criticisms of the very restrictive concept of fraud, for the purpose of these actions, is partly met by the new head of liability under the 1990 Act for 'reckless trading'.[66]

21 days report   Among the matters which the examiner must deal with in the 21 days report is to express an opinion on whether, on the basis of the facts he has learned, further enquiries are warranted into the questions of fraudulent or reckless trading.[67] In expressing this opinion, it would seem that the examiner is not required to set out in detail the reasons for his views. But occasions could arise where detailed reasons for his conclusions is one of the 'other matters' he deems relevant to put in the report. If the report expresses the opinion that there is evidence of a substantial disappearance of property from the company, which has not been sufficiently accounted for, or evidence of other serious irregularities regarding the company's affairs, the court is required to hold a hearing into the report relatively promptly after having received it.[68]

Recovering property   As has been explained, where the company's property has been disposed of in a manner that perpetrated a fraud on either the company, its creditors or its members, the examiner may apply to the court.[69] If the court

63.   1963 Act. 213(f); see *Company Law*, pp. 363-365.
64.   1963 Act s.213(f); see *Company Law*, pp. 363-365.
64.   1963 Act s.299 and 1990 Act s.179.
65.   See post pp. 258-261.   66. See post pp. 261-267.
67.   S.16(1).   68. S.17(1)(d0.
69.   1990 Act. s.139.

is satisfied that company property was applied in that manner and it is just and equitable to do so, it may direct that the property be delivered to the examiner or that the sum be paid to him.

Vetoing agreed scheme   The 1990 Act does not state whether the existence of fraudulent practices within the company, or the fact that its management was fraudulently or recklessly trading, should have any bearing on whether a scheme or compromise, agreed by most of the interested parties, should receive the sanction of the court. Account is taken of culpable conduct when considering schemes of arrangement under the Bankruptcy Act, 1988.[70] For instance, in *Re McKeown*,[71] which involved two auctioneers who had converted several of their clients' money for their own purposes, Hanna J rejected their creditors' scheme because their 'business was carried on fraudulently, contrary to the principles of commercial morality. . . .'[72] The argument could be made that, since the Companies Act, 1990, enables civil and indeed criminal proceedings to be brought for fraudulent trading, normally past frauds by the management should not have a decisive effect on an arrangement which secured extensive support from the creditors and the members.

Scheme procured by fraud   As has been explained, if within 180 days of a scheme having been confirmed it is found that the scheme was procured by fraud, the company or any creditor or member may apply to the court to have the scheme revoked.[73]

---

70. See *Bankruptcy Law*, pp. 34-35.
71. [1934] IR 225.
72. Id. at pp. 230-231.
73. S.27.

PART III

Winding up/Liquidation

Companies go out of existence through the formal process of winding up or liquidation; the two expressions are coterminous. Companies also go out of existence by being struck off the register of companies,[1] but this procedure is somewhat exceptional. Unless it is duly wound up or else de-registered, a company continues in existence for year after year, while all of its shareholders or members may die. One of the characteristics of corporate personality is perpetual succession, until the corporate entity is extinguished through the statutory procedures. As Blackstone observed of corporations, they 'have perpetual succession until they are formally dissolved. They are . . . a person that never dies; in like manner as the River Thames is still the same river, though the parts which compose it are changing every instant.'[2] Winding up or liquidation is by far the most important and common of the procedures for achieving dissolution, which takes place some time after the liquidation has concluded.

Originally, companies could be wound up for insolvency only, although inability to pay their debts is not the only reason why companies are wound up today. The Winding Up (Ireland) Act, 1845,[3] provided that certain circumstances shall be deemed to constitute acts of bankruptcy by a company and, on their happening, the company shall be wound up by order of the High Court of Chancery; many of the then rules and practices regarding bankruptcy were applied to companies in liquidation. In 1848 provision was made whereby a company's members could petition the court for a winding up order on grounds other than insolvency.[4] In 1856 the voluntary winding up mechanism was adopted,[5] which did not require any court proceedings; the members could simply pass a special resolution for a winding up and the liquidation commenced from that time

Nature of liquidation   In his excellent treatise on the subject,[6] Judge McPherson describes liquidation or winding up as

> a process whereby the assets of a company are collected and realised, the resulting proceeds are applied in discharging all its debts and liabilities, and

1. 1963 Act s.311, amended by 1982 Act ss.11 and 12.
2. W. Blackstone, *Commentaries on the Laws of England*, Vol. 1, ch. 18 (1765).
3. 8 & 9 Vic. c. 98.   4. 11 & 12 Vic. c. 45.
5. 19 & 20 Vic. c. 47.
6. B. H. McPherson, *The Law of Company Liquidation* (3rd ed., 1987), ed. J. O'Donovan. See too E. Bailey et al., *Corporate Insolvency—Law and Practice* (1992).

any balance which remains after paying the costs and expenses of winding up is distributed among the members according to their rights and interests, or otherwise dealt with as the constitution of the company directs.[7]

The essential features of a winding up, both voluntary and compulsory (i.e. by order of the court), were summarised by Lord Diplock as follows:

> the making of a winding up order brings into operation a statutory scheme for dealing with the assets of the company that is ordered to be wound up. The scheme is now contained in Part VI of the Companies Act [1963] and extends to voluntary as well as to compulsory winding up; but in so far as it deals with compulsory winding up its essential characteristics have remained the same since it was first enacted by the Companies Act 1862. The procedure to be followed when a company is being wound up varies in detail according to whether this is done compulsorily under an order of the court or voluntarily pursuant to a resolution of the company in general meeting, and, in the latter case, whether it is a members' voluntary winding up or a creditors' voluntary winding up; but the essential characteristics of the scheme for dealing with the assets of the company do not differ whichever of these procedures is applicable. They remain the same as those of the original statutory scheme in the Companies Act 1862. . . .

Upon the making of a winding-up order:

> (1) The custody and control of all the property and choses in action of the company are transferred from those persons who were entitled under the memorandum and articles to manage its affairs on its behalf, to a liquidator charged with the statutory duty of dealing with the company's assets in accordance with the statutory scheme. Any disposition of the property of the company otherwise than by the liquidator is void.

> (2) The statutory duty of the liquidator is to collect the assets of the company and to apply them in discharge of its liabilities. If there is any surplus he must distribute it among the members of the company in accordance with their respective rights under the memorandum and articles of association. In performing these duties in a compulsory winding up the liquidator acts as an officer of the court, and if the company is insolvent the rules applicable in the law of bankruptcy must be followed.

> (3) All powers of dealing with the company's assets, including the power to carry on its business so far as may be necessary for its beneficial winding up, are exerciseable by the liquidator for the benefit of those persons only who are entitled to share in the proceeds of realisation of the assets under the statutory scheme. The company itself, as a legal person, distinct from its members, can never be entitled to any part of the proceeds. Upon completion of the winding up, it is dissolved.[8]

7.   At p. 1.
8.   *Ayerst v C. & K. Construction Ltd* [1976] AC 167, at pp. 176-177.

Sources of the law—bankruptcy regime The principal sources of the law on winding up are Part VI of the 1963 Act (ss.200-313), as amended, especially by Part VI of the 1990 Act (ss.122-179). Order 74 of the Rules of the Superior Courts[9] contains the Winding Up Rules, which apply mainly to compulsory liquidations. The only other statutory instrument of significance is S.I. No. 42 of 1964 on the recognition of other countries' winding up jurisdiction.[10]

The various principles and rules governing bankruptcy were revised and consolidated in the Bankruptcy Act, 1988.[11] Because the liquidation of an insolvent company resembles the administration of a bankrupt's estate in many respects, several of the rules of bankruptcy law extend to such liquidations. These rules are applied in two major ways and, it is important to note, not every rule of bankruptcy law applies to winding up insolvent companies; it is only those rules rendered applicable by the Companies Acts that so apply.

In the first place, several of the provisions in Part VI of the 1963 Act have identical or closely comparable provisions in the Bankruptcy Act, 1988; to that extent, it may be said that these bankruptcy rules apply in liquidations. Among the principal examples are the rules regarding disclaimer of onerous property and contracts,[12] the prohibition of fraudulent preferences,[13] priority amongst creditors and preferential creditors,[14] and the prohibition of forms of execution against the insolvent estate.[15] Often the bankruptcy cases are of assistance in construing comparable provisions in the Companies Acts.

Secondly, there is the direct incorporation of various bankruptcy rules in s.284(1) of the 1963 Act, according to which,

> In the winding up of an insolvent company the same rules shall prevail and be observed relating to the respective rights of secured and unsecured creditors and to debts provable and to the valuation of annuities and future and contingent liabilities as are in force for the time being under the law of bankruptcy relating to the estates of persons adjudged bankrupt. . . .

This provision was first contained in s.28(1) of the Judicature (Ireland) Act, 1877, which also applied the bankruptcy rules to the administration of deceased persons' insolvent estates.[16] Before then, company and also deceased insolvencies were governed by Chancery rules, some of which differed from those being administered in the Bankruptcy Court. The principal reason for aligning the practice for all kinds of insolvencies was to abolish the rule in Mason v Bogg[17] whereby, in Chancery, a secured creditor could prove for his entire debt and receive a dividend before ever realising his security; although if the proceeds of realisation yielded him more than 100 pence in the pound, he was obliged to pay over the excess to the estate.

---

9. S.I. No. 15 of 1986, made under 1963 Act s.312.
10. Made under 1963 Act s.250.
11. See generally, M. Forde, *Bankruptcy Law in Ireland* (1989).
12. 1963 Act s.290. 13. Id. s.286.
14. Id. s.285. 15. Id. ss.291 and 292.
16. Cf. *Moore v Smith* [1895] 1 IR 512.
17. (1837) 2 My. & G. 443.

Thenceforth, in all insolvencies, the bankruptcy rule prevails, such as the secured creditor must realise or value his security and prove only for the difference.

It is only the bankruptcy rules regarding the three matters specified in s.284(1) that apply in this context. One concerns the 'debts provable', i.e. what debts of and claims against the company can be discharged by the liquidator.[18] It has been held that the rule requiring the set-off of mutual liabilities and credits before lodging claims against the insolvent falls within this heading.[19] The second matter is closely related to proving debts, 'the valuation of annuities and future and contingent liabilities', i.e. valuing these in order to determine how much should be paid by the liquidator. Thirdly, there is the 'respective rights of secured and unsecured creditors'. The full extent of this provision has not been determined. It has been held that the bankruptcy rules apply to the rights of secured creditors inter-se as well as vis-à-vis unsecured creditors.[20]

What may be termed the Bankruptcy Act's 'asset- swelling' measures are not incorporated by reference in this way into insolvent liquidations.[21] In Gorringe v Irwell India Rubber and Gutta Pecha Works[22] *it was held that the old 'reputed ownership' rule in s.313 of the Bankruptcy (Ireland) Act, 1857, did not apply in a winding up. According to Cotton LJ, s.284(1) was 'not intended to bring into the assets of the estate being administered, or of the company being wound up, any property which would not be otherwise assets, but to regulate the mode of dealing with the assets which are proved to belong to the company.'[23] In* Re Irish Attested Sales Ltd[24] *it was held that what is now s.51 of the Bankruptcy Act, regarding priority of judgment mortgages, did not so apply because s.284(1) of the 1963 Act does not import into the winding up of companies 'the bankruptcy rules which have the effect of increasing the assets of a person adjudged bankrupt which are available for his creditors.'[25] However, a comparable rule is now contained in s.284(2) of the 1963 Act. Similarly, in* Re Withernsea Brickworks[26] *it was held that what is now s.50 of the Bankruptcy Act, regarding execution against the bankrupt's property prior to adjudication, also was not incorporated in this manner because it relates to 'bringing in property which [otherwise] would not be liable to be administered in bankruptcy';[27] a comparable rule was subsequently inserted in the Companies Acts.[28]*

In determining whether a company is insolvent for the purpose of applying s.284(1), generally, the relevant time is the time application of this section is being invoked. In several instances where the company was insolvent when it was ordered to be liquidated but, during the winding up, transpired to become solvent, it was

---

18. Considered in Ch. 19.
19. *Mersey Steel & Iron Co. v Naylor Benzon & Co.* (1884) 9 HLC 434.
20. *Re Leinster Contract Corp.* [1903] 1 IR 517.
21. Supra n. 11, Ch. 7.   22. (1886) 34 Ch D 128.
23. Id. at p. 133.   24. [1962] IR 70.
25. Id. at p. 73.   26. (1880) 16 Ch D 337.
27. Id. at p. 342; followed in *Re Whiterock Quarries Ltd* [1933] IR 363.
28. 1963 Act s.291.

held to be a solvent company and accordingly s.284(1) no longer could be applied.[29] *This approach was endorsed by the Supreme Court in* Re Hibernian Transport Companies Ltd,[30] *where interest accruing on bank deposits held by the liquidator overy many years enabled an original insolvent liquidation to become a solvent one. Both in principle and for practical reasons, it is only at the end of many liquidations that it is truly possible to say whether or not they are solvent.*

29. E.g. *Re Lines Bros. Ltd* [1984] BCLC 215.
30. [1990] ILRM 42 overruled by Supreme Court, 13 May 1993.

12

The Modes of Winding Up

There are three main methods of winding up companies—the members' voluntary winding up, the creditors' voluntary winding up and winding up by order of the court, otherwise known as an official liquidation. The main distinction between them is that the latter is carried out entirely within the court system whereas the two types of members' windings up in principle take place away from the court. Nevertheless, provision is made to facilitate court involvement in the members' and the creditors' voluntary windings up in several ways; s.276(1)(a) of the 1963 Act enables a voluntary liquidator to obtain court sanction for several kinds of transactions[1] and s.280 of that Act authorises application to the court to determine any question arising out of the liquidation or for the voluntary liquidator to exercise any of the powers available in a compulsory liquidation.[2] Except where the Companies Acts provide otherwise, their winding up provisions apply to all modes of liquidations.[3]

A fundamental distinction exists between the winding up of companies which are solvent and which are insolvent. The members' voluntary winding up is designed for solvent companies. Although the great majority of compulsory liquidations involve insolvent companies, as is explained below, that mode is also used to wind up companies which are solvent, especially the petition to wind up on 'just and equitable' grounds, which at times is used in order to seek redress against the oppression of minority shareholders.[4] If the company being wound up is insolvent, then s.284(1) of the 1963 Act applies certain bankruptcy law rules to the process. But not all of the bankruptcy rules are rendered thereby applicable,[5] although several other provisions of the 1963-1990 Acts apply rules to insolvent liquidations which have parallels in bankruptcy.

MEMBERS' VOLUNTARY WINDING UP

Members can take steps to voluntarily wind up their company, provided the company is registered under the Companies Acts, 1963-90, or one of the

---

1. Enumerated in 1963 Act s.231(1)(d)-(f).
2. Cf. *Re Campbell Coverings Ltd* [1953] Ch 488.
3. 1963 Act s.206(2).
4. E.g. *Re Murph's Restaurants Ltd (No. 2)* (Gannon J, 31 July 1979); see *Company Law*, pp. 363-368.
5. See ante pp. 125-126.

previous Companies Acts. The members' voluntary winding up is a pre-dominantly extra-curial process to enable a company's members or share-holders to bring its existence to an end. There are numerous reasons why they may want to wind up their company. For instance, they may be dissatisfied with the way in which it is being run; they may be unable to raise the additional funds it needs to stay in business; they may want to liquidate their investment but there is no ready market for their shares.

Resolutions   Section 251 of the 1963 Act lays down how the members may wind up their company, viz.:

    i.   by passing a special resolution for a winding up, or

    ii. where the company was formed for a fixed duration and that period has expired, by passing an ordinary resolution for a winding up, or

    iii. if the company is insolvent, by passing an ordinary resolution for a winding up. On account of the insolvency, this must be a creditors' voluntary winding up.[6]

A special resolution is one which was passed by a majority of at least three quarters of the votes cast, at a meeting of which at least 21 days notice was given.[7] However, if the holders of more than 90 per cent in value of the voting shares so agree, a special resolution may be passed by a three-quarters majority notwithstanding shorter notice.[8] As has been explained elsewhere, the notices of that resolution must sufficiently describe what is being proposed, so that all the company's members can form a reasoned judgment of the proposals.[9] An ordinary resolution, which is all that is needed if the company is insolvent, means a simple majority of the votes cast.

The meeting to consider the proposals must have been properly convened, either by the directors or else under s.132 (default powers)[10] or s.135 (court-ordered meetings)[11] of the 1963 Act. In one instance, where the meeting was convened by the company's secretary purportedly for the board, but without their clear authority to do so, the meeting and ensuing winding up resolution were held to be invalid;[12] that departure from proper procedures would not be considered a 'mere irregularity'. By analogy with the position in official liquidations, it has been held that the court has jurisdiction to annul a winding up resolution in an appropriate case.[13]

Within fourteen days of the resolution being passed a notice thereof must be published in the *Iris Oifigiúil*.[14] A copy of that resolution and of the statutory declaration of solvency must be delivered to the registrar of companies.[15]

6.   See infra p. 132.   7. 1963 Act s.141.   8. Id. s.141(2).
9.   See *Company Law*, pp. 88-89.
10. See id. p. 86.   11. See id. pp. 86-87.
12. *State of Wyoming Syndicate* [1901] 2 Ch 431.
13. *Re Oakthorpe Holdings Ltd* [1987] IR 632.
14. 1963 Act s.252.   15. Id. s.143(4)(e) and s.256(6).

Declaration of solvency   In order for the members themselves voluntarily to wind up their company, s.256 of the 1963 Act, as amended,[16] requires a majority of the directors to have made a statutory declaration that, upon having made full inquiry, they are of the opinion that the company will be able to pay its debts in full within at least 12 months from when the winding up commences. This declaration must have been made not more than 28 days before the time the winding up resolution was passed. It must contain a statement of the company's assets and liabilities as of not more than three months before that declaration was made. It must be accompanied by a report by an 'independent person' stating that the directors' opinion regarding the company's solvency and the statement of affairs they drew up are reasonable. Formerly, directors often made unduly optimistic declarations of solvency but the requirement of independent verification should put an end to that practice. In order to be independent for this purpose, the person verifying the declaration must be qualified to be the company's auditor.[17] If it later transpires that the company was insolvent, the directors who made the declaration risk being held personally liable for all of the company's unpaid debts unless they can show that there were reasonable grounds for the view which they held.[18]

Appointing liquidator   A duly qualified liquidator must be appointed by the shareholders, who may fix his remuneration.[19] The liquidator's function is 'winding up the affairs and distributing the assets of the company. . . .'[20] This appointment puts an end to the directors' powers but the shareholders or the liquidator may permit them to continue exercising some or all of those powers.[21] Where the liquidator's office becomes vacant it may be filled by the general meeting.[22] If for any reason the members do not select a liquidator, he can be appointed by the court.[23] He also may be removed by the court for 'cause shown' and be replaced.[24]

Conduct of liquidation   A voluntary winding up commences from the time the resolution to wind up is passed.[25] The company must then cease to carry on business except in so far as is necessary to facilitate the liquidation.[26] Although this mode of winding up is entirely controlled by the company's members, s.280 of the 1963 Act authorises any creditor to apply to the court to determine any matter and s.309 of that Act provides that the court shall have regard *inter alia* to the creditors' wishes.

If at any time the liquidator forms the opinion that, contrary to the directors' declaration, the company will not be able to pay its debts in full, he must publicly

16. By 1990 Act s.128.
17. See *Company Law*, pp. 260-263.
18. 1963 Act s.256(8).   19. Id. s 258(1).
20. Ibid.   21. Id. s.258(2).
22. Id. s.259.   23. Id. s.277(1).
24. Id. s.277(2); see post pp. 189-190.   25. Id. s.253.
26. Id. s.254.

advertise and call a meeting of the company's creditors and provide them with a statement of the company's assets and liabilities and such further information as they may reasonably require.[27] A general meeting of the company must be summoned by the liquidator every year following the decision to wind up;[28] those attending should be given a statement of what the liquidator has done. A copy of this statement should be sent to the registrar of companies.[29]

When the company's assets have been collected and the creditors and shareholders are paid off, the liquidator must call a publicly advertised general meeting and provide it with an account of the winding up.[30] A copy of this account, together with a return of the holding of the terminal meeting, must be sent to the registrar of companies.[31] The company is deemed to be dissolved three months following the registrar receiving these documents, although the court has power to defer the date of dissolution.[32]

CREDITORS' VOLUNTARY WINDING UP

One form of winding up under the Companies Act, 1862, was a hybrid of voluntary and official liquidation—winding up subject to the supervision of the court.[33] This mode was mainly designed to protect creditors' rights where the liquidation was strictly outside of the court; it also facilitated access to the court by contributories. It fell into disuse and was not continued by the 1963 Act; a similar procedure was abolished in Britain more recently.[34] It was replaced by the creditors' voluntary winding up—in 1929 in Britain[35] on the recommendation of the Greene Committee[36] and here in ss.265-273 of the 1963 Act.

The policy underlying this mode of liquidation is that control over the winding up should rest with those who are most affected by it. When the company is insolvent, those persons are its creditors. Accordingly, it is their wishes which are consulted when important questions arise. Thus, they appoint the liquidator and fix his remuneration,[37] they appoint a committee of inspection to advise and assist him in carrying out his functions,[38] they sanction certain exercises of his powers.[39] At any time a creditor may apply to the court for directions[40] and the court must take due account of the creditors' wishes and have regard to the value of each creditor's debt.[41] By contrast, the members are virtually excluded from any say in the liquidation, although they too can apply to the court for directions under s.280 of the 1963 Act.

If the company is insolvent, the position under the voluntary liquidation is practically no different from that in a compulsory liquidation; for instance, the normal bankruptcy rules govern the proof of debts, the assets available for

27. Id. s.261, amended by 1990 Act s.129.
28. Id. s.262.   29. Ibid.
30. Id. s.263.   31. Id. s.263(3).
32. Id. ss.263(4) and (5).   33. Ss.147-152.
34. Insolvency Act 1986.   35. Companies Act 1929.
36. Cmd. 2657 (1926).   37. 1963 Act s.267; see post p. 191.
38. Id. s.268; see post p. 193.   39. Id. s.276(1)(a).
40. Id. s.280.   41. Id. s.309.

division among the creditors and priorities between creditors.[42] The conduct of these liquidations and of insolvent official liquidations is the subject of the next eight chapters.

WINDING UP BY THE COURT

Winding up by order of the High Court—or compulsory or official liquidation—is a more formal process which can be slower and more expensive than the voluntary modes. Here, instead of the machinery being administered by the members or the creditors, as the case may be, the actual administration of the process is by the court; the liquidator carries out his duties under its direct supervision and the Companies Acts provide for a greater degree of court control. The fact that a company is already in voluntary liquidation does not prevent the court from ordering that it be wound up. Most official liquidations are initiated by creditors who have not been paid what is owing to them; the rules regarding creditors' petitions are considered in the next chapter. The position regarding court winding ups initiated by other parties may be summarised briefly as follows, although many of the points made apply just as much to creditors' petitions.

'Any company'   The High Court's power under s.213 of the 1963 Act to order a winding up applies to 'any company'.[43] This does not mean every conceivable kind of association and corporation. What are companies for the purpose of the Companies Acts, 1963-90, are companies which have been registered under those Acts or under any of the earlier Companies Acts—those of 1908, of 1862 and of 1844.

Unregistered companies   Part X of the 1963 Act (ss.344-350) establishes a procedure for winding up certain unregistered companies, including indigenous partnerships with at least eight members. The High Court has an inherent power to dissolve partnerships.[44] It can hardly be doubted that a deed of settlement company, if any still exist, is an unregistered company for the purposes of Part X of the 1963 Act. The winding up jurisdiction has been held to apply to friendly societies[45] and to industrial and provident societies.[46] That jurisdiction was given to the court in the case of building societies[47] and credit unions[48] and also

42. Id. s 284(1).   43. Id. s.212.
44. See E.H. Scammell & R.C. l'A. Banks, *Lindley on the Law of Partnership* (13 ed., 1984) pp. 687-709.
45. *Re Independent Protestant Loan Fund Soc.* [1895] 1 IR 1. and *Re Irish Mercantile Loan Soc.* [1907] 1 IR 78. Cf. s.78 of the Friendly Societies Act 1896, on the dissolution of societies.
46. *Re Belfast Tailors' Co-partnership* [1909] 1 IR 49. Cf. ss.58-61 of the Industrial and Provident Societies Act 1893, on the dissolution of societies.
47. Building Societies Act 1989, s.109. Cf. *The King (McClean) v Recorder of Londonderry* [1911] 2 IR 553.
48. Credit Union Act 1966, s.33.

certified trustee savings banks.[49] In *Re Commercial Buildings Company of Dublin*[50] it was held that the court could order the winding up of a company incorporated by royal charter.

This jurisdiction may not invariably apply to companies established by statute either directly or, indirectly, by way of royal charter or an order in council or instrument issued under statutory authority. In *Re Portstewart Tramway Co.*,[51] the court acceded to a judgment creditor's petition to wind up a company that was established by order pursuant to the Tramways (Ireland) Acts. It was held that the winding up jurisdiction was not precluded because the Act there authorised the appointment of a receiver over the company's assets. There is conflicting authority regarding whether a public utility company established by a private Act of Parliament could be dissolved in this fashion.[52] It is unlikely that the court's winding up jurisdiction applies to companies established by a public act of the Oireachtas or of its predecessors.

Foreign companies   Part XI of the 1963 Act deals with foreign-registered companies which have a presence in Ireland but it does not lay down any winding up procedure for those companies. However, in Britain it is accepted that such companies are unregistered companies, within the equivalent of Part X, and accordingly there is a jurisdiction to wind them up.[53] That power will only be exercised where there are sufficient contacts between the company in question and the forum. Indeed, it is not essential that the company has a business presence in the State to bring it within Part X, which defines an unregistered company as 'includ[ing] any association or any company', other than a registered company.[54] In *Re Compania Merabello San Nicholas S.A.*[55] the prerequisites for winding up foreign-registered companies were summarised by Megarry J as follows:

> (1) There is no need to establish that the company ever had a place of business here. (2) There is no need to establish that the company ever carried on business here, unless perhaps the petition is based upon the company carrying on or having carried on business. (3) A proper connection with the jurisdiction must be established by sufficient evidence to show (a) that the company has some asset or assets within the jurisdiction, and (b) that there are one or more persons concerned in the proper distribution of the assets over whom the jurisdiction is exercisable. (4) It suffices if the assets of the company within the jurisdiction are of any nature; they need not be 'commercial' assets, or assets which indicate that the company formerly carried on business here. (5) The assets need not

49. 1963 Act s.344.   50. [1938] IR 477.
51. [1896] 1 IR 265.
52. See cases considered in the *Commercial Buildings Co.* case [1938] IR 477 and *Buckley on the Companies Acts* (14th ed., 1981) pp. 857-858.
53. See generally, I. Fletcher, *The Law of Insolvency* (1990) ch. 29.
54. 1963 Act s 344.   55. [1973] Ch 175.

be assets which will be distributable to creditors by the liquidator in the winding up; it suffices if by the making of the winding up order they will be of benefit to a creditor or creditors in some other way. (6) If it is shown that there is no reasonable possibility of benefit accruing to creditors from making the winding up order, the jurisdiction is excluded.[56]

PETITIONERS FOR A WINDING UP ORDER

The procedure for obtaining a winding up order requires the presentation of a petition to the High Court, which is verified on affidavit. Procedural requirements regarding presenting the petition, advertisement, service and verification, the hearing and appearances are set out in Rules 7-13 and 15-18 of the Winding Up Rules.[57] Section 215 of the 1963 Act states who may petition to have a company wound up, viz. any creditor, the company, any member or contributory, or the Minister. A petition by a contingent or prospective creditor will not be heard unless security for costs is given and a satisfactory prima facie case has been established.[58]

The company   As regards a petition by the company itself, unless they have clear authority in its articles of association to do so, the directors may not present a petition without the shareholders' consent;[59] but the general meeting can ratify the directors' unauthorised action in so doing. In exceptional circumstances, a receiver and manager appointed over the company's assets may be entitled to present a petition on the company's behalf.[60] The court is not obliged to order a winding up because an ordinary resolution of the company was passed; the mere desire of a majority of members to wind up is not sufficient reason to make an order on 'just and equitable' grounds.[61]

A contributory/member   A contributory, in brief, is an existing member of the company or a previous member who is liable to contribute to the company's assets in the event of it being wound up.[62] There is an extensive case law on who precisely are contributories, which deals principally with actual liability to make a contribution.[63] As regards petitioning for a winding up, the contributory must either be an original allottee of the shares or else have been the registered owner of the shares for at least six of the eighteen months before the winding up commences.[64] The purpose of this restriction is to prevent persons seeking to put a company into liquidation by the mere device of acquiring some shares in it and straight away presenting a winding up petition. If the con-

56.   Id. at p. 91. See too *Re A Company* (No. 00359 of 1987) [1988] Ch. 210 and *Re Wallace Smith Group Ltd* [1992] BCLC 989.
57.   See post pp. 482-504.   58.   1963 Act s.215(c).
59.   *Re Galway & Salthill Tramways Co.* [1918] 1 IR 62.
60.   *Re Emmadart Ltd* [1970] Ch 540.
61.   *Re Angulo Continental Produce Co.* [1939] 1 All ER 99.
62.   1963 Act s.208.
63.   See post p. 146.   64.   1963 Act s.215(a).

tributory/member has died, then his personal representative or trustee or legatee may present the petition.[65] Where a dispute arises about whether the petitioner is the owner of the shares he has registered in his name or claims to own, the petition to wind up will be postponed until this matter has been resolved.[66] If that dispute is raised by the company, then entirely separate proceedings must be instituted in order to determine the matter.[67] A bankrupt member cannot petition for a winding up,[68] but the Official Assignee can do so provided the shares were registered in his name for at least six months previously.[69]

If the company is solvent, a contributory/member can present a petition to wind it up if a special resolution to wind up was passed or if it is 'just and equitable' that the company be wound up.[70] Because there are several other modes of redress for dissatisfied shareholders, the court will not readily accede to an application under the 'just and equitable' grounds.[71] But the Companies Acts do not contain an explicit provision that, where the grievance could be remedied by an order under s.205 of the 1963 Act for 'oppression', redress should be given under s.205 instead.[72] If the company is insolvent, then because there will be no surplus for the contributory, the court tends to reject his petition because he no longer has any tangible interest in the company's fate.[73]

The Minister   Following an investigation by inspectors into a company's affairs under Part II of the 1990 Act, the Minister may petition that the company be wound up on 'just and equitable' grounds or for 'oppression' and the like under s.205 of that Act, or both.[74] Section 45 of the Insurance Act, 1936, empowers the Minister to petition for the winding up of an assurance company on the grounds of insolvency.

The Central Bank   Section 48 of the Central Bank Act, 1989, empowers the Central Bank to petition to have a licensed bank wound up because it is insolvent, that it has contravened directions from the Bank, that its licence has been revoked and it has ceased doing business, or that the Bank considers it to be in the interests of the company's depositors that it be wound up.

The Attorney General   There is no express authority in the Companies Acts for the Attorney General to seek the winding up of a company. But it would seem that he has some inherent authority to apply to the court to have a company

65. Id. s.210.
66. *Re Garage Door Associates Ltd* [1984] 1 WLR 35.
67. *Re J.N.Z. Ltd* [1978] 1 WLR 183.
68. *Re Wolverhampton Iron & Steel Co.* [1977] 1 WLR 860.
69. 1963 Act s.211 and *Re H.L. Bolton Engineering Co.* [1956] Ch 577.
70. *Re Emmadart Ltd* [1979] Ch 540 at p. 543.
71. See generally, *Company Law*, pp. 363-368.
72. E.g. British Insolvency Act 1986, s.125(2).
73. See post pp. 146-147.
74. Cf. *Re Lublin Rosen & Associates Ltd* [1975] 1 WLR 122 and *Re Golden Chemical Products Ltd* [1976] Ch 300.

dissolved because it was formed for an unlawful purpose.[75] It is possible that he has a more extensive power to seek the dissolution of charitable companies.[76]

GROUNDS FOR ORDERING A WINDING UP

Section 213 of the 1963 Act sets out the grounds on which the court may order that a company be wound up, viz.:

- where by a special resolution the company resolves to be wound up in this way;

- where the company does not commence business within a year of being incorporated or suspends its business for a year;

- where the membership falls below the statutory minimum of two or seven, as the case may be;

- where the company is unable to pay its debts;

- where there is 'oppression' and the like that would justify making an order under s.205 of the 1963 Act; and

- where it is 'just and equitable' to order a winding up.

Some of these grounds are self-explanatory. Oppression and the like under s.205 has been dealt with elsewhere in considering minority shareholder protection and some of the principal applications of the 'just and equitable' heading are also treated there.[77] Other examples include where the main object for which the company was formed has become impracticable,[78] where its internal decision-making procedures are deadlocked[79] and where the majority have committed a significant fraud on the company.[80] As is explained in Chapter 13, by far the most common ground on which orders for a winding up are sought is under s.213(e), that the company is 'unable to pay its debts'; a frequent petitioner under this head are the Revenue Commissioners.

At the hearing of the petition, or even earlier, the company or any creditor or contributory may apply to the court to stay the proceedings or to have further proceedings restrained;[81] the court may grant that application on such terms as it thinks fit. If the court is satisfied that the applicant is a qualified petitioner

---

75. *R. v Registrar of Companies, ex p. Attorney General* [1991] BCLC 476.
76. See generally R. Keane, *Equity and the Law of Trusts in the Republic of Ireland* (1988) p. 133.
77. See *Company Law*, pp. 354 et seq.
78. E.g. *Re German Date Coffe Co.* (1882) 20 Ch D 169 and *Re Dublin & Eastern Regional Tourism Organisation Ltd* [1990] 1 IR 579.
79. E.g. *Re Yenidje Tobacco Co.* [1916] 2 Ch. 426 and *Re Vehicle Buildings & Insulations Ltd* [1986] ILRM 239.
80. E.g. *Loch v John Blackwood Ltd* [1924] AC 783 and *Re Newbridge Steam Laundry Ltd* [1917] 1 IR 167.
81. See post pp. 152-153.

and that the alleged grounds exist, it may order that the company be wound up and appoint a liquidator. Since, however, it has a discretion in the matter, it may refuse to make that order where there are good reasons for doing so.[82] Or the court may adjourn the hearing, make an interim order or make such other order as it thinks fit. A provisional liquidator may be appointed by the court pending appointment of the liquidator proper.[83]

Whenever a winding up order is made, a copy must be delivered to the registrar of companies.[84] On being appointed, the liquidator must publish that fact in the *Iris Oifigiúil* and deliver to the registrar of companies a copy of the court's appointing order.[85]

CONDUCT OF THE LIQUIDATION

Where a compulsory liquidation is ordered, it is deemed to have commenced not as of the date of the court's order but from the time the winding up petition was filed in the Central Office.[86] Accordingly, several kinds of transaction which took place between those dates may be void or voidable and may require to be sanctioned by the court.[87] A statement of the company's affairs which is verified by one or more of the company's officers must be filed by them in the court.[88] It must show the particulars of the company's assets, debts and liabilities; the names, addresses and occupations of its creditors; the securities held by its creditors and the dates when those securities were given; and any additional information that the court may stipulate. Every creditor or contributory is entitled to inspect the company's books and papers.[89]

Conduct of the winding up is then left in the hands of the liquidator.[90] Usually the court will direct the liquidator to call a meeting of the creditors, or meetings of the creditors and contributories, to appoint a committee of inspection whose function it is to act with the liquidator.[91] Where at any time it is proved to the court's satisfaction that the winding up should be stayed or the winding up order should be annulled, the court may direct a stay or an annulment on such terms as it thinks fit.[92]

As soon as may be after the winding up order is made, the court must settle a list of contributories with a view to making calls, where shares are not fully paid up, and to adjusting rights between contributories.[93] At the same time the court must 'cause the assets of the company to be collected and applied in discharge of its liabilities.'[94] To this end, the court may *inter alia* order that any money, property or papers to which the company is *prima facie* entitled to be transferred to the liquidator and order that any money owing to the company

82. *Re Bula Ltd* [1990] 1 IR 440.
83. 1963 Act s.226; see post pp. 162-163.
84. Id. s.221.
85. Id. s.227.
86. Id. s.220(2).
87. Id. s.218.
88. Id. s.224.
89. Id. s.243.
90. Id. s.231.
91. Id. ss.232 and 233.
92. Id. s.234; see post p. 301-302.
93. Id. ss.235, 238 and 237.
94. Id. s.235(1).

be paid into a designated bank account.[95] The court may fix a time or times within which creditors must prove their debts or claims against the company;[96] those not proven in time are excluded from the benefit of any distribution. The court is empowered to order that any officer of the company attend a meeting of the creditors, contributories or committee of inspection in order to give them such information about the company as they need.[97] It moreover may summon before it and examine on oath any company officer or debtor, or person it believes is capable of providing information regarding the company;[98] what may be referred to as the liquidation *inquisitionsprozess*. And where it suspects that any contributory is about to abscond or to remove or conceal property, so as to evade paying calls or avoid being examined about the company, the court may order that he be arrested and detained, and that his property, books and papers be seized.[99]

Those creditors who have proved their debts or claims must be paid off in accordance with the priorities that are explained below.[1] Any rights between the contributories must then be adjusted and if there is a surplus it must be distributed among those persons who are entitled to it.[2] On the application of the liquidator and provided that the winding up is complete, the court will order that the company be dissolved and will direct how the company's books and papers are to be disposed of.[3]

INFORMAL LIQUIDATION

Companies will not be allowed to short-circuit the statutory procedures by seeking to in effect wind themselves up without going through the requisite formalities. In *Davidson v King*[4] the company had not traded for several years but was never wound up. The shareholders then decided to dispose of its entire assets and, from the proceeds, to pay themselves a dividend of 330%. All that remained in the company thereafter was an amount equivalent to its issued share capital. Dealing with the question whether that large dividend should be treated as income or capital coming into a settlement, it was held that it was capital. This was because 'the whole operations of this company . . . were realisation and liquidation and not trading or carrying on the business of the company authorised by their memorandum of association.'[5] According to Wilson J, he could 'find no case where a limited company has been held entitled to realise its entire assets and after setting aside its nominal capital and paying its liabilities, to divide the surplus as income or profits under the guise of declaring a dividend.'[6] Taking such steps, it was said, 'would be a fraud on the winding up provisions of the Companies Act.'[7]

95. Id. s 239; cf. s.237.
96. Id. s.241.
97. Id. s.246.
98. Id. s.245.
99. Id. s.247.
1. Id. s.285.
2. Id. s.242.
3. Id. ss.249 and 305(1)(a).
4. [1927] NI 1.
5. Id. at p. 11.
6. Id. at p. 12.
7. Ibid.

Notwithstanding these remarks, the practice is quite common of share-holders leaving behind their companies as defunct shells with hardly any assets in them and not liquidating them. Usually, they do not want to incur the cost of having a liquidator appointed. And if the company has creditors, usually it has so few assets that there seems little point in the creditors petitioning the court to have it wound up. Eventually the company will be struck off the companies' register for failure to file the usual returns.[8] Usually that will be the end of the matter for all practical purposes, although companies which have been struck off in this manner can be restored to the register in an appropriate case within twenty years of the strike off date.[9]

Section 251 of the 1990 Act now discourages this practice by applying several of the main liquidation rules to companies which have been practically abandoned in this manner. A company comes within s.251 if it is insolvent or an attempt to execute a judgment against its property was unsuccessful and the reason, or main reason, why it is not being wound up is the insufficiency of its assets. Where it appears to the court that a company meets this description, the following provisions of the Companies Acts, which normally apply only in liquidations, are made applicable to the company, its officers and property:

1963 Act

s.243	Inspection of books by creditors and members.
s.245	Examination of persons on oath.
s.245A	Order against person examined under s.245.
s.247	Arresting absconding contributory.
s.295	Frauds by company officers.
s.297	Offence of fraudulent trading.
s.297A	Liability for fraudulent or reckless trading.
s.298	Liability for misfeasance.

1990 Act

s.139	Ordering return of assets wrongly taken.
s.140	Contribution to debts of related companies.
s.203	Offence of not keeping proper accounts.
s.204	Liability for not keeping proper accounts.

8.   1963 Act ss.311 and 312.
9.   Ibid.

13

Commencing the Winding Up

Only the company's members can commence a creditors' voluntary winding up. Where the company is insolvent and official liquidation is being contemplated, usually it is a creditor who petitions to have it wound up. Exceptionally a contributory or the company itself will present the petition.

CREDITORS' VOLUNTARY WINDING UP

Although a creditors' voluntary winding up is almost entirely under the control of the company's creditors, they cannot commence a winding up of this nature; the initiative is throughout with the members and the creditors' entitlements only take effect once the members' resolution has been passed.

Resolution to wind up Section 251(1)(c) of the 1963 Act enables a company to be wound up by ordinary resolution on the grounds that 'it cannot by reason of its liabilities continue on its business'. Previously a special or extraordinary resolution was needed for this purpose. Once a winding up resolution has been passed, the members cannot change their minds and revoke that resolution. Because the Companies Acts deem the liquidation to have commenced once that resolution is passed, with several important immediate effects on the company and persons dealing with it, the passing of the resolution 'immediately confers the irrevocable status of being in liquidation, with all the legal incidents thereof.'[1] But in exceptional circumstances, the court may annul that resolution.[2]

Where a special resolution to wind up was passed under s.251(1)(b) of the 1963 Act, with the intention of having a members' voluntary winding up, but no statutory declaration of solvency has been made, this cannot then be a members' winding up; it must proceed as a creditors' winding up. In *Re Oakthorpe Holdings Ltd*[3] it was held that the court does not have jurisdiction to extend the period of time laid down in s.256 of the 1963 Act for making this declaration, so that there could be a members' winding up. According to Carroll J, a 'time limit was provided by statute and no discretion was given to the court to extend it.'[4]

1. *Ross v P.H. Heeringa Ltd* [1970] NZLR 170, at p. 172.
2. *Re Oakthorpe Holdings Ltd* [1987] IR 632.
3. Ibid.   4. Id. at p. 636.

The legal minimum notice periods for convening extraordinary general meetings are set down in s.133 of the 1963 Act; they and the rules regarding convening and the location of meetings generally are considered elsewhere.[5] In companies with Part I of Table A, at least 14 days written notice must be given, exclusive of the date of service and the date fixed for the meeting.[6] Although generally seven days notice would suffice for companies with Part II of Table A,[7] because creditors must be given at least 10 days notice, in effect the members' meeting cannot take place before that period expires. The notices must specify the place, the day and the hour of the meeting; also the general nature of the business to be transacted.[8]

Because of the exceptional significance of what is being proposed, there should be no room for ambiguity in the notices sent out. It has been said that it is 'of great importance that the steps taken in a matter of such consequence as the resolving to wind up a company should be perfectly regular.'[9] For instance, in *Re Haycroft Gold Reduction & Mining Co.*,[10] the members' meeting was convened by the company secretary without the directors having first met and decided that a meeting should be held to wind up the company. The court refused to regard that departure from the normal lines of authority as a mere irregularity; the meeting was not properly called and the resolution was invalid. In a later similar instance, it was again stressed that 'proceedings of this kind ought to be conducted with substantial propriety.'[11]

Within 14 days of its being passed, a notice of the resolution to wind up must be published in the *Iris Oifigiúil*;[12] if that is not done any officer of the company responsible for the default and also the liquidator can be prosecuted. Within 15 days of its being passed, a copy of the resolution must be given to the registrar of companies.[13]

Creditors' meeting   Either for the day of the members' meeting or the following day, a meeting of the company's creditors must be duly convened and held; s.266 of the 1963 Act sets out the requirements.[14] This meeting must be summoned by the company, meaning its directors. At least 10 days before the date of the members' meeting, notices convening the creditors' meeting must be posted to the creditors[15] and also those notices must be advertised in two daily newspapers circulating in the district where the company's registered office or its principal place of business is located.[16] Accordingly, persons who are owed or who believe they are owed money by the company have reasonable

5.   See *Company Law*, pp. 83 et seq.
6.   Table A, art. 51.
7.   Part II of Table A, art. 4.   8. Art. 51.
9.   *Re Bridport Old Brewery Co.* (1867) LR 2 Ch App 191, at p. 194.
10. [1900] 2 Ch 230.
11. *Re State of Wyoming Syndicate* [1901] 2 Ch 431, at p. 436.
12. 1963 Act s.252   13. Id. s.143.
14. Amended by 1990 Act s.130.
15. 1963 Act s.266(1).   16. Id. s 266(2).

notice of what the company proposes to do and opportunity to make preparations for selecting a liquidator and otherwise. Prosecutions can be brought against either the company, the directors or a director for failure to give proper notice of the meeting.

Where no creditors' meeting has been convened or that meeting was not properly convened, it is debatable what the consequences are for the liquidation or for what is purported to have happened at any creditors' meeting. In 1981 the comparable British legislation was amended to provide that failure to send out notice of the meeting shall not invalidate any resolution passed or other thing done at whatever meeting did occur.[17] There is no similar provision in the 1963-1990 Acts.

The directors must choose one of their number to preside at this meeting.[18] They also must arrange to provide the meeting with the following information:

> a full statement of the position of the company's affairs, together with a list of [its] creditors . . . and the estimated amount of their claims. . . .

It is preferable if the statement of affairs is in the form contained in Form No. 13 of the High Court Rules for official liquidations.

Often these meetings are attended by creditors' solicitors or financial advisers. The High Court rules regarding official liquidations permit representation of creditors by proxy[19] and it seems that those provisions would apply by analogy to these meetings. Usually the chairman will explain to those assembled why the company finds itself in the predicament it is in and how the various categories of creditors stand to fare in the winding up. The High Court Rules probably will also be applied by analogy to determine who is entitled to vote at the meeting.[20] However, the requirement that, for the purposes of voting, a secured creditor must either surrender his security or give particulars of it to the liquidator does not apply to meetings held under s.266.[21] Exactly how this exemption affects rule 69, which states that a creditor who votes in respect of his entire debt is deemed to have surrendered his security, remains to be clarified.

Appointing liquidator and committee of inspection   The main business transacted at these meetings is appointing a duly qualified liquidator and a committee of inspection. Often the members will have chosen the same person as the creditors select. Where both meetings nominate different persons, s.267 of the 1963 Act gives precedence to the creditors' choice. Because resolutions of the creditors require a majority in number *and* in value,[22] it is possible that they may be deadlocked about who to select; in which case, the members' nominee gets appointed. There is no provision in the 1963-1990 Acts which deals directly with this eventuality but any aggrieved creditor can apply to the

17. Cf. *Re E.V. Saxton & Sons Ltd v R. Miles (Confectioners) Ltd* [1983] 1 WLR ...
18. 1963 Act s.266(4); cf. *Re Salcombe Hotel Development Co. Ltd* [1991] BCLC 44.
19. Rules 74-83.   20. Rules 67-71.
21. Rule 72.   22. Rule 62.

court for directions under s.280 of the 1963 Act or indeed petition for a compulsory winding up. Where the members and the creditors nominate different liquidators, any member, director or creditor may apply to the court, within 14 days, seeking either to have both members' nominee or some third party appointed to the office.[23] Either the creditors or the committee of inspection fix the liquidator's remuneration.[24]

At that meeting or later on, the creditors may decide to appoint a committee of inspection,[25] consisting of not more than five of their nominees. Ordinarily, the company can appoint three additional names to this committee; but the creditors can veto individual company nominees unless the court otherwise directs.

'Centrebinding' powers   The powers of any liquidator who was appointed prior to the holding of the creditors' meeting are greatly circumscribed by s.131 of the 1990 Act.[26] Except for taking custody of company property, disposing of perishable goods and goods of diminishing value, and taking such steps as are necessary to protect the company's assets, he may not exercise any of the normal liquidators' powers without obtaining the sanction of the court. Furthermore, that liquidator is required to attend the s.266 creditors' meeting and report to it on how he has exercised any of his powers.

Creditor's s.256(5) application   Where a resolution for a members' voluntary liquidation is passed, a creditor is not precluded from petitioning the High Court for a compulsory liquidation.[27] Alternatively, if a creditor believes that the company is indeed insolvent, notwithstanding the directors' statutory declaration, s.256(5) of the 1963 Act enables the liquidation to be converted into a creditors' voluntary winding up. To do this, the aggrieved creditor and those supporting him must represent one fifth in number or in value of the company's creditors, they can apply within 28 days and must provide the court with evidence which indicates that the company will not be able to pay its debts in full within the time stated in the directors' declaration. The court may then order that the liquidation shall take the form of a creditors' voluntary winding up. A copy of that order must be delivered to the registrar of companies within 15 days. As is explained next below, the liquidator must then convene a meeting of the company's creditors.

Members' liquidator decides the company is insolvent   Where at any time a liquidator appointed by the members forms the opinion that the company is insolvent, s.261 of the 1963 Act[28] requires him to convene a creditors' meeting to deal with the situation. This meeting must be summoned within 14 days of

23. 1963 Act s 267(2)   24. Id. s.269.
25. Id. s.268.
26. Which was a response to *Re Centrebind Ltd* [1967] 1 WLR 377.
27. See infra pp. 158-160.
28. Amended by 1990 Act s.129.

him reaching that conclusion; notices must be posted to the creditors at least seven days before that meeting; at least ten days before that meeting, notices thereof must be published in two daily newspapers circulating in the company's locality and also in the *Iris Oifigiúil*. Those notices must inform the creditors that, prior to the meeting, the liquidator will supply them free of charge with such information concerning the company's affairs as they may reasonably require.

The ensuing creditors' meeting must be presided over by the liquidator. He must furnish the meeting with a statement of affairs, conforming with Form No. 13, including a statement of the company's assets and liabilities, a list of its outstanding creditors and estimated amounts of their claims. This meeting can then exercise all the powers as if it were convened under s.266 of the 1963 Act, as described above.

Conduct of the liquidation The winding up commences once the members' resolution has been passed;[29] thenceforth the company must cease to carry on its business except in so far as is necessary to facilitate the liquidation.[30] As is clear from the procedures outlined above, the creditors almost entirely control the process, although any contributory can apply to the court for directions under s.280 of the 1963 Act. Meetings of members and of creditors must be summoned by the liquidator each year following the decision to wind up.[31] The liquidator's account must be presented to terminal meetings of members and of creditors.[32] The company will be deemed to be dissolved three months following delivery of the liquidator's account and a return of these meetings to the registrar of companies, although the court may defer the date of dissolution.[33]

COMPANY'S OWN PETITION TO WIND UP

The company itself can petition for a winding up under any of the grounds set out in s.213 of the 1963 Act.[34] However, petitions of that nature are extremely rare because, ordinarily, the company will elect for a voluntary liquidation. Exceptionally, where the requisite majority for a special resolution cannot be obtained, the company might then petition the court. But if it is insolvent, a simple majority of the members' votes will commence a creditors' voluntary winding up.

Whatever the grounds being invoked, the company's decision to seek a winding up cannot be made by the directors without reference to the members, who are entitled to be properly consulted before their company can be brought to an end. In *Re Galway & Salthill Tramways Co.*,[35] the directors of a transport undertaking petitioned to have it wound up on 'just and equitable' grounds because it was loosing money, its net assets were steadily diminishing and it

---

29. 1963 Act. s.253.
31. Id. s.272.
33. Id. s.273(4) and (5).
35. [1918] 1 IR 62.

30. Id. s.254.
32. Id. s.273.
34. Ante p. 137.

could not pay its debts as they were falling due. The argument that the equivalent of article 80 of Table A empowered the directors to make this application was rejected by O'Connor MR, who observed that 'the object of management is the working of the company's undertaking, while the object of a winding up is its stoppage.'[36] There the petition was adjourned in order that the members could meet and decide if they would support it.

Neither a receiver nor an examiner, under the Companies (Amendment) Act, 1990, are empowered by legislation to petition for a winding up. However, in his report to the court, an examiner can recommend liquidation. Circumstances can arise where a receiver and manager appointed over a company's assets is entitled to petition for a winding up, on the company's behalf. That happened in *Re Emmadart Ltd*,[37] where a receiver had been appointed over a company with one asset remaining, an unoccupied shop held under a 25 year lease. A rate demand was presented by the local authority. There was an exemption from rates for companies being wound up. In order to gain the benefit of that exemption, a petition was presented by the receiver and the court ordered that the company be wound up. Because of the insolvency and the effect of a winding up order would be to protect the company's remaining assets, it was held that the receiver was entitled to petition on its behalf.

CONTRIBUTORY'S/MEMBER'S PETITION TO WIND UP

A contributory is someone who is obliged to contribute to a company's assets when it is being wound up, most notably a member with partly paid up shares. But for the purpose of presenting a winding up petition a fully paid up member or shareholder is also deemed to be a contributory.[38] In principle the contributory's petition can be based on any of the grounds set out in s.213 of the 1963 Act[39] but usually his application will be based on alleged 'oppression' or 'just and equitable' grounds. It is most unusual for a contributory to be seeking a winding up on the grounds of insolvency; if his shares are fully paid he would be in effect throwing away his investment and if they are partly paid he would be triggering his liability to pay what remains due on them. Moreover, it is far more convenient and cheaper to seek to have a members' meeting convened to consider a winding up resolution.

There is some doubt about whether an order would ever be made, on a contributory's petition, winding up his company for being insolvent because insolvency is a matter which primarily concerns creditors and, if they are content to do nothing about the company, a contributory on his own is unlikely to be successful in the application. In *Re Chesterfield Catering Co.*[40] the court confirmed the 100-year-old principle that 'where a fully paid shareholder petitions for a compulsory winding up he must show, on the face of his petition, a *prima facie* probability that there will be assets available for distribution

---

36. Id. at p. 65. Compare *Re Equitycorp International plc* [1989] BCLC 597.
37. [1979] 2 WLR 868.   38. 1963 Act s.207.
39. See ante p. 137.   40. [1977] Ch. 373.

among the shareholders'[41] or some other 'tangible interest' for the petitioner.[42] An example of such other tangible interest would be in an unlimited company; the shareholder may desire liquidation in order to put some cap on his liability for the company's debts. But that tangible interest must arise by virtue of the petitioner's membership of the company; he must show that the liquidation will deliver him some advantage or minimise a disadvantage *qua* member. In *Re Instrumentation Electrical Services Ltd*,[43] it was held that two contributories lacked standing to seek a winding up of their insolvent company because their petition disclosed neither any advantage they might obtain from a liquidation or any disadvantage they might suffer if the company continued in being. The judge there gave the petitioners opportunity to amend their petition so that they could show some benefit or detriment but no amendment was made.

An exception of sorts is made where the petition is based on the failure of the company to supply accounts and information. If as a result the petitioner is not able to demonstrate that he will be able to share in a surplus, he will not be deprived of *locus standi.*[44]

CREDITOR'S PETITION TO WIND UP

Where the company is insolvent, in most cases it is a creditor who petitions to have it liquidated. Often the threat of liquidation is made in order to exact payment of a debt owed by the company. For if the statutory demand for payment is made and the money due is not received within three weeks,[45] the creditor can proceed with a winding up petition—usually on the grounds of insolvency and exceptionally on 'just and equitable' grounds.

Bowen LJ once compared winding up as a form of equitable execution—a process through which the liquidator takes control of the company's assets and realises them for the benefit of its creditors.[46] Before a liquidation commences, the normal creditors' remedies are available to them. As is explained below, once the winding up order is made, those modes of redress virtually lapse[47] and the creditor is then left to prove in the winding up and receive his proportionate share from such assets as are realised. *Prima facie*, a creditor is entitled to have a company which does not pay its debt wound up,[48] although the court occasionally rejects petitions where insolvency has been established. Creditors are not expected to exhaust alternative remedies before seeking a winding up order; once the stipulated sum is due or owing, the creditor can present his petition even where that is done mainly as a means of exerting pressure to obtain payment. Even the presence of a collateral motive, like the desire to eliminate a competitor, does not disentitle an unpaid creditor to a winding up order.[49] But

41. *Re Othery Construction Ltd* [1966] 1 WLR 69, at p. 72.
42. *Re Costa Rica Gold Washing Co.* (1879) 11 ChD 36. 43. [1988] BCLC 550.
44. *Re Newman & Howard Ltd* [1962] Ch. 257. 45. 1963 Act s 214(a).
46. *Re Chapel House Colliery Co.* (1883) 24 Ch D 259, at p. 269.
47. See post pp. 180-185.
48. Supra n.2 and *Bowes v Hope Life Insurance Co.* (1865) 11 HL Cas 389.
49. *Bryanston Finance Ltd v de Vries (No. 2)* [1976] Ch 63.

if many of the unsecured creditors are against liquidation, the court may hold its hand.

'Any creditor'   According to s.215 of the 1963 Act, a petition to wind up a company may be brought by 'any creditor' but there is no statutory definition of this term. It means any person who is owned money by the company, including the present assignee of a previous creditor[50] and a creditor by subrogation.[51] It must be a valid enforceable debt, which is not barred by the Statute of Limitations[52] and which remains owing by the company at the time the petition was presented.[53] Every person who will be admitted to prove a debt in the liquidation[54] is entitled to present the petition—including a tort creditor and a creditor whose claim is not statute barred at the time of presentation but has become barred by the date of the hearing.[55] Secured creditors are not prevented from petitioning for a winding up.[56] Where a garnishee order has been obtained, the garnishor is not a creditor of the garnishee and accordingly cannot petition for the garnishee's winding up.[57]

When the petition is based on a debt which is disputed on substantial grounds, the petitioner is deemed not to be a creditor for these purposes and accordingly lacks *locus standi* to make the application, even if the company is insolvent.[58] To present a petition where the debt is clearly disputed has been described as 'scandalous abuse of process'.[59]

Section 215 defines a creditor as including any 'contingent or prospective' creditor. Prospective creditors are those who are owed money except that the debt has not yet actually fallen due, such as where there is a loan that is repayable at some future date or rent falling due at some future date. A contingent creditor is someone to whom the company owes certain duties under which it will or even may become obliged to pay money in the future. A contingent creditor is 'a person towards whom, under an existing obligation, the company may or will become subject to a present liability on the happening of some future event or at some future date';[60] for instance, a person who under a contract with the

---

50. *Re Steel Wing Co.* [1921] 349. Cf. *Perak Pioneer Ltd v Petroliam Nasional Bhd.* [1986] AC 849, where the petitioning creditor's debt was assigned after the petition was presented.
51. *Re Healing Research Ltd* [1991] BCLC 716.
52. *Re Karnos Pty.* [1989] BCLC 340.
53. *Re W. Hockley Ltd* [1962] 1 WLR 555.
54. See Ch. 19.
55. *Motor Terms Pty. v Liberty Insurance Ltd* (1967) 116 CLR 177
56. *Moore v Anglo-Italian Bank* (1879) 10 Ch D 681 and *Re Borough of Portsmouth etc. Tramway Co.* [1892] 2 Ch 362.
57. *Re Combined Weighing etc. Co.* (1889) 43 Ch D 99.
58. *Mann v Goldstein* [1968] 1 WLR 1091.
59. *Re Gold Hill Mines* (1883) 23 Ch D 210.
60. *Re William Hockley Ltd* [1962] 1 WLR at p. 558; compare *Re A Company (No. 006273 of 1992)* [1993] BCLC 131.

company may have a claim against it for damages or compensation. It has never been established whether this term includes a contingent tort creditor.[61] However, the court will not hear a prospective or contingent creditor's petition until that creditor provides such security for costs as the court deems reasonable and, additionally, a *prima facie* case for a winding up has been made out.[62] Accordingly, in such applications there should first be a preliminary hearing as to whether there is a *prima facie* case to allow the petition to go forward to a hearing;[63] although the court may consider the petition immediately after it finds that there is a *prima facie* case.

Insolvent Apart from the very exceptional petition on 'just and equitable' grounds, the creditor's petition will be based on the grounds in s.213(e) of the 1963 Act, that the company is 'unable to pay its debts' or, for short, is insolvent.[64] Because of obvious administrative difficulties for many creditors establishing as a matter of evidence that a company is insolvent, s.214(a) and (b) of the 1963 Act lay down two simple mechanisms for showing that the company cannot pay its debts. Once the requirements of either of these procedures have been satisfied the company will be deemed to be insolvent. But a petitioner is always free to prove insolvency by any other means.

The statutory demand The most frequently used of these mechanisms is the s.214(a) statutory demand for payment, which does not require to be preceded by any final judgment. If a creditor who at the time is owed more than £1,000[65] serves on the company a written and signed demand to pay the sum due and, within the following three weeks, that sum was not paid or satisfactorily secured, then the company is deemed to be insolvent. A demand may be served by an assignee of a debt but not by an assignee in equity, at least of part of a debt, because the company cannot know whether meeting the demand would discharge the liability for that part of the debt.[66]

Service must be at the company's registered office and, it would seem, must be made by hand. Because of the drastic consequences that can follow not satisfying the statutory demand, the prescribed procedures must be strictly complied with. Sending the demand by way of telex has been held not to be a good service because it was not left at the company's office.[67] The sum due by the company must be specified. No special form for the demand is required but it must be unequivocal, peremptory and unconditional.[68] In one instance where the demand had been posted but the court was satisfied it had been received by

---

61. See post p. 281.
62. 1963 Act s.215(c).
63. *Re Fitness Centre (South East) Ltd* [1986] BCLC 518.
64. See generally, Samuels, 'Winding Up a Company for Inability to Pay its Debts', 28 *Conv* 121 (1964).
65. 1990 Act s.123.
66. *Re Steel Wing Co.* [1921] 1 Ch 349.
67. *Re A Company* [1985] BCLC 37.
68. Ibid.

the company, it was held that s.214(a) had been sufficiently complied with.[69] A clear three weeks must have been allowed to make the payment.[70]

The debt in question must be 'then due' and payable at the time the demand is served, in the sense that the petitioner is entitled to be paid immediately.[71] Consequently, this method of establishing insolvency is not open to prospective or contingent creditors. Nor may this method be used where there is a bona fide dispute about the debt, be it about its existence or the amount which is owing.[72] In those circumstances, it cannot be said that the company 'neglected to pay' a debt 'then due', since the company has good grounds to contest it. As Jessel MR once observed,

> It is very obvious, on reading that enactment, that the word 'neglected' is not necessarily equivalent to the word 'omitted'. Negligence is a term which is well known to the law. Negligence in paying a debt on demand . . . is omitting to pay without reasonable excuse. Mere omission by itself does not amount to negligence. Therefore, . . . where a debt is bona fide disputed by a debtor, and the debtor alleges, for example, that the demand for goods sold and delivered is excessive, and says that he, the debtor is willing to pay such sum as . . . he himself considers a fair sum for the goods, then in that case he has not neglected to pay, and is not within s.214(a).[73]

Where only the quantum of the debt is disputed but the company refuses to tender any payment in respect of what undoubtedly is owed, the court may order a winding up if other evidence of insolvency is adduced.[74] Although the company may seem to be solvent, if it persistently refuses to pay an undisputed debt, the creditor is entitled to present the winding up petition on foot of the statutory demand.[75]

A petition to wind up must not be presented until at least 21 full days after this demand was served. Once that time has elapsed, the creditor is not obliged to present his petition forthwith.[76] But the debt must remain unpaid at the date the petition is heard.

Unsatisfied execution   The other simple mechanism for establishing insolvency is under s.214(b)—where some creditor has sought to levy execution or equivalent process against the company which has been returned unsatisfied. For instance, the sheriff may have made a return of *nulla bona*. Even partly

---

69. *Re A Company* [1991] BCLC 561.
70. *Re Lympne Investments Ltd* [1972] 1 WLR 523.
71. *Re Bryant Investments Co.* [1974] 1 WLR 826.
72. *Re A Company* [1984] 1 WLR 1090.
73. *Re London & Paris Banking Corp.* (1874) 19 Eq. 444, at p. 446; See to *Re Lympne Investments Ltd* [1972] 1 WLR 523.
74. *Re Tweeds Garage Ltd* [1961] Ch 407.
75. *Cornhill Insurance plc v Improvement Services Ltd* [1986] 1 WLR 114.
76. *Re Imperial Hydropathic Hotel Co.* (1882) 49 LT 147.

unsatisfied execution is sufficient for these purposes. It seems that the court may go behind the sheriff's return to ascertain whether he really did attempt to levy execution, which was unsatisfied.[77]

Unable to pay debts   Alternatively, the creditor may choose to demonstrate by other means that the company 'is unable to pay its debts'. The question then arises, what exactly is meant by this phrase; does it mean inability to meet demands as they fall due or excess of liabilities over assets, or whatever? In a case which was not directly concerned with liquidation, Barron J observed that

> Insolvency is essentially a matter of assets and liabilities. If liabilities exceed assets, the position is one of insolvency. But the reverse is not necessarily true. A company is not solvent because its assets exceed its liabilities. It cannot for example take into account assets which it requires to remain in existence save in so far as they may be used as security to raise finance. The text is ultimately, can it pay its debts as they fall due.[78]

In *Re Capital Annuities Ltd*,[79] it was held that inability to pay debts occurs where the company's present, contingent and prospective liabilities exceed the present value of its assets. In other words, the balance sheet shows that its assets are less than its liabilities. If needs be, expert evidence can be advanced as to the reliability of the balance sheet and valuations contained in it. Before 1871 the court could not take account of prospective or contingent liabilities in making this assessment.[80] Since those liabilities are particularly important for insurance companies,[81] in that year it was provided that account should be taken of such liabilities in determining the solvency of those companies. In 1907 these liabilities were made applicable to assessing the solvency of all other companies.[82]

Insolvency can also be established where the company has insufficient current assets to meet its current liabilities, i.e. it does not have sufficient readily realisable assets to meet its immediate debts. This situation can be proved by the petitioner showing that he sought payment of a debt which the company did not pay within a reasonable time, even though that request was not the statutory demand as described above. Slade J has observed that a 'failure by the company to pay an admitted creditor within a reasonable time after demand would be likely to provide ample evidence of such inability.'[83] On the other hand, a temporary shortage of liquid assets in the company does not establish inability

77. *Re Alexander* [1966] NI 128.
78. *H. Albert de Barry & Co. N.V. v O'Mullane* (2 June 1992) at pp. 54-55.
79. [1979] 1 WLR 170.
80. *Re European Life Assur. Soc.* (1869) 9 Eg 122.
81. S.21 of the Life Assurance Companies Act 1871.
82. S.28 of the Companies Act 1907. For a full account, see *Re Capital Annuities Ltd* [1979] 1 WLR 170, at pp. 182-186. See too, *Byblos Bank SAL v Al-Khudhairy* [1987] BCLC 232 at pp. 247-249.
83. Id. at p. 187. See too *Taylor Industrial Flooring Ltd v Plant Hire (Manchester) Ltd* [1990] BCLC 216.

to pay.[84] Nor is such inability established when the petitioner is relying on accounts that are some years out of date. Among the circumstances from which courts have concluded that there was inability to pay is the existence of many outstanding judgments against the company,[85] the absence of any assets against which execution can be levied,[86] dishonouring a bill of exchange,[87] having a receiver appointed over all of the company's assets.[88] Ultimately the court must decide on the basis of what evidence is placed in front of it whether the company is indeed insolvent.

Just and equitable   Often a creditor who is petitioning to have a company wound up on the grounds of insolvency will include in his petition a claim that the company should also be wound up on 'just and equitable' grounds. Formerly, where prospective and contingent claims did not count in determining if a company was insolvent, there was some practical advantage in adding this claim; otherwise companies could in effect engage in fraudulent or reckless trading by purchasing stocks on credit without any real prospect of eventually paying for them.[89] Practices of that nature are now expressly proscribed by s.297A of the 1963 Act. At present, although adding the 'just and equitable' grounds may be construed as inviting the court to consider the surrounding circumstances, it would seem that the petitioning creditor will not succeed under this ground unless he shows that the company is indeed insolvent.[90]

Intervention prior to the hearing   Before the actual hearing of the petition takes place, the company may apply to the court to have the proceedings blocked in one way or another. Four main forms of application may be made, viz.

i. to restrain the creditor from even presenting the petition in the Central Office,[91]

ii. to restrain the petition being advertised, or being otherwise published or presented,[92]

iii. for a stay on the hearing of the petition, although the court is very reluctant to grant stays,[93]

iv. to have the petition struck out.[94]

---

84. Ibid. See *Re a Company* [1986] BCLC 201.
85. *Re Tweeds Garages Ltd* [1962] Ch 406.
86. *Re Douglas Griggs Engineering Ltd* [1963] Ch 19.
87. *Re Globe New Patent Iron Co.* (1875) 20 Eq. 337.
88. *Re Chic Ltd* [1905] 2 Ch 345.
89. E.g. *Re A. Melson & Co.* [1906] 1 Ch 801.
90. *B. Karsberg Ltd* [1956] 1 WLR 57.
91. E.g. *Stonegate Securities Ltd v Gregory* [1980] Ch 576.
92. E.g. *Mann v Goldstein* [1968] 1 WLR 1091 and *Re A Company* [1986] BCLC 127.
93. E.g. *Re A Company* [1991] BCLC 514.
94. E.g. *Re A Company* [1973] 1 WLR 1566.

Where it can be shown that presenting the petition is an abuse of the process of the court, it will be struck out on much the same grounds as ordinary proceedings can be struck out for being frivolous and vexatious or as showing no cause of action.[95] A common example is where there is a substantial and bona fide dispute about the petitioner's debt; in that event, the question of whether he is indeed a creditor of the company is not a matter to be determined by the winding up court. Another form of intervention prior to the hearing is by the creditor applying to have a provisional liquidator appointed.[96]

DISCRETION TO REFUSE WINDING UP

Section 213 of the 1963 Act does not oblige the court to order a winding up if any of the circumstances set out in (a)-(g) of that section have been established. Instead, it is provided that a company 'may be wound up' in any of these circumstances. Thus, even if insolvency as defined in any of s.214's heads has been proved, the court nevertheless can decline to make the order. But it does not have a complete discretion where the petitioner demonstrates insolvency, as provided. Generally, a petitioner who satisfies any of s.214's requirements is entitled to the winding up order; an unpaid creditor 'is entitled *ex debito justitiae*' to a winding up order.[97] Nevertheless, there are several well established circumstances in which that order will not be made and there may be other special circumstances about a particular case which justifies the court in declining to make the order, or adjourning the matter for some time and subject to appropriate conditions. The court does not lean in favour of adjournments because they prevent other petitions being presented.

In *Re Bula Ltd*,[98] following consideration of many of the reported cases on this point, McCarthy J summed up the position as follows:

> The section . . . gives to the court a true discretion which should be exercised in a principled manner that is fair and just. . . . A creditor is *prima facie* entitled to his order so as to shift the initial burden to those who oppose the winding up; the petitioner does not have to demonstrate positively that an order for winding up is for the benefit of the class of creditors to which he belongs, but, if issue is joined on the matter, and the case made that the petition is not for that purpose but for an ulterior, though not in itself improper object, then the burden shifts back to the petitioner.[99]

Payment or tender to the petitioner   In the past, a petitioning creditor at any time could withdraw his petition, for instance where the company paid his debt

95.   E.g. *Re A Company* [1991] BCLC 235 and *Re A Company (No. 0013734 of 1991)* [1993] BCLC 59.
96.   See post pp. 162-163
97.   *Western of Canada Oil etc. Co.* (1873) LR 17 Eq 1, at p. 7.
98.   [1990] 1 IR 440.
99.   Id. at p. 448.

prior to the date of the hearing. However, since 1910 if that person drops out of the proceedings the court has had a discretion to substitute him with another willing petitioner. On account of this power, it would seem that payment or tender to the petitioner gives the court only a discretion to decide what should happen to his application; it may dismiss the application, adjourn it or allow another creditor to take it up. An important consideration is the financial state of the company. There is some risk for the petitioner accepting the company's offer of payment at this stage because, if another creditor proceeds with the application and the company is wound up, that payment is strictly an invalid disposition;[1] unless the court sanctions that payment, it must be refunded.[2]

Disputed debt   The court has a general discretion to decline the order where the petitioner's debt is subject to bona fide dispute on reasonable grounds.[3] In those circumstances, the appropriate procedure for the petitioner is first to bring a claim in the courts and thereby establish that the debt indeed exists. As Megarry J has observed, the winding up court

> must not be used as a debt-collecting agency, nor as a means of bringing improper pressure to bear on a company. The effects on a company of the presentation of a winding up petition against it are such that it would be wrong to allow the machinery designed for such petitions to be used as a means of resolving disputes which ought to be settled in ordinary litigation, or to be kept in suspense over the company's head while the litigation is fought out.[4]

In another instance, Buckley LJ observed that

> The whole of the doctrine of this part of the law is based upon the view that winding up proceedings are not suitable proceedings in which to determine a genuine dispute about whether or not a company does or does not owe the sum in question; and equally . . . it must be true that the winding up proceedings are not suitable proceedings in which to determine whether [a] liability is an immediate liability or only a prospective or contingent liability.[5]

Thus, for instance, in *Re Pageboy Couriers Ltd*,[6] the petitioner had instituted proceedings against the company claiming payment of two years' directors' fees. Subsequently, he petitioned to have the company wound up for not paying

1.   See post p. 176.
2.   *Re Webb Electrical Ltd* [1988] BCLC 382.
3.   *Re Catholic Publishing & Bookselling Co.* (1864) 2 De G. J. & S.116, *London and Paris Banking Corp.* (1874) L.R. 19 Eq. 444, *Cadiz Waterworks v Barnett* (1874) 19 Eg. 182 and *Re Gold Hill Mines* (1882) 23 Ch D 210. For an exception to this principle, see *Re Russian and English Bank* [1932] 1 Ch 663.
4.   *Re Lympne Investments Ltd* [1972] 1 WLR 523.
5.   *Re Stonegate Securities Ltd* [1980] 1 Ch 576, at p. 587.
6.   [1983] ILRM 510. Similarly *Re Prime Link Removals Ltd* [1987] NZLR 512.

those fees. On the grounds that this debt had been disputed on all occasions by the company in good faith and on substantial grounds, O'Hanlon J refused to order a winding up. In cases like this costs are often awarded against the petitioner on a solicitor and client basis.[7]

Nature of the dispute It depends on the entire circumstances whether the dispute about the existence of a debt is bona fide and substantial, rather than spurious or trivial. There should be evidence before the court supporting the defence which the company is relying on.[8] In some cases, where it has all the relevant evidence, the winding up court should decide the substantive dispute.[9] More often this matter is left to be resolved in separate proceedings. Some of the old authorities suggest a test similar to that for obtaining an interlocutory injunction; has the company brought forward 'a *prima facie* case . . . that there is something which ought to be tried.'[10] On account of the rights of parties to negotiable instruments, it is only in the most exceptional circumstances that the court will refuse to entertain a winding up petition based on a dishonoured cheque.[11] The court may even refuse the petition where the company demonstrates that it has a substantial counter-claim against the petitioner.[12]

At times, instead of dismissing a petition, the court may adjourn the hearing until other proceedings are resolved, for instance, where it is claimed that the judgment against the company was obtained by fraud.[13] Generally, it will not adjourn the hearing where a judgment which establishes the existence of the debt is subject to appeal.[14]

Amount only in dispute A winding up order will not be refused where the company is insolvent and all that is in dispute is the amount of the debt. This is because 'it would, in many cases, be quite unjust to refuse a winding up order to a petitioner who is admittedly owed moneys which have not been paid merely because there is a dispute as to the precise amount owing.'[15] In *Re A Company*[16] it was held that where the amount in the statutory demand is disputed, if the petitioner, without serious argument, can satisfy the court that a particular sum in excess of £1,000 is owing and has not been paid, the court can go ahead and make the order. But there, where the company paid over the amount which it

7. *Cadiz Waterworks Co. v Barnett* (1874) LR 19 Eg 182, at p. 197 and *Re A Company (No. 0012209 of 1991)* [1992] 2 All ER 797 at p. 800.
8. *Re Welsh Brick Industries Ltd* [1946] 2 All ER 197.
9. *Brinds Ltd v Offshore Oil NL*, 60 ALJR 185 (1986).
10. *Re Great Britain Mutual Life Assur. Soc.* (1880) 16 Ch D 246, at p. 253.
11. *Re A Company* [1991] BCLC 464; contrast *Re A Company* [1991] BCLC 737.
12. *Re L.H.F. Wools Ltd* [1970] Ch. 27; compare *Re Douglas Griggs Engineering Ltd* [1963] Ch. 19 and *Re F.S.A. Business Software Ltd* [1990] BCLC 825. Cf. *Re Julius Harper Ltd* [1983] NZLR 215.
13. *Bowes v Hope Life Insurance Soc.* (1865) 11 HLC 389.
14. *Re Amalgamated Properties of Rhodesia Ltd* [1917] 2 Ch 115.
15. *Re Tweeds Garage Ltd* [1962] 1 Ch 406, at p. 413.
16. [1984] 1 WLR 1090.

conceded was owing and a serious question remained about the existence and/or quantum of the balance being demanded, the petition was dismissed.

Creditors opposed to winding up   The right of a creditor to obtain a winding up order is, to an extent, a collective right that must be exercised on behalf of all unsecured creditors and, accordingly, where many of these creditors are opposed to winding up, generally the court should not make the order. According to Buckley J in *Re Crigglestone Coal Co.*,

> the order which the petitioner seeks is not an order for his benefit, but an order for the benefit of a class of which he is a member. The right (to have the company wound up) is not his individual right, but his representative right. If a majority of the class are opposed to his view, and consider that they have a better chance of getting payment by abstaining from seizing the assets, then . . . the court gives effect to such right as the majority of the class desire to exercise.[17]

Reasons for opposition   The opposing majority must be able to demonstrate some good reason why the company should not be wound up, for instance, they genuinely expect to get paid or a proposed reorganisation of the company would be jeopardised. As Willmer LJ put it in *Re P. & J. Macrae Ltd*,

> before a majority of creditors can claim to override the wishes of the minority, they must at least show some good reason for their attitude. ...
>
> [W]here a majority of creditors do for good reason oppose a petition for the winding up of a company, then prima facie they are entitled reasonably to expect that their wishes will prevail, in the absence of proof by the petitioning creditor of special circumstances rendering a winding up order desirable in spite of their opposition.[18]

There, it was held that the trial judge was correct in ordering a winding up even though the vast majority in number and amount of the creditors, mostly trade and business creditors, opposed the petition. The opposing creditors had not advanced any reasons, good or otherwise, why the petition should not be granted.[19]

One reason that will weigh heavily with the court is that the unsecured creditors expect to get paid by the company without having to resort to a winding up, and they can point to circumstances which lend credence to their belief.[20] In the past, the court held to the view that the absence of unencumbered assets in the company to satisfy the general creditors was sufficient reason for acceding to their opposition.[21] However, abstaining from ordering a winding

17.   [1906] 2 Ch 327, at pp. 331-332.
18.   [1961] 1 All ER 302, at p. 307.
19.   Similarly in *Re Vuma Ltd* [1960] 1 WLR 1283.
20.   *Re S.O.S. Motors Ltd* [1934] NZLR s.129.
21.   *Re Chapel House Colliery Co.* (1883) 24 Ch D 259.

up in such situations often encourages abuses within companies, so that the 1963 Act now provides that a winding up should not be refused merely because there are no free assets.[22] In *Re St. Thomas' Dock Co.*,[23] the petitioner was the secured creditor, to whom all the company's assets were charged, and there was opposition from many of the unsecured creditors. There was no evidence that the liquidation would generate any surplus beyond the amount of the petitioner's debenture. The court directed that the petition should stand over for six months, subject to several conditions.

Evaluating the opposition: In ascertaining the creditors' wishes, account should be taken of the value of the debts in question[24] as well as the actual number of creditors who are opposing liquidation. Account will be taken of the status of the creditors and it seems the view of the preferential creditors may weigh heavily with the court.[25] In *Re P. & J. Macrae Ltd*, Upjohn LJ observed that

> Although the statute provides that it is the wishes of the creditors to which the court may have regard [and it] gives a complete discretion, the weight to be given to those wishes . . . varies according to the number and value of the creditors expressing wishes, and the nature and quality of their debts. I [reject] the proposition that it is merely a matter of counting heads and that a majority of fifty one per cent opposing a petition will outweigh the views of the forty-nine per cent. . . .
>
> Apart altogether from prospective or contingent creditors whose position may be difficult to assess, a judge may properly take the view that greater weight should be given to the wishes of a large number of small creditors against the wishes of one or two very large creditors, even though the latter are larger in amount in the aggregate. Then there may be differences in the quality of the creditors. The circumstances may be such that the court is rightly suspicious of the opposing creditors and motives which are activating them.[26]

Secured creditors opposing Where it is the secured creditors who oppose the winding up, generally the court will not accede to their views because the process of liquidation is designed primarily to benefit the general creditors. Thus in *Re Crigglestone Coal Co.*,[27] the secured creditors opposed the petition because commencement of a winding up would seriously jeopardise their security, which was a lease that was subject to re-entry where, *inter alia*, winding up commenced. It was held that this was not a sufficient reason for

22. 1963 Act s.216(1).   23. (1876) 2 Ch D 116.
24. 1963 Act s.309(2).
25. *Re Camburn Petroleum Products Ltd* [1980] 1 WLR 186.
26. [1961] 1 WLR 229, at pp. 238, 239. See too *Re Jacobs River Sawmilling Co.* [1961] NZLR 602, *Re J.R.S. Garage Ltd* [1961] NZLR 632 and *Re Restaurant Chevron Ltd* [1963] NZLR 225.
27. [1906] 2 Ch 327.

rejecting the petition; the secured creditors had accepted a security that by its very terms became worthless in the event of winding up, and 'it does not lie in their mouth to say that their debtor must, therefore, for their benefit be relieved from the legal consequences which result in favour of other creditors from incurring debts and not paying them.'[28] Yet it is conceivable that where winding up will cause very grave damage to secured creditors, but will inflict little damage on the other creditors, the formers' wishes will prevail.

Voluntary liquidation in progress   The position where a voluntary liquidation has already commenced was explained in *Re George Downes & Co.*[29] as follows:

> if the petitioner proves he will be prejudiced by a continuance of the voluntary winding up then he is entitled to a compulsory order *ex debito justitiae*, and the court cannot refuse it. If, on the other hand, he fails to establish prejudice by the continuance of the voluntary winding up, the court still has power to make the order if the court forms the opinion that the rights of creditors will be prejudiced by a voluntary winding up. This has been interpreted to cover many different sets of special circumstances.[30]

Overend J there instanced various circumstances where the creditors would be sufficiently prejudiced to warrant ordering a compulsory liquidation, such as where the voluntary liquidator is the same person as was appointed receiver in a debenture-holders' action,[30] where a *prima facie* case was established of fraud in connection with forming the company or running its business,[31] where there was undue delay or some other unsatisfactory feature in conducting the voluntary liquidation,[32] where the company's liabilities are very large,[33] where the reason for having a voluntary liquidation no longer obtains[34] and where certain features of the company are such as to demand public investigation.[35] In the *Downes & Co.* case there were several matters pertaining to the company that might very well have required investigation, where it was likely that the liquidator might have to make several applications to the court, and where all the creditors had not been properly notified of the creditors' meeting, it was held that the winding up should be made compulsory.

28. Id. at p. 335.
29. [1943] IR 420, at p. 423. See too *Re New York Exchange Ltd* (1888) 39 Ch D 415.
30. *Re Medical Battery Co.* [1894] 1 Ch 444 and *Re Wicklow Textile Industries Ltd*, 87 ILTR 72 (1971).
31. *Re Varieties Ltd* [1893] 2 Ch 235.
32. *Re Manchester Queensland Cotton Co.*, 16 LT 583 (1867) and *Re Caerphilly Colliery Co.* (1875) 32 LT 15.
33. *Re Barned's Banking Co.* (1866) 14 LT 451.
34. *Re Guta Percha Corp.* [1900] 2 Ch 665.
35. *Re Consolidated South Rand Mines Deep Ltd* [1909] 1 Ch 491. Compare *Re B Karsberg Ltd* [1956] 1 WLR 57; matters could be adequately investigated in the context of a voluntary winding up.

If an overwhelming majority of the creditors want a compulsory liquidation then, generally, they will get the order to wind up.[36] The fact that the voluntary liquidation commenced after the petition to wind up was presented is not in itself grounds for having a compulsory liquidation,[37] except for example where operation of the 'relation back' rule would be advantageous. Where the petitioner is a contributory, s.282 of the 1963 Act requires the court to be notified that he will be prejudiced by the voluntary liquidation.

The criterion articulated in the *Downes & Co.* case has been reformulated somewhat in England, where the courts now take particular account of the views of the independent trade creditors, i.e. ordinary business creditors who are not closely connected with the company in question. According to Hoffman J in one instance,

> it is . . . proper to discount the opposition of those opposing creditors who are clearly associated with the management of the company, particularly when .. it is said that the main reason why there should be an order for compulsory winding up is the necessity for an independent investigation into their management. . . . [T]he public interest requires that the liquidator should not only be independent, but be seen to be independent.[38]

In another instance, the same judge observed that

> Even if the creditors in favour of a continuation of the voluntary liquidation are a minority in value, the court may refuse a compulsory order if there appears to be no advantage to creditors in making one. . . . The court may also take into account not only the value of the debts but the possible or probable motives of the creditors in making their choice. Thus, creditors who are also shareholders or connected with the former management may have less weight given to their views than those who have no interest except in their capacity as creditors.
>
> Besides counting debts, . . . I am also entitled to have regard to the general principles of fairness and commercial morality which underlie the details of the insolvency law as applied to companies. A judicial exercise of discretion should not leave substantial independent creditors with a strong and legitimate sense of grievance.[39]

In these and other recent cases winding up orders were made in circumstances where most of the opposition to the orders came from creditors who were associated with the company in one form or another, or who had given the directors their proxies, and where it was those opposing the order who had selected the voluntary liquidator. Some of these cases also contained indications of assets being improperly transferred out of the company and *prima facie* evidence of fraud. As Vinelott J put it,

36. *Re E. Bishop & Sons Ltd* [1900] 2 Ch 254.
37. *Re J.D. Swain Ltd* [1965] 1 WLR 909.
38. *Re Lowestoft Traffic Services Ltd* [1986] BCLC 81 at p. 84.
39. *Re Palmer Marine Surveys Ltd* [1986] 1 WLR 573 at p. 578.

It would be wrong to refuse a compulsory order if the refusal would leave a majority of trade creditors with a justified feeling of grievance, a feeling that is that they have been unfairly deprived of the opportunity of ensuring that an independent liquidator, that is a liquidator not chosen by the directors, is given the charge of the winding up.[40]

Company in receivership Ordinarily a winding up petition will not be refused just because a receiver has already been appointed over all or part of the company's assets. Where, however, it was the petitioner for a winding up who appointed the receiver and his security attaches to the entire assets of the company, liquidation will not readily be directed. In *Re Bula Ltd*,[41] several banks appointed a receiver over all the assets of a mining company, which was very heavily insolvent. Some time later, one of its major unsecured creditors registered a judgment mortgage against the company's assets. Then, when three months from that time had almost expired, the banks petitioned to wind up the company in order to prevent that judgment mortgage becoming in any way effective.[42] The receiver was having some difficulty selling the charged assets and the banks claimed that it might be easier to dispose of those assets if an official liquidator were appointed. Little credence was given to that contention by the Supreme Court, which dismissed the petition as an abuse of process. McCarthy J's judgment suggests that petitioners like the bank in this instance have quite a strong onus to show why a winding up order should be made.

ABUSING THE RIGHT TO PETITION

If the petitioner is indeed owed money by the company which the company declines to pay, it would seem that the petition may be presented regardless of the creditor's motives for doing so. A distinction has been drawn between motives and the actual purpose of presenting a petition. As was observed in one case, the court is 'not concerned with his motives or with the past conduct of the company, [whether] deplorable or worse and which may have led the petitioner to have justified dislike for and a desire to see the downfall of some person such as the main protagonist in the company.'[43] The governing principle here is that 'malice or bad motive does not make unlawful that which is otherwise lawful.'[44] But where the very object of commencing the procedure is to gain some collateral advantage for the petitioner, then the court will order the proceedings to be struck out because 'the only proper purpose for which a petition can be presented is for the proper administration of the company's assets for the benefit of all in the relevant class' of creditors.[45] In *Re A*

40. *Re M.C.H. Services Ltd* [1987] BCLC 535, at p. 538. See too, *Re Falcon R,J. Developments Ltd* [1987] BCLC 737. *Re H.J. Tomkins & Son Ltd* [1990] BCLC 76 and *Re Hewitt Brannan (Tools) Co. Ltd* [1991] BCLC 80.
41. [1990] 1 IR 440.   42. 1963 Act s.284(2); see post p. 181.
43. *Re A Company* [1983] BCLC 492, at p. 495.
44. Id.; also *Bryanston Finance Ltd v de Vries (No. 2)* [1976] Ch. 63 at p. 75.
45. [1983] BCLC 492 at p. 495. Cf. *McGinn v Beagan* [1962] IR 364.

Company,[46] the petition was based on taxed costs awarded in proceedings and the petitioner stood to benefit significantly from a forfeiture clause, in a lease of property to the company, if a winding up order was made before a specified date. It was held that the petitioner's primary purpose was to reap the benefit of that clause and, accordingly, the petition was not properly presented. A creditor petitioning for a winding up 'is invoking a class right and his petition must be governed by whether he is truly invoking that right on behalf of himself and all others of his class rateably, or whether he has some private purpose in view.'[47] Similarly, a petition merely in order to put pressure on a company is not properly presented.[48]

Preliminary motion or injunction One way of confronting what may be termed an 'abusive' petition is to oppose it at the hearing. Another approach is a preliminary motion for an order to have the petition struck out with costs.[49] Another still is to seek an injunction restraining presentation of the petition or to restrain taking any further steps with it.[50] It would seem that an injunction of this nature will not be given merely where the grounds for opposing the petition are grounds on which, exercising its discretion, the court could reject it, such as that the company has a substantial claim against the petitioner.[51] But where it is reasonably clear that the petition is bound to fail, an injunction might be granted. As a New Zealand judge explained, '[i]n such circumstances, rather than leave it to the Companies Court to dismiss the petition when it is brought on for hearing, the court in the exercise of its inherent jurisdiction will intervene at an earlier stage because the presentation and advertising of the petition are likely to do such serious, if not irreparable, harm to the company, and no good at all—or at least no legitimate good—to the petitioner.'[52]

Thus, if the debt in question is disputed on substantial grounds, presentation of the petition will be enjoined as an abuse of the process of the court,[53] at least when the company is not insolvent.[54] Where the parties agreed to submit a dispute to arbitration and an interim award was made, it was held to be an abuse of process in the circumstances there for one party to petition for a winding up because the other party had not complied with that award.[55] But it is not sufficient if the dispute is only as to the quantum of the claim or to some other

46. Ibid.   47. Id. at p. 495.
48. *Re A Company* [1894] 2 Ch 349.
49. E.g. *Re Gold Hill Mines* (1883) 23 Ch D 210 and *Re Garage Door Associates Ltd* [1984] 1 WLR 35.
50. E.g. *Re Cadiz Waterworks v Barnett* (1874) 19 Eq. 182 and *Bryanston Finance* case, supra.
51. *Re Julius Harper Ltd* [1983] NZLR 215.
52. Id. at p. 218.
53. *Cadiz Waterworks* case, supra n. 50 and *Stonegate Securities Ltd v Gregory* [1980] 1 Ch 576.
54. Compare *Niger Merchants Co. v Capper* (1881) 18 ChD 557n (injunction refused) with *Mann v Goldstein* [1968] 1 WLR 1091 (injunction granted).
55. *Wilsons (NZ) Portland Cement Ltd v Gatx-Fuller etc. Ltd (No. 2)* [1985] 2 NZLR 33.

aspect which does not affect the petitioner's status as a debtor.[56] In some Australian cases, injunctions have been given where the company had a right of set-off for the balance of the debt and at least once where the company had a counter- claim.[57]

Damages In exceptional circumstances, the company may even recover damages against a petitioner for abuse of the legal process. While, generally, it is not an actionable wrong to institute legal proceedings without reasonable or probable cause, there are exceptions to this rule,[58] such as presenting a bankruptcy petition against a trader. In *Quartz Hill Mining Co. v Eyre*,[59] it was held that presenting a winding up petition was also an exception to the rule, where the objective was to wreck the company's credit. Of such proceedings, Bowen LJ remarked that he 'should be sorry to think that since they involve a blow against the credit of those against whom they are instituted, the law did not afterwards place in the hands of the injured and aggrieved persons who have been wrongfully assailed, a means of righting themselves and recouping themselves, as far as can be, for the mischief done to them.'[60] It will depend on the circumstances whether there was malice and no reasonable and probable cause. It has not been determined whether such an action would lie where the company is indeed insolvent and, consequently, no longer has a credit or trading reputation to protect.[61]

PROVISIONAL LIQUIDATOR

At times the petitioning creditor or creditors may fear that those in control of the company may improperly dispose of its assets or put them in jeopardy in one way or another before the petition is even adjudicated. Accordingly, they may wish the court to intervene in the company's affairs pending the appointment of a liquidator. Section 226 of the 1963 Act empowers the court to appoint a provisional liquidator, who is a hybrid of interlocutory injunction and interim receiver designed to protect the company's assets in the intervening period.

Appointment Section 226 does not stipulate the circumstances in which a provisional liquidator may be appointed and it would seem that an appointment will be made whenever it is deemed appropriate by the court to do so. The older cases confined appointments to a very limited set of circumstances, for instance, where the company was clearly insolvent or it was inevitable that a winding up order would be made. More recently, the tendency has been not to so restrict the court's power.[62]

---

56. *Holt Southey Ltd v Catric Components Ltd* [1978] 2 All ER 276.
57. See cases referred to in *Re Julius Harper Ltd* [1983] NZLR 215.
58. *Dorene Ltd v Suedes (Ireland) Ltd* [1981] IR 312.
59. (1883) 11 QBD 674.   60. Id. at p. 693.
61. Cf. *Niger Merchants Co.* case, supra n.54.
62. E.g. *Re Highfield Commodities Ltd* [1984] 1 WLR 149.

An application can be made once the petition has been presented[63] but, if a petition is struck out, the court no longer has jurisdiction to appoint one.[64] The grounds for appointment, on a creditor's application, will be that the company's assets are in some serious jeopardy. Usually because such an appointment has the effect of taking control of the company's affairs out of the directors' and shareholders' hands before the petition is adjudicated, the creditor has to establish on affidavit sufficient grounds for a provisional liquidator. Moreover, great urgency would need to be demonstrated for the court to make such an appointment on an *ex parte* application. The mere fact that the company is insolvent would rarely justify having a provisional liquidator.

Effects of appointment The appointment of a provisional liquidator deprives the company's directors of all powers to deal with the assets described in the court's order.[65] But he may ratify, either expressly or by implication, unauthorised acts of the directors. It has been held that, notwithstanding the appointment, the board retains some residual powers and are not entirely *functus officio*; for instance, they can give instructions to apply to discharge the provisional liquidator, to oppose the winding up petition and, where granted, to appeal against the winding up order.[66]

Powers and duties A provisional liquidator's general functions are to take control of and to preserve the company's assets until an official liquidator is appointed. The order appointing him is required to set out the nature of and a brief description of the property to be taken into possession and also the duties to be performed.[67] These powers can be as extensive as those of a liquidator but, usually, the court will restrict the powers to protecting the assets and preserving the *status quo* until the petition is adjudicated.[68] It has been observed that the Companies Acts do 'not differentiate the powers of the two' kinds of liquidator and that 'the word "provisional" in this context seems . . . to imply a qualification not of the liquidator's powers, but of the tenure of his office; he is a liquidator but his appointment is temporary. . . . How far it is expedient for a provisional liquidator to exercise his powers is, of course, a different question which must depend on the circumstances of the case.'[69] Thus, for instance, unless prevented by the court from doing so, a provisional liquidator can apply to disclaim onerous property. Occasionally, a provisional liquidator may be empowered to carry on all or part of the business or he may apply to the court to have a special manager appointed for the interim.

63. 1963 Act s.226(1).
64. *Re A Company* [1974] 1 WLR 1566.
65. *Re Mawcon Ltd* [1969] 1 WLR 78.
66. *Re Union Accident Insurance Co.* [1972] 1 WLR 640.
67. Winding Up Rules, r. 14(2).
68. 1963 Act s.226(2).
69. *Re ABC Coupler & Engineering Co. Ltd (No.3)* [1970] 1 WLR 702, at p. 715.

14

Effects of Winding Up

When the members resolve to wind up their company or when the court orders that it shall be wound up, a liquidator will be appointed, either by the members, by the creditors or by the court, as the case may be. It is then the liquidator's task to get in all the company's assets, to realise them for as good a price as can reasonably be obtained, to pay off the creditors and to distribute any surplus remaining among the shareholders. As in the law of bankruptcy,[1] the commencement of a winding up is of great significance and affects a variety of matters. It terminates the power of the company to dispose of its property,[2] it fixes the status and liability of contributories,[3] it deprives creditors of their ordinary remedies against the company,[4] and it is the critical time for the purpose of determining the validity or otherwise of preferences[5] or of floating charges[6] given by the company prior to winding up. All these may be treated as effects, though in some instances retrospective effects, of winding up. There are, however, a number of other important consequences of liquidation which are not directly related to the commencement of a winding up, but which may nevertheless be regarded as directly or indirectly attributable to the winding up. In the majority of these cases the relevant date or event is the occurrence of the winding up itself, and this is so in relation to the effect of liquidation upon the contracts of the company, the powers of a receiver previously appointed, and in some circumstances the right to commence or continue actions or proceedings against the company.

COMMENCEMENT OF WINDING UP

The various impacts described below take effect from when the winding up commences; hence, knowing the precise time of commencement is vitally important. Section 253 of the 1963 Act stipulates that a voluntary winding up commences, for these and other purposes, the moment the shareholders pass their resolution to wind up. Section 220(2) of the 1963 Act provides that a compulsory winding up commences, not when the court makes the relevant order, but when the petition to wind up is presented, i.e. is lodged in the Central

---

1. See *Bankruptcy Law*, ch. 5.
2. 1963 Act s.218.
3. Id. ss.218 and 255.
4. Id. ss.219, 291 and 292.
5. Id. s.286.
6. Id. s.288.

Office of the High Court. But if the company had previously resolved to wind up, the liquidation began at that time.[7] Certain anomalies arise because a compulsory liquidation commences perhaps before many of the shareholders and even the company itself were aware of the fact; these anomalies are compounded by the fact that if, in the event, the court does not accede to the petition, there still would have been a period of time when the company was deemed to be in liquidation. In at least one instance, receipt of a notice convening a meeting to consider a voluntary liquidation is the relevant time for determining the validity of prior transactions.[8] In compulsory winding ups, for certain purposes the relevant time of commencement is when the petition was presented.[9] As in the present bankruptcy law, there is no general doctrine of 'relation back'.

MEMBERS

The principal effect that the liquidation of a company has on its shareholders or members is that they no longer can freely transfer their shares. In the case of a voluntary winding up, s.255 of the 1963 Act stipulates that any purported transfer of the shares shall be void unless the liquidator sanctioned the particular transfer. In the case of a compulsory liquidation, s.218 of the 1963 Act provides that every post- commencement transfer of shares in the company is void; but application can be made to the court to validate any particular transfer. There is scant authority on the criteria that should be applied by the liquidator or the court, as the case may be, in approving proposed transfers of shares. In the case of shares which are partly paid, one obvious requirement would be that the proposed transferee be in a position to pay any calls that the liquidator might make[10] or, alternatively, that the transferor guarantees payment of any calls made by the liquidator.[11] Where the company's members are not shareholders, notably in many companies limited by guarantee, ss.255 and 218 provide that, when a liquidation commences, there shall be no alteration in the status of the members without the approval of the liquidator or the court, as the case may be.

This prohibition also applies where shareholders seek to alter their status within the company, to its detriment, other than by seeking to transfer their shares.[12] The courts have not yet defined what is an alteration in status for these purposes. Authority on any other effects that a liquidation has on the shareholders is scantier still. For instance, are they still entitled to have convened general meetings and must they still be circulated with annual accounts?

Where persons have acquired shares in the company as a result of some

---

7. Id. s.220(1).
8. Id. s.291(2). Cf. *Re London, Hamburg & Continental Exchange Bank* (1866) LR 2 Eq 231.
9. E.g. *Re Amalgamated Investment & Property Co.* [1985] Ch 349.
10. E.g. *Re National Bank of Wales* [1897] 1 Ch 298.
11. E.g. *Cleve v Financial Corp.* (1873) 16 Eq 363.
12. *Re Oriental Commercial Bank, Barge's Case* (1868) 5 Eq 420.

misrepresentation and they wish to rescind their agreement to take those shares, they cannot rescind once a winding up has commenced. This principle is not based on the above statutory provisions but seems to have an independent foundation, that rescission should not be allowed where third parties' rights would be affected. In *Tennant v City of Glasgow Bank*,[13] where the company was insolvent (the deficit was enormous), the court would not permit rescission once a notice was circulated convening a meeting to resolve on a voluntary winding up. Even where the creditors have all been paid off in full, rescission will not be allowed where it still remains necessary to adjust creditors' rights *inter se*. But the statutory right to apply to rectify the register of members does not cease once a liquidation has commenced. It has been said that a member cannot sue for 'fraud on the minority' once the company goes into liquidation because, from then on, the liquidator has entire control of the company's affairs and the minority cannot any longer be at the mercy of the majority.[14]

DIRECTORS

Sections 258(2) and 269(3) of the 1963 Act provide that, in a voluntary liquidation, the directors' powers shall cease except so far as, in a creditors' voluntary liquidation, the committee of inspection or the creditors shall allow. No identical provision exists for compulsory winding ups, but the extensive powers that s.231 vests in the liquidator operate to deprive the directors of any say in the company's affairs.[15] Indeed, it would appear that liquidation not alone deprives the directors of their powers but in consequence they cease to hold their offices as directors. There is some Canadian authority to the effect that, once a liquidator is appointed, the directors no longer owe fiduciary duties to the company and are free to purchase company property from the liquidator.[16] There is South African authority to the effect that criminal provisions dealing with directors do not apply to persons who were directors of companies presently in liquidation.[17] However, in one instance, directors of such a company were ordered to answer interrogatories in their capacity as company 'officers'.[18]

Opposing petition   When a winding up petition is presented, the directors can authorise the company to oppose it. Notwithstanding the appointment of a provisional liquidator, the directors have some residual powers, for instance, to instruct solicitors and counsel to oppose the petition, and to appeal against a winding up order where one was made.[19]

13.   (1879) 4 App Cas 615.
14.   *Ferguson v Wallbridge* [1935] 3 DLR 66.
15.   *Re Oriental Bank Corp.* (1884) 28 Ch D 643.
16.   *Chatham National Bank v McKeon* (1895) 24 SCR 348. Cf. 1963 Act, s.231(1)(a).
17.   *Attorney General v Blumenthal* (1961) 4 SA 313 (T).
18.   *Madrid Bank v Bayley* (1866) LR 2 QB 37.
19.   *Re Union Accident Insurance Co.* [1972] 1 WLR 640.

Former directors of insolvent companies   An objective of the 1990 Act was to deal with the so-called 'phoenix syndrome', meaning directors liquidating one company, leaving substantial unpaid debts behind, and then going on and setting up a new company, often in the very same or a similar business. It was felt that certain restrictions should be placed on former directors of insolvent companies. Except where permitted by the court under s.150 of the 1990 Act, the court may declare that a person who was the director of a company which is wound up and is found to be insolvent cannot be a company director for a period of five years, unless the company meets certain minimum capital requirements. This restriction applies to anyone who was a director or a 'shadow director' of the company within twelve months prior to the winding up commencing, including foreign-registered companies with an established place of business in Ireland.[20] And it extends to being appointed or acting in any way, either directly or indirectly, as a company director or secretary, and even being concerned in or taking part in the promotion or formation of any company. This prohibition is founded on the assumption that the former company probably would not have become insolvent if it had been adequately capitalised.

Accordingly, any company which these restricted persons now wish to manage should have a substantial capital basis. Any p.l.c. must have a minimum capital of £100,000 which, along with any premium on those shares, must be fully paid up in cash. In the case of a private limited company, that minimum is £20,000. Additionally, that company is not allowed to avail of s.60(2)-(11) of the 1963 Act,[21] which permits it to lend money or otherwise assist persons to purchase the company's own shares. Also, the company must comply with the requirements in ss 32-36 of the 1983 Act,[22] regarding having certain acquisitions of substantial assets by the company subjected to independent valuation, as if it were a p.l.c. An allottee of shares in a p.l.c. or a private company which are not fully paid up in cases as required above, remains liable for the outstanding sum.

The above restrictions do not apply in the following circumstances. If the directorship was held solely by reason of the person being nominated by a licensed bank or other financial institution, in connection with that institution providing credit facilities to the company, ordinarily he will escape the restriction. However, he must have acted 'honestly and responsibly' in the office and, additionally, the institution must not hold any personal guarantee from any of the company's directors in respect of the company's liabilities. Directors nominated by prescribed venture capital companies also can be excluded. Apart from these, if the director can satisfy the court that he acted 'honestly and responsibly' in connection with the company and there is no other reason why, in fairness, these restrictions should apply to him, the court can exonerate him. Finally, within one year of the court declaring the restriction applicable, s.152 of the 1990 Act enables the person to apply to the court to be relieved of the restriction in whole or in part.

20. 1990 Act s.149(4).   21. See *Company Law*, pp. 248-249.
22. See id. pp. 198-199.

Any director who contravenes a restriction commits an offence and, additionally, is deemed to be subject to a 'disqualification order' under s.160 of the 1990 Act.[23] If at the time he was subject to a disqualification order, the period of the order is extended by an additional ten years and he may not then apply to the court under s.160(8) to have that order relaxed or lifted. Moreover, the court is empowered to impose unlimited liability on him in respect of any debts incurred by the company during the period he acted as its director or officer while disqualified or, if the company was not adequately capitalised, subject to the restriction.

Disqualifications orders   One of the earliest declared objectives of what became the 1990 Act was to strike at so-called 'rogue directors', meaning persons who had been involved in company frauds or had committed other wrongs when managing a company. In order to deter wrong-doing, these persons would be banned from managing companies for a prolonged period. Section 160 of the 1990 Act empowers the court to ban persons who are convicted of any offence involving fraud or dishonesty from acting as directors for up to five years or indeed for a longer period in an appropriate case. This ban is called a 'disqualification order' and it prohibits the person affected from being appointed or acting as a director or other officer of the company or being in any way, whether directly or indirectly, concerned with or taking part in the management or the promotion or formation of any company. The ban therefore is wide-ranging and indeed extends to being a shadow director, a secretary or other officer of the company, or a company auditor, receiver, liquidator or manager. It extends to any of the above positions in an industrial and provident society.

Directors can similarly be disqualified in the following circumstances. In any proceedings whatsoever, the Director of Public Prosecutions, any member, officer, employee, creditor, receiver, liquidator or examiner of the company may apply for a disqualification order. If the court is then satisfied of the following, it may make the order and indeed may do so of its own motion: while an 'officer' of the company, the person committed a fraud in relation to it, its members or creditors, or was in breach of any of the duties attaching to his office, or was held to have committed fraudulent trading or reckless trading, or whose conduct as such officer made him 'unfit to be concerned in the management of a company', or who was 'persistently in default' of his obligations under the Companies Acts. Those company officers whose acts may result in disqualification here are any director, including *de facto* director,[24] promoter, auditor, receiver, liquidator and examiner and, presumably, secretary. There is a substantial body of case law in Britain dealing with the circumstances where disqualification orders will be made. Several of them deal with what constitutes conduct indicating unfitness to manage a company, which has been held to

23.   1990 Act s.161(2); infra.
24.   *Re Lo Line Motors Ltd* [1988] Ch. 477.

extend even to gross negligence without any suggestion of dishonesty or contravening commercial morality.[25]

A register of disqualified persons is kept at the registry of companies.[26] Contravention of a disqualification order is a criminal offence and the court can impose unlimited liability for debts incurred by the company during the period a disqualified person was involved in managing its affairs in the manner proscribed.[27]

CONTRACTS

Commencement of a liquidation can affect contracts with the company in four principal ways.[28] It may have no legal effect at all; it can operate as a breach of contract; it may be an event that frustrates the contract; or the contract may expressly stipulate how liquidation is to affect it, for instance, a forfeiture provision in a lease. Precisely what effect a liquidation will have depends on all the terms of the contract in question, express and implied. It is most exceptional for liquidation to frustrate the entire contract.[29]

It has been held that s.218 of the 1963 Act,[30] which voids dispositions of property made after a winding up has commenced, subject to the court directing otherwise, does not apply to contracts entered into at that time; that 'dispositions of property only are affected by the section, and that contracts are left untouched.'[31]

Breach of contract At times a liquidation will operate as a breach of contract. For instance, in *Reigate v Union Manufacturing Co.*,[32] the company had a contract designating the plaintiff as its sole agent for a seven years period and, thereafter, until the agreement was determined by six months notice in writing. When the company discovered it was insolvent, it resolved to be wound up, whereupon the plaintiff sued it for breach of contract. It was held that the proper approach in such cases is first to see whether the contract's express terms throw any light on the question and then to see whether it is an implied term that the contract shall come to an end on a winding up. In the event, it was concluded that, by winding itself up, the company there had repudiated the contract and, therefore, had to pay damages. A compulsory winding up operates as a breach of any employment contract but, generally, employment contracts are not broken by the company going into voluntary liquidation.[33]

25. See generally, Finch, 'Disqualification of Directors: A Plea for Competence', 53 *Mod L Rev* 385 (1990).
26. 1990 Act s.167.   27. Id. s.163.
28. See generally, A.G. Guest ed., *Chitty on Contracts* (26th ed., 1989) pp. 911 et seq.
29. Compare *Re Award Dairy Co.* [1938] NZLR 411 with *Re Premier Products Ltd* [1963] NZLR 368.
30. See infra p. 176.
31. *Re Oriental Bank Corp.* (1884) 28 ChD 634, at p. 639.
32. [1918] 1 KB 592.   33. See post pp. 384-385.

Disclaiming and rescinding onerous contracts Mention has already been made of the power liquidators possess under s.290 of the 1963 Act, similar to that in bankruptcy law, with the consent of the court to disclaim onerous property and contracts. But for this power, at times the company would be confronted with a continued drain on its resources in honouring a contract, without obtaining any comparable benefit, thereby reducing further the net assets available for payment to the creditors or for distribution to the members in the event of there being a surplus. Although the other party to the contract and third parties must be compensated for any ensuing loss, disclaimer is designed to lead to a reduction in the company's aggregate liabilities.[34]

Section 290(6) of the 1963 Act empowers the other party to any contract with a company, which is being wound up, to apply to the court for an order rescinding the contract and for the payment of damages for not performing the contract. The court may make whatever order it 'thinks just' in the circumstances.

Leases Leases are often the subject of disclaimer applications and consequent vesting orders under s.290 of the 1963 Act. Apart from that matter, the liquidation may in the circumstances operate to terminate the lease by way of forfeiture; leases often designate the commencement of a liquidation or the appointment of a receiver or of an examiner as grounds upon which the lease may be forfeited.[35] In the absence of an express stipulation to that effect, the insolvency of a tenant does not entitle a landlord to forfeit the lease where there is no other breach, although special circumstances may warrant implying a forfeiture clause in some commercial leases. Because the effect of forfeiture is often to penalise the tenant, a right of this nature will be strictly construed against the landlord and can readily be waived by him. Moreover, under s.2 of the Conveyancing Act, 1892, the general statutory power to obtain relief against forfeiture[36] is applied to forfeiture provisions in leases of most kinds of property when the tenant becomes bankrupt or is put into liquidation. Relief must be sought within one year of the liquidation commencing;[37] if the lease is sold within that period, there is no time limit on seeking relief. In an application under s.2 of this Act, the burden is on the landlord to show that there are good grounds for excluding the insolvent tenant from its statutory right to relief.[38]

Any assignment otherwise than by the liquidator of a lease, following commencement of the liquidation, is a void disposition of property unless the agreement is declared valid under s.218 of the 1963 Act. Pre-liquidation assignments may in certain circumstances come under attack as fraudulent conveyances or fraudulent preferences. Where the lease so provides, it cannot be assigned without the landlord's consent, because the liquidator is the agent

34. See post pp. 224-229.
35. See generally, P. McLoughlin, *Commercial Leases and Insolvency* (1992).
36. Under s.14 of the Conveyancing Act 1881.
37. *Official Custodian for Charities v Parway Estates Developments Ltd* [1988] 1 Ch 151.
38. *Monument Creameries Ltd v Carysfort Estates Ltd* [1967] IR 462.

of the company which has agreed to that restriction on its freedom of disposition.[39] In an appropriate case, however, under s.66 of the Landlord and Tenant Act, 1980, the court may override the landlord's veto where his consent is being unreasonably withheld.

Once the liquidation commences, there are restrictions on the landlord's resort to distress in order to get payment of outstanding rent.[40] Rent due up to the time of the liquidation is a debt of the company which must be proved in the winding up.[41] It depends on the circumstances whether rent claimed following that time is an expense of the liquidation, which gets priority over unsecured debts of the company. Murphy J summarised the position in *Re G.W.I. Ltd* as follows:

> where a liquidator takes possession or remains in possession of leasehold property for the purpose of the winding up, the rent of the premises ought to be regarded as a debt contracted for the purpose of winding up the company and ought therefore to be paid in full like any other debt or expense properly incurred by the liquidator for the same purpose.[42]

LITIGATION

Commencement of a liquidation does not automatically affect litigation and proceedings to which the company is a party. But once a provisional liquidator has been appointed or a winding up order has been made, s.222 of the 1963 Act provides for an automatic stay:

> no action or proceedings shall be proceeded with or commenced against the company except by leave of the court and subject to such terms as the court may impose.

Thus, once a compulsory liquidation has got fully in train, proceedings cannot be brought against the company or even be continued without leave of the court. Indeed, once the petition is presented, s.217 of the 1963 Act provides that any creditor or contributory can apply to the court for an order staying proceedings against the company. There is no statutory provision on the effect of a voluntary liquidation on litigation but, by virtue of s.280 of the 1963 Act, the liquidator, or any creditor or contributory, can apply to the court to stay any proceedings against the company. Under its general equitable jurisdiction, the court can enjoin parties from bringing proceedings in a foreign court aimed at obtaining some prior right over part of the assets of a company which is being wound up.[43]

39. *Re Farrow's Bank Ltd* [1921] 2 Ch 164.
40. *Re Lancashire Cotton Spinning Co.* (1887) 35 Ch D 656; see infra p. 185.
41. *Re South Kensington Co-Op. Stores* (1887) 17 Ch D (1881); see post p. 280.
42. Unrep., 16 November 1987, at p. 4, referring *inter alia* to *Re ABC Coupler & Engineering Co. (No. 3)* [1970] 1 WLR 362 and *Re Downer Enterprises Ltd* [1974] 1 WLR 146.
43. *Re Belfast Shipowners' Co.* [1894] 1 IR 322.

The object of ss.217 and 222 of the 1963 Act is not so much to preserve as much of the company's assets as possible, for rateable division among the creditors, as to avert the inconvenience of defending actions and to channel all claims against the company into the liquidation machinery. In *Re David Lloyd & Co.*[44] it was said that '[t]here being only a small fund or a limited fund to be divided among a great number of persons, it would be monstrous that one or more of them should be harassing the company with actions and incurring costs which would increase the claims against the company and diminish the assets which ought to be divided among all the creditors.'[45] Of course, if the company is solvent *pro rata* division among the creditors is even a less relevant consideration; the statutory restrictions on proceedings apply as much to solvent as to insolvent companies.

'Action or proceedings'   The courts have given an expansive interpretation to the concept of what is an 'action or proceedings' for these purposes. Most mechanisms for execution of judgments come within the concept, although the 1963 Act has special provisions for freezing execution once a winding up has commenced.[46] Interpleader and counter claim have been held to be 'proceedings';[47] seeking to establish a set-off, on the other hand, is not.[48] Nor, would it seem, are prosecutions for offences or statutory enquiries 'proceedings'.

Leave to proceed   In determining whether, in a compulsory liquidation, leave should be given to proceed with a claim, the court has an extensive discretion; it is free 'to do what is right and fair in the circumstances.'[49] Generally, leave will only be given where some question arises that cannot properly be determined in the winding up and where litigation is needed to resolve matters.[50] Leave is almost always refused where the claim is for a simple contract debt which can be proved in the usual way. Where a creditor first sought to prove in the liquidation but then instead sought to bring proceedings to establish the amount of his claim, leave was refused because, 'having selected one method of having his claim adjudicated upon, which gives him the right to question the decision of the liquidator, [he] ought not to then to be in a position to select another method. . . .'[51] Ultimately it is a question of the balance of convenience—are there circumstances which render it just and reasonable that the matter should be resolved outside the winding up.

There are several circumstances where, generally, the court will allow the action to proceed. One is when the plaintiff is seeking to enforce his security, because a secured creditor is in a position where he can fairly claim that he is

---

44. (1877) 6 Ch D 339.
45. Id. at p. 334.   46. See infra pp. 182-183.
47. *Langley Constructions (Brixham) Ltd v Wells* [1969] 1 WLR 503.
48. Ibid.
49. *Re Aro Ltd* [1980] 1 Ch 196, at p. 209.
50. *Re Exchange Securities & Commodities Ltd* [1983] BCLC 186.
51. *Craven v Blackpool Stadium Ltd* [1936] 3 All ER 513.

independent of the liquidation, since he is enforcing a right, not against the company, but to his own property.[52] But leave will be refused where the mortgagee is offered all he is entitled to without instituting or continuing proceedings. Leave to proceed with an Admiralty action will readily be given where the applicant has issued a writ *in rem* against a ship.[53] Leave will also be given where the plaintiff has an unimpugnable claim for specific performance of an agreement by the company to sell property.[54] Leave was granted to proceed in an action by the social security authorities to recover unpaid social welfare contributions, on the grounds that 'the court should be slow to exercise its discretion by making an order that would prevent the recovery in criminal proceedings of a penalty imposed by an Act of Parliament.'[55] In proceedings against others to which the company is a necessary party, leave will readily be given if the plaintiff undertakes not to enforce against the company any judgment he may obtain, without leave of the court.[56]

Stay on proceedings   Proceedings are not automatically stayed in a voluntary winding up but the liquidator can apply to have a stay put on them. Between the time a winding up petition is presented and heard, a creditor or contributory can apply to have proceedings stayed. The onus is on the applicant to show why the matter should not be dealt with in court in the ordinary way—for instance 'the existence of a debt or liability was substantially admitted, though there might be some question of the exact amount due. . . .'[57] The court must be satisfied that it is 'just and beneficial' to order a stay.[58] Thus, where a former managing director sought to prove a claim for outstanding remuneration but, when dissatisfied with the amount which the liquidator admitted, commenced an action for damages, the court directed that those proceedings be stayed.[59] And where, while a scheme of arrangement with creditors was being put together, a winding up petition was lodged, a stay was put on a claim brought by one of the company's unpaid suppliers.[60]

COMPANY PROPERTY

Unlike the position in bankruptcy law,[61] commencement of a winding up does not operate to vest the title to the company's property in the liquidator; instead

52. *Re David Lloyd & Co.* (1877) 6 Ch D 339.
53. *Re Aro Ltd* [1980] Ch 196.
54. *Re Coregrange Ltd* [1984] BCLC 453.
55. *Re Burrows (Leeds) Ltd* [1982] 1 WLR 1177, at p. 1185.
56. Ibid.
57. *Currie v Consolidated Kent Collieries Corp.* [1906] 1 KB 134 at p. 139.
58. Supra n 13, at p. 1181.
59. *Craven v Blackpool Stadium Ltd* [1936] 3 All ER 513; compare *Currie* case, supra n. 57 and *Cook v 'X' Chair Patents Co. Ltd* [1960] 1 WLR 60.
60. *Bowkett v Fullers Utd. Electric Works Ltd* [1923] 1 KB 160.
61. Bankruptcy Act 1988 s.44(1).

the liquidator gets custody and control of that property, which remains in the name of the company. By virtue of his powers, the liquidator is able to sell or otherwise dispose of the property.[62] But the liquidator can apply to the court to have the property put in his own name.

Ownership   Section 229(1) of the 1963 act stipulates that, when a winding up order has been made, the liquidator 'shall take into his custody or under his control all the property and things in action to which the company is or appears to be entitled.' The same principle applies in voluntary liquidations and also where a provisional liquidator has been appointed. Thus, neither the members nor the creditors acquire any proprietary interest whatsoever in the company's property; it continues to belong, legally and beneficially, to the company. Nor are the creditors the *cestuis que trust* or beneficiaries under a type of trust arrangement. In *Ayerst v C. & K. (Construction) Ltd*[63] Lord Diplock explained the position as follows:

> the concept of legal ownership of property which did not carry with it the right of the owner to enjoy the fruits of it or dispose of it for his own benefit, owes its origin to the Court of Chancery. The archetype is the trust. . . . But it [does] not follow even in equity that a person could only be the legal owner without being at the same time the beneficial owner in cases where it was possible to identify some other person or persons in whom the beneficial ownership had become vested. . . . [One of the characteristics of trust properties is] vesting the beneficial ownership of any part of the undistributed property in those persons who will eventually become entitled to share in the proceeds of realisation.

> [T]he property of the company ceases upon the winding up to belong beneficially to the company. . . . [But t]he statutory scheme for dealing with the assets of a company in the course of winding up its affairs differ[s] in several aspects from a trust of specific property created by the voluntary act of the settlor. Some respects in which it differ[s are] similar to those which distinguish the administration of estates of deceased persons and of bankrupts from an ordinary trust: another peculiar to the winding up of a company is that the actual custody, control, realisation and distribution of the proceeds of the property which is subject to the statutory scheme are taken out of the hands of the legal owner of the property, the company, and vested in a third party, the liquidator, over whom the company has no control. His status . . . differs from that of a trustee 'in the strict sense' for the individual creditors and members of the company who are entitled to share in the proceeds of realisation. He does not owe to them all the duties that a trustee in equity owes his *cestuie que trust*.[64]

62. See post pp. 210-214.   63. [1976] AC 167.
64. Id. at pp. 177-178 and 180.

Vesting order   The liquidator can apply to the court to transfer title to the company's property to him. Section 230 of the 1963 Act empowers the court to direct that all or part of the property shall vest in the liquidator, thereby enabling him to participate in his own name in legal proceedings involving that property. It is most exceptional for liquidators to apply for an order of this type.

Disclaiming and vesting onerous property   Section 290 of the 1963 Act empowers liquidators to apply to the court for permission to disclaim company property which is or will impose undue burdens on the company. A similar power is given to Official Assignees in bankruptcy.[65] Disclaimer can apply to

> any part of the property of the company which . . . consists of land of any tenure burdened with onerous covenants, of shares or stock in companies, of unprofitable contracts, or of any other property which is unsaleable or not readily saleable by reason of its binding the possessor thereof to the performance of any onerous act or to the payment of any sum of money.[66]

Because the source of onerous burdens on the company usually is stipulations in the agreement under which the company holds the property in question, such as a repairing covenant in a lease[67] or the obligation to pay calls on shares, consideration of this section is best left to the discussion of the various 'asset-swelling' measures in the Companies Acts.[68] An excellent example of where a company was permitted to disclaim freehold property is *Re Nottingham General Cemetery Co.*[69] The company had been established under a private Act of Parliament to run a cemetery but, due to various developments in local government, its business practically came to an end and eventually it was decided to wind it up. At the time, it had assets of about £5,000 but the cost of keeping up the graves was approximately £2,000 per annum, so that it would have no more funds if it continued in business for another two and a half years. Consequently, the liquidator applied for and was given consent to disclaim the cemetery and the various contracts regarding the upkeep of the graves. Wynn Parry J. there described the right to disclaim as a right which the liquidator 'exercises by writing under his hand, and he can exercise it only in relation to property which in effect has ceased to be an asset and had become a liability.'[70]

Any person who claims an interest in the property in question or who is subject to some liability in connection with the property may apply to the court for an order vesting the property in himself.[71] This is in accordance with the general policy that disclaimer shall cause the very minimum disturbance to the

---

65. Bankruptcy Act 1988, s 56. Formerly leave of the court was necessary only to disclaim leases.
66. 1963 Act s.290(1).
67. E.g. *Grant v Aston Ltd*, 103 ILTR 39 (1969).
68. Post pp. 224-229.   69. [1955] 1 Ch 683.
70. Id. at p. 695.
71. 1963 Act s.290(7) and (8) and Winding Up Rule 85; see post p. 228.

rights and liabilities of third parties.[72] In the absence of such an order, it would seem that freehold property which is disclaimed vests in the State.[73]

Invalid dispositions of property   Because a compulsory liquidation is deemed to have commenced once the winding up petition has been presented, it is not uncommon for dealings to take place with the company's property between that time and when the liquidator gets control of it. Especially when the success of the petition is not assured, the directors may wish to continue trading, in the expectation that there probably will be no winding up. Even if a liquidation is very likely, entering into certain transactions prior to the court hearing may on balance be to the company's advantage. Although in a voluntary liquidation the liquidator would have taken control almost immediately after being appointed, it is conceivable that directors or employees of the company entered into some transactions without his prior authority.

Where any of the transactions being considered here constitutes a 'disposition' of the company's property, then it is deemed void in an official liquidation. And on the basis of general principles, it may also be void or voidable in a voluntary winding up. Section 218 of the 1963 Act provides that, in a winding up by the court,

> any disposition of the property of the company, including things in action, . . . made after the commencement of the winding up, shall, unless the court otherwise orders, be void.

The purpose of this is to ensure that, at the time of the liquidation, all the assets are 'frozen' within the company in order that they may be rateably divided among the creditors. Because, however, some dispositions which take place may be beneficial to the company and its creditors, on application, the court may direct that those transactions should not be avoided.[74] There is no equivalent statutory provision for voluntary liquidations but, since only the liquidator is entitled to determine what shall happen to company assets, a disposal of company property by anybody else is inconsistent with the liquidator's exclusive rights regarding that property.

'Disposition'   The term 'disposition of the property' has been given a wide meaning in this context and includes virtually all transactions that involve the company parting with anything of value. It, therefore, includes all sales of property,[75] charges given over company assets[76] and all payments of company money, whether by the company or by a third party and whether directly or indirectly.[77] Because of this rule, banks adopt the practice of freezing the

---

72. Id. s.290(3).   73. State Property Act 1954, ss.27 and 30.
74. See generally, Furey, 'The Validation of Transactions Involving the Property of Insolvent Debtors', 46 *Mod. L. Rev* 257 (1983).
75. *Re Wiltshire Iron Co.* (1868) 3 Ch App 443.
76. *Re Steane's (Bournemouth) Ltd* [150] 1 All ER 21.
77. E.g. the cheque cases, considered infra.

company's bank account once they learn that a winding up petition has been presented.

But the disposition by a receiver of property which is subject to a charge is not caught by s.218 because that property beneficially belongs to the debenture-holder and not the company.[78] Nor does s.218 in any way invalidate contracts entered into by the company; 'dispositions of property only are affected by the section and contracts are left untouched.'[79] Where the company has made an unconditional contract for the sale of property, which it duly completes after the liquidation commenced, that disposition is not caught by s.218.[80] If that contract was conditional or if its terms were varied, then it depends on the circumstances whether or to what extent s.218 applies.[81]

Cheques and banks   In the case of transactions with cheques the disposition happens when the cheque is paid, not when it is drawn.[82] And when a bank pays a cheque into its customer's account, the disposition is made to the customer and not to the bank.[83] It was held in *Re Pat Ruth Ltd*[84] that, not alone are payments from a company's bank account dispositions but, in certain circumstances, so too are lodgments to that account. Costello J there followed the reasoning of the Court of Appeal in *Re Gray's Inn Construction Ltd*,[85] where it was held that lodgments to a bank account which is in debit are dispositions because the effect of each lodgment is to discharge all or part of the company's indebtedness to the bank. As Buckley LJ explained,

> When a customer's account with his banker is overdrawn he is a debtor to his banker for the amount of the overdraft. When he pays a sum of money into the account, whether in cash or by payment in of a third party's cheque, he discharges his indebtedness to bank pro tanto. There is clearly in these circumstances . . . a disposition by the company to the bank of the amount of the cash or of the cheque. It may well be the case . . . that in clearing a third party's cheque and collecting the amount due on it, the bank act as the customer's agent, but as soon as it credits the amount collected in reduction of the customer's overdraft, as in the ordinary course of banking business it has authority to do in the absence of any contrary instruction from the customer, it makes a disposition on the customer's behalf in its own favour discharging pro tanto the customer's liability on the overdraft.[86]

78. *Sowman v David Samuel Trust Ltd* [1978] 1 WLR 22, at p. 30. In *Re Clifton Palace Garage Ltd* [1970] Ch. 477 it was erroneously assumed that a receiver's disposition falls within s.218.
79. *Re Oriental Bank Corp.* (1884) 28 Ch D 634, at p. 639.
80. *Re French's (Wine Bar) Ltd* [1987] BCLC 499.
81. Ibid.   82. *Re Ashmark Ltd (No. 2)* [1990] ILRM 455.
83. *Westpac Banking Corp. v Merlo* [1991] 1 NZLR 560.
84. [1981] ILRM 51.   85. [1980] 1 WLR 711.
86. Id. at pp 715-716.

The court there declined to rule on whether lodgments to a bank account which is in credit are dispositions, although Buckley LJ ventured that he 'doubt[ed] whether even in those circumstances it could be properly said that the payment did not constitute a disposition of the amount of the cheque in favour of the bank.'[87]

Buckley LJ in the *Gray's Inn Construction* case advised bankers of the best procedure to be followed on learning that a petition has been presented to wind up a customer which is a company. On the one hand the bank may simply freeze the company's account or accounts. But if the bank wants to continue providing facilities to the company until the court has ruled on the petition, and the account is then in debit,

> the bank can itself freeze that account and insist upon all subsequent dealings being dealt with on a separate account. It can require personal assurances from the directors of the company that no payments out of the new account will be made in discharge of pre-liquidation debts and that all payments out of the new account shall be in respect of liabilities incurred in the ordinary course of business subsequent to the presentation of the petition.[88]

Validation   An application can be made to the court under s.218 of the 1963 Act by the liquidator or by the disponee, or by anyone with a tangible interest in the void transaction, to have it validated. Sometimes those applications are made even before the winding up order is made and before the proposed disposition occurs.[89] Everyone with notice of the petition will be very hesitant to have any dealings in the company's property because there is no assurance that any particular transaction will get approval under s.218. Where the company is insolvent, the proposed disposition will be considered very carefully by the court and will only be sanctioned where clearly it will benefit the creditors or there is some other very good reason for doing so. In *Re Tramway Building Soc.*,[90] it was stressed by Scott J that the court's discretion is very much at large, subject to the general principles applicable to discretions and the general context of the statutory provisions on liquidation:

> The discretion . . . is not fettered by any statutory criteria. [It] should not be exercised so as to permit an unauthorised disposition to reduce the assets available for the unsecured creditors. But, subject thereto, it should . . . be exercised so as to enable equity to be done as between the unsecured creditors on the one hand and the claimants under the unauthorised disposition on the other. . . . [The law] does not require that validation be refused in order to allow a windfall [to the liquidation. There is no] authority for the proposition that if the assets available in a winding up

87. Id. at p. 716.   88. Id. at p. 720.
89. E.g. *Re Sugar Properties (Derisley Wood) Ltd* [1988] BCLC 146.
90. [1988] Ch. 293.

would be greater if an *ex post facto* validation order were not made than if one were made, then the validation order should not be made.[91]

The court's power to validate post-liquidation dispositions is founded on the assumption that there can be advantages for the company in engaging in certain transactions even though its winding up has commenced. This is especially so where there is the distinct likelihood that the petition will be rejected by the court; for if the company's activities were completely frozen between when the petition was presented and the winding up order was refused, that paralysis could very well have the most disastrous consequences for the company.[92] Or the transaction itself may be one that enhances the value of the company's assets, for instance the transfer of a lease that otherwise would be forfeited because the company had gone into liquidation,[93] or giving a charge in order to raise funds so as to make the assets more saleable.[94] In one instance,[95] where a company in the road haulage business paid for supplies of fuel obtained just before liquidation, in order to continue obtaining supplies of fuel, it was held that, in the circumstances, the company had benefited. At least, there was no evidence before the court that the company had not benefited. In another instance it was said that approval will be given 'if it can be seen that the payment was made perhaps to enable the company to obtain supplies on a contract which looked profitable, to pay wages which would have had to be paid in any event, though above the subrogation level permitted, or in some way properly and responsibly paid out under the threat of a winding up petition with a bona fide view to the assistance of the company.'[96] It is far easier to get entirely post-liquidation transactions validated because, generally, they do not deplete the assets available for the general creditors; for instance, the sale of an asset at full market value.[97] Where the company is solvent the court 'will . . ., normally sanction the disposition notwithstanding the opposition unless [there is] compelling evidence proving that the disposition is in fact likely to injure the company.'[98]

But where the company is insolvent, s.218's object has been described as 'to protect the interest of the creditors from the possibly unfortunate results which would ensue from the presentation of a petition, and to protect their interests as much during a period when the petition was pending as after an order has been made on it.'[99] One of the main themes of insolvency law is to procure, so far as practical, rateable payment of the unsecured creditors' claims. Consequently, in exercising its discretion, 'the court should not validate any transaction or

---

91. Id. at pp. 304, 305.
92. E.g. *Sugar Properties* case, supra n. 89.
93. E.g. *Re A.I. Levy (Holdings) Ltd* [1964] Ch 19.
94. E.g. *Re Steane's (Bournemouth) Ltd* [1950] 1 All ER 21.
95. *Denny v John Hudson & Co. Ltd* [1992] BCLC 901.
96. *Re Webb Electrical Ltd* [1988] BCLC 382, at p. 386.
97. *Re Gray's Inn Construction Co.* [1980] 1 WLR 711, at p. 719.
98. *Re Burton & Deakin Ltd* [1977] 1 All ER 631, at p. 639.
99. *A.I. Levy* case, supra n. 93.

series of transactions which might result in one or more pre-liquidation creditors being paid in full at the expense of other creditors, who will only receive a dividend, in the absence of special circumstances making such a course desirable in the interests of the unsecured creditors as a body.'[1] Thus, it is only when discharging some pre-liquidation obligation would bring some tangible benefit to the creditors generally that the court will give its sanction; for instance, 'a transaction which . . . has increased the value of the company's assets . . . or has preserved the value of the company's assets from harm which would result from the company's business being paralysed.'[2] Many of these instances could be labelled as salvage cases.

Apart from what is best for the general creditors, another consideration that guides the court's discretion is 'what would be just and fair in each case . . ., having regard to the question of good faith and honest intention of the persons concerned.'[3] Good faith on its own is not enough to justify validation.[4] But if the disposition was a bona fide business transaction carried out in the ordinary course of business and the parties were not aware of the liquidation, the tendency is to validate it if the transaction seems to have benefited the company, absent special circumstances.[5] On the other hand, where the parties were aware of the liquidation then, to a considerable extent, they should be treated as entering into the transaction very much at their own risk.[6] The courts are more inclined to validate a single transaction in contrast with a whole series of transactions. Where a composite transaction or a series of transactions resulted in some loss to the general creditors, the court may validate those parts that did not result in such loss.[7] The best advice is to apply for validation before completing the transaction but, at times, that may not be possible or practical.

CREDITORS' REMEDIES

Commencement of a winding up is a crystallising event which converts any floating charge on all or part of the company's property into a fixed charge.[8] A winding up does not prevent the appointment of a receiver under a debenture, nor does it affect the receiver's entitlement to dispose of the charged assets.[9] But it puts an end to the receiver's express authority to manage the business and to enter into contracts binding on the company for that purpose.

The law lays down several execution procedures through which creditors can recover what is owing to them, be their debtors companies or individuals, notably, registering a judgment mortgage on the debtor's land, *fieri facias*, garnishment, receivership by way of equitable execution and distress. There are

1.   *Re Grays's Inn* case, *supra* n. 24, at p. 718.
2.   Id. at p. 719.   3.   *Supra* n.94 at p. 25.
4.   *A.I. Levy* case, supra n. 20 at p. 304.
5.   E.g. *Denny v John Hudson & Co. Ltd* [1992] BCLC 901.
6.   E.g. *Re Ashmark Ltd* [1990] IR 10.
7.   E.g. *Re Tramway Building & Construction Co.* [1988] Ch. 293.
8.   See *Company Law*, p. 508.
9.   See ante pp. 73-75.

several provisions in the 1963 Act regarding how these remedies affect companies being wound up by the court. Section 222 of the 1963 Act bars any action or proceedings against the company unless the court directs otherwise, and 'proceedings' in this context has been held to embrace most of the creditors' remedies. Furthermore, s.219 of the 1963 Act provides that:

> any attachment, sequestration, distress or execution (that thereafter is) put in force against the property or effects of the company . . . shall be void to all intents.

Both of these provisions can be applied to a voluntary liquidation by an application to the court under s.280 of the 1963 Act; in such applications the liquidator has the burden of convincing the court that, in the circumstances, enforcement of the remedy should be blocked. Section 291 of the 1963 Act, which applies to all forms of liquidation, provides that any creditor who is in the process of issuing execution against the company's property or attaching any debt due to the company cannot keep the benefit of the process unless it was completed at the time the liquidation commenced. But the court has a discretion to allow the process to be completed in an appropriate case.

Judgment mortgage If a judgment mortgage is registered against a company's property,[10] then it is a specific charge on the land in question and is treated in essentially the same way as other fixed charges. However, since this mortgagee is not a purchaser for value and the registration system is really no more than a mode of executing judgments, the judgment mortgagee's interest is subject to all equities subsisting at the time of its registration.[11] Once a company goes into liquidation, judgment mortgagees are affected by three provisions of the 1963 Act.

Section 284(2) of that Act applies the rule in bankruptcy law[12] where the company being wound up is insolvent. In that event, in order for the judgment mortgage to be at all effective against the company's contract creditors, the affidavit must have been registered more than three months before the winding up commenced. Unless the affidavit is registered before that time, it does not confer 'any priority or preference over simple contract creditors'.[13] It would seem that a simple contract in this context means any contract which is not made under seal or not deemed to be a sealed contract; there does not appear to be any authority squarely on this section. Accordingly, the virtual invalidation of judgment mortgages registered within three months of the liquidation commencing does not seem to apply to creditors with sealed contracts, tort creditors and creditors under some statutory, fiduciary or equitable obligation.

Nor does there seem to be any authority squarely on the question of whether a judgment mortgage is a form of execution for the purposes of ss.219 and 291

10. See ante pp. 9-10.
11. *Tempany v Hynes* [1976] IR 101.
12. See generally, *Bankruptcy Law*, p. 88.
13. Bankruptcy Act 1988, s.51.

of the 1963 Act. It can hardly be doubted that the answer is yes. On several occasions it has been said that 'a judgment mortgage is a process of execution and is not a charge. . . .'[14] And in *Re Overseas Aviation Engineering (G.R.) Ltd*,[15] it was held that the modern English charging order, which is very similar to our judgment mortgage, is a form of execution for these purposes, because it is a means of enforcing a debt. Three consequences, therefore, appear to follow.

Under s.219 of the 1963 Act, regardless of the financial state of the company, registration of the mortgage cannot be 'put in force' once a compulsory winding up has commenced, unless the court consents to that being done. In a voluntary winding up, an application can be made to the court to block enforcement of the mortgage. And under s.291 of that Act, unless enforcement of the charge was 'completed' before the winding up commenced, the judgment mortgagee is not entitled to retain the benefit of his interest in the property affected. There does not seem to be any authority either on what constitutes 'putting in force' a judgment mortgage under s.219. But under s.291(5), execution against land is deemed to be completed by seizure of the land or, in the case of an equitable interest, by the appointment of a receiver. Accordingly, it seems that the judgment mortgagee must have obtained an order for possession of the land or got a receiver appointed over it, before the liquidation commenced. And for this purpose, a voluntary liquidation is deemed to have commenced once the judgment mortgagee gets notice of the meeting at which a resolution to wind up will be voted on.[16] However, s.291(4) gives the court a discretion, in an appropriate case, to set aside the benefit which a liquidator may obtain through the operation of this section.

Seizure by the sheriff   Levying execution by way of *fi. fa.*[17] has been held to be a 'proceeding' for the purposes of s.222 of the 1963 Act[18] and, in any event, falls within s.219 of that Act. Accordingly, without the court's consent, *fi. fa.* cannot be levied once a compulsory winding up has commenced.[19] Application can be made to the court to have these provisions apply to a voluntary winding up,[20] but the court will not invariably stay execution when a members' voluntary liquidation begins because it is assumed that the company can pay all its debts.[21] Sections 291 and 292 of the 1963 Act have deprived these provisions of much of their practical relevance.

According to s.291, where a liquidation, whether compulsory or voluntary, commences while *fi. fa.* is being levied but has not been completed, the creditor

---

14. E.g. *Tempany v Hynes* [1976] IR 101, at p. 110.
15. [1963] 1 Ch 24.   16. S.291(2).
17. See ante pp. 11-12.
18. *Re Great Ship Co.* (1863) 4 De GJ & Sm 63,
19. Ibid., *Re London Cotton Co.* (1866) 2 Eq 53 and *Re London & Devon Biscuit Co.* (1871) 12 Eq 190.
20. Under 1963 Act s.280.
21. Cf. *Gerard v Worth of Paris Ltd* [1936] 2 All ER 905.

cannot retain the benefit of the execution unless the court directs otherwise.[22] For the purpose of this provision, a voluntary winding up is deemed to commence once the judgment creditor gets notice of a meeting at which a resolution to wind up will be voted on or of the creditors' meeting fixed for around that time.[23] Execution is deemed to be completed by the seizure and sale of the goods.[24] Section 291 does not render an uncompleted execution void but states that the execution creditor cannot retain the 'benefit of the execution'— which means the security or charge that the creditor acquires on levying execution as opposed to the fruits of execution.[25] This section entitles the liquidator to recover the proceeds of any sale of the goods which took place after the critical date—be it the presentation of the petition or receipt of notice of the proposed resolution to wind up. But the court has a discretion to set aside the rights that the liquidator thereby acquires in an unfinished execution; although the court will require cogent reasons to permit an execution to be completed, thereby departing from the principle of rateable distribution among the creditors.[26]

Section 292(1) of the 1963 Act deals with where goods are taken but either are not yet sold or the proceeds of a sale are not handed over to the execution creditor, and the sheriff is notified that a winding up has commenced. On being so required, the sheriff must deliver up to the liquidator those goods or proceeds. Where under an execution goods are sold or money is paid to avoid a sale, the sheriff must retain the proceeds or the money paid for up to fourteen days.[27] If in the meantime the sheriff is notified of a winding up being initiated, the liquidator is entitled to be paid over what is in the sheriff's hands and apply it rateably for the creditors.

Attachment of debts Attachment of debts or garnishment[28] is a 'proceeding' for the purposes of s.222 of the 1963 Act and, in any event, falls within s.219 of that Act. Accordingly, without the court's consent, this process cannot be levied once a compulsory winding up commences. In a voluntary liquidation an application may be made to the court to have these provisions apply.[29] While the court will usually grant a stay of execution where it is a creditors' voluntary winding up, because otherwise the *pro rata* distribution among all the general

---

22. Overruling *Re Whiterock Quarries Ltd* [1933] IR 363. First introduced by the English 1929 Act modelled on the Bankruptcy Act 1988, s.50.

23. Subs (2) and see *Re Eros Films Ltd* [1963] Ch 565; *Engineering Industry Training Board v Samuel Talbot (Engineers) Ltd* [1969] 2 QB 270, and *Hellyer v Sheriff of Yorkshire* [1974] 2 WLR 844.

24. Sub s.(5).

25. Cf. *Re Caribbean Products (Yam Importers) Ltd* [1966] 2 Ch 331, and infra p. 184.

26. E.g. *Re Grosvenor Metal Co.* [1950] 1 Ch 63; *Re Suidair International Airways Ltd* [1951] 1 Ch 165; *Re Redman (Builders) Ltd* [1964] 1 WLR 542, and *Re Caribbean* case, supra n.25.

27. *Re Walkden Sheet Metal Co.* [1960] 1 Ch 170 and *Marley Tile Co. v Burrows* [1978] 1 QB 291.

28. See ante pp. 14-16.   29. Under 1963 Act s.280.

creditors would be disturbed,[30] a stay will not be granted where it is a members' voluntary winding up.[31] Section 291 of the 1963 Act has deprived these provisions of much of their practical relevance. Apart entirely from particular provisions of the Companies Acts, where a court has made an order *nisi* attaching a debt due to a company, which then goes into liquidation, ordinarily an order absolute will not then be made. It has been held that if 'the statutory scheme for dealing with the assets of a company has been irrevocably imposed on the company, by resolution or winding up order. Before the court has irrevocably determined to give the creditor the benefit of [the remedy], the statutory scheme should prevail.'[32]

According to s.291, where a liquidation commences and a creditor has attached some of the company's debts he is not entitled to retain the benefit of his attachment unless that process was completed before the winding up started. In a voluntary winding up, this means the time when that creditor got notice of the meeting at which the winding up resolution was to be voted on or of the creditors' meeting called for around that time.[33] In *Re Caribbean Products (Yam Importers) Ltd*,[34] the Court of Appeal ruled on the meaning of the term 'entitled to retain the benefit' in that section and on the court's discretion to permit an execution creditor to keep the benefit of an uncompleted garnishment. A creditor obtained judgment against the company and, twelve months later, obtained a garnishee order *nisi* over a claim that the company had against an insurer. But in order to thwart that creditor obtaining those funds, notice of a resolution to wind up the company was given. What then happened was that the garnishee order was made absolute and, four days later, the insurer paid the money over to the creditor-garnishor. Two hours later, the company resolved to wind itself up. Therefore, execution was not completed when the creditor learned of the intention to wind up the company, but was completed when the actual winding up commenced. It was held that the creditor was not entitled to keep the money it got from the insurer because, under s.291, at the critical time the attachment had not been completed. Completion for these purposes is defined as receipt of the debt. Harman J observed that this is in accordance with 'the policy of the law, both in bankruptcy and in the liquidation of companies, that all unsecured creditors shall be treated alike from the date when there comes to their notice an act which . . . in the case of a limited company amounts to notice of an intention to liquidate.'[35] From that critical time, the creditor 'loses his right to enforce his security. If he improperly obtains payment by wrongfully enforcing the security, this is a wrong against the liquidator.'[36]

Charging and attaching stocks and shares   There is no provision in the Companies Acts, comparable to s.291 of the 1963 Act, which deals with

30. *Anglo-Baltic & Mediterranean Bank v Barber & Co.* [1924] 2 KB 410.
31. *Gerard v Worth of Paris Ltd* [1936] 2 All ER 905.
32. *Roberts Petroleum Ltd v Bernard Kenny Ltd* [1983] 2 AC 193, at p. 208.
33. 1963 Act s.291(2).   34. [1966] 1 Ch 331.
35. Id. at pp. 345-346.   36. Id. at p. 354.

attaching and charging stocks and shares as a mode of enforcing judgments.[37] This procedure may very well be a 'proceeding' for the purposes of s.222 of the 1963 Act and may also be an 'execution' within s.219 of that Act. If an order *nisi* is made and the company then goes into liquidation, the court will not make an order absolute.[38]

Equitable execution Having receiver appointed by the court is a 'proceeding' for the purposes of s.222 of the 1963 Act but, because that appointment does not create any charge on the company's property so as to make the execution creditor a secured creditor,[39] the appointment is not a 'putting in force' of execution for the purposes of s.219 of that 1963 Act. Accordingly, it has been held, the court should not normally refuse a request to have a receiver appointed merely because the company is being wound up.[40]

Distress Distress, which is a remedy mostly used by lessors,[41] is an extra-judicial process whereby the creditor/lessor is entitled to take the debtor's /tenant's and others' property, and to sell it and keep the proceeds of disposal in reduction of the debt/rent. Powers to distrain are occasionally contained in mortgage debentures and there are statutory provisions that give some public authorities the power of distress, notably the Revenue.[42] The constitutionality of this form of self-help is questionable.

Curiously distress has been held to be a 'proceeding' within s.222 of the 1963 Act[43] and in any event falls within s.219 of that Act. Accordingly, without the court's consent, distress cannot be levied once a compulsory winding up commences. In a voluntary liquidation an application can be made to the court to have these provisions applied.[44] Where what is owed is rent outstanding at the time of the compulsory or creditors' voluntary winding up, leave to distrain will rarely be given.[45] But rent accruing thereafter will be treated differently where it is effectively a cost of the liquidation.[46] Where the distress is partly completed before the winding up commenced, s.291 of the 1963 Act does not apply and the court, in the exercise of its discretion under s.219, has refused to apply s.291 by analogy.[47]

---

37. See ante pp. 17-18.
38. *Roberts Petroleum* case, supra n.25.
39. *Re Lough Neagh Ship co., ex p. Thompson* [1896] 1 IR 29.
40. *Crowshaw v Lyndhurst Ship Co.* [1897] 2 Ch 154.
41. See generally, J.C.W. Wylie, *Irish Landlord & Tenant Law* (1990) p. 367 et seq.
42. Finance Act 1963, s.480. Cf. *Re Herbert Berry Associates Ltd* [1977] 1 WLR 1437.
43. *Re Exhall Coal Mining Co.* (1864) 4 GS & Sm 377 and *Re Memco Engineering Ltd* [1986] Ch 86.
44. Under 1963 Act s.280.
45. *Re Oak Pitts Colliery Co.* (1882) 21 Ch D 322.
46. *Re Downer Enterprises Ltd* [1974] 1 WLR 1460.
47. *Re Bellaglade Ltd* [1977] 1 All ER 319.

15

Appointment of Liquidator, Status and Supervision

Before the winding up commences, the management of the company's affairs would have been in the hands of the directors. Following the decision or order to wind up, the directors (and also the shareholders, to the extent that they had a say in dealings in the company's property) are displaced by a liquidator, who takes control of the entire company with a view to winding it up. The company as a corporate entity will continue to exist and, unlike the position in bankruptcy, there is no *cessio bonorum* of the company's property to the liquidator. But the actual administrative control of a winding up is placed in the hands of a liquidator who, on being appointed, assumes control of the company's property and business and who then realises the company's assets and distributes the proceeds among the creditors and, if there remains a surplus, among the shareholders. A liquidator in a compulsory winding up is called the official liquidator, being an officer of the court, to which he is always answerable. Often a committee of inspection is appointed to assist the liquidator in his task and to whom he is answerable to an extent. On certain matters, the wishes of the creditors, reached in general meetings of creditors, can be decisive. Generally the liquidator must act impartially and even-handedly among the different interests in the liquidation and, while he must take account of the views of the creditors, he is not bound to carry out the wishes of any majority of them.

APPOINTMENT

In a compulsory winding up, the liquidator is appointed by the court, usually on the nomination of the petitioning creditor. It is the members or the creditors, as the case may be, who appoint the liquidator in a voluntary winding up.

Disqualifications The law in Ireland does not require liquidators to possess any professional qualifications, although most liquidators tend to be experienced accountants. Bodies corporate are prohibited from being liquidators and it is a criminal offence for a body corporate to act as a liquidator.[1] Section 300A of the 1963 Act[2] disqualifies a wide category of persons who were already

1. 1963 Act s.300.
2. Inserted by 1990 Act s.146.

closely connected with the company's management. These are any person who, within the twelve months prior to his purported appointment as liquidator, was an 'officer', employee or auditor of the company or of one of its closely associated companies. These persons include any parent, spouse, brother, sister or child of any company officer or its auditor; but anyone whose connection is only through this family relationship can apply to the court for leave to act as a liquidator. A present partner or employee of any of the company's present officers or employees is disqualified. If any of the above people would be disqualified from being a liquidator of any of the company's closely related companies, then they are disqualified too as regards the company being wound up. These companies are any of the company in question's subsidiaries or its holding company,[3] or any other subsidiary of its holding company. A creditor of the company or a mortgagee of its property is not prohibited from accepting the appointment.

Apart from any formal disqualifications, the court will decline to appoint or will veto an appointment of a person who is shown not to be independent, such as by having conflicts of interest that could seriously jeopardise the shareholders' or the creditors' interests in the company.[4]

Any liquidator who becomes disqualified by virtue of the above provisions is required, within 14 days of such time, to vacate the office and, in a compulsory winding up, notify the court and, in a voluntary liquidation, notify the company and the creditors too in the case of a creditors' voluntary winding up.[5] Disqualified persons who act as liquidators can be fined up to £10,000 on indictment.

Creditors' voluntary winding up In a members' voluntary winding up, the appointment is made by the shareholders and is usually done at the meeting which resolves to wind up the company.[6] In a creditors' voluntary winding up, if the company's members in general meeting select a liquidator who is acceptable to the creditors, that person is appointed.[7] But the creditors can choose somebody else, who then becomes the liquidator.[8] Since, however, in order to override the shareholders' choice there must be a majority both of the number of creditors and the value of the creditors,[9] often the management can defeat the principal creditors' choice by winning over support of a numerical majority of the small creditors. Where the members and the creditors nominate different persons, any director, member or creditor of the company can apply to the court for an order that, instead of the creditors' nominee being the

3.   Defined in sub (i)(d).
4.   *Re Corbenstroke Ltd (No. 2)* [1989] BCLC 496.
5.   S.300A(3). Cf. *Re A.J. Adams (Builders) Ltd* [1991] BCLC 359.
6.   Cf. *Re London Flats Ltd* [1969] 1 WLR 711: appointment held invalid because only one member was present at meeting.
7.   1963 Act s.258.   8. Id. s.267.
9.   *Re Caston Cushioning Ltd,* [1955] 1 WLR 163.
10. 1963 Act s.267(2).

liquidator, the office should be held by the members' nominee, or by both persons, or by somebody else entirely.[10]

Section 301A of the 1963 Act[11] is aimed at preventing abuses by having liquidators appointed who are too closely connected with some of the creditors. In the first place, any creditor's representative who is present at the meeting deciding the matter is not allowed to vote on the proposal that he shall be the liquidator. Secondly, whenever the proposed liquidator is connected with any creditor's representative at the meeting, in the sense of being the latter's partner, employee or close relative, the details of that connection must be revealed to the chairman, who must disclose them to the meeting. It is an offence, under s.301 of the 1963 Act, to pay consideration to a creditor or member in order to serve appointment as a liquidator.

A nominee must have consented in writing to act before the appointment becomes effective.[12] The chairman of the meeting must notify the chosen liquidator within seven days. Within 14 days of being appointed, the liquidator must notify the registrar of companies of that fact.[13]

Compulsory winding up   In a compulsory winding up it is the court which appoints the liquidator.[13a] The court has a complete discretion who to appoint but, in the absence of special circumstances, will appoint the petitioner's nominee.[14] Rules 29 et seq. of the Winding Up Rules lay down the procedure. The extent of the court's discretion in this matter is stressed by rule 29. Normally, the court registrar gives a date for the petition to be heard or, in the case of filling a vacancy, for hearing an application to appoint the replacement. A newspaper advertisement of the hearing should be published between fourteen days and seven days of the date fixed. The order of appointment will direct when the liquidator's accounts shall be passed on to the court examiner's office and will provide for the opening and operation of the liquidator's bank account. Directions may be given about advertising the appointment.

Within 21 days of being appointed, the liquidator must have published a notice to that effect in the *Iris Oifigiúil* and, as well, must provide the registrar of companies with a copy of the court order making the appointment.[15]

Indemnity bond   Every official liquidator must get an indemnity in the form of a bond,[16] although in exceptional circumstances the court may allow him to act without being bonded. Usually that bond is provided by an authorised insurance company which has money deposited in the court under the Insurance Acts. Where a bond is not provided at the time of appointment, the court will direct a time within which one must be given. The bond must be filed in the Central Office.

11. Inserted by 1990 Act s.147.   12. 1963 Act s.276A, inserted by 1990 Act s.133.
13. 1963 Act s.278.   13a. 1963 Act s.225.
14. *Re Albert Average Assur. Assn.* (1870) LR 5 Ch App 597 and *Northern Assam Tea Co.* (1870) LR 5 Ch App 644.
15. 1963 Act s.259.   16. Winding Up Rules 31-33.

Filling a vacancy   If for some reason there is no liquidator acting the court can appoint a liquidator in a members' or a creditors' voluntary winding up;[17] although before doing so the court will usually direct that the members and the creditors shall meet in order to indicate their wishes in the matter. The procedure for filling a vacant official liquidator is the same as for the initial appointment.

RESIGNATION

The 1963 Act does not prohibit a liquidator from resigning. In appropriate circumstances in a voluntary liquidation, however, resignation may constitute a breach of contract with the appointing shareholders or creditors, as the case may be. While official liquidators are expressly empowered by s.228(c) to resign if they so choose, any such resignation is not fully effective until they have been released by the court and had their bond vacated.

In *Re Northern Waterproofs Ltd*[18] it was held that resignation does not of itself release official liquidators from their obligations. There, Lowry J. pointed out that although the equivalent of s.228(c) of the 1963 Act 'clearly stated' the official liquidator's right to resign, and that right may well be exercisable without the court's leave, it nevertheless is for the court to release him from his obligations and to vacate the bond that secures those obligations. Before the court will grant that release, it will insist on an acceptable successor being designated to whom the company's books and the like can be delivered, as required by the Winding Up Rules. In deciding whether to grant that release, the creditors' consent is relevant but not conclusive, because there is also the public interest involved in the proper investigation of the affairs of insolvent companies.' In that case, where there would be no money left over for the liquidator's costs or for the creditors after the receiver's claim was satisfied, a release was refused until, at the least, the liquidator lodged a report and final account in chambers. Lowry J referred to several unreported judgments of instances where, on consent, liquidators were released,[19] and he called for the adoption of a provision along the lines of s.251 of the British 1948 Act concerning the release of liquidators. There is no statutory provision for the release of liquidators in voluntary winding ups.

REMOVAL

A liquidator who is disqualified under s.300A of the 1963 Act must vacate the office within 14 days. The court may remove any liquidator 'on cause shown' and can appoint a replacement.[20] In *Re Sir John Moore Gold Mining Co.*[21] it was held that this power of the court 'cannot mean that it is to be a pure matter of judicial discretion whether a liquidator is to be removed or not';[22] as a general

---

17.   E.g. *Re A.J. Adams (Builders) Ltd* [1991] BCLC 359.
18.   [1967] NI 17.
19.   See too, *Re Palgrave Murphy Ltd*, 112 ILTR 30 (1978).
20.   1963 Act ss.228(c) and 277(2).
21.   (1879) 12 Ch D 325.   22. Id. at p. 332.

rule, there must be 'some unfitness of the person, it may be from personal character, or from his connection with other parties, or from circumstances in which he is mixed up—some unfitness in a wide sense of the term.'[23] In that case a liquidator who had sought to prevent misfeasance proceedings being taken against himself was removed. The court may also remove a liquidator where it is satisfied that it is in the interests of the liquidation to do so; where the company is insolvent the court will pay particular heed to the unsecured creditors' wishes in this respect.[24] According to Cotton LJ 'it is not necessary in order to justify the court . . . in removing the liquidator that there should be anything against the individual. [A]lthough of course unfitness discovered in a particular person would be a ground for removing him, yet the power of removal is not confined to that.'[25] Although the burden of proof is on the applicant to have a liquidator removed, Millet J observed that 'the words of the statute are very wide and it would be dangerous and wrong for a court to seek to limit or define the kind of cause which is required. Circumstances vary widely, and it may be appropriate to remove a liquidator even though nothing can be said against him, either personally or in his conduct of the particular liquidation.'[26]

For instance, in *Re Corbenstoke Ltd (No. 2)*,[27] the liquidator was removed because he was in a conflict of interest situation. A liquidator cannot 'place himself in a position where his duty and his interest conflict, without the fullest disclosure of the conflict and the approval of his continuing to hold that position despite the conflict.'[28] Some judges take the view that it is undesirable that the receiver for the debenture-holder should become the liquidator because the interests of the secured and of the unsecured creditors may very well diverge. In *Re Keypak Homecare Ltd*,[29] the liquidator was removed because he did not carry out his duties with sufficient vigour and also because he exhibited a relaxed and complacent attitude to wrongdoing by the directors. During his three months in office he had not examined the sales and purchases ledgers, he had not checked if stock was missing, he did not interview employees about the events shortly before the winding up. Moreover, he assumed that the directors had done nothing wrong by closing down the company's business and restarting it immediately in a new company but on the same premises and with the same employees.

REMUNERATION

Before accepting the appointment, the intended liquidator usually will want to know how much he will be paid for his services. The remuneration will be paid from the company's assets in priority to the preferential creditors[30] and possibly

23. Id. at p. 331.
24. *Re Kamarelli & Barnett Ltd* [1917] 1 Ch 203.
25. *Re Adam Eyton Ltd* (1887) 36 Ch D 299, at p. 303.
26. *Re Keypack Home Case Ltd* [1987] BCLC 409 at p. 164.
27. [1990] BCLC 60.   28. Id. at p. 62.
29. [1987] BCLC 409.   30. 1963 Act s.281.

the holders of any floating charge.[31] But it can happen that the company is so hopelessly insolvent that it does not have sufficient assets to cover the other costs of liquidation and the remuneration. In that event, absent special circumstances, the costs and expenses of getting in and realising the assets take precedence over the liquidator's remuneration.[32] The best that a liquidator can do in such a case is to refuse to continue with the liquidation until one or more of the creditors agrees to pay him.

Creditors' voluntary winding up   In a creditors' voluntary winding up the liquidator's remuneration is fixed by the creditors or by the committee of inspection,[33] if there is one. But if any creditor or shareholder believes that the amount so fixed is 'excessive', they can apply within 28 days for the court to fix the remuneration.[34] It is the shareholders who determine the remuneration in a members' voluntary winding up.[35]

Compulsory winding up   Section 228(d) of the 1963 Act provides that the compulsory liquidator's remuneration shall be fixed by the court; that he shall receive such salary or remuneration by way of percentage or otherwise as the court may direct. There is no official scale of remuneration; various methods for determining it exist, such as a lump sum, a salary, payment on the basis of the time devoted to the task and a percentage of the assets collected. The practice in Ireland, as summarised in Mr Justice Keane's book on Company Law and approved by the Supreme Court is as follows:

> The Court directs what remuneration the liquidator is to receive. There is no scale of fees fixed for remuneration: the Court considers the circumstances of the particular case and determines what is fair: the Court is in no sense bound by the scales of fees fixed for accountancy work by professional institutions, although it may take such scales into account in determining what is fair remuneration if it thinks proper. In practice, the Court will naturally seek to ensure that there is reasonable uniformity in the fixing of remuneration for accountancy work of similar types. In order to achieve this result, a practice has developed in recent times of appointing a creditor—usually for Revenue—to represent the general body of creditors in an inquiry into the liquidator's charges before the Examiner. The procedure is not dissimilar to the taxation before a Taxing Master of a successful litigant's costs. The Examiner then submits a report on the inquiry to the the judge.[36]

Stopping payment   A sanction occasionally used by the court against liquida-

---

31. See post p. 62.
32. *Re Beni-Felkai Mining Co.* [1934] Ch 406; see post pp. 357-359.
33. 1963 Act s.269(1).
34. Id. s.269(2).   35. Id. s.258(1).
36. Endorsed by McCarthy J in *Re Merchant Banking Ltd* [1987] ILRM 260, at p. 261.

tors who were in breach of duty is to order that they shall not be paid all or some of the remuneration which would be due to them.[37]

STATUS

Official liquidators are officers of the court. Voluntary liquidators may be described as fiduciary agents of the company. It has been said that a voluntary liquidator 'in many respects undoubtedly acts as the agent for the company; but . . . in some respects he certainly is in the position of a trustee. His office is a statutory office under which he has statutory duties to perform, including the getting in of the assets and the payment of the liabilities of the company and distribution of the surplus among the shareholders.'[38] While the position of voluntary liquidators is very similar to that of trustees, they are not trustees in the strict sense. It has been observed that '[o]f course, the position of a liquidator is not the same as the position of a trustee, but the duty cast upon him' to distribute the company's assets among the creditors and among the members, if there is a surplus, 'is very much the same duty as that cast upon an executor,'[39] who is a trustee of the estate for the benefit of the beneficiaries. However, 'a liquidator may, from some points of view be treated as a trustee, just as a director may be treated as a trustee.'[40]

A liquidator is the agent of the company in the sense that the liquidator's acts bind the company in the same way as its directors' acts did. A liquidator in a voluntary winding up owes the company a duty of care and skill, and the same kind of fiduciary duties as are owed by company directors. Moreover, the liquidator is an officer of the company for the purposes of any misfeasance claims against him under s.298 of the 1963 Act.[41] As yet there is no definition of the general relationship that exists between liquidators on the one hand and the company's contributories and creditors on the other. Unlike an executor of an estate and the Official Assignee in bankruptcy, the liquidator does not become the legal owner of the company's property automatically. It would seem that the liquidator owes fiduciary duties to the creditors and contributories but, during the course of the liquidation, these duties may only be enforced through the company. Official liquidators are directly responsible to the court for the due performance of their duties.

SUPERVISING THE LIQUIDATOR

The principal way in which the actions of liquidators are supervised is through the committee of inspection, which is selected by the creditors. Provision is also made for general meetings of the creditors to deal with several matters. Official liquidators are always directly accountable to the court. Liquidators in voluntary

37. E.g. *Re Brook Cottage Ltd* [1976] NI 78.
38. *Re Windsor Steam Coal Co.* (1901) Ltd [1929] 1 Ch 151, at p. 167.
39. *Butler v Broadhead* [1975] 1 Ch 97, at p. 108.
40. Supra n.37 at p. 161.
41. See post pp. 253-258. Cf. *Re X & Co.* [1907] 2 Ch. 92.

liquidations are indirectly accountable to the court in that, under s.280 of the 1963 Act, any member of the company or creditor can apply to the court to have it determine any question arising in the course of the winding up. One way of obtaining judicial supervision of liquidators is to contest the remuneration, costs and expenses which they may claim. Another is to bring a claim, under s.298 of the 1963 Act, against a liquidator for misfeasance.

Committee of inspection   For reasons of convenience, often a committee of inspection is appointed by the creditors and also by the members to supervise the liquidator's activities and to give him practical assistance and advice. A committee of this nature is very useful in large liquidations, especially where there are a great many creditors and where difficult and complex questions arise. For instance, a liquidator may be considering bringing a claim against former officers for misfeasance or for reckless trading and may be anxious to discuss the matter with creditors' representatives before going ahead with the action. Having obtained the committee's approval for such course of conduct may provide the liquidator with protection if later on he is sued for misfeasance or negligence. Members of this committee occupy a fiduciary position. For instance, without the prior approval of the court they should not purchase the company's assets from the liquidator.[42]

Appointment   The appointment and composition of this committee is provided for in ss.232 and 268 of the 1963 Act. In a voluntary winding up, the creditors at the meeting held under s.266 or later can appoint no more than five persons to this committee. The members then can appoint no more than three persons to represent their interests. But the creditors can veto any person so chosen by the members unless the court directs otherwise. In a compulsory winding up, the court may direct the liquidator to summon meetings of the creditors and the members for the purpose of appointing a committee. Those meetings designate who ought to go on that committee but the appointment is made by the court, which is not obliged to abide by the meetings' wishes, although it would be most unusual for the court to depart from them. Persons with a general power of attorney from the members or from the creditors can be appointed by them, as well as any member or creditor.[43]

Members of the committee can be removed by an ordinary resolution of the members or the creditors, as the case may be.[44] Provision is made for filling vacancies on the committee. Any member may resign.[45] There is no power in the court to remove a member of this committee.[46]

Powers   In voluntary winding ups, the liquidator's remuneration is fixed by the committee of inspection.[47] Several powers can be exercised by the liquida-

---

42. *Liquidators of North British Locomotive Co. v Lord Advocate* (1963) SC 272.
43. 1963 Act s.233(1).
44. Id. s.233(7) and (8).   45. Id. s.233(4).
46. *Re Rubber & Produce Investment Trust* [1915] 1 Ch 382.
47. 1963 Act s.269.

tor only after getting the consent of this committee—or of the creditors themselves or the court, as the case may be. These include the power to carry on the business and to make calls in compulsory liquidations; it also includes the powers to pay any class of creditors in full, to reach a compromise with creditors or debtors and to disclaim onerous property. When he is administering the company's assets, the liquidator should have regard to the directions of this committee. But he is not bound by those directions; if he disagrees with them, he can refer the matter to general meetings of the creditors and the members. He can apply to the court for directions, although there is some authority to the effect that a court application should not be made until the matter was first put before the general meetings.[48]

Procedures How the committee of inspection should act is governed by s.233 of the 1963 Act and rules 50-53 of the Winding Up Rules, which are made expressly applicable to voluntary liquidations.[49] The quorum is a majority of the committee's members and decisions are made by a majority of those present.[50] Either the liquidator or any committee member can call a meeting as he deems necessary.

General meeting of creditors and members In a creditors' voluntary liquidation the liquidator should be especially attentive to the wishes of the creditors as a body. In a compulsory liquidation, since the liquidator is primarily answerable to the court, the duty to pay heed to the creditors' concerns is not quite as strong. Where the company is solvent, the liquidator must also take account of the wishes of the members. Where a committee of inspection was appointed the creditors' and members' wishes are conveyed primarily through that committee. Where there is no such committee then meetings of the members and of the creditors should be convened for that purpose. But there is no express statutory obligation on a liquidator to abide by any directions given by the members or the creditors, as the case may be; he must always exercise his independent discretion but should not disregard their wishes.

When any matter comes before the court concerning the liquidation, be it voluntary or compulsory, s.309 of the 1963 Act provides that the court 'may', not must, 'have regard to the wishes of the creditors or contributories', and for that purpose may direct that meetings be convened and held. In considering any decision made by the creditors, regard must be had to the value of each creditor's debt.[51]

How these meetings should be conducted is regulated by rules 56-83 of the Winding Up Rules, which apply to all types of liquidation,[53] but these by no means lay down an exhaustive code of procedure. Many questions are determined by the general law regarding meetings. What the rules deal with are summoning meetings, place of meetings, the chairman, resolutions, adjourn-

48. *Re Consolidated Diesel Engine Manufacturing Ltd* [1915] 1 Ch 912.
49. 1963 Act s.268(3).   50. Id. s.233(3).
51. Id. s.309(2).   52. Rule 56.

ment, the quorum, creditors who may and who may not vote, the position of secured creditors, minutes and proxies. There is very little reported case law dealing directly with the application of these rules.

At creditors' meetings, the quorum is at least three creditors who are entitled to vote or, if there are fewer, all of the creditors.[54] A proof of the debt must be lodged before any creditor becomes entitled to vote.[54] Proxy voting is allowed and there are detailed rules regarding proxies.[55] A creditor may not vote in respect of any unliquidated or contingent or unascertained debt.[56] A secured creditor must either surrender his security or value it; if he votes in respect of his entire debt, he is deemed to have surrendered his security, unless the court finds that he acted inadvertently.[57] Where the chairman is in doubt about admitting a proof, he should allow the creditor in question to vote subject to that vote being declared invalid later if any objection is upheld.[58] For a resolution to be passed by the creditors, it must have secured a majority of those voting in number *and* in value.[59] A minute of every meeting must be kept by the chairman.

53. Rule 66.   54. Rule 67.
55. Rules 74-83.   56. Rule 68.
57. Rule 69   58. Rule 71.
59. Rule 62.

16

Liquidator's Powers and Duties

Liquidators' powers derive principally from the Companies Acts; s.231 of the 1963 Act sets out most of the official liquidator's powers, s.276 of that Act enumerates the voluntary liquidator's powers and, under s.280(1) of that Act, a voluntary liquidator can apply to the court for permission to use any power which is not specifically conferred on him but which a compulsory liquidator possesses. All of the powers enumerated in these provisions are there to facilitate the liquidator getting in the company's assets, realising them and paying the proceeds of disposals to the creditors and, if there is a surplus, to the shareholders. There is also a general power to this end; to 'do all such other things as may be necessary for winding up the affairs of the company and distributing its assets.'[1] This power is extremely wide and presumably encompasses every transaction that reasonably might be thought necessary to facilitate the winding up.[2] The Winding Up Rules spell out in considerable detail how many of these powers are to be exercised.

Liquidators' duties fall into several categories; they must perform their task with reasonable care, skill and promptitude, they are subject to the same kind of fiduciary obligations as are company directors, and the Companies Acts and other legislation lay various duties on their shoulders. Some of these duties have already been dealt with briefly above when considering the effects of liquidations.[3] Disclaiming onerous property and contracts[4] might be regarded as a liquidator's duty as well as a power, subject of course to the court's consent. The official liquidator's principal duties are formulated in s.235(i) of the 1963 Act as, on the directions of the court, to 'cause the assets of the company to be collected and applied in discharge of its liabilities.' Section 276(2) of the 1963 Act states that the voluntary liquidator 'shall pay the debts of the company and shall adjust the rights of the contributors among themselves.'

CONSENT TO EXERCISING POWERS

Exercise of some of the official liquidator's statutory powers requires the consent of the court or of the committee of inspection, if there is one, viz.[5]

1. 1963 Act s.231(20(i).
2. *Re Cambrian Mining Co.* (1881) 20 Ch D 376.
3. Especially, by inference, seeking to put a stay on litigation and challenging invalid dispositions of company property.
4. See post pp. 224-229.
5. 1963 Act s.231(1).

paying a class of creditors in full, compromising with creditors or with share-holders in respect of calls, appointing a solicitor, carrying on the business and bringing and defending actions. Indeed, exercise of all of the official liquid-ator's powers deriving from s.231 of the 1963 Act is 'subject to the control of' the court.[6] Any creditor or shareholder can apply to the court in relation to the exercise or proposed exercise of these powers but, in any such application, the court will not readily direct the liquidator to act in a manner contrary to what in his view is best for the liquidation. As Barwick J observed in one instance, an official liquidator 'is subject only to the orders of the court . . . by which his duties are defined, and it would militate against the due discharge of his proper functions if duties were thrown upon him other than those prescribed by the Rules of the Court.' Voluntary liquidators need the sanction of the committee of inspection in order to pay a class of creditors or to compromise with creditors or in respect of unpaid calls.[8] Consent to exercising these powers, which requires court or creditors' approval, should be obtained in advance, although consent can be given retrospectively.[9]

It is not entirely clear whether transactions which did not obtain the requisite consent bind the company or the liquidator. Unless the other party knew or should have known that consent was not given, the most likely position is that the transaction is effective and binds the company.[10] Nevertheless, creditors or shareholders may be able to bring a claim against the liquidator for exceeding his statutory authority.

APPOINTING A SOLICITOR

One of the matters for which the official liquidator must get the prior consent of the court or the committee of inspection, as the case may be, is to appoint a solicitor.[11] Because the conduct of a liquidation usually will give rise to legal questions and will require the execution of conveyances, liquidators, who generally are not lawyers, will want to employ a solicitor. But they must not employ someone whose independence may be unduly prejudiced.[12] Unless he is willing to act without remuneration, a partner of the liquidator should not be employed as solicitor. The solicitor's remuneration is a cost of the winding up and, accordingly, has priority over other debts, but he is not entitled to any lien over the company's money and documents which he acquired in the course of the winding up.[13] The liquidator is not personally responsible for those costs.

---

6. Id. s.231(3).
8. 1963 Act s.276(1)(a).
9. *Re Associated Travel Leisure & Services Ltd* [1978] 1 WLR 547.
10. Cf. *Dublin Distillery Co. v Doherty* [1914] 1 IR 398.
11. 1963 Act s.231(1)(c).
12. *Re Universal Private Telegraph Co.* (1870) 23 LT 884.
13. *Re Motor Cabs Ltd* [1911] 1 IR 398.

COLLECTING ASSETS AND PROTECTING THEM

One of the liquidator's principal powers and duties is to 'cause the assets of the company to be collected' and to protect them;[14] many of the specific powers are given for this purpose. In carrying out this task the official liquidator is 'in the same position as if he were a receiver of the property appointed by the court. . . .'[15] Therefore, interference with the official liquidator's exercise of these powers can amount to contempt of court.[16] Winding Up Rules 117-123 regulate the operation of the official liquidator's bank account.

Section 236 of the 1963 Act lays down a summary delivery order procedure for obtaining possession of property that belongs to the company and which is being held by any shareholder, trustee, receiver, banker, agent or officer of the company. This empowers the liquidator to serve on such persons a written notice ordering them to 'pay, convey, surrender or transfer' to him any money or property, books or papers in their hands to which the company is 'prima facie entitled.' But these powers do not apply where there is some dispute about ownership of the property in question; they do not empower the court to adjudicate contested ownership.[17] The Companies Acts also contain what may be described as several 'asset-swelling' measures which are designed to augment the company's assets, principally by ensuring that property which was improperly disposed of is recovered, such as the prohibition against fraudulent preferences.[18] The Acts also provide for unlimited liability for directors and others who were involved in fraudulent or reckless trading.[19] These and related matters are dealt with in detail later.

INVESTIGATION AND EXAMINATION ON OATH

Liquidators are empowered and indeed have a duty to investigate the company's affairs to ascertain the full extent of its assets and liabilities. A liquidator may embark on such enquiries starting with the statement of affairs that has been prepared by the directors,[20] although often this statement will raise far more questions than it answers. An official liquidator must 'with all convenient speed after he is appointed proceed to make up, continue, complete, check and rectify the books of account. . . .'[21] At the beginning or shortly after the liquidation commences, the liquidator will be given the directors' statement of affairs. He also will take charge of all the company's books and records. He may interview some of the company's officers in order to have a fuller picture of its circumstances. At times, however, persons involved in managing the company or in certain dealings with it may not be fully forthcoming with answers and may indeed seek to conceal certain facts.

14. 1963 Act s.235(1).   15. Rule 90.
16. See generally, C.J. Miller, Contempt of Court (1989) pp. 388-391.
17. *Re Ilkley Hotel Co.* [1893] 1 QB 248.
18. See post pp. 236-246.   19. See post pp. 258 et seq.
20. Under ss.224 or 266(3)(a) if the 1963 Act.
21. Rule 37.

One of the most effective instruments in the liquidator's entire armoury is the examination under oath in court of a wide category of people who had dealings with that company. Sections 245 and 280 of the 1963 Act[22] empower the court to conduct a veritable inquisition into the affairs of the company that is being compulsorily or voluntarily wound up. The court may summon before it any person it knows or suspects possesses company property or is indebted to the company, and any person it deems capable of giving information about the company's formation, promotion, trade, property, dealings or affairs. These persons may be required to produce any documents relating to the company that they possess. They may be examined on oath and required to set out in a written statement an account of transactions between themselves and the company. Information gained from these examinations frequently provides the foundation for misfeasance suits and for proceedings for fraudulent trading. The object of this examination has been described as 'for the sole purpose of enabling a thorough and searching examination to be conducted to ascertain the truth as to the property of' the insolvent.[23] A similar examination power is contained in the Bankruptcy Act, 1988, and many of the major authorities on this topic are bankruptcy law cases.[24]

There are at least five situations where a liquidator would be advised to apply to have persons examined under s.245;

(1) where he has reason to suspect that there may be a claim for misfeasance;

(2) where he thinks there may be grounds for taking proceedings against promoters or others;

(3) where proceedings are pending by or against the company and he desires to ascertain whether he can prudently proceed with or defend the action;

(4) where the circumstances in which a person became or ceases to be a member are material; and

(5) where a contributory cannot be found or is in default.

This list should not be regarded as exhaustive.

Persons and documents Those who can be examined under s.245 are not alone officers and former officers of the company but any 'person known or suspected to have in his possession any property of the company or supposed to be indebted to the company, or any person whom the court deems capable of giving information relating to the promotion, formation, trade, dealings, affairs or property of the company.'[25] As was observed some 120 years ago, '[t]he practice in these cases has been assimilated to the practice in bankruptcy, and in bankruptcy a very wide net is thrown to obtain evidence.'[26] It is for the court and not the liquidator to decide whether a person falls into this category.

22. Amended by 1990 Act s.126.
23. *Hollinghead v M'Loughlin* [1917] 2 IR 28, at p. 34.
24. See *Bankruptcy Law*, pp. 110 et seq.
25. S.245(1).
26. *Re Bank of Hindustan, China and Japan* (1871) 13 Eq 178, at p. 182. See too *Massey v Allen* (1878) 9 Ch D 164 and *Re Land Credit Co. of Ireland* (1872) 14 Eq 8.

A witness can be required to produce 'any accounting records, deed, instrument, or other document or paper',[27] provided they are in his custody or power. A company's secretary is ordinarily regarded as having the company's books.[28] Whether any of the directors can be required to produce those books is an open question.[29] The witness, on attending, may take any objection he may have to permitting inspection of all or part of the books, for instance a banker;[30] he is in the same position as an ordinary witness served with a *subpoena duces tecum*. A banker will not be required to disclose anything that may affect the account of a person not directly connected with the investigation.[31] Production of documents will be directed notwithstanding the existence of a lien over them, even though production may deprive the lien of much of its practical value.[32]

Discretion to refuse order   Almost always the applicant for an examination order is the liquidator but s.245 does not prevent other interested parties from seeking such an order, although it is most exceptional for parties other than the liquidator to get an order. The court has a discretion to refuse or to postpone any examination if it would be oppressive or vexatious, or an abuse of process. Bowen J once described s.245's predecessor as

> an extraordinary section. It is an extraordinary power; it is a power of an inquisitorial kind which enables the court to direct to be examined—not merely before itself, but before the examiner appointed by the court— some third person who is not party to a litigation. That is an inquisitorial power, which may work with great severity against third persons, and it seems to me to be obvious that such a section ought to be used with the greatest care, so as not unnecessarily to put in motion the machinery of justice when it is not wanted, or to put it in motion at a stage when it is not clear that it is wanted, and certainly not to put it in motion if unnecessary mischief is going to be done or hardship inflicted upon the third person who is called upon to appear and give information.[33]

Almost 100 years later Hoffman J remarked that many of the

> Victorian cases on [s.245] contain emotive language which invokes the images of the Inquisition and the Court of Star Chamber. This language was used against a background of company law which required very little public disclosure and placed a much higher value than today on the protection of the privacy of business transactions and a lower value on the protection of creditors and shareholders. Today we have no difficulty with the proposition that persons who have had what perhaps was no more

27. S.245(3).
28. *Gladstone v McCallum* (1896) 23 R. (C. Sess.) 783.
29. *Re Maville Hose Co.* [1939] Ch 32.
30. *Re Smith Knight & Co.* (1869) LR 4 Ch App 421.
31. *Re Contract Corp.* (1872) 14 Eq 6.
32. *Re South Essex Estuary & Reclamation Co.* (1869) LR 4 Ch App 215.
33. *Re North Australian Territory Co.* (1890) 45 Ch D 87, at p. 93.

than the misfortune to be involved in the affairs of an insolvent company owe a public duty to assist the liquidator to investigate the affairs of that company in the interests of the creditors.[34]

In *Cloverbay Ltd v Bank of Credit and Commerce and International S.A.*,[35] the following general criteria were stated by Browne-Wilkinson VC as governing the exercise of the court's discretion whether or not to order an examination:

The words of the [statute] do not fetter the court's discretion in any way. Circumstances may vary infinitely. It is clear that in exercising the discretion the court has to balance the requirements of the liquidator against any possible oppression to the person to be examined. Such balancing depends on the relationship between the importance to the liquidator of obtaining the information on the one hand and the degree of oppression to the person sought to be examined on the other. If the information required is fundamental to any assessment of whether or not there is a cause of action and the degree of oppression is small (for example in the case of ordering premature discovery of documents) the balance will manifestly come down in favour of making the order. Conversely, if the liquidator is seeking merely to dot the i's and cross the t's of a fairly clear claim by examining the proposed defendant to discover his defence, the balance would come down against making the order. Of course, few cases will be so clear: it will be for the judge in each case to reach his own conclusion.

That said that are a number of points which . . . should be borne in mind in exercising the discretion. First, the reason for the inquisitorial jurisdiction contained in s.245 is that a liquidator . . . comes into the company with no previous knowledge and frequently finds that the company's records are missing or defective. The purpose of s.245 is to enable him to get sufficient information to reconstitute the state of knowledge that the company should possess. . . . Its purpose is not to put the company in a better position than it would have enjoyed if liquidation or administration had not supervened. In many cases an order under s.245 may have the *result* that the company is in such improved position, e.g. an order for discovery of documents made against a third party in order to reconstitute the company's own trading records may disclose the existence of claims which would otherwise remain hidden. But that is the *result* of the order not the *purpose* for which it is made.

Second, as a corollary to the first point, I do not think that the test of absolute 'need' as opposed to a reasonable requirement for the information is a workable or appropriate test. . . . If the applicant has to show an absolute 'need' this would lead to endless argument about whether the circumstances of each case disclose such need and would lead

34. *Re J. T. Rhodes Ltd* [1987] BCLC 77, at p. 80.
35. [1991] Ch. 90.

to the order being refused even in cases where the information would be of great utility to the applicant (short of absolute need) and could be obtained (e.g. by discovery of documents) without any great oppression to the person sought to be examined.

Third, . . . the case for making an order against an officer or former officer of the company will usually be stronger than it would be against a third party. Officers owe the company fiduciary duties and will often be in possession of information to which the company is entitled under the general law. . . . The enforcement of these duties owed by its officers to the company may require an order under s.245 even though it exposes such officers to the risk of personal liability. No such considerations apply when an order is sought against a third party. He owes no duty to the company. In an otherwise proper case he may be required to disclose documents or answer questions so as to provide the liquidator with the information necessary to carry out his functions even though this may have unfortunate repercussions for him. But he owes no general duty to give such information (apart from an order under s.245) and if by giving the information he risks exposing himself to liability this involves an element of oppression. That is not to say that an order cannot or should be made against a third party. But it should be borne in mind that the degree of possible oppression is greater in his case.

Fourth, although the section treats the production of documents and the oral examination of witnesses together, an order for oral examination is much more likely to be oppressive than an order for the production of documents. An order for the production of documents involves only advancing the time of discovery if an action ensues: the liquidator is getting no more than any other litigant would get, save that he is getting it earlier. But oral examination provides the opportunity for pre-trial depositions which the liquidator would never otherwise be entitled to: the person examined has to answer on oath and his answers can both provide evidence in support of a subsequent claim brought by the liquidator and also form the basis of later cross-examination.[36]

Where liquidators have commenced proceedings against the person they want to interrogate or are just about to begin proceedings, the court will be somewhat hesitant about permitting an examination because that may give the liquidator an unfair litigation advantage. But there are no hard and fast rules in this regard; account must be taken of the entire circumstances of each case. The authorities on the matter are carefully analysed by Slade J in *Re Castle New Homes Ltd*,[37] who concluded that once the liquidator has taken a firm decision to bring the action, he then would have to show special grounds why he should

36. Id. at pp. 102-103. See too, *British & Commonwealth Holdings plc v Spicer & Oppenheim* [1992] 4 All ER 876 and *Re Northrop Instruments & Systems Ltd* [1992] 2 NZLR 361.
37. [1979] 1 WLR 1075.

be permitted to conduct an examination of the intended defendant. However, in the *Cloverbay Ltd* case,[38] that approach was criticised because it gives rise to undesirable disputes of fact about the true state of the liquidator's mind. In that instance, two appeal judges found that the examination being sought of the company's bankers would be oppressive in the circumstances. What the court must reconcile is the principle that all information must be made available to the liquidator, to assist the beneficial winding up of the company, against the principle that a party should not be forced to reveal the strengths and weaknesses of his case. Even where proceedings have commenced, an examination order will not always be refused, although the scope of the questioning may then be restricted so as to prevent questioning of a purely fishing nature.

There is no requirement that the person to be examined should first be furnished with a list of the questions that will be asked,[39] although in an appropriate case the court may direct that such a list be provided. One matter of which the court may take account is the existence of an alternative source of the information being sought, which is readily accessible to the liquidator.[40]

Public or private hearing? Under the Constitution, justice must be administered in public unless the law provides otherwise, and even then there is a strong judicial preference for public hearings.[41] Under the Companies (Consolidation) Act, 1908, two forms of examination were provided for. One, which did not apply in Ireland, was to be held in open court[42] and was designed principally to ascertain whether the company's officers had defrauded the company, as a preliminary to launching prosecutions. The other form could be heard privately in chambers or in public, at the discretion of the court,[43] and its primary purpose was to assist the liquidator in locating assets. But the chambers procedure was abolished in Ireland in 1926. It was held by the Supreme Court in *Re Redbreast Preserving Co. Ltd*[44] that this latter procedure was not strictly the administration of justice and, in consequence, at the court's discretion, could be carried out *in camera*. Subsequently, in that instance, it was held that persons being interrogated under s.174 of the 1908 Act were entitled to invoke the privilege against self-incrimination.

It is not entirely clear whether *in camera* examinations are permissible under s.245 of the 1963 Act. Rule 125 of the Winding Up Rules speaks of '[i]f a witness is examined in private. . . .' That the court is empowered to direct that a person being examined shall pay the costs of the entire process, that he cannot any longer claim the privilege against self-incrimination and, especially, because failure to attend one's examination is stated to be a contempt of court all suggest that the legislature envisages a full judicial proceeding. It therefore

38. [1991] Ch. 90   39. *Re Rolls Razor Ltd (No. 2)* [1970] 1 Ch 576.
40. *Re Castle New Homes Ltd* [1979] 1 WLR at p. 1093.
41. *Re R. Ltd* [1989] IR 126.
42. 1906 Act s.175; later s.270 of Companies Act 1948 (U.K.).
43. 1906 s.174; later s.268 of Companies Act 1948 (U.K.).
44. 91 ILTR 12 (1957).

would seem that the hearing must always be held in public. In the light of this it is possible that some of the authorities on private examinations under s.268 of the English 1948 Act might not be followed in all respects in this jurisdiction..

Conduct of the examination Although the examination can be conducted by the judge or by the Master, usually the questions are put by the applicant for the examination, through his solicitor or counsel. The person being examined is entitled to be legally represented and be questioned by his solicitor or counsel in order more fully to explain his position. Questions may be put in the form of interrogatories. What the liquidator or applicant will be seeking to ascertain, principally, are the reasons for the insolvency, whether the statement of affairs is indeed a complete account of the company's financial situation, whether claims can be brought against third parties to recover property which was improperly transferred, such as fraudulent preferences and void dispositions. Another matter is whether any of the criminal laws relating to insolvency have been contravened. It has been said that the object of these examinations is 'not merely for the purpose of collecting the debts on behalf of the creditors or of ascertaining simply what sum can be made available for the creditors who are entitled to it, but also for the purpose of the protection of the public in the cases in which the liquidation proceedings apply. . . .'[45] To concentrate attention on the mere debt collecting and distributing assets aspects is to disregard one very important side of liquidation proceedings and law. Evidence is usually recorded in shorthand and a transcript is made which the examinee may be required to sign[46] but which he is entitled to peruse before signing, adding any corrections which he may wish to make in pencil in the margin.

The actual tenor of questioning a bankrupt under a similar provision in bankruptcy law has been described in *Hollingshead v M'Loughlin* as follows:

> that examination . . . ought to be conducted in such a way as to avoid any kind of concussion upon the bankrupt to make him give evidence in one direction rather than another. A bankruptcy examination ought not to be converted into a torture chamber. The sanctions of the law behind the evasions or concealments or untruths of bankrupts are strong enough without concussions in the course of the examination being practised.[47]

Ronan LJ observed that

> The object of such examinations is to get at the truth, and the judge must be guided in the exercise of his discretion as to the mode of examination by this. He has a perfect right to form his own opinion as to whether a witness is telling the truth or not, and to put such questions himself, and to allow counsel to pursue such method of examination as the judge thinks necessary for the purpose of ascertaining the truth.[48]

In the *Hollingshead* case the House of Lords rejected the contention that, in

45. *Re Paget* [1927] 2 Ch. 85, at p. 87. 46. 1963 Act s.245(2).
47. [1917] 2 IR 28, at p. 36. 48. [1916] 2 IR 583, at p. 605.

conducting the examination, the judge adopted an unduly partisan approach. It was held that, in the circumstances, he acted properly in committing the bankrupt and his spouse to jail because their answers were so unsatisfactory that it was not possible to believe they were making a candid disclosure. In *Re Poulson*,[49] the inquisitorial nature of the proceedings under the bankruptcy law was referred to by Walton J:

> although doubtless the procedure can be used in an accusatorial manner if that is what will best serve the trustee's overriding purpose, it is also capable of being used, and frequently is used most fruitfully, in an inquisitorial manner. And when so used, many answers given by a witness who is prepared to be co-operative and prepared to volunteer information may be of the utmost assistance to the trustee although they might well not be proper answers, or even admissible answers, in the more normal proceedings.[50]

Questions cannot be put simply in order to build up a case or with a view to probing defences in a case which is already in train. Where an action is pending between the liquidator and the witness, while the liquidator is entitled to 'reasonable information', the court will not permit 'anything like a dress rehearsal of the cross examination in the action'.[51] Questions which are mere 'fishing' exercises also will be disallowed.[52]

Evidential privileges   Formerly, persons summoned before the court could refuse to answer questions where the answer would implicate them in criminal offences.[53] The common law privilege against self-incrimination is now abrogated by s.245(6). However, although that privilege may no longer be claimed, the witness is protected to some extent in that his answers may not be used against him in any subsequent proceedings, be they civil or criminal. The only exception is a prosecution for perjury for having given false answers. However, proceedings being brought by a liquidator in the winding up are not always 'other proceedings' for this purpose. Accordingly, it was held in *Re Aluminium Fabricators Ltd*[54] that answers obtained in a s.245 examination may be used against the witness in fraudulent trading proceedings in the same liquidation and, presumably, in a misfeasance claim as well. In another instance, it was held that there is nothing which prevents those answers being used against persons other than that witness, including a company of which the witness is an officer.[55]

---

49. [1976] 1 WLR 1023.   50. Id. at p. 1032.
51. *Re Franks* [1892] 1 QB 646, at pp. 647-648. See too *Re Castle New Homes Ltd* [1979] 1 WLR 1075.
52. *Re Gregory* [1935] 1 Ch 65.
53. *Re Redbreast Preserving Co. Ltd*, 91 ILTR 12 (1957).
54. [1984] ILRM 399.
55. *Irish Commercial Soc. Ltd v Plunkett* [1986] ILRM 624. Compare *Re Keypack Homecare Ltd* [1990] BCLC 441, at p. 447.

Other privileges that can be claimed in the examination include the legal professional privilege,[56] which covers all communications between the witness and his legal advisor which are directly referable to litigation. A lawyer who is a witness can equally claim this privilege.[57] In bankruptcy cases where the witness is the bankrupt's own solicitor and the questions are being put on behalf of the Assignee or trustee, this privilege has a far narrower compass.[58]

Committal for non-cooperation   If, without having a reasonable excuse, a person fails to attend the court for examination, s.245(7) states that he is guilty of contempt of court and that he may be punished accordingly. A person summoned must attend the court, whether or not he believes he has information which may assist the liquidator or he has the documents specified in the order. If there are reasonable grounds for believing that he has absconded or is about to abscond, the court may order his arrest and that all or any of his property be seized, including any books and documents in his possession.[59] Unlike the position under the Bankruptcy Act, 1988,[60] there is no statutory authority to commit or impose other sanctions on a witness who refuses to answer fully questions being put to him.

Costs   Ordinarily the costs of conducting the examination would form part of the costs of the liquidation. But in an appropriate case, the court may direct that the witness bears all or part of those costs himself.[61]

CONDUCT OF LITIGATION

Liquidators are authorised to 'bring or defend any action or other legal proceedings in the name or on behalf of the company.'[62] In order to institute or defend proceedings, an official liquidator is required to get the consent of the court or of the committee of inspection, as the case may be. A liquidator who proceeds with a case without having first obtained such consent and who then looses the case risks being made personally liable for the costs awarded against the company.[63] Actions commenced by liquidators are usually brought in the name of the company in liquidation, with the writ identifying who the liquidator is. Proceedings being brought against a company in liquidation are often subject to a stay.[64]

---

56. See generally, C. Fennell, *The Law of Evidence in Ireland* (1992) pp. 166 et seq.
57. *Ex p. Campbell* (1870) LR 5 Ch. 703.
58. *Re Wells* (1892) 9 Mor 116.
59. 1963 Act s.245(8). Cf. *Re Oriental Credit Ltd* [1988] 2 WLR 17.
60. S.24.   61. S.245(5).
62. 1963 Act s.231(1)(a).
63. *Re Silver Valley Mines* (1882) 21 Ch D 381.
64. See ante pp. 171-173.

Security for costs   In any case where the plaintiff is a limited company and there is good reason for believing that it will not be able to pay the costs if it looses, s.290 of the 1963 Act enables the judge to order that the company shall give security for costs.[65] Almost invariably, such an order will be made against a company which was wound up on foot of a creditor's petition or which is in a creditors' voluntary liquidation. But an order requiring security for costs will not be made where the defendant in the case was the cause of the company's financial difficulties and he is being sued for those very actions;[66] in that event, the court can decline to require the security. It is not enough for the company to assert that the defendant caused its impecuniosity; a *prima facie* case to that effect must be made out. Thus, in *Irish Commercial Society Ltd v Plunkett*,[67] the Supreme Court held that the plaintiff was not within this exception to the general rule because the evidence concerning the defendant's actions were blurred, unsatisfactory and too contradictory to constitute a *prima facie* case of wrong-doing by him. Liquidators are authorised 'to give security for costs in any proceedings commenced by the company or by' them.[68] Where in an inter-locutory application a liquidator consented to an order for security for costs but events subsequently come to light which show that he gave his consent under a misapprehension about the true state of affairs, the court may set aside the interlocutory consent order.[69]

Insolvent defendants will not normally be required to give security for costs. However, where the steps being taken by the defence go beyond mere defence, security will usually be required; for instance, in an action for possession by mortgagees, where the company seeks to declare the mortgage invalid.[70]

Liquidator's costs   Regarding costs incurred in litigation involving the company, one question is the extent to which those costs must be borne by the liquidator personally rather than the company itself. A related matter, considered later,[71] concerns the priority status of costs which are payable by the company or in respect of which the liquidator is entitled to be indemnified against the company. Generally, if the company or the liquidator succeed in the action then their costs are payable by the loosing party. Where an action brought against the insolvent company succeeds, although the plaintiff in principle is entitled to his costs against the company, on account of the insolvency he will not recover those costs; so he litigates at his own risk. He cannot sue the liquidator personally

---

65.   E.g. *D. Peppard & Co. Ltd v Bogoff* [1962] IR 180; *Comhlúcht Paipéar Piomhaireachta Teo v Udarás na Gaeltachta* [1990] 1 IR 320 and *Lismore Homes Ltd v Bank of Ireland Finance* [1992] ILRM 798.
66.   *Personal Service Laundry Ltd v National Bank* [1964] IR 49; *Bula Ltd v Tara Mines Ltd* [1987] IR 494 and *Weld Street Takeaways & Fisheries Ltd v Westpac Banking Corp.* [1986] NZLR 741.
67.   [1986] IR 258.   68.   1963 Act s.231(2)(g).
69.   *Irish Commercial Soc. Ltd v Plunkett* [1986] IR 258.
70.   *City of Moscow Gas Co. v International Financial Soc. Ltd* [1872] 7 Ch App 225.
71.   See post pp. 356-359.

in connection with any dispute he has with the company, no more than directors can be made personally liable for the wrongs of their insolvent companies.

Where it is the liquidator who is the plaintiff or applicant and he looses, the order for costs is against him personally. It was held in *Re Wilson Lovatt & Sons Ltd*,[72] where the authorities in this area were analysed carefully, that the court will not direct that his liability for those costs shall be limited to such sums as he may recover from the company. Liability for costs is personal and unqualified. However, in an appropriate case, the court handling the liquidation may direct that his costs should be treated as costs of the liquidation. If there are sufficient unencumbered assets, he may then be able to recover that sum from the company.

In deciding whether the liquidator's cost's were properly incurred for this purpose, the same general approach is taken as in the case of remunerated trustees' costs. In *Re Silver Valley Mines Ltd*,[73] Jessell MR remarked that 'an official liquidator who (though no doubt in a sense he is a trustee) is a paid agent of the court, is [not] entitled to the same indulgence as an ordinary gratuitous trustee. . . . [T]he cases in which he may properly be deprived of costs for a mistake, or a blunder, are more numerous. . . .'[74] There the liquidator was denied his costs because the proceedings he had launched were a 'manifest mistake'. A prudent step would be to make a prior application to the court for leave to bring the action; the *Re Beddoe*[75] application. In a voluntary liquidation, approval from the committee of inspection should be sought and, indeed, it would be wise for the liquidator to seek an indemnity in respect of his costs before going any further.[76] If it is the case that a liquidator's costs are recoverable from assets which are subject to a floating charge,[77] it was held in *Re M.C. Bacon Ltd*[78] that the test for the court approving those costs is more demanding than that they were properly incurred. Before allowing those costs, the court must be satisfied that in all the circumstances it is just to do so. It was pointed out there that in all the previous cases, where the general point being considered here arose, the fund from which approved costs would be payable was the money available for the unsecured creditors.

Other party proving costs against the company Where costs of litigation have been awarded against the company, as opposed to the liquidator, the other party to the action may be able to lodge a proof in respect of them. In *Re British Gold Fields of West Africa*[79] Lindley MR stated the governing principles in liquidations as follows:

> If an action is brought against a person, who afterwards becomes bank-

---

72. [1977] 1 All ER 274.   73. (1882) 21 Ch D 381.
74. Id. at p. 386.
75. [1893] 1 Ch 547. Cf. *Re Movietex Ltd* [1990] BCLC 785.
76. E.g. in *Re M.C. Bacon Ltd* [1991] Ch. 127.
77. See post p. 359.
78. [1991] Ch 127.   79. [1899] 2 Ch 7.

rupt, for the recovery of a sum of money, and the action is successful, the costs are regarded as an addition to the sum recovered and to be provable if that is provable, but not otherwise. . . .

If the action against the person who becomes bankrupt is unsuccessful, no costs becomes payable by him or out of his estate, and no question as to them can arise. But if an unsuccessful action is brought by a man who becomes bankrupt, then, if he is ordered to pay the costs, or if a verdict is given against him before he becomes bankrupt, they are provable. On the other hand, if no verdict is given against him and no order is made for payment of costs until after he becomes bankrupt, they are not provable. In such a case there is no provable debt to which the costs are incident, and there is no reason to pay them by reason of any obligation incurred by the bankrupt before bankruptcy; nor are they a contingent liability to which he can be said to be subject at the date of his bankruptcy.[80]

COMPROMISE CLAIMS AND CALLS

As well as being entitled to bring and assert claims, and also to make calls, on behalf of the company, a liquidator can 'make any compromise or arrangements with creditors' and can 'compromise all calls and (other) liabilities' to the company from its shareholders or members.[81] In order to make compromises, an official liquidator must get the consent of the court or of the committee of inspection, as the case may be; in a creditors' voluntary winding up such compromises must get the consent of the creditors, the committee of inspection or the court, as the case may be.[82] But failure to obtain that consent does not render a compromise which has been reached invalid. In *Cyclemakers Co. Op. Supply Co. v Sims*[83] it was held that 'a compromise between a creditor of a company and its liquidator, which is otherwise binding on both, cannot be objected to by the creditor merely on the ground that the liquidator did not obtain the sanction of the court to the compromise; and if the liquidator can say that the other party to such a compromise is bound by it, it follows that the liquidator himself must also be bound.'[84] A bona fide compromise of a claim against the company which has been duly effected will not readily be set aside by the court on the grounds that the claim could never have been enforced, for instance, because the company had a good defence under the Moneylenders Acts.[85]

CHARGE ASSETS

Where it is necessary to raise funds or otherwise incur credit, the liquidator can charge the company's assets as security.[86]

---

80. Id. at p. 11; see post pp. 285-286
81. 1963 Act s.231(1)(e) and (f).
82. Id. s.276(1)(a).
83. [1903] 1 KB 4777.
84. Id. at pp. 480-481.
85. *Binder v Alachovzos* [1972] 2 QB 151.
86. 1963 Act s.231(2)(e).

CARRY ON THE BUSINESS

Liquidators are authorised to 'carry on the business of the company so far as may be necessary for the beneficial winding up thereof.'[87] In order to carry on the business, the official liquidator must get the consent of the court or the committee of inspection, as the case may be. It was held in *Re Wreck, Recovery and Salvage Co.*[88] that the necessity to continue the business to assist the winding up does not 'import . . . something which would be highly expedient under all the circumstances of the case for the beneficial winding up of the company.'[89] Carrying on the business 'must be with a view to winding up the company, not with a view to its continuance.'[90] There, the court refused to permit the liquidator to continue the business in order to reconstruct the company by making its shares more valuable, although the court agreed that circumstances could arise where continuing in business with a view to selling it as a going concern can be for the benefit of the winding up. In a voluntary winding up the court will not readily reject the liquidator's conclusion that, in the circumstances, the company's business ought to be continued.[91] All invoices and business letters issued for the company must state that it is in liquidation.[92] Debts incurred by the liquidator for this purpose have priority over other debts because they are a cost of the liquidation.[93]

There are several other specific powers that are particularly relevant to carrying on the business, such as to draw, accept, make or endorse any bill of exchange or promissory note in a company's name,[94] to raise money on the security of the company's assets[95] and to appoint an agent to do any business which the liquidator himself cannot do.[96]

REALISE THE ASSETS

One of the liquidator's principal functions is to realise the company's assets with a view to paying out and distributing the proceeds. His power of sale is formulated in s.231(2) in very wide terms: it is

> (a) to sell the real and personal property and things in action of the company by public auction or private contract, with power to transfer the whole thereof to any person or company or to sell the same in lots and for the purpose of selling the company's land or any part thereof to carry out such sales by fee farm grant, sub fee farm grant, lease, sub-lease or otherwise, and to sell any rent reserved on any such grant or any reversion expectant upon the determination of any such lease;

> (b) to do all acts and to execute, in the name and on behalf of the company,

87. Id. s.231(1)(b).
89. Id. at p. 362.
91. Ibid.
93. See post pp. 355-359.
95. Id. s.231(2)(e).

88. (1880) 15 Ch D 353.
90. Id. at p. 360.
92. 1963 Act s.303.
94. 1963 Act s.231(2)(d).
96. Id. s.231(2)(h).

all deeds, receipts and other documents, and for that purpose to use, when necessary, the company's seal.

In a compulsory winding up, sales of assets must have the court's approval and the court can give directions regarding the mode of sale and what shall be done with the proceeds.[97] Unless the court directs otherwise, any deposit must be paid into a joint deposit account in the name of the official liquidator and the examiner, and the purchase money must be paid into the official liquidator's bank account. But in a voluntary liquidation, exercise of the power of sale does not require the consent of the creditors, or of the shareholders if the company is solvent. Nor will the court readily interfere with the voluntary liquidator's decisions regarding the conduct of a sale. It has been held that the court will intervene, at the instigation of a creditor or a shareholder, only where the liquidator was acting fraudulently or had not exercised his discretion bona fide, or was 'doing that which was so utterly unreasonable and absurd that no reasonable man would so act.'[98]

Sale to ex-officer   Section 231(1A) of the 1963 Act[99] strikes at an abuse of liquidators' powers by selling some of the company's assets to one or more of its former directors or officers, often at a knock-down price. Before a valuable asset can be sold to anyone who was an officer of the company in the three years before the winding up, at least fourteen days notice of the liquidator's intention must be given to all the creditors who are known to him. An officer here includes a 'shadow director' and any 'connected person' for the purpose of the rules regarding the company contracting with its directors.[1] A valuable asset in this context has the same meaning as that in the rule regarding substantial property transactions between the company and any of its directors.[2]

Duties of care and good faith   Liquidators' duties generally are dealt with below but it is convenient to consider here their duties in connection with selling the company's assets. Being fiduciaries, liquidators must exercise this power bona fide and for the benefit of the liquidation. Thus, without leave of the court, they must not sell these assets to themselves or to a company they established for this very purpose.[3] Presumably, where the purchaser is a company in which the liquidator has a significant direct or indirect financial interest, the manner in which the sale was carried out would be scrutinised carefully by the court in order to ensure that the liquidator did what was best for the winding up.[4]

---

97.   Rule 124.
98.   *Leon v York-O-Matic. Ltd* [1966] 1 WLR 1450 and *H.M. Pitman & Co. v Top Business Systems (Nottingham) Ltd* [1984] BCLC 593.
99.   Inserted by 1990 Act s.124.
1.   1990 Act s.26; see *Company Law*, pp. 108 and 162.
2.   1990 Act. s 29; see *Company Law*, pp. 161-162.
3.   *Silkstone & Haigh Moor Coal Co. v Edey* [1900] 1 Ch 167.
4.   Cf. the position of the receivers in equivalent circumstances; ante pp. 59-60.

Unlike receivers,[5] liquidators do not have an express statutory obligation to take all reasonable care to obtain the best price reasonably possible in the circumstances. But the general law subjects them to a similar duty, the full extent of which has not been articulated by the courts. This duty was described by Murray J in *Re Brook Cottages Ltd*[6] as a 'statutory fiduciary duty to obtain the best possible price' and that the assets should not be 'sold at an undervalue.'[7] In *Van Hool McArdle Ltd v Rohan Industrial Estates Ltd*,[8] Kenny J said that '[t]he primary duty of the court and of the liquidator in a court winding up is to get the maximum price for the assets.'[9]

Re Brook Cottage Ltd[10] provides an excellent example of what liquidators ought not to allow happen. The company's main asset was a hotel at Newcastle, Co. Down, which the liquidator sought to sell. It was not put up for auction and was advertised for sale only once, and that advertisement was not in a local newspaper circulating in the Newcastle area. Bidding started at £60,000 and, in the space of one week, reached £75,000. Negotiations were being handled by an estate agent, but he left for England on the Friday afternoon of that week, instructing his secretary that, if the bidder who had offered £75,000 put in a higher bid then that bid should be accepted. This bidder telephoned the secretary that very evening, offering £75,500, and was told that his bid was accepted. During the following week one of the other bidders offered £80,000, subject to contract, but the liquidator decided to sell to the previous bidder. Proceedings were then brought by one of the disappointed bidders, who also was a shareholder in the company, to have the contract for sale set aside. It was held that the liquidator had acted improperly and that the contract should be set aside. No substantial explanation was given why the bidding closed on the Friday evening, only after a week, when obviously there were other potential purchasers in the market.

Murray J found that 'the probabilities are that the decision' to close the bidding then 'prevented the highest available price being obtained'.[11] The arrangement between the estate agent and his secretary about accepting a bid was described as 'open to the severest criticism.'[12] It was held that 'the liquidator was in breach of his statutory fiduciary duty to get the best price and can[not] escape vicarious responsibility for the[se] very slack arrangements. ...'[13] Moreover, the liquidator was not 'entitled to excuse himself on the basis of the professional advice he received'.[14] It was ordered that the contract for sale be set aside even though there was no suggestion that the other party had acted wrongly in any way. Murray J. observed that 'a third party who contracts with a liquidator in a compulsory winding up has to remember that the liquidator

5.   1963 Act s.316A.   6. [1976] NI 78.
7.   [1976] NI 78 at pp. 115 and 116.
8.   [1980] IR 237.
9.   [1980] IR 237 at pp 242-243.
10. [1976] NI at p. 114.   11. Ibid.
12. Ibid.   13. Id. at p. 115.
14. Id. at p. 117

is under the control of the court and if the third party wishes to be absolutely sure of his ground he should stipulate for the approval of the court to the contract being obtained by the liquidator.'[15] Because of his negligence, the liquidator was ordered to pay his costs and also half of the applicant's costs there; since he had relied on his solicitor's and estate agent's advice to reject the £80,000 bid, half of the applicant's costs and also the third party's costs were decreed to be costs of the winding up.

It was contended in *Re Brook Cottages Ltd* that, because the agreement to sell at £75,500 had been made by an officer of the court and had obtained the approval of the clerk of the court (equivalent to the examiner), the court ought not to set aside the contract and probably agree to sell the property to some other bidder. But the clerk of the court had not been given all the relevant information about the transaction. Furthermore, there was no legal principle which prevented the court or the liquidator from accepting higher bids.

A somewhat similar situation arose in *Van Hool McArdle Ltd v Rohan Industrial Estates Ltd*.[16] There the official liquidator received an offer for the company's assets of £750,000, conditional on exchange control consent being obtained. Two days later he was offered £730,000 but that offer was open for only one day. On the advice of two firms of estate agents, he accepted the latter offer and entered a contract to sell the property for that price, subject to the consent of the court being obtained, which is the usual stipulation in these circumstances. But three days later the first offeror returned with a new offer of £850,000, again subject to getting exchange control consent. It was held by the Supreme Court that, despite acceptance of one offer, the highest bid should be accepted even if that meant reneging on the contract for sale. The provision in this contract for the court's consent, it was held, 'requires the court to consider whether . . . its consent should be given to the sale, having regard to the circumstances obtaining not merely at the time when the sale was effected but also at the time of the application for such consent.'[17] Kenny J observed that a system 'under which a bid of £730,000 is accepted when one of £850,000 has been made would bring the court into well deserved ridicule.'[18] If the liquidator had sold by public auction and not by private treaty the court most likely would not then have rejected the terms which had been agreed. O'Higgins CJ said that, had the liquidator done this instead, 'the court would only have been concerned to see whether he acted bona fide and in due discharge of his duties as liquidator.'[19]

The Supreme Court distinguished this case from its previous decision in *Re Hibernian Transport Ltd*,[20] which also involved acceptance of one bid even though a significantly higher bid was made subsequently. The court ordered the company's official liquidator to offer its property for sale by auction but no bid was made then, so the property was withdrawn. A bank then offered to buy the premises for £80,000, subject to contract, but that offer was open for only two

15. Id. at p. 119.   16. [1980] IR 237.
17. Id. at pp. 240-241.   18. Id. at p. 243.
19. Id. at p. 240.   20. [1972] IR 190.

days. This figure was close to the reserve price at the auction. Because the offer was open for just two days and also because the company had no money to pay the next instalment of rent on its premises, which could lead to the lease being forfeited, the liquidator sought the consent of the judge in charge of the case. Kenny J agreed to selling the premises to the bank at this price and contracts were drawn up. But then another bidder arrived on the scene and offered £101,000. Because he had sanctioned a sale to the first offeror, Kenny J held that the second offer should not be accepted and his decision was upheld by the Supreme Court. Walsh J for the court, said that 'if all other things were equal then there should no be doubt but that the larger sum should be accepted.'[21] However, 'all other things were not equal' in the circumstances. Since the earlier offer was near the reserve price and as no other offer had been made at the time and this offer was accepted in a situation of great urgency, with the approval of Kenny J, there was 'nothing unreasonable in the judge taking the course which he did when the initial application for prior approval was made to him. . . .'[22] Here the court was 'bound, if not in law certainly in honour, to permit the liquidator to complete the contract already executed. . . .'[23]

CALLS ON MEMBERS

In unlimited companies, the members are liable without limit for their company's unpaid debts. In limited companies that liability is only in respect of the amounts which have not been paid up on the shares.[24] In companies limited by guarantee, the members are liable to contribute the amounts which they have guaranteed to do.[25] Accordingly, one of the liquidator's tasks is to call in and recover all sums due to the company from its members as such. A member's liability as a contributory may not be set-off against a debt which the company owes that member.[26] Persons who hold shares in trust for others are personally liable as contributories in respect of those shares.[27]

Past members Section 207 of the 1963 Act provides that every present and past member of the company is liable to contribute towards its debts and to its expenses in a winding up, subject to qualifications. If the shares are fully paid up, that is the end of the matter. The fact that a person has sold or otherwise transferred his shares does not completely exempt him from liability. If he was a member within one year of the winding up commencing and those shares are still not fully paid, he can be held liable as a contributory. But that liability does not apply to debts of the company which were contracted since his membership ceased; and then he is only so liable if the existing members are unable to satisfy whatever calls are made on them. When drawing up the list of persons against

---

21. Id. at p. 202.   22. Id. at p. 203.
23. Ibid. *Munster & Leinster Bank v Munster Motor Co.* [1922] 1 IR 15 is a similar instance.
24. 1963 Act s.207(1)(d).   25. Id. s.207(1)(e).
26. *Re Hiram Maxim Lamp Co.* [1903] 1 Ch 70.

whom calls can be made, the past members who are liable as described here are placed on what is referred to as a 'B list' of contributories. Every contributory's liability is declared by s.209 to be a debt to the company which is subject to a 12 years limitation period. There is still some doubt whether B contributories can be held liable for part of the liquidation costs and expenses when the company has 'old debts'.

Settling the list The process of identifying which contributories are liable for calls is known as settling the list of contributories. Liquidators are required by s.235(1) of the 1963 Act to settle that list with reasonable speed.[28] To that end they are empowered to rectify the register of members in all cases where rectification can be done under the Companies Acts. Persons whose names are placed on the list must be given an opportunity to contest that listing and, should they choose, require the court to rule on the matter. A liquidator may always draw up a supplementary list which varies or adds to the original list.

Making calls In a compulsory liquidation, ss.237 and 238 of the 1963 Act empower the court to make calls on contributories.[29] Liquidators in voluntary winding ups are authorised by s.276(1)(d) to exercise the power of making calls. Even if the company is solvent, the liquidator may have to make calls in order to adjust rights between the contributories. Where there are a large number of contributories against whom calls have been made, instead of bringing separate actions against them, the usual mode of enforcing the call is what is known as the 'balance order' procedure.[30] This is a direction by the court to pay the liquidator or his accountant the sum specified in the order. It does not have the effect of a judgment.[31]

RESPONSES TO WRONG-DOING

In the course of his investigations, the liquidator may come across evidence of wrong-doing on the part of the company, its officers or other agents or otherwise. Those wrongs may range from serious frauds, through failure to keep adequate books and records to incurring credit in a reckless manner. In an appropriate case, he may bring proceedings against persons involved in those actions. As is explained in Chapter 18, the court may sanction those responsible for fraudulent or reckless trading or inadequate record-keeping by making them personally liable for the company's debts. The power to conduct examinations on oath under s.245 of the 1963 Act can be most valuable when deciding whether or not proceedings should be brought on these or other grounds.

If an official liquidator comes across wrong-doing, he must bring the matter

27. *Re City of Glasgow Bank* (1879) 4 App Cas 583.
28. See Rules 86-89.
29. See Rules 92-94.
30. *Ex p. Whinney* (1884) 13 QBD 476.
31. *Westmoreland Green & Blue State Co. v Fielden* [1891] 3 Ch 15.

to the court's attention. Where it appears in the course of a voluntary winding up that any past or present officer or member of the company has been guilty of a criminal offence in relation to the company, s.299 of the 1963 Act requires the liquidator to report the matter to the Director of Public Prosecutions. In the circumstances, the liquidator must give the Director 'such information . . . and access to and facilities for inspecting and taking any copies of any documents' he possesses or controls and relating to the suspected offence. Where the Director decides to prosecute, the liquidator must 'give all assistance . . . which he reasonably can' in connection with the prosecution. Where without good cause a liquidator does not furnish that assistance, the Director can apply to the court for a direction to provide assistance in such manner as the court indicates, and the costs of that application may be given against the liquidator personally. The fact that he has made such a report to the DPP must be revealed in the liquidator's next periodic return, statement, abstract or account.

Where a liquidator finds that a person who was disqualified or restricted by Part VII of the 1990 Act from managing a company's affairs had been involved in the management of the company, he is required forthwith to inform the court of that fact if it appears that the creditors' or the company's interests may be jeopardised. A liquidator who contravenes this duty can be prosecuted under s.151 of the 1990 Act.

DISCHARGING LIABILITIES

One of the main functions of the liquidator and, in a creditor-initiated or controlled winding up, his predominant function is to discharge the company's liabilities. Doing this will require notifying the various creditors and submitting proofs of their debts and, also, dealing with the secured creditors. Payment must be made by cheque to the creditor or to such other person as the liquidator has been authorised by the creditor to be paid.[33] Where others have some claims against the creditor regarding those funds, it is not the liquidator's function to seek to resolve those claims. As was observed in *Re Dublin Cattle Market Co.*, 'the Legislature intended to confine [the liquidator's] duties to the realising of the assets of the . . . estate, and the distribution of them amongst the creditors of that estate, and . . . it never was intended that he should be embarrassed with any claims on or equities affecting the parties entitled to these dividends.'[34]

Secured creditors may very well choose to stand outside the liquidation and instead realise their security, giving over to the liquidator any surplus between the amount of their debt and the proceeds of sale. Preferential creditors must be paid before the general creditors get a penny.[35] In order to pay off any class of creditor in full, the liquidator must obtain consent—either from the court, the

---

32. Cf. *Re Merchant Banking Ltd* [1987] ILRM 260 concerning payment for work done preparing a report on wrong-doing.
33. Winding Up Rule 121.   34. (1867) Ir Eq 153, at p. 157.
35. See post ch. 25.

committee of inspection, the creditors or the members, as the case may be.[36] Liquidators must also secure such consent before entering into any compromise or arrangement with the company's creditors or persons claiming to be owed money by the company.[37]

DISTRIBUTION TO MEMBERS

If the company happens to be solvent there will be a surplus to be distributed among its members or shareholders. Where the shares are divided into several classes, such as ordinary shares and preference shares, the question of who is entitled to any surplus left over after the capital has been returned often gives rise to difficulties.[38]

OTHER AND INCIDENTAL POWERS

The 1963 Act confers several other powers on liquidators which may be regarded as incidental to the above powers and also a general incidental power.[39] Liquidators can apply to the court for permission to disclaim onerous property or contracts.[40] Liquidators can do all acts and execute deeds in the company's name, use the company's seal, deal with bills of exchange on the company's behalf, borrow on the security of the company's assets, give security for costs in litigation involving the company, appoint agents to do any business that the liquidator cannot do, take out letters of administration in the name of any deceased contributory, and prove in the bankruptcy of any contributory. Liquidators in voluntary winding ups are empowered to summon general meetings of the company for obtaining the members' sanction or for any other purposes, to exercise the court's power of settling a list of contributories and making calls, to pay the company's debts and to adjust the rights of contributories,[41] and to sanction a transfer of shares made after the winding up commences.[42] A liquidator in a voluntary winding up can also apply to the court for permission to exercise any or all of the powers that the Companies Acts confers on official liquidators.[43] Finally, the liquidator can 'do all such other things as may be necessary for winding up the affairs of the company and distributing its assets.'[44] This incidental power is extremely wide, and has been said to cover everything that a reasonable person might consider and to empower the liquidator to do anything which may be thought expedient with reference to the company's assets, such as mortgaging company property.[45]

36. 19763 Act s.231(1)(d).
37. Id. ss.231(1)(e) and (f).
38. See *Company Law* pp. 304-307.
39. Mainly in 1963 Act s.231.   40. Post pp. 224-229.
41. 1963 Act s 276.   42. S.255.
43. S.280. Cf. *Re Campbell Coverings Ltd* [1953] Ch 488.
44. Id. s.231(2)(i) and 276(1)(b).
45. *Re Cambrian Mining Co.* (1882) 48 LT 114.

TAXATION

Usually, when the winding up commences, the business activities will come to an end and no further trading or income generating activities will take place. However, the liquidator may very well chose to carry on business for a short while for the benefit of the winding up. Also, cash in hand and the proceeds of realisations may be put on deposit and start earning interest. Indeed, in at least one well-known instance, a company which was insolvent when it went into liquidation ended its winding up as a solvent company by virtue of the interest earned on the liquidator's bank deposits over many years.[46]

Under the Corporation Tax Act, 1976, corporation tax is chargeable on all 'profits arising in the winding up.'[47] Once a winding up begins, the company's present accounting period comes to an end and a new one commences;[48] a new accounting period then lasts for twelve months, followed by another twelve months period from then and so on. One consequence of this change in accounting periods is that trading losses being brought forward cannot be set-off against capital gains which arise during the course of the liquidation. Following the winding up, it is permissible to raise assessments before the end of any accounting period.[49] Appointment of a liquidator does not break up a group for capital gains tax purposes; in a group, therefore, capital losses can be set-off against capital gains.

Formerly a dilemma facing liquidators was whether they should register for value added tax (V.A.T.). Since 1983, they have had no choice in the matter as, under s.78 of the Finance Act, 1983, all disposals of 'goods forming part of the assets of the business' are deemed to be supplied by a taxable person in furtherance of the business and are subject to V.A.T. Therefore, liquidators must charge V.A.T. and make the normal V.A.T. returns; they can recover V.A.T. paid on goods and services purchased in the course of the liquidation. Where the liquidator disposes of the business as a going concern to another V.A.T.-registered person, ordinarily the transaction is exempted from V.A.T.[50] Relief may be obtained from V.A.T. in respect of bad debts; the rate of relief applicable is the current rate when the bad debt is deemed to be uncollectable.

FIDUCIARY DUTIES

Being officers of the court or agents of the company, as the case may be, liquidators are fiduciaries and are subject to the general fiduciary duties.[51] These duties include not taking unfair advantage of, or profiting from, their office and also avoiding all undue conflicts of interest. The only gain that liquidators can make from their office is whatever remuneration has been authorised; they have no right to retain any other profit that fell to them in the course of their duties. In the words of one judge, '[t]here is between . . . liquidators on the one side

46. *Re Hibernian Transport Ltd* (Supreme Court, 13 May 1993).
47. S.6(2).   48. Id. s.9(7).   49. Id. s.7.
50. Value Added Tax Act 1972, s.3(5).
51. See generally, P. Finn, *Fiduciary Obligations* (1977).

and the shareholders or creditors of the company on the other a fiduciary relationship which prevents the liquidators making a profit out of their trust [and] prohibit[s] any arrangement by which a liquidator may receive extra remuneration to that allowed by the Act and Rules.'[52] Rule 38 of the Winding Up Rules proscribes a particular form of profiteering by liquidators, viz. to 'accept from or arrange to accept from any solicitor, or auctioneer or other person connected with the company any gift, gratuity, remuneration, emolument, or pecuniary or other consideration or benefit whatever in addition to' the properly fixed remuneration. The general principle against trustees (liquidators) buying trust (company) property and selling their own property to the trust (company)[53] is reflected in Rules 39 and 40 of the Winding Up Rules. A liquidator may not 'either directly or indirectly, by himself or any employer, partner, clerk, agent or servant, become purchaser of any part of the company's assets.' And no liquidator who carries on the company's business may 'purchase goods for the carrying on of such business from any person whose connection with him is of such nature as would result in his obtaining any portion of the profit (if any) arising out of the transaction.' However, the court may give its consent to a transaction that falls within either of these two rules. Breach of fiduciary duty can result in the liquidator being deprived of his remuneration and indeed of him having to compensate the victim of the breach.

Being officers of the court, official liquidators are subject to what is often referred to as the 'rule in *Ex p. James*',[54] which also applies to the Official Assignee in bankruptcy.[55] Under this, circumstances can arise where they are bound to act in a particularly high-mined manner, beyond what the ordinary principles of equity might require. In those circumstances, 'where it would be unfair for [him] to take full advantage of his legal rights as such, the court will order him not to do so, and, indeed, will order him to return money which he may have collected.'[56]

LIABILITY OF LIQUIDATOR

Like all professionals doing a job, liquidators run a risk of being held liable in damages for errors they make in carrying out their duties, as well as for more serious wrong-doing.

Contracts Unless they agree to assume such liability, liquidators are not personally liable on contracts they make in the course of the winding up. Whether the contract is made in the name of the company or of the liquidator, he is not bound by it, absent his consent to be so bound.[57]

---

52. *Re R. Gertzenstein Ltd* [1937] 1 Ch 117, at p. 117.
53. *Silkstone & Haigh Moor Coal Co. v Edey* [1900] 1 Ch 167.
54. *Re Condon, ex p. James* (1874) 9 Ch App 609.
55. See *Bankruptcy Law*, pp. 73-74.
56. *Re Clark* [1975] 1 WLR 559, at p. 563. Cf. *Re Wyvern Developments Ltd* [1974] 1 WLR 1097 and *Re T.H. Knitwear Ltd* [1987] 1 WLR 371.
57. *Stead Hazel Co. v Cooper* [1933] 1 KB 840.

Tort and misfeasance Liquidators who intermeddle with other persons' property, such as selling chattels which are subject to retention of title, may be liable for trespass or conversion; intermeddling with trust property may in the circumstances render them liable as constructive trustees.[58] Liquidators are also subject to the same general duty of care, to avoid foreseeable loss, as are all others who are involved in a company's affairs. The breach by liquidators of several of the obligations imposed by the Companies Acts are at times characterised as actionable breaches of statutory duty, such as the duty to ascertain who a company's creditors are and to pay what is owing to them.[59]

Liquidators must exercise a reasonably high degree of care and skill,[60] and complete their task within a reasonable time.[61] Like company directors, liquidators are not in the position of insurers in that they will not be held liable for each and every error of judgment.[62] It has never been established that liquidators owe a direct duty of care to the company's creditors or shareholders but the usual mechanism for holding liquidators responsible for negligence is the misfeasance procedure under s.298 of the 1963 Act,[63] which can be initiated by any creditor or member. Although the courts usually will not hold company directors liable for mere negligence in proceedings brought under this section (generally brought by liquidators), on the grounds that misfeasance as defined there requires at least mala fides or breach of trust, it would seem that liquidators can be held liable under s.298 for serious negligence even though their actions did not have the other connotations. A possible explanation for this may be that there would seem to be no other way of proceeding against negligent liquidators—except applying to disallow them their costs, expenses and remuneration on account of their having been so careless, or applying to have them removed from the office.

Because they are paid for doing their job, often quite handsomely, and because their remuneration is virtually guaranteed, the courts have subjected professional liquidators to a stringent standard of care. Thus in *Re Home & Colonial Insurance Co.*,[64] the liquidator was found liable for having admitted to proof and paying a debt which, in law, could not have been enforced against the company. There, the court rejected the view that 'the liquidator is a mere agent liable only if negligence of a gross kind is established'; on the other hand it would not hold that 'a voluntary liquidator is personally liable if, notwithstanding every care on his part he admits a proof which is ill founded.'[65] Maugham J, would

> not ... accept the view that the liquidator in the matter of admitting proofs is practically in the same position as an insurer so that, in any event, and

58. Cf. *Competitive Insurance Co. Ltd v Davies Investments Ltd* [1975] 3 All ER 254.
59. E.g. *Pulsford v Devenish* [1903] 2 Ch. 625, infra p. 221.
60. *Re Windsor Steam Coal Co.* (1901) Ltd [1929] 1 Ch 151.
61. *Re House Property & Investment Co.* [1954] Ch 576.
62. *Re Home & Colonial Ins. Co.* [1930] 1 Ch 102, at pp. 124-125.
63. See post pp. 253-258.
64. [1930] 1 Ch 102.   65. Id. at pp. 125 and 124.

under all circumstances, he is liable if a debt is subsequently shown to have been wrongly admitted. On the other hand . . . there can be no doubt that, in the circumstances of the case, a high standard of care and diligence is required from a liquidator in a voluntary winding up. He is of course paid for his services; he is able to obtain wherever it is expedient the assistance of solicitors and counsel; . . . he is entitled, in every case of serious doubt or difficulty in relation to the performance of his statutory duties, to submit the matter to the court, and to obtain its guidance.[66]

The debt in question in the *Home & Colonial* case was a very large claim under a policy of marine insurance. But the policy there was not valid because it did not set out in writing certain particulars which were required for stamping purposes.[67] The liquidator was a chartered accountant and was not aware of this legal flaw in the claim. Indeed, the liquidator had suggested to the creditor there that the compromise they were negotiating should be sanctioned by the court but the creditor's response was that sanction was not necessary and, consequently, the liquidator did not pursue the matter further. At that stage, there was no suggestion that the claim might be invalid. In all the circumstances, it was held that the liquidator had been negligent. Because he was being paid, because he could have referred the entire matter to the court for a ruling on it and, especially, because of the magnitude of the claim, Maugham J found that 'it was the duty of the liquidator carefully to investigate the validity of the proof put in. . . . This duty he did not discharge and . . . he can[not] fully escape liability by pointing out that other persons—the contributories, the creditors, his solicitors and other persons with whom he came into contact during the liquidation—failed to give him a warning. He chose to navigate in these narrow seas, to him unaccustomed and unknown, without either chart or pilot; and for this temerarious conduct he must bear the responsibility.'[68] However, since the company was solvent, any damages the liquidator paid would enure to the benefit of the shareholders and, since it would seem that most of the shareholders there felt that the liquidator should not have to pay compensation in the circumstances, the judge exercised the discretion he has in misfeasance proceedings and held that the liquidator should not be required to pay any damages.

As well as being personally responsible for paying claims that should not have been paid, liquidators also have been held responsible in circumstances for not paying debts which ought to have been paid. Thus, in *Pulsford v Devenish*[69] the liquidator agreed to sell the company's entire undertaking to another company and he then proceeded to dissolve the company. The consideration paid was shares in the transferee company and those were distributed to the transferor's shareholders. But the liquidator did not advertise sufficiently for creditors to put in their claims and took no other steps to see who they were

66. Id. at p. 125.
67. Marine Insurance Act 1906.
68. [1930] 1 Ch at p. 126.
69. [1903] 2 Ch. 625.

or that they get paid. He was held to be in breach of his duty under the Companies Act, 'not merely to advertise for creditors, but to write to the creditors of whose existence he knows, and who do not send in claims, and ask them if they have any claim. . . .'[70]

---

70. Id. at p. 631. Similarly, *Re Armstrong, Whitworth Securities Co.* [1947] 1 Ch 673.

17

Asset-swelling Measures

One of the liquidator's principal powers and duties is to 'cause the assets of the company to be collected. . . .'[1] Before all the creditors can be paid off, in full or in part, and before any surplus as may exist can be distributed, it is necessary to get in all the company's property. Getting in that property in this context includes bringing proceedings to defeat improper transfers of company property and also against persons, often directors, who have done wrong to the company. Where the company is insolvent, certain transactions in company property that took place prior to the winding up commencing will be defeated by special statutory provisions regarding voidable dispositions, recent floating charges and fraudulent preferences. The objective underlying the various rules and principles discussed here is to augment as much as possible the company's assets for division among its creditors and distribution to its members. Some of these procedures have already been considered above, most notably voiding transactions in the company's assets after the winding up commenced[2] and the extremely useful power of liquidators to examine on oath persons who had dealings with the company or its property,[3] often with a view to then commencing proceedings.

As was explained earlier, although s.284(1) of the 1963 Act applies, by analogy, several rules of bankruptcy law to winding up insolvent companies, what may be termed the Bankruptcy Act's 'asset-swelling' rules are not rendered applicable in this way. In *Re Irish Attested Sales Ltd*[4] Kenny J observed that s.284(1)

> does not import into the . . . winding up of companies the bankruptcy rules which have the effect of increasing the assets of a person adjudged bankrupt which are available for his creditors. . . . The basis in principle for the exclusion of these sections in the Bankruptcy Acts is that the Companies Acts have, since 1862, contained provisions dealing with these matters and it could not, therefore, have been the intention of the Legislature that the provisions of the Companies Acts and of the Bankruptcy Acts should apply to the winding up of a company.[5]

Unlike the position in some countries, the Companies Acts do not contain a

---

1. [1963] Act s.235(1).
2. See ante p. 176.
3. See ante pp. 199-206.
4. [1962] IR 70.
5. Id. at p. 73.

general provision which applies to companies all the 'asset swelling' devices in the bankruptcy law. Instead, the Companies Acts lay down several procedures which are almost identical to those in bankruptcy law.

AVAILABLE ASSETS

All property belonging to the company at the commencement of the winding up constitutes its available assets. Whether a company owns a particular item of property depends on the general law of ownership—of land, of chattels and of choses in action—which is outside the scope of this book. There is no definition in the Companies Acts for the terms 'property' or 'assets' in this context. It has been said that the word 'property' here means all property, rights and powers of any description;[6] as well as obvious items of tangible property, the term includes goodwill,[7] rights of action for compensation or damages[8] and unpaid calls on shares.[9] Excluded is property held in trust and property which is properly mortgaged or charged, and non-assignable rights under contracts, for instance, contracts of employment and probably contracts for services.[10]

DISCLAIMER OF ONEROUS PROPERTY AND CONTRACTS

It frequently happens that the company's assets include property and certain obligations which are a substantial drain on its resources. For example, they may include leasehold property held at a relatively high rental which is no longer really needed but which, because of the rental and repairing and other obligations, cannot be sold. In such cases, continuance of the onerous obligations seriously deplete the company's net assets. Section 290 of the 1963 Act applies the bankruptcy rule about disclaiming onerous obligations[11] to companies in liquidation, whether or not they are insolvent. It was in 1929 in Britain[12] that this rule was first made applicable to companies being wound up; in bankruptcy it went back to 1872.[13] No amendments were made to s.290 in the 1990 reforms. Many of the decisions on this topic are bankruptcy law cases.[14]

A major objective of disclaimer is simply to enable the liquidator to realise and dispose of the company's assets without needlessly protracting the winding up. Indeed, one way of viewing disclaimer is as an aspect of the liquidator's duty to discharge the company's debts. Within 12 months of the winding up commencing and with the court's consent, the liquidator may in a sense

6. *Noakes v Doncaster Amalg. Collieries Ltd* [1940] AC 1014.
7. *Re Leas Hotel Co.* [1902] 1 Ch 332.
8. *Re Cyona Distributors Ltd* [1966] 2 WLR 761, overruled [1967] Ch 889.
9. *Webb v Whiffin* (1872) LR 5 HL 711.
10. Supra n.6.
11. Bankruptcy Act 1988, s.56(1).
12. Companies Act 1929, s.267.
13. Bankruptcy (Ireland) Amendment Act 1872, s.97.
14. See *Bankruptcy Law*, pp. 106-110.

discriminate against particular creditors by disclaiming the company's obligations to them, on the grounds that performance would be unduly burdensome for the company. The court is empowered to make appropriate orders to give effect to the disclaimer. However, those persons to whom the company owed the disclaimed obligations need not shoulder the entire cost of thereby benefiting the general creditors; any person damaged by the disclaimer is deemed to be a creditor for the amount of that loss and may prove it as a debt in the winding up.

What can be disclaimed The property and interests which are capable of being disclaimed are defined in s.290(1) of the 1963 Act as

> land of any tenure burdened with onerous covenants, of shares or stock in companies, of unprofitable contracts, or any other property which is unsaleable or not readily saleable by reason of its binding the possessor thereof to the performance of any onerous act or to the payment of any sum of money.

Thus, a very extensive range of matters can be disclaimed in appropriate circumstances, leases being the commonest subject matter.[15] Another is shares which are not fully paid up.[16] Another still is a contract to continue works in a mine that do not appear to have any immediate benefit.[17] Provided that the proprietary interest is 'onerous' or the contract is 'unprofitable', it is inherently disclaimable. Even freehold property burdened by obligations can be disclaimed, the classic instance being where a company in liquidation owned a cemetery in respect of which there were expensive duties regarding the upkeep of the graves and the like.[18] It would seem that the covenant in the property may even be an affirmative one,[19] as contrasted with an obligation to refrain from making certain uses of the property.

In *Re Potters Oils Ltd*,[20] it was held that chattels could not be disclaimed simply because they are onerous in a general sense. The company there owned 46,000 gallons of chlorinated waste oil, which was worthless and would cost the liquidator over £14,000 to remove. Because the oil was potentially hazardous, the liquidator contended that the company was thereby obliged to keep it safe, which meant performing onerous acts. But there was no evidence before the court that, if the company remained owner of the oil, it would incur some present liability in respect of it. Accordingly, s.290 did not authorise disclaimer of this asset.

The entire of the property or contract must be disclaimed; a liquidator will not be allowed to disclaim part only and keep the remainder.[21] However, where

---

15. E.g. *Grant v Aston Ltd*, 103 ILTR 39 (1969).
16. E.g. *Re Hallett* (1894) 1 Mans 380.
17. E.g. *Re Grundy* (1829) Mont & M 231.
18. *Re Nottingham General Cemetery Co.* [1955] Ch 683; see ante p. 175.
19. *Re Mercer & Moore* (1880) 14 Ch D 287.
20. [1985] BCLC 203.   21. *Re Fussell* (1882) 20 Ch D 321.

the company has contracted to purchase land and has also entered into a sub-contract to sell that land, with a building to be erected on it, the subcontract can be disclaimed without also disclaiming the contract.[22]

Effects of disclaimer Before dealing with matters which influence the court's discretion to permit disclaimer, the effects of disclaimer should be considered with regard to the position of the other contracting party and that of third parties who are not directly involved in the insolvency. The position is set out in s.290(3) of the 1963 Act. As regards the company and its property, disclaimer will

> operate to determine, as from the date of disclaimer, the rights, interests and liabilities of the company and [its] property in or in respect of the property disclaimed. . . .

Thus, as well as being absolved from all future liabilities[23] arising from the property or contract in question, the company will have no further rights regarding them. For instance, rent does not have to be paid, calls do not have to be paid, guarantees the company gave do not have to be honoured. As Lindley LJ explained, dealing with 'the simple case of a lease . . . and the lessee becomes bankrupt, the disclaimer determines his interest in the lease. . . . He gets rid of all of his liabilities, and he loses all his rights by virtue of the disclaimer.'[24] Failure by a liquidator to disclaim a particular contract does not render him personally liable on it.[25]

Third parties A major source of difficulty in the cases has been the effects of disclaimer on third parties, i.e. on persons other than the immediate parties to the lease, contract or whatever was disclaimed. Sub-section (3), which deals with the effects generally, concludes by stipulating that disclaimer

> shall not, except so far as is necessary for the purpose of releasing the company and the property of the company from liability, affect the rights or liabilities of any other person.

In other words, third parties' entitlements and obligations must not be adversely affected except were so affecting them is essential in order to realise the insolvent estate. Where impinging on their position is necessary to dispose of the property, they can prove as unsecured creditors for the amount of their loss. But in heavily insolvent bankruptcies, that redress is of little value to them. They also can apply for a vesting order or for an order delivering to them the property disclaimed.

Most of the cases dealing with the impact of disclaimer on third parties have concerned leases, the third party being, for instance, the sub-lessee or the

22. *Re Gough* (1927) 90 LJ Ch 239.
23. Cf. *Re No. 1 London Ltd* [1991] BCLC 501.
24. *Re Finley* (1888) 21 QBD 475, at p. 485.
25. *Stead Hazel & Co. v Cooper* [1933] 1 KB 840.

mortgagee of the lease. Where the bankrupt is the assignee of the lease, disclaimer does not exonerate the original lessee's liability to the landlord for future rent.[26] Where the assignor of the lease became bankrupt, i.e. where he is the sub-lessor, disclaimer will extinguish his rights and liabilities *vis-à-vis* his lessor;[27] but the sub-lessee in turn can apply for an order vesting the head lease in him on terms of his assuming the covenants and conditions in the original lease. Special works on landlord and tenant law should be consulted for treatment of the entire spectrum of issues which arise when it is sought to disclaim a lease or where a lease has been disclaimed.[28]

There was some conflict of authority regarding the position of the guarantor of covenants in a lease until the matter was resolved by Keane J in *Re Farm Machinery Distributors Ltd.*[29] It was decided in 1882 in England[30] that the surety remains liable. There, the assignee of a lease went bankrupt and his trustee disclaimed the lease. Having then paid rent to the lessor, the original lessee claimed reimbursement from a person who had covenanted with him to be surety for the rent for the remainder of the term. The surety was held liable to the original lessee who, despite the disclaimer, was liable for the rent. However, it was held in England in 1900 in a bankruptcy case[31] and thirty years later in a company case[32] that, where the disclaimer absolves the lessee from liability, the lessee's surety also becomes released from liability, on the grounds that once the primary obligation is extinguished there remains nothing to guarantee.[33] In the *Farm Machinery* case Keane J declined to follow those two decisions because they departed from the principles in the earlier authorities and did not take account of the statutory requirement that third parties shall be prejudiced by a disclaimer only where that is necessary. Although the legislation under which the English cases were decided contained a similar requirement, the Court of Appeal there nevertheless concluded that disclaimer discharges a guarantee on account of the surety's right of indemnity. As A.L. Smith MR explained, '[i]f the surety is liable to pay rent *in futuro* on his guarantee, he would be entitled to indemnity against the bankrupt or his property. It is therefore necessary in order to release the bankrupt and his property from liability under the lease subsequently to the disclaimer that' the surety's liability be determined.[34] An answer to this point in a liquidation case is that, unlike a bankrupt, when the winding up is concluded the company will not be anticipating a full discharge and rehabilitation in the commercial world.

---

26. *Hill v East & West India Cock Co.* (1884) 9 HLC 448 and *Warnford Investments Ltd v Duckworth* [1979] 1 Ch 127.
27. *O'Farrell v Stephenson* (1879) 4 LR Ir 151.
28. E.g. P. McLoughlin, *Commercial Leases and Insolvency* (1992) Ch. 6.
29. [1984] ILRM 273.   30. *Harding v Preece* (1882) 9 QB D 281.
31. *Stacey v Hill* [1901] 1 QB 660.
32. *Re Katherine et Cie* [1932] 1 Ch 70.
33. See generally, J. O'Donovan & J.C. Phillips, *The Modern Contract of Guarantee* (1985) pp. 253-255.
34. *Stacey v Hill* [1901] 1 QB at p. 664.

Bona vacantia   Freehold property which is disclaimed will vest in the State as *bona vacantia*[35] unless the court orders that it should vest in someone else. However, s.31 of the State Property Act, 1954, authorises the Minister for Finance to waive, in whole or in part, and on such terms as he thinks proper, any right acquired by the State in this manner. Section 32 of that Act authorises the Minister to disclaim a lessee's interest under a lease which devolved to the State by way of *bona vacantia*.

Compensating adverse effects   It does not follow that the other party to the contract, such as the lessor, the company making the calls, the primary creditor whose entitlements have been guaranteed by the insolvent, must bear the entire cost of the burden being lifted from the company's shoulders. For s.290(9) of the 1963 Act provides that they, or any other 'person damaged' in consequence of the disclaimer, can prove as a creditor in the winding up for the amount of such loss or damage. Where that person's loss is contingent then a valuation must be placed on the loss. In *Re Ranks Ireland Ltd*,[36] the matter to be determined was the measure of damages payable to a party whose contract was being disclaimed. The contracts there were equipment leases and one of the terms was that, in the event of their being repudiated, a stipulated sum shall become payable as damages. Murphy J. held that this was not the proper measure of compensation in these circumstances. That measure was the difference between the rent which the company would have paid the lessor and the rent that the lessor is likely to earn during the unexpired residue of the leases.

Vesting order   Another form of compensation or redress is the court ordering, under s.290(7) of the 1963 Act, that the disclaimed property shall vest in or be delivered to the applicant. A vesting order can be made in favour of any person claiming an interest in the disclaimed property or who is under a liability in respect of that property which was not discharged by the disclaimer.[37] The court is given a wide discretion, which operates to vest the title to the property without the need for any conveyance or transfer. Generally, the court will give a duly qualified applicant a vesting order and, where there are competing applicants, to the one with a prior right of possession.[38] A matter which has interested the courts in recent years is the circumstances in which vesting orders should be made in favour of mortgagees of the disclaimed property.[39] Section 290(8) contains special provisions for making vesting orders in connection with leasehold property.[40]

---

35. State Property Act 1954, s.28; cf. *Re Mercer & Moore* (1880) 14 Ch D 247.
36. [1989] IR 1.
37. Cf. *Re No. 1 London Ltd* [1991] BCLC 501.
38. *Re Finley* (1888) 21 QBD 475.
39. E.g. *Re David James & Co.* [1991] NZLR 219 and *Rural Banking etc. Ltd v Official Assignee* [1991] 2 NZLR 351.
40. For background to this, see *Re A.E. Realisations (1985) Ltd* [1988] 1 WLR 200.

Procedure   Disclaimer requires the leave of the court and the liquidator has 12 months in which to apply for leave.[41] In the case of property or contracts that did not come to his notice until more than a month had elapsed from the date of the liquidation, the 12 months period runs from when he became aware of them, and that period may be extended by the court in an appropriate case.[42] If the liquidator does not take the initiative, other persons interested in the property or contract can compel him to make up his mind and, if then he elects not to disclaim, he is thenceforth prevented from doing so.[43] For this purpose, an application in writing must have been made to him and he has 28 days, or such further period as the court may allow, to decide on the matter. If by that time he has not disclaimed a contract, he is deemed to have adopted it. Indeed a party to a contract with the company or, more exactly, a person 'entitled to the benefit or subject to the burden' of such contract, can apply directly to the court for an order to have it rescinded.[44]

Before giving leave to disclaim, the court will usually require that any other 'persons interested' in the matter be duly notified so that they can appear in the proceedings. In deciding to give leave, the test is 'the balance of the advantages and disadvantages of the disclaimer to be gained' by the estate and by the persons who would be affected by disclaiming.[45] It is for the applicant to satisfy the court that the balance of advantages lies with disclaimer.[46] Thus in England and Northern Ireland, where (unlike here) disclaimer of a lease releases the guarantor of covenants in the lease, leave has been refused where the loss to the lessor of his guarantee far outweighs the benefits to the estate.[47]

The court is not expressly authorised to attach conditions to the disclaimer but, since it has a general discretion in such cases, its inherent jurisdiction includes imposing conditions. But when it orders that a contract shall be rescinded, it is empowered to impose terms as to payment of damages for non-performance.[48]

RECOVERY OF ASSETS WRONGLY DISPOSED OF

Section 139 of the 1990 Act facilitates recovery of company property which had been disposed of in any way that defrauded the company, its creditors or its members. Any creditor or contributory of the company or the liquidator can apply and, if they satisfy the court that the property was disposed of in that manner, the court is empowered to order its repayment or recovery. That order can be made against any person who appears to have the use, control or possession of such property or of the proceeds from its sale or any development of the property. In deciding to make any order of this nature, account must be taken of the interests of any bona fide purchaser for value of the property. Mention has already been made of purported disposition of the company's

41. 1963 Act s.290(1).
42. Id. s.290(2).
43. Id. s.290(5).
44. Id. s.290(6).
45. *Re Madeley Homecare Ltd* [1983] NI 1.
46. Ibid.
47. Ibid.
48. 1963 Act s.290(6).

assets which are invalid because they were made following the commencement of the liquidation.[49]

FRAUDULENT CONVEYANCE

For hundreds of years it has been a principle of bankruptcy law that where, with the object of defeating his creditors, a debtor who shortly afterwards becomes bankrupt transferred his property to a third party, the courts can intervene and set aside that transfer.[50] In England this principle was incorporated into what is commonly known as the Statute of Elizabeth I;[51] the equivalent measure in Ireland is the Fraudulent Conveyances Act, 1634, which is entitled 'An Act against covenous and fraudulent conveyances'.[52] Section 10 of the 1634 Act provides that:

> for the avoiding and abolition of fained, covenous and fraudulent feoff-ments, gifts, grants, alienations, conveyances . . . as well of lands and tenements, as of goods and chattels . . ., which . . . are devised and contrived of malice, fraud... to the end, purpose and intent to deal, hinder or defraud creditors and others of their just and lawful actions, suits, debts, accounts, damages, . . . and reliefs; Be it therefore . . . enacted . . . that all and every feoffment, gift, grant, alienation, bargain and conveyance . . . for any intent or purpose before declared and expressed, shall be from henceforth deemed and taken only as against that person [so prejudiced] to be clearly and utterly void, and of no effect. . . .

Whether s.10 of the Act of 1634 applies to transactions entered into by insolvent companies does not seem to have been the subject of sustained legal argument and a plausible case could be made that it does not so apply. In England[53] and in New Zealand[54] more recent versions of that Act are assumed to apply to liquidations. Murphy J in *Re Kill Inn Motel Ltd*[55] held that the 1634 Act so applies, remarking that 'this is the first occasion in which I have ever heard of [this] Act being invoked in the case of a corporate body but I see no reason why it should not be done.' Counsel for the defence, in this case, does not seem to have argued that the Act does not apply to insolvent companies, which, therefore, leaves the matter in some doubt. This is compounded by the fact that Murphy J in the *Kill Inn* case also based his judgment on the fact that the conveyance being challenged there was in any event a gift by the company and accordingly *ultra vires*. The argument could be made that only those rules of bankruptcy law which are expressly rendered applicable to company insol-

---

49. See ante p. 176.
50. See generally, H.W. May, *The Law of Fraudulent and Voluntary Conveyances* (3rd ed., 1908), D.L. McDonnell & J.G. Monroe eds., *Kerr on the Law of Fraud and Mistake* (7th ed., 1952) and Langstaff, 'The Cheat's Charter', 91 *LQR* 86 (1975).
51. 13 Eliz. c.5.   52. 10 Car. I, sess. II, c. 3.
53. *Re Shilema Hosiery Co. Ltd* [1980] Ch 219.
54. *Re Green's Grocery Stores Ltd v Morris* [1928] 8 LR 334.
55. *Ex tempore* 16 Sept. 1987, summarised in [1987] *Ir Tax Rev* 404.

vencies apply; since this Act is not one of those rules it, therefore, does not apply. That the 1963 Act specifically applies to companies the bankruptcy rule regarding fraudulent preferences lends some support to this view. The counter-argument would say that the 1634 Act is not a bankruptcy provision as such. There also is the forceful point made by Murphy J, that while 'it is true that when this early Irish Act was passed there was no such thing as a commercial company but the principles to which it applies, which it was created, were in fact merely declaratory of the common law . . .'. In 1983 the Scots Outer House came to a similar conclusion.[56]

General The power to set aside a transfer of property on the grounds of fraud under the 1634 Act is not an exclusively bankruptcy or liquidation jurisdiction; the courts can just as easily set aside a transaction in non-insolvency proceedings. Also, it is not essential that the transferor of the property be insolvent, although fraudulent intent will more readily be inferred where he was insolvent at the relevant time. Section 10 of the 1634 Act applies to transfers of all kinds of property; it is not confined to land or interests in land, although the bulk of the cases on its interpretation relate to conveyances of land. Thus, an assignment of an insurance policy[57] and even a payment of money[58] have been held to be 'conveyances' for these purposes. Moreover, s.10 applies to all types of transfers; it is not confined to conveyances by deed or even to written instruments of transfer. Thus, a transfer of goods or chattels by delivery[59] or even the payment over of cash[60] are potentially impeachable as fraudulent. So too is permitting a charge on property to merge.[61]

Fraud for these purposes has a more extensive connotation than for the tort of deceit. As has been pointed out, 'in every case under this section the debtor has done something which in law he has power and is entitled to do; otherwise it would never reach the section. If he disposes of an asset which would be available to his creditors with the intention of prejudicing them by putting it (or its worth) beyond their reach, he is in the ordinary case acting in a fashion not honest in the context of the relationship of debtor and creditor. And in cases of voluntary dispositions that intention may be inferred.'[62] On a number of occasions it has been observed that s.10 should be given a liberal construction and that transactions that offend against the spirit or intent of the section should be set aside.[63] Nevertheless, in determining whether a transfer of property was indeed fraudulent the burden of proof lies on the party alleging fraud.

Perhaps the most exhaustive exposition on the thrust of s.10 by an Irish judge

56. *Johnstone v Peter Irvine Ltd* (1984) SLT 209.
57. E.g. *Rose v Greer* [1945] IR 503.
58. E.g. *Re Moroney*, 21. LR Ir Ch 27(1887).
59. E.g. *Re Eicholz* [1959] Ch 708
60. Supra n.8.
61. *Re Godley's Estate* [1896] 1 IR 45.
62. *Lloyds Bank v Marcan* [1973] 3 All ER 754, at p. 759.
63. *Cadogan v Kennett*, 98 Eng Rep 1171 (1776) at p. 1172.

is Palles CB's observations in *Re Moroney*.[64] In that case, in accordance with the Land League's 'Plan of Campaign', agricultural tenants would not pay rent to their landlord but instead paid over to Land League trustees what they deemed to be a reasonable rent for their farms. Around the time Mr Moroney's rent of £85 fell due, he sold cattle for £117 and then paid £25.10 to his local trustees, which represented his rent as abated in accordance with the Land League's formula. If this payment contravened s.10 and he was insolvent at the time, he would have committed an act of bankruptcy. What the Chief Baron had to say of the section was as follows:

> to bring a conveyance within the statute, first, it must be fraudulent; secondly, the class of fraud must be an intent to delay, hinder, or defraud creditors. Whether a particular conveyance be within this description may depend upon an infinite variety of circumstances and considerations. One conveyance, for instance, may be executed with the express intent and object in the mind of the party to defeat and delay his creditors, and from such an intent the law presumes the conveyance to be fraudulent, and does not require or allow such fraud to be deduced as an inference of fact. In other cases, no such intention actually exists in the mind of the grantor, but the necessary or probable result of his denuding himself of the property included in the conveyance, for the consideration, and under the circumstances actually existing, is to defeat or delay creditors, and in such a case . . . the intent is, as matter of law, assumed from the necessary or probable consequences of the act done; and in this case, also, the conveyance, in point of law, and without any inference of fact being drawn, is fraudulent within the statute. In every case, however, no matter what its nature, before the conveyance can be avoided, fraud, whether expressly proved as a fact, or as an inference of law from other facts proved, must exist. What, then, is the nature of this fraud which will avoid a conveyance? The object of the statute was to protect the rights of creditors, as against the property of their debtor. It was no part of its object to regulate the rights of creditors *inter se*, or to entitle them to an equal distribution of that property. One right, however, of the creditors taking them as a whole, was that all the property of the debtor should be applied in payment of the demands of them, or some of them, without any portion of it being parted with without consideration, or reserved or retained by the debtor to their prejudice.[65]

There are two main types of case; one involves voluntary transfers of property, the other transfers for consideration. For obvious reasons, courts more readily strike down voluntary transfers. Where the consideration is natural love and affection, the transfer is deemed voluntary for these purposes.

---

64.   21 LR Ir Ch 27 (1887).
65.   Id. at pp. 61-62.

Voluntary transfers On numerous occasions it has been said that 'a man must be honest before he is generous'.[66] Where a debtor disposes of property for no consideration, the courts readily presume a fraudulent intent where, at the time or in consequence of the disposition, the debtor was insolvent.[67] Thus in *Re Moroney*, the Court of Appeal showed little hesitancy in holding that the insolvent tenant's paying £25.10 to the Plan of Campaign trustees was a fraudulent conveyance; the fact that the payment was made to defeat one particular creditor did not save the transaction from being declared invalid. But there can be circumstances where the courts will not draw that inference.[68] In *Graham v O'Keeffe*[69] the governing principle was stated as follows:

> With respect to voluntary settlements, the result of the authorities is, that the mere fact of a settlement being voluntary is not enough to render it void against creditors; but there must be unpaid debts which were existing at the time of making the settlement; and the settlor must at the time not have been necessarily insolvent, but so largely indebted as to induce the court to believe that the intention of the settlement, taking the whole transaction together, was to defraud the persons who, at the time of making the settlement, were creditors of the settlor. The mere fact of a man making a voluntary settlement, and thereby parting with a large portion of his property, has never been held to make such a settlement fraudulent against subsequent creditors.[70]

Unless a fraudulent intent is proved, subsequent creditors will never succeed in impeaching a voluntary transfer where, at the time, the transferor was not insolvent. As Holmes J put in *Re Kelleher*, 'once the creditors' debts that existed at the date of the deed were discharged, this later creditor cannot take advantage of what might have been relied on by the previous creditors as an implied fraud on them.'[71]

Transfers for valuable consideration Even though valuable consideration is paid, the transfer may still be voided under s.10 of the 1634 Act. To do so, it must be shown that the transferee was privy to the intention to delay or defeat the transferor's creditors. Section 14 of the 1634 Act provides that, even where the transferor was intending to defeat, hinder or delay his creditors, the transfer will be upheld where it was made 'upon good consideration and bona fide' to a person not having knowledge of the transferor's objective. While the

---

66. *Smith v Tatton* (1879) 6 LR Ir 32, at p. 41.
67. E.g. *Murphy v Abraham* (1863) 15 Ir Ch 371 and *Freeman v Pope* (1870) 5 Ch App 538.
68. E.g. *Graham v O'Keefe* (1864) Ir Ch Rep 1 and *Ex. p. Mercer* (1886) 17 QBD 290.
69. (1864) Ir. Ch Rep 1.
70. Id. at p. 17, quoting Wood V.C. in *Holmes v Penny* (1856) 3 K & J 96.
71. [1911] 2 IR 1, at p. 9.

transaction may well be an act of bankruptcy on the transferor's part, the bona fide transferee for value and without notice cannot be deprived of the property. For instance, in *Bryce v Fleming*[72] the plaintiff got a judgment against the defendant, who owned land, and the judgment was registered. Three days later, the defendant sold his land to the second defendant. Some weeks later the sheriff arrived at the farm to levy execution but was obliged to return *nulla bona*. The plaintiff then sought, unsuccessfully, to impeach the sale as a fraudulent conveyance. According to Meredith J,

> If a man has lands, and can only pay his debts by selling his lands, the honest thing for him to do is to sell them. It is also the prudent thing to do; for if he sells them himself he will probably get a better price, and avoid unnecessary costs. Consequently, the mere fact that a man in such a position is selling his land is no evidence whatever that his intention is to defeat his creditors rather than to obtain the wherewithal to pay his debts. . . . [Moreover] where there is a bona fide purchase for valuable consideration the transaction cannot be impeached . . . unless the purchaser is shown to have been privy to the vendor's intention.[73]

There are certain circumstances where the court will readily presume fraud, which are commonly referred to as the 'badges of fraud'. In the famous *Twyne's* case,[74] the first leading case on this Act, the court itemised several of these indicia of fraudulent intent:

> 1st. That this gift had the signs and marks of fraud, because the gift is general, without exception . . .; for it is commonly said, *quod dolus versatur in generalibus*,
> 2nd. The donor continued in possession and used them as his own; and by reason thereof he traded and trafficked with others, and defrauded and deceived them.
> 3rd. It was made in secret, *et dona clandestina sunt semper suspiciosa*.
> 4th. It was made pending a writ.
> 5th. Here was a trust between the parties, for the donor possessed all, and used them as his proper goods and fraud is always apparelled and clad with a trust, and a trust is the cover of fraud.
> 6th. The deed contains, that the gift was made honestly, truly and bona fide; *et clausuloe inconsuet semper inductunt suspicionem*.

In the light of the subsequent cases, the following is a more complete list, i.e. the circumstances from which the courts tend as a rule to infer that there was a fraudulent intent.

Generality of the transfer   Where the debtor disposed of all or virtually all of his property. Entering into a deed of arrangement, within the terms of the 1887

---

72. [1930] IR 376.   73. Id. at pp. 380 and 383.
74. (1602) 3 Co. Rep. 80b.

Act, is an act of bankruptcy[75] but the assignment of property under such a deed would not be a fraudulent conveyance.[76]

Continuance in possession Where the transferor remains in possession of the property. Of course a mortgage of land is not necessarily fraudulent because it is the very essence of the transaction that the mortgagor remains in possession of the property.[77] And remaining in possession of goods and chattels is only *prima facie* evidence and not conclusive of fraud.

Pendente lite Where the property is disposed of just before a creditor is about to enforce judgment. But it has been held that a sale of property for sufficient consideration is not fraudulent even though the vendor's motive was to prevent execution being levied.[78]

Secrecy The secrecy of the transaction is closely related to the vendor continuing in possession.

Trust or reservation for grantor's benefit Palles CB has said that 'if the conveyance reserve, either expressly or by some collateral or secret arrangement, any interest, no matter how small, to the grantor, under such circumstances as to make it impossible or difficult to resort to it if the deed be binding, the conveyance would be a fraud within the statute, because by it that interest in the debtor would be reserved for him in preference to his creditors, and so withdrawn from the fund to which they were entitled to resort.'[79]

Power of revocation If the terms of the sale give the vendor a power to revoke the transaction, that is a badge of fraud.

False statements Another such badge is false statements in the instrument of transfer. Especially when it proclaims the honesty and bona fide nature of the transaction, the judge is bound to be suspicious.

Inadequate consideration When the consideration is inadequate then, as regards the deficiency, the transfer was voluntary. But in the circumstances the court may find that there was 'sufficient' consideration to save the transaction from invalidity;[80] there is no rule which requires the consideration to be adequate.[81]

Closely related parties Another matter which is bound to arouse suspicion is where the transferor and transferee are closely related, such as a close family relationship or closely connected companies. In such circumstances the courts

---

75. I.e. the Deeds of Arrangement Act 1887. Registered companies cannot make such arrangements: *Re Rileys Ltd* [1903] 2 Ch. 590.
76. Cf. *Re David & Adlard* [1914] 2 KB 694.
77. *Re Ryan* [1937] IR 367.
78. *Nolan v Neill*, 33 ILTR 129 (1899).
79. *Re Moroney*, 21 LR Ir Ch 27 (1887) at p. 64.
80. E.g. *Myers v Duke of Leinster* (1844) 7 IR Eg 146.
81. Cf. *Rose v Greer* [1945] IR 503.

may want to scrutinise the transaction carefully in order to be entirely satisfied of its bona fides.[82]

Fraudulent preference   A 'fraudulent preference', in the sense of paying one creditor or giving him security in preference over all the other creditors, is not itself a fraudulent transaction under the 1634 Act.[83] This Act was aimed at transfers intended to defeat, delay or hinder creditors, not at distributing the debtor's property *pari passu*. But such preferences may fall foul of s.57 of the Bankruptcy Act 1988. As Palles CB explained, in connection with giving security to a single creditor, 'security given by a debtor to one creditor, upon a portion or upon all his property although the effect of it, or even the intent of the debtor in making it may be to defeat an expected execution of another creditor, is not a fraud within the statute; because notwithstanding such an act, the entire of the property remains available for the creditors, or some or one of them, and as the [1634] statute gives no right to rateable distribution, the right of the creditors by such an act is not invaded or affected.'[84] Thus in *Re Ryan*,[85] where the bankrupt mortgaged his public house in order to raise the funds to pay a settlement on a personal injuries action which was brought against him, Johnston J rejected the contention that this 1634 Act applied 'where a debtor under pressure mortgages a portion of his property to secure a bona fide debt due to a single creditor, the debtor gaining nothing for himself out of the transaction.'[86] And in *Rose v Greer*,[87] where the debtor assigned a life insurance policy to secure an existing debt, Overend J held that there is no fraudulent intent where a debtor 'gives his creditor security with the intention of preferring him to other creditors or another creditor, and consequently defeating or delaying such other creditors or creditor. . . .'[88]

FRAUDULENT PREFERENCE

A bankruptcy law rule which is made directly applicable to company liquidations is that regarding what is termed fraudulent preference,[89] although the term fraud here is something of a misdescription. A more appropriate name might be improper or unfair preference. The Eleventh Schedule of the 1963 Act amended the old Bankruptcy Act's definition of fraudulent preference[90] and s.286 of the 1963 Act, as amended,[91] applies this bankruptcy rule to companies in liquidation. Many of the leading decisions on this topic are bankruptcy law cases.[92] In recent years the law regarding fraudulent preference has received

---

82. *Koop v Smith*, 25 DLR 355 (1915) and *Re O'Neill* [1989] IR 544.
83. *Re Sarflax Ltd* [1979] 1 Ch 592 and *Re Lloyds Furniture Palace Ltd* [1925] 1 Ch 853.
84. *Re Moroney*, 21 LR Ir Ch 27 (1887) at p. 62.
85. [1937] IR 367.   86. Id. at p. 374.
87. [1945] IR 503.   88. Id. at pp. 513-514.
89. See generally, Farrar, 'The Bankruptcy of the Law of Fraudulent Preference', [1983] *J Bus L* 390.
90. Bankruptcy (Ireland) (Amendment) Act 1872; now s.57 of the Bankruptcy Act 1988.
91. By 1990 Act s.135.   92. See *Bankruptcy Law*, pp. 121-129.

considerable criticism and has been amended significantly in many common law jurisdictions, with the emphasis being focused on objective preferential treatment as opposed to proving a subjective purpose of unfairly discriminating.[93] Section 58 of the Bankruptcy Act, 1988, was a move in this direction, striking at certain 'improvident dispositions', but it does not have an equivalent in the Companies Acts. All that the 1990 Act did by way of reform was to extend the relevant period and reverse the burden of proof for transactions with 'connected persons'.

The underlying principle is that it is 'unjust to permit a party, on the eve of bankruptcy, to make a voluntary disposition of his property in favour of a particular creditor, leaving the mere husk to the rest, and therefore, that a transfer made at such a period, and under such circumstances, as evidently showed that it was made in contemplation of bankruptcy and in order to favour a particular creditor, should be void.'[94] What s.286 of the 1963 Act renders void is every transfer and the like by a company of its property, occurring within *six months* of its being wound up, that was made

> in favour of any creditor . . . with a view to giving such creditor, or any surety or guarantor for the debt due to such creditor, a preference over the other creditors. . . .

Unlike the position under the 1634 Act, s.286 of the 1963 Act can only be invoked in insolvency proceedings in order to invalidate a transaction; it does not confer on the courts a general jurisdiction to strike down fraudulent preferences. A transfer of property which is fraudulent under s.286 is void only against the liquidator. But a person taking title 'in good faith and for valuable consideration', through or under a creditor, to property that was fraudulently conveyed is not expressly affected by this rule.[95]

For these purposes a compulsory liquidation is deemed to have commenced when the petition was presented.[96] Except for dealings with 'connected persons', transfers of property made more than six months before the liquidation are not affected by s.286. There is scant authority on determining whether a particular transaction took place inside or outside the six months period, although useful guidance can be derived from cases dealing with whether a company charge was created within a specified period for the purposes of s.99 of the 1963 Act.[97] Nor are post-liquidation transactions so affected, but usually those will be void dispositions under s.218 of the 1963 Act.[98]

Insolvency   In order for the transfer of property to be caught by this pro-

93. E.g. in Britain; see E. Bailey et al., *Corporate Insolvency—Law and Practice* (1992) pp. 363-372 and cf. *Re M.C. Bacon & Co.* [1990] BCLC 324.
94. *Ex. p. De Tastet v Carroll* (1813) 1 Stark. 88, at p. 89.
95. 1963 Act s.286(4).
96. *Re Port Supermarket Ltd* [1978] 1 NZLR 330, at p. 349.
97. See *Company Law*, pp. 512 et seq.
98. See ante p. 176.

hibition, the company must have been insolvent at the time the transfer was made, meaning that it was unable to pay its debts as they fell due. It matters not that the directors believed that the company was solvent, or that its financial position would shortly improve and it would not have to be wound up. The company's entire financial position must be taken into account in ascertaining whether it was insolvent, including the nature of its debts, the type of business it is carrying on and whether its assets are easily realisable.[1] A mere temporary liquidity crisis or an occasional dishonouring of cheques, which are shortly afterwards paid, will not suffice. When calculating the company's liabilities for this purpose, all liabilities which could be proved in its winding up must be taken into account.

Nature of transaction   Although most preferences falling within this section involve cash payments, transfers of any kind of property made with the prohibited intention are caught by s.286 of the 1963 Act. The term transaction may be a little misleading because what is avoided is not an instrument but the very preference itself, whatever form it may have taken. There is comparatively little authority on the kinds of property and the types of transfers that are caught by s.286. The term property is defined very extensively to include 'every description of property', including property located abroad and also obligations, easements and every description of interest in property.[2]

Those modes of transfer, which are capable of being caught by s.286, are set out as

> any conveyance, mortgage, delivery of goods, payment, execution or other act relating to property made or done by or against the company.
> ...[3]

It has been held that a company's not opposing an application to the court to extend the time for registering a charge it gave is suffering a judicial proceeding regarding its property and, therefore, comes within s.286.[4] However, certain acts can be done with regard to property which can involve the owner being divested of that property but without a disposition of any of the kind enumerated here taking place. An example is a set-off arising before the debtor was adjudicated a bankrupt or was wound up.[5] The reason why set-off is treated differently, and not as an 'obligation incurred', is that the Bankruptcy Act, 1988, expressly stipulates that all mutual obligations between a bankrupt and others should be set-off.[6]

---

1.   *Bank of Australasia v Hall*, 4 CLR 1514 (1907); see post p. 248 on insolvency for the purpose of s.288 of the 1963 Act, which invalidates certain floating charges.
2.   Bankruptcy Act 1988, s.3.
3.   1963 Act s.286(6)(1).
4.   *Peat v Gresham Trust Ltd* [1934] AC 252.
5.   *Re A Debtor* [1927] 1 Ch 410.
6.   Schedule to the 1988 Act par. 17(1); see post pp. 339-342.

It is the company itself which must have given the preference and not some third party. As Blayney J remarked in one instance, '[w]hat the section is concerned with is the bankrupt giving one of his creditors a preference over his other creditors. It is not concerned with someone other than the bankrupt paying off one of the bankrupt's creditors because such a person would have no obligation towards the other creditors. . . .'[7] Where a creditor holds money or property belonging to the company and, instead of returning it, pays itself out of those assets in respect of a debt by the company, the company is regarded as having given him a preference.[8]

The person preferred must have been a creditor of the company when the preference was made; he must be owed money by the company at that time. A contingent creditor, for instance a surety, is a creditor in this context.[9] If the company pays him far more than is actually owing, the entire payment can be contested under s.286 and not just the sum which was actually due.[10] What must not be preferentially diminished is past indebtedness and s.286 does not prohibit a company from entering into fresh transactions with a person merely because he is owed money by the company.

Scienter/'fraud' The term 'fraud' in this context is a complete misdescription of what s.286 of the 1963 Act strikes at and, for that reason, in many jurisdictions comparable provisions have been labelled as rules against 'unfair' or 'improper' preferences. What the court will declare void are dispositions of property to one creditor, or to just some creditors, in circumstances where it is intended that they should secure an advantage at the expense of the other creditors. The general policy underlying insolvency law is that all creditors should be treated equally and share *pari passu* in the estate. Paying off one or only some creditors, on the eve of adjudication or liquidation, undermines this objective. Unless there was indeed a good reason for paying one or some creditors, or for otherwise giving them an advantage over the generality of the creditors, such as giving them security, the court will hold the disposition to be unfair and voidable under the terms of s.286. In determining whether a particular payment or disposition contravened the section, the bona fides of the preferred creditor are not relevant.

In several common law jurisdictions the law on preferences in this context has been amended, by applying the prohibition to all payments made within the six months period unless the payee can show that the payment was made in good faith, for valuable consideration and in the ordinary course of business.[11]

7. *John C. Parkes & Son Ltd v Hong Kong & Shanghai Banking Corp.* [1990] ILRM 341, at p. 345.
8. *Re Peter Austin Ltd* [1990] 2 NZLR 245.
9. *Re Blackpool Motor Car. Co.* [1901] 1 Ch 77.
10. *Re Clasper Group Services Ltd* [1989] BCLC 143.
11. E.g. in Australia; see B.H. McPherson, *The Law of Company Liquidation* (3rd ed., 1987) pp. 320-325 and cf. *National Australia Bank Ltd v KDS Constructions Services Pty. Ltd* 62 AJLR 63 (1987/8).

In New Zealand the prohibition has been extended to all payments made by the company within one month of its liquidation, except for liabilities either incurred or accruing due within that one month period.[12] When enacting the 1990 Act, the Oireachtas resisted the temptation to change the law in that general direction, in the face of strong criticism of s.286, except for transactions with 'connected persons'.

'View to giving a preference over' Except for dealing with 'connected persons', what has to be established under s.286 is that the company's predominant intention when transferring the property to the creditor in question was to prefer that creditor, i.e. was deliberately to place that creditor at an advantage over the others. It is not enough that the effect or consequence of what was done places him at an advantage. As Halsbury LC observed, '[n]othing could have been easier than to have enacted, if they had thought proper to do so, that any preference to one creditor over another creditor, or any . . . advantage given by previous payment to one creditor, to which advantage all the other creditors were not a party, should of itself be preference which should be void under the statute.'[13] If the company's intention was other than simply to place the creditor in an advantageous position, the payment or disposition will not be avoided. To a degree, what actually motivated the company to make the particular payment is not relevant because what is prohibited is simply selecting one or some creditors for preferential treatment over the others. But motives or objectives will frequently show whether the dominant intention was one of preference.

In *Re John Daly and Co. Ltd*,[14] Porter MR explained what is meant by 'with a view to giving . . . a preference' as follows:

> 'view to prefer' is produced in one man's mind by the fact that the creditor is his brother or near relation; in another's because the creditor has been kind to him in the past; in that of a third, because he expects that after his bankruptcy the creditor (if now preferred) will aid him in business once again; in that of a fourth, because it is a first transaction with the creditor, and he thinks his a specially hard case; in that of a fifth, because he thinks his other creditors have treated him harshly. There is always some motive behind the 'view to prefer'. Yet, in cases where there is no trust, no pressure, and no obligation other than contract, neither natural love and affection, gratitude, expectation of benefit, sympathy, vindictiveness, or any other mental condition, can in such cases eliminate the view to prefer, which is the statutory condition of liability, however strongly the debtor may be convinced that he is doing what is fair and right in according the preference.[15]

12. Cf. *Re Peter Austin Ltd* [1990] 2 NZLR 245.
13. *Sharp v Jackson* [1899] AC 419, at p. 423. See generally, Coutts, 'Proof of Intent to Defeat or Delay Creditors' [1952] *Conv* 459.
14. (1886) 19 LR Ir 83.   15. Id. at p. 97.

When seeking to have a payment or disposition set aside under s.286, the burden of proof is on the liquidator; he must satisfy the court, on the balance of probabilities, that the company's intention was to prefer the creditor in question. Holmes LJ described this burden, in *Re Oliver*,[16] in the following terms:

> unless it can be made clearly apparent, and to the satisfaction of the court which has to decide, that the debtor's sole motive was to prefer the creditor paid to the other creditors, the payment cannot be impeached, even though it be obviously in favour of a creditor. The act of the debtor is alone to be considered—the object and purpose for which the payment is made can alone be inquired into—and although it is perfectly legitimate, and in all cases requisite, that all the attending circumstances should be carefully investigated, yet if the act done can be properly referred to some other motive or reason than that of giving the creditor paid a preference over the other creditors, . . . neither the statute, nor any principle of law or policy, will justify a court of law in holding that the payment was fraudulent or void.[17]

Dealing with the burden of proof, O'Brien LC held that

> it must be established that the dominant motive of the debtor was to 'prefer'; this dominant motive is one to be inferred or rejected by the court on an examination of the evidence, and . . . there is no presumption against the creditor, the onus not being on him.[18]

Because it can be difficult to ascertain precisely what was the dominant motivation for making a particular payment or disposition, the court is frequently forced to rely on inferences from the evidence produced. As was observed in a recent instance, the court must 'look at the circumstances as a whole and draw the appropriate inferences from the evidence, such as it is. [For] in a a case like this, the liquidator, not having been a participant in the relevant events, is faced with the difficulty that he knows only what appears from the books and papers of the company and what he is told by the participants in those events.'[19] On account of the fraudulent connotation, the court will not too readily infer an improper motivation. It has been said that it must 'be remembered that the inference to be drawn is of something which has about it, at the least, a taint of dishonesty, and, in extreme cases, much more than a mere taint of dishonesty. The court is not in the habit of drawing inferences which involve dishonesty or something approaching dishonesty unless there are solid grounds for drawing them.'[20] In the same vein, 'the inference should not be drawn, having regard to the situation of the onus of proof, unless the inference is the true and proper inference from the facts proved. Thus, it will not be drawn if

16. [1914] 21 Ir 356.
17. Id. at p. 370, quoting Bacon V.C. in *Ex p. Blackburn* (1871) LR 12 Eg 358.
18. Id. at p. 362.
19. *Re Clasper Group Services Ltd* [1989] BCLC 143.
20. *Re M. Kushler Ltd* [1943] 1 Ch 248, at p. 252.

the inference from the facts is equivocal and, in particular, it will not be drawn from the mere circumstance that the creditor paid was in fact "preferred" in the sense that he was paid when other creditors were not paid and could not be paid.'[21]

Intention to prefer proved   An improper intention was established in *Re John Daly & Co. Ltd*[22] where the company, which was in serious financial difficulties, borrowed a substantial sum from its auditor. It was understood that the company would then raise funds, from which the auditor would be repaid. In the event, when the shareholders refused to issue any debentures and following remonstrations by the auditor, he was repaid the loan. Shortly afterwards the company was wound up. It was held that this payment was unlawful because the payee was fully aware of all the circumstances of the company and no actual pressure was exerted by him on the company to make payment; accordingly, the reasonable inference was an intention to benefit the auditor especially.[23]

An improper intention was also found in *Re Clasper Group Services Ltd*,[24] where a one-person company paid £2,000 to the 17-year-old son of its owner and managing director. The son, who was employed by the company as a trainee manager, was dismissed one month before the company went into liquidation. Because he had not been given proper notice of his dismissal, he would have been a creditor of the company for a relatively small sum. On his father's instructions, he paid the £2,000 cheque into his own bank account but immediately withdrew £3,000 and lent it to another company, which he and his father had just acquired. Although the ultimate purpose of the £2,000 payment was to channel that money to the new company, it was held that the payment was a fraudulent preference of the son. Moreover, even though the son's actual claim against the company was for a much smaller sum, the entire payment was caught by s.286. Even if the payment was outside s.286, it was held that a tracing order could be made against the son insofar as he still had the money or its traceable proceeds.

In *Re Cutts*,[25] the debtor was a solicitor who acted for a building society. When he sold his house, which was mortgaged to the society, he kept the entire proceeds of the sale for his own purposes. Another solicitor, a Mr W. who was a director of the society, learned of what happened and exhorted the debtor to pay what he owed the society under the mortgage. Shortly afterwards, the Law Society inspected his books, whereupon the debtor paid £3,000 to the building society. The debtor had an agreement with Mr W. that, should he survive the Law Society investigation unscathed, they would set up in partnership. However, he was struck off the roll of solicitors and was then adjudicated a bankrupt. A divided appeal court held that the bankrupt had the requisite improper intent. In order for him to survive at all, he needed Mr W. and, in order to secure Mr

21. *Re T.W. Cutts* [1956] 2 All ER 537, at p. 541.
22. (1886) 19 LR Ir 83.
23. Now he would be a 'connected person'; see infra p. 246.
24. [1989] BCLC 143.   25. [1956] 2 All ER 537.

W.'s support, he had to repay the building society, which was his best client and of which Mr W. was a director. Jenkins LJ, dissenting, found that enough evidence had not been placed before the court to warrant the inference of a motive to prefer the society.

There are certain stock situations where the courts readily infer an improper intention, most notably where a consequence of the payment is to release or reduce exposure on guarantees given by some of the company's officers and also where the payee had a charge which was not entirely complete at the time.

Officers' guarantees Perhaps the commonest of these is where a company's directors have given personal guarantees in respect of the company's debts and, shortly before its winding up, they arranged to have the guaranteed debt paid off or they arranged for the company to give security for that debt. Nearly 50 years ago, in *Re Kushler Ltd*,[26] it was observed that there was

> the type of case which is extremely familiar nowadays, where the person (such as a director) who makes the payment on behalf of the debtor is himself going to obtain by means of it a direct and immediate personal benefit. These cases of guarantees of overdrafts and securities deposited to cover overdrafts are very common indeed, and where, for example, you have directors who have given guarantees, the circumstances of that strong element of private advantage may justify the court in attaching to the other facts much greater weight than would have been attached to precisely similar facts in a case where that element did exist.[27]

On numerous occasions,[28] the courts have declared invalid payments made or securities given by companies where, in consequence, directors would no longer be exposed under their guarantees for the company's debts or other obligations. For example, in *Re Station Motors Ltd*,[29] the company's directors and shareholders were a husband and wife, who had given joint and several guarantees for its overdraft with the bank. In the light of the company's financial situation, they convened a shareholders' meeting to consider a winding up resolution and they also convened a creditors' meeting for around the same time. Between then and when the resolution to wind up was passed, they caused about £23,000 to be lodged to the company's bank account, thereby reducing the debt to the bank. No evidence was given by the two defendants to explain their actions. Because this was a 'guarantee case', because when the lodgements were made the directors knew that the company was insolvent and would shortly be liquidated, and there could not then have been normal trading, Carroll J found the inference overwhelming that those lodgements were made to prefer the bank and, indirectly, to prefer the directors as guarantors of the overdraft.

26. [1943] 1 Ch 248. 27. Id. at p. 251.
28. E.g. *Re F.P. & C.H. Matthews Ltd* [1982] Ch 257 and *Corran Construction Ltd v Bank of Ireland* [1976-7] ILRM 175.
29. [1985] IR 756.

Incomplete charges   Another stock situation, especially in the company context, is where the company agreed to give a charge once the creditor calls for one. One of the reasons for such an arrangement is that, once its other creditors learn that the company has charged its assets, they may press for payment. For so long as the charge is not executed, the other creditors may be content to carry on business with the company on normal terms in ignorance of what was being done. Regarding these arrangements, the position was stated in *Re Eric Holmes Property Ltd*[30] as follows:

> Where a creditor making an advance takes from the debtor a promise to execute a charge at the request of the creditor, the court will, in the absence of any other circumstances, readily infer that the purpose of the parties— i.e. the debtor as well as the creditor—was to give the creditor the right to be preferred on request. Such an arrangement, although for value, is fraudulent and unenforceable, and when the debtor, in performance of his promise, in fact creates the charge at the request of the creditor, the court again, in the absence of any other circumstances will readily infer that the intention of the debtor is to prefer the creditor. Obviously an intention to perform a promise to prefer is no less an intention to prefer than is an intention to prefer without any antecedent promise.[31]

Where the arrangement between debtor and creditor is of this nature but there are other conditions as well, then account must be taken of the entire circumstances in order to ascertain the company's motivation.[32]

Intention to prefer not proved   In several leading cases, it was held that the Assignee or trustee or liquidator, as the case may be, did not succeed in establishing the requisite motive for avoiding the payment or other disposition. Unlike the position in some countries, s.286 of the 1963 Act does not contain any detailed description or catalogue of the type of transactions which fall outside the prohibition.

Pressure   One factor which negatives any discriminatory intent is pressure. What constitutes pressure for these purposes depends on the entire circumstances, Also, the pressure must be genuine and not a cloak for preferring the creditor. In *Sharp v Jackson*,[33] the debtor was a solicitor who had converted trust monies to his own account. Knowing that his firm was insolvent, he conveyed property to trustees to raise money, in order to rectify his breaches of trust, and he also deposited share certificates with them for that purpose. It was held that, in the circumstances, his motive was not so much as to prefer the trust as to protect himself from criminal prosecution, which almost certainly would ensue once his breaches of trust came to light in the course of his bankruptcy examination. As Halsbury LC put it, 'he made this conveyance not with the

---

30. [1965] 1 Ch 1052.   31. Id. at p. 1067.
32. See infra p. 245.   33. [1899] AC 419.

"intention" or "view" or "object" or whatever it may be called.'[34] But in the somewhat similar *Re Cutts* case,[35] the court came to the contrary conclusion; it was found that the predominant motive in paying the building society, which the debtor had defrauded, was to attempt to establish a law partnership with one of the society's directors and to retain the society as a major client.

Ordinary course of business: The fact that the transaction was carried out in the ordinary course of business is also a strong indication that the company's motive was not simply to prefer. For instance, in *Re Oliver*,[36] where the debtor was the Dublin agent for a cattle dealer who was based in Manchester, in the usual course of business the debtor sent the dealer a cheque for a large sum, but the dealer omitted to cash the cheque. Shortly afterwards he came to Dublin where he learned that his agent was in serious financial difficulties. He thereupon demanded that the agent give him a replacement cheque and immediately cashed it. Not long afterwards, the agent was adjudicated bankrupt. It was held that an improper motive had not been established, because the agent believed that the dealer was legally in a different position from his other creditors, with regard to the cheque, and also that the dealer would have done nothing wrong if he had brought the original cheque to Dublin and, on learning of the agent's financial position, cashed it immediately. Giving the replacement cheque should be regarded a making a fresh payment.

Giving a charge: Although arrangements whereby the company agrees to execute a charge on request tend, generally, to be regarded as fraudulent preferences, in *Re William Hall (Contractors) Ltd*[37] it has been held that this is not so where title deeds are pledged under a deed of deposit, one of the terms of which is that a legal charge shall be executed forthwith. In *Re F.L.E Holdings Ltd*,[38] where a defective charge was registered, at the bank's request the company executed a legal charge and had it registered. The contention that the bank had thereby been improperly preferred was rejected on the grounds that 'the dominant intention was not to confer an advantage on the bank, but to benefit the company by keeping on good terms with the bank.'[39] In *Re M.I.G. Trust Ltd*,[40] where the company withdrew its opposition to an application by its bankers to extend the time for registering a charge over its property, thereby facilitating rendering the charge effective, it was held that an intention improperly to prefer the bank had not been established. This was because the company and its directors could face criminal penalties for not duly registering such charges.[41]

Payments to connected persons   In many of the instances where payments were challenged under s.286 the 1963 Act, the company had discharged a debt owing to one of its officers or some other person or body which was closely

34. Id. at p. 422.
35. [1956] 2 All ER 537.
36. [1914] 2 IR 356.
37. [1967] 1 WLR 948.
38. [1967] 1 WLR 1409.
39. Id. at p. 1420.
40. [1933] 1 Ch 542.
41. 1963 Act s.100.

connected with them. For instance, in *Re Port Supermarket Ltd*,[42] the creditor's managing director was a member of the board of an insolvent company which gave additional securities for money owing, almost six months before the liquidation commenced. It was said there that 'it is impossible to accept that the presence of this creditor's managing director on the company's board can be disregarded. His duty to his principal clearly required him to look after its interest, he must have exercised a considerable, if indirect, influence on his fellow directors in this company.'[43] The only realistic inference which could be drawn was an intention to prefer that creditor. Even where the circumstances would warrant drawing the inference of an improper intention, if the payment was made more than six months before winding up commenced, it could not be challenged on these grounds; the only possibility then would be an attack based on the 1634 Act against fraudulent conveyances.

In the 1990 Act, s.286 was amended to deal with this kind of situation. Where a payment was made to a 'connected person' then the relevant period is extended to *two years* prior to the liquidation and, additionally, the payment is *deemed to be improper* unless the contrary is shown. Thus, it is for the connected payee to demonstrate a genuine commercial justification for the company preferring him over all the other creditors. A connected person for these purposes is a director or a shadow director[44] of the company, a person connected with a director as defined in s.26 of the 1990 Act,[45] a 'related company' as defined in s.140 of that Act[46] and also a trustee or surety or guarantor for the debt due to any of those parties.

Preferring secured creditor   Section 287 of the 1963 Act is designed to protect, principally, banks that extend credit to a company by an overdraft, that is guaranteed by a director, from unfairly suffering loss in consequence of the fraudulent preference rule.[47] If the company in the circumstances defined in s.286 reduced the overdraft, it may very well thereby prefer the bank; the guarantor and the bank will then be obliged to repay those sums to the liquidator. This provision gives the bank a statutory right of action against the guarantor as if he had undertaken to be personally liable to the extent of the interest in the security given.

Effects of voiding the transaction   Where the court declares that a disposition was void under s.286, the preferred creditor will be obliged to return what he got to the liquidator. However, a person who acquired such property in good faith and for valuable consideration cannot have his title impeached because of the earlier preference.[48]

---

42. [1978] 1 NZLR 330.   43. Id. at p. 349.
44. 1963 Act s.286(5); see *Company Law*, p. 108.
45. See *Company Law*, pp. 108 and 134.
46. See id. p. 459.   47. See too Bankruptcy Act 1988, s.57(2).
48. 1963 Act s.286(4).

INVALID FLOATING CHARGE

There is always a danger that, when a company is beginning to run into financial difficulties, one or more unsecured creditors who are in a very strong bargaining position, like the company's bankers or main suppliers, may be able to obtain a charge over its assets and thereby improve their position if the company proves to be insolvent. Since that charge would usually cover the company's entire assets, which were not otherwise charged, the general unsecured creditors are at risk of recovering nothing at all if the company is liquidated and there is a large deficiency. In order to give some protection to creditors, in 1907 the legislature introduced a requirement that every floating charge given by a company must be registered at the registry of companies within 21 days;[49] that rule is now contained in s.99 of the 1963 Act.[50] At the same time the legislature declared invalid every floating charge given by an insolvent company shortly before it was wound up.[51]

Under ss.288 and 289 of the 1963 Act, as amended,[52] a floating charge created by a company within *12 months* of its being wound up is invalid unless it is proved that the company was solvent immediately after the charge was given. Where the floating charge is given to a 'connected person' as defined in s.288(4)[53] (for instance Mr Salomon in the *Salomon & Co.* case),[54] the relevant period for invalidation is extended to *two years*.[55] The purpose of s.288 has been explained as 'to prevent companies on their last legs from creating floating charges to secure past debts or for moneys which do not go to swell their assets and become available for creditors.'[56]

An exception is made for money paid to the company at the time when the charge was given or subsequent thereto and, since 1990, for the price paid for goods purchased or services supplied. An interest cap of 5% per annum is put on any charge falling within this exception.

Despite the above rule, if the chargee moves quickly and enforces his security before the company goes into liquidation, he can retain the entire proceeds of realisation. In *Mace Builders (Glasgow) Ltd v Lunn*[57] a company gave the defendant a floating charge and, within twelve months of that time, it went into liquidation. In the meantime, however, the chargee had demanded repayment of the sum owing to him, which was not done. He promptly appointed a receiver who quickly realised the security and paid off the debt. It was held that s.288 did not operate retrospectively to invalidate what was done under that charge. In this case the chargee was a related company and, being a 'connected person', the relevant period would now be two years before the liquidation. But that circumstance would not have affected the outcome in the case.

49. Companies Act 1907, s.10.
50. See *Company Law*, pp. 512 et seq.
51. Companies Act 1907, s.13.
52. By 1990 Act s.136.
53. See *Company Law*, pp. 108-109.
54. [1897] AC 22.
55. 1963 Act s.288(3).
56. *Re Orleans Motor Co.* [1911] 2 Ch 41, at p. 45.
57. [1986] Ch 459.

Floating charge   What is a floating charge, as contrasted with a fixed or specific security, has been considered elsewhere.[58] The old 'reputed ownership' rule in bankruptcy did not apply in company insolvencies and creditors could easily get the wrong impression when dealing with a company that had charged all its stock, work in progress, debtors and the like. Section 288 does not apply to eve of liquidation fixed charges, but in an appropriate case they could be avoided under s.286 of the 1963 Act as fraudulent preferences.[59] A floating charge which crystallised prior to the liquidation can fall within s.288. It was held in *Re Port Supermarket Ltd*[60] that s.288 applies once the security was created as a floating charge; the section 'is concerned with the status of advances relative to the creation of the security, and it logically follows that the nature of the security as a floating charge is to be determined at the date of its creation.'[61]

Insolvent   In *Crowley v Northern Bank Finance Corp.*,[62] it was held that, once the charge was created within the specified period, it is for the chargee to demonstrate that the company was solvent at that time. Solvency in this context means that the company was able to pay its debts as they fell due and not that its assets exceeded its liabilities or whether a business person would have regarded the company as solvent. In order to ascertain if the company was solvent, an examination of its financial history, both before and after the charge was given, may be required. Where at that time the directors had intended to carry on the company's business, the company's fixed and movable assets must not be taken into account in determining solvency. But against that, account may be taken of the company's capacity to raise additional funds by borrowing after the charge was given.[63]

Money paid   An exception to the above rule is made for a charge that is given in consideration for 'money actually advanced or paid' to the company either when the charge was created or later. In other words, a charge is not invalid where it was given, not to secure existing debts, but to raise additional funds. It was held in *Re Daniel Murphy Ltd*[64] that the critical time here is not the date the charge was actually executed but when the company agreed to create the charge, provided however that any delay in executing the charge was not intended to deceive creditors and was not unreasonably culpable. In other words, advances made at the time or after the company agreed to create the floating charge are effectively secured by it. An interest rate cap of 5% per annum is placed on money paid under a charge which is saved by this exception.

Making a payment   It always is a question of fact whether the chargee paid

---

58. See *Company Law*, pp. 494-504.
59. See supra pp. 236-246.   60. [1978] 1 NZLR 330.
61. Id. at p. 340.   62. [1981] IR 353.
63. See too *Smurfit Parisbas Bank Ltd v A.A.B. Export Finance Ltd (No. 2)* [1991] 2 IR 19 at p. 27.
64. [1964] IR 1.

money to the company. The court is concerned with the substance of any transaction that took place, not simply its form. In *Revere Trust Ltd v Wellington Handkerchief Works Ltd*[65] Andrews LJ observed that the courts duty is 'to look, not at the mere form but at the reality of the transaction. The object of the section was to prevent companies which were *in extremis* giving charges on their property for past debts to the prejudice of other creditors. . . . [C]ash cannot be said to be "paid" . . . if it is only received by right hand to be paid back to the lender with the left.'[66] There are several reported instances of apparent payments to companies which were subterfuges for obtaining a security for an existing debt. In *Re Orleans Motor Co.*,[67] the directors got a floating charge for advancing money to the company, but that money was to be used for repaying its overdraft, which the directors had guaranteed. The court had little hesitation in invalidating their charge. In the *Revere Trust Ltd* case,[68] when the company got the cash, it immediately paid it back to the lender. In *Re Port Supermarket Ltd*,[69] which concerned a series of transactions within a group of companies, it was held that the charge given was simply a device to transfer a debt from one subsidiary to its parent under the colour of receiving new cash. And in *Re G.T. Whyte & Co.*,[70] where a very large advance was made by a bank's subsidiary, to be secured by a charge, it was held that this advance was in substance made by the bank and that the charge merely substituted a better security for the company's existing indebtedness to the bank.

However, the fact that the money was advanced to be used in a specified manner does not always lead to the charge being struck down. According to Romer LJ,

> Where . . . a man advances money to a company on the security of a debenture on the terms that the money . . . is to be applied by the company in discharge of one of its existing liabilities or in the acquisition of some asset which the company does not at the moment possess, the money paid by the lender does not . . . cease to be cash paid to the company merely by reason of the imposition of that condition. There are, of course, certain considerations for the issue of a debenture which plainly do not amount to payments in cash. Where, for instance, an existing creditor of a company takes a debenture . . . to secure the amount of his debt, . . . on the terms that the debt itself be extinguished, obviously no cash passes. . . .[71]

It was held in *Re Destone Fabrics Ltd*[72] that the test of whether the company indeed received funds in exchange for the security is whether the transaction benefited the company or those behind it:

65. [1931] N.I. 55.   66. Id. at p. 61.
67. [1911] 2 Ch. 41.
68. [131] NI 55. Similarly *Re Destone Fabrics Ltd* [1941] 1 Ch 319.
69. [1978] 1 NZLR 330.   70. [1983] BCLC 311.
71. *Re Matthew Ellis Ltd* [1933] 1 Ch 458, at p. 477.
72. [1941] 1 Ch 319.

The ultimate test in such cases may well be whether the transaction is to be regarded as one intended bona fide for the benefit of the company, or whether it is intended merely to provide certain moneys for the benefit of certain creditors of the company to the prejudice of other creditors of the company.[73]

Time of Payment   In order to come within this exception the cash must be paid to the company 'at the time of or subsequent by to the creation of, and in consideration for, the charge. . . .'[74] But it is not essential that execution of the charge and the payment should be simultaneous. The phrase 'in consideration for' a charge means not consideration in the formal legal sense but by reason of the charge, or having regard to its existence. Cash paid to the company after the charge was given but which is referable to the charge comes within the exception. Depending on the circumstances, payments made shortly before the charge was given, in anticipation of it, may validate the charge. In *Re Olderfleet Shipbuilding Co.*,[75] Powell J observed that

> As a general rule, a payment made on account of the consideration for the charge and in anticipation of its execution, and in reliance on a promise to execute it, although made some days before its execution, is made at the time of its creation, within the meaning of the section.[76]

The judge approved the view expressed in an earlier instance, that

> Time in this connection is not . . . a matter to be decided by the clock, but in accordance with the substance of the transaction and upon the determination of the question of whether the advance was or was not a present advance.[77]

In *Smurfit Parisbas Bank Ltd v A.A.B. Export Finance Ltd (No. 2)*,[78] Barron J summarised the position in these terms:

> In order to treat payments made to the company before the execution of the charge as payments made at the time of the charge, the necessary elements to be established are:—an honest transaction; advances made before the execution of the charge and reasonable expedition in and about the preparation and execution of the charge.[29]

In a recent instance, where a charge was given to a 'connected person', Hoffman J observed that

> The degree of contemporaneity which [the] words connote must depend upon the context. It might not be unreasonable to say that two species of dinosaur became extinct 'at the same time' when millions of years

73. Id. at p. 324.   74. 1963 Act s.288(1).
75. [1922] 1 IR 27.   76. Id. at p. 39.
77. *Re Columbia Fireproofing Co. Ltd* [1910] 1 Ch 758, at p. 765.
78. [1991] 2 IR 19.   79. Id. at p. 30.

separated their last known representatives. On the other hand, one would not say that the winner of a one hundred meters race crossed the tape at the same time as the runner-up, even though separated by less than a tenth of a second.[80]

Often, some delay between paying the money and executing the charge cannot be avoided and both transactions will be regarded as having happened at the same time, provided there is a satisfactory explanation for the delay. In the *Olderfleet* case,[81] there were protracted discussions between the bank and the company's shareholders, who resolved that a charge should be given. Some money was then advanced and later the directors gave the charge. It was held that all of the parties there had acted bona fide, that in the circumstances the delay was quite understandable and, accordingly, the money was paid when the charge was created and in consideration of it. By contrast, in the *Smurfit Parisbas*[82] case, three different banks had made secured loans to the company and it was anticipated, when the defendant advanced its money, that its security would be postponed to the plaintiff's floating charge. Although the company agreed to give that charge in March 1984 and the plaintiff's first advance was made in June 1984, the plaintiff's draft debenture was not prepared until July 1985 and was not executed until July 1986. Because the reason for the delay here was not that arrangements could be put in train to have the charge executed, Barron J had little hesitation in concluding that the money was not advanced when the charge was given. In an instance where periods of 18 months and 70 days intervened between the original agreement to give the charges and their execution, it was held that the delays were excessive.[83]

Running accounts   In the case of banks and other creditors with a running accounts, the operation of the rule in *Clayton's* case[84] often enables them to virtually nullify the effects of s.288. Under that rule, where payments out are being made and lodgments are being made at the same time, the lodgments are regarded as first paying off the earlier withdrawals, according to the priority in order of the entries. It was held in *Re Daniel Murphy Ltd*[85] that *Clayton's* rule applies in this context. For an ordinary overdraft, this means that all subsequent lodgments first pay off the debit balance, and all subsequent withdrawals are fresh payments by the bank. Accordingly, if enough funds are turned over in the bank account during the twelve months period the bank will have obtained a valid charge in respect of substantially what the company owed it at the outset.

In the *Smurfit Parisbas Bank Ltd*[86] case Barron J criticised the application of *Clayton's* rule in this manner, observing that 'application of the rule defeats the intention of the legislature and the proviso [about fresh advances] would be

---

80. *Re Shoe Lace Ltd* [1992] BCLC 636, at pp. 638-639.
81. [1922] 1 IR 27.   82. [1991] 2 IR 19.
83. *Re Port Supermarket Ltd* [1978] 1 NZLR 330.
84. (1861) 1 Mer 572.   85. [1964] IR 1.
86. [1991] 2 IR 19.

better construed where there is an unbroken account between the company and the debenture-holder by deeming that it had been broken and a new account opened.'[87] A similar view was expressed in one of the recommendations made by the Cork Committee in Britain[88]—that payments into the overdrawn account should be treated as discharging debit items incurred after the creation of the floating charge before they discharge the debts incurred prior to the creation of the charge.

Goods or services acquired   In 1990 another exception was established, for 'the actual price or value of goods or services sold or supplied' to the company in exchange for the charge.[89] As with the 'money paid' exception, the goods or services here must have been acquired by the company after the charge was given and in consideration of it. Presumably the principles discussed above concerning precisely why and when the payment was made also apply to charges given for goods and services. For the purpose of this exception, the value of any goods or services is defined as the amount that, at the time, could reasonably have been expected to be obtained for them in the ordinary course of business and on the same general terms.[90] An interest rate cap of 5% per annum is placed on any money recoverable under the charge.

Charges given to officers and to 'connected persons'   Section 289 is an application of the above 12/24 months rule to floating charges created in favour of an 'officer' of the company. But the exception for cash paid or goods or services acquired on or after the charge being given does not apply here. This provision is designed to prevent evasion of s.288 by directors and the like, to whom the company was indebted, arranging to have the debt discharged and then obtaining a floating charge to secure fresh advances that the officer would make to the company.

---

87. Id. at pp. 28-29.											88. Cmnd. 8558 (1982) at p. 353.
89. 1963 Act s.288(1).											90. Id. s.288(2).

18

Redress against Wrong-doing and Unlimited Liability

The asset-swelling measures described in the previous chapter all have parallels in the law of personal bankruptcy. In Company Law, these measures are supplemented by provisions which enable the liquidator to obtain redress against persons involved in running the insolvent company, that redress often being holding those individuals personally liable for all or part of the company's unpaid debts. To an extent, these provisions are an exception to the principle of limited liability in limited companies. However, they do not go to the extent of imposing additional liability on shareholders whose company has collapsed; generally, the individuals being rendered accountable must have been involved in some active wrong-doing against the company or its creditors. There may, however, be very exceptional circumstances where the limited liability of members principle will not be applied.

MISFEASANCE

Section 298 of the 1963 Act, as amended,[1] provides a summary procedure whereby a company which is being wound up can obtain redress against officers and several others who have wronged it in particular ways. One way of securing redress is for the liquidator to bring an ordinary action against the wrongdoer. But under the misfeasance procedure, it is not necessary to launch an entire action and the initiative to start proceedings is not exclusively with the liquidator. Section 298 does not create any new head of liability; instead it provides a swift and simple procedure for obtaining redress against certain categories of wrong done to the company.[2] This procedure applies only where the company is in liquidation or where s.251 of the 1990 Act (on dormant companies) has been declared applicable to the company.

Parties Usually, it is the liquidator who takes the proceedings under s.298 of the 1963 Act. Any creditor or contributory (but not an examiner) may also initiate proceedings. It has been held that, where a company is so insolvent that there is no reasonable prospect of its members ever getting back any part of

1. By 1990 Act s.142.
2. *Re B. Johnson & Co. (Builders) Ltd* [1955] 1 Ch 634, at p. 648.

their investment, a court will not entertain a misfeasance claim brought by a fully paid up contributory, on the grounds that it was not 'contemplated by the legislature, that a contributory who could have no possible interest in the result of the application and could obtain no benefit whatsoever as a contributory— even if to the fullest extent to which the claim was advanced it proved good—should have the right to apply under this section.'[3]

The defendant in such proceedings can be 'any person who has taken part in the formation or promotion of the company, or any past or present officer, liquidator, or receiver, or any examiner of the company. . . .'[4] It would seem that a person whose involvement in the promotion of a company was in a purely ministerial capacity, such as a solicitor who was instructed to do exclusively legal work,[5] cannot be made a party to misfeasance proceedings.[6] *De facto* directors have been held to fall within the section. Who is an 'officer' of the company for these purposes has been construed broadly to include, for example, a company's duly appointed auditors,[7] but not accountants who were casually appointed to prepare the company's annual accounts,[8] nor the company's solicitors or bankers.[9] Before 1990, receivers were not deemed to be officers for these purposes.[10] Under s.148 of the 1990 Act, any director of a holding company of the company being wound up can be held liable for misfeasance of the insolvent subsidiary.

Scienter/'misfeasance'   The misfeasance procedure is not a remedy for each and every claim that a company may have against any present or former officer and others. The section applies where any officer etc.

> misapplied or retained or became liable or accountable for any money or property of the company, or has been guilty of any misfeasance, or other breach of duty or trust in relation to the company.[11]

The scope of s.298 was said to be

> limited to cases where there has been something in the nature of a breach of duty by an officer of the company as such which has caused pecuniary loss to the company. Breach of duty, of course, would include a misfeasance or breach of trust in the stricter sense, and the section will apply to a true case of misapplication of money or property of the company, or a case where there has been retention of money or property which the officer was bound to have paid or returned to the company.[12]

3.   *Cavendish Benthick v Fenn* [1887] 12 HLC 652, at p. 665.
4.   S.298(1).
5.   *Re Great Wheal Polgooth Co.* (1883) 53 LJ Ch 42.
6.   *Coventry and Dixon's case* (1880) 14 Ch D 660.
7.   *Re London & General Bank* [1895] 2 Ch 166 and *Re John Fulton & Co.* [1932] NI 35.
8.   *Re Western Counties Steam Bakeries Ltd* [1897] 1 Ch 617.
9.   Supra n.5; compare *Re Liberator Permanent Benefit Bldg. Soc.* (1894) 71 LJ 406.
10. *Re Imperial Land Co. of Marseilles* (1870) LR 10 Eg 298.
11. S.298(1).   12. *Re Ethic Ltd* [1928] Ch. 861, at p. 875.

Thus the section has provided a remedy for misappropriating company property or funds,[13] retention of secret profits,[14] preferring certain creditors[15] and several other abuses of directors' powers.[16] Dishonesty or *mala fides* is not a necessary condition for liability; for instance, directors who honestly but improperly paid dividends from the company's capital have been held liable.[17]

The misfeasance claim does not provide a remedy for mere negligence. In *Re Mont Clare Hotels Ltd*[18] Costello J reiterated the view that

> It is not every error of judgment that amounts to misfeasance in law and it not every act of negligence that amounts to misfeasance in law. . . . [S]omething more than mere carelessness is required, some act that, perhaps, may amount to gross negligence in failing to carry out a duty owed by the director to his company.[19]

In this case the director of the company in question had arranged for it to make a substantial loan to another company, of which he was a director as well, but there was nothing in writing about that loan and no security was given. In the event the borrower failed and, largely because the company could not recover the loan, if got into financial difficulties and eventually had to be wound up. In the light of all the circumstances, it was held that the director was not guilty of misfeasance for not ensuring that the loan was repaid. The misfeasance claim for having actually made the loan and not getting any security was barred by the Statute of Limitations.

It seems however that where the negligence is particularly gross or where it was compounded by recklessness, proceedings under s.298 will be entertained. In *Re Welfab Engineers Ltd*,[20] the directors of a small engineering company sold the undertaking for £110,000 to a firm which agreed to take on the entire workforce, including the directors. There was a distinct possibility of the company getting £125,000 from another purchaser. While holding that, in the circumstances, no misfeasance was committed, Hoffman J did not suggest that the claim should never have been brought under that heading. Redress has been given against negligent auditors[21] and also against negligent liquidators in misfeasance proceedings.[22]

Failure to perform a duty that leads to the company's property being misapplied can constitute misfeasance. In *Re George Newman & Co.*,[23] for

13. *Walker v Wimbourne* (1976) 50 ALJR 446.
14. *Re North Australian Territory Co.* [1892] 1 Ch 323 and *Gluckstein v Barnes* [1900] AC 240.
15. *Re Washington Diamond Mining Co.* [1893] 3 Ch 95.
16. *Re Englefield Colliery Co.* (1878) 8 Ch D 388.
17. *Re Exchange Banking Co., Flitcroft's case* (1882) 21 Ch D 519.
18. Costello J, 2 December 1986.
19. Id. at p. 4.   20. [1990] BCLC 833.
21. E.g. *Re John Fulton & Co.* [1932] NI 35.
22. E.g. *Re Home & Colonial Ins.Co.* [1930] 1 Ch 102.
23. [1895] 1 Ch 674.

example, it was held to be misfeasance for directors of a company that was heavily in debt to permit one or their number, without charge, to use company property for his own private ends. According to Lindley LJ, 'the presents made by the directors . . . there were made out of money borrowed by the company for the purposes of its business; and this money the directors had no right to apply in making presents to one of themselves.'[24] In *Re John Fulton & Co.*,[25] the company's auditor who certified erroneous accounts, on the strength of which the company improperly paid dividends, was ordered to compensate the company for those amounts. The company's directors there were made jointly responsible. And it was held that a paid director there could not plead in his defence that he was entirely ignorant of his duties, that he only saw what reports were submitted to the annual general meeting and that he relied entirely on the auditor to look after the company's financial affairs. What saved the directors in the *Welfab*[26] case was that, at the time they sold the undertaking, there was a severe recession in the trade and a sale of the business probably could not have been made unless they had acted fast; also it was far from certain that the higher offer could have been obtained. While 'directors are not entitled to sell the business to save their jobs and those of other employees on terms which would clearly leave the creditors in a worse position than on a liquidation',[27] in the circumstances there the directors had acted completely honestly and in good faith.

Defences   There is some authority to the effect that the Statute of Limitations does not provide a defence to a wrong-doer who retained secret profits or who otherwise acted fraudulently or in breach of trust.[28] At times, ratification of the wrong by a majority of the shareholders is a defence, especially when every one of the shareholders approved of what was done and the company was solvent at the relevant time. Thus in *Re S.M. Barker Ltd*[29] the ex-directors being accused of misfeasance were also the company's sole shareholders and, *qua* shareholders, had consented to the company in effect giving them presents of its property. It was held by Gavan Duffy P that making their presents cannot constitute officer misfeasance. There the directors-owners of a then solvent company had agreed to sell their shares in it and, at the same time, resolved in general meeting that they should be released from a substantial debt they owed the company. That resolution was described as improvident and as regrettable, in that it did not observe various formalities. It nevertheless was concluded that the directors could not be held liable for misfeasance

because they were the owners, they were the complete masters of the

24.   Id. at p. 685.
25.   [1932] N.I. 35.
26.   *Re Welfab Engineers Ltd* [1990] BCLC 833.
27.   Id. at p. 838.
28.   *Re Lands Allotment Co.* [1894] 1 Ch 616.
29.   [1950] IR 123.

company's situation; it is as such that they were in a position to profit and did profit, and not as directors or trustees for the shareholders.

> [Their release], whether valid in law or void or voidable, was the act of the company in general meeting. . . . There was . . . no concealment by the directors-owners, no trickery and no fraud.[30]

The outcome would have been different if at the time of the resolution the company had been heavily in debt to outsiders and probably insolvent. In *Re George Newman & Co.*,[31] it was said that

> The shareholders at a meeting duly convened for the purpose, can, if they think proper, . . . make presents to directors for their services out of assets properly divisible amongst the shareholders themselves. . . . But to make presents out of profits is one thing and to make them out of capital or out of money borrowed by the company is a very different matter. Such money cannot be lawfully divided amongst the shareholders themselves, nor can it be given away by them for nothing to their directors so as to bind the company in its corporate capacity.[32]

That distinction was again drawn in a more recent instance[33] on the grounds that, once a company is insolvent, the interests of its creditors override those of its owners because, for practical purpose, the corporate assets belong to the creditors.

Court's discretion Where the court finds that there has been misfeasance, it can make two kinds of order. One is to repay the money or restore the property, or any part of it, which has been misappropriated; such rate of interest as the court thinks just can be imposed. Alternatively, the court can order payment of compensation to the company. It has been held that there is no right of set-off in respect of sums awarded in such proceedings.[34] Even where the company has sustained no financial loss from the misfeasance, the court may order the defendants to pay the costs of the proceedings.[35] Property or money recovered in such proceedings forms part of the company's general assets and, accordingly, if the entire undertaking was covered by a floating charge what the company recovered from the document must be held for the chargee.

The broad discretion which the court possesses under s.391 of the 1963 Act to exonerate company officers from liability for breach of duty, where they acted 'honestly and reasonably' and 'ought fairly to be excused',[36] can also be applied in misfeasance cases. For instance, in *Re Home & Colonial Insurance*

---

30. Id. at p. 138. Cf. *Multinational Gas and Petrochemical Co. v Multinational Gas & Petrochemical Services Ltd* [1983] 1 Ch 258.
31. [1895] 1 Ch 674.   32. Id. at p. 686.
33. *West Mercia Safewear Ltd v Dodd* [1988] BCLC 250.
34. *Re Anglo French Co-Op Soc.* [1882] 21 Ch D 492.
35. *Re David Ireland & Co.* [1905] 1 IR 133.
36. *Company Law*, pp. 173-174.

Co.,[37] where a liquidator was found liable in misfeasance for having paid a claim in respect of which the company was not legally liable, he was ordered to contribute only such amount as would ensure that the company's creditors were paid in full.[38] There was no suggestion that the liquidator had acted other than in good faith as many of the shareholders knew that he was going to pay that claim and many others would have sought to reimburse him if he had been ordered to pay compensation. If the company is insolvent the court would consult the creditors' wishes before exonerating a defendant under s.391[39] and it is only in the most exceptional circumstances that an officer who benefited personally from the wrong would be relieved from liability in this manner.[40]

FRAUDULENT TRADING

Sections 297 and 297A of the 1963 Act,[41] which deal with fraudulent trading, were among the most important protections for creditors of insolvent companies. What constitutes fraudulent trading is defined, as

> knowingly [being] a party to the carrying on of any business of the company with intent to defraud creditors of the company, or creditors of any other person or for any fraudulent purpose.[42]

Put briefly, if it is shown that the company was being managed with the intention of defrauding its creditors or others, then those who were then running the company can be made responsible. Fraudulent trading is a criminal offence, with a maximum penalty of a £50,000 fine or seven years imprisonment, or both, were there is a conviction on indictment.[43] It is also a civil wrong, the sanction for which is imposing unlimited liability for all or part of the company's debts.[44] These sections apply when the company is in liquidation or under the protection of the court and also where s.251 of the 1991 Act (on dormant companies) has been declared applicable to the company.

Parties   An application for civil redress under s.297A can be made by a liquidator. That application can also be made by an examiner to the company, by a receiver and by any creditor or contributory. Unlike the new wrong of 'reckless trading', liability for fraudulent trading is not confined to officers of the company. Those who can be held responsible under ss.297 and 297A are any person who at the time was involved in carrying on its business and was knowingly a party to the fraud. A company's creditors—even its bankers—can

37. [1930] 1 Ch 102; for details, see ante pp. 220-221.
38. See too, *Re V.G.M. Holdings* [1942] Ch 235.
39. *Re Barry & Staines Linoleum Ltd* [1934] 1 Ch 227.
40. *Re Sunlight Incandescent Lamp Co.* (1900) 16 TLR 535 and *Re Franklin & Son Ltd* [1937] 4 All ER 43.
41. As amended by 1990 Act ss.137 and 138.
42. Ss.297(1) and 297(A)(1)(b). See generally, Farrer, 'Fraudulent Trading' [198] *J. Bus. L.* 336 and Ussher , 'Fraudulent Trading,' [1984] *Dub. U. L. J.* 8.
43. S.297(2).   44. S.297(A)(1); see infra.

conceivably be caught by ss.297 or 297A. In *Re Cooper (Gerard) Chemicals Ltd*[45] it was held that 'a creditor is party to the carrying on of a business with intent to defraud creditors if he accepts money which he knows full well has in fact been procured by carrying on the business with intent to defraud creditors for the very purpose of making the payment.'[46]

Scienter/'fraud' In contrast with what is described as a 'fraudulent pre-ferences', the word fraud in this present context signifies fraud in its generally accepted meaning and has no special connotation. The dictionary meaning is 'deliberate deception, trickery, or cheating intended to gain an advantage.' In *Re Patrick & Lyon Ltd*[47] it was said that to come within s.297 of the 1963 Act requires 'actual dishonesty involving, according to current notions of fair trading among commercial men, real moral blame.'[48] In *R. v. Grantham,*[49] which was an appeal against a conviction for fraudulent trading, the requirement of actual dishonesty was stressed:

> there is nothing wrong in the fact that directors incur credit at a time when, to their knowledge, the company is not able to meet all its liabilities as they fall due. What is manifestly wrong is if directors allow a company to incur credit at a time when the business is being carried on in such circumstances that it is clear that the company will *never* be able to satisfy its creditors. However, there is nothing to say that directors who genuinely believe that the clouds will roll away and the sunshine of prosperity will shine upon them again and disperse the fog of their depression are not entitled to incur credit to help them to get over the bad time.[50]

Although it was said in *Re W.C. Leitch Bros. Ltd*[51] that 'if a company continues to carry on business and to incur debts at a time when there is to the knowledge of the directors no reasonable prospect of the creditors ever re-ceiving payment of those debts, it is, in general, a proper inference that the company is carrying on business with intent to defraud,'[52] the court was dealing with what constitutes evidence of fraud. Since usually it is extremely difficult to prove an actual fraudulent intent, a court often can only draw inferences from facts which do not unambiguously constitute fraud. It remains to be seen how s.40 of the 1983 Act on 'capital haemorrhages' will affect establishing liability for fraudulent trading.[53]

Re Aluminium Fabricators Ltd (No. 2)[54] provides a typical example of what is outlawed. In the course of its winding up, it was discovered that all cash payments made to the company were not recorded in the accounts made available to the auditors, but were instead recorded in a secret register which

45. [1978] Ch 262.   46. Id. at p. 268.
47. [1933] Ch 786.   48. Id. at p. 790.
49. [1984] 2 WLR 815.
50. Id. at p. 820. In the same vein, *Re Augustus Barnett & Son Ltd* [1986] BCLC 170.
51. [1932] 2 Ch 71.   52. Id. at p. 77.
53. See *Company Law*, p. 08.   54. O'Hanlon J, 13 May 1983.

ultimately disappeared unaccountably from the company's premises. The cash was siphoned off by the company's two directors to their bank accounts in the Isle of Man. At the time of the action the company was hopelessly insolvent. O'Hanlon J had no hesitation in concluding that the directors should be personally liable without limit for all the company's debts and liabilities. He observed that '[t]he privilege of limitation of liability which is afforded by the Companies Act . . . cannot be afforded to those who use a limited company as a cloak or shield beneath which they seek to operate a fraudulent system of carrying on business for their own personal enrichment and advantage.'[55]

Re Kelly's Carpetdrome Ltd[56] is a similar instance, which concerned a carpet retailing business which was owed and managed by two brothers. At first, the business was in the name of one company, 'Supermarket Ltd'; its stock was then transferred to another of their companies, 'Carpetdrome Ltd', and later still the stock was transferred again to one more of their companies, 'Drive Inn Ltd'. On the occasion of each of these transfers, the transferor companies were heavily insolvent; they got paid sufficient by the transferees to pay off their trade creditors but very large liabilities to the Revenue remained. The third of these companies sold off the stock it had purchased but again left large debts to the Revenue. It was found that there were inadequate records kept and indeed records were destroyed for the purpose of avoiding tax. Cash received in some of the above transactions was never recorded and there was no commercial justification for transferring stock from one of their companies to the other. Costello J had little hesitation in concluding that the two brothers had been involved in fraudulent trading. In a later instance where proceedings were brought against those companies' auditors for fraudulent trading,[57] O'Hanlon found that there was insufficient evidence to show that the defendants were knowingly a party to carrying on the business of any of these companies with the intention of defrauding their creditors.

Simply to prefer one creditor of an insolvent company over another does not contravene ss 297-297A, not even when the creditor who is preferred is the company's dominant shareholder or its parent company, provided of course that the indebtedness is genuine and bona fide.[58] Nor will directors be held liable under this heading where the company continues trading at a loss, even for a prolonged period, provided they took some steps to ensure that creditors' claims would be satisfied. It is not necessary that those steps always ensure that the creditors do get paid. The tendency to construe the sections' *scienter* and *mens rea* requirements narrowly is often criticised because, as a result, it is only in the most blatant instances that individuals are held responsible under this head.

Trading   In order to be convicted or to be held civilly liable, the defendant in an action under ss.297-297A of the 1963 Act must have been 'a party to the carrying on of any business of the company'[59] with the proscribed intent. This

---

55. Id. at p. 17.
56. Costello J, 1 July 1983.
57. O'Hanlon J, 13 July 1984.
58. *Re Sarflax Ltd* [1979] Ch 592.
59. S.297(A)(1)(a).

suggests that he must have played quite a decisive role in the events which have come under scrutiny. What constitutes carrying on business has been given an extensive meaning. It includes, for example, engaging in simply one significant commercial transaction, even collecting the assets acquired in the course of the business and distributing the proceeds among the company's debtors. For instance in *Re Hunting Lodges Ltd*[60] directors and the secretary of a company that was insolvent and that owed a large sums to the Revenue Commissioners arranged for the sale of the company's principal undertaking, a well known public house called 'Durty Nellies'. But the full consideration was not paid to the company; part of the consideration was diverted into the directors' and the secretary's own bank accounts. Carroll J. held that disposing of the undertaking constituted carrying on business for these purposes and that, in the circumstances, the defendants had requisite fraudulent intent.

Burden of proof Because the civil wrong is also a crime, it was suggested in *Re Kelly's Carpetdrome Ltd (No. 2)*,[61] where the defendants were the company's auditors, that the burden of proof on plaintiffs under s.297A is the criminal standard, beyond all reasonable doubt, and not the usual civil standard of the balance of probabilities. It is mainly for this reason and because of the narrow concept of *scienter* in these cases that few claims for fraudulent trading are brought and even fewer succeed. Where a defendant can show any reasonably plausible explanation for his actions, the claim would usually fail.

Unlimited liability A person who is held responsible for fraudulent trading risks being made liable personally for all or part of the company's debts. It depends entirely on the circumstances of the case how extensive a liability will be imposed. For instances in *Re Hunting Lodges Ltd*[62] the precise extent to which the defendants should be rendered liable for the company's debts was held to depend on their particular circumstances. Two of the defendants were directed to be liable without limit for the company's entire debts, but two others were made jointly liable only for £12,000, which was the amount diverted to their own benefit. So far criteria have not been laid down for determining how extensive a personal liability should be imposed on those who have committed fraudulent trading.

RECKLESS TRADING

The 1990 Act introduced the concept of 'reckless trading', which is intended to answer many of the criticisms made against the narrow scope of fraudulent trading. It is probable that henceforth, when creditors or others are seeking to render persons who managed a company personally responsible for its unpaid debts, applications ordinarily will be brought under this heading rather than for

60. [1985] ILRM 75.   61. O'Hanlon J, 13 July 1984.
62. [1985] ILRM 75.

fraudulent trading. It is only in the clearest instances of unquestionable fraud that persons would be pursued on that ground rather than for reckless trading. However, where the alleged wrongdoer was not an 'officer' of the company, he can only be pursued for fraudulent trading; an officer for these purposes is defined as including 'any auditor, liquidator, receiver or shadow director.'[63] Mere employees and agents of the company and third parties, therefore, cannot be held accountable for reckless trading. This provision applies when the company is in liquidation or is under the protection of the court and also where s.251 of the 1990 Act (on dormant companies) has been declared applicable to the company. The fact that the action being complained of was performed outside the State or that the respondent may be held criminally responsible for what he has done is no bar to a claim for reckless trading by him.[64]

The kind of conduct which would constitute reckless trading is defined by s.297A of the 1963 Act as

> any person [who] was, while an officer of the company, knowingly a party to the carrying on of any business of the company in a reckless manner, ...
>
> Without prejudice to the generality of [this definition] an officer of the company shall be deemed to have been knowingly a party to the carrying on of any business of the company in a reckless manner if
>
> (a) he was a party to the carrying on of such business and, having regard to the general knowledge, skill and experience that may reasonably be expected of a person in his position, he ought to have known that his actions or those of the company would cause loss to the creditors of the company or any of them, or
>
> (b) he was a party to the contracting of a debt by the company and did not honestly believe on reasonable grounds that the company would be able to pay the debt when it fell due for payment as well as all its other debts (taking into account the contingent and prospective liabilities).

Because of the very serious consequences which can flow from a finding under s.297A, notably unlimited liability and possibly a lengthy disqualification from acting again as a company officer, liability here must be clearly and unequivocally established.

Any analysis of these provisions would commence with the 'Cork Report' on Insolvency Law,[65] which recommended introduction of a similar concept in Britain, under the name 'wrongful trading'. Comparable measures have been introduced in Australia,[66] New Zealand[67] and South Africa[68] and cases from

---

63. S.297(A)(10).   64. S.297(A)(9).
65. Insolvency Law and Practice (1982, Cmnd. 8558) Ch 14. See generally, Oditah, 'Wrongful Trading' *LLl. J. M & C* 5 (1990) 205.
66. Companies Code, s.556.
67. Companies Act 1955, s.320.
68. See generally, Williams, 'Liability for Reckless Trading by Companies; the South African Experience', *33 Int'l & Comp LQ* 684 (1984).

those jurisdictions might throw some light on what exactly constitutes reckless trading.

Parties   An application to hold a person accountable for reckless trading may be made by a liquidator, receiver or examiner, or by any creditor or contributory of the company. The applicant in the proceedings must have suffered loss or damage in consequence of the alleged reckless conduct, or he must be representing someone who has so suffered. Because of this requirement, it will be very exceptionally, if ever at all, that an examiner will make an application under s.297A. The respondent must have been an 'officer' of the company.

Contracting unpayable debt   Three categories of situation arise. One ((b) above) is where the officer was directly involved in contracting a debt on behalf of the company, for instance, by ordering supplies. If it can be shown that, at that time, he did not honestly believe on reasonable grounds that the company could repay that debt when it fell due, then he was trading recklessly. In *Re Hefferon Kearns Ltd (No. 2)* Lynch J remarked that 'paragraph (b) of subsection (2) appears to be a very wide ranging and indeed draconian measure and could apply in the case of virtually every company which becomes insolvent and has to cease trading for that reason. If, for example, a company became insolvent because of the domino effect of the insolvency of a large debtor, it would be reasonable for the directors to continue trading for such a time thereafter to assess the situation and almost inevitably they would incur some debts which would fall within paragraph (b) before finally closing down. It would not be in the interests of the community that whenever there might appear to be any significant danger that a company was going to become insolvent, the directors should immediately cease trading and close down the business. Many businesses which might well have survived by continuing to trade coupled with remedial measures could be lost to the community'.[69] The following points arise regarding this heading.

Party   There must have been a significant direct involvement by the defendant or respondent in contracting the debt; that he was just an officer when the debt was incurred would not suffice.

Belief   To avoid liability, it is not enough that the defendant believed the debt could have been repaid by the company; he must have held that belief honestly and on reasonable grounds. In determining which grounds are reasonable in this context, the test applied may be entirely subjective, completely objective or some combination of these. In New Zealand the courts have adopted a mainly objective test—the standard of an officer of the company of reasonable competence.[70] The exact significance of the phrase 'honestly believe' here is not

69. Unrep., 14 January 1993, at p. 47.
70. *Vinyl Processors (N.Z) Ltd v Cant* [1991] 2 NZLR 416.

clear; does it mean that the person did not really believe that the debt could be repaid or is it necessary to go further and establish that he had some dishonest intention at the time? Indeed, it is questionable whether a belief can be either honest or dishonest; whether a belief is held is a pure question of fact about which the good or evil intentions of the believer do not have any bearing.

Condoning the risk   A matter which the court is required to take into account here is whether the creditor in question was aware of the company's financial predicament at the time and, notwithstanding that knowledge, he went ahead and incurred the debt. If the creditor indeed acted recklessly or possibly negligently in allowing the debt to arise, then the court is free to find that in all the circumstances the defendant had not acted recklessly.

Carrying on business and causing loss to creditor   Secondly ((a) above), there is where the officer was involved in carrying on the company's business in circumstances where either his very actions or those of the company damaged the creditors or any one of them. For instance, he may have contracted a large debt which was repaid but at the expense of several of the creditors. The following points arise.

Carrying on business   Use of this phrase suggests that the defendant should have been involved to a significant extent in managing the company's business. It is likely that his involvement in a single transaction (other than incurring a debt) does not suffice.

Loss to creditor   A loss suffered by one creditor alone, for instance the Revenue, is enough for (2)(a) to apply.

Knowledge   In order to be made liable, it must be shown that, at the time, the defendant knew or ought to have known that his or the company's actions would damage those creditors. Account will be taken of what general knowledge, skill and experience may reasonably be expected of him in determining whether he should have anticipated that damage. According to Lynch J in *Re Hefferon Kearns Ltd (No. 2)*, 'It is not sufficient that there might be some worry or uncertainty as to the ability to pay all creditors. The requirement is that the defendant knew or ought to have known that his actions or those of the company would cause loss to the creditors.'[71]

Carrying on business recklessly   Thirdly, there are other situations which do not fall within (a) or (b) but which still amount to acting recklessly. A possible example may be the company not keeping proper records or having proper accounts. Indeed, s.204 of the Companies Act, 1990, expressly provides for unlimited liability for officers who do not ensure that proper accounts are kept, which contributed to the company's inability to pay its debts.

71. Unrep., 14 January 1993, at p. 45.

Carrying on business The points raised above in connection with this matter also apply here.

'Reckless' There is abundant authority on the meaning of the word 'reckless' in the criminal law,[72] although those cases can hardly be described as models of consistency. There are also cases on the meaning of this word in statutory provisions which impose civil liability. As was observed in one of these cases, however, 'not . . . much assistance is to be gained from decided cases where the meaning of statutes containing the words "recklessly" or "recklessness" has to be discovered. In construing a statute, the first thing to do is to consider the meaning of the words themselves. While decided cases may be resorted to for assistance in the case of doubt, it must always be remembered that a word will have a different meaning or a shade of meaning depending on its context. It is therefore dangerous to examine the meaning of a word in isolation and then to adopt an isolated meaning given to it in a previous case where it has been considered as a step in the solution of the meaning of some different phrase.'[73]

The first decision to be given on the substance of these provisions, *Re Hefferon Kearns Ltd (No. 2)*[74] concerned a firm of heating and plumbing contractors which ran into difficulties in the severe recession of 1990, the year after it had been incorporated. When the management accounts showed there was a substantial deficiency, the directors met and agreed on an informal compromise with its principal creditors, involving disposal of most of its existing projects, each of which was in the ownership of separate related companies. Attempts were made to secure the creditors' consent and eventually a creditors' meeting was called, which approved proposals to have an examiner appointed. Allegations were made that the company's directors had profitted personally from several transactions involving the company, but those claims were rejected by the court. Because several of the directors had given personal guarantees to the company's bank, the entire enterprise had been a financial disaster for them as much as for the unsecured creditors. In concluding that the directors were not liable for reckless trading, Lynch J, made the following general observations about this new head of liability:

> At the outset s.297A does not impose a collective responsibility on a board of directors as such in respect of the manner in which a company has been run. [I]t operates individually and personally against the officers (which includes the directors) of a company and the onus rests on the plaintiffs to prove in relation to each of the defendants . . . that his conduct falls within the ambit of the conduct prohibited or liable to be penalised by s.297A. . . . The meaning of the expression 'reckless' has been considered under different branches of the law, including the criminal law and the law of tort. . . . [T]he best and most realistic test of recklessness which

72. Note, 'Recklessness in Assault—and in General?', 107 *LQR* 187 (1991).
73. *Goldman v Thai Airways Int'l Ltd* [1983] 1 WLR 1186, at p. 1193.
74. Lynch J, 14 January 1993.

has yet been propounded in cases of torts [is]: . . . Recklessness is gross carelessness—the doing of something which in fact involves a risk whether the doer realises it or not: and the risk being such having regard to all the circumstances that the taking of that risk would be described in ordinary parlance as reckless. The likelihood or otherwise that damage will follow is one element to be considered, not whether the doer of the act actually realised the likelihood. The extent of the damage which is likely to follow is another element, not the extent which the doer of the act in his wisdom or folly happens to foresee. If the risk is slight and the damage which will follow if things go wrong is small it may not be reckless, however unjustified the doing of the act may be. If the risk is great and the probable damage great recklessness may readily be a fair description, however much the doer may regard the action as justified and reasonable. Each case has to be viewed on its own particular facts and not by reference to any formula. The only test in my view is an objective one. Would a reasonable man knowing all the facts and circumstances which the doer of the act knew or ought to have known describe the act as reckless in the ordinary meaning of the word in ordinary speech? . . . [T]he ordinary meaning of that word is a high degree of carelessness.

The inclusion of the word 'knowingly' in s.297A requires that the [defendant] is a party to carrying on the business in a manner which [he] knows very well involves an obvious and serious risk of loss or damage to others and yet ignores that risk because he does not really care whether such others suffer loss or damage or because his selfish desire to keep his own company alive overrides any concern which he ought to have for others.[75]

Unlimited liability   A declaration of personal liability will not be made if the company is solvent. If the court finds that the respondent had indeed traded recklessly, it may declare him personally responsible, in whole or in part, for the company's debts. Presumably, in most cases the court would not impose personal liability beyond the amount which was lost as a result of the respondent's activities. No doubt, in time criteria will be adopted for determining the extent to which personal liability should be imposed.

Exoneration   When declaring someone personally liable under this heading, the court may make various ancillary orders. It is provided that if in all the circumstances the respondent acted honestly and responsibly in relation to the actions being complained of, the court may relieve him, either wholly or in part, from personal liability for the company's debts.

As Lynch J pointed out in *Re Hefferon Kearns Ltd (No. 2)*,[76] because the definition of reckless trading, and especially para b (i.e. contracting an unpayable debt) is so wide-ranging, the power of exoneration was incorporated

75. At pp. 38-42, quoting from Donovan v Landys Ltd [1963] IR 441, at pp. 460-462.
76. Unrep., 14 January 1993.

into s.297A. The scope of the court's power here is somewhat more extensive than under corresponding provisions of the English Act; the court may relieve a defendant from any personal liability whatsoever. Since one defendant in that case had been a party to the company contracting a debt when it was insolvent and when there was no real prospect of repayment, his actions were caught by para b. However, because in all the circumstances he had acted honestly and responsibly, he was relieved from all personal liability without imposing any terms.

Retrospection These provisions do not expressly purport to apply retrospectively. On account of the drastic consequences of being held liable for reckless trading, s.297A of the 1963 Act, will not be applied retrospectively, i.e. to events which occurred prior to the enactment of the Companies Act, 1990, on 22 December 1990. To apply this section retrospectively might very well contravene Article 15.5 of the Constitution. For that reason, it was held in *Re Hefferon Kearns Ltd*,[77] which was an examinership case, that directors could not be made liable for reckless trading by virtue of events which took place before 29 August, 1990, the day the 'Goodman' Act was passed. The present version of s.297A was not brought into force until 1 August 1991 and a strong argument could be made that, in a winding up, liability for reckless trading cannot be imposed for things done before that date. Against that, it could be argued that possible liability for reckless trading existed from 29 August 1990 for companies in examination and that liability still applied if the company in question was forced into liquidation, following a period of court protection. Accordingly, a case could be made that, as regards companies which never went into examination, the anti-retrospection principle does not apply to events occurring since the Companies Act, 1990, was passed.

PIERCING THE CORPORATE VEIL

It would seem that limited liability is not a necessary attribute of corporations, although there does not appear to be any authoritative statement that members of a corporation are personally liable for its debts unless the grant of incorporation includes some express limitation on their liability.[78] Some early laws provided that shareholders were liable to pay to the statutory corporation sums assessed on them by the corporation; the power to make these 'levitations' or assessments took a prominent place in some charters. In *Salmon v Hamborough*,[79] the House of Lords decided that unpaid corporate creditors could get an order from a court that the company should make levitations and, thus, by a sort of subrogation, the creditors could use the powers of the corporation against the individual members and so make these individuals indirectly liable to the extent necessary to satisfy the corporate debts. This was

---

77. [1992] ILRM 51.
78. Cf. *J.H. Rayner (Mincing Lane) Ltd v Dept of Trade & Industry* [1990] 2 AC 418.
79. 1 Ch Cass 204 (1671).

not the same thing as shareholder liability for corporate debts, however. If the corporation had no power to make these levitations, the creditor had no rights against shareholders; if the charter contained no provision making the shares subject to assessment, individual liability on shares could be limited in any way agreed upon by the corporation. Other early statutes, as in the case of banks,[80] declared that in certain events shareholders were to be personally liable for certain debts, from which it may be inferred that no personal liability existed in the absence of those sipulations.

The Act which first enabled companies freely to be registered, by lodging their constitutive documents in a registry of companies, expressly provided for making the shareholders liable for the company's unpaid debts.[81] A decade later, that policy was changed and the Limited Liability Act of 1855[82] permitted companies to be registered with the liability of their members limited. The significance of *Salomon v Salomon & Co.*,[83] decided forty years later still, was that it underwrote the principle that shareholders, even in 'one person' companies, can entirely insulate their own financial positions from that of their company, in that they themselves are not in jeopardy of being bankrupted if the company is wound up without being able to pay its debts. In the absence of any agreement to the contrary[84] or such exceptional circumstances as are indicated below, shareholders in a limited company are liable to it only in respect of the amounts, if any, remaining unpaid on their shares.[85]

Where the legislature decrees or a court decides to identify the company with its owners, it is said that the law 'pierces the corporate veil'. Although the *Salomon & Co.* case lays down a broad principle of segregation of the company from its owners, there are statutory and other qualifications to that principle,[86] especially in regard to wholly-owned subsidiaries.[87] Indeed, the further we move from 1896 the less reluctant courts are to take account of the economic reality behind the corporate facade.[88] Hard and fast rules for this purpose have not been laid down and perhaps are incapable of being developed. Where two or more companies are being wound up by the court, s. 141 of the 1990 Act, enables their assets to be pooled in an appropriate case and they be wound up as one.

Agency   A person will be held responsible for all or part of a company's debts where the company was acting as his agent or *alter ego*. But that agency must

80. E.g. Bank of Ireland Act 1781-82, 21 & 22 Geo. III, s.20.
81. See ante p. 3.   82. 18 & 19 Vic. c. 133.
83. [1897] AC 22; see *Company Law*, par. 3.09-10.
84. Cf. 1963 Act s.27.   85. Id. s.207(1)(d).
86. See generally, *Company Law*, pp. 56 et seq., Gallagher & Zeigler, 'Lifting the Corporate Veil in the Pursuit of Justice' [1990] *J. Bus. L.* 292 and Ottolenghi, 'From Peeping Behind the Corporate Veil to Ignoring it Completely', 53 *Mod. L. Rev* 338 (1990).
87. Cf. *Re Irish Commercial Society Group Ltd* (Lynch J, 12 February 1987), concerning dealings in assets of a building society group which became insolvent.
88. Perhaps the most extensive judicial analysis is in *Adams v Cape Industries plc* [1990] 1 Ch 433.

be clearly proved. It will not be inferred from the mere fact that the person owns and controls the company;[89] additional factors must be established that point compellingly to that relationship.[90] But it is not absolutely essential to point to an express agency agreement. There are no reported instances of persons being held liable for all the debts of an insolvent company because it acted throughout as their agent.

Fraud In appropriate circumstances the courts will pierce the corporate veil on the grounds that the company is a mere puppet of its controllers, especially where it is being used for fraudulent purposes. What exactly is meant by fraud in this context has not been defined. Does it mean that the corporate structure, being attacked, was established or was continued predominantly in order to perpetrate a fraud, or are other forms of wrong-doing or misbehaviour sufficient? Where equitable relief is being sought, it is likely that a more expansive concept of fraud will be adopted.[91] Company controllers who in effect give themselves presents of company assets, with the consequence that the company is unable to pay its debts, can be compelled to disgorge those sums to the company's creditors. In *Re George Newman & Co.* it was pointed out that 'to make presents out of profits is one thing [but] to make them out of capital or out of money borrowed by the company is a very different matter. Such money cannot be lawfully divided amongst the shareholders themselves. . . .'[92] That is to say, such payments are *ultra vires*.

Repayment of capital Where capital is repaid to any shareholder other than by the methods set out in s.72 of the 1963 Act or Part XI of the 1990 Act, the funds must be repaid if the member knew or ought to have known that there was a prohibited 'distribution'. For instance, in *Re Halt Garage (1964) Ltd*,[93] the first defendant acquired a shelf company and thereafter carried on a garage business through the company. He and his wife owned the only issued share capital in the company and were its only directors. Its articles of association incorporated article 76 of Table A, which gave the company an express power to remunerate a director, the amount to be determined in general meeting; they also included express power for the company to determine and pay directors' remuneration for the mere assumption of the post of director. The husband and wife built up the company together and drew weekly sums from the business as remuneration. Then the wife became ill. She remained a director of the company but soon afterwards it became apparent that she would not be active again in the business. The husband continued to work virtually fulltime in the business for several years apart from two periods of three and six months when he was away because of his wife's illness and an accident he sustained. At the start of the business was making a substantial trading profit but from then on

89. *Stewarts Supermarkets Ltd v Secretary of State* [1982] NI 286.
90. E.g. *Munton Bros. Ltd v Secretary of State* [1983] NI 369.
91. E.g. *Jones v Lipman* [1962] 1 WLR 832.
92. [1895] 1 Ch 674 at p. 686.   93. [1982] 3 All ER 1016.

the profits began to decline and, despite an increase in turnover, the company became insolvent. It went into voluntary liquidation and was subsequently compulsorily wound up. Throughout the entire period the husband and wife drew director's remuneration. The liquidator brought proceedings against both of them, claiming to recover the whole of the remuneration drawn by the wife from the very beginning and such part of the husband's remuneration as exceeded the market value of his services to the company, on the grounds that they were guilty of misfeasance and breach of trust in making the drawings. The liquidator submitted that, although the amounts drawn were either formally determined by the company in general meeting as directors' remuneration or were otherwise sanctioned as such by the company, and although they were made in goods faith, nevertheless they were *ultra vires* the company as being gratuitous payments made out of capital otherwise than for consideration, unless it could be show that they were made for the benefit of the company and to promote its prosperity. He further submitted that, having regard to the amount of the drawings, they could not have been made for the company's benefit when it was suffering a loss and the money was needed for the business.

Regarding the husband's drawings, it was held that there was no evidence that, in the light of the company's turnover, those payments were patently excessive or unreasonable as director's remuneration. Accordingly, the court would not inquire into whether it would have been more beneficial to the company to have paid him less, since that was a matter for the company alone to determine. As for the wife's drawings, it was held that, although the company's articles included power to award remuneration for the mere assumption of the office of director, even where the director was not active in the conduct of the business, the mere fact that the label of directors' remuneration was attached to her drawings did not preclude the court from examining their true nature. Having regard to her inactivity during the period in question, it could not be said that the whole of the amounts drawn by her in that period were genuine remuneration for holding office as a director, That part of her drawings in excess of what would have been a reasonable award of remuneration amounted to a disguised gift of capital or payment of dividends in recognition of her co-proprietorship of the business; it therefore was *ultra vires* the company and repayable to the liquidator.

Equity and 'justice'   Courts exercising equitable jurisdiction at times rely on the amorphous criterion of 'justice' to determine whether the corporate veil should be lifted in particular instances. Thus in *Power Supermarkets Ltd v Crumlin Investments Ltd*,[94] where it was sought to identify a subsidiary with its holding company and where the evidence indicated that both companies were merely instruments for carrying out the wishes of their controlling family, Costello J concluded that

> a court may, if the justice of the case so requires, treat two or more related

94. Costello J, 22 June 1981.

companies as a single entity . . . if this conforms to the economic and commercial realities of the situation. It would [moreover] be very hard to find a clearer case than the present one for the application of this principle. [In the circumstances here, [t]o treat the two companies as a single economic entity . . . accord[s] fully with the realities of the situation. Not to do so could involve considerable injustice to the plaintiffs as their rights under [contract] might be defeated by the mere technical device of the creation of a company with a £2 issued capital which had no real independent life of its own.[95]

Whether 'justice' alone warrants imposing unlimited liability has not yet been finally determined.

Under-capitalisation It is sometimes overlooked that the core contention in the *Salomon & Co.* case was not that the unsecured creditors should have a direct claim against Mr Salomon but merely that whatever claim he had against his company should be postponed until other claims were satisfied first. In support of this, it was argued that Mr Salomon had established an insufficiently capitalised entity and that, accordingly, he should suffer some of the adverse consequences of its over-trading, especially when he exercised complete control over its management and stood to benefit virtually exclusively from any profits arising from the venture. More particularly, it was said that, in return for securities in it, the company had acquired assets from him at a considerable over-valuation, that in consequence the actual capital possessed by the company was seriously over-stated and, therefore, it was unfair for unsecured creditors to bear the entire loss when they were led to believe they were doing business with a much more substantial entity. This line of argument foundered on one of the House of Lords' leading cases on promoters' liability.[96] It was cited as supporting that proposition that, where the price paid by a company for a business is an exorbitant one but 'all the shareholders are perfectly cognisant of the conditions under which the company is formed and the conditions of the purchase, it is impossible to contend that the company is being defrauded.'[97] It furthermore was said that the unpaid creditors 'if they had thought fit to avail themselves of the means of protecting their interests which the Act provides, could have informed themselves of the terms of the purchase';[98] and that 'the law does not lay any obligations . . . to warn those members of the public who deal with [a company] on credit that they run the risk of not being paid.'[99]

Nevertheless is conceivable that in exceptional circumstances at least the controlling shareholders might be held liable for the debts of their inadequately capitalised companies[1]—as where the creditor is of the 'involuntary' category,

95. Id. at pp. 8 and 9.
96. *Erlanger v New Sombrero Phosphate Co.* (1878) 3 App Cas 1218.
97. [1897] AC at p. 33.　　　　　98. Id. at p. 40.　　　　　99. Ibid.
1. See generally, Hackney & Benson, 'Shareholder Liability for Inadequate Capital', 43 *Univ Pittsberg. L. Rev* 837 (1982) and Halpern et al., 'An Economic Analysis of Limited Liability in Corporation Law', 30 *Univ Toronto L.J.* 117 (1980).

or where there was some misrepresentation about the company's true worth or the shareholders had 'milked' the company of substance. Such an outcome is especially likely where the company is a wholly-owned subsidiary being operated in fact as an integral part of the parent's business. Indeed, s.140 of the 1990 Act empowers a court, in appropriate case, to order that a company contribute towards paying the debts of its insolvent related company.[2]

Involuntary creditors In the *Salomon & Co.* case the argument that, in the circumstances, it would be unjust to give the plaintiff priority over the company's unsecured creditors was also met with the answer that they 'may be entitled to sympathy, but they have only themselves to blame for their misfortunes. [For] they had full notice that they were no longer dealing with an individual, and they must be taken to have been cognisant of the memorandum and of the articles of association.'[3] The authorities, however, do not appear to deal with what is called the involuntary creditor, like the pedestrian who is injured by a company-owned vehicle and has a right of action in negligence. The victim does not choose to be struck by a vehicle owned by an insolvent limited company as opposed to being owned by an individual trader or partnership.[4]

Under the bankruptcy rules, which also apply to winding ups, the position used to be that claims for damages in tort were not provable debts against the insolvent tort-feasor.[5] At common law, those claims simply could not be asserted against the company, thereby precluding the argument that the company's shareholders should be rendered responsible for those debts because of the very special circumstances of the case. In Britain, this rule was embodied in the bankruptcy legislation (s.30(1) of the 1914 Act). In Ireland, however, the rule was abolished by s.61 of the Civil Liability Act, 1961. Consequently, involuntary creditors are now entitled to maintain claims against insolvent companies, thereby making it at least possible to argue that the company's shareholders should be held responsible to them because of the special circumstances of the case.

There would be little difficulty in distinguishing the *Salomon & Co.* case. The argument would be made that the public policy supporting limited liability must be reconciled with, if not forced to make way for, the broad principle that persons who, through no fault whatsoever of their own, suffer damages as a result to another's fault ought not to go uncompensated. It may even be possible to demonstrate that the economic and social goals that limited liability was intended to achieve are not unduly compromised by allowing recourse in this context against the shareholders, who in any event stand to benefit from the company's risky activities. An inevitable problem with any involuntary creditor doctrine is separating the voluntarily-assumed legal relationships from those

2. See infra p. 274.   3. [1897] AC at p. 53.
4. See generally Hansmann & Kraakman, 'Toward Unlimited Shareholder Liability for Corporate Torts', 100 *Yale L.J.* 1879 (1991).
5. See post p. 281.

imposed by events. Take a Canadian case concerning against whom costs should be awarded when a 'one-person' company loses a wholly unmeritorious legal claim brought by it, and is then discovered to be insolvent.[6]

In *Sweeney v Duggan*,[7] the plaintiff might be regarded as an involuntary creditor. He was an unskilled labourer employed by a one-person company, which was owned and managed by the defendant. He was injured in an accident at his workplace and brought an action for damages against the company but, shortly before his case came on for hearing, the company went into a creditors voluntary liquidation and the action was not defended. He got judgment for around £23,000 but, as the company was heavily insolvent, recovered very little of that from the liquidator. He then brought fresh proceedings in negligence against the defendant, contending that the defendant in the circumstances owed him a duty of care—either to ensure that the company had adequate employers liability insurance to cover his loss or, alternatively, to warn him that there was no such insurance covering the workplace. It was argued that these duties applied in the circumstances there because all but one of the company's £1000 issued shares were owed by the defendant, the other shareholder being his wife; he and his wife were company's directors and he carried out all the management; the business was quarrying and, under the Mines and Quarries Act, 1965, he was designated as manager of the quarry. Also, there was expert evidence that quarries are exceptionally dangerous workplaces and that, at the time the accident occurred, the company's finances were in a precarious position because its accounts for that year had to be qualified under s.40 of the 1983 Act, dealing with capital haemorrhages. Following two English decisions rejecting claims that defendants (a school and an employer, respectively) owed a duty to insure the plaintiffs, Barron J held that there was no duty in the above circumstances to ensure that the company would have sufficient insurance to cover injuries the plaintiff might suffer in the course of his employment.[8] The judgment does not deal with the alternative argument, that there was a duty on the defendant to warn employees at the quarry that there was no third party insurance. This decision is under appeal.

Groups of companies   There is no major reported instance in these islands of a holding or parent company being held liable for its insolvent subsidiary's debts on the grounds that it controlled the subsidiary.[9] In the absence of fraud or wholly exceptional circumstances, the principle in *Salomon & Co.* would insulate the parent from liability.[10] It could be argued that the justifications for limited liability do not obtain in these circumstances;[11] for instance, that limited

6.   *Rockwell Developments Ltd v Newtonbrook Plaza Ltd* (1972) 30 OR (2d) 199.
7.   [1991] 2 IR 274.
8.   In *Trevor Ivory Ltd v Anderson* [1992] 2 NZLR 517, a client of an insolvent 'one person' company lost his negligence claim against the company's owner and managing director.
9.   On groups generally, see *Company Law*, pp. 457 et seq.
10. E.g. *Adams v Cape Industries plc* [1990] 1 Ch 433.
11. See generally, Landers, 'A Unified Approach to Parent, Subsidiary and Affiliate

liability was designed to insulate individual investors and not organisations that already possess limited liability. It could also be contended that, when the subsidiary is being run as an arm of the group enterprise, then loans advanced to it by the parent or by another subsidiary should not be treated as debts that must be preferred over outside unsecured creditors, on the grounds that those advances are more akin to equity investment. This is because funds placed by a parent in its subsidiary are made over in the expectation of enhancing the entire group's profit and, accordingly, are more in the nature of equity than debt. The fact that the subsidiary was left seriously under-capitalised and was never given the opportunity to grow into an independently profitable unit might give credence to such arguments in an appropriate case.

Contribution from related companies   Provision to this effect is now made in s.140 of the 1990 Act for 'related companies' as defined there. Before a contribution to the company's unpaid debts can be ordered, the court must be satisfied that 'the circumstances that gave rise to the winding up of the company are attributable to the actions or omissions of the related company'; in other words, the related company had some decisive role in the events that triggered the winding up. Additionally, the court is required to have regard to certain aspects of the relationship between both companies, notably, involvement of one in the other's management, the conduct of one towards the other's creditors, as well as the effect of a contribution order on the related company's own creditors.[12]

Piercing the veil   In *Albert de Barry & Co. N.V. v O'Mullane*,[13] where a foreign bank had lend money to two companies owned by the first defendant and incorporated abroad, Barron J held that he and his Irish-registered companies were liable for fraud and for the repayment of those loans. All of these companies were involved in the first defendant's business, butter dealing. Seven companies in all were involved; his old family company, O'Mullane Bros. Ltd, which had been trading in butter for many years until it became insolvent in 1987; a warehousing company, which owned a premises that was destroyed by fire in 1979; two wholly-owned subsidiaries of O'Mullane Bros. Ltd, which were incorporated in the early 1970s and through which exports were channelled, in order to get the benefit of export sales tax relief; a British-registered company, owned by Mr O'Mullane himself, which imported butter products from the Continent into England; finally a Dutch registered company, which was also owned by Mr O'Mullane. This latter company was established

Questions in Bankruptcy', 42 *U. Chicago L. Rev* 589 (1975); Posner, 'The Legal Rights of Creditors of Affiliated Corporations: An Economic Approach', 43 *U. Chicago L. Rev* 449 (1976); Landers, 'Another Word on Parents Subsidiaries and Affiliates in Bankruptcy', 43 *U. Chicago L. Rev* 527 (1976). Cf. Prentice, 'Group Indebtedness' in C. Schmitthoff & F. Woolridge eds., *Groups of Companies* (1991) ch. IV. and Schmitthoff, 'The Wholly Owned and Controlled Subsidiary' [1978] *J. Bus. L.* 218.

12.   E.g. in *Re Dalhoff & King Holdings Ltd Ltd* [1991] 2 NZLR 296.
13.   Barron J, 2 June 1992.

at the instigation of the plaintiff, an Amsterdam-based bank, so that loans could be made in foreign currency to finance butter trading, without the necessity of obtaining exchange control permission from the Central Bank of Ireland. Loans were also made to the British-registered company for that purpose. Those companies would then use the money lent to purchase butter, mainly from the export sales company, which in turn purchased butter from O'Mullane Bros. Ltd and it, in turn, bought the butter from creameries. When this company (the 'first company') became insolvent, the first defendant incorporated another company (the 'successor company') to take over its business and which adopted the same name as the first company; at the same time the successor adopted a new name, O'Mullane (Holdings) Ltd.

One of the main matters in dispute was the arrangements for securing the loans. Barron J held that the principal security was that stocks of butter should be actually in existence which were directly referable to the funds borrowed and when those stocks were sold, the security would then extend to the sums receivable on the sales. The first company's insolvency in 1986 resulted mainly from foreign exchange losses when the pound was devalued; further substantial losses were incurred by the other companies in 1989 due to another devaluation and also a fall in the price of butter. By that time, the bank was under new management and representatives of the bank came to Ireland to clarify the position. When they learned of these losses and that there were no stocks of underlying butter for security and, also, that forward sales contracts for butter had been rescinded by purchasers, due to the fall in the price of butter, the bank became alarmed. A *Mareva* injunction was obtained.

In the trial of the action, Barron J held that, firstly, the bank was entitled in the circumstances to call in the loans and that the two borrowers were in breach of contract for not repaying them. Secondly, it was held that the first defendant and his companies had defrauded the bank; three of these frauds were failures to disclose certain details about the group companies and their finances and one was failure to use the money to purchase actual stocks of butter. Barron J's third conclusion was reached before addressing the question of fraud.

Having found that the Dutch and British companies had defaulted on the loans, it was necessary to consider the remedy to which the bank was entitled. The bank argued that, because of the way the butter trading business was conducted through the group, as a single economic unit, every company in the group should be held responsible. There was no evidence that the group structure had been established with any fraudulent design; the two exporting companies were set up for tax planning reasons and the two foreign companies on account of exchange control difficulties and to an extent for V.A.T. reasons. There was no evidence to suggest that proper books and accounts for each separate company had not been kept, although there was expert evidence that many inter-group transactions were not at arms length and often were recorded after the event. The bank were aware of the group structure and how the business in general was being managed, except that it always believed there were actual stocks of butter in existence representing funds lent and it was never told about the first company's insolvency in 1986. The argument for lifting the veil and imposing unlimited liability was that 'justice requires that all the companies in the group should be treated as one entity'.

Barron J accepted that argument, giving the following reasons:

> there was only one organisation at all times relevant to the proceedings and only one business. There had in the past been several aspects to the business which had been segregated among the several companies. These had ceased and were no longer being carried on. The entirety of the business was that of butter trading. Mr O'Mullane was the sole trader who carried on that trade from his office in Cork.
>
> The business was in reality carried on by the [the first] company although the documentation relating to the trade also to [the export sales company and the English and Dutch companies]. What happened here was a succession of inter-company invoices came into being when the invoice to the ultimate purchase was being prepared. There was no commercial reason for all these invoices. They came into being as part of a tax planning exercise. [The exporting companies] were both entitled to export sales relief. Transactions were routed through these companies so that the paper profits generated might be free from liability to tax. Sales lost its full exports sales relief in . . . 1987 and thereafter the majority of the sales were put through Highland Traders. [The British company] was incorporated in the United Kingdom and was used to take the benefit of unrestricted foreign exchange regulations in that country and also lower VAT rates. [The Dutch company] was incorporated in Holland and was used solely to take the benefit of unrestricted foreign exchange regulations there. . . .
>
> Neither [the British nor Dutch companies] were genuine overseas companies. Both were beneficially owned in this jurisdiction and were being used to circumvent exchange control regulations and to a much lesser extent to lessen liability to VAT. Indeed [the Dutch company] was set up specifically to avoid exchange control regulations.
>
> All of this was occurring in the context of borrowing by the foreign currency companies from the bank where such borrowing was being used to keep the entire Group running. All the companies were inextricably intertwined and living off one another. In my view, it is intolerable that a court should even be asked to sanction what was being done, which it would have to do, if it was to hold the assets of the foreign currency companies alone should be available to meet the sums owing to the bank. Those assets are ultimately dependent upon how many invoices Mr O'Mullane had prepared for each transaction and in which names and for what amounts they were completed. I am not prepared to sanction that. It is clearly in the interest of justice . . . to make each company jointly and severally liable on the debt to the bank.
>
> There were very considerable losses on forward currency transactions

in the name of the two foreign currency companies. The business was totally dependent upon foreign exchange dealings for its survival. Its margin on butter sales was said to be around 1% whereas that on its foreign exchange dealings was said to raise this level of profitability to between 6 and 7%. Clearly these transactions in the manner in which they were entered into were made for the benefit of the group as a whole. However, the avowed reason for these forward contracts was to protect the purchase moneys payable in foreign currencies. Whichever way the dealings were looked at, it would be an injustice to the bank to limit recourse in respect of these losses to the assets of the foreign currency companies.[14]

This decision is presently under appeal. Among the legal issues being raised in the appeal include the circumstances when non-disclosure of information constitutes fraud and also when does the 'justice' exception to the principle of separate legal personality warrant imposing liability on inter-related companies for the unpaid debts of connected companies when all of those companies were involved in the same business. Among the arguments being advanced on this point are that s.140 of the 1990 Act 'occupies the field' in this regard; that the veil should not be pierced when foreign companies are involved and no evidence is given of when, under their law, separate personality can be disregarded; that the appropriate way of doing justice to all of the company's creditors is through the normal insolvency machinery, which is finely tuned to that end, rather than a civil action for deceit based on non-disclosures of information; that the bank was a sophisticated lender which knew or was in a position to know the risk the borrowers were running (dealings in foreign currencies without having any forward exchange cover), that the bank always could have and should have insisted on obtaining far more financial information about the entire group and could have insisted on a more satisfactory security and careful monitoring of adherence to the security conditions.

14. At pp. 42 and 45-47.

19

Proving Debts and Paying Claims

Proving a debt in a winding up is the process of establishing that the creditor in question was owed a certain sum by the company. If the company is solvent, then the full amount of all debts proved will be paid; if it is insolvent then at most a dividend can be paid to the unsecured creditors and to secured creditors who were not fully satisfied out of any security they held. Where the company is insolvent s.284 of the 1963 Act applies the general rules in bankruptcy law to 'debts provable and to the . . . future and contingent liabilities. . . .' A detailed set of rules regarding proof of debts is contained in the first schedule of the Bankruptcy Act, 1988,[1] and many of the cases on the topic are bankruptcy law decisions.[2] Several aspects of proving debts are governed by the Winding Up Rules.[3]

The liquidator's function here is to ensure that the claims of all creditors will be satisfied rateably, regardless of when the company incurred the debt or the degree of pressure particular creditors were exerting on the company. Once the liquidation commences, creditors are precluded from levying execution on the company's assets[4] and legal proceedings against the company may be stayed.[5] In place of their usual legal remedies, creditors become entitled to share proportionately in the fund which the liquidator will distribute. When deciding whether to admit a claim to proof, the liquidator is described as acting in a quasi-judicial capacity, meaning that his standards are as exacting as those of a court or a judge.[6] He must take care that only legally enforceable claims are admitted to proof and are paid. His failure to take proper steps to investigate a claim can amount to misfeasance or breach of duty, rendering him personally liable for a claim which he improperly paid.[7]

Although the principles which determine what debts can be proved are in the main the same as those applicable in an action brought against the company to enforce a debt or claim, this is subject to a qualification. Because the parties whose interests are affected by admitting a proof are the general body of creditors and the contributories, not just the company itself, there are some liabilities of the company which a liquidator should not admit to proof lest the

1.   Paras. 1-23.   2. See *Bankruptcy Law*, ch.8.
3.   Rules 102-111.   4. See ante pp. 180-185.
5.   See ante pp. 171-173.
6.   *Tanning Research Laboratories Inc. v O'Brien*, 64 ALJLR 21 (1990).
7.   E.g. *Re Home & Colonial Insurance Co.* [1930] 1 Ch 102; ante pp. 220-221.

interests of the creditors and contributories be unfairly prejudiced. For instance, there is the rule against 'double proof', which applies even where there are separate contracts for what in substance is the same debt.[8] And if what purports to be a liability of the company is founded on some act or omission on its part which unjustly prejudices its creditors, for instance fraud or collusion, the liquidator can reject a proof on grounds additional to those available to the company under the general law.[9]

CLAIMS PROVABLE

What can be proved in bankruptcy is defined in s.75(1) of the Bankruptcy Act, 1988, as

> Debts and liabilities, present or future, certain or contingent, by reason of any obligation incurred by the bankrupt . . . before the date of adjudication . . . and claims in the nature of unliquidated damages for which [he] is liable at that date by reason of a wrong. . . .

Thus, liabilities under nearly every conceivable legal category, such as breach of contract, tort, equitable obligation and statutory duty, can be proved. The terms of that section are virtually reproduced by s.283(1)of the 1963 Act:

> All debts payable on a contingency, and all claims against the company, present or future, certain or contingent, ascertained or sounding only in damages, shall be admissible to proof against the company, a just estimate being made, so far as possible, of the value of such debts or claims which may be subject to any contingency or which sound only in damages, or for some other reason do not bear a certain value.

Of s.283's predecessor, s.158 of the 1862 Act, Buckley LJ observed that it

> admitted to proof, in the winding-up, debts and claims under very large words of description. Under other provisions of the Act, it resulted that when a company went into liquidation its assets were to be got in and realised, and the resulting fund was to be divided in satisfaction *pro rata* of its debts. Sections 98 and 107 of the Act of 1862 are sufficient for reference to show that in respect of debts existing at the time of the winding-up there was to be a right of proof and distribution. But s.158 rendered admissible to proof debts payable on a contingency and claims against the company, present or future, certain or contingent, ascertained or sounding only in damages, and went on to say how obligations or liability of that kind were to be dealt with. The relevant words are 'a just estimate being made, so far as is possible, of the value of all such debts or claims as may be subject to any contingency or sound only in damages, or for some other reason do not bear a certain value.' Any liability falling within the words of the section which was not a debt at the winding-up

8. See infra pp. 294-295.
9. *Re Van Laun* [1907] 2 KB 23.

was by that section admissible to proof, and the proof was to be of 'the value' of the debt or claim, to be estimates if it was subject to a contingency or did not bear a certain value.[10]

Liabilities incurred after the liquidation commenced may not be proved, except for those which are referable to obligations which the company had incurred before that time. Post-liquidation liabilities, however, may be costs of the liquidation itself and thereby obtain a preferential status.[11] The following types of debts and claims call for special attention. The question of set-offs when proving debts is dealt with below in the section on priorities.[12]

Periodic payments   In the case of periodic payments, for example rent and instalments which accrue, formerly a sum falling due shortly after the winding up commenced could not be recovered if the period in respect of which it was due straddled that date.[13] The sums were not deemed to accrue due until the date for payment arrived and, since the company was then wound up, they were deemed not to have fallen due. Now the creditor is entitled to claim the proportionate part between the previous payment date and the time of the liquidation.[14] If the liquidator continues to occupy a premises for the benefit of the winding up, then the landlord is entitled to receive his rent in full as a cost of the liquidation.[15]

Future debts   All debts, 'present or future', are made admissible to proof by s.283(1) of the 1963 Act. Future debts here signifies liquidated sums which have not actually fallen due or payable at the time of the winding up. Examples include a loan which is repayable at some later date, instalments due on hire purchase or credit sale agreements (which do not provide for accelerated payment on a winding up), rent due under a lease (which has not been disclaimed) and annuities. The winding up is in effect treated as rendering those sums immediately payable, so that the full amount of principal and interest falls due on the winding up, regardless of the stipulated due date.[16] However, the liquidator must deduct a rebate of interest, at 6% per annum, from the winding up date to the time the sum or sums were due to be paid under the contract.[17]

Where, as a result of terminating a lease or other contract, the landlord or contracting party obtains an advantage, that advantage must be valued and be deducted from the amount of the proof in respect of the future payments.[18] Accordingly, where a landlord can re-let the property at the same or a better rent than the company would have to pay, he has no future claim in respect of his rent.[19]

10.   *Re Law, Car & General Insurance Corp.* [1913] 2 Ch 103, at pp. 120-121.
11.   See post pp. 356-357.   12. See post pp. 339-342.
13.   *Re South Kensington Co Operative Stores* (1881) 17 Ch D 161.
14.   Rule 106; also schedule to Bankruptcy Act 1988, reg. 16.
15.   *Re Downer Enterprises Ltd* [1974] 1 WLR 146.

Unliquidated claims   An unliquidated debt or claim is a present existing liability where the actual amount due cannot yet be ascertained; it is necessary to resort to legal proceedings in order to determine exactly how much must be paid. Examples include most claims in tort and some claims for breach of contract and for breach of fiduciary duty. The converse is a liquidated debt, i.e. a liability the full extent of which can readily be calculated.

A claim that formerly could not be proved in a bankruptcy was in tort; in other words, a person who would have a good case in negligence or for some other tort could not prove against an insolvent defendant's estate.[20] Frequently, this somewhat anomalous rule could be avoided by framing the claim in contract rather than in tort; for instance, in an employer's liability situation, the employee would claim damages for breach of contract.[21] Also, persons with alternative remedies in contract and in tort could waive the tort and sue in contract.[22] But if the claim was exclusively in tort, it could not be proved in bankruptcy or against an insolvent company. Unless the tort claim had been liquidated either by agreement or by entry of a judgment before the winding up commenced, it lapsed.[23] But if the company was solvent, such claims could be proved.

This rule preventing tort creditors from proving in an insolvency was abolished by s.61 of the Civil Liability Act, 1961, according to which,

> Notwithstanding any other enactment or any rule of law, a claim for damages or contribution in respect of a wrong shall be provable in bankruptcy where the wrong out of which the liability to damages or the right of contribution arose was committed before the time of the bankruptcy.

Section 75(1) of the Bankruptcy Act, 1988, provides that 'claims in the nature of unliquidated damages for which the bankrupt . . . is liable . . . by reason of a wrong within the meaning of the Civil Liability Act, 1961,' can be proved. A 'wrong' under the 1961 Act is defined most extensively, as meaning a 'tort, breach of contract or breach of trust . . . whether or not the act is also a crime, and whether or not the wrong is intentional.'[24] An application can be made to the court to assess the amount of the unliquidated liability and it is provided that, if all the necessary parties agree, the court can make that assessment even where the claim is one that must be brought in some other court.[25]

A contract which purports to fix how much damages should be paid on a

---

16. Schedule to Bankruptcy Act 1988, reg. 15.
17. Rule 108. Cf. *Re Browne & Wingrove* [1891] 2 QB 574.
18. *Jones Smith & Sons (Norwood) Ltd v Goodman* [1936] Ch. 216.
19. *Re House Property & Investment Co.* [1954] Ch 576.
20. *Re Pen-Y-Van Colliery Co.* (1877) 6 Ch D 477.
21. Cf. *Matthews v Kuwait Bechtel Corp.* [1957] 2 QB 57.
22. *Watson v Holliday* (1882) 20 Ch D 780.
23. *Re Islington Metal & Plating Works Ltd* [1984] 1 WLR 14. Cf. *Turner v Derham* [1958] Ir Jur Rep 78.
24. S.2(1).   25. Bankruptcy Act 1988, s.75(3).

winding up is not binding on the court.[26] Where the liquidator has disclaimed an onerous lease, the damages which may be proved are the difference between the rent which the lessor would have got under the lease and the rent he is now able to obtain in the open market.[27] A similar principle applies to employment contracts for a fixed duration.[28]

Contingent claims   A contingent claim is in respect of a liability that might very well occur but nevertheless may never occur. The liability of a surety under a guarantee, for instance, is contingent because it will only arise if the principal debtor defaults. There are, however, certain contingencies in a general sense that are not regarded as giving rise to provable claims, for instance, costs incurred by the company in an action up to the date of the liquidation[29] and the surety's right of indemnity against the principal debtor, under his guarantee.[30] Formerly a proof could not be lodged in respect of a liability while it remained a contingency but that too is no longer the case. Sections 257 and 258 of the Bankruptcy Act, 1857, distinguished contingent debts from contingent liabilities, and were interpreted somewhat restrictively,[31] as was s.46 of the 1872 Act concerning unliquidated damages.[32]

Section 75(1) of the Bankruptcy Act, 1988, provides that '[d]ebts and liabilities, present or future, certain or contingent' can be proved. In the event of there being difficulties in placing a value on the contingent claim, the court can make an estimate of its value and it is that sum which then can be proved.[33] As well as those under guarantees, the commonest contingent liabilities are those arising from covenants contained in leases[34] and in annuities.[35] Calls on shares are another such liability.[36] Another is claims under insurance policies; special rules for valuing these are contained in the Assurance Companies Act, 1909.[37] That it may be very difficult to value a particular contingency is no reason for not admitting it to proof.

The way of dealing with contingent claims has been described as follows:

> There is no doubt that a contingent claim for unliquidated damages is a provable debt, and its amount has to be estimated as at the date of the [liquidation]. That, however, does not mean that the effect of the [liquidation] is to accelerate the happening of the contingency so as to fix

26. *Re London & Scottish Bank* (1870) 9 Eg 149.
27. *Re Hide* (1871) 7 Ch App 28.
28. *Re English Joint Stock Bank* (1867) LR 4 Eg 350.
29. *Re A Debtor (No 68 of 1911)* [1911] 2 KB 652.
30. *Re An Arranging Debtor No. A 1076* [1970] NI 96.
31. Id. pp. 108-111.
32. *Cinnamond v Curdy* [1909] 2 IR 185.
33. Bankruptcy Act 1988, s.75(4).
34. Cf. *Hardy v Fothergill* (1888) 13 HLC 351.
35. Cf. *Re Rothermere* [1945] Ch 72.
36. Cf. *Re Bolton* [1930] 2 Ch 48.
37. Cf. *Re Law, Car & General Insurance Corp.* [1913] 2 Ch 103.

the amount of the claim on the basis of the contingency having happened on the day of the [liquidation]. . . . The claim must be stated as on the day of the [liquidation]; if when the proof is lodged the contingency has not happened the amount of the claim must be estimated as accurately as possible; if the contingency happens before the proof is lodged, that fact is *pro tanto* evidence of the true value of the claim as at the date of the [liquidation], and there will, as a rule, be no difficulty in arriving at the amount of the claims; if the contingency happens after the proof is lodged, and it appears that the amount at which the damages have been estimated is below the true value, the creditor will be allowed to amend the proof or lodge a fresh proof at any time during the continuance of the bankruptcy, but not so as to disturb prior dividends.[38]

With regard to contingent claims by lessors, frequently it will not be necessary to place a value on these. If the company's lease is valuable, unless there is some effective forfeiture clause, usually the liquidator will sell and assign it. In that event, the position is the same as if the lease had been assigned by the company before the winding up commenced and the lessor is entitled to compensation for any loss he stands to suffer. He can prove for a sum equal to the difference between the value of the lease with and without the benefit of the company's covenants following dissolution.[39] If, on the other hand, the lease is onerous, usually the liquidator will apply to disclaim it, with the leave of the court,[40] and the lessor can then prove for the loss he suffered in consequence of the disclaimer.

Interest Interest cannot be recovered in respect of the period following a bankrupt's adjudication or the winding up commencing, which causes some injustice in periods of very high interest rates and where the administration of the insolvent estate takes a long time. As Costello J said in *Daly v Allied Irish Banks*, '[i]t has long been established that in the case of an insolvent company which is being wound up creditors whose debts carry interest are entitled to dividends only upon what was due for principal and interest at the commencement of winding up and interest ceases to run from that date.'[41] This rule of convenience is confirmed by s.75(2) of the Bankruptcy Act, 1988, and is extended to any other financial 'consideration in lieu of interest'. Where, however the debt was secured, the contractual right to be paid interest out of the security continues beyond the liquidation date.[42] If the company was solvent, then even an unsecured existing right to interest continues beyond the date of the liquidation.

38. *Ellis & Co.'s Trustee v Dixon Johnson* [1924] Ch 342, at pp. 356-357.
39. *Re House Property & Investment Co.* [1954] 1 Ch 576.
40. See ante pp. 224-229.
41. Unrep., 27 January 1987, at p. 2, referring to *Re Humber Ironworks and Shipbuilding* (1869) 4 Ch App 643.
42. *Re McCairns (P.M.P.A.) plc* [1991] 2 IR 465; see infra p. 293.

Interest can be proved in the following circumstances up to the time of liquidation.[43] First, there is where the contract or agreement with the debtor by its very terms provides for paying interest. Some statutes expressly provide for paying interest, notably s.57 of the Bills of Exchange Act, 1882. The Money-lenders Acts place certain restrictions on the amount of interest that licensed moneylenders can charge.[44] Even if there is no agreement or stipulation regarding interest, s.22 of the Courts Act, 1981, empowers the courts, when awarding a sum of money or damages against a person, to award interest on all or part of that sum at the then prevailing rate for judgment debts.[45] Finally, the provisions of s.53 of the Debtors (Ireland) Act, 1840, are incorporated into the rules for proving debts and provide as follows.[46] Those deal with where there was no agreement between the parties regarding interest but the debt is overdue at the date of adjudication or liquidation. Interest at the rate currently payable for judgment debts can be proved in two circumstances. One is where the debt or sum due is payable 'by virtue of a written instrument at a certain time.' If the debt is not so payable, such as if the agreement is oral or the amount due is not payable at a fixed time, interest can be proved if the creditor makes a written demand for payment and notifies the debtor that interest will be claimed from the date of that demand until the debt is paid.

Following a thorough analysis of the authorities on interest in insolvencies, it was held in *Re Amalgamated Investment & Property Co.*[47] that, where a creditor in a compulsory liquidation is entitled to interest, the cut-off period is when the petition was presented and not the date of the winding up order. A New Zealand court has opted instead for the date of the order because it is 'anomalous, and without logical or practical justification, that interest should be separated from other claims in the selection of the date for proof.'[48] Interest can be awarded against a bankrupt up to the time of adjudication and, since a liquidation's equivalent to adjudication is the making of the order, there was also some legal justification for that conclusion. Where interest is payable under any of the above-mentioned headings and the debt was overdue when the liquidation commenced, interest at not more than six per cent can be paid down to that date.[49] Where the sum became payable following service of a written demand for payment, together with interest, this time runs from when the demand was made.

Foreign currency debts For practical reasons, the liquidation cannot be carried out in several currencies. Where one or more of the debts are in a foreign

---

43. Bankruptcy Act 1988, s.75(2)
44. Cf. SI No. 167 of 1993, exempting a wide category of money lenders from these Acts.
45. Being 8 per cent: SI No. 12 of 1989.
46. Bankruptcy Act 1988, schedule, reg. 14.
47. [1985] Ch. 349.
48. *U.D.C. Finance Ltd v P.J. Bradey Ltd* [1983] NZLR 481, at p. 483.
49. Cf. the 3rd question in *Re Amalgamated Property & Investment Co.* [1985] Ch at pp. 386 et seq.

currency, they must be converted into the currency of the liquidation as of the date when the winding up commenced. As Brightman LJ explained in *Re Lines Bros Ltd*,[50] in an insolvent company,

> The sterling creditors are not in default *vis-à-vis* the foreign currency creditors. Therefore, there is no obvious reason why the risk of depreciation in the value of sterling pending distribution of the assets should be borne by the sterling creditors. The company is the wrong-doer towards both the sterling creditors and the foreign currency creditors. There is no particular reason, in the field of abstract justice, why the currency risk should be borne by one description of creditor rather than by another description of creditor when they are all directed to rank pari passu. They do not rank pari passu if the sterling creditors are required to underwrite the exchange rate of the pound for the benefit of the foreign currency creditors. The just course . . . is to value the foreign debt once and for all at an appropriate date, and to keep to that rate of conversion throughout the liquidation until all debts have been paid in full. The loss and the benefit from changes in exchange rates will then lie where they fall. In terms of sterling, if that is the currency of the liquidation, the amount of the debts will be unaffected by movements on the foreign exchange market. In the case of a debt expressed in a depreciating currency the other creditors will stand to gain nothing from a protracted liquidation. In the case of a debt expressed in an appreciating currency, the liquidator will not be faced with the question whether expedited payment of such foreign debt, if that can be effected, might be to the advantage of sterling creditors. All the creditors will be treated alike. No re-calculations will have to be made of the company's indebtedness, and no forecasts of distributions will need to be revised on account of exchange factors. The position will be stabilised and all creditors will be treated alike.[51]

That case concerned a creditors' voluntary liquidation. It has not been authoritatively determined whether, in a compulsory liquidation, the relevant time for the conversion is when the petition was presented or when the winding up order was made.

Costs Where costs were awarded against the company in proceedings, whether they can be proved in the liquidation turns principally on whether the costs order was made before or after the winding up commenced.[52] If, prior to his adjudication, the bankrupt was the unsuccessful party in an action and costs were awarded against him, s.78 of the Bankruptcy Act, 1988, entitles the successful party to prove for the costs, whether or not they were taxed or ascertained at the date of adjudication. Where taxation of costs was provided

50. [1983] Ch 1.
51. Id. at pp. 16-17.
52. *Re British Gold Fields of West Africa* [1899] 2 Ch 7; see summary of position by Lindley MR there at pp. 11-12, set out ante pp. 208-209.

for and they are not yet measured, in order to be entitled to vote, the creditor may swear to a certain amount 'and upwards'.[53] Even if the basis of the action is a claim which is not provable, entry of judgment against the debtor with an order for costs renders those costs provable.[54] Once the winding up commences, any action against the company may be stayed.[55] The creditor may then instead seek to prove for the debt, which was the subject of his claim, or he may seek leave of the court to continue prosecuting the action.

Any award of costs against the company made after the winding up commenced is not provable, Although possible liability for costs 'is just as much a contingency as any other contingency in the action, but it is not a contingency in the sense of being a contingent liability which gives rise to a provable debt';[56] this is because '[i]f a man brings an action he does not place on himself an obligation to pay the costs, that obligation arises when judgment is given against him.'[57] An order in an interlocutory application making the costs of that application 'costs of the action' does not give rise to a provable debt.[58]

Negotiable instruments The principal kinds of negotiable instruments are cheques, bills of exchange and promissory notes. In an official liquidation, where a creditor seeks to prove a debt based on any of those instruments, the instrument must be produced to the liquidator and marked by him before that creditor is allowed to vote or for any other purpose.[59] But the court may make some other order regarding this matter. The following are the main principles applicable to what can be proved; almost all of the reported cases are bankruptcy law decisions.[60]

Where the instrument has not been transferred to a third party, it is the payee of the cheque or bill who is entitled to lodge the proof. Where the instrument has been transferred, then it is the indorsee and holder who is entitled to prove against any prior party who would be liable on the instrument. The holder's claim is subject to the same equities as could have been raised by the party liable against those through whom the holder acquired the instrument. If the insolvent discounted the bill at a small fraction of its nominal value, the circumstances may warrant setting aside the transaction as a fraud on the creditors. An excellent illustration is *Jones v Gordon*[61] which concerned several bills of exchange drawn by two parties, each of whom was insolvent and contemplating bankruptcy. Each drew bills on the other, which were then discounted to finance

53. *Ex p. Ruffle* (1873) LR 8 Ch 997.
54. *Re Newman* (1876) 3 Ch D 494.
55. See ante pp. 171-173.
56. *Re A Debtor (No 68 of 1911)* [1911] 2 KB 652, at p. 656.
57. Id. at p. 657. See too, *Re Pitchford* [1924] 2 Ch 260.
58. *Ex p. Bluck* (1887) 56 LJ QB 607.
59. Rule 111.
60. See generally, F. Ryder & A. Bueno eds., *Byles on Bills of Exchange* (26th ed., 1988) pp. 461-470.
61. (1877) 2 HLC 616.

their failing businesses. The plaintiff purchased four bills, in the sum of £1,727, for £200 and then sought to prove in the bankruptcy for their face value. He had given value for the bills and all the other prerequisites for a holder in due course were present. But it was held that, from his knowledge of the parties and the enquiries he made, he must have known of the embarrassed circumstances of the acceptor and the drawer. As Lord O'Hagan remarked, 'could any man of intelligence—any commercial man—any man conversant with bill trans-actions—. . . have failed to believe that the offer of such terms was clouded with suspicion and suggestive of fraud?'[62]

There can be only one proof in any one insolvency in respect of the instrument; there can be no double proof and only one dividend will be paid.[63] Where more than one party to the instrument is insolvent, the holder may prove against all of them, who are liable, although he may not receive more than 100p. in the pound.[64] Where the creditor has been paid part of his debt or where a dividend has been declared by the liquidator, he may thereafter prove only for the balance.[65] But if he has properly proved for the whole debt and he then receives part from another party liable on the bill, his proof stands.[66] A particular source of difficulties is where there has been mutual accommodation between the insolvent and other parties to the instrument, with or without a specific exchange of securities.

Guarantees A guarantee is a contract whereby one person (the guarantor or surety) agrees to meet the present or future debt of another person (the principal or principal debtor) due to another party (the creditor) in the event and to the extent that the principal debtor does not make payment when required to do so. As with negotiable instruments, most of the cases on proof of debts connected with guarantees are bankruptcy law decisions.[67] Before the 1988 consolidation of bankruptcy law, there was a special statutory provision regarding proving claims where debts have been guaranteed.[68] Two main situations arise—where the principal debtor becomes insolvent (also involving the surety proving against him) and where the insolvent is the guarantor himself.

Creditor's proof against principal debtor A creditor holding a guarantee is not a secured creditor for the purpose of the Bankruptcy Act, 1988, or for most aspects of the parts of the Companies Acts which deal with liquidations.[69] Once

62. Id. at p. 624.
63. *Carey v Harper* [1897] 2 IR 92, at p. 109 and *Re Oriental Commercial Bank* (1871) 7 Ch App 99.
64. *Re Scholfield* (1879) 12 Ch D 337.   65. *Cooper v Pepys* (1741) 1 Atk 107.
66. *Ex p. Cama* (1874) LR 9 Ch 686.
67. See generally, J. O'Donovan & J.C. Phillips, *The Modern Contract of Guarantee* (1985) pp. 364-373 and 461-470 and R.M. Goode, *Legal Problems of Credit and Security* (2nd ed., 1988) ch. 7.
68. Irish Bankrupt & Insolvent Act 1857, s.253.
69. *Midland Banking Co. v Chambers* (1868) 7 Eq 179.

the principal debtor goes into liquidation, the creditor's rights against the guarantor are not profoundly affected. The creditor can prove in the liquidation and, at the same time, proceed against the guarantor; the liquidator cannot require that the creditor first exercise his rights against the guarantor before seeking a dividend in the insolvency.

Where the creditor submits his proof against the principal debtor, there is some uncertainty about whether he must always give credit for any sums he has received from the guarantor or another co-surety. It would seem that generally the creditor is not obliged to first deduct from his proof any such sums received,[70] but there are instances where a deduction is called for, most notably negotiable instruments, where credit must always be given for payments received before the proof is lodged.[71] In *Ulster Bank Ltd v Lambe*,[72] where the defendant owed the bank more than £900, the bank obtained £766 from sureties for that debt, which it placed in a suspense account. When the defendant then declined to pay the balance of his debt, the bank sued him for the full amount of the debt. It was held that, since the payments received from the sureties did not discharge the entire debt guaranteed, they did not discharge *pro tanto* the defendant's liability to the bank. According to Lowry J, the

> true principle is that where the entire debt is guaranteed, with or without a limit, the creditor can sue the principal debtor, or claim in his bankruptcy, for the full amount of the debt, despite any payments on foot of a guarantee, whether they are made before or after the principal debtor's bankruptcy, provided those payments in the aggregate fall short of the full amount of the debt. The benefit to the guarantor is that money recovered in excess of the full amount of the debt is held in trust for him. The rights of other creditors of the principal debtor are not infringed, since the bank was at all times entitled to rank equally with other unsecured creditors in the principal debtor's bankruptcy, and has independently of this right contracted to receive from the guarantor payment to supplement the dividend on the entire debt. If the entire debt is discharged, the creditor has no further interest, and the guarantor stands in his shoes. If the principal debtor remains solvent, the question of justice among his creditors does not arise.[73]

But the creditor may not receive more than 100p in the pound; once he is paid in full he cannot have any further dividend.[74]

Surety's proof against principal debtor   Where a surety makes any payment under a guarantee, he has an implied right of indemnity against the principal debtor for that sum. Under ss.257 and 258 of the 1857 Act, which provided for

---

70. *Re Sass* [1896] 2 QB 12 and *Re Houlder* [1929] 1 Ch 205.
71. *Re Houlder*, supra, at pp. 210-211.
72. [1966] NI 161.
73. Id. at p. 169.   74. *Re Melton* [1918] 1 Ch 37.

proving contingent debts and liabilities, it was held that this claim by a surety could not be proved until he had made payment discharging the entire sum which he had guaranteed. In *Re an Arranging Debtor,*[75] the insolvent had an overdraft of £2,600, which was guaranteed by the applicant up to a limit of £1,700. Following the petition being presented and demand for payment being made, the surety paid £1,700 to the bank. Lowry J held that the surety could not then prove for that sum because he had not discharged the entire debt, notwithstanding the limited liability under his guarantee.[76]

Furthermore, because of the rule against 'double proof', the extent to which the surety can prove in the debtor's liquidation depends on what the creditor has done in that regard. It was held in *Re Fenton*[11] that, where the creditor has lodged a proof, the guarantor cannot prove his claim until he has paid the creditor in full. As Lawrence LJ explained,

> When ... the principal debtor is bankrupt, ... the claim of a surety, who has been called upon to pay but has not yet paid anything to the principal creditor, is in effect a claim for damages for the breach by the principal debtor of his obligation to indemnify the surety on the ground that his bankruptcy has rendered it impossible for him to perform his obligation and has made it possible to estimate the amount which the surety can properly claim by way of damages. . . . [S]o long as the estate of the principal debtor remains liable to the principal creditor the surety will not be permitted to prove ... as such a proof would be a double proof for the same debt.
>
> [Where] the surety has guaranteed the whole of the debts of the principal creditors, although he has limited his liability ... to a fixed amount, . . . the principal creditors have the right to prove against the estate of the principal debtor for the whole of their debts, and until they have received 20s. in the pound on those debts the surety cannot prove against the estate of the principal debtor, even although he may have paid the full amount for which he is liable under his guarantees.[78] Even where the principal creditor has been paid in full partly by a dividend from the estate of the insolvent surety and partly by a dividend from the estate of the insolvent principal debtor, the trustee of the insolvent surety will not be allowed to prove against the estate of the principal debtor for the amount which the estate of the surety has contributed towards the payment of the debt, as it is only when the surety has paid the full amount of the debt that he will be subrogated to the rights of the principal creditor:[79]

A surety who has paid off the full debt covered by his guarantee is entirely subrogated to the rights of the principal creditor. He is entitled to the benefit of any securities held by that creditor in respect of the debt.[80] If the creditor enjoyed

75. [1970] NI 96.
76. Following *Ulster Bank v Lambe* [1966] NI 161.
77. [1931] 1 Ch 85.   78. Citing *Re Sass* [1896] 2 QB 12.
79. [193] 1 Ch at pp. 114-115.   80. *Re Whitehouse* (1887) 37 Ch D 683.

preferential status, the surety acquires an equivalent status.[81] He may succeed to that creditor's proof and receive any further dividends paid by the liquidator. His payments under the guarantee may be set-off against debts due to him by the principal debtor. However, because of the no 'double proof' rule, that set-off extends only to payments actually made and not to his prospective liabilities under the guarantee.[82]

Insolvency of the guarantor   Where the surety has been put into liquidation, the creditor can prove in respect of the liability under the guarantee, whether it is absolute (e.g. the debtor has defaulted) or is contingent (e.g. no demand has yet been made by the creditor).[83] The fact that the creditor has obtained a judgment or award against the debtor is not in itself sufficient to establish the surety's liability; it is necessary to prove that liability independently.[84] The amount of the guaranteed debt will be reduced by any payments made by the debtor or by a co-surety, provided one of them appropriated the payment to that debt.[85]

Taking first payments made before the liquidation commenced; where the guarantor is liable for the whole debt, without limit to his liability, which is the commonest case, any appropriation of payments made will accordingly reduce the proof in the guarantor's insolvency. Where there is liability for the whole debt but subject to a limit, the appropriated payments will only reduce that proof if the payments are such that they reduce the total amount of the debt below the expressed limit of liability. Where the guarantor is liable for only part of the debt, then, in the absence of specific appropriation of any payments made or express provision in the guarantee, the liquidator cannot insist that those payments be applied solely to reduce the guaranteed part of that debt.[86]

Where, after the liquidation commenced, the creditor receives part-payment from the principal debtor or a co-surety, he may still prove for the full amount of the guaranteed debt; he can do so whether the payment was received before or after he lodged his proof.[87] But the creditor cannot receive in aggregate more than 100p in the pound. Special rules apply to this matter where the debt is in respect of a negotiable instrument.[88]

Secured creditors   Before 1887, when the winding up of companies was governed by Chancery rather than bankruptcy practice, a secured creditor could retain his security and, at the same time, prove for the full amount of his debt.[89]

---

81. *R. v Fay* (1878) 4 LR Ir 606 and *Re Lamplugh Iron Ore Co* [1927] 1 Ch 308.
82. *Re Fenton* [1931] 1 Ch 85.
83. *Re Fitzgeorge* [1905] 1 KB 462.
84. *Ex p. Young* (1881) 17 Ch D 668.
85. *Commercial Bank of Australia v Official Assignee* [1893] AC 181.
86. *Re Sherry* (1883) 25 Ch D 692.
87. *Re Houlder* [1972] 1 Ch 205; see *Re Amalgamated Investment & Property* [1985] Ch 349.
88. See supra.   89. *Mason v Bogg* (1834) 2 My. & Cr. 443.

The position regarding proofs lodged by secured creditors is now set out in considerable detail in rule 24 of the Bankruptcy Act, 1988's first schedule. A secured creditor is defined in s.3 of that Act as meaning 'any creditor holding any mortgage, charge or lien on the debtor's estate or any part thereof as security for a debt due to him.' A creditor who has legal title to property held by the company, for instance under a leasing agreement, is not a secured creditor for these purposes. Nor is a creditor who has a guarantee or indemnity from a third party, a secured creditor within this definition even if the guarantor has given a supporting charge over his property.[90] Nor is a creditor who obtained a court order appointing a receiver by way of equitable execution a secured creditor, except to the extent that actual possession was taken of the property.[91]

Rule 24 retains, with considerable elaboration, the traditional bankruptcy rule, which is that secured creditors could not both prove for the entire debt and also realise their security. Three options are open to the secured creditor,[92] viz. surrender the security and prove for the entire debt, realise the security and prove for the balance or value the security and prove for the balance.

Surrendering the security   He may surrender his security for the benefit of the general creditors; in that event, he can then prove for the entire debt. Surrendering the security does not discharge a guarantee.[93] Surrendering a first mortgage does not accelerate the rights of subsequent mortgagees; it simply substitutes the liquidator for the first mortgagee.[94] Once a surrender is made, presumably the creditor cannot then change his mind and rely on the security he had.

Realising the security   Alternatively, he can realise the security; on doing that, he can prove for the balance due to him after deducting the proceeds of sale of the security. He is not however permitted to disturb any dividend already declared, i.e. all payments which the liquidator has already made to other creditors cannot be disturbed because the secured creditor has chosen this option. Where the secured creditor has several claims against the company, he can appropriate the proceeds of realisation between those claims as he thinks fit. He may even appropriate that money between claims which are provable and are non-provable,[95] or between preferential and non preferential claims.[96] Where there was a surplus on the realisation but the company also has an unsecured debt with that creditor, he may set-off the balance in his hands against that debt.[97] Where several securities are held in respect of separate debts, the proceeds of realisation must be applied to each security's particular debt; a

90. *Re National United Investment Corp.* [1901] 1 Ch 950.
91. *Crowshaw v Lindhurst Ship Co.* [1897] 2 Ch 154.
92. *Moore v Anglo Italian Bank* (1879) 10 Ch D 681.
93. *Rainbow v Juggins* (1880) 5 QBD 422.
94. *Cracknall v Janson* (1877) 6 Ch D 735.
95. *Re William Hall (Contractors) Ltd* [1967] 1 WLR 948.
96. *Re Fox & Jacobs* [1894] 1 KB 438.
97. *Re H.E. Thorne & Son* [1914] 2 Ch 438.

surplus on any one realisation may not be applied to make up the deficiency on another secured debt.[1]

Valuing the security The third choice is to value his security; if he does that he can prove for the balance over what value he put on the security. When taking this option, on submitting the proof he must state the particulars of the security, the date it was acquired and its estimated value. Creditors should exercise some care when valuing their security because they cannot easily alter whatever value they gave initially. Formerly an amendment would be allowed only in 'some very extreme instance' but this rule has now been relaxed somewhat. Amendment will be permitted if it is proved that the earlier value was 'made bona fide on a mistaken estimate'.[2] Where such amendment is allowed, that creditor's proof must be appropriately adjusted and, if an excess has been paid to him, that must be reimbursed.[3] He is entitled to be paid more if the value was adjusted downwards, subject to the proviso that any payments already made to creditors should not be disturbed. The court will not readily set aside the estimate of the security submitted by a creditor. Vaughan Williams LJ once remarked that 'when one arrives at the conclusion that the estimate is real and not a sham, we ought not to go into the question what is the true value after the declaration of the estimated value.'[4] In any event, there are several deterrents against a creditor knowingly placing a wrong value on the security. He will not without good reason be permitted to amend his valuation. Furthermore, the liquidator is given the option to redeem the security at the value which the creditor has assigned to it;[5] the possibility of this happening is a strong incentive against under-valuing the security. Instead of redeeming it, if dissatisfied with the estimated value, the liquidator also has the choice of putting the security up for sale.[6] The actual form and methods of sale should be agreed with the security-holder; absent such agreement, these matters will be determined by the court. It is provided that, if the sale is by public auction, the mortgagee is permitted to bid for and to buy the property.[7]

Redemption of security by liquidator While the liquidator can decide to redeem or to offer for sale any security which the creditor has valued, if the creditor so chooses he can compel the liquidator to decide whether he will do either of these things.[8] At any time, by notice in writing, the secured creditor can require him to make this election; the liquidator then has three months within which to decide. On the expiry of that period, the security belongs entirely to that creditor and he is entitled to prove for the balance due on the debt after the estimated value of the security has been deducted. However, if that creditor subsequently realises the security and obtains a different price from

1. *Re Newton* (1836) 2 Deac 66.
2. Bankruptcy Act 1988, schedule reg. 24(5).
3. Id. reg. 24(6).   4. *Re Button* [1905] 1 KB 602, at p. 605.
5. Supra n.12, reg. 24(4)(a).   6. Ibid.
7. Bankruptcy Act 1988, s.53.   8. Id. schedule, reg. 24(4)(b).

his earlier valuation, he is required to adjust his proof to fully take account of the price he got.[9]

Surrender for non-disclosure   When submitting a proof, the secured creditor must state that he is secured. If subsequently it is discovered that there was a security which was not stated, it must be surrendered to the liquidator for the benefit of the creditors generally.[10] However, the court is given a broad discretion to allow the proof to be amended by stating the security, on such terms as the court deems proper in the circumstances. An amendment will not be permitted if the other creditors would be prejudiced.[11] A creditor who did not disclose his security and who then did not surrender it or comply with the court's directions, as the case may be, is excluded entirely from sharing in any distribution.

Interest on the secured debt   It was held by the Supreme Court in *Re McCairns (P.M.P.A.) plc*[12] that, where the secured creditor was entitled to interest, his right does not end once the company is liquidated; that creditor is entitled to continuing interest as well as the principal from the proceeds on realisation of the security. Section 136 of the Bankruptcy Act, 1988, which restricts various forms of enforcement against the bankrupt's assets, is subject to the proviso that it does 'not affect the power of a secured creditor to realise or otherwise deal with his security' as if this section did not exist. There is no express provision in the Companies Acts that secured creditors shall not be entitled to recover interest from their security and the Court declined to imply such a rule into those Acts. According to McCarthy J, 'not having brought the property the subject of the charge into the winding up and not having sought to prove any claim in the winding up, the bank is entitled to be paid interest up to the date of redemption, in accordance with the terms of the charging documents.'[13]

REJECTING CLAIMS

There are several grounds on which a liquidator will not admit a claim to proof.

Indebtedness to shareholders   Debts to shareholders or members of the company in that very capacity cannot be the subject of proof. Section 207(i)(g) of the 1963 Act stipulates that any sum due to a member 'in his character of a member, by way of dividends, profits or otherwise', shall not be deemed to be a debt of the company for these purposes. It is only when all the other creditors are paid off that the liquidator can contemplate repaying these particular debts. But the mere fact that a creditor is also a shareholder of the company does not

9.   Id. reg. 24(7).   10. Id. reg. 24(8).
11. Cf. *Re Robinson* [1958] NI 166 and *Re Sythes* [1962] NI 38.
12. [1991] 2 IR 465.
13. Id. at p. 493. See too, *Re Norman Holdings Co. Ltd* [1991] 1 WLR 10: no set-off against secured creditor who does not prove in the insolvency.

debar him from proving his debt.[14] It is only when the sum in question is owed to the member *qua* member that it cannot be the subject of proof. As Kay J observed, the words 'or otherwise' in s.207(i)(g) 'must mean something analogous to dividends or profits on his shares. That shows the meaning. Dividends are due to him in character of member; profits are due to him in his character of member; there may be something else equally due to him in his character of member which this clause was intended to include.'[15]

The most common example of such sums are dividends which have been declared but which have not been paid. Several of the reported cases concern arrears of what were categorised as remuneration voted to directors-shareholders, the issue being whether those sums were really remuneration for services or were they a share of the company's profits. *Re Cinnamond Park Ltd*[16] is an excellent example. Each of the directors there held one fifth of the shares in the company. At the relevant time some of them were employed under contracts for a ten years duration whereby, in addition to a fixed salary, they were to be paid one fifth of the net profits of the business for so long as they held their shares. Wilson J found, in the circumstances, that the sums due under these contracts were genuine remuneration and, therefore, could be the subject of proof. Another director used to have a similar agreement but, when he became ill and could no longer work for the company, that was replaced by a new agreement under which, so long as he or his personal representatives held one fifth of the company's capital, they would be paid one fifth of the net profits of the business. It was held '[t]his is not an agreement for remuneration for work done at all. It is simply an agreement to pay him the extra one fifth of the net profits so long as he keeps his share interest in the capital of the company in one holding. . . .'[17] Any money payable to him under this agreement was due to him *qua* member and, therefore, could not be proved. Under a provision in the articles of association, the company's shareholders had voted for the directors a substantial amount by way of a bonus for one year. These sums were held not to be in the nature of dividends but were 'voted . . . for good work done . . . over and above being a member, as director and manager of the company.'[18] Difficulties could arise in applying the distinction here to dealings between co-operative societies and their members.[19]

Double proof Persons will not be permitted to prove more than once for what in substance is the one and the same debt. The leading authority on the rule against double proof is *Deering v Bank of Ireland*[20] where, as security for a loan, the debtor assigned a life insurance policy to the bank and made a covenant to pay the annual premiums on that policy as they fell due. On being adjudicated a bankrupt, he owed the bank £980 and his life policy was worth £180. The

14. E.g. *Salomon v Salomon & Co.* [1897] AC 22.
15. *Re Dale & Plant Ltd* (1889) 43 Ch D 255, at p. 259.
16. [1930] NI 47.   17. Id. at p. 54.
18. Id. at p. 56.   19. See *Company Law*, pp. 474-476.
20. (1886) 12 HLC 20.

bank lodged a proof for £800, which was the balance owing after valuing its security. But the bank also sought to prove for £400, which was the actuarial value of the debtor's covenant to continue paying the premiums on this policy. It was held that the rule against double proof precluded paying for both liabilities. As Porter MR explained,

> if the creditor proves for his debt, he cannot also prove for the bankrupt's contract to keep up [the] policy . . . as security for the same debt. To do so, would be to admit a double proof; because the security cannot, for purposes of proof in bankruptcy, be deemed a debt distinct and separate from the thing secured, and the creditor's interest in the security is the same thing as the debt itself. In the substance, a covenant to pay premiums on a policy . . . is only a covenant to pay the debt, by keeping alive something which will ultimately pay it; and to allow the creditor to prove both for the debt and for the contract to secure the debt, is to admit a double proof. The creditor can choose either, but cannot . . . have both.[21]

Whenever two or more debts, which are apparently distinct, are in reality the one and the same debt, only one of those will be admitted to proof. The criterion of identity is not the technical legal characterisation of the liability but whether 'in substance' both are the same, in the sense that it obviously would be unjust on the general creditors if both claims were admitted to proof. As Oliver LJ observed in one instance, 'the rule against double proofs in respect of two liabilities to an insolvent debtor is going to apply wherever the existence of one liability is dependent upon and referable only to the liability of the other and where to allow both liabilities to rank independently for dividend would produce injustice to the other unsecured creditors.'[22] Thus, in *Re Fenton*,[23] it was held that a surety for the bankrupt's debts cannot prove his claim unless he has paid the principal creditor in full under the guarantee. Romer LJ could not 'agree that a surety who has not paid off the principal creditor can prove in the bankruptcy of the principal debtor . . . unless the principal creditor has re-nounced in some way his right to lodge a proof himself while preserving . . . his rights against the surety. To allow such a sharing in the assets would be to subject the assets to two claims in respect of the same debt, and this is contrary to the well established rule in bankruptcy against double proof.'[24] For the same reason, there cannot be a proof against the drawer and also against the acceptor of a bill of exchange.

Unenforceable debts   Debts which could not have been enforced against the debtor cannot be proved against his estate in bankruptcy or a liquidation. In *Government of India v Taylor*,[25] Viscount Simonds observed that

21. *Sub nom. Re Killen* (1885) 15 LR (Ir) Ch 388, at p. 393.
22. *Barclays Bank v T.S.O.G. Trust Fund* [1984] 2 WLR 49, at p. 58.
23. [1931] 1 Ch 85.
24. Id. at pp. 118-119.   25. [1955] AC 491.

it is the duty of the liquidator to discharge out of the assets in his hands those claims which are legally enforceable, and to hand over any surplus to the contributories. I find no words which vest in him a discretion to meet claims which are not legally enforceable. It will be remembered that, so far as is relevant for this purpose, the law is the same whether the winding up is voluntary or by the court, whether the company is solvent or insolvent, and that an additional purpose of a winding up is to secure that creditors who have enforceable claims shall be treated equally, subject only to the priorities for which the statute provides. It would be a strange result if it were found that the statute introduced a new category of creditors to compete with those who alone, apart from it, could enforce their claims.[26]

There are various reasons why the debt might be unenforceable. The contractual obligation to pay the money could be unlawful, such as for breach of the Gaming Acts,[27] of exchange control regulations[28] or other statutory provisions. Or the obligation may be unenforceable because it contravenes public policy, such as in integral aspect of an agreement which is an unreasonable restraint of trade[29] or a debt owed to some foreign revenue authority.

Ultra vires transactions   Formerly, *ultra vires* debts could not be enforced against a company and could not be proved.[30] But, by virtue of s.8(1) of the 1963 Act, such a debt is now enforceable provided that the creditor, at the time the debt was incurred, was not 'actually aware' that it was *ultra vires*.[31]

Pre-incorporation contracts   Formerly, pre-incorporation contracts could not be enforced against the company and debts arising under them could not be proved.[32] But, under s.37(1) of the 1963 Act, those contracts can now be enforced against the company whenever it has ratified the contract.[33]

Statute barred claims   Limitation periods cease to run against the debtor as from the date of his adjudication as a bankrupt.[34] In liquidations, limitation periods cease to run from the time of the winding up order or, if earlier, from the time the company resolved to wind up.[35] In the case of the petitioning creditor, however, time ceases to run against him from the time he presented the petition.[36]

26. Id. at p. 509.
27. Cf. *Lipkin Gorman v Karpnale Ltd* [1991] 3 WLR 10.
28. Cf. *Westpac Banking Corp. v Dempsey* (Morris J, November 1992).
29. Cf. *Stenhouse (Australia) Ltd v Phillips* [1974] AC 391.
30. *Re Jon Beauforte (London) Ltd* [1953] Ch 1331.
31. See *Company Law*, pp. 428-431.
32. *Re National Motor Mail Coach Co.* [1908]. 2 Ch 515.
33. See *Company Law*, p. 426.
34. *Re Benzon* [1914] 2 Ch 68.
35. *Re General Rolling Stock Co.* (1872) LR 7 Ch App 646.
36. *Re Cases of Taffs Well Ltd* [1992] Ch 179.

Foreign revenue claims   In *Re Gibbons*,[37] Walsh J refused to give assistance to English bankruptcy proceedings, which were commenced by the Revenue authorities there to collect unpaid taxes, because providing assistance in those circumstances would contravene the public policy against enforcing the claims of foreign revenue authorities. Walsh J followed the principles laid down by the former Supreme Court in *Buchanan v McVey*,[38] where claims brought by a Scots liquidator who was appointed in similar circumstances were not enforced. It was held that '[i]t is not a question whether the plaintiff is a foreign State or the representative of a foreign State or its revenue authority. In every case the substance of the claim must be scrutinised and if it then appears that it is really a suit brought for the purpose of collecting the debts of a foreign revenue, it must be rejected.'[39] The position may very well be different where the foreign revenue authority is one, albeit a significant one, of the creditors. In *Re Ayres*[40] an Australian court permitted a New Zealand assignee in bankruptcy to continue proceedings in Australia, even though approximately 60% of the bankrupt's debts were owed to various New Zealand revenue authorities.

Liabilities improperly incurred   There are certain kinds of liabilities which could be enforced against the company itself but which a liquidator nonetheless will not admit to proof because to do so would unfairly prejudice the general body of creditors and the contributories. The governing principle was stated by the High Court of Australia as follows:

> A liquidator may properly reject a proof of debt if the liability, though enforceable against the company, is not a true liability of the company but is founded merely on some act or omission on the part of the company which unjustly prejudices the interests of the creditors or contributories in the assets available for distribution. In this respect there is no reason to distinguish between the position of a liquidator and that of a trustee in bankruptcy. . . . The occasions when it is right to reject a proof of debt in respect of what is not a true liability of the company may not be susceptible of exhaustive definition.[41]

One type of instance where a claim would be rejected is where the circumstances are similar to those in which a court of bankruptcy would go behind a judgment, which were summarised as

> Circumstances tending to show fraud or collusion, or miscarriage of justice or that a compromise was not a fair and reasonable one, in the sense that even if not fraudulent it was foolish, absurd or improper, or resulted from an unequal position of the parties.[42]

Accordingly, in an appropriate case the liquidator may go behind a judgment

---

37. [1960] Ir Jur Rep 60.   38. [1954] IR 89.
39. Id. at p. 107.   40. (1981) FLR 235.
41. *Tanning Research Laboratories Inc. v O'Brien*, 64 ALJLR 211 (1990), at p. 214.
42. Ibid. See *Bankruptcy Law* pp. 138-139.

or may re-open a compromise. Nor is he bound by a statement of affairs submitted on behalf of the company.[43] But he cannot go behind a proof from the Revenue for assessed taxes;[44] the most he can do is seek a re-assessment or to appeal the assessment.

PROCEDURE FOR PROOF

How creditors go about proving their debts is as follows.

Ascertaining the liabilities   In order to ensure that all debts are proved within a reasonable time, the liquidator may fix a time by which all proofs must be lodged.[45] Usually, he will publish a notice in the prescribed form to that effect; he also should give written notice to every creditor mentioned in the statement of affairs who has not lodged a proof. In a compulsory winding up, s.241 of the 1963 Act enables the court to fix a time within which proofs must be lodged; any subsequent claims by creditors may be excluded from any distribution which has been made. But the court cannot prevent a late proof which may be satisfied from any subsequent distribution. Where in all the circumstances a liquidator ought to have been aware of a claim but does not pursue the matter, he risks being held liable in negligence to that creditor if no proof is submitted.[46]

If, after the liquidation has been completed, a person finds that he is owed money by the company, it is then too late for him to enforce payment, either against the company or its contributories if the company had been solvent.[47]

Modes of proof   How debts or claims are to be proved in a liquidation is set out in rules 102-111 of the Winding Up Rules. In voluntary liquidations formal proofs are not essential but the liquidator may require that the claim be submitted in writing. In compulsory liquidations ordinarily furnishing the liquidator with particulars of the claim will suffice. But he may insist on the proof being made by affidavit, in the prescribed form. That affidavit must[48] be made by the creditor himself or by someone duly authorised by him; it should contain or refer to a statement of account showing the particulars of the debt and specify any vouchers with which the debt can be substantiated. If the creditor has security, that fact must be stated[49] but there is no express requirement to state the nature of the security. Unless the liquidator requires a creditor to attend and prove his claim, he must bear the costs of his proof.[50]

Normally, each individual creditor must prove his own debt; somebody else cannot make the proof for him. But in the case of arrears of wages due to company employees, their trade union official or foreman or other designated

---

43. *Re Browne* [1960] 1 WLR 692.
44. *Re Calvert* [1899] 2 QB 145.   45. Rule 95.
46. *Re Armstrong Whitworth Securities Co.* [1947] Ch. 678 and *Pulsford v Devenish* [1903] 2 Ch 625.
47. *Butler v Broadhead* [1975] Ch 97.   48. Rule 103.
49. Rule 69.   50. Rule 104.

person may put in the proof on their behalf, on the prescribed form.[51] In the case of proof of a debt under a negotiable instrument, that instrument must be produced to the official liquidator.[52] As was explained above, there are rules for proving debts in the form of periodical payments and debts payable at some future time.[53]

Dealing with the proofs   Whether or not a proof will be admitted is for the liquidator to decide in the first place. In making that decision he should consider the grounds of the debt and the existence of any set-off.[54] In official liquidations, the liquidator must leave in the Examiner's office a list of the debts which may be admitted without any further evidence and a list of those which he believes ought to be proved.[55] He should also file with the Examiner an affidavit in the prescribed form setting out the debts and claims which should be allowed without any further evidence.[56] He should notify those creditors whose claims he has decided to disallow. Even in respect of a debt which he has allowed, the Examiner may still require the creditor to prove his claim. Creditors may be required by the liquidator to attend to have their claims adjudicated on; they are entitled to their costs of proof. The outcome of the adjudication will be set out in a certificate which the examiner makes up. Any creditor who is dissatisfied with the outcome of the adjudication may appeal the matter to the court. That appeal is a re-hearing *de novo* and both sides may adduce fresh evidence.[57] Usually the costs of a successful appeal against the liquidator's rejection of a proof will be directed to be paid out of the company's assets.[58]

PAYMENT OF DIVIDENDS

One of the fundamental rules in company insolvency is the equal treatment of creditors. This is embodied in s.275 of the 1963 Act, according to which 'the property of a company shall . . . be applied in satisfaction of its liabilities *pari passu*. . . .' But there are several exceptions to the principle of equality, which are dealt with in detail in Part IV of this book. In brief, there are, firstly, secured creditors and others with some proprietary right in the company's assets; generally, they are entitled to the full value of their security or other right and may then prove for the balance as ordinary unsecured creditors. Secondly, there are preferential creditors who, under the Companies Acts, must be paid before the ordinary unsecured creditors; mainly certain Revenue debts and certain debts to company employees. Thirdly, there is a small category of creditors who rank after the general unsecured creditors; these are described as deferred creditors. In 1990, s.275 of the 1963 Act was amended to enable creditors to

51. Rule 110. 52. Rule 111.
53. Rules 106-108; see supra p. 280. 54. For set-off, see post pp. 339-342.
55. Rule 97. 56. Ibid.
57. *Re Kentwood Constructions Ltd* [1960] 1 WLR 646 and *Re Trepca Mines Ltd* [1960] 1 WLR 1273.
58. *Re National Wholemeal Bread & Biscuit Co.* [1892] 2 Ch 457.

agree that some of them shall rank after other creditors; consequently, the former mandatory rule of equality may now be contracted out of.

Generally the liquidator will not wait until the entire liquidation has been concluded before paying any dividend. Because it is important that creditors should get at least some of their money back as soon as possible, usually the liquidator will seek to pay them a dividend as soon as he has made substantial realisations of assets. Before an official liquidator may pay a dividend, he must obtain the sanction of the court.[59] When paying an interim dividend, the liquidator should be satisfied that there is enough to pay the statutorily preferred debts. Although the court may permit him to pay a particular class of creditors in full, an application for such consent ought not be made unless the liquidator is satisfied that the preferred creditors will be paid in full.

Any creditor who is late putting in his proof after the deadline notified by the liquidator cannot disturb any dividends which have been paid already and must take his chance in the liquidator finding further realisations in order to finance a payment to him. It has not been established whether, if such assets come to hand, he is entitled to an equalising dividend or he simply ranks *pari passu* in the remaining dividends being paid. When the winding up has been entirely concluded, there may have been further realisations to enable an additional and final dividend to be paid, again on a *pari passu* basis, except of course for creditors who have agreed to be subordinated to the ordinary unsecured creditors.

59. Rule 112.

20

Termination and Aftermath of Winding Up

In appropriate circumstances it is possible to have a liquidation annulled by the court or to have its progress stayed. Otherwise the liquidator is required to conclude the process, which leads to the company's dissolution. Within two years of the date of dissolution, it is possible to have the company resuscitated in a fashion.

ANNULLING THE WINDING UP

Section 234(1) of the 1963 Act empowers the court to annul an official liquidation on such terms as the court deems fit. Either the liquidator, any creditor or a contributory may apply for an annulment and the order will be made 'on proof to the satisfaction of the court' that the winding up should be terminated in this manner. There are no reported cases which deal with the circumstances in which an order will be made under s.234(1) or the terms such an order might include. It was held by Carroll J in *Re Oakthorpe Holding Ltd*[2] that s.280 of the 1963 Act gives the court jurisdiction to annul a voluntary winding up. There an annulment was granted because the company's directors had not filed the statutory declaration of solvency in accordance with the requirements laid down.

STAYING THE WINDING UP

Section 234(2) of the 1963 Act empowers the court to stay an official liquidation on such terms as it deems fit. On several occasions this power has been applied to voluntary winding ups via s.280 of the 1963 Act. It would seem that a voluntary winding up cannot be stayed by the members of the company passing a resolution to that effect—or by such a resolution from the members and the creditors.

Applications for a stay are usually made in order to give effect to some scheme of arrangement with the creditors or agreed plan for reconstruction of the company; also where the company has succeeded in paying off all of its debts in full. A stay will be granted 'on proof to the satisfaction to the court'

1. Cf. *Re Calmey Ltd* [1989] BCLC 299.
2. [1987] IR 632.

that an order under s.234(2) should be made. In exercising its jurisdiction under this section, the court is guided by the criteria it follows when ordering that a bankruptcy sequestration should be annulled. This order will not be made merely because that is what all the creditors want or support. According to Buckley J in *Re Telescriptor Syndicate Ltd*, before it would grant a stay the court must consider 'not only whether what is proposed is for the benefit of the creditors, but also whether it is conducive or detrimental to commercial morality and to the interests of the public at large.'[3] For instance, if the company's affairs are or ought to be under investigation or misfeasance proceedings ought to be commenced, a stay will not be ordered. At least in Australia it has been held that a stay will never be granted if there is a substantial deficiency between the company's assets and liabilities, even where a scheme of arrangement has been put together which would render the company no longer insolvent.[4] However, these cases may have turned on the fact that the objective of the reorganisation schemes there was to obtain a substantial tax windfall.

CONCLUDING THE WINDING UP

When all the assets have been realised and the creditors have been paid whatever dividend was due to them, in full if they were that fortunate, and any surplus is appropriately distributed, the liquidator will take steps to being the liquidation to an end. In the case of official liquidations, there is no express requirement to hold final meetings of the company's creditors or members. Of course the liquidator could always convene such meetings. Usually what happens is that, having passed his final account, the official liquidator applies to the court for directions regarding how the balance should be disposed of. Then, once the Examiner has certified that the balance was dealt with in the manner so directed, the liquidator will then apply to the court for an order dissolving the company.

In creditors' voluntary liquidations, final meetings of the members and of the creditors must be convened in accordance with s.273 of the 1963 Act. Details of those meetings must be advertised in two daily newspapers circulating in the district where the company's registered office is located. An account of the liquidation must be given at those meetings and any questions about it must be answered by the liquidator. Within a week of those meetings, a return must be made to the registrar of companies, stating that they were held, which should be accompanied by the liquidator's account presented at them.

A compulsory liquidation is deemed to have ended when the court's order dissolving the company has been notified to the registrar of companies.[5] A voluntary winding up ordinarily ends at the date of dissolution.[6] However, it continues if the liquidator retains funds which remain to be claimed or distributed, until they are either distributed or are paid into the Companies Liquidation Account provided for in s.307 of the 1963 Act.

3.   [1903] 1 Ch 174 at p. 180. Cf. *Re Calgary & Edmonton Land Co.* [1975] 1 WLR 355.
4.   *Re Data Homes Pty. Ltd* [1972] 2 NSWLR 23.
5.   1963 Act. s.273.   6. Ibid.

DISSOLUTION OF THE COMPANY

Dissolution of the company is the final step in the liquidation; from that time onwards, the company has ceased to exist, although s.310 of the 1963 Act gives the court a power of resuscitation.

Procedure The procedure for dissolving a company varies depending whether the liquidation is compulsory or is voluntary. Where the company is being wound up by the court and its affairs have been 'completely wound up', s.249 of the 1963 Act authorises the liquidator to apply to the court for the company's dissolution. An order may then be made that it be dissolved as from that date.

In the case of voluntary liquidations, dissolution occurs three months from the time the registrar of companies has received the liquidator's return and account, as provided for in s.273 of the 1963 Act.[7] This rule applies even if in fact the company's affairs had not been fully wound up if, so far as the liquidator was aware, they had been wound up. Once 'the liquidator has done all that he can to wind up the company, when he has disposed of the assets as far as he can realise them, got in the calls as far as he can enforce them, paid the debts as far as he is aware of them, and has done all that he can do in winding up the affairs, so that he has completed his business so far as he can, and is *functus officio*',[8] the prerequisites for s.273 have been fully met.

Effects of dissolution Dissolution destroys the company's very existence. According to Blackstone,[9] the debts either to or by the corporation are entirely extinguished by its dissolution. Actions cannot any longer be brought by the company or against it. An application made in the course of a winding up cannot be dealt with by the court, which no longer has any jurisdiction to wind it up. Formerly, the company's remaining real property devolved to the Crown by way of *escheat* and its personal property by way of *bona vacantia*. Under s.28 of the State Property Act, 1954, the property now vests in the State. An exception, of course, to this principle is property which the company was holding in trust or had given as security.

Unclaimed amounts It occasionally happens where a company is being wound up that, after paying off the creditors and distributing the surplus, it still has funds because all the liabilities that were admitted to proof have not been claimed or some of the surplus has not been claimed. Where that occurs in the case of a company that is being wound up voluntarily, s.307 of the 1963 Act provides that the unclaimed sum be lodged to the Companies Liquidation Account which is kept at the Bank of Ireland, and which is under the court's

7. Id. s.273(4).
8. *Re London & Caledonian Marine Insurance Co.* (1878) 11 Ch D 140, at p. 144. See too, *Re Cornish Manures Ltd* [1967] 1 WLR 807.
9. *Commentaries on the Laws of England*, Vol. I, Ch. 18 (1765).

control. Rule 132 of the Winding Up Rules sets out the procedure for lodging funds to that account and how claims made in respect of such sums are dealt with. Where a sum is not claimed within seven years of its being lodged, it must be paid into the Exchequer. However, if later the court is satisfied that an applicant is entitled to money paid over in this manner, it will order the Minister for Finance to pay that money to the applicant.

Disposing of company records Where the company is being wound up compulsorily,[10] the court will direct how the liquidator shall dispose of the company's records. In the case of a voluntary winding up,[11] the ultimate disposal of the records is determined by a special resolution of the company if it is a members' voluntary winding up. In a creditors' voluntary winding up, the determination is by the committee of inspection or by the creditors, if there is no committee; in the absence of any such determination the decision is the liquidator's, who can dispose of the records 'as he thinks fit'. However, during the three years immediately following the company's dissolution the records must be kept by the liquidator, who has absolute control over them.

RESUSCITATING DISSOLVED COMPANIES

If the company's affairs had not in fact been fully wound up, the dissolution of the company and the drastic ensuing effects often cause considerable hardship. Some time after the dissolution took place a person may discover that he had a claim against the company, for instance, for a disease or other damage that had not actually manifested itself previously.[12] Occasional suggestions were made that a dissolution might be set aside where it was caused by fraud or possibly where no reasonable liquidator would have concluded that the company's affairs had been fully wound up. In 1907 a procedure was introduced for in effect resuscitating dissolved companies.[13] It is now s.310 of the 1963 Act, which empowers the court to declare a dissolution void in an appropriate case; this power should not be confused with s.12(6) of the 1982 Act for re-registration, within 20 years, of companies which were struck off for failure to make annual returns or are otherwise defunct.

The court's resuscitation power under s.310 is entirely discretionary and no guidance of any kind is contained in the section. Its primary function is to revive the company in order to complete the winding up of its affairs by getting in any outstanding assets, discharging so far as is possible any remaining liabilities and distributing whatever capital and surplus there is. It was held in *Re Servers of the Blind League*[14] that this resuscitation power would not be exercised where, as a result, persons would be deprived of a vested interest in an asset acquired otherwise than through the medium of the dissolved company. An

10. 1963 Act s.305(1)(a).   11. Id. s.305(1)(b).
12. E.g. *Bradley v Eagle Star Insurance Co.* [1989] AC 957.
13. Companies Act 1907, s.31.
14. [1960] 1 WLR 564.

application under s.310 can be made by the liquidator, presumably meaning the former liquidator, and by any other person 'who appears to the court to be interested'. Thus a wide category of person are given *locus standi*. Perhaps the main defect with the section is its application for a comparatively short period; the application under it must be made within two years of the date of dissolution. Especially now that tort claims can be proved in a liquidation and the limitation period for undiscovered torts has been extended appreciably, this period may be far too short.[15]

Once a company is revived under s.310, proceedings may be brought as if it had never been dissolved. But it is not stipulated whether the company returns to life in liquidation or in an unliquidated form; presumably the latter. It perhaps is an exaggeration to say that the effect of the court's order is to render the dissolution void *ab initio*, for all that s.310 says is that, following the court's order, proceedings may then be taken. It would seem that the shareholders and directors cannot simply return and assume control of the company.

After the two years from the dissolution date expires, it would seem that persons with claims against the company cannot obtain any redress, not even if the winding up yielded a large surplus for the shareholders. For instances, in *Butler v Broadhead*,[16] the company conveyed land to the plaintiffs and some time later it went into a members' voluntary liquidation. Several years later, the plaintiffs discovered that the company never had good title to the land. They sought to sue the shareholders, claiming restitution from the substantial distributions which were made by the liquidator. It was held that their claim should be struck out because statute lays down a procedure for enforcing a company's debts. It would be inconsistent with the rule that all proofs must be lodged in time if redress could be given in an instance like this. The outcome might be different, however, if fraud was involved.

---

15. See generally, Note, 'Recognising Product Liability Claims at Dissolution', 87 *Columbia L.J.* 1048 (1987).
16. [1975] Ch 97.

PART IV

Priorities among Creditors

Where a company is solvent, then all the creditors will be paid off in full and no question can arise of competition between them for shares in the realisations. If a company is insolvent, there are statutory provisions that certain creditors be paid in priority to others and that certain other creditors be paid only after the remainder have received payment in full. The fund from which these payments are to be made is greatly influenced by proprietary and equivalent rights which some creditors may have in the company's assets;[1] generally those prior rights must be met in full from designated assets before the proceeds of sale of those assets can be divided among the other creditors. For instance, creditors with specific security are entitled to be paid the full market value of their security before the preferential and the ordinary creditors can get paid.

Section 284(1) of the 1963 Act provides that, in an insolvent liquidation, 'the same rules shall prevail and be observed relating to the respective rights of secured and unsecured creditors . . . as are in force . . . under the law of bankruptcy . . . .' The full extent of this provision has not been determined.[2] It has been held that the bankruptcy rules apply to the rights of secured creditors inter-se as well as vis-à-vis *unsecured creditors. Thus in* Re Leinster Contract Corp.,[3] *it was held that judgment creditors who have taken no active steps to enforce their security are not entitled to any priority over the ordinary or unsecured creditors; the Chancery rule was that judgment creditors should be so preferred. But it is only the bankruptcy matters referred to in s.284(1) which are rendered applicable in winding ups, except where some other express provision to that end so provides. For instance, in* Re Albion Steel & Wire Co.[4] *it was held that the preferential payments provisions of the Bankruptcy Act were not thereby rendered applicable in a company insolvency. Shortly afterwards the preferential debts legislation was amended to extend to companies being wound up[5] and some time later to where a receiver is appointed over a company's assets.[6]*

1. See generally, Oditah, 'Assets and the Treatment of Claims in Insolvency', 108 *LQR* 459 (1992) and Milman, 'Property Rights on Corporate Insolvency', in A. Clarke ed., *Current Issues in Insolvency Law* (1991) ch. 57.
2. See ante pp. 125-126.
3. [1903] 1 IR 517.
4. (1878) 7 Ch D 547.
5. Preferential Payments in Bankruptcy (Ireland) Act 1889.
6. Preferential Payments in Bankruptcy (Amendment) Act 1897.

21

Absolute Title

Property that is not owned by a bankrupt individual does not vest in the Official Assignee or in his trustee in bankruptcy and, therefore, is not available for distribution among his creditors.[1] The position is broadly the same with insolvent companies; assets which are in the company's possession but which it does not own cannot be seized by a receiver or a liquidator and, instead, must be delivered up to their true owner when due demand is made. As Henchy J observed of the situation where a company's assets vest in a liquidator,

> To say that when the liquidator takes over, the assets of the company vest in him is a less then complete statement of the legal position. The general rule is that he acquires only such title to the assets as the company had—no more, no less. He cannot take any better title to any part of the assets than the company had. This means that he takes the assets subject to any pre-existing enforceable right of a third party in or over them. If that were not so, equities, liabilities and contractual rights validly and enforceably created while the assets were in the hands of the company would be unfairly swept aside and an unjust distribution of the assets would result.[2]

A major qualification to this principle in the law of bankruptcy was the doctrine of 'reputed ownership', under which property which a bankrupt possessed for the purpose of his trade or business, which apparently belonged to him, vested in the Official Assignee even though somebody else in fact was the owner.[3] This rule, however, did not apply to insolvent companies, which is one of the main reasons why floating charges are given mainly by companies and the like and not by private individuals. The rule was repealed entirely in 1988.[4]

There are certain 'absolute title' situations which call for some comment in that, under them, for most practical purposes the company is the owner of the property in question but, legally, it is not the owner. As was explained earlier, where a company obtains the protection of the High Court under the Companies (Amendment) Act, 1990, property which the company holds under hire

---

1. Bankruptcy Act 1988, s.44(1); see *Bankruptcy Law*, pp. 71 et seq.
2. *Dempsey v Bank of Ireland* (Supreme Court, 6 December 1985) at p. 8.
3. Irish Bankrupt and Insolvent Act 1857, s.313; see e.g. *Re McClemens* [1960] IR 141.
4. Repealed by Bankruptcy Act 1988.

purchase, retention of title or equivalent arrangements cannot be repossessed by its owner without the prior consent of the examiner.[5]

LEASING

Assets in a company's possession and being used by it in the course of its business may be held under a lease. There are three main types of lease—leases of land, which are governed by the law of landlord and tenant,[6] 'operating' leases of chattels, whereby the company is simply making temporary use of another's chattels, and 'finance' leases, which in fact are a form of secured lending.

Operating lease   This is an ordinary bailment of chattels at a market rent which bears no direct relationship with the cost of purchasing the asset. It is usually for a comparatively short duration. The leased asset belongs to the bailor and cannot be realised for the benefit of the company's creditors. At times the terms of the lease will stipulate what is to happen in the event of the company becoming insolvent. Where there is no such express clause, it unlikely that liquidation or receivership automatically constitute a repudiation of the contract,[7] but non-payment of the rent due for any appreciable period would have that effect.

Finance lease   Many companies do not own significant parts of their capital equipment but instead lease it from finance companies which specialise in that business—for instance machinery, office furniture and motor vehicles.[8] Under these leases the 'rent' is calculated with reference to the price of the asset— usually to represent the asset's cost to the finance company and its financing charge over the lease period, ordinarily being the asset's useful life. Although this arrangement resembles hire purchase, it is different because it does not involve any option by the lessee to purchase the goods. Once the lease has expired, in principle the finance company remains the goods' owner. In practice, however, those goods will have relatively little commercial value and, if machinery, may be too expensive to repossess. Accordingly, the finance company tends to abandon the goods once all the lease payments have been made.

   Ordinarily, it is a very straightforward matter to ascertain whether any particular asset is being leased. The lessee company is a bailee of those assets and they cannot be used for paying its liabilities to its secured or general creditors. Unless the finance company abandons those assets, it is entitled to have them returned if there has been a breach of the terms of the lease. Under the terms of the lease, the lessor may be entitled to enter the company's premises

---

5.   Companies (Amendment) Act 1990, ss.5(2)(e) and 11(8).
6.   See ante pp. 56-57 and pp. 170-171 on landlord and tenant questions.
7.   See A.G. Guest ed., *Chitty on Contract* (26th ed., 1989) Vol. 1, p. 919.
8.   See generally, A. Membal et al., *Equipment Leasing* (1992).

and repossess the goods. Of course, the assets cannot be repossessed from a company under court protection without the consent of the examiner.[9]

Attractions for lessees using finance leases include fiscal considerations[10] and treatment in the accounts.[11] One of the main features of modern hire purchase legislation is that, where the hirer has made substantial payments but then defaults, he must be given credit for those sums. There is no similar provision for leases, which is one reason why financiers prefer this mode of lending. Accordingly, if the full amount due under the lease is say £30,000 and the company has paid £20,000 but then defaults, the lessor is entitled to keep that £20,000 and still insist on the goods being returned to it. A liquidator or receiver may choose to pay or undertake to pay the outstanding amount, so that the company can continue using those assets.

Can the finance company stipulate in the lease that, in the event of insolvency, the lease is determined—thereby entitling it to retain what has been paid on the lease and also recover the goods, even though a liquidator or receiver is prepared to continue paying the instalments under the lease? Where the lessee is a private individual, a clause of this nature is void under s.49 of the Bankruptcy Act, 1988. It is possible that this rule is made applicable to insolvent liquidations by s.284(1) of the 1963 Act, depending on what exactly is meant by 'the respective rights of secured and unsecured creditors'.[12] Apart entirely from statute, an argument could be made that a clause of that nature is void because it contravenes the principle that an insolvent person cannot by contract provide for a different distribution of his assets than the law allows.[13] But for this argument to succeed, the company must have some proprietary interest in the leased asset. There is slender authority to suggest that such an interest exists—that a hirer's interest under a hire purchase agreement is a proprietary interest of sorts.[14] It could also be argued that equity will protect the company under its jurisdiction to grant relief against forfeiture.[15] But that power is also conditional on the existence of proprietary or possessory rights as opposed to purely contractual rights.

HIRE PURCHASE

Hire purchase is one form of leasing; the main difference from leases generally is that the hirer has an option to purchase the property in question once the lease has expired. The great majority of hire purchase arrangements are consumer contracts, involving the disposal of goods to individuals who do not want them for exclusively commercial purposes. However companies occasionally acquire motor vehicles and certain other types of equipment on hire purchase,

9. Supra n.5; see ante pp. 92-93.
10. See generally, S. Keegan, *Butterworth (Ireland) Tax Guide, 1992-93*, pp. 412-415.
11. See generally, P. Clarke, *Financial Accounting* (1990) pp. 260-263.
12. See ante p. 307.
13. *Ex p. Mackay* (1873) LR 8 Ch App 643.
14. *Wickham Holdings Ltd v Brooke House Motors Ltd* [1967] 1 WLR 295, at p. 300.
15. *Re Piggin* (1962) 106 SJ 768.

although more often those goods would be supplied under straight leases. Hire purchase transactions are now regulated by the Hire Purchase Acts, 1946-1980;[16] many provisions of these Acts also apply to conditional sale agreements and to other letting arrangements of a consumer nature.

Terminating the agreement   Where, by his conduct, the hirer repudiates the agreement, the lessor is entitled at common law to terminate it. It depends on the circumstances of each case whether the hirer's conduct amounts to a repudiation. Mere failure to pay one or more instalments promptly ordinarily will not suffice. If the agreement makes prompt payment 'of the essence', then failure to pay any one instalment on time entitles the lessor to terminate the agreement.[17] Most hire purchase agreements stipulate that the agreement and the hiring come to an end in the event of the hirer's insolvency. Where the hiring is so determined, the bailor can repossess the goods (subject to restrictions set out below) and sue for any unpaid arrears of hire. Moreover, it would seem that the hirer is not entitled to any credit for sums already paid under the agreement, either as deposit, first payment or instalments. Clauses of this nature are declared void by s.49 of the Bankruptcy Act, 1988; whether under s.284(1) of the 1963 Act this rule applies to company insolvencies can be debated.[18] It was held by a County Court judge in England[19] that these clauses contravene the rule against bankrupts stipulating for a different distribution of their assets than the law allows and, moreover, are subject to the equitable jurisdiction to grant relief against forfeiture. The current trend in the case law is to regard the hirer under a hire purchase agreement as possessing some proprietary interest in the goods in question, which co-exists with the hirer's ownership of those goods pending exercise of the option to purchase them. Although a lessor is entitled to recover damages where the hirer wrongfully repudiates the agreement, the Hire Purchase Acts considerably restrict any contractual rights he has to repossess the goods or to obtain a court order for their specific delivery.

Repossession   Repossession involves the lessor or his agent going out and actually recovering the goods. The agreement may give an express right to repossess, such as for the hirer's failure to pay instalments or failure to safeguard the goods. Any stipulation purporting to authorise entry upon any premises for this purpose is declared void.[20] An exception is made for lessors of motor vehicles. A clause in the agreement may permit them to enter a premises and repossess the vehicle, other than any house which is used as a dwelling or any building within its curtilage.[21]

One of the principal protections given to hirers is the prohibition in s.12 of

16. See generally, M. Forde, *Commercial Law in Ireland* (1990) ch. 2.
17. *Lombard North Central plc v Butterworth* [1987] QB 527.
18. See ante p. 307.
19. *Re Piggin* (1962) 106 SJ 768.
20. Hire Purchase Act 1946, s.6(a).
21. Hire Purchase Act 1960, s.16(1).

the 1946 Act against repossession once one-third of the purchase price has been paid or tendered. In that event, the owner may only recover the goods by taking court proceedings. If, in breach of s.12, the goods are repossessed, the hirer not alone is relieved from all liability under the agreement, but all sums paid to the lessor on foot of the agreement can be recovered, including any sums paid by a guarantor.

This prohibition against repossession does not apply in two circumstances. One is where the hirer has exercised any right he has to terminate the agreement.[22] The other is where the goods in question are a motor vehicle for which the lessor has commenced proceedings to recover possession, but the vehicle is found abandoned or left unattended in such circumstances as causes, or is likely to cause, damage to the vehicle, other than its ordinary depreciation. For instance, a car is abandoned in circumstances where it is likely to be stolen and vandalised. In such cases, the vehicle may be repossessed prior to the court hearing the proceedings being brought by the lessor.[23] In order to ensure that the lessor does not abuse the right given to him here, he must apply to the court within fourteen days of having taken possession of the goods and must satisfy it that, in the circumstances then obtaining, he was entitled to repossess the goods. Of course, the hirer always may voluntarily return the goods, thereby waiving all rights he has under s.12. As Davitt P observed in one instance, 'it would surely be an intolerable hardship upon a hirer if, in every case in which one-third of the hire-purchase price had been paid, he could not safely allow the owner to resume possession of goods until he had initiated and prosecuted to judgment an action at law for their recovery.'[24]

Return of the goods Where goods have been wrongful detained or converted, at common law the court has a discretion, instead of just awarding their owner damages, to direct that the goods be returned to him and that he be paid damages for the detention.[25] But where one-third of the purchase price has been paid or tendered to the lessor of hired goods, any proceedings he brings specifically to secure a return of the goods is subject to ss.13-15 of the 1946 Act. In those cases, the lessor may only obtain whatever sum is owing to him under the agreement. On hearing the action, however, the court has a discretion to order that the goods he delivered up to their owner,[26] thereby depriving the hirer of the option to buy the goods on tendering the balance due. A stay may be put on such an order pending payment of money by the hirer.[27] The court order may be to return only a part of the goods proportionate to the amount paid by or for the hirer.[28] A judgment for the recovery of goods hired may only be given by a judge or by the Master of the High Court, and may not simply be entered in the Central Office of the High Court.[29]

22. 1946 Act s.12(3).   23. 1960 Act s.16(2)-(5).
24. *McDonald v Bowmaker (Ireland) Ltd* [1949] IR 317, at p. 320.
25. *British Wagon Co. Ltd v Shortt* [1961] IR 164.
26. 1946 Act s.13(4).   27. Id. s.14 and 1960 Act s.15.
28. 1960 Act s.29.   29. Id. s.27.

RETENTION OF TITLE

Since the mid 1970s, retention of title arrangements have become a common feature of commercial life.[30] The idea behind these clauses is very simple. Generally, ownership of specific goods passes to the buyer once the sale contract is made[31] and ownership of unascertained goods passes when they are appropriated to the contract.[32] These *prima facie* rules can be displaced by specific provision in the sales contract regarding when the buyer shall become the owner of the goods. Section 19(1) of the Sale of Goods Act, 1893, recognises that the passing of title in the goods to the seller can be made subject to various conditions, such as the goods are first paid for in full. According to s.19(1),

> the seller may, by the terms of the contract or appropriation, reserve the right of disposal of the goods until certain conditions are fulfilled. In such a case, . . . the property in the goods does not pass to the buyer until the conditions imposed by the seller are fulfilled.

The main attraction of retention of title clauses is that they provide sellers with extensive protection in the event of buyers becoming insolvent before the goods are paid for. In the absence of such a proviso, if the property vested in a buyer at the time of the sale or the appropriation and shortly afterwards he becomes insolvent, the seller is merely one of his many general creditors and quite likely will receive only a small proportion of the price, if even that, from the receiver or liquidator. But for so long as the seller retains title to the goods, then ownership does not pass to the buyer and, accordingly, they cannot be taken by a liquidator or by a receiver appointed by a debenture holder over the buyer's assets. Those persons can only seize and sell off property actually owned by the insolvent. The *Interview Ltd* case[33] and the similar *Romalpa* case,[34] which were decided around the same time, both concerned unsuccessful attempts by receivers appointed over the buyers' assets to get the proceeds from sales by those buyers of goods which were subject to retention of title clauses. As is explained below, there is a great variety of such clauses. Advantageous as they are to sellers who doubt their buyers' willingness or ability to pay, they have some drawbacks. Since the risk in goods generally follows their title,[35] the seller will be exposed to the risk of the goods being accidentally damaged or destroyed while in the buyer's hands. That snag is often overcome by a clause stating that the buyer must bear the risk. If the retention of title clause is not carefully drafted, it may be construed as a charge on the goods rather than as a full reservation of title; in that event, the clause may be ineffective either as an unregistered bill of sale or as an unregistered company charge.

---

30. See generally, G. McCormack, *Reservation of Title* (1990) and M. Forde, *Commercial Law in Ireland* (1990) pp. 200-209.
31. Sale of Goods Act 1893, ss.17 and 18 rule 1.
32. Id. ss.16 and 18, rule 5.   33. [1975] IR 382.
34. *Aluminium Indistrie Vaassen BV v Romalpa Alunimium Ltd* [1976] 1 WLR 676.
35. Sale of Goods Act 1893, s.20.

A feature of the first modern Irish and English cases on these clauses is that the sellers were continental European firms, one being German and the other Dutch. Several of the recent cases also involved Continental suppliers. As a result, some of the cases raise questions of the conflict of laws. In the *Interview Ltd* case,[36] for instance, the contract of sale was expressly subject to German law. According to the expert witness there, reservation of title was being used extensively in Germany under the name of 'current account clauses.' It was the prominence given to *Interview Ltd* and to the *Romalpa* case[37] in England that reminded many sellers of this extremely useful device for ensuring that they should get paid for their goods. Over the last ten years or so reservation of title clauses have proliferated. In 1989, the entire phenomenon was considered by the Law Reform Commission,[38] which proposed that resort to those devices should be curbed, by requiring that they be specially registered somewhat like bills of sale and floating charges.

The clause Subject to one qualification, in order to have effect, the seller must demonstrate that the retention of title clause is a part of the sale contract. This gives rise to the more general question of ascertaining what are the terms of a contract, such as when a term will be implied from a course of dealing and the 'battle of the forms.'[39] Often the invoice with which the goods are dispatched will make it clear that terms were already agreed regarding when the property in the goods can vest in the buyer. Where the goods being sold are un-ascertained, s.19(1) of the Sale of Goods Act, 1893, permits a seller to reserve his title to them when appropriating goods to the contract. Accordingly, it would seem, in breach of the sale contract, the seller can subsequently protect his interest up to the appropriation stage. Of course he will be liable in damages for doing so but, against that, he can repossess the goods and re-sell them in the event of the buyer becoming insolvent.

Section 19(1) does not place any limit on what circumstances the passing of title to the buyer can be conditioned upon. In a one- off transaction, the common stipulation is that title shall pass once the goods are paid for. Where goods are being sold over a period, it is common to provide for the title to pass only when the entire quantity supplied have been paid for. At times even the title to goods might be reserved until 'all moneys' owed by the buyer have been discharged, i.e. every form of indebtedness by the buyer to the seller. For there to be an effective reservation of title, it must be abundantly clear from the contract that the seller shall remain owner of the goods until the designated condition has been satisfied.

The goods If, by virtue of the clause, the supplier retains title to the goods, then in the event of the buyer becoming insolvent it may be necessary to identify which goods on the buyer's premises are captured by the clause. The seller may

36. [1975] IR 382.   37. [1976] 1 WLR 676.
38. Report, *Debt Collection (2): Retention of Title* (1989).
39. E.g. *Somers v James Allen (Ireland) Ltd* [1985] IR 340.

even want to be in a position to enter the buyer's premises at an earlier stage in order to verify that the goods are in a sound condition or to recover them if they were not paid for. In such a case, the clause should expressly stipulate exactly what rights of entry and otherwise are being conferred on the seller and also that the goods shall be stored where they may be readily identified.

Proceeds of sale   Although the goods may be subject to a reservation of title clause, the buyer in possession can re-sell them and give his sub-buyer a good title to them. Many reservation of title clauses are adopted on the assumption that the buyer shall be entitled to re-sell the goods; that right may even be made explicit in the clause. Unless a clause proscribes re-sale, it is generally accepted that the buyer has implicit authority to re-sell. Provided the sub-buyer is not aware that his seller is not in fact entitled to sell the goods, being subject to the clause, s.25(2) of the 1893 Act gives him title to the goods, being someone who purchased from a buyer in possession. The most that original sellers can do to prevent unauthorised dispositions of their goods to sub-buyers is to try their best to bring the existence of the clause to the notice of potential sub-buyers.

A common feature of reservation of title clauses is for them to stipulate that the buyer-cum sub-seller holds the proceeds of any sub-sale in trust for or in a fiduciary capacity for the original seller. Such a provision ordinarily creates an effective trust (or a fiduciary relationship) and prevents the proceeds of sub-sales from falling into the hands of the original buyer's receiver or liquidator. When drafting provisions of this nature, it is regarded as advisable to require that the proceeds of all sub-sales be held in a separate account and shall not be mixed with the sub-seller's own money. For if the sub-seller is not obliged to keep those proceeds separate and is able to use the money for his own purposes until called upon to hand it over, that money cannot be subject to a trust.

In *Re Sugar Distributors Ltd*[40] Carroll J held that the proceeds of a sub-sale are so held in trust even though there was no express stipulation in the contract regarding ownership of the proceeds or that they should be segregated. Because the goods there were still the seller's goods, it was held that the sub- seller was liable to account in a fiduciary capacity for the proceeds of any sale by him which could be traced. However, there does not seem to have been a sustained argument there that a trust over the proceeds could be implied merely from the fact that the seller retained title to the goods; nor does it seem to have been argued that, for there to be a trust of proceeds, there must be an agreement to keep those funds entirely separate. The position in Ireland, therefore, is unclear regarding who owns the proceeds of sub-sales when the matter is not dealt with expressly in the clause.

English courts do not readily imply a trust obligation from the existence of a clause merely reserving title to the goods or simply declaring that the proceeds are to be held in trust. For instance, in *Re Andrabell Ltd*,[41] the company was supplied with travel bags on credit terms and on condition that the property in

40. [1982] ILRM 399.   41. [1984] 3 All ER 407.

them should not be transferred until the entire quantity had been paid for. Those goods were sold in the course of the company's business shortly before it went into liquidation. The question then arose of whether the proceeds of those sales were held in trust for the supplier or belonged to the company, to be divided up among its creditors generally. It was held that there was no trust or fiduciary relationship for the following reasons: (a) the passing of the property in the goods was postponed only until full payment was made for the particular consignment rather than the total indebtedness, (b) there was no provision obliging the company to store the bags in a manner which manifested the supplier's ownership of the bags, (c) there was no express acknowledgement of a fiduciary relationship and no provision that the supplier should obtain the benefit of claims against purchasers from the company, (d) the company was not selling as agent for the supplier or on its account, (e) there was no obligation on the company to keep the proceeds from the sales of bags supplied separately from its own money, (f) it was to be inferred from the fixed 45-day period of credit that the company was free during that period to use the proceeds received from sale of the bags as it liked, and that was not compatible with the supplier having an interest in the proceeds of sale, and (g) it was not necessary to imply a term in the contract that the company was under a duty to account to the supplier because, having regard to the detailed express provisions relating to payment, such a term was not necessary to give business efficacy to the contract.[42] In the absence of a fiduciary relationship, the relationship was one of creditor and debtor and, therefore, the company was not under a duty to account to the supplier in respect of those proceeds. Even where the clause expressly stipulates that the proceeds of sub-sales shall be held in trust and be segregated into an entirely separate bank account, as is explained below, the clause may in the circumstances amount only to a charge on the proceeds.

Products Where the goods supplied subject to retention of title are incorporated into other goods, as in a manufacturing process, as a rule the clause ceases to have effect with regard to those goods. For those goods no longer exist; they have become absorbed into entirely different goods, which are not the subject of any restrictive clause. But until the goods are so absorbed in a composite product, they will remain the seller's property in accordance with the clause. Thus in one instance,[43] where resin was sold to a chipboard manufacturer, to become part of the board, it was held that a simple reservation of title clause gave the seller no rights with regard to the manufactured boards. Even if the clause purported to give rights in the manufactured product, generally any such right would be no more than a charge, as opposed to an outright retention of title. For instance,[44] leather was supplied to a handbag manufacturer subject to the usual clause and the added stipulation that owner-

---

42. Compare *Romalpa case* [1976] 1 WLR 676, where a fiduciary relationship was implied.
43. *Borden (U.K.) Ltd v Scottish Timber Products Ltd* [1981] 1 Ch 25.
44. *Re Peachdart Ltd* [1984] 1 Ch 131.

ship of any goods made from the leather would also vest in the seller. It was held that the clause did not give the supplier title to the manufactured products but was construed as creating a charge over them.

An appropriately worded clause might extend the seller's title to the manufactured goods. To do that would require the buyer to agree, for a consideration, that, once manufactured, ownership of the new goods shall vest in the seller. Any such arrangement, however, might not be possible where other components of the manufactured item were themselves subject to other retention of title arrangements.

Retention of title or charge?   At times clauses which ostensibly reserve the title to goods do not achieve that result and instead amount to charges. If the clause expressly states that the seller reserves some interest in the goods by way of security or charge, there can be no doubt about the matter. One of the provisions of the clause in *Re Interview Ltd*[45] was that any claims the buyer had against sub-buyers of the goods would be assigned to the original seller by way of security. That stipulation only constituted a charge and, accordingly, the original seller could not claim actual title to the proceeds of the sub-sales. If there is any ambiguity about the clause in question, the courts tend to regard it as a charge. Unless it is abundantly clear that title was to be retained by the seller, title to the goods will be deemed to have passed to the buyer and that he then gave a charge over the goods, or over the proceeds of sub-sales or over manufactured products, to secure the indebtedness. If the clause indeed only creates a charge, then in order to be fully effective it will have to be registered as company charge under s.99 of the 1963 Act.[46]

Whether an effective retention of title or else a charge was created in respect of the goods depends entirely on the construction of the particular contract, including other clauses in the agreement which bear on the retention clause. Although the parties' intention in a very general sense may have been to provide the seller with security, that is of no special significance. The issue is the form of security they intended to create. As was observed when seeking to determine if an agreement was one for the sale or for the hire of goods,

> the substance of the agreement must ultimately be found in the language of the contract itself. The duty of a court is to examine every part of the agreement, every stipulation which it contains, and to consider their mutual bearing on each other; but it is entirely beyond the function of a court to discard the plain meaning of any term in the agreement unless there can be found within its four corners other language and other stipulations which necessarily deprive such term of its primary significance.[47]

Where an unpaid vendor is laying claim to the proceeds of sub-sales, there

45. [1975] IR 382.
46. See *Company Law*, pp. 512 et seq.
47. *McEntire v Crossley & Co.* [1895] AC 457, at p. 467.

must be no doubt whatsoever that the sub-seller was to hold those proceeds in trust for or as fiduciary agent of the vendor. Where such an obligation is not spelt out in the contract, the normal inference is that the sub-seller is free to use the proceeds of the sales for his own account. In *Re W.J Hickey Ltd*[48] Barron J held that stipulating that the proceeds shall 'be held in trust for the seller' in a manner which enables those proceeds to be identified as such gave the vendor the property in, not just a charge over, those proceeds. The leading English case *Re Bond Worth Ltd*[49] was distinguished because, in that case, there was no express obligation to keep either the goods or the proceeds of their sale entirely separate from the sub-seller's own property.

The extent to which retention of title clauses can capture the proceeds of sub-sales has been substantially diminished by *Carroll Group Distributors Ltd v G. & J.F. Bourke Ltd.*[50] The clause there applied to tobacco products purchased by a retailer over a period and it provided that the proceeds from all sub-sales should be held in trust for the supplier in a separate bank account, the details of which account shall be provided to the seller. Murphy J pointed out that it was very likely that the aggregate amount of those proceeds at various times would exceed the sum actually owing to the supplier, because those proceeds would include the retailer's mark-up on the goods and sums in respect of some goods which already had been paid for. Accordingly, it was held, the 'substance of the transaction as ascertained from the words used by the parties and the context in which the document [was] executed'[51] was to confer a charge on those proceeds in substitution for the property rights the supplier had retained in the goods. It is not entirely clear from the judgment whether it was this feature of the clause alone or whether it was several other aspects of the clause that proved decisive.

Reference was made to three characteristics of a mortgage or charge identified by Romer LJ in a case decided in 1933[52] concerning a dealer discounting hire purchase agreements to a finance company. The first of these characteristics would not appear to have any bearing on the matter. The others are that

> if the mortgage realises the subject matter of the mortgage for a sum more than sufficient to repay him [what he is owed], he has to account to the mortgagor for the surplus. . . . Thirdly, if the mortgagee realises the mortgage property for a sum that is insufficient to repay him the money [owing to him], then the mortgagee is entitled to recover from the mortgagor the balance of the money. . . .[53]

The apparent inference is that if the fund or proceeds which is captured by the clause exceeds the amount owed to a supplier, it is to be implied that the supplier's right to that fund is confined to the amount due to him and that the remainder belongs to the sub-seller; this being so, the arrangement is more in

48. [1988] IR 126.
49. [1980] 1 Ch 228.
50. [1990] 1 IR 481.
51. Id. at p. 486.
52. *Re George Inglefield Ltd* [1933] Ch 1.
53. Id. at p. 27.

the nature of a charge. Conversely, if the fund is not sufficient to cover the entire debt, the supplier is still entitled to claim the balance from the sub-seller, which also is a feature of a charge. Although the full title to a designated fund can be transferred outright by way of assignment, title to only a portion of that fund cannot be transferred outright.[54] That being so, a retention clause capturing so much of the fund as represents what is owed to the supplier is intrinsically a charge. But it would seem that is a charge is not necessarily created by a clause assigning an entire fund merely because more than the amount in that fund is owed to the assignee. Perhaps a clause which seeks to secure those two outcomes in the alternative is a charge. Perhaps what made the difference in the *Carroll Group Distributors Ltd* case was the combination of such a clause and several other stipulations in the agreement between the parties, notably that all risks in the goods passed to the retailer and that, when selling the goods, the retailer would 'act on their own account and not as agent for' the suppliers, together with the fact that no separate bank account was opened as was stipulated for and the suppliers were aware of that omission but they took no steps to rectify the position.

On several occasions reservation clauses which applied to products manufactured from the goods supplied were held to create only charges.[55] Only the most unambiguous language can in effect extend retention of title to new products made from the goods, especially where the goods were mixed with other goods in the manufacturing process. Indeed as of yet there is no reported authority where it was held that a retention of title clause captured products made from the goods in question. So far, all attempts to extend the vendor's title to them have foundered, with the retention clause usually being construed as a charge. And because those clauses had not been appropriately registered, they were virtually ineffective.

FACTORED DEBTS

Especially with companies in financial difficulty, factoring debts is a mode of financing trading which has become quite common. From a legal point of view, what is involved is straightforward.[56] The company simply assigns or sells its debtors, or a designated portion of its debtors, to a finance company and agrees to assign future debtors of that description. Where the debts have been actually assigned, then the finance company will be the legal owner of them. For there to be an outright legal assignment, it must be made in writing and the debtor must have been notified in writing of the transfer of title.[57] It was held by the former Supreme Court that an assignment of a debt by a company must be done

---

54. *Conlon v Carlow County Council* [1912] 2 IR 535.
55. E.g. *Re Peachdart Ltd* [1984] 1 Ch 131; compare *Somers v James Allen (Ireland) Ltd* [1985] IR 340.
56. See generally, F. Salinger, *Factoring Law and Practice* (1991) and A.P. Bell, *Modern Law of Personal Property* (1989) ch 15.
57. Supreme Court of Judicature (Ireland) Act 1877, s.28(6).

under the company seal.[58] Formerly, assignments of debts were subject to 6% *ad valorem* stamp duty but, under s.207 of the Finance Act, 1992, stamp duty was lifted from most kinds of assignments of debts.

In *Pfeiffer G.m.b.h. v. Arbuthnot Factors Ltd*,[59] the question arose whether the proceeds of re-sales, under a retention of title clause, belonged to the initial seller of the goods or whether they should be paid to a factoring company, to whom that money had also been factored. In other words, both the retention of title clause and the factoring agreement purported to give different parties title to the same money. In the event, it was held that the retention clause gave only a security interest in the proceeds, which was void for non-registration under s.99 of the 1963 Act.

Even if in the *Pfeiffer G.m.b.h.* case the interest in the money created by the retention clause was not an unregistered charge, Phillips J went on the consider what the position would be. He concluded that, although a full assignment of a debt enables the assignee to acquire title in the debt, that it not the complete title of a bona fide purchaser without notice. Instead, the assignee 'acquire[s] a title that has all the procedural advantages of a legal title, but so far as priorities are concerned his position is no better than if the assignment had been effected prior to the [Judicature Act]. It follows that, even if the assignment is effected for value without notice of a prior equity, priorities fall to be determined as if the assignment had been effected in equity, not in law.'[60] Accordingly, the priority between competing claimants to the money depends on the application of what is called the rule in *Dearle v Hall*.[61] Under this rule, priority turns on the order in which notices of the assignment were given to the person affected—in this instance, were given to the company's debtors affected by the factoring agreement.[62]

Where the requisite formalities (i.e. writing and notice to the debtor) were not complied with, or where there is merely an agreement to assign which has not been carried out, or only a portion of the debt is being assigned, an equitable assignment of the debts has taken place. That equitable assignee is in much the same position as a chargee of the company's land or chattels. In the case of book debts, that charge must have been registered under s.99 of the 1963 Act for it to be effective in an insolvent liquidation.

INCOMPLETE SALES TRANSACTIONS

At the time the receivership or liquidation commenced, the company may have been a party to a sales transaction. In that event, it is important to know whether the property in what was being sold vested in the company at the very moment the receiver was appointed or the winding up commenced because, if it did, then generally it can be realised by the receiver or the liquidator, as the case

---

58. *Re A Debtor's Summons* [1929] IR 139.
59. [1988] 1 WLR 150. 60. Id. at p. 162.
61. (1823) 3 Russ 1.
62. See too, *Compaq Computer Ltd v Abercorn Group Ltd* [1991] BCLC 484.

may be. If the property did not vest, or no longer vested in the company at that time then, generally, all that the receiver or liquidator may be entitled to is a portion of the price the buyer agreed to pay for that property or of the money the insolvent paid for the property. A major exception to this principle is sales of land: equity will intervene to compel completion of contracts to sell or to buy land and other forms of property in respect of which specific performance will be granted.[63] Thus, if the company agreed to sell land, the purchaser on paying the price (to the receiver of liquidator) can compel a transfer of the land, by way of an order for specific performance. Where the company was the purchaser, on tendering the price the receiver or liquidator can compel completion of the sale of land.

But for the vast majority of sales of goods and chattels, equity will not intervene to compel performance of a sales agreement. For sales of goods, the critical time is when the property in them actually passed, which may be when the sale agreement was made, when the goods were delivered or when they were paid for, depending on the terms of the agreement and the nature of the transaction.[64] It was said in *Re Wait*[65] that the Sale of Goods Act, 1893, contains an exhaustive statement of the various rules regarding the transfer of property in goods and that Act, by implication, excludes any equitable rights which might otherwise arise in such transactions. According to Atkin LJ,

> These rules [in the 1893 Act] for transfer of property as between seller and buyer, performance of the contract [and the like] appear to be complete and exclusive statements of the legal relations both in law and equity. They have, of course, no relevance when one is considering rights, legal or equitable, which may come into existence dehors the contract for sale. A seller or a purchaser may, of course, create any equity he pleases by way of charge, equitable assignment or any other dealing with or disposition of goods, the subject matter of sale; and he may of course create such an equity as one of the terms expressed in the contract of sale. But the mere sale or agreement to sell or the acts in pursuance of such a contract mentioned in the [1893] Code will only produce the legal effects which the Code states.[66]

Transfer of property   The rules regarding the transfer of property in sale of goods transactions are set out in ss.16-18 of the Sale of Goods Act, 1893, and are exhaustively dealt with elsewhere.[67] For these purposes, goods are divided into 'specific' goods and 'unacertained' goods; specific goods are the actual

---

63. See generally, R. Keane, *Equity and the Law of Trusts in the Republic of Ireland* (1988) ch. 16.
64. See generally, M. Forde, *Commercial Law in Ireland* (1990) pp. 67-74.
65. [1927] 1 Ch 606.   66. Id. at pp. 635-636.
67. Supra n.64 and R.M. Goode, *Proprietary Rights and Insolvency in Sales Transactions* (1985). Cf. *Re Anchor Line (Henderson Bros.) Ltd* [1937] 1 Ch 1 and *Howden Bros. v Ulster Bank* [1924] 1 IR 117.

goods which the parties agreed to sell. With regard to sales of specific goods, the governing rule is that the property in them changes hands whenever the parties agreed that the change of ownership should take place. Where such an intention cannot be clearly established, s.18 of the 1893 Acts lays down various rules for the purpose of establishing that intention, for instance, when the goods are put into a deliverable state and the buyer is notified of that fact. Unless the parties otherwise agreed, property in specific goods will not pass at the very time the buyer pays for them or at the time of their delivery to the buyer.

A sale of unascertained goods is a sale where the particular goods to be delivered to the buyer have not yet been identified; at some later stage, goods will be selected and 'appropriated' to the buyer. An example is an agreement to sell a ton of coal or a new BMW car. Until the particular ton of coal or the car to be delivered to the buyer has been identified, the agreement remains one for the sale of unascertained or non-specific goods. Thus the act of appropriation is very important because, unless the parties otherwise agreed, property in unascertained goods passes when the goods 'are unconditionally appropriated to the contract' with the assent of the buyer or of the seller, as the case may be.[68] That is to say, if the actual appropriation was done by the seller or his agent, that appropriation must have been unconditional and have been assented to by the buyer. Conversely, where it was the buyer or his agent who performed the act of appropriation, the seller must have consented.

An excellent example of the operation of these rules in the insolvency context is *Re London Wine Co. (Shippers) Ltd*[69] which concerned a wine dealer which kept stocks of wine in various warehouses. Under a 'Claret Investment' scheme the company operated, persons could 'invest' in stocks of claret by buying a designated quantity of the wine, and each buyer got a certificate from the warehouse stating that he was the beneficial owner of a stated quantity of wine being held there. Each certificate described the wine and the cases where it was being held. However, no bottles of wine were physically segregated and set aside for named individuals. Buyers of the wine concluded several transactions and the principal question for the court was whether the wine belonged to them, when the company went into liquidation, or whether the company owned it. It was held that, because there had been no actual unconditional appropriation of bottles by the company to the buyers and with their assent, the property in the wine remained throughout in the company. Accordingly, the wine belonged to the liquidator and the buyers merely had claims in damages against the company for breach of the agreements to sell the wine. Oliver J rejected the contention that stocks of wine were being held in trust for the various persons who bought them.

Stoppage in transit An unpaid seller of goods is given a lien over them in certain circumstances by ss 41-43 of the Sale of Goods Act, 1893. Section 44 of that Act then gives the unpaid seller an extension of that lien by entitling him

68. *Healy v Howlett & Sons* [1917] 1 KB 337.
69. Unrep.: Oliver J, 7 November 1975, in appendix to R.M. Goode, supra n.67.

to stop the goods while they are in transit to the purchaser, notwithstanding that the buyer has acquired title to them. This right is exercised either by the seller repossessing the goods or by notifying the carrier of his claim to them.[70] But the exercise of the right does not re-transfer the property in the goods back to the seller. He cannot immediately re-sell the goods but an exception is made for goods which are perishable.

Forfeiture clause   Once a purchaser acquires title to property, he is not free to stipulate how it is to be allocated in the event of his insolvency; to do so is regarded as a form of fraud on the bankruptcy laws. Thus where standing timber was sold to a trader, with a proviso that the vendor may retake it in the event of the trader's bankruptcy, that proviso was held to be void.[71] Where a patentee sold a patent to manufacturers in consideration of them paying him royalties and, at the same time, they lent him money on terms that they were entitled to retain half of the royalties towards the satisfaction of the loan, with a proviso that they could retain the entire royalties if he became bankrupt, that proviso was declared to be void.[72] Similarly, a provision in a building contract that if the builder becomes insolvent his plant and materials shall be forfeited to the employer, was not enforced because it contravened the principle that an owner of property cannot limit his interest in it by a condition which is to take effect on his insolvency.[73]

70. See supra n.67, pp. 104-105.
71. *Holroyd v Gwynne* (1809) 2 Tarant. 176.
72. *Ex p. Mackay* (1873) LR 8 Ch App 643.
73. *Ex p. Jay* (1880) 14 Ch D 19.

22

Trust Property and Equities

Where a person holds property in trust for another then the company cannot create a charge over that property nor can any receiver or liquidator appropriate that property. While trust property is treated in substantially the same way as if it were another's 'absolute title' property, the beneficiary's interest in the property is defeated by its sale to a bona fide purchaser without notice of the trust. Because of this vulnerable feature of the beneficial owner's interest, the prudent course is to have that interest recorded in an appropriate register—for instance, the registry of deeds or the land registry in the case of land.[1] But beneficial interests in shares may not be recorded in the company's share register,[2] nor may beneficial interests in patents be registered in the patents' register.[3] There is no special register for recording beneficial interests in goods—other than as individuals' 'bills of sale'[4] and agricultural chattel mortgages.[5] Beneficial interests in insurance policies are often noted on the policy. Where the beneficial interest is by way of security, then it constitutes a charge and must comply with the registration and other requirements for fixed or floating charges under s.99 of the 1963 Act.

Whether or not a company is holding property in trust for another is a matter of law and of fact.[6] There are two main types of situation. The commonest is the express trust, where the owner of property expressly provides that either he or some third party will hold it in trust. Trusts can also be deemed to exist as a matter of law; there are several situations where, regardless of persons' intentions, the law will regard property as being held in trust. Trusts in favour of particular creditors give them many of the advantages of a charge in their favour, yet may avoid publicity as to that fact.[7]

---

1. See generally, J.C. Wylie, *Irish Land Law* (2nd ed., 1986) chs. 21 and 22.
2. 1963 Act s.123; see *Company Law*, pp. 312-313.
3. Patents Act 1992, s.84(5).
4. Bills of Sale (Ireland) Acts, 1879-1883.
5. Agricultural Credit Act 1978, Part III.
6. See generally, R. Keane, *Equity and the Law of Trusts in the Republic of Ireland* (1988) chs. 7 and 8.
7. See generally, Anderson, 'The Treatment of Trust Assets in English Insolvency Law', in E. McKendrick ed., *Commercial Aspects of Trusts and Fiduciary Obligations* (1992) pp. 166 et seq.

COMPANY CONSTITUTING ITSELF AS TRUSTEE

For an express trust, no particular form of words or legal instrument is required; a trust has been created once the 'three certainties' are established. These three requirements have been described as follows:

> in order that a trust may be created, the subject matter must be certain, the objects of the trust must be certain and words relied upon as creating the trust must have been used in an imperative sense, so as to show that the testator intends to create an obligation.[8]

A company can expressly constitute itself a trustee of certain funds for one or some of its creditors. Thus, in *Re Kayford Ltd*[9] a company, the business of which was supplying consumer goods by way of mail order, was in financial difficulties and was anxious to protect the position of customers who in advance would pay deposits and even the full purchase price of goods, which were not yet supplied to them. To that end, it opened a separate bank account called a 'Customers' Trust Deposit Account' and paid into it sums sent by customers; that money would be withdrawn only when the goods were supplied to them. Megarry J had 'no doubt that the intention was that there should be a trust'; there was 'no doubt about the so-called "three certainties" of a trust.'[10] In a subsequent instance where money collected from customers was paid into a special joint bank account but there was no detailed agreement about the terms for making withdrawals, it was held that the company never manifested a sufficient intention to create a trust.[11] Accordingly, the money formed part of the company's general assets. It is unlikely that a company would be allowed to constitute itself a trustee of funds which had no close connection with the intended beneficiary—for instance, a declaration that its book debts would be held in trust for one supplier or one lender. An agreement of this nature most likely would be regarded as a charge or as an 'illusory trust' which is revocable.[12]

LOAN OR TRUST?

In certain circumstances, money which is lent to a company for a specified purpose is deemed to be held by it in trust for that purpose or, where the objective has not been achieved, on a resulting trust for the lender. Accordingly, in an insolvency those funds are not available for division among the other creditors; although no charge has been created in favour of the purpose in question or the lender, a receiver or liquidator must hold the money separately. The leading case is *Barclays Bank v Quistclose Investments Ltd*,[13] where the company was

8.   *Chambers v Fahy* [1931] IR 17, at p. 21.
9.   [1975] 1 WLR 279.   10. Id. at p.282.
11. *Re Multi Guarantee Co. Ltd* [1987] BCLC 257.
12. D.J. Hayton ed., Underhill & Hayton, *Law Relating to Trusts* (14th ed., 1987) p. 99-100.
13. [1970] AC 567. In *Shanahan Stamp Auctions Ltd v Farrelly* [1962] IR 386, certain 'investors' who put money into the company to finance certain transactions were held

in financial difficulties but was anxious to pay shareholders a dividend which it had declared. To that very end, it borrowed money from another company, which had the same controlling shareholder as itself; that loan was made for no other purpose. Consequently, it was held that the company held that money in trust. This was because '[t]he mutual intention . . . and the essence of the bargain, was that the sum advanced should not become part of the assets of [the company] but should be used exclusively for the payment of a particular class of its creditors, namely those entitled to the dividend. A necessary consequence of this . . . must be that if, for any reason, the dividend could not be paid, the money was to be returned to the [lender].'[14]

This principle was extended somewhat in *Re McKeown*[15] where the debtor, who was a building contractor, borrowed money from the applicant in order to pay the costs and fees of an arbitration and thereby take up the arbitrator's award. They agreed that this loan should be repaid from money paid to the debtor under the award. He was then adjudicated bankrupt and the question arose whether all of the money payable under that award must be distributed among his general creditors or whether a portion of it, equivalent to the loan, should be held in trust for the lender. It was held that the amount of the original loan was impressed with a trust. As Lowry LCJ put it, the debtor's agreement to repay the loan from the proceeds of the award 'raises as clear an equity as would have been attracted by a breach of the [undertaking] to use the loan to obtain the award. What the bankrupt was in effect saying was that having used the loan to obtain the award he would hold an equal part thereof in trust for the applicant.'[16] Furthermore, had the bankrupt not used the loan for the agreed purpose and the funds remained in his bank account, they would still be affected by the trust.

The rationale for not permitting receivers or liquidators to appropriate payments made in these circumstances has been described as the principle 'that equity fastens on the conscience of the person who receives from another property transferred for a specific purpose only and not, therefore, for the recipient's own purposes, so that such person will not be permitted to treat the property as his own or to use it for other than the stated purposes.'[17] A critical question, therefore, is whether it was envisaged that the recipient of the money could mix it with his general funds or, instead, the intention was that the money should be specially appropriated to that purpose, for instance, by designating a special account to hold the money. Otherwise, nearly every loan for a designated purpose might give rise to a trust. But as *Re McKeown* illustrates, this special appropriation does not always have to be a designated account.

In these kind of cases, two distinct trusts arise. There is a primary trust for the designated purpose; the parties' common intention is that the money should

not to be secured creditors but were persons on whose behalf the funds were to be held in trust.
14. Id. at p. 580.   15. [1974] NI 226.
16. Id. at p. 231.
17. *Carreras Rothmans Ltd v Freeman Matthews Treasure Ltd* [1985] Ch 207, at p. 222.

be used for that objective. But there is no requirement that the indirect 'beneficiaries' of that trust share that common intention or, indeed, even have any knowledge of the trust before it becomes effective to bind the company. The trust can be enforced by the provider of the money[18] and he probably can restrain any breach of trust by the transferee. It can also be enforced by the immediate 'beneficiaries' so as to acquire, by the transfer of the money or other property to them, absolute title. This trust comes to an end once it is performed or wherever it becomes impossible to perform. Once the trust is performed, the provider of the funds simply becomes an unsecured creditor of the company for that amount. If that trust is not possible to perform, a secondary 'resulting' trust arises in favour of the provider of the funds. What have become known as *'Quistclose* trusts' have generated a large academic literature,[19] some of it critical of the decided cases, which show that the law in this rapidly developing area is far from being entirely settled.

In certain circumstances, however, a purported creation of a trust may be void as a fraudulent preference.[20] This is where the company, which shortly before it goes into liquidation and finds itself insolvent, has declared that it holds certain assets in trust for particular creditors. It would seem that the facts in the *Kayford* case[21] do not disclose such circumstances; at lest, it seems to have been assumed that beneficial ownership in the payments made to the company there had throughout been retained by the payers. There might very well have been an unlawful preference if the company became the complete owner of those funds but then decided to appropriate them to a special trust account. In the *Quistclose* case,[22] by contrast, the creation of the trust in no way placed one of the company's creditors at an advantage vis a vis the other creditors in that, if the objects of the trust were achieved, the lender of the money would have been substituted for the shareholders who were paid their dividend whereas, if those payments were never made, the lender was entitled to be reimbursed, but all the company's other creditors would thereby be no worse off.

TRUST OR LIENS BY OPERATION OF LAW

Trusts can also arise by operation of law[23]—either because the law presumes that the original owner of property intended that it should be held in trust or because the law regards it as inequitable in certain circumstances that persons should be permitted to retain property for their own benefit just because it is being held in their name. These trusts are known as 'resulting' trusts and 'constructive' trusts, and are sometimes referred to as 'equitable liens'. They arise in several situations, the most common of these being the unpaid vendor of land's 'lien' in respect of the purchase price and the purchaser of land's 'lien'

18. Ibid.
19. E.g. Rickett, 'Different Views on the Scope of the *Quistclose* Analysis: English and Anitpodean Insights', 107 *LQR* 608 (1991).
20. See ante p. 236-246.
21. [1975] 1 WLR 279.   22. [1970] AC 567.
23. See generally, R. Keane, supra n.1, Ch.'s 12 and 13.

where he has paid for the property but the conveyance has not yet been executed.[24] An equitable lien is something which exists independently of possession and gives rise to a charge, but it arises by operation of law out of the relationship between the parties and not out of an express contract. Because these security interests arise by operation of law instead of being directly created by the company, they are not registerable under s.99 of the 1963 Act. While these liens arise by operation of law, they can be waived or abandoned.[25] Such trusts or liens as can be asserted against a company's property can be asserted when the company is in receivership or is being wound up.

Some lawyers contend that property should be regarded as being held in trust whenever permitting a party to retain that property would cause him to be 'unjustly enriched'; that a broad restitutionary objective should be achieved through the technique of the deemed trust. However, it appears that the Irish courts tread cautiously in this area and will not readily resort to trust terminology in order to provide redress against inequity. Thus in *Re Barrett Apartments Ltd*,[26] intending purchasers of apartments from a building company paid it what were referred to as 'booking deposits' in respect of the flats each of them intended to purchase. When the company went into liquidation, they claimed that those deposits were subject to a trust or a lien. That contention was rejected by the Supreme Court on the grounds that the deposits there did not come within the traditional purchaser's lien.[27] Those deposits were not made under any contract to purchase property; no contract of purchase had been made and the deposits were accepted expressly on the basis that they would be returnable upon notification by either party. It was argued that the scope of the lien should be extended to cover this situation. But to do that, it was held, would be 'unfairly and unjustifiably discriminatory *vis-à-vis* other creditors.'[28] McCarthy J posed the rhetorical question, 'how does the doing of justice demand that those who pay advances in respect of an anticipated contract should be put in a position better than that of trading creditors or professional creditors who have put their goods or their services at the disposal of the self same debtor without payment and whose claims can only rank as those of unsecured creditors?'[29]

An unpaid vendor of land who has conveyed it and thereby no longer owns the property, nevertheless, by virtue of equity, has a charge over that land in respect of the purchase price;[30] until that is paid, the vendor can intervene and enforce this equitable mortgage. This lien is available against all except the bona fide purchaser for value of the legal estate without notice of the fact of non- payment. The extent to which a company's secured creditors' claims can be disappointed by such liens is illustrated by *Wilson v Kelland*.[31] There the

---

24. See generally, P.V. Baker & P. St.J. Langan, *Snell's Principles of Equity* (28th ed., 1982) pp. 457-462.
25. *Re Aluminium Shop Fronts Ltd* [1987] IR 419.　　26. [1985] IR 350.
27. Distinguishing *Tempany v Hynes* [1976] IR 101.
28. [1985] IR at p. 358.　　29. Id. at p. 361.
30. *Rose v Watson* (1864) 10 HLC 672.
31. [1910] 2 Ch 306.

company granted a floating charge which contained the usual covenant against creating other charges ranking in priority of *pari passu* to it. Subsequently the company bought property but, since it could not pay the full price at the time, it was agreed that the outstanding purchase money should be secured by way of a mortgage on that property. Shortly afterwards the mortgage deed was executed. In a foreclosure action, the question arose whether this mortgage took priority over the debenture, and it was held that it did. According to Eve J,

> it is . . . immaterial whether the mortgagees had, or had not, notice of the [earlier] debentures. . . . Any equity which attached to the property contracted to be purchased . . . and conveyed to the company . . . in favour of the debenture-holders . . . was, throughout, subject to the paramount equity of the unpaid vendors and the [subsequently executed] legal mortgage which secures the unpaid purchase-money must . . . take priority over any charge to persons claiming through the purchaser.[32]

The evidence showed that the unpaid vendor- mortgagee had no actual notice of the company's debenture. But Eve J added that, even if he had such notice, it was merely notice that the floating charge existed and not of any particular restrictive clause contained in the charge.[33]

SUBJECT TO EQUITIES

When the bankrupt's property vests in the Official Assignee, his title is 'subject to equities', meaning all equitable claims against that property continue, despite the change in ownership.[34] An extension of this principle is that where certain contractual rights exist with reference to some of the insolvent's assets, those rights may still be exercisable following commencement of the bankruptcy or winding up. In that event, the person with those rights may gain a distinct advantage over all the other creditors. In *Dempsey v Bank of Ireland*[35] it was held by the Supreme Court that contractual rights to apportion a company's funds can be exercised even after the company has gone into liquidation because exercising those rights is not the same as proving a debt. The case concerned the bonding arrangements sponsored by the Irish Travel Agents' Association and the issue was whether a bank, which made payments under one travel agency's bond, could reimburse itself from that agency's bank account even though by then the agency had gone into liquidation. Under the arrangement, the bank entered into a guarantee to pay £75,000 towards the costs of catering for travellers who were stranded whenever the agency in question had insufficient funds. At the same time, the agency agreed to indemnify the bank against whatever was owing by the bank under that indemnity. The agency here, Eurotravel Ltd, had gone into liquidation before the bank sought to debit the account with £75,000, having paid that amount under its guarantee.

32. Id. at p. 312.   33. Id. at p. 313.
34. See *Bankruptcy Law* pp. 72-74.
35. Supreme Court, 6 December 1985.

Giving judgment for the Court, Henchy J held that this debit could be made because what was being claimed was not a right to prove a debt in the winding up but an entitlement to enforce a contractual right notwithstanding a winding up. For this reason, several leading cases on set-offs claimed by guarantors, which were applied in the court below,[36] were distinguished. Applying first principles, the bank's claim succeeded because an insolvent company's assets are subject to the same burdens and equities as existed immediately prior to the winding up. The liquidator 'takes the assets subject to any pre-existing enforceable right of a third party in or over them. If that were not so, equities, liabilities and contractual rights validly and enforceably created while the assets were in the hands of the company would be unfairly swept aside and an unjust distribution of the assets would result.'[37] When the travel agency's winding up commenced the bank had paid the £75,000 on the guarantee and, consequently, the company's bank account was subject to the bank's contingent right to debit that sum, which it did shortly afterwards. If, immediately before the winding up, the bank had debited that sum the debit could not have been questioned because 'it would have been done under the terms of a guarantee which was entered into in good faith and which in no way offended the statutory provisions applicable in a winding up.'[38] It therefore does not matter for these purposes that the bank exercised its contractual right to debit the account after the winding up had commenced.

The *'Eurotravel'* case should be contrasted with *Re Tullow Engineering Ltd*[39] Once a floating charge crystallises, the property covered by it immediately passes to the chargee.[40] It was held in the *Tullow* case that where the company had given a third party an option to purchase property and a floating charge over that property then crystallises, the option immediately lapses. That option was to purchase certain shares held by the company. According to Blayney J,

> The effect of the crystallisation . . . was that there was an immediate equitable assignment of the shares to the debenture-holder so that in equity they became the owners of the shares. [The Company] was divested of its ownership in favour of the debenture-holders. Accordingly, it no longer had the capacity to enter into a contract to sell the shares in pursuance of the option which it granted. Its ownership had been terminated and its irrevocable offer to sell became a dead letter. No longer having the ownership of the shares, it could contract to sell them. The only person who could do that was the receiver under the powers given in the debenture. And the purported exercise of the option did no alter the position.[41]

However, it does not seem to have been argued there that the principle stated in *Dempsey* should have applied, i.e. that a liquidator cannot take a better title

36. *Re Euro Travel Ltd* (Murphy J, 28 May 1984).
37. At pp. 8-9.   38. At p. 10.
39. [1990] 2 IR 452.   40. See *Company Law*, p. 511.
41. [1990] 2 IR at p. 458.

to the assets than the company itself had. Accordingly, it could be contended, since the company's title to the shares was subject to an option, the receiver's title remained subject to that clause.

THIRD PARTY INSURANCE

Formerly, a most unjust situation could arise where the insolvent company had been responsible for injuring someone or his property. Where the company was insured for that particular liability, the proceeds of the insurance policy would form part of the company's general assets and would be distributed in accordance with the priorities and preferences being considered here.[42] Accordingly, if the company were heavily insolvent, the injured party would receive next to nothing, notwithstanding the insurance. That state of affairs was rectified by s.62 of the Civil Liability Act, 1961, which provides that money paid under the insurance must be used to discharge the injured party's claim and none of that money shall form part of the company's assets for the purpose of distribution among its other creditors.[43]

42. *Re Harrington Motor Co.* [1928] Ch 105.
43. See post pp. 370-371.

23

Set-off

Subject to the various qualifications set out below, where A owes B money but B also owes A money, both debts can be set-off against and cancel out each other, so that A or B, as the case may be, is entitled to claim against the other only for the net amount. Set-off has been defined as 'something which provides a defence because the natural equity of the sum so relied upon are such that it is a sum which is property to be dealt with as diminishing the claim which is made, and against which the sum so demanded can be set-off.'[1] Set-off, therefore, is a defence to a claim for money and, to an extent, is a counter-claim.[2] However, the mere fact that several sums are owing between A and B does not invariably entitle the net debtor to set-off those sums and pay over only the balance. The right to set-off debts is not an equitable security interest and does not confer any right *in rem* to funds; it is merely a right to set up one personal claim against another in reduction or discharge of the defendant's liability.

The question of set-off is of no great significance in the case of solvent debtors since their creditors are assured of being paid in full. But the matter becomes extremely important in a receivership or liquidation[3] since the effect of permitting a set-off is to relieve the company *pro tanto* of the duty of paying a dividend on a debt and, on the other hand, to enable the creditor *pro tanto* to pay himself in full out of a debt which he owes the company.

TYPES OF SET-OFF

Set-off in bankruptcy must be distinguished from set-off at common law, in equity and arising under a contract. Common law set-off[4] is a statutory pro-cedure which permits cross-claims to be pleaded as a defence in an action; it originated in a Statute of 1751,[5] and was endorsed by ss.40 and 58 of the Common Law Procedure Amendment Act (Ireland), 1853.[6] Equitable set-off[7] is a substantially similar defence against cross-claims which was developed in

1. See generally, S.R. Derham, *Set-Off* (1987).
2. *Re A Bankruptcy Notice* [1934] Ch 431, at p. 437.
3. Cf. *Stooke v Taylor* (1880) 5 QBD 569.
4. See generally, Derham, supra no. 1, pp. 5-8.
5. 25 Geo. II c. 8; cf. *Sheehan v National Bank* [1937] IR 783.
6. 16 & 17 Vic. c. 113.
7. See generally, supra n.1, pp. 9-52; cf. *Hanak v Green* [1958] 2 QB 9.

the Chancery Courts and was expanded beyond circumstances analogous to those provided for in the Act of 1751. Set-off is now provided for in Order 19, r.2 of the Rules of the Superior Courts. Common law and equitable set-off merely provide a procedural shield and are not substantive defences in an action, although the modern practice is to plead set-off as a defence. Parties can contract out of their right to invoke set-off, for instance by issuing securities that are stated to be free from equities.

Parties to a contract may stipulate expressly for a right of set-off between them. Set-off also arises in certain contractual relationships, such as between landlord and tenant, employer and employee, solicitor and client and between partners. Those set-offs may be regarded as implied terms of the contracts between the parties. One such set-off, that has been the subject of much litigation, is the right of set-off between banker and customer[8]—often referred to as the right to combine accounts or, misleadingly, as the banker's lien. A contractual right of set-off is a substantive defence to an action and not just a procedural shield. But it is not a charge or other security interest because it is a purely personal right and does not confer any proprietary interest in a monetary claim. The set-off is merely a countervailing claim for a sum of money in reduction or discharge of a liability on the plaintiff's claim.

Bankruptcy set-off has a more ancient lineage, originating in England in the Statute of 4 Anne c.17, 1705,[9] and in Ireland in s.43 of the Bankruptcy Act, 1772.[10] Its objective has often been described as doing justice between the parties on the basis that, where there are cross-claims, it is most unfair to a creditor for him to be obliged to pay over everything owing by him to the bankrupt and then to prove against the estate for a dividend on whatever sum the bankrupt owes him. Because setting off in this manner in effect prefers particular creditors, it is surprising that the rule has attracted so little criticism. There is nothing in the Bankruptcy Act, 1988, comparable to 'the proviso' in the British legislation whereby, once the creditor has notice of the debtor's act of bankruptcy, sums which fall due from the debtor following that time cannot be the subject of set-off.[11] The rules regarding proofs in bankruptcy stipulate that

> Where there are mutual credits or debts as between a bankrupt and any person claiming as a creditor, one debt or demand may be set-off against the other and only the balance found owing shall be recoverable on one side or the other.[12]

---

8. See generally, supra n.10, ch. 10; cf. *Bank of Ireland v Martin* [1937] IR 189.
9. See generally, Derham, supra no. 1, ch. 3 and R.M. Goode, *Legal Problems of Credit and Security* (2nd ed., 1988) Ch 6.
10. 11 & 12 Geo. II. c. 8.
11. Insolvency Act 1986, s.323(3).
12. Bankruptcy Act 1988, schedule, reg. 17(1).

RECEIVERSHIP

In their brief account of the application of set-off when a company is in receivership, eminent Australian commentators observe that

> This has been a vexed area of the law, in which differing views, difficulties of classification and difficulties in reconciling decided case abound. In those circumstances, it may be thought over-optimistic to hope that most of the problems vanish upon resort to first principles, rather than to the multitude of instances. . . . This is, however, an instance where optimism may be justified. . . .
>
> [T]here is not a peculiar, self-contained body of doctrine know as receivership set-off. There is a body of legal rules and equitable principles relating to set-off which may become relevant to transactions with which a receiver is concerned or to which he is a party.[13]

However, these commentators' elaboration of the law diverges somewhat from the law as it is stated in the leading Irish and English authorities.

When a company goes into receivership and claims are then brought either by or against the receiver, and one of the parties asserts a right of set-off, a crucial matter is whether the debts or claims in question arise between the same or different parties. For if they arise between different parties there can be no set-off. Subject to their right of indemnity, receivers are 'personally liable on any contract entered into' by them.[14] But if one debt arose before the receivership commenced and the other debt arises afterwards, there can be no set-off between those debts because the receiver cannot be held answerable for the pre-receivership debt.[15] This is the case, it has been held, even where the receiver is designated as the company's agent, on the grounds that the receiver's principal concern is the debenture-holder, for whom he acts. This is so, it has been held, even where the receiver also manages the company's business, in the course of which liabilities are incurred by the company. Because the floating charge has crystallised, post-receivership liabilities to the company are immediately assigned to the debenture-holder, to whom they beneficially belong; accordingly, the requisite mutuality does not exist for setting off those liabilities against the company's pre-receivership debts. Indeed, if set-off were permitted in those circumstances, the unsecured pre-receivership creditor of the company could obtain priority over the secured creditor by purporting to set-off what is owed to him against sums he becomes bound to pay the company in receivership. However, this unfair preference would not arise where it is the company, in receivership, and not the pre-receivership debtor, is claiming the set-off. Australian commentators[16] take the view that the above reasoning is faulty in that mutuality of debts is not an essential prerequisite to a set-off but never-

---

13. R.P Meagher et al., *Equity Doctrine and Remedies* (2nd ed., 1984) at pp. 674-675. See generally, Derham, supra n.1, ch. 12.
14. 1963 Act s.316(2).
15. See ante pp. 40-41. 16. Supra n.13, at p. 680.

theless, generally, the courts will not permit setting off pre-receivership debts against post-receivership debts were that would give the company's unsecured creditor an unfair preference.

Absence of mutuality   An excellent example of the absence of mutuality is *Lynch v Ardmore Studios Ltd*,[17] which concerned two sets of taxed costs awarded in separate cases involving the company and the other party. In the first instance, costs were awarded against the company but in the later instance, after the company had gone into receivership, costs were awarded in its favour. The issue to be decided was whether the first set of costs would be set-off against the post-receivership costs. It was contended that the intervening receivership did not affect the right of set-off, which otherwise would have existed, because the receiver and manager, who was the plaintiff in the second action, was an agent of the company, which was the plaintiff in the earlier action. Adopting the reasoning expounded in an earlier English case,[18] Budd J rejected this argument on the grounds that the right to post-receivership costs vested in the debenture-holder once the charge crystallised, whereas it was the company alone which was obliged to pay the pre-receivership costs. Under the debenture,

> There is . . . a charge on all future assets of the [company] without restriction; that amounts to an agreement for valuable consideration to charge all such future assets which agreement enables equity to fasten a charge on those future assets, when they arise; and every such equitable charge as it arises operates as an equitable assignment to the debenture-holder of that asset. . . . The fact that this charge is a floating charge cannot . . . operate to exclude assets from the agreement to charge. That particular quality of the charge (or agreement to charge) only means that its full operation is so to speak in suspense until certain events occur, and when such an event occurs the charge (or agreement to charge) loses that suspended quality. That in no way justifies the conclusion that the field of the charge is in any way restricted: it only means that after this particular quality disappears equity will fasten the charge directly on all assets thereafter coming into existence as soon as they do so. . . . [Consequently,] the choses in action consisting of the debts now sued on became as they arose subject to an equitable charge—an equitable assignment—to the debenture holder.[19]

Additionally, set-off would not be permitted in the circumstances if the receiver had been appointed by the court, and there was no overwhelming reason why the position in this regard should be entirely different when the receiver was appointed by a creditor:

> if the receiver and manager had been appointed by the court and set-off

17. [1966] IR 133.
18. *N.W. Robbie & Co. v Witney Warehouse Co.* [1963] 1 WLR 1324.
19. Id. at pp. 1337.

in this case could not have been successfully asserted, because, since such receiver and manager would not have been agent of the plaintiffs, there would be no 'mutuality'. It would . . . be a defect in the law if there was in the present context such a distinction between a receiver and manager appointed by the debenture-holder under the common form which makes him agent for the company and a receiver and manager appointed by the court, more especially since at any time the latter may be substituted for the former, and where possible the costs of litigation should be avoided. In both cases the receiver and manager is a piece of administrative machinery designed to enforce a charge, in the present case (as in most) an equitable charge on property of the company. I am not prepared to accept this distinction in the field of set-off; and this would work both ways. In each case proceedings necessary to enforce a claim would be brought by the company, the writ being issued in the name of the company by solicitors instructed by the receiver and manager. In each case the purpose is to recover that which is the property of the company subject to the fact that it is also the beneficial concern of the debenture-holder to whom it has been assigned in equity by way of charge. The substance of the situation is the same in each case, and it is, I venture to think, by the substance and not by the form that the existence or non-existence of a right to set-off is to be ascertained.[20]

Another such case is *Rendell v Doors & Doors Ltd*[21] where the receiver sold goods to the plaintiff, who was owed money by the company before the receivership commenced. Set-off again was denied because

the debt owing by the company to the [plaintiff] in no way involved the debenture holder. The [plaintiff] was the legal and beneficial owner of that debt or chose in action. When the [plaintiff] purchased goods from the company during the receivership those goods were impressed with a charge in favour of the debenture holder. Likewise when the goods were sold to the [plaintiff] the choses in action consisting of the several debts owing by [him] for the purchase price on such sale of goods were impressed with the same charge in favour of the debenture holder. The legal title to those choses in action was vested in the company; the beneficial title in the debenture holder until it had been paid off in full. . . . [T]here was no mutuality of beneficial interest until the debenture holder had been paid in full.[22]

Set-off allowed   If, before the floating charge crystallised and a receiver was appointed, a right of set-off existed between the company and its debtor or creditor, the advent of the receivership does not destroy that right. This is because there was 'an inchoate right to set-off at the time when the receiver was appointed' and the debenture 'must be regarded as an incomplete assignment

20. Id. at p. 1340.
21. [1975] 2 NZLR 191.   22. Id. at pp. 201-202.

[of assets] until the time when the receiver is appointed.'[23] In addition there are a number of instances where it was held that liabilities that might be regarded as arising before and after the receivership could be set-off.[24] One was *Parsons v Sovereign Bank of Canada*[25] where, following his appointment by the court, the receiver supplied goods on credit to the plaintiff under contracts subsisting with the company when he was appointed. Later he renounced those contracts, thereby rendering the company liable in damages to the plaintiff. It was held that both liabilities could be set-off against each other because the goods supplied were delivered, not under new contracts made by the receiver, but under the old contracts with the company, and the damages were in respect of breach of those very contracts. In *Rother Iron Works v Canterbury Precision Engineers Ltd*[26] the company, which already owed money to the defendant, agreed to sell it goods; following the appointment of a receiver, those goods were delivered. Because both obligations arose before the receivership commenced, it was held that there was a set-off between amounts due on them. It was said that the right of the company to sue for the debt due 'was embraced, when it arose, in the [floating] charge. But if this was because the chose in action consisting of the rights under the contract became subject to the charge on the appointment of the receiver, then the debenture-holder could not be in a better position to assert those rights than had been the assignor [company].'[27]

The principle to be derived from these and similar cases was summarised by Templeman J as follows:

> a debt which accrues due before notice of assignment [to the debenture-holder] has been received, whether or not it is payable before that date, or a debt which arises out of the same contract as that which gives rise to the assigned debt, or is closely connected with that contract, may be set-off against the assignee [e.g. the receiver]. But a debt which is neither accrued nor connected may not be set off even though it arises from a contract made before the assignment.[28]

The outcome of one case lends some support to the Australian thesis that, in principle, there can be set-off even between entirely pre-receivership and entirely post-receivership debts, although in many circumstances the courts will not enforce that set-off because to do so would be inequitable. In *Re Harrex Ltd, Murphy v Revenue Commissioners*,[29] at the time a receiver was appointed over its business, the company owed the Revenue a sum in respect of outstanding corporation profits tax. Eventually, when the company discontinued trading permanently, it became entitled to a larger sum from the Revenue in

---

23. *Biggerstaff v Rowatt's Wharf Ltd* [1896] 2 Ch 93, at p. 106.
24. *Government of Newfoundland v Newfoundland Rly. Co.* (1888) 13 HLC 199.
25. [1913] AC 160.   26. [1974] 1 QB 1.
27. Id. at p. 6. See too the £1,477 claim in *Business Computer Ltd v Anglo-African Leasing Ltd* [1977] 1 WLR 578.
28. *Business Computers* etc. case [1977] 1 WLR at p. 586.
29. [1976] IR 15.

respect of its terminal trading losses. Kenny J held that the amount of unpaid tax could be set-off against the terminal credit on the grounds that, when the receiver was appointed, the assignment to the debenture-holders of the company's future assets, including any receipts for terminal trading losses, 'was subject to the right of any creditor to whom a debt was then due to set it off against the sum which that future asset might realise. . . . [T]he debt due to the [Revenue] was in existence when the receiver was appointed, and so the equitable assignment of the . . . right to payment of a terminal loss was always subject to the right of set-off'.[30]

LIQUIDATION

In contrast with the position in receiverships, there is a special self-contained body of rules governing set-offs when a company is being wound up and is insolvent. This 'code' was contained in s.251 of the Irish Bankruptcy and Insolvency Act, 1857, and is now in the first schedule (para. 17(1)) of the Bankruptcy Act, 1988:

> Where there are mutual credits or debts as between a bankrupt and any person claiming as a creditor, one debt or demand may be set off against the other and only the balance found owing shall be recoverable on one side or the other.

For over one hundred years it has been well established that this is one of the rules of bankruptcy law which are applicable in company insolvencies.[31] Whatever may be the position with set-off in receiverships, it is abundantly clear that there must be mutual debts or credits or other mutual dealings for set-off to operate when winding up insolvent companies. It would seem that para.17(1) displaces common law, equitable and contractual set-off in insolvency and, as is explained below, probably the parties cannot contract out of the statutory set-off in this context. It has been said that set-off in insolvency is somewhat more extensive than in the general law because its purpose in the former is not merely to avoid cross-actions but to do substantial justice between the parties.[32] Companies' bankers frequently assert rights to set-off and combine accounts during winding ups.

Mutuality   What can be set-off under para. 17(1) in an insolvent liquidation are 'mutual credits or debts' between the company and its creditor. Mutuality in this context does not require that the debts arise at the same time nor that they should be connected in any way or that they should be of the same nature. Debts arising at different times in unconnected transactions, be they written, oral, under seal or whatever, can be mutual debts. The focus instead is on the parties

30. Id. at p. 19.
31. *Mersey Steel & Iron .Co. v Nayler Benzon & Co.* (1884) 9 HLC 434. See generally, Derham, supra n.1, ch's. 3-7.
32. *Forster v Wilson* (1843) 12 M. & W. 191, at pp. 203-204.

to the debts and the relationship between each other, not on the nature of the claims being asserted. If the debts are between the same parties and in the same capacity, they are mutual debts which can be set- off in the liquidation. This identity must be between those who are beneficially entitled to the debt. It is the beneficial owner of a debt who may set-off that debt against an obligation he owes the debtor. Generally, a joint liability may not be set-off against an individual debt or vice versa, although there are some exceptions to this principle.[33] But there can be set-off between an individual debt and joint and several liabilities, because each party is severally as well as jointly liable. Money obtained for a particular purpose may, in the circumstances, be excluded from set-off.[34] The case law on when agency relationships give rise to mutual rights and liabilities is very complex.[35]

Debts capable of set-off   Provided the mutual debt in question is one which can be proved in a winding up, it can be the subject of set-off under para. 17(1). Accordingly, debts and claims which arise after the liquidation has commenced cannot be the subject of set-off. There can be no set-off in respect of a debt which, at the time of liquidation, has been assigned to some other person, except to the extent of any residue which remains. Where, at that time, a right of set-off does not exist, it cannot be acquired through a subsequent assignment.

The debt or claim in question need not have arisen out of a contract; 'any mutual demand capable of being proved in bankruptcy can be the subject matter of set-off whether or not arising out of contract.'[36] Unliquidated damages can be the subject of set-off[37] and so too can amounts owing to and by the Revenue in respect of taxes.[38] Since they can be proved, contingent claims can give rise to a set-off, provided that the debt or claim in question came into existence prior to the winding up commencing. There even can be a set-off between a money debt and goods being held, provided that those goods were entrusted for sale and that the proceeds were to be handed over to the debtor.[39] But even though both parties had mutual dealings, a debt cannot be set off against a liability in respect of a judgment for detinue.[40] The primary obligations between the parties must have been to pay each other money. Lord Esher MR observed that '[i]f the claim on one side in the action and the counter-claim on the other were such as would both result in a money claim, so that for the purposes of the action there would be merely a pecuniary liability on each side, the case would . . . come within the section. [One should] give the widest possible scope to the section.'[41]

---

33. Cf. E.H. Scammell & R.C. Banks, *Lindley on the Law of Partnership* (15th ed., 1984) pp. 890-915.
34. *Re Mid Kent Fruit Factory* [1896] 1 Ch 567. Cf. *Re Johnson & Co.* [1902] 1 IR 439.
35. See generously, Derham, 'Set-Off and Agency', 44 *Cam. L.J.* 834, (1985).
36. *Re D.H. Curtis (Builders) Ltd* [1978] 1 Ch 162, at p. 173.
37. Supra n.24.   38. *Re Harrex Ltd* [1976] IR 15.
39. *Rolls Razor Ltd v Cox* [1967] 1 QB 552.
40. *Eberle's Hotel & Restaurant Co. v Jonas Bros.* (1887) 18 QBD 459.
41. Id. at p. 465.

Secured and preferential debts It is only unsecured debts that must be proved in a liquidation. Accordingly, the company cannot set-off against its liabilities to a secured creditor unless he elects to prove in the liquidation.[42] Where the company owes both preferential debts and non-preferential debts to a particular creditor, for instance the Revenue, it cannot select which element of these debts shall be the subject of set-off. Instead, its set-off operates rateably, in proportion to the amounts of the two kinds of debt.[43]

Peremptory or optional? Whether set-off is a peremptory rule in bankruptcy that cannot be contracted out of or waived is a debatable matter. In *Deering v Hyndman*,[44] which dealt with set-off under s.251 of the 1857 Act, it was held that the right was optional, or at least was not compulsory in all circumstances. There, all the creditors, including the defendant, agreed that the debtor should continue trading. At that time, the defendant was owed £2,000 and, following the agreement, he became indebted to the debtor for £1,190. When shortly afterwards the debtor was adjudicated bankrupt, the defendant sought to set-off these two amounts and to prove for the balance. It was held that, by agreeing that the debtor could trade on, in the circumstances, the defendant purported to waive any set-off he may have had and that such an agreement was not precluded by 1857 Act nor by the general law. According to Johnson J,

> I have always understood the settled law to be—*quilibet potest renunciare juri pro se introducto*—that a person who has a benefit given to him by statute may waive it if he thinks fit, but that an individual cannot waive a matter in which the public have an interest. . . . The right of set-off is a benefit to the individual creditor, and it in no way concerns the public or society whether he relies on it or waives it. And even if an individual creditor agrees for sufficient consideration to waive the right, I fail to see why he should not be at liberty to do so either without bankruptcy or in bankruptcy; and if a number of creditors of a firm which has suspended payment agree together, and with the firm, to buy the goods of the firm on hands for cash, and not to rely on set-off of antecedent debts, even in the event of bankruptcy supervening, I fail to see why such agreement should not be valid and binding, the mutual promises being the consideration.[45]

May CJ, however, emphasised that the case concerned 'a special agreement entered into. . . , not by any particular creditor, but by the general body, to exclude a set-off,'[46] although he did not expressly reject the contention that any creditor could 'commute the right of set-off for sufficient consideration.'[47]

In Britain and in New Zealand it has been held that the right of set-off under the relevant insolvency legislation cannot be contracted out of. In *National*

---

42. *Re Norman Holding Co.* [1991] 1 WLR 10.
43. *Re Unit 2 Windows Ltd* [1985] 1 WLR 1383.
44. (1886) 18 LR Ir 323.
45. Id. at p. 340.
46. Id. at p. 332.
47. Id. at p. 338, O'Brien J.

Westminster Bank v Halesowen Presswork & Assembles Ltd,[48] the House of Lords held that the parallel though not absolutely identical provision of the British 1914 Act[49] was peremptory. Instead of 'may be' set off, s.31 of the 1914 Act stated that mutual debts 'shall be' set off; and it was held that s.31's legislative history and its surrounding sections showed that the word 'shall' in it was used 'in its directory and mandatory sense, prescribing the course to be followed in the administration of the bankrupt's property.'[50] It was said that this part of the Act 'lay[s] down a code of procedure whereby bankrupts' estates (and, by reference, insolvent companies) are to be administered in a properly and orderly way; this is a matter in which the commercial community generally has an interest, . . . [is] a matter where the public have an interest.'[51] It remains to be seen whether or in what circumstances the Irish courts would follow *Halesowen Presswork*. The New Zealand Bankruptcy Act's formulation of the set-off rule is practically identical to para.17(1) of the 1988 Irish Act and, in *Rendell v Doors & Doors Ltd*,[52] the New Zealand Supreme Court choose to follow the House of Lords and held that the statutory provision there was peremptory. Pointing out that the section also said that an account 'shall be stated' and that only the balance 'shall be claimed or paid', Chilwell J reasoned that he 'cannot conceive how these mandatory provisions can be complied with unless one debt or demand is set-off against another. This [is] a classic instance where the word 'may' should be given mandatory effect.'[53] One reason for making the set-off rule mandatory in Britain was that often it would be very difficult to determine if there was an agreement to by-pass set-off and that it was desirable to prevent liquidators from being badgered by arguments about the existence of such agreements.

Rule in *Cherry v Boultbee*   There is in equity what is know as the rule in *Cherry v Boultbee*,[54] which applies principally in the area of wills and inheritances but is not confined to there. In the case which gave rise to the rule, a bankrupt owed money to his sister, who then died leaving money in her will; this led to a dispute between the Assignee in bankruptcy and her executors. The rule has been formulated as follows:

> Where a person entitled to participate in a fund is also bound to make a contribution in aid of that fund, he cannot be allowed to participate unless and until he has fulfilled his duty to contribute.[55]

This rule is very similar to equitable set-off but is regarded as a distinct principle because it is wider and applies even if the debt is one that cannot be set-off, whether under the general law or in an insolvent liquidation.

48. [1972] AC 785.   49. Bankruptcy Act 1914, s.31.
50. [1972] AC at p. 805.   51. Id at p. 809.
52. [1975] 2 NZLR 191.   53. Id. at p. 198.
54. (1839) 4 My. & Cr. 442. See generally, Derham, supra n.1, ch. 9 and Meagher et al.,
     Equity Doctrine and Remedies (2nd ed., 1984) pp. 784-789.
55. *Re Peruvian Rly. Construction Co.* [1915] 2 Ch 144, at p. 150.

Where this rule could apply in an insolvency is where two companies are being wound up as insolvent and each owes the other money but those debts cannot be set-off. For instance, one of the debts is in respect of unpaid calls or is damages for misfeasance or is a sum repayable as a fraudulent preference. The rule here prevents either company from receiving a dividend until it has paid the full amount due from it to the other.

24

Secured Creditors

Frequently banks, suppliers and others will not lend money or otherwise extend credit to persons without having first obtained security. Without some security, it is possible that no credit will be extended to particular individuals or that such credit as is given is at extravagant rates of interest or is subject to extensive restrictions regarding its use. Additionally, when the borrower or debtor is a company, the creditors' only recourse is against its assets and, as a rule, the management and shareholders cannot be held accountable to the lender—unless, of course, they are parties to the loan agreement or commit a tort or some other actionable wrong, or have guaranteed the liability themselves.

There are two main types of security. One is proprietary; the creditor is given some legally enforceable interest in property, most notably a mortgage. The other is a personal security; a third party can be made accountable for the debt, for instance under a guarantee or an indemnity. Several eminent books that deal with securities do not discuss guarantees. Sykes defines security in his excellent treatise as

> an interest vested in a person called the 'creditor' in certain property owned by another called the 'debtor', whereby certain rights are made available to the creditor over such property in order to satisfy an obligation personally owed or recognised as being owed to the creditor by the debtor or some other person. This is wide enough to comprehend the case of a security [given] by a guarantor but not wide enough to embrace a personal promise [to pay] given by him.[1]

The subject matter of the proprietary security can be land, chattels or choses in action. While security often is specific, in the sense that the creditor gets an equitable interest in the charged property and the debtor is no longer free to deal with that property without the creditor's consent, in circumstances the security may be a 'floating' charge. On account of provisions in the Bills of Sale Acts and previously in the Bankruptcy Acts, floating charges are used mainly in connection with corporate finance. Floating charges rank after fixed charges in order of priority and, by virtue of s.285(7)(b) of the 1963 Act, rank even after statutorily preferred debts,[2] notably certain unpaid taxes, rates and remuneration for company employees. The discussion here first concerns fixed or

1.   E.I. Sykes, *The Law of Securities* (4th ed. 1986) at p. 12.
2.   See post p. 365.

specific charges, i.e. charges which have originally been given as such or floating security which, prior to the examination, receivership or liquidation, has crystallised into a fixed security. For an account of the law relating to security in land, mainly legal and equitable mortgages and equitable charges, the reader is referred to Professor Wylie's *Irish Land Law*.[3] For an account of the law concerning security in chattels and in choses in action (meaning stocks and shares, insurance policies, debts etc.), the reader is referred to A.P. Bell's *Modern Law of Personal Property*[4] and F. Oditah's *Legal Aspects of Receivables Financing*.[5] A comprehensive account of the whole question of charges from a company law point of view is contained in W.J. Gough's excellent *Company Charges*.[6]

REGISTRATION OF COMPANY CHARGES

In order to be fully effective in an insolvency, practically every proprietary security must have been duly registered in the registry of companies, as required by s.99 of the 1963 Act. As is explained elsewhere,[7] this system of registration was introduced in 1907[8] in order to answer some of the criticisms made of the *Salomon & Co.* case,[9] decided ten years earlier. It will be remembered that the principal shareholder of the company in that case was owed £10,000 by his company and that debt was secured by a floating charge on its assets. It was held that, in an insolvency, he was entitled to be paid out of the company's charged assets before any of the unsecured trade creditors could recover a penny. The registration of charges system here was introduced so that persons dealing with companies can ascertain the extent to which a company's assets are already charged. However, the system is not all- embracing; it only applies to charges given by the company and its catalogue of registerable charges does not cover every conceivable security a company can give, for instance, fixed charges over stocks and shares and over funds other than book debts.

Registration under s.99 of the 1963 Act is not absolutely essential for the charge to be valid. Nor does that registration fix the priority ranking of the charge against other charges over the same property. But a charge which has not been registered within 21 days of its being given is, by s.99(1),

> so far as any security on the company's property or undertaking is conferred thereby, void against the liquidator and any creditor of the company. . . .

Accordingly, whether the company is solvent or not, an unregistered charge can be disregarded entirely by a liquidator and by a receiver. But it has been held that the non-registration of a charge does not prevent the chargee from appointing a receiver.[10] The efficacy of an unregistered charge in an examination under

3. 2nd ed., 1986.   4. 1989.   5. 1991.   6. 1978.
7. *Company Law*, pp. 512 et seq.   8. Companies Act 1907, s.10.
9. [1897] AC 22.
10. *Alexander Hull & Co. v O'Carroll Kent & Co.*, 89 ILTR 70 (1955).

the Companies (Amendment) Act, 1990, can be debated. Even though s.99(1) deprives an unregistered charge of most of its effect, the underlying debt covered by the charge is not affected. Once a charge becomes 'void' under s.99(1), the money secured by it becomes immediately repayable.

Late registration As is explained elsewhere,[12] in an appropriate case and subject to certain conditions, the court will permit the late registration of a charge which was not filed in the registry within the required 21 days period. The court has a wide discretion in this matter. Generally an application to extend the time will be refused when the company is in liquidation[13] and even where an insolvent liquidation is imminent and manifestly cannot be avoided.[14] Nevertheless, special circumstances may warrant allowing registration in those cases. That happened in *Re O'Carroll Kent Ltd*,[15] where in an earlier proceeding the applicant for the extension of time got the court to appoint a receiver and manager to protect the assets charged under the debenture. However, Dixon J added, when granting the extension of time, that if the company were indeed wound up, if the liquidator felt that his interests had been prejudiced by the court's order, he could take appropriate proceedings.

If late registration were permitted without any proviso, intervening chargees would be very seriously prejudiced. For the unregistered charge is always a valid charge, except that it was rendered practically unenforceable for not being registered. If it becomes registered without any qualification, its priority position is based on the date the charge was granted. Accordingly, it would rank before subsequent charges which were obtained by persons who were completely unaware of its existence; even if they searched the company's register, no evidence of that charge would be disclosed. Accordingly, where an application for late registration is granted, almost always it is without prejudice to the rights of the parties acquired during the period between when the charge was created by the company and the date of its actual registration. This formula protects all intervening secured creditors.

It is not regarded as protecting unsecured creditors.[16] However, the actual words used in the common formula do not expressly or by necessary implication confine its scope to secured creditors. An Irish court, in an appropriate case, might interpret it more generously. An obviously deserving case would be an unsecured creditor who gave the company substantial advances because he had consulted its file in the companies' office and saw that there was no recorded charge over its assets. The practice in Australia is for the court to stipulate that

---

11. 1963 Act s.99(1).
12. *Company Law*, pp. 524-525.
13. *Re Ashpurton Estates Ltd* [1983] Ch 110 and *Re Farm Fresh Frozen Foods Ltd* [1980] ILRM 131.
14. *Re Barrow Burrough Transport Ltd* [1990] 1 Ch 227.
15. 89 ILTR 72 (1955); also *Re Braemer Investments Ltd* [1989] 1 Ch 54.
16. *Watson v Duff Morgan & Vermont Holdings Ltd* [1974] 1 WLR 450.

unsecured creditors too should not be prejudiced where the circumstances so require.[17]

Other registration systems   In order for the security to be fully effective, or indeed to be an enforceable security, it may be necessary to have it also registered under some other legislative provision, depending on the nature of the property in question. If it is land, it ought to be registered either in the registry of deeds or in the land registry, as the case may be;[18] most urban property is registerable under the former and rural property under the latter. Where the security is an Irish registered ship, then it must be registered under s.50 of the Mercantile Marine Act, 1955, at the ship's port of registry. Priority of ship mortgages turns entirely on the times they were so registered.[19] There are no special provisions for registering charges on aircraft. Where the land is outside the State or the ship or aircraft are registered abroad, the registration requirements of the State where the land is or where the ship or aircraft is registered must be followed. Where a person acquires a security interest in a patent which is registered under the Patents Act, 1992, he is required by s.85 of that Act to apply to have his interest registered with the registrar of patents. It is only the registered owners of interests in patents who are empowered to deal with them.

Because the Bills of Sale Acts do not apply to companies,[20] it is not necessary to register charges over chattels under those Acts. Although shares in companies are a very common form of security, the 1963 Act does not allow the existence of a charge on a company's shares to be entered in its own register of members.[21] Where debentures are issued in a series, a similar prohibition is often contained in the debenture, thereby enabling the issuer in many respects to disregard any security interests in its debentures.[22]

PLEDGES AND LIENS

It is convenient here to mention liens and pledges, which are forms of possessory security. Most securities used in the commercial world are non-possessory, or hypothecations, in that the secured creditor does not have physical control of the charged assets. Instead, they remain in the possession of the company, or some third party on its behalf and, to an extent, the chargee must rely on the company adhering to the restrictions on dealing with the security contained in the debenture or other charging instrument. Those concerns simply do not arise when the chargee also has the security in his possession. What distinguishes pledges from liens is that it is always a term of the pledge that the property being held as security can be sold in the event of default.

17. *Re Flinders Trading Co. Pty. Ltd* (1978) 3 ACLR 218.
18. See generally, J.C. Wylie, *Irish Land Law* (2nd ed., 1986) chs. 21 and 22.
19. Cf. *The Ship 'Betty Ott' v General Bills Ltd* [1992] 1 NZLR 655.
20. *Re Royal Marine Hotel Co.* [1895] 1 IR 368.
21. 1963 Act s.123; cf. *Rearden v Provincial Bank* [1896] 1 IR 532.
22. E.g. *Re Goy & Co.* [1900] 2 Ch. 149.

Where a person has a lien over another's property,[23] he is entitled to retain possession of its until he is paid what is owing—either in respect of that property or otherwise, depending on the kind of lien it is. Most liens are particular, in the sense that the right to retain the item of property in question only applies where money is owed in respect of that property, for instance, the unpaid seller of goods, the unpaid carrier of goods and the unpaid accountant who has possession of his clients' books and papers. Certain professions and occupations enjoy more extensive liens, most notably bankers, solicitors and stockbrokers.

Liens can also be given by express contract. It depends on exactly what was intended whether the contract granted a lien or went further and constituted a pledge or even gave a charge over the property. For instance in *De Lorean Motor Cars Ltd v Northern Ireland Carriers Ltd*,[24] the plaintiffs, car manufactures, agreed that the defendants should transport their cars from their Belfast factory to the dock side. A clause in the agreement provided that the defendants would have a 'general lien' over goods carried for 'all moneys whatsoever due from the plaintiffs.' The agreement went on to confer a power of sale on the defendants if they were not paid within a reasonable time, which suggests that the real intention was to pledge the goods and not simply give a lien.

PRIORITIES BETWEEN SPECIFIC CHARGES

Because they are possessory securities, the question of priority doesn't really arise with regard to pledges and liens. A security interest of that nature will subsist in the property in question only for so long as the creditor retains possession of it—although possession for this purpose is not always confined to permanent immediate possession. If the pledgee, when accepting the property as security, actually knew that it had been charged to a third party, presumably equity would insist on that pledgee ranking behind the chargee. It is in respect of non- possessory securities that issues of priority feature so prominently.[25]

Land Where the security constitutes a charge over land, the question of priorities between persons with competing security interests in that land is a complex matter of land law. This often involves the qualification of common law rules by equitable principles, with the further complication that registration of the charge in either the Land Registry or the Registry of Deeds can often be decisive. Of particular significance here is the doctrine of notice, especially of constructive or imputed notice.

Chattels Where the security constitutes a charge over chattels, the same

23. See generally, A.P. Bell, *Modern Law of Personal Property* (1989) ch. 6.
24. [1982] N.I. 163.
25. See generally, R. Keane, *Equity and the Law of Trusts in the Republic of Ireland* (1988) ch. 5, E.I. Sykes, *The Law of Securities* (4th ed., 1986) chs. 11 and 17 and Bell, supra n.23, ch. 22.

general common law and equitable principles as apply to land determine who has the prior security interests.[26] In the case of charges on ships, which must be registered under the Mercantile Marine Act, 1955, priority is determined exclusively by reference to the time the charge was registered under that Act, even where the chargee has actual notice of a prior mortgage on the ship.[27] The doctrine of constructive notice does not apply to chattels,[28] in the sense of notice being deemed to derive from failure to search a register which would have shown the existence of the charge.

Choses   The security may be a charge over a chose in action, for instance a debt, stocks and shares, insurance policies, copyrights and the like. As regards certain choses, the basic rule, that priority is determined by reference to when the charge was granted, gives way to the time when notice of the security was given to the debtor.[29] Under what is known as the rule in *Dearle v Hall*,[30] whoever first notified the debtor, trustee or fund-holder gets priority. Originally this 'rule' was based on negligence, that by not notifying the fund-holder the subsequent chargee was misled, but it has now become an absolute rule of priority, regardless of the parties' conduct. It therefore is no longer material that the subsequent chargee was somehow prevented from giving notice. Another difference as regards choses is that assignments of choses in action are 'subject to equities',[31] unless the chose expressly provided that it is not subject to this principle.

FLOATING CHARGES

The question of what is a floating charge and the difference between it and a fixed charge, or specific security, has been examined in some detail elsewhere.[32] While there is no accepted definition of the floating security, it is helpful to reiterate the widely accepted criteria for identifying it, the test adopted by Romer LJ in *Re Yorkshire Woolcombers Ass'n Ltd*:

> I certainly do not intend to attempt to give an exact definition of the term 'floating charge', nor am I prepared to say that there will not be a floating charge . . . which does not contain all the three characteristics that I am about to mention, but I certainly think that if a charge has the[se] three characteristics, . . . it is a floating charge.

26. See generally, ibid. and M. Forde, *Commercial Law in Ireland* (1990) pp. 200-229.
27. Mercantile Marine Act 1955, s.52
28. *Joseph v Lyons* (1884) 15 QBD 280.
29. See generally, F. Oditah, *Legal Aspects of Receivable Financing* (1991) chs. 5 and 6, Keane, *supra* n.25, pp. 63-65, Bell, supra n.23, pp. 528-535, and Forde, *supra* n.26 at pp. 230-238.
30. (1823) 3 Russ 1.
31. E.g. *Re Gwelo (Matabeleland) Exploration & Development Co.* [1901] 1 IR 38; see generally, Oditah, *supra* n.29, ch.8.
32. See *Company Law*, pp. 494 et seq.

(1) If it is a charge on a class of assets of a company present and future;
(2) if that class is one which, in the ordinary course of the business of the company, would be changing from time to time; and
(3) if you find that by the charge it is contemplated that, until some future step is taken by or on behalf of those interested in the charge, the company may carry on its business in the ordinary way as far as concerns the particular class of assets I am dealing with.[33]

It is possible, by appropriate drafting to create a fixed charge over a company's debts and other receivables. However, the Irish law in this regard has diverged significantly from the position in England and it now appears that in Ireland one can have a fixed charge over assets which the company remains free to use in the ordinary course of its business. That was the reasoning of the Supreme Court in *Re Wogans (Drogheda) Ltd*[34] involving a debenture which *inter alia* purported to create a fixed charge on book debts, which provided that at any time the chargee could designate a bank account into which those debts would be paid but, until that has been done, the company is free to realise its debtors in the course of its business. Finlay CJ, giving the only judgment, concluded that the clear intention was to grant a fixed charge and the chargee should not be disadvantaged merely because, as a temporary measure, he allowed the company to deal with the assets in a manner apparently incompatible with a fixed charge. This analysis has been rejected in England in *New Bullas Trading Ltd*,[35] where the classic test of a floating charge was re-affirmed, viz. up to the time a special account is designated, was the company left free to deal with its book debts and proceeds if and when collected. Prohibitions or restrictions on factoring, assigning or selling the debtors are not enough to create a fixed charge; an obligation to pay the money into a special account suffices. But until that obligation actually arises, the company remains free to deal with the debts and, accordingly, they are not subject to a fixed charge. It remains to be seen whether the peculiar logic in the *Wogans* case will be extended to other forms of current assets and, if it is, whether for most practical purposes the floating charge will become defunct in Ireland.

When a floating charge 'crystallises' it immediately becomes a fixed charge and the company is no longer at liberty to deal with the assets covered by the charge in the ordinary course of its business. The chargee is then the equitable owner of those assets. Frequently floating charges contain what are called 'negative pledge' clauses whereby, during the currency of the charge, the company is restricted from certain forms of dealing in the charged assets, for instance creating a specific security in some or all of them.

Registration of floating charges   The system of registration of charges given

---

33. [1903] 2 Ch 284, at p. 295.
34. [1993] ILRM XXX.
35. [1993] BCLC 251.

by companies under s.99 of the 1963 Act, as described briefly above, applies to all floating charges. In order to be enforceable against any creditor or in a liquidation, every floating charge must be duly registered under that section, although late registration may be allowed in an appropriate case but subject to conditions which protect any intervening chargees.

Registration might affect priorities of floating charges if the contents of negative pledge clauses were entered in the companies' registry when the charge is being registered. The argument would be that the entire world is then fixed with notice of any restrictions in those clauses, for instance, a ban on granting additional security. However, Form No. 47[36] makes no provision for entering the existence or details of any such restrictions. And it was held in *Welch v Bowmaker (Ireland) Ltd*[37] that persons who have dealings with the charged property will not be deemed to have notice of any of these restrictions. Simply because negative pledge clauses are a common feature of floating charges does not place a duty on creditors to ascertain if the debtor is thereby restricted from creating an additional security interest in the charged assets. According to Henchy J '[a]ctual or express notice of the prohibition must be shown before the subsequent mortgagee can be said to be deprived of priority' by the equitable doctrine of notice.[38]

Early crystallisation When setting out the preferential status of certain revenue and employees' claims, s.285(7)(b) of the 1963 Act says that they have priority over claims by the 'holders of . . . any floating charge' and shall be paid from the assets governed by that charge. It has been held in England that a similar principle applies to the liquidation expenses.[39] If, however, the floating charge crystallises some time prior to the time of liquidation, it seems that the s.285 preferences, described in the next chapter, must no longer be paid from the assets that are subject to the charge. For the secured creditor is not then enforcing a right under a floating charge. It is for this reason that the legislation in Britain has been amended to extend those preferences to 'a charge which, as created, was a floating charge'.[40]

The statutory preferences under s.285 apply to receivers as well as in liquidations. Section 98 of the 1963 Act provides that when, under a floating charge, a receiver is appointed over property or the chargee otherwise takes possession of it, sufficient funds must be held from the sale of that property in order to pay the debts which are preferred in every winding up.[41] The security must still be a floating charge when the receiver is appointed or possession was otherwise taken. In *Re Brightlife Ltd*,[42] it was held that if the charge actually crystallised before a receiver was appointed or possession was otherwise taken of the security, the property is no longer caught by s.98 for the benefit of the

36. In SI No. 45 of 1964.
37. [1980] IR 251.   38. Id. at p. 256.
39. See post p. 359.
40. Insolvency Act 1986, ss.40 and 251.
41. See post p. 365.   42. [1987] Ch. 200.

preferred creditors. There the debenture contained an 'automatic crystallisation' clause, under which the creditor could crystallise the security at any time on delivering a notice to the company. Ten days before the company resolved to wind itself up and a receiver was appointed, a notice of that nature was delivered to the company. That was enough to prevent the preferred creditors from being paid out of the proceeds from the sale of assets subject to this charge. Section 98 has no application where a receiver was appointed under a fixed charge, not even where the security is sold, the chargee is paid off in full and there is a surplus on the disposal.[42a]

Priority between charges   Priority conflicts can arise between a fixed and a floating charge and between two or more floating charges.[43] A fixed charge takes priority over a floating charge on the same assets, no matter how long after the floating charge it was created. As James LJ observed, 'it would be a monstrous thing to hold that the floating security prevented the making of specific charges or specific alienations of property, because it would destroy the very object for which the money was borrowed, namely, the carrying on of the business of the company.'[44] Thus in *Re Castell and Brown Ltd*,[45] the company gave a floating charge over its entire assets but some time later it deposited title deeds to part of its land with its bankers as security for a loan. Although both charges there were equitable, it was held that the charge over the land took precedence. For the floating charge, by its very terms, 'authorised the mortgagor, the company, to deal with its property as if it had not been enumbered, and left with the mortgagor the deeds in order to enable the company to act as owner.'[46] As is explained below, however, if the floating charge actually forbids giving a specific charge over the already-charged assets, and if the later mortgagee was in fact aware of that prohibition at the time he obtained his charge, then the prior floating charge takes precedence.

Where the conflict is between two floating charges, each of which are over the entire undertaking (or which are over an identical category or categories of assets), then the first in time takes precedence, in accordance with the maxim that where the equities are equal the first in time prevails. As between two floating charges, one over the company's entire assets and the other over part of those assets (or one over a category of assets and the other over part of those assets), the first in time does not invariably prevail. Instead, a later charge over the limited range of assets takes precedence except where the earlier more extensive charge forbade the company from further charging those assets and the subsequent chargee knew of that restriction. Thus in *Re Automatic Bottle Makers Ltd*,[47] some months after the company gave a floating charge over its

---

42a. *Re G.L. Saunders Ltd* [1986] 1 WLR 215.
43. See generally, R.M. Goode, *Legal Problems of Credit and Security* (2nd ed., 1988) ch. 4 and Farrar, 'Floating Charges and Securities', 38 *Conv* 315 (1974).
44. *Wheatley v Silkstone & Haigh Moor Coal Co.* (1885) 29 Ch D 715. at p. 724.
45. [1898] 1 Ch 315.
46. Id. at p. 321.   47. [1926] Ch. 412.

entire assets, it gave a floating charge over specific categories of assets (dock warrants, bills of lading, raw materials and stocks). It was held that the later charge took precedence over the former because, 'by creating a charge upon its assets generally by way of floating security the company is not, in the absence of any stipulation to the contrary, prohibited from creating specific charges on specific portions of its assets in the ordinary course of its business, as otherwise it would be prevented from effectively carrying on that business the carrying on of which was contemplated by the parties to the security.'[48]

LIQUIDATION

The position of secured creditors in a liquidation has already been described when discussing the proof of debts.[49] It was summarised in *Moor v Anglo Italian Bank* as follows:

> if a secured creditor wants to prove, he must do one of three things; he may give up his security altogether and prove for the full amount, or he may get his security valued and prove for the difference, or he may sell and realise his security and then prove for the difference. If without doing either of the latter two things, he proves for the full amount, . . . he shows by that an intention to give up his security; and if he so proves or receives a dividend or votes, he shows pretty conclusively that he has finally given up his security.[50]

Usually the secured creditor will choose to stand entirely outside the liquidation and realise his security and, if the proceeds of sale do not discharge his debt, then prove for the balance.

Whether the chargee is entitled to deduct the costs of selling the security from the proceeds of sale depends on the terms of the debenture. As has been pointed out, in a common mode of disposal, appointing a receiver and manager, it is usually provided that the entire expense of the process shall be defrayed from the proceeds of sale of the assets. At times, by agreement, the liquidator may sell the charged assets on behalf of the secured creditor. It was held in *Re Northern Milling Co.*[51] that the liquidator is entitled to be paid from the proceeds of sale the costs he properly incurred in connection with that disposal.[52] But that amount is all he is entitled to; if he incurred substantial other expenses in the course of his office and now finds that there are no unencumbered assets to cover those expenses, he cannot then look to the charged assets. As James LJ once said, where a liquidator found himself in that predicament,

> No doubt it is a very hard case for [liquidators] that they have to deal with an insolvent company, but they ought to have looked into that matter before they incurred expenses and made themselves liable. Those who render services to an insolvent company, or an insolvent person, fre-

---

48. Id. at p. 421.
49. Ante pp. 290-293.
50. (1879) 10 Ch D 681, at pp. 689-690.
51. [1908] 1 IR 473.
52. Similarly *Re Berkeley Applegate (Investment Consultants) Ltd* [1989] Ch 32.

quently find they have to go without payment, and the liquidators should not have incurred disbursement which they had no means of being reimbursed.[53]

Where, under the security instrument, the chargee is entitled to interest on the debt, that right continues after the liquidation until the security has been realised. In *Re McCairns (P.M.P.A.) plc*,[54] where this point was decided for the first time, the security was a mortgage of registered land—which the liquidator had realised with the bank's consent. There does not seem to be any compelling reason why the same principle does not apply to other forms of security, such as an equitable deposit of title deeds. Where the interest charges stipulated for exceed the usual market rate for that kind of transaction, it is possible that the agreed rate of interest does not survive the liquidation.

53. *Re Regents Canal Ironworks Co.* (1876) 3 Ch D 43, at p. 46.
54. [1991] 2 IR 465; see ante p. 293.

25

Statutorily Preferred Debts

If the Bankruptcy Act, the Companies Acts and other legislation made no special provision for treating some groups of creditors differently from others then all unsecured creditors would be treated equally. In an insolvent liquidation, assuming there were some funds left over after set-offs have been exercised and secured creditors have realised their security, this means that the remaining creditors would all be paid the same *pro rata* amount, i.e. the same number of pence for each pound's worth of their proved debts. One of the fundamental principles of insolvency law is that of equality among creditors, except where statute provides otherwise. However, statute goes further than putting some unsecured creditors in front of others in a distribution by the liquidator or by a receiver. It also places one category of secured creditors—the holders of a floating charge—behind those preferred creditors.[1] It is most unlikely that this interference with secured creditors' property rights, by subordinating them to the Revenue and the company's employees, is an unconstitutional infringement of those rights.[2]

EXPENSES OF WINDING UP

If the liquidator's own costs and expenses in the winding up were not given some preferential treatment, it could be difficult at times to find persons prepared to wind up insolvent companies. Even with the present preference, if almost all of the company's assets are caught by charges, there may be insufficient funds in the winding up to attract a liquidator, unless he can get some of the creditors to indemnify his costs. Section 281 of the 1963 Act, which deals with voluntary liquidations, provides that

> All costs, charges and expenses properly incurred in the winding up, including the remuneration of the liquidator, shall be payable out of the assets of the company in priority to all other claims.

Section 244 of that Act, which deals with compulsory liquidations, provides that

1. 1963 Act s.285(7)(b).
2. Cf. Rogers, 'The Impairment of Secured Creditors' Rights in Reorganization: A Study of the Relationships Between the Fifth Amendment and the Bankruptcy Clause', 96 *Harvard L. Rev* 973 (1963).

The court may, in the event of the assets being insufficient to satisfy the liabilities, make an order as to the payment out of the assets of the costs, charges and expenses incurred in the winding up in such order of priority as the court thinks just.

It was held in *Re Readbrest Preserving Co. (Ireland) Ltd*[3] that these sections place liquidation expenses before the s.285 preferential revenue and employee debts.

Costs, charges and expenses   Although there is no complete definition of what these liquidation expenses are, rule 128 of the Winding Up Rules, which sets out the priority between the expenses, identifies many of them. The term 'expenses of the liquidation' is not a term of art and has been held to cover 'any expense which the liquidator might be compelled to pay in respect of his acts in the course of a proper liquidation of the company's assets.'[4] It includes the costs of recovering, preserving and realising the company's assets. It also includes a variety of debts incurred when carrying on the business for the purposes of the winding up, for instance, employees' wages and salaries[5] and rent and rates on property being occupied by the company.[6] The liquidator's reasonable remuneration is another such cost; determining the quantum of his remuneration has been considered above.[7] Litigation expenses and taxes arising from the company's activities call for special comment.

Litigation expenses   Costs in legal proceedings are costs of the liquidation in two main circumstances. One is where the action was brought by the liquidator and, even though he lost, the court directs that those costs were properly incurred by him. The other is where the company itself, in liquidation, was the plaintiff. Where, on the other hand, an action was brought or continued against a company in liquidation and the plaintiff succeeds, he must look to the company's general assets for his costs *pari passu* with the unsecured creditors; he litigates at his own risk. The circumstances in which the court will rule that a liquidator's costs were properly incurred and also when it will order security for costs have been considered earlier in the discussion of litigation in the winding up.[8]

In *Comhlucht Páipear Ríomhaireachta Teo. v Udarás na Gaeltachta*,[9] the Supreme Court confirmed the line of authority that costs awarded to a defendant in an action brought by the company, in liquidation, are not alone costs of the liquidation but rank before the liquidator's own properly incurred costs in the winding up. This rule applies in voluntary and in compulsory liquidations. Generally, those costs will rank after the petitioner's costs and costs incurred

3.   [1958] IR 234.
4.   *Re Beni-Felkai Mining Co.* [1934] 1 Ch 406, at p. 419.
5.   *Re English Joint Stock Bank* (1867) 3 Eq 341.
6.   *Re Downer Enterprises Ltd* [1974] 1 WLR 146.
7.   See ante p. 191.   8.   See ante p. 207-209.   9.   [1990] IR 320.

by the liquidator in realising the assets. Costs which the liquidator has been allowed then rank next, before his remuneration and the claims of preferential creditors.

Taxes It was held in *Re Beni-Felkai Mining Co.*[10] that, where profits were earned by the company when it was being wound up, income tax chargeable on those profits is an 'expense' of the liquidation and, accordingly, enjoys the priority under s.281 of the 1963 Act. The view expressed there, that 'rates and taxes . . . falling due subsequently to the winding up are part of the expenses of the winding up',[11] has been endorsed by the Irish courts on several occasions.[12] And in *Re A. Noyek & Sons Ltd*,[13] which concerned corporation tax on interest accruing on bank deposits of a company being voluntarily wound up, it was held that the tax was a 'charge properly incurred' under that section. The word charge was 'sufficiently wide to encompass any imposition, such as tax or whatever constitutes a burden or duty, on land or property, and income tax and corporation tax are . . . clearly charges.'[14] Formerly, there was no statutory provision requiring corporation tax, falling due during the post-liquidation period, to be paid over to the Revenue before distributions were made to other creditors,[15] but that was changed by s.56 of the Finance Act, 1983. It has been held that, ordinarily, stamp duty is not a 'cost or expense' of an official liquidation but,[16] in the light of the *Noyek* case, stamp duty would seem to be a 'charge' incurred in a liquidation.

Order of priority Where there are insufficient assets in the liquidation to pay all of the winding up expenses, the Companies Acts give no indication about in what order of priority the different kinds of expenses ought to be paid, other than s.244's statement that, in compulsory liquidations, they be paid 'in such order of priority as the court thinks just.' Rule 128 of the Winding Up Rules lays down an order of payment which should be followed in compulsory liquidations unless the court directs otherwise. In a voluntary liquidation, the court may apply this list by way of analogy.[17]

According to rule 128(1)

> The assets of a company in a winding up by the court remaining after payment of the fees and expanses properly incurred in preserving, realising or getting in the assets, including where the company has previously commenced to be wound up voluntarily such remuneration, costs and expenses, as the court may allow to a liquidator appointed in such voluntary winding up, shall, subject to any order of the court, be

10. [1934] Ch 406. 11. Id. at p. 418.
12. Cf. *Re McMeekin* [1973] NI 191.
13. [1988] IR 772. 14. Id. at p. 776.
15. *Re Hibernian Transport Companies Ltd* [1984] ILRM 583 at p. 586.
16. *Michael Orr (Kilternan) Ltd* [1986] IR 273.
17. E.g. in *Re Redbreast Preserving Co. (Ireland) Ltd* [1958] IR 324; contrast *Re A. Noyek & Sons Ltd* [1958] IR 234.

liable to the following payments which shall be made in the following order of priority, namely:

First—The costs of the petition, including the costs of any person appearing on the petition whose costs are allowed by the court.

Next—The costs and expenses of any person who makes or concurs in making the company's statement of affairs.

Next—The necessary disbursements of the Official Liquidator, other than expenses properly incurred in preserving, realising or getting in the assets hereinbefore provided for.

Next—The costs payable to the solicitor for the Official Liquidator.

Next—The remuneration of the Official Liquidator.

Next—The out-of-pocket expenses necessarily incurred by the committee of inspection (if any).

This catalogue is far from being exhaustive.

The issue to be decided in *Re Beni-Felkai Mining Co.*[18] was whether the liquidator's remuneration should be paid before income tax assessed in respect of profits made in the liquidation. The quantum of his remuneration had been agreed by the committee of inspection when they believed the company was entirely solvent. Applying rule 128(i) by analogy, It was held that generally the liquidator's remuneration will be paid last, because

> in the normal case, expenses which he has incurred, whether by the employment of agents or, for example, in respect of gas and electric light or for rents, or any other of the numerous expenses which he may incur in the winding up of a company, are things for which he is bound to provide out of the assets of the company as far as he is enabled to recover them. If his position is that, having provided for them, there will be no remuneration left for him, then he is entitled to say: 'I cannot go on unless the creditors or shareholders or others will put up a fund for my benefit'. He is the person who can see what the position is. The people to whom the company in liquidation has incurred a liability for expenses have not got the materials which he has for ascertaining the true position.[19]

However, the court has a discretion here and would deviate from this principle in respect of remuneration for 'services which he has rendered by way of salvage, in a case where the realisation of property has long been delayed or has become impossible.'[20] An exception might also be made for remuneration already paid when there was no reason to believe there would be such a large deficiency.

Formerly, liability for corporation tax, whether on capital gains or on income, was regarded as not being a 'necessary disbursement' of an official

18. [1934] Ch 406.   19. Id. at p. 422.   20. Ibid.

liquidator for the purposes of rule 128(1)(3rd para).[21] What is envisaged by that term is, for instance, necessary maintenance of buildings or wages for care-taking or other purposes. However, under s.56 of the Finance Act, 1983, all 'referable' taxes on chargeable gains, as defined there, are treated as a 'necessary disbursement out of the proceeds of the disposal' and are recoverable from the liquidator. Taxes on income are still not 'necessary disbursements'.

From assets subject to floating charge? It is expressly provided that pre-ferential debts under s.285 of the 1963 Act payable to the Revenue and employees, can be paid from the assets which are subject to a floating charge when a receiver was appointed or when the liquidation commenced.[22] But there is no similar provision about liquidation expenses and floating charges. It was held in *Re Barleycorn Enterprises Ltd*[23] that the word 'assets' used in the English equivalent of ss.244 and 281 of the 1963 Act shall be deemed to include assets which are subject to a floating charge. The reasoning of the Court of Appeal there is questionable and, in the light of the Supreme Court's decision regarding post-liquidation interest,[24] might not be followed here. According to Lord Denning MR, for much of the last century the word 'assets' in this general context meant the company's free, i.e. unencumbered, property; property subject to a floating charge which had crystallised was not free. However, in the 1889 and 1897 measures on preferential debts[25] the legislature gave the word 'assets' a restricted meaning, to include property subject to a floating charge. Consistency therefore demands, he said, that the word should be given the same restrictive meaning in the sections equivalent to ss.244 and 281. His reason for changing the clear meaning of a word, without express statutory warrant (like s 285(7)(b)), is to make sense of the legislation as a whole, although it is not shown that there would be a nonsense if the word assets were given its normal meaning. For many years before the *Barleycorn* decision there was a practice of the floating chargee ranking before the liquidation expenses, other than expenses referable to realising the charged assets.[26]

In *Re M.C. Bacon & Co.*[27] a floating chargee objected to being in effect compelled to pay for the costs of litigation brought by the liquidator against him, contesting the validity of his charge and accusing him of wrongful trading. It was held that those expenses are not costs of the liquidation unless they obtained the court's sanction. Not alone must they have been properly incurred but, when the chargee is being asked to pay them, it must be just that he should do so. All parties in that case accepted the correctness of the *Barleycorn* decision.

21. *Revenue Commissioners v Donnelly* [1983] ILRM 329 and *Re Hibernian Transport Companies Ltd* [1984] ILRM 583.
22. 1963 Act s.285(7)(b).   23. [1970] 1 Ch 465.
24. *Re McCairns (P.M.P.A.) plc* [1991] 2 IR 465; see ante p. 293.
25. 52 & 53 Vic. c.60 and 60 & 61 Vic. c.19.
26. *Re Redbreast Preserving Co.* [1958] IR 234. The *Barleycorn* decision 'came as a surprise to the (insolvency) profession': *Re M.C. Bacon Ltd* [1991] Ch 127 at p. 134.
27. [1991] Ch. 127.

TAXES

At common law debts to the Crown, in particular outstanding taxes, had to be paid in an insolvency before the other unsecured creditors could get any payment. In 1924 that principle was incorporated into s.38(2) of the Finance Act of that year, but that extensive preference was repealed in the Finance Act, 1967. In the meantime, the Supreme Court ruled that the common law preference, to the extent to which it may not have been displaced by statute, was unconstitutional. According to Kingsmill Moore J in *Re Irish Employers Mutual Insurance Ass'n Ltd*, 'the Central Fund of Saorstát Éireann did not possess the characteristics of a royal exchequer, . . . the king owned no property in Ireland and . . . therefore the prerogative of priority payment which is dependent on the existence of a royal property claim or title had ceased to exist' when the 1937 Constitution came into force.[28] In 1878 it was held that the provisions of the Bankruptcy Acts, which gave certain taxes and other debts preferential status in a bankruptcy, did not apply to company liquidations, through the then equivalent of s.284 of the 1963 Act.[29] That led to the Companies Act, 1883,[30] being passed which extended those preferences to liquidations. That Act was amended in 1897 to place those preferences in front of assets which are subject to a floating charge. Post-liquidation taxes do not enjoy any of the s.284 preferences.

The Revenue's preference here is not compulsory in the sense that it cannot be waived by them. In *Re M.F.N. Construction Co.*,[31] where the court had approved a scheme for distribution in an arrangement under s.201 of the 1963 Act, it was held that all the parties remained bound by that scheme when the company was being liquidated. This was the case even though in consequence there would be a divergence from the priorities laid down in s.285(2).

Preferential The principal basis of the Revenue's preference is s.285(2)(a) of the 1963 Act, which covers the following matters. All 'assessed taxes' up to 5 April before the liquidation commenced are preferred, but not more than any one year's assessed tax in respect of each category of tax of each kind.[32] In other words, as regards all kinds of assessed taxes, a preference exists for any one year's tax of each kind. The Revenue can select which particular year shall be taken for this purpose and it can select different years for the different kinds of assessed taxes.[33] Understandably, the Revenue will select the largest outstanding year of each tax. If the company is insolvent, often there will be little or no liabilty under these headings.

28. [1955] IR 76, at p. 231.
29. *Re Albion Steel & Wire Co.* (1878) 7 Ch D 547. Cf. *Re Oriental Bank Corp., ex p. The Crown* (1884) 28 Ch D 643.
30. 46 &·47 Vic. c.28. Cf. *Re Thompson & Co. (Carriers) Ltd* [1932] IR 45 and *Food Controller v Cork* [1923] AC 647.
31. Supreme Court, 12 May 1988.
32. 1963 Act s.285(2)(a)(ii); cf. *Gowers v Walker* [1930] 1 Ch 262.
33. *Re Pratt* [1951] 1 Ch 229.

Unpaid value added tax or V.A.T. (less V.A.T. refundable) is preferred in relation to taxable periods ending within 12 months before the company was wound up;[34] preference is also given in respect of any interest payable on outstanding V.A.T.

Employers' P.R.S.I. contributions which were payable during the 12 months preceding the winding up are preferred,[35] but not interest payable on those sums. Unpaid income tax which a company, as employer, has or should have deducted from its employees' remuneration during the 12 months preceding the liquidation is preferred,[36] as is interest payable on those sums. Finally, there is a preference for deductions made by employers in the construction industry from payments made to non-exempt sub-contractors.[37]

Super-preferential In 1976 a new category of preference was introduced, the so-called 'super-' or 'pre'-preferential debt,[38] which impresses a form of trust on the funds in question and they rank before all the other preferential debts. That provision is now embodied in s.120(2) of the Social Welfare (Consolidation) Act, 1981, as amended in 1991,[39] with regard to P.R.S.I. contributions which an employer has or should have deducted from employees' remuneration—as contrasted with the employer's own P.R.S.I. contributions, which are simple preferential debts.[40] According to the 1991 version of s.120(2), the 'assets of a limited company in a winding up . . . shall not include' employees' P.R.S.I. contributions which the company has or should have deducted from their pay. Instead, a sum equal to this amount 'shall notwithstanding anything in [the Companies] Acts be paid to the Social Insurance Fund in priority to the debts specified' in s.285(2) of the 1963 Act. The precise import of this section has yet to receive judicial elaboration. Among the matters awaiting resolution are whether this super-preferential debt must be paid before the liquidator's remuneration and expenses and whether any charge on the company's assets is subject to the Revenue's entitlement under this section.

Fixed charge on book debts It was held in *Re Keenan Bros. Ltd*[41] that it is possible to create a fixed charge over book debts and, in that case, that the bank had succeeded in creating such a charge. The practical consequences of the decision was that banks and other creditors, who normally would have a floating charge over debts, could rank in front of the Revenue by persuading the debtor company to give them a fixed charge over all or some of its book debts. However, s.115 of the Finance Act, 1986, substantially closed off this option

34. Finance Act 1976, s.62(2); cf. *Re Liverpool Commercial Vehicles Ltd* [1984] BCLC 587.
35. 1963 Act s.285(2)(e), as amended by Social Welfare Act 1991, s.37.
36. 1963 Act s.285(2)(a)(iii) and Finance Act 1989, s.10.
37. Finance Act, 1970, s.17 and Finance Act 1976, s.14.
38. Social Welfare (No.2) Act 1976, n.7.
39. Social Welfare Act 1991, s.36.
40. Supra n.35.   41. [1985] IR 401.

for those charges given after 27 May, 1986. Under s.115, where the Revenue are owed outstanding P.A.Y.E. and also value added tax, they are entitled to call on a creditor who has a fixed charge over the debtor company's book debts to pay a sum to the Revenue. The amount that the chargee is made liable to pay is an amount equivalent to that owing by the company to the Revenue under the above heading, subject to the following. The total amount payable should not exceed whatever sums, following receipt of the Revenue's notice, the chargee received from the company, directly or indirectly, in payment of any debts due by the company to the chargee. Thus, following receipt of the Revenue's notice, the secured creditor can be obliged to pay over to the Revenue all or part of whatever funds it obtained from the company in discharging indebtedness.

RATES

Local rates have enjoyed preferential status for many years in bankruptcy and were expressly dealt with in the 1872 Bankruptcy legislation. In 1888 they also were given preferential status in company liquidations. Section 285(2)(a)(i) of the 1963 Act gives priority to 'all local rates due from the company' at the date of the liquidation and which were due and payable during the 12 months preceding the winding up. The term 'local rates' is not defined but must mean the rates struck by the local authorities under the various Local Government Acts. It has been held to include levies which the legislature treats in the same way as rates.[42]

EMPLOYEES

Because company employees were not in as strong a bargaining position as other creditors of the insolvent estate, such as banks and suppliers, in 1883 the legislature gave clerks, servants and labourers preferential claims in respect of up to £50 of their unpaid remuneration.[43] At that time trade unions and collective bargaining were not at all as prevalent as they have since become. The main basis for employees' preferred debts today is s.285(2)(b)-(i) of the 1963 Act, as amended in 1982. Only those who work with the company under a contract of employment benefit from these provisions. Thus, in *Re Sunday Tribune Ltd*,[44] where several journalists with a Sunday newspaper claimed to be preferential creditors, some of the claims were rejected on the grounds that those journalists were independent contractors. In *Stakelum v Canning*,[45] it was held that executive directors of companies, other than managing directors, can be employees for the purpose of this preference.

Remuneration   First and foremost are unpaid wages and salaries owing for

42. *Re Baker* [1954] 1 WLR 1144, *Re Ellwood* [1927] 1 Ch 455 and *Re An Arranging Debtor* [1921] 2 IR 1.
43. 46 & 47 Vic. c. 28.   44. [1984] IR 505.
45. [1976] IR 314.

services rendered to the employer, up to a maximum of £2,500 for every claimant.[46] There is no general definition of what is a 'wage' or a 'salary' for these purposes but it must mean remuneration for work done; it includes remuneration for periods of absence from work for 'good cause' and for holidays.[47] In *Re M.*[48] it was held that amounts deducted from earnings and credited to a holiday stamp scheme in the construction industry were wages, even though the employees were only entitled to have the sums deducted paid into what was described as a suspense account. The services in question must have been rendered during the four months immediately preceding the commencement of the liquidation. Where the arrangement with a 'farm labourer' is to pay him a lump sum at the end of his hiring or at the end of the year, the court is empowered to apportion how much of what is owing should be preferred. The Minister is empowered by order to vary the ceiling here of £2,500, which was fixed in 1982,[49] but no such order has yet been made.

Sick and holiday pay, and pension contributions   Accrued holiday remuneration at the date of the liquidation is preferred.[50] Outstanding amounts due under an arrangement for sick pay are preferred.[51] Outstanding pension contributions, under any scheme or arrangement made for superannuation, are preferred, whether they are employer's contributions or those deducted from the employee's remuneration.[52] There is no financial ceiling on the sums preferred under these provisions.

Compensation for dismissal   Three major statutory schemes exist for compensating employees who have been dismissed from their jobs in specific circumstances, viz. where they were not given the requisite statutory minimum notice, where they were made redundant and where their dismissal was held to be unfair. Compensation which is awarded to a dismissed employee under any of these schemes is a priority debt.[53] Where the employer is unable to pay that compensation, the Protection of Employees (Insolvency) Act, 1984, requires those amounts to be paid by the Minister for Labour.[54] In that event, the Minister is subrogated for the employee in respect of the amounts paid.[55]

Damages for accidents at work   If the employee was injured in the course of his employment and has been awarded or stands to be awarded damages and costs in respect of that injury, the amount of those damages and the costs are a preferred debt.[56] However, this preference does not exist where the company

46. 1963 Act s.285(2)(a)-(b) and (3), as amended in 1982 Act s.10(b).
47. S.285(11).   48. [1955] NI 182.
49. Sub. (13), added by 1982 Act. s.10(e).   50. Sub. (2)(d).
51. Sub. (2)(h), inserted by 1982 Act s.10(a).
52. Sub. (2)(i), inserted by 1982 Act s.10(a).
53. Minimum Notice and Terms of Employment Act 1973, s.13, Redundancy Payments Act 1979, s.42, Unfair Dismissals Act 1977, s.12.
54. See post pp. 387-389   55. 1984 Act s.10.
56. 1963 Act s.285(2)(g).

is effectively indemnified by insurers against the liability. In such a case, the injured employee is in effect subrogated for the company and is entitled to be paid the full amount forthcoming on the policy.[57] Before they were repealed in 1966, a preference also existed for compensation payable under the Workmen's Compensation Acts.[58]

Money advanced to pay preferential debts   Where money was advanced to the company for the purpose of paying employees' wages or salary, holiday remuneration or pension benefits, the lender is preferred to the extent that those employees would have been preferred if they had not been paid what was owing to them.[59] Thus, if a bank lends £20,000 to meet the payroll at the end of the week or the end of the month, the bank is a preferred creditor for that amount if the company is shortly afterwards wound up. Any form of 'advance' to the employer comes with this preference; it need not strictly be a loan but connotes furnishing money for a specific purpose.[60] In *Re Station Motors Ltd*,[61] Carroll J endorsed the view that s.285(6) 'should be given a benevolent construction'; that the object of this sub-section 'was to establish a principle of subrogation in favour of banks (although its operation, of course, is not confined to banks), and . . . should therefore . . . be given a benevolent construction rather than one which narrows the limits of its operation.'[62] There, money needed for wages was paid from the company's general overdraft account to the probable knowledge of the bank, which did not open a special wages account, as is often done to get maximum benefit from s.285(6). Because the bank advanced the money knowing that part of it would be used for wages, it was held that the bank was entitled to be subrogated for the employees. But the fact that a bank debits wages cheques to a separate wages account does not always entitle it to the preference.[63]

Where the money in question is paid from a current or running account it is subject to the rule in *Clayton's* case.[64] Accordingly, earlier wages cheques can get cleared by the subsequent lodgments.[65]

RECEIVERS UNDER FLOATING CHARGE

Where a receiver is appointed under or takes possession under a floating charge, s.98(1) of the 1963 Act requires him to pay the s.285(2) preferential debts before the proceeds of selling the charged assets can be paid to the debenture-holder.[66]

57. Civil Liability Act 1961; see post pp. 370-371.
58. 1963 Act s.285(2)(f); cf. *Re Farmer Bros.* [1964] IR 505 and 513.
59. Id. s.285(6) and 1982 Act s.10(c).
60. *Waikato Savings Bank v Andrews Furniture Ltd* [1982] 2 NZLR 520.
61. [1985] IR 756.
62. *Re Rampgill Mill Ltd* [1967] Ch. 1138, at p. 1145.
63. *Re E.J. Morel (1934) Ltd* [1962] Ch. 21.
64. (1816) 1 Mer. 572.
65. *Re Station Motors Ltd* [1985] IR 756.
66. See ante p. 65. Cf. *Inland Revenue Cmrs. v Goldblatt* [1972] Ch. 498.

And s.285(7)(b) of the 1963 Act provides that, where there are insufficient unencumbered assets from which the preferential debts can be paid, those debts have priority over the claims of any floating chargee and must be paid from the assets covered by that charge. Section 285(8) then allows the costs and expenses of the liquidation to rank before the preferential debts. But no reference is made to the remuneration, costs and expenses of a receiver appointed under a floating charge. Presumably a receiver in these circumstances would be entitled to deduct from the charged assets a reasonable sum in respect of the costs of realising them and a reasonable remuneration on a *quantum meruit* basis.

The duty under s.98(1) to pay the preferred debts arises once the receiver is appointed and is not affected by the company subsequently being put into liquidation.[67] But this duty does not apply to a receiver who was appointed after the charge crystallised, for instance by the previous operation of an automatic crystallisation clause[68] or by the previous presentation of a winding up petition.[69] Where the debenture grants a fixed and a floating charge, any surplus obtaining after the assets subject to the fixed charge where disposed of is not immediately caught by the floating charge and thereby payable by the receiver to the preferential creditors.[70] Instead, satisfaction of the debt covered by the fixed charge releases the security and the surplus becomes payable directly to the chargeor, being the company or the liquidator if there is a winding up.

As was observed above, the decision in *Re Barleycorn Enterprises Ltd*[71] has not been formally accepted in Ireland and an argument could be made that it is wrongly decided. If that view is right, the question then arises of what priority debts come under s.98 of the 1963 Act. In particular, does s.98 cover liquidation expenses? This has been answered in Britain in the affirmative,[72] provided the expenses were incurred in realising or getting in the company's assets or the court otherwise directs that they be paid from those assets. Sections 244 and 281 of the 1963 Act, concerning liquidation expenses etc., do not strictly provide that they shall be paid from the company's assets before all other claims; they instead confer a priority only in so far as those expenses etc. are payable from the company's assets. Ordinarily a court will approve payment of the litigation expenses, provided the liquidator has not acted improperly. But where the only source for paying those expenses is the assets subject to a floating charge, it was held in *Re M.C. Bacon Ltd*[73] that there can be circumstances where it would be unjust for the court to approve that payment. In that case, the liquidator had brought expensive proceedings, seeking to upset the floating charge, which on the twelfth day of the trial were abandoned by the liquidator.

---

67. *Re Eisc Teo.* [1991] ILRM 760.
68. *Brightlife Ltd, Re* [1987] Ch. 200. Cf. *Herde v Mahabirsingh* [1991] 1 WLR 867.
69. *Re Christonette International Ltd* [1982] 1 WLR 1245.
70. *United Bars Ltd v Revenue Cmrs.* [1991] 1 IR 396, following *Re G.L. Saunders Ltd* [1986] 1 WLR 215.
71. [1970] Ch. 465.
72. *Re M.C. Bacon Ltd* [1991] Ch. 127.   73. Ibid.

26

Remaining Creditors

After the creditors with various proprietary rights in the company's assets, including secured creditors, and then the preferred creditors, there comes the unsecured creditors. As has been mentioned earlier, subject to certain quali-fications, the principle applicable to them is equality of treatment. Section 275 of the 1963 Act provides that, in a voluntary liquidation, 'the property of the company shall . . . be applied in satisfaction of its liabilities *pari passu*. . . .' It has been held that this rule also applies to compulsory liquidations; that *pari passu* distribution is a fundamental rule in insolvency law and it is inconceivable that, the legislature in failing to provide so expressly in the case of compulsory liquidations, the court would permit an unequal distribution.[1] It was mainly on account of the equality principle that, in *Webb v Whefin*,[2] the leading case on the liability of contributories, it was held that payment from the B contributories could not be directed exclusively to paying off past debts; that instead, those payments formed part of the general assets available to pay off all the general unsecured creditors. There are, however, exceptions to the equality principle.

DEBT SUBORDINATION

Formerly, the *pari passu* distribution principle was regarded as a peremptory rule that could not be contracted out of, except perhaps where each and every creditor had agreed to waive his right to equal participation. In *British Eagle International Airlines Ltd v Air France*[3] a narrowly divided House of Lords concluded that the equivalent to s.275 of the 1963 Act was peremptory and that view was accepted by Costello J in the *Glow Heating Ltd*[4] case. However, in 1990, this section was amended to permit contracts to subordinate certain unsecured debts to others.

The 'British Eagle' principle The *British Eagle* case concerned a 'clearing house' system for airlines which were members of the International Air Transport Association, whereby payments made via travel agents could be settled between the various carriers. It contained quite complex provisions, involving a form of set-off (but not strictly set-off), whereby whenever a

1. *Attorney General v McMillan & Lockwood Ltd* [1991] 1 NZLR 53.
2. (1872) LR 5 HL 711.
3. [1975] 1 WLR 758.   4. [1988] IR 110.

company's account with the clearing house was closed only net balances under the scheme were payable to its creditors, even though strictly those creditors may have been owed more money or less money than the account stated. It was contended that this system contravened s.275 because credits to which the company was entitled and debits to which it became liable in respect of trading in an account period were, in substance, debts due to and from the company. Therefore, to give effect to the clearing house arrangement with regard to them would result in what were in substance debts owing to the company being applied, not for the benefit of all its creditors, but exclusively for the benefit of what may be called the clearing house creditors. Against this, it was argued that what passes into the liquidation is the company's property, subject to any rights created in respect of that property in good faith while the company was a going concern.

It was held that the clearing house system contravened the *pari passu* principle and accordingly did not apply in a liquidation. It has been a long-standing rule of bankruptcy law that

> a man is not allowed by stipulation with a creditor to provide for a different distribution of his effects in the event of bankruptcy from that which the law provides.[5]

If the clearing house scheme were to apply here, the defendant (Air France) would be treated as if in effect it had a charge over the insolvent company's book debts. However, the intention underlying that scheme was not to create charges and, if this were the intention, those charges would have been void for non-registration. The equal distribution rule was one of public policy and applied to all creditors, and it was irrelevant that there were good business reasons for entering into the clearing house arrangement. The principle decided in the *British Eagle* case has been summed up in these terms:

> where the effect of a contract is that an asset which is actually owned by a company [including a debt] at the commencement of its liquidation would be dealt with in a way other than in accordance with [s.275 of the 1963 Act], then to that extent the contract as a matter of public policy is avoided, whether or not the contract was entered into for consideration and for *bona fide* commercial reasons and whether or not the contractual provision affecting that asset is expressed to take effect only on in-solvency.[6]

In that case the asset in question, the company's interest in the scheme, was an innominate chose in action having some but not all the characteristics of debts.

The principle as summed up above was followed in *Glow Heating Ltd v Eastern Health Board*,[7] which concerned retention moneys held under a scheme

5. *Ex p. Mackay* (1873) 8 Ch App 643, at p. 647.
6. *Carreras Rothmans Ltd v Freeman Matthews Treasure Ltd* [1985] Ch.207, at p. 226. See too the *McMillan* case, supra n.1.
7. [1988] IR 110.

for making payments to building contractors and sub-contractors under a common form building contract. But it was stressed by Costello J there that s.275 should

> not be interpreted as meaning that every contract is void by which a party to it obtains rights over a company's assets superior to those given to ordinary creditors under the section. Such an interpretation would mean, for example, that retention of the title clauses in contracts for the sale of goods, and clauses in building contracts conferring rights on building owners over retention moneys would be void—which is obviously not the case. [*British Eagle*] in no way conflicts with the well established principle . . . that the liquidator takes the company's property subject to liabilities which affected it in the company's hands.[8]

It was held that the clause in question there did not contravene s.275 because, on a correct analysis, it could not be regarded as part of a contract for the disposal of assets of the company. Instead, the clause imposed 'a contingent liability on an asset of the main contractor, the moneys in the retention fund, namely, a liability to suffer a reduction in the event of a specified default on the contractor's part.'[9] The liquidator took the retention fund subject to that very liability.

As is illustrated by the *Glow Heating* case,[10] and by the *Carreras Rothmans* case[11] which was followed there and indeed by the *British Eagle* case itself, very fine distinctions can be drawn in determining whether what is being claimed is no more than an asset of the company which the creditor is claiming to have in effect charged to his benefit. Indeed, of the nine judges in all who heard the *British Eagle* case at its different stages, six of them (the trial judges, the Court of Appeal and two Law Lords) were of the view that the money in the I.A.T.A. clearing account was not an asset of the insolvent company and, accordingly, the question could not arise of a stipulation about how a company's asset should be disposed of when the company's account there was cleared.

Subordination agreements   Section 275(2) of the 1963 Act, as amended in 1990,[12] provides for one exception to the *pari passu* rule, whereby unsecured creditors may agree that other unsecured creditors shall be paid off before them, either entirely or in part. Such arrangements are known as subordination agreements. According to s.275(2), the *pari passu* principle does not

> affect any rights or obligations . . . arising as a result of any agreement entered into . . . under which any particular liability of the company to any general creditor is postponed in favour of or subordinated to the rights or claims of any other person to whom the company may be in any way liable.

8. Id. at pp. 119-120.   9. Id. at p. 120.
10. [1988] IR 110.   11. Supra n.6.
12. 1990 Act s.132.

In other words, it is permissible for a creditor to waive his entitlement to be treated in exactly the same way as the other unsecured creditors. But s.275(2) would not now render enforcible the I.A.T.A. scheme in *British Eagle*.

DEFERRED CREDITORS

Deferred creditors are members of the company who are owed money by it in their capacity as members. According to s.207(1)(g) of the 1963 Act,

> a sum due by any member of the company, in his character of a member, by way of dividends, profits or otherwise, shall not be deemed to be a debt of the company, payable to that member in a case of competition between himself and any other creditor not a member of the company. . . .

In other words, all 'outside' creditors must be paid off in full before debts due to members *qua* members can be paid. The prime example is a dividend which has been declared; once a proper declaration of a dividend is made it becomes a debt of the company but, in an insolvency, falls into this deferred category. It was held by Kenny J in *Re Belfast Empire Theatre of Varieties Ltd*[13] that, by virtue of s.25(3) of the 1963 Act, which treats a company's memorandum and articles of association as if it were a sealed contract, the appropriate limitation period for unpaid dividends is twelve years from the time of their declaration. In a later English case it was held that the period is six years.[14]

Ordinarily, directors' remuneration is outside of the deferred category because the money is not owing to them by virtue of being members of the company.[15] But merely to describe a liability as directors' remuneration is not sufficient to have it classified as an ordinary unsecured debt or a preferred debt. The liability must actually be in respect of services rendered or to be rendered. Thus in *Re Cinnamond Park Ltd*,[16] claims by two directors in respect of remuneration were rejected because, under the agreements there, their entitlement to the sums claimed really was because they were a proportion of the profits.

INSURANCE AND CREDITOR PROTECTION FUNDS

Insurance can play two main roles in insolvencies. The creditor may have taken out bad debts insurance, in which case he can recoup from his insurers whatever he has lost in the liquidation. Alternatively, the company itself may have purchased insurance against some contingency or another, which then occurred. For instance, it might have purchased employer's liability insurance or products liability insurance and either an employee was injured at work or a consumer of its products was injured by the product. Most drivers of motor vehicles being used on the public highways are required, to have the vehicle suitably insured.

13. [1963] IR 41.
14. *Re Compania de Electriciadad de la Provincia de Buenos Aires Ltd* [1980] Ch 146.
15. *Re Dale & Plant Ltd* (1889) 43 Ch D 255.
16. [1930] NI 47.

Every operator of a travel agency or tour operator is required to take out insurance in respect of losses his customers may incur. Depositors with licensed banks and holders of insurance policies with authorised insurers benefit from special provisions which significantly reduce the losses they may suffer if their bank or insurer becomes insolvent.

Insurance generally   At times the victims of accidents caused by companies which have third party insurance, but which then became insolvent, were most unfairly treated because they had no right, direct or indirect, to the proceeds of the insurance policy. Instead, what money the insurers paid to the company would be divided among the general creditors and, indeed, if the policy was charged the money would be paid to that secured creditor. As was explained in *Re Harrington Motor Co.*,[17] where this anomaly was highlighted,

> a third party in a case like [this] has no claim in law or in equity of any sort against the insurance company, or against the money paid by the insurance company, nor has he any claim against the person who injures him, the assured, to direct the assured to pay over the sum of money received under the insurance policy to him. The amount that the insured in fact received is part of his general assets. . . . It obviously would disturb the whole practice of insurance if the claimant against the assured who caused the risk had a direct right of recourse against the insurance company. . . . [18]

An exception to this principle was contained in the old Workmens' Compensation Acts and, while they were in force, was continued by s.285(2)(f) of the 1963 Act.

In 1961 this principle was virtually overridden by s.62 of the Civil Liability Act, 1961, according to which,

> Where a person (hereinafter referred to as the insured) who has effected a policy of insurance in respect of a liability for a wrong . . . is wound up . . . , moneys payable to the insured under the policy shall be applicable only to discharging in full all valid claims against the insured in respect of which those moneys are payable, and no part of the those moneys shall be part of the assets of the insured or applicable to the payment of [its] debts . . . in the winding up. . . .

In other words, the liquidator is required to apply the insurance money to discharge the liability which triggered the insurance payment. For practical purposes, that money must be held in trust for the injured party. In *Dunne v P.J. White Construction Co.*[19] the view was expressed that the injured party has a direct right of action against the insurer to be paid that money, with the qualification that this is a matter to be argued fully before it is finally determined.

17. [1928] 1 Ch 105.   18. Id. at p. 118.   19. [1989] ILRM 803.

Legislation was enacted in Britain in 1930 to the same general effect[20] but that measure differs in several respects from s.62 of the Civil Liability Act, so that cases on the British Act cannot always be treated as reliable guides to the position here. For instance, in Britain there is transferred to and vested in the third party the insured's 'rights against the insurers under the contract.' Accordingly, it has been held that, before the victim can have any claim in the liqduiation to the insurance moneys, it must have been established by an action, arbitration or agreement with the insured company that it is liable in damages for the injury or loss caused.[21] It is only then that the insured's right of indemnity against the insurers will arise. Until the primary liability has been determined, the victim has no rights under the 1930 Act. All that s.62 of the 1961 Act says is that 'moneys payable to the insured' shall be used to discharge the debt due to the victim. It could be argued that this also means that the liability of the insured must first be established before the third party can have any claim in respect of the money, either against the insured, the liquidator or the insurers.

This analysis gave rise to considerable hardship in *Bradley v Eagle Star Insurance Co.*,[22] where the plaintiff had contracted a serious industrial disease during the 37 years she had worked in a cotton mill. It was not until nearly eight years after her former employer had been wound up and dissolved that she sought compensation in respect of that disease. Because the time during which a dissolved company can be resuscitated under s.310 of the 1963 Act (two years) had long expired, there was no legal procedure through which she could sue the company to have the primary liability established. Instead she sued the company's former insurers, who would have had to indemnify the company if her claim against it could have succeeded. It was held that the requirement that the primary liability of her employer in damages must first be established in an action or arbitration between them, or by agreement, prevented her from recovering from the insurers. For until that liability was established, the insured's statutory right of indemnity does not arise. The British 1930 Act was passed to deal with a particular state of affairs, evidenced by the *Harrington Motor Co.* case[23] and another similar instance.[24] That problem was victims getting judgment against an insolvent company but the liquidator then applying the insurance money to pay off the unsecured creditors or even a secured creditor. The 1930 Act was 'not passed to remedy any injustice arising from other matters; in particular, it was not passed to remedy any injustice which might arise as a result of the dissolution of a company making it impossible to establish the existence and amount of the liability of such company to a third party.'[25] It could hardly be said that s.62 of the Civil Liability Act has so narrow an objective.

20. Third Parties (Rights Against Insurers) Act 1930.
21. *Post Office v Norwich Union Fire Insurance Soc.* [1967] 2 QB 363.
22. [1989] 1 AC 957.   23. [1928] 1 Ch 105.
24. *Hood's Trustees v Southern Union etc. Co.* [1928] 1 Ch 793.
25. [1989] 1 AC at p. 968; followed in *Dickson v Blackstaff Weaving Co.* [1988] NI 197.

Motor insurance   Before most persons may be allowed to use a motor vehicle in a public place, they must be covered by an approved insurance policy or an approved guarantee in respect of liability for negligence arising from the use of that vehicle. The general scope of this obligation is adequately dealt with elsewhere.[26] Where the insured user of the vehicle is a corporate body and is wound up, s.76(4) of the Road Traffic Act, 1961, is in terms almost identical to s.62 of the Civil Liability Act of that year, which has been considered in the preceding paragraphs. There do not appear to be any reported cases which deal with the effects of s.76(4).

Tour operators and travel agents   Tour operators and travel agents frequently are forced into liquidation, often leaving their customers stranded in foreign countries and causing other customers to loose a much anticipated foreign holiday. Under the Transport (Tour Operators and Travel Agents) Act, 1982, a fund know as the Travellers Protection Fund was introduced to provide financial assistance to customers who suffered loss in that manner when the agency they had contracted with became insolvent. This fund is financed by contributions made by licensed tour operators in accordance with criteria laid down by the Minister. In addition, under that Act every licensed travel agent and tour operator must take out an insurers' bond to cover certain liabilities to their customers in the event of an insolvency. The nature and extent of that bond is also prescribed by the Minister. Payments from the Fund are discretionary, although it is likely that the Minister's discretion here must be used reasonably and with some consistency. However, no payment can be made from the Fund until all money payable under the agent in question's bond have been paid.

Bank depositors   Banking is a highly regulated industry. Special provision is made in ss.48-52 of the Central Bank Act, 1989, dealing mainly with the involvement of the Central Bank in the liquidation of banks. Sections 53-73 of that Act then go on to establish a deposit protection system whereby a 'deposit protection account' is maintained by the Central Bank for the benefit of bank depositors. This is financed mainly by contributions from licensed banks in the manner set out in that Act, which also prescribes what deposits are eligible for protection and the extent of the payments that will be made to depositors with banks which become insolvent.

Insurance policy holders   Insurance is another highly regulated industry. Under the Insurance Act, 1964, an Insurance Compensation Fund was established to compensate the policy holders with insurance companies which became insolvent. It is financed mainly by contributions from authorised insurers and is controlled by the President of the High Court. Under this scheme, the payments are made to the liquidator of the insolvent insurer to be paid on to the policy holders.[27]

26.   B. McMahon & W. Binchy, *Irish Law of Torts* (2nd ed., 1990) p. 24.
27.   See Insurance Act 1989, s.31.

PART V

Administration of Insurance Companies

The Insurance (No.2) Act, 1983, was a precursor of the Companies (Amendment) Act, 1990, which it resembles in many ways. Just as enactment of the 1990 Act was brought about by the crisis that hit the Goodman group of companies in August 1990, enactment of the 1983 Act was provoked by the troubles in the P.M.P.A. group of companies. The 1983 Act is confined to non-life Insurance companies, meaning the holders of an authorisation to carry on insurance business under the European Communities (Non-Life Insurance) Regulations, 1976; only companies with such an authorisation can be protected under the 1983 Act. Indeed, the 1990 Act too applies to insurance companies as well as to other companies, except that only the Minister can petition to have 'an insurer' placed under court protection under the 1990 Act.[1] The principal difference between the 1983 Act and that of 1990 are that, under the former, there is no time scale built into the Act, so that administration, as it is called, can exist for years on end; the scope of protection given against creditors and third parties is far less extensive; the administrator's primary function is to run the insurance business and not to draw up proposals to be put before the creditors.

1. S.3(2)(a). There is a similar provision for petitions to have a licen? ?rk place under court protection.

27

Administration of Insurance Companies

Only the Minister can petition the High Court for the administration of a non-life insurer under the 1983 Act.[2] a petition for this purpose may be presented even though the Minister may possess some other mode of redress against the events which prompted his application. For instance, under the Insurance Act, 1989, the Minister has very extensive powers of supervision over insurers.

Grounds for administration The grounds on which an administration order may be made are far more extensive than by reason of the insurance company's insolvency. Three grounds are specified.[3] One is that the insurer has failed to make adequate provision for its debts, including contingent and prospective liabilities, in the manner in which it has conducted its business. Another is that the rights or interests of its policy-holders are or have been jeopardised by the way the company did its business. The third is that the company, in a material respect, has not complied with the E.C. Non-Life Insurance Regulations. Accordingly, court administration is central to the whole process of regulating the non-life insurance industry. Before the court will make an administration order, it must be shown that placing the company under administration 'would assist in the maintenance, in the public interest, of the proper and orderly regulation and conduct of, non-life insurance business.[4] Where the court makes such an order, it appoints the person nominated by the Minister to act as administrator.[5]

Provisional administrator Unlike the 1990 Act, there is express authority to appoint a provisional administrator of an insurer within the 1983 Act.[6] That appointment can be made on an *ex parte* application by the Minister, without anybody being notified in advance, if a *prima facie* case is made out that any of the grounds referred to above exist.

Group enterprises There is no express power to extend the administration to companies which are related to the insurer. However, s.4 of the 1983 Act enables the court to make a very extensive range of orders in respect of connected

2. S.2(1).   3. S.2(2)(a).   4. S.2(2)(b).
5. s.2(2).   6. S.2(4).

companies. In addition to several specified orders, the court may make 'such order as it thinks fit', which may possibly be construed as including orders bringing those companies entirely within the administration.

EFFECTS OF PROTECTION

A company is deemed to be under administration from the very time the Minister's petition has been presented.[7] However, the various forms of protection which the 1983 Act gives non-life insurers apply only 'for so long as an administrator stands appointed'.[8] It, therefore, is not certain whether, as in the case under the 1990 Act, protection applies from the moment the petition has been presented to the court or whether an administrator must first have been appointed. It is expressly provided that the appointment has no direct effect on the company's business as such; according to the proviso to s.3(1),

> the business of the insurer concerned shall be continued without interruption as a going concern and no contract (including a contract of employment or service), policy, transaction, bank account or bank mandate, right, title, claim, debt, proceeding or obligation of the insurer, right, claim or proceeding against the insurer, shall be avoided, cancelled, stayed or otherwise affected by reason only of the order for administration. . . .

Accordingly, administration does not have as profound an impact on insurance companies as does protection under the 1990 Act. The extent of protection given by the 1983 Act is as follows.

Non-application of Companies Acts   The following provisions of the Companies Act, 1963, do not apply to an insurer which is under administration:[9]

S.131	Requirements to hold annual general meetings.
S.132	Shareholders requisitioning extraordinary general meetings.
S.159	Circulating annual accounts and directors' report to members.
S.161	Resolutions for appointing and for removing auditors.
S.205	Oppression of members or disregard of their interests: proceedings can only be commenced or proceeded with in respect of events which occurred before the administration.
S.218	Avoidance of dispositions of company property and of transfer of company's shares made after a winding up.
S.219	Avoidance of execution, attachment, sequestration and distress put into force after a winding up.
S.222	Stay on proceedings against the company being wound up.
S.228	General provisions regarding liquidators.

7.   S.2(5).   8. S.3(2).   9. S.3(1)(ii).

S.231(3)   Control by the court of certain powers of liquidators.

S.234   Power to annul or to stay order for a winding up.

S.283   Proving debts.

S.284   Application of bankruptcy rules to aspects of winding up.

S.285   Preferential debts in a winding up.

S.291   Restriction on rights of creditor as to execution or attachment when company is being wound up.

S.292   Duties of sheriff when company is being wound up.

S.302   Enforcement of liquidator's duty to make returns.

S.306   Filing with registrar of companies information about progress of a liquidation.

Additionally, the Minister is empowered, by order, to amend the Companies Acts, or rules made under those Acts or any other instrument or the rules of court relating to companies, where he considers such changes 'necessary or appropriate ... to facilitate the performance of the functions of an administrator. . . .'[10] However, the apparent scope of this power is restricted in that the objective of the alteration being made must be to 'give full effect' to s.3(1) of the Act. Under this section, the administrator is given the powers of a liquidator and the court has the same powers regarding the company as if it were being wound up, subject to the above sections of the Companies Acts which are expressly excluded.

Directors   All of the directors' functions, or those of any of the company's committee of management, become vested in the administrator.[11] He then can exercise those powers. In the case of powers which, under the company's rules, can be exercised by the directors only with the sanction of the members, the administrator can exercise those powers if he obtains the sanction of the court.

Execution, attachment, sequestration and distress   The usual creditors' remedies of execution (*fi.fa.*), attachment (or garnishment), sequestration or distress cannot be 'put in force' against the company's property.[12] But, on application, redress of this nature may be obtained with the prior sanction of the court.

Receiver   A receiver may not be appointed over any part of the company's property or undertaking.[13] But, on application, the court may give its prior sanction to such appointment.

Winding-up   Similarly, a resolution to wind up the company cannot be passed and proceedings to have it wound up cannot be commenced.[14] But, on application, the court may give its prior consent to taking any such step.

10. S.3(6).   11. S.3(2)(g).   12. S.3(2)(d).
13. S.3(2)(b).   14. S.(2)(i).

ADMINISTRATOR'S STATUS, POWERS AND FUNCTIONS

An administrator's task is very different from that of an examiner under the 1990 Act.

Appointment and terms   In the same way as is an examiner under the 1990 Act, the administrator appointed over a non-life insurer is an officer of the court. On application to the Minister, he may resign.[15] He may be removed by the court on 'cause shown'.[16] His remuneration, expenses and costs are determined by the court.[17] He is entitled to be indemnified in respect of those amounts and, to that end, may retain from the funds of the company or from the proceeds of disposal of any assets such amount as is owing to him.[18]

Application to the court   If any matter arises in the course of the administration which requires resolution, an application may be made to the court to have it determined.[19] Such application may be made by the administrator, any member or contributory of the company, any of its directors or creditors and its liquidator.

One matter which can be the subject of an application is that the administrator shall not be bound by any rules or regulations which limit the types of insurance business which the company may engage in.[20] Those limitations are any provision 'restricting or defining the classes or categories of persons to whom the insurer may issue policies or the terms upon which it may issue policies.' A declaration made under this power can be varied or annulled by the court.

Manage the business   The administrator's principal function is to manage the company's business with a view to putting the company's affairs in order. According to s.2(3) of the 1983 Act,

> An administrator shall take over the management of the business of the insurer and shall carry on that business as a going concern with a view to placing it on a sound commercial and financial footing. . . .

In order to manage the business in that manner, the administrator is given, in relation to the company, 'all such powers as may be necessary for or incidental to his functions', including sole authority over the company's officers and employees.[21] All functions which are vested in the company's directors can only be performed by the administrator.[22]

Sale of assets   The administrator can sell or dispose of any or all of the company's assets. To avoid any doubt on this matter, s.33(1) of the Insurance Act, 1989 states that he has:

15.   16. Ibid.   17. S.3(4)(b).
18. S.3(4)(a). Cf. *Re P.M.P.A. Insurance Co.* [1988] ILRM 109.
19. S.3(2)(h).   20. S.3(3).   21. S.2(3).
22. S.3(2)(g).

power to dispose of all or any part of the business, undertaking or assets of the insurer and to carry on any remaining business including the settlement of liabilities, with a view to the orderly completion of the administration.

Liquidator's powers The administrator possesses all the powers of a liquidator although, in the light of the proviso to s.3(1), he may not be entitled to disclaim onerous contracts. According to s.3(1)(a) of the 1983 Act, he has

all the powers (including the power to sell the real and personal property and things in action of the insurer concerned) that he would have, and there shall apply in relation to him all the statutory provisions that would so apply, if he were a liquidator appointed by the court. . . .

The court is given, in relation to the company, all the authority it would possess if the company were being wound up.[23] However, several sections of the Companies Acts dealing *inter alia* with winding up are not applicable to an insurer which is under administration.[24]

Affairs of connected bodies The court can direct that the administrator shall exercise a very wide range of powers in relation to companies and other bodies which are connected with the insurer.[25] Orders can be made in relation to any such body if the court considers that its affairs are or may be conducted in a manner which may jeopardise or prejudice the interests of the insurer, its policy-holders or its creditors; or that it is expedient for preserving the insurer's assets or safeguarding the insurer's interest that the connected body's affairs be regulated; or having regard to the relationship between the insurer and the body, any part of its property should be preserved or controlled.[26] But before making any order under s.4 of the 1983 Act, the court must consider whether doing so would be 'just and equitable' and would further the 'proper and orderly regulation and conduct of non-life insurance business'.[27]

The court's powers regarding these companies are far more extensive than those under the 1990 Act regarding related companies. Among the kinds of orders specified in s.4, without prejudice to the wide-ranging order power, are orders conferring powers on the administrator in relation to the connected body's affairs; appointing him as receiver and manager of all or part of the connected body's property and assets; appointing additional directors or managers to the body; providing that the administrator shall have direct control over the functions of its officers and management. What bodies are connected with the insurer for this purpose are defined in s.4(4).

TERMINATION OF ADMINISTRATION

An insurance company's administration comes to an end when the court orders

23. S.3(1)(b) and (c). 24. S.3(1)(ii).
25. S.4(1). 26. S.4(1)(a). 27. S.4(1)(b).

that the company be wound up or when, on the Minister's or the administrator's application, the court directs that the position shall terminate.[28] Additionally, if it is established that, once the administration would end, the company's affairs will be run in an entirely satisfactory manner and any debt due to the Compensation Fund has been paid, and it would be unjust and inequitable not to terminate the position, the court must order that it shall be terminated.[29] Who may apply for such an order is not specified.

28. S.2(7)(a) and (b).   29. S.2(7)(i).

PART VI

Employees and Insolvency

For many years, the only special protection for employees, when their employer became insolvent,[1] was the preferential debts which they are entitled to be paid before the general creditors can get a penny. The extent to which the 1980 Transfer of Undertakings Regulations apply to disposals made in the context of insolvency proceedings has not been fully clarified. As a result of a 1980 E.C. initiative, an insolvency fund was established to meet various debts to employees who an insolvent employer is unable to pay.

1. This Part is adapted from M. Forde, *Employment Law* (1992) ch.10.

28

Employees and Insolvency

IMPACT ON THE EMPLOYMENT CONTRACT

An important preliminary question is the effect, under the general principles of contract law, of the insolvency in question on the workers' contracts of employment. Does the insolvency operate to frustrate those contracts or otherwise terminate them, or do the contractual rights and obligations survive the onset of insolvency? There may be express or implied terms in a contract which provide answers to these questions. In the absence of such terms, the matter turns on the nature of the insolvency proceedings involved.

Court-supervised examination   There is no reason in principle why the appointment of an examiner into a company's affairs, under the Companies (Amendment) Act, 1990, should bring an end to the employment contracts of the company's workforce. Even where the court directs the examiner to take over the function of the company's directors,[2] that should not affect the employee's contracts.

Receivership   The effect on the employment relationship of the appointment of a receiver was analysed in *Griffiths v Secretary of State*,[3] where the plaintiff was a managing director of a company when a debenture-holder appointed a receiver and manager over its entire assets. The position was explained by Lawson J as follows:

> the appointment by debenture-holders of a receiver and manager as agent of the company (the commonest case) . . . does not of itself automatically terminate contracts of employment previously made and subsisting between the relevant company and all its employees. There are three situations in which this may be qualified.
>
> The first situation is where . . . the appointment is accompanied by a sale of the business; that will operate to terminate contracts of employment . . . because . . . there is no longer any business for which the employees can work.[4]

---

2.   S.9 of that Act.   3.   [1974] 1 QB 468.
4.   E.g. *Re Foster & Clarke Ltd's Indenture Trusts* [1966] 1 WLR 125.

The second situation is where . . . a receiver and manager enters into a new agreement with a particular employee that may be inconsistent with the continuation of his old service contract. . . .[5]

The third situation . . . is where . . . the continuation of the employment of a particular employee is inconsistent with the role and functions of a receiver and manager. The mere fact that he is labelled 'managing director' does not . . . indicate that because he is so labelled his employment in that capacity or office is inconsistent with the position, role and functions of a receiver and manager. . . .[6]

Where it its the court which appoints the receiver and manager, 'the result of such an appointment is to discharge the servants from their service to their original employer and that [may be] a wrongful dismissal for which an action would lie.'[7] The reason for this rule perhaps is that this receiver is the agent of the court.

Liquidation   The effects of a liquidation on contracts similarly depends on whether it is an official or a voluntary process.[8] Where the winding up is by order of the court, publication of the winding up order is deemed to be notice to the entire world, including the company's employees, that they are dismissed.[9] That order operates retrospectively to when the petition was presented,[10] so that the deemed notice of dismissal would also operate retrospectively in this manner. If, under their contracts, the employees were entitled to advance notice of termination, they would be entitled to damages for breach of that requirement. This rule applies regardless of the employee's status within the company and regardless of whether the job is subject to a specified notice period or is for a fixed term or indeed for life.[11] Strictly, publication of the winding up order does not terminate the contract because, in principle, an employee can refuse to accept the unlawful repudiation of the contract; but for all practical purposes the contract is brought to an end at that time.

However, the liquidator may want to carry on the business for the time being and to continue all or some of the employees in their jobs. He therefore is entitled to waive the deemed notices of dismissal and to continue employing the relevant employees under their existing contracts.[12] Unless there has been an unequivocal waiver, the company's employees will be treated as having been dismissed, although they may be re-employed by the liquidator on new terms for the purpose of the winding up.

5.   E.g. *Re Mack Trucks (Britain) Ltd* [1967] 1 WLR 780.
6.   [1974] 1 QB at pp. 485-486.
7.   *Reid v Explosives Co.* (1887) 19 QBD 264, at p. 267.
8.   See generally, Graham, 'The Effect of Liquidation on Contracts of Service', 15 *Mod. L. Rev* 48 (1952).
9.   *Re General Rolling Stock Co.* (1866) ILR Eg. 346.   10.   1963 Act s.220(2).
11. *Fowler v Commercial Timber Co.* [1930] 2 KBI. Cf. *Re R.S. Newman Ltd* [1916] 2 Ch. 309 and *Re T.N. Farrer Ltd* [1937] Ch. 352.
12. *Re English Joint Stock Bank* (1867) 3 Eq 341.

Occasionally, a provisional liquidator is appointed by the court prior to ordering a winding up, whose task is to safeguard the company's assets. If that provisional liquidator is authorised to carry on the company's business for the time being, his appointment does not operate to discharge the employment contracts of the workforce.[13]

A creditor's voluntary liquidation commences when the members of the company pass a resolution that it be wound up because it cannot pay its debts. It has been held that the passing or indeed the publication of such resolution does not invariably operate as a notice of dismissal.[14] In particular circumstances, depending on the terms of the contract, the resolution to wind up may constitute notice of termination. The test is whether in all the circumstances the employee is justified in regarding the winding up as indicating an intention by the company to repudiate its obligations under the employment contract.[15] If employees are retained by the liquidator or are re-hired shortly after the resolution was passed, they are deemed to be still employed by the company.[16]

TRANSFER OF UNDERTAKINGS REGULATIONS

The strict contract law position of employees of insolvent businesses may be significantly modified by the European Communities (Safeguarding of Employees' Rights on Transfer of Undertakings) Regulations, 1980.[17] These Regulations apply only to persons employed by the business in question at the date of the transfer. Therefore, if the insolvency operated as a dismissal before any transfer took place, the Regulations would not apply. This, of course, is not the case where the employee was dismissed in order to facilitate the transfer, other than for the specified 'economic' etc. reasons.[18] It furthermore would seem that if the transfer took place before the expiry of the employee's notice period, the employment relationship continued in existence after the dismissal took place provided the employee did not accept the repudiation of his contract.[19] In such a case, the Regulations would apply to any transfer of all or part of the business.

It was contended before the European Court of Justice that the 1977 E.C. Directive, which gave rise to these Regulations, does not apply where the transfer is being made in the context of insolvency administration. That view received some support from the European Commission and from Advocate

---

13. *Donnelly v Gleeson* (Hamilton J, 11 July, 1978) and *Re McEvanhenry Ltd* (Murphy J, 15 May 1986).
14. *Midland Counties Bank v Attwood* [1905] 1 Ch357.
15. *Reigate v Union Mfg. Co.* [1918] 1 KB 592.
16. *Collman v Construction Industry Training Board* (1966) 1 ITR 52.
17. SI No. 306 of 1980, implementing Directive No. 77/187, OJ No. L61/26 (1977). See generally, Collins, Transfer of Undertakings and Insolvency', 18 *Ind. L.J.* 144 (1989).
18. Reg. 5(1).
19. *Quare* where employee accepts money in lieu of notice? Cf. *Gothard v Mirror Group Newspapers Ltd* [1988] ICR 729.

General Slynn in the *Abels* case,[20] which concerned a transfer made by a Dutch company that was in *surseance van betaling*—a status resembling a stay on proceedings imposed by s.201 of the Companies Act, 1963. It was argued that, insolvency being a very technical field, which will be the subject of E.C. approximating measures at some stage, the 1977 Directive should not be regarded as applying in those circumstances unless it explicitly provides otherwise, which it does not. Should they so choose, Member States remain free, under the Directive, to apply its provisions to insolvent businesses. There were also practical considerations, that the Directive's actual objects would be frustrated rather than advanced if it applied to insolvency disposals. It was said that

> a potential purchaser may be deterred from buying up businesses which are insolvent, but which might be capable of rescue, if they are obliged to take on all the employees. The only way to save the business may be to reduce the number of staff. It is in the interests of the labour force as a whole that such rescue attempts should be made, even if some staff have to go. In fact, rather than in theory, more jobs may be lost if purchasers are deterred by a rule that they must take on the employees and satisfy all obligations to them.[21]

But the court declined to be guided by this analysis in its entirety. Some insolvency disposals fall within the Directive, for instance the disposal in the instant case. The fact that a court has authorised an employer to suspend payments to his creditors does not take him outside the Directive.

In *Mythen v Employment Appeals Tribunal*,[22] Barrington J held that a sale of part of the business by a receiver, appointed under a debenture, came within the Directive. If receivers' disposals fell outside the Directive, its requirements could easily be avoided, because the most common form of receivership is an 'entirely extra-judicial process . . . which might be employed much more easily than a liquidation . . . to defeat the purposes of the Directive'.[23] The *Litster* case[24] in Britain, where the Directive was held to apply, also involved a sale by a receiver. Because a creditors' voluntary liquidation could relatively easily be used to avoid the Regulations' requirements, it would seem that a disposal in that situation also falls within the Regulations. Of course, the Regulations will not apply where all that is transferred is the bare assets and not the going concern or the goodwill of all or part of the business.

If, however, the High Court ordered that the employer be wound up as being insolvent, it was held that the Directive does not apply. According to the European Court in the *Abels* case,

> Article 1(1) of (the) Directive . . . does not apply to the transfer of an

---

20. *Abels v Administrative Board of the Bedrijfsverreinging Voor de Metal-Industrie (Case 135/83)* [1985] ECR 469.
21. Id. at p. 474.   22. [1989] ILRM 844.   23. Id. at p. 853.
24. *Litster v Forth Dry Dock & Engineering Co.* [1990] 1 AC 546.

undertaking, business or part of a business where the transferor has been adjudged insolvent and the undertaking or business in question forms part of the assets of the insolvent transferor. . . .[25]

It remains to be determined whether the Directive applies in situations where the High Court is involved in the case but has not made a formal adjudication of insolvency, notably a scheme of arrangement under ss.201-203 of the Companies Act, 1963, and the supervised examination under the Companies (Amendment) Act, 1990.

PREFERENTIAL DEBTS

There are certain creditors who are entitled to be paid out of the insolvent estate before any payments can be made to the general creditors. The traditional justification for preferring employees of the insolvent in this manner is that they are very much in an unequal position when dealing with an employer who is in financial difficulties. Preferential treatment was first accorded to them in an era when there was no welfare state and trade unions hardly existed. Under the Preferential Payments in Bankruptcy (Ireland) Act, 1889,[26] arrears of salary owed to the bankrupt's employees, up to a specified amount, were made a preferential debt. The position is now covered by s.285(2) of the Companies Act, 1963, as amended in 1982.[27] Only employees who work under a contract of employment benefit from these debts provisions.[28] The State is also a preferred creditor in respect of certain unpaid taxes. Employers are affected by these provisions in that unpaid tax deducted from the employee's remuneration and unpaid P.R.S.I. are preferred debts.[29]

THE INSOLVENCY FUND

At times an employer may be so heavily insolvent that there is not enough in his entire estate to satisfy even the preferential debts. Whatever assets he possessed may have been captured by a prior charge or be subject to leasing, hire purchase or retention of title arrangements. Even if there are enough assets to cover the preferential debts, the employees may have to wait years for the liquidator to make a distribution. It was to deal with these eventualities that the Protection of Employees (Employers' Insolvency) Act, 1984, was passed. This Act sets up a fund, administered by the Minister, from which the equivalent of certain debts to employees can be paid to them from the fund; the Minister is then subrogated for those employees. This Act is based on the E.C. Directive 80/987 on the protection of employees in the event of the insolvency of their

---

25. [1985] ECR 469.
26. 46 & 47 Vic. c.28. For 'clerks and servants', the period was four months and the maximum was £50; for 'labourers and workmen', the period was two months and there was no ceiling on the amount.
27. See ante pp. 362-364.   .28. *Re Sunday Tribune Ltd* [1984] IR 505.
29. See ante p. 361, n.'s 35 and 36.

employer.[30] The fund was known as the Redundancy and Employers Insolvency Fund but in 1991 was amalgamated with the general Social Insurance Fund.

Employees covered   Like the redundancy payments legislation, the 1984 Act applies only to employees who are insurable for all benefits under the Social Welfare Acts.[31] But the Minister, by order, can extend or restrict the personal scope of the Act. In 1988 employees over 66 years of age who otherwise would be insured for all benefits were brought within the Act.[32]

Debts payable   Those debts which eligible employees may recover from the fund are listed in s.6(2) of the 1984 Act. These are:

> Arrears of 'normal weekly remuneration'[33] not exceeding £250 per week and for a duration of no more than eight weeks.
> Arrears under a sick pay scheme, subject to the same £250 per week[34] and eight weeks ceiling; but also subject to a ceiling measured by reference to the injury or disability benefit and pay related benefit payable under the Social Welfare Acts.35
> Arrears of holiday pay, subject to the same £250 per week and eight weeks ceiling.
> Money in lieu of the minimum notice periods for dismissal prescribed by the Minimum Notices etc. Act, 1973, again subject to the same ceilings. Damages, compensation, awards and fines payable under the Unfair Dismissals Act, 1977, the Redundancy Payments Acts 1967-79, the Anti-Discrimination (Pay) Act, 1974, the Employment Equality Act, 1979, and also remuneration payable under Part VI of the Industrial Relations Act, 1946. Where the amount payable under any of these heads is calculated on the basis of normal remuneration, the Fund will not pay out any more than what represents £250 a week. The amount payable under some of these heads is subject to several other qualifications.

It was held by the House of Lords in the *Westwood* case[36] that payments made from a similar fund in Britain are subject to the collateral benefits principle. There the amount of unemployment benefit an employee drew immediately following his dismissal was deducted from the amount due to him in principle under the insolvency fund legislation and only the net sum was payable to him. This was because the mode or redress for not giving the minimum notice of dismissal required by statute is deemed to be an action for breach of contract. That being so, the successful plaintiff has a duty to mitigate his damages and it was previously held that, under the duty to mitigate, unemployment benefit received during the relevant period must be deducted

30. OJ No. L283/23 (1990).   31. S.3.
32. SI No. 48 of 1988.   33. As defined s.6(9).
34. S.6(4)(a), as amended by SI No. 17 of 1990.
35. S.6(4)(b).
36. *Westwood v Secretary of State for Employment* [1985] AC 20.

from the overall sum due.[37] The legislative mechanism for recovery under the Minimum Notice etc. Act, 1973, is different from that in Britain but s.12(1) of that Act speaks of 'recovering compensation for any loss sustained'. In *Irish Leathers Ltd v Minister for Labour* Barrington J[38] declined to follow *Westwood* because it was unsafe to follow the English precedents where there are differences of detail in the legislation. It was held that the fund should pay the full amount of the outstanding salary without deducting any unemployment benefit the employee had received. Under the 1973 Act, he has a right to be paid a specified sum of money and whether at the same time he received unemployment benefit is outside that Act's concerns; it is entirely a matter between the employee and the social welfare authorities. More recently it was held in Britain that the amount payable from the insolvency fund is the net amount after deducting income tax.[39]

Obtaining payment Payment from the Fund is obtained principally by making an application by or on behalf of the employee to the Minister.[40] If the Minister is satisfied that the employee falls within the Act, that his employer is insolvent and that all or part of any debt, described above, is owed to the employee, the Minister shall make the payment. What constitutes insolvency for these purposes is defined as a company being put into receivership or being wound up, or possession being taken of company assets under a floating charge.[41] The Minister is empowered to require information regarding the debt in order to ascertain if the claim is well founded.[42] If there was some agreement between the employer and the applicant that an application should be made to the Fund in respect of a debt but the employer then had the means to pay that sum, the Minister can refuse to make a payment.[43]

In the case of an application for arrears of remuneration, sick pay or holiday pay, if the sum has been awarded by a court to the employee, then the obligation to make a payment from the Fund is immediate.[44] Where there has not been a court award under either of these heads, if an application for payment from the Fund is refused by the Minister the matter can be appealed to the Employment Appeals Tribunal.[45] Moreover, if the Minister is in doubt whether any particular claim should be paid, he may refer the matter to the Tribunal for its determination.[46]

37. *Parsons v B.N.M. Laboratories Ltd* [1964] 1 QB 95.
38. [1986] IR 177.
39. *Secretary of State for Employment v Cooper* [1987] ICR 766.
40. S.6(1).   41. S.1(3); cf. s.4.   42. S.8.
43. S.6(8).   44. S.6(3).
45. S.9(1) and (4). Cf. *Re Solas Teo* [1990] ILRM 180.
46. S.9(3).

APPENDIX

An Act against Convenous and Fraudulent Conveyances, 1634

10 Car. I, sess. II, c.3

X. AND furthermore for the avoyding and abolishing of fained, convenous and fraudulent feoffments, gifts, grants, alienations, conveyances, bonds, suites, judgements and executions, as well of lands, and tenements, as of goods and chattels more commonly used and practised in these daies, then hath been seen or heard of heretofore; which feoffments, gifts, grants, alienations, bonds, suits, judgements and executions have been and are devised and contrived of malice, fraud, covin, collusion or guile, to the end, purpose and intent to delay, hinder or defraud creditors and others of their just and lawfull actions, suits, debts, accompts, dammages, penalties, forfeitures, herriots, mortuaries, and reliefs, not only to the lette or hindrance of the due course or execution of law and justice, but also to the overthrow of all true and plaine dealing, bargaining and chevisance between man and man, without the which no common wealth or civill society can be maintained or continued; Be it therefore further declared, ordained and enacted, by the authority of this present Parliament, That all and every feoffment, guift, grant, alientation, bargaine and conveyance of lands, tenements, hereditaments, goods and chattels, or any of them, or of any lease, rent, common, or other profit or charge out of the same lands, tenements, hereditaments, goods, and chattels, or any of them, by writing or otherwise and all and every bond, suit, judgement and execution at any time had or made, sithence the beginning of the raign of his said late Majesty King James of blessed memory, or at any time hereafter to be had or made, to or for any intent or purpose before declared and expressed, shall be from henceforth deemed and taken onely as against that person or persons, his or their heires, successors, executors, administrators and assignes, and every of them, whose actions, suits, debts, accompts, dammages, penalties, forfeitures, herriots, mortuaries and reliefs, by such guilefull, convenous and fraudulent devises and practices, as is aforesaid, are, shall, or mought be in any wise disturbed, hindred, delayed or defrauded to be clearly and utterly void, and of none effect: any pretence, colour, fained consideration, expressing of use, or any other matter or thing to the contrary notwithstanding.

XI. PROVIDED also, and be it enacted by the authority aforesaid, That this act, or any thing therein contained, shall not extend to any state or interest in lands, tenements, hereditaments, leases, rents, commons, profits, goods or chattells, had, made, conveyed or assured, or hereafter to be had, made, conveyed or assured; which estate or interest is or shall be upon good consideration and bona fide lawfully conveyed or assured to any person or persons, or bodies politique or corporate, not having at the time of such conveyance or assurance to them made, any manner of notice or knowledge of such covin, fraud, or collusion, as is aforesaid; any thing before mentioned to the contrary hereof notwithstanding.

Debtors (Ireland) Act, 1840

3 & 4 Vic. c.105

XXIII. And be it enacted, That if any person against whom any Judgement shall have been entered up in any of Her Majesty's Superior Courts at Dublin shall have any Government Stock, Funds, or Annuities, or any Stock or Shares of or in any public Company in Ireland (whether incorporated or not), standing in his Name in his own Right, or in the Name of any Person in trust for him, it shall be lawful for the Court of Chancery, or the Court of Exchequer at the Equity Side thereof, on any such Petition as aforesaid, and also for any of the Superior Courts of Law, or a Judge thereof, on the Application of any Judgment Creditor, to order that such Stock, Funds, Annuities, or Shares, of such of them or such Part thereof respectively as he shall think fit, shall stand charged with the Payment of the Amount for which Judgment shall have been so restored and Interest thereon; and such Order shall entitle the Judgment Creditor to all such Remedies as he would have been entitled to if such Charge had been made in his Favour by the Judgment Debtor, and the Provisions last aforesaid shall extend to the Interest of any Judgment Debtor, whether in Possession, Remainder, or Reversion, and whether vested or contingent, as well in any such Stocks, Funds, Annuities, or Shares as aforesaid, as also in the Dividends, Interest, or annual Produce of any such Stock, Funds, Annuities, or Shares; and whenever any such Judgment Debtor shall have any Estate, Right, Title, or Interest, vested of contingent, in Possession, Remainder, or Reversion, in, to, or out of any such Stock, Funds, Annuities, or Shares as aforesaid which shall be standing in the Name of the Accountant General of the Court of Chancery or the Accountant General of the Court of Exchequer, or in, to, or out of the Dividends, Interest, or annual Produce thereof, it shall be lawful for such Court or Judge to make any Order as to such Stock, Funds, Annuities, or Shares, or the Interest, Dividend, or annual Produce thereof, in the same Way as if the same had been standing in the Name of a Trustee of such Judgment Debtor: Provided always, that no Order of any Court of Judge as to any Stock, Funds, Annuities, or Shares standing the Name of the Accountant General of the Court of Chancery or the Accountant General of the Court of Exchequer, or as to the Interest, Dividends, or annual Produce thereof, shall prevent the Governor and Company of the Bank of Ireland, or any public Company, from permitting any Transfer of such Stocks, Funds, Annuities, or Shares, or Payment of the Interest, Dividends, or Annual Produce thereof, in such Manner as the Court of Chancery or the Court of Exchequer respectively may direct, or shall have any greater Effect than if such Debtor had charged such Stock, Funds, Annuities, or Shares, or the Interest, Dividends, or annual Produce thereof, in favour of the Judgment Creditor, with the Amount of the Sum to be mentioned in any such Order: Provided also, that no Proceedings shall be taken, save by the presenting of such Petition as aforesaid, to have the Benefit of such Charge until after the Expiration of Six Calendar Months from the Date of such Order.

Judgment Mortgages (Ireland) Act, 1850

13 & 14 Vic. c.29

VI. And be it enacted, That where any Judgment shall be entered up after the passing of this Act in any of Her Majesty's Superior Courts at Dublin, or any Decree of Order in any Court of Equity, Rule in any Court of Common Law, or Order in Bankruptcy or Lunacy, to which the Effect of a Judgment in One of the Superior Courts of Common Law is given by the Debtors (Ireland) Act, 1840, shall be made after the passing of this Act, or any Judgment, Rule, or Order shall be obtained or made in or by any Inferior Court of Record after the passing of this Act, and shall, under the Provisions of the said Act of 1840, be removed into One of Her Majesty's Superior Courts of Record at Dublin, and the Creditor under any such Judgment, Decree, Order, or Rule shall know or believe that the Person against whom such Judgment, Decree, Order, or Rule is entered up, obtained, or made is seised or possessed at Law or in Equity of any Lands, Tenements, or Hereditaments, of any Nature or Tenure, or has any disposing Power over any such Lands, Tenements, or Hereditaments which he may without the Assent of any other Person exercise for his own Benefit, and where any Judgment has been entered up before the passing of this Act in any of Her Majesty's Superior Courts at Dublin, or any Decree of Order in any Court of Equity, Rule in any Court of Common Law, or Order in Bankruptcy or Lunacy, to which the Effect of a Judgment in any of the Superior Courts of Common Law is given by the said Act of the Fourth year of Her Majesty, has been made before, the passing of this Act, or any Judgment, Rule, or Order has been obtained or made in or by an Inferior Court of Record before the passing of this Act, and has been or shall be, under the Provisions of the said Act of the Fourth Year of Her Majesty, removed into one of Her Majesty's Superior Courts at Dublin, and the Creditor under any such Judgment, Decree, Order, or Rule shall know or believe that the Person against whom such Judgment, Decree, Order, or Rule is entered up, obtained, or made is seised or possessed as aforesaid of, or has such disposing Power as aforesaid over, any Lands, Tenements, or Hereditaments which by virtue of this Act are exempted from being taken in execution under any Writ or Execution to be issued upon such Judgment, Decree, Order, or Rule, it shall be lawful for such Creditor, at any Time and from Time to Time after the entering up or Removal of such Judgment in or into such Superior Court, or the making of such Decree, Order, or Rule, or the passing of this Act, whichever shall last happen, to make and file in the Superior Court in, by, or into which such Judgment, Rule, or Order is entered up, made, or removed, or in the Court of Equity by which such Decree or Order is made, or in the Case of such Order in Bankruptcy or Lunacy as aforesaid, in the Court of Chancery in Ireland, an Affidavit stating the Name or Title of the Cause or Matter, and the Court in which such Judgment, Decree, Order, or Rule has been entered up, obtained, or made, and the Date of such Judgment, Decree, Order, or Rule, and the Names, and the usual or last known Place of Abode, and the Title, Trade, or Profession of the Plaintiff (if there be such), and of the Defendant or Person whose Estate is intended to be affected by the Registration, as herein-after mentioned, of such Affidavit, and the Amount of the Debt, Damages, Costs, or Monies recovered or ordered to be paid by such Judgment, Decree, Order, or Rule, and stating that, to the best of the Knowledge and Belief of the Deponent, the Person against whom such Judgment, Decree, Order, or Rule is entered up, obtained, or made is at the Time of the swearing of such Affidavit so seised or possessed, or has such disposing Power as aforesaid, of or over such Lands, Tenements, or Hereditaments, and such Affidavit shall specify the County and Barony, or the Town or County of a City, and Parish, or the Town and Parish, in which the Lands to which the Affidavit relates are situate, and where such Lands lie in Two or more Counties or Baronies, or Parishes or Streets, or partly in One Barony, Parish, or Street and partly in another, the same shall be distinctly stated in such Affidavit; and it shall be lawful for the Creditor making such Affidavit to register the same in the Office for registering Deeds, Conveyances, and Wills in Ireland, by depositing in such Office an Office Copy of such Affidavit; and such Copy shall be numbered and transcribed, and shall be entered in the Books and Indexes kept in the said Office, in like Manner as if the same were a Memorial of a Deed; and for the Purpose of such Entries the Creditor under such Judgment, Decree, Order, or Rule shall be deemed the Grantee, and the Debtor thereunder shall be deemed the Grantor; and the Amount of the Debt, Damages, Costs, or Monies recovered or ordered to be paid thereby be deemed the Consideration; and the like Fee shall be paid on such Registration as in the Case of registering a Memorial of a Deed.

VII. And be it enacted, That the Registration as aforesaid as such Affidavit shall operate to transfer to and vest in the Creditor registering such Affidavit all the Lands, Tenements, and Hereditaments mentioned therein, for all the Estate and Interest of which the Debtor mentioned in such Affidavit shall at the time of such Registration be seised or possessed at Law or in Equity, or might at such Time create by virtue of any disposing Power which he might then without the Assent of any other Person exercise for his own Benefit, but subject to Redemption on Payment of the Money owning on the Judgment, Decree, Order, or Rule mentioned in such Affidavit; and such Creditor, and all Persons claiming through or under him, shall, in respect of such Lands, Tenements, and Hereditaments, or such Estate or Interest therein as aforesaid, have all such Rights, Powers, and Remedies whatsoever as if an effectual Conveyance, Assignment, Appointment, or other Assurance to such Creditor of all such Estate or Interest, but subject to Redemption as aforesaid, had been made, executed, and registered at the Time of registering such Affidavit.

Common Law Procedure Amendment (Ireland) Act, 1853

16 & 17 Vic. c.113

CXXXII. If any Person against whom such Judgment shall be entered as aforesaid shall have any Government Stock, Funds, or Annuities, or any Stock or Shares in any public Company in Ireland, whether incorporated or not, and standing in his own Name and in his own Right, or in the Name of any Person in trust for him, or any Interest in the Dividends, Interest, or annual Produce of such Stock, Funds, Annuities, or Shares, it shall be lawful for the Court or a Judge, on Application of the Party having recovered such Judgment, to make an Order ex parte in the Form No. 7. in the Schedule B. to this Act annexed, to attach such Stock, Funds, Annuities, or shares, and such Dividends, Interest, or annual Produce shall be attached in the Books of the Governor and Company of the Bank of Ireland or any public Company, to answer the Purposes of such Execution, and such Stock, Funds, Annuities, and Shares shall not be suffered to be transferred, nor shall such Dividends, Interest, or annual Produce be paid, until such Order of Attachment shall be withdrawn or discharged or disposed of, and no Disposition in the meanwhile of such Debtor shall be valid or effectual as against such Party recovering such Judgment and obtaining such Order of Attachment.

CXXXIII. A Copy of such Order of Attachment shall be served on the Debtor or his Attorney or Agent, and unless the said Debtor or some other person interested shall within the Space of Twenty Days from the Service of such Order of Attachment and Copy, or from the Date of the last Service, or such other Time as the Court or a Judge may think reasonable, show sufficient Cause to the contrary, it shall be lawful for the Court or a Judge, if he shall so think fit, on Proof of the Service of such Order of Attachment and copy, to make an Order on all Persons, Corporations, and public Companies whose Act of Consent is thereto necessary, to transfer the said Government Stock, Funds, Annuities, or Shares belonging to the said Judgment Debtor, and standing in his own Name, or in the Name of any trustee for him for his own Benefit, into the Name of the said Sheriff or other Officer as aforesaid, or to make Payment of such Dividends, Interest, and annual Produce to said Sheriff, and all such Person whose Act or consent is so necessary as aforesaid are hereby required to obey such Order, and are indemnified for all Things done or permitted pursuant to such Order: Provided also, that it shall be lawful for such Court or a Judge, on the Application of the Debtor or any Person interested, to discharge or vary such Order for Attachment, and to award such Costs, on such Application, as to the said Court or a Judge shall seem just.

Bankruptcy Act, 1988

Number 27 *of* 1988

AN ACT TO CONSOLIDATE WITH AMENDMENTS THE LAW RELATING TO BANKRUPTCY AND TO PROVIDE FOR RELATED MATTERS. [13*th July*, 1988]

Interpretation

3.—In this Act, unless the context otherwise requires,—

"property" includes money, goods, things in action, land and every description of property, whether real or personal and whether situate in the State or elsewhere; also obligations, easements, and every description of estate, interest, and profit, present or future, vested or contingent, arising out of or incident to property as above defined;

"secured creditor" means and creditor holding any mortgage, charge or lien on the debtor's estate or any part thereof as security for a debt due to him.

Amount of fraudulent preferences.

(1872, s. 53; 33/1963, sch. 11, para. 1.)

57.—(1) Every conveyance or transfer of property or charge made thereon, every payment made, every obligation incurred and every judicial proceeding taken or suffered by any person unable to pay his debts as they become due from his own money in favour of any creditor or of any person in trust for any creditor, with a view to giving such creditor, or any surety or guarantor for the debt due to such creditor, a preference over the the other creditors, shall, if the person making, incurring, taking or suffering the same is adjudicated bankrupt within six months after the date of making, incurring, taking or suffering the same, be deemed fraudulent and void as against the Official Assignee; but this section shall not affect the rights of any person making title in good faith and for valuable consideration through or under a creditor of the bankrupt.

(2)   (*a*) Where a person is adjudicated bankrupt and anything made or done is void under *subsection (1)* or was void under the corresponding provisions of the law in force immediately before the commencement of this Act as a fraudulent preference of a person interested in property mortgaged or charged to secure the bankrupt's debt, then (without prejudice to any rights or liabilities arising apart from this section) the person preferred shall be subject to the same liabilities and shall have the same rights as if he had undertaken to be personally liable as surety for the debt to the extent of the charge on the property or the value of his interest, whichever is the less.

(*b*) The value of the said person's interest shall be determined as at the date of the transaction constituting the fraudulent preference, and shall be determined as if the interest were free of all encumbrances other than those to which the charge for the bankrupt's debt was then subject.

(*c*) On any application made to the Court in relation to any payment on the ground that the payment was a fraudulent preference of a surety or guarantee, the Court shall have jurisdiction to determine any questions relating to the payment arising between the person to whom the payment was made and the surety or guarantor, and to grant relief in respect thereof notwithstanding that it is not necessary so to do for the purposes of the bankruptcy, and for that purpose may give leave to bring in the surety or guarantor as a third party as in the case of an action for the recovery of the sum paid.

(*d*) *Paragraph (c)* shall apply, with the necessary modifications, in relation to transactions other than the payment of money as it applies to payments.

75.—(1) Debts and liabilities, present or future, certain or contingent, by reason of any obligation incurred by the bankrupt or arranging debtor before the date of adjudication or order for protection and claims in the nature of unliquidated damages for which the bankrupt or arranging debtor is liable at that date by reason of a wrong within the meaning of the Civil Liability Act, 1961, shall be provable in the bankruptcy or arrangment.

(2) Where interest or any pecuniary consideration in lieu of interest is reserved or agreed for on a debt which is overdue at that date of adjudication, the creditor shall be entitled to prove or be admitted as a creditor for such interest or consideration up to the date of adjudication.

(3) Where all necessary parties agree, an order for assessment of damages or contribution under section 61(2) of the Civil Liability Act, 1961, may be made by the Court, notwithstanding that it may not be the court by or before which the claim for damages or contribution fails to be determined.

(4) An estimate may be made by the Court of the value of any debt which, by reason of it being subject to any contingency or for any other reason, does not bear a certain value and the amount of the estimate shall be proved as a debt.

Debts provable in bankruptcy and arrangements.
(*cf.* 1857, ss. 247, 249, 252 to 258; 1872, ss. 45-47)

76.—The provisions of the *First Schedule* shall apply in relation to the proof of debts.

Proof of debts. (*cf.* 1857, s. 246 in pt.)

77.—Section 12(1) of the Factories Act, 1889 (which regulates the rights of an owner of goods in the case of the bankruptcy of a mercantile agent to whom they have been entrusted) shall have effect with the substitution for the reference to a trustee in bankrupty of a reference to the Official Assignee.

Bankruptcy of mercantile agent
(New)

78.—Where a party to any cause or matter has obtained a judgment or order against a person who is afterwards adjudicated bankrupt or is granted an order for protection for any debt for which he proves or is admitted a creditor, he shall also be entitled to prove or be admitted a creditor for the costs of the judgment or order, whether or not the costs have been taxed or ascertained at the date of the adjudication or order for protection.

Proof for costs of judgment.
(1857, s. 261)

79.—The Court may, on the application of the Official Assignee or any creditor of the bankrupt or arranging debtor, disallow, in whole or in part, any debt already proved or admitted.

Disallowance of debts already proved.
(1857, s. 263)

FIRST SCHEDULE

PROOF OF DEBTS

Section 76

General

1. Every creditor shall prove his debt and a creditor who does not do so is not entitled to share in any distribution that may be made. (New)

2. (*a*) A creditor may prove his debt by delivering or sending by post to the Official Assignee particulars of his debt (in this Schedule referred to as a "proof of debt").

    (*b*) *Subparagraph (a)* is without prejudice to the entitlement of a creditor to prove his debt at a sitting of the Court.

3. The Official Assignee may fix a time within which proofs of debt shall be sent to him. A proof submitted thereafter shall not be allowed except by order of the Court.

4. Proof of debt may be furnished by way of a detailed statement of account, an affidavit of debt or other prescribed means.

5. The creditor shall specify the vouchers or any other evidence by which the debt can be substantiated. He shall also give particulars of any counterclaim that, to his knowledge, the bankrupt or arranging debtor may have, and he shall indicate whether or not he is a secured creditor.

6. Proof of debt in respect of money lent by a moneylender shall have annexed thereto the particulars required by section 16(2) of the Moneylenders Act, 1933.

7. An affidavit shall be required in any case where the debt is disputed or the Court or the Official Assignee thinks fit.

8. Proof of debt may be given by the oath or affidavit of the creditor himself or by the oath or affidavit of some person authorised by or on behalf of the creditor and, if made by a person so authorised, shall state his authority and means of knowledge.

9. Subject to *paragraph 24(5)*, a creditor may, with the consent of the Official Assignee, amend his proof of debt.

10. Every creditor who has lodged a proof of debt is entitled to see and examine the proofs of other creditors.

11. A husband and wife may prove a debt against each other as if they were not married.

12. A sole trustee (including a personal representative) who is a bankrupt or an arranging debtor shall be entitled, without leave of the Court, to prove in his own bankruptcy or arrangement in respect of a debt due from him to the trust estate. Any dividend in respect of such a debt shall be paid to the Accountant of the High Court for credit of the trust estate.

13. If any bankrupt or arranging debtor, at the date of the adjudication or order for protection, is liable in respect of distinct contracts, as a member of two or more distinct firms, or as a sole contractor, and also as member of a firm, the circumstance that such firms are, in whole or in part, composed of the same individuals, or that the sole contractor is also one of the joint contractors, shall not prevent proof in respect of such contracts against the properties respectively liable upon such contracts.

14. On any debt or sum certain, payable at a certain time or otherwise, whereon interest is not reserved or agreed for, and which is overdue at the date of the adjudication, the creditor may prove for interest at the rate currently payable on judgment debts to that date from the time when the debt or sum was payable, if the debt or sum is payable by virtue of a written instrument at a certain time, and if payable otherwise, then from the time when a demand in writing has been made, giving notice that interest will be claimed from the date of the demand until the time of payment.

15. In respect of debts due after the adjudication or order for protection, the liability for which existed at the date of such adjudication or order for protection, a creditor may prove for the value of the debt at that date.

16. Where a person who is liable to make any periodical payment (including rental) is adjudicated bankrupt or is granted an order for protection on a day other than the day on which such payment becomes due, the person entitled to the payment may prove for a proportionate part of the payment for the period from the date when the last payment became due to the date of the adjudication or order for protection as if the payment accrued due from day to day.

17. (1) Where there are mutual credits or debts as between a bankrupt and any person claiming as a creditor, one debt or demand may be set off against the other and only the balance found owing shall be recoverable on one side or the other.

(2) Section 36 of the Civil Liability Act, 1961 (which provides for the set-off of claims)

as amended by section 5 of the Civil Liability (Amendment) Act, 1964, shall apply with the substitution in section 36(3) of a reference to *subparagraph (1)* for the reference to section 251 of the Irish Bankrupt and Insolvent Act, 1857.

18. This Schedule is without prejudice to section 61 of the Civil Liability Act, 1961 (which provides for proof of claims for damages or contribution in respect of a wrong) and section 62 of the said Act (which provides for the application of moneys payable under certain policies of insurance where the insured becomes a bankrupt).

19. A creditor shall, unless the Court otherwise orders, bear his own costs of proving a debt.

20. Any person seeking to prove a debt or from whom additional proof is required, or any other person, may be examined by the Court in relation thereto.

21. Where a creditor or other person with intent to defraud makes any false claim or any proof, declaration or statement of account before the Court or in his affidavit which is untrue in any material particular in connection with the proof of debts, the Court may, in addition to any other penalty provided in this Act, disallow the claim in whole or in part.

22. Before deciding on a claim, the Official Assignee may require a creditor to furnish additional information or proof or to attend before him.

23. The Official Assignee shall deal in the following manner with claims:

    (*a*) He shall prepare a list certified by him of the claims.

    (*b*) This list shall record—

        (i) the claims allowed by him, which shall be deemed to be admitted, and

        (ii) the claims either disallowed by him or which he considers should not be admitted without reference to the Court.

    (*c*) He shall refer disputed debts to the Court for adjudication.

    (*d*) The decision of the Official Assignee in regard to a claim shall be confirmed in writing to the creditor.

    (*e*) Any person aggrieved by the decision of the Official Assignee may appeal to the Court.

    (*f*) The Official Assignee shall place a copy of the list on the Court file.

    (*g*) The list shall be open to public inspection on payment of a prescribed fee but no fee shall be charged to creditors inspecting the list.

Secured Creditors

24. (1) If a secured creditor realises his security, he may prove for the balance due to him after deducting the net amount realised and receive dividends thereon but not so as to disturb any dividend then already declared. If he surrenders his security for the general benefit of the creditors, he may prove for his whole debt.

(2) If a secured creditor does not either realise or surrender his security, he shall, before ranking for dividend, state in his proof the particulars of his security, the date on which it was given and the value at which he assesses it and he shall be entitled to receive a dividend only in respect of the balance due to him after deducting the value so assessed.

(3) A secured creditor shall not be entitled to surrender his security after the time fixed by the Official Assignee for receipt of proofs of debt, except by order of the Court.

    (4)   (*a*) Where a security is valued by the creditor, the Official Assignee may at any time redeem it on payment to the creditor of the assessed value. If the Official Assignee is dissatisfied with the assessed value he may require that the property comprised in any security so valued be offered for sale at such time and on such terms and conditions as may be agreed upon between him and the creditor or, in default of agreement, as the Court may direct. If the

sale be by public auction the creditor, or the Official Assignee on behalf of the estate, may bid or purchase.

(*b*) The creditor may, however, at any time by notice in writing require the Official Assignee to elect whether he will or will not exercise his power of redeeming the security or requiring it to be offered for sale, and if the Official Assignee does not, within three months after receiving the notice, signify in writing to the creditors his election to exercise the power, he shall not be entitled to exercise it; and the equity of redemption, or any other interest in the property comprised in the security which is vested in the Official Assignee, shall vest in the creditor and the amount of his debt shall be reduced by the amount at which the security has been valued.

(5) Where a creditor has valued his security he may at any time amend the valuation and proof on showing to the satisfaction of the Official Assignee, or the Court, that the valuation and proof were made *bona fide* on a mistaken estimate, but every such amendment shall be made at the cost of the creditor, and upon such terms as the Court shall order, unless the Official Assignee allows the amendment without application to the Court.

(6) Where a valuation has been amended in accordance with *subparagraph (5)*, the creditor shall forthwith repay any surplus dividend which he may have received in excess of that to which he would have been entitled on the amended valuation or, as the case may be, shall be entitled to be paid, out of any money for the time being available for dividend, any dividend or share of dividend which he has not received by reason of the inaccuracy of the original valuation before the money is made applicable to the payment of any future dividend but he shall not be entitled to disturb the distribution of any dividend declared before the date of the amendment.

(7) If a creditor having valued his security subsequently realises it, or if it is realised under the provisions of *subparagraph (4)*, the net amount realised shall be substituted for the amount of any valuation previously made by the creditor, and shall be treated in all respects as an amended valuation made by the creditor.

(8) If it is found at any time that the affidavit made by or on behalf of a secured creditor has omitted to state that he is a secured creditor, such creditor shall surrender his security to the Official Assignee for the general benefit of the creditors unless the Court on application otherwise orders, and the Court may allow the affidavit to be amended upon such terms as to repayment of any dividend or otherwise as the Court may consider just.

(9) If a secured creditor does not comply with *subparagraph (8)*, he shall be excluded form all share in any dividend.

(10) Subject to the provisions of *subparagraph (4)*, the creditor shall in no case receive more than one pound in the pound and interest, where the creditor is entitled to prove for interest.

(11) Where a mortgagee holds as security a policy of assurance on the life of a bankrupt or an arranging debtor which in the event of the non-payment of premiums provides for their automatic discharge out of moneys payable under the policy, the value of the policy for the purpose of proving in the bankruptcy or arrangement shall be taken to be not less than the value as at the date of adjudication or order for protection; provided that, if the bankrupt or arranging debtor dies before the policy is surrended, the mortgagee may apply to the Court for the purpose of revaluing his security.

Companies Act, 1963
(as amended)

Number 33 *of* 1963

2.—(1) In this Act unless the context otherwise requires—

"company" means a company formed and registered under this Act, or an existing company;

"the court" used in relation to a company means the High Court;

"debenture" includes debenture stocks, bonds and any other securities of a company whether constituting a charge on the assets of the company or not;

"director" includes any person occupying the position of director by whatever name called;

"existing company" means a company formed and registered in a register kept in the State under the Joint Stock Companies Acts, the Companies Act, 1862, or the Companies (Consolidation) Act, 1908;

"Joint Stock Companies Acts" means the Joint Stock Companies Act, 1856, the Joint Stock Companies Acts, 1856, 1857, the Joint Stock Banking Companies Act, 1857 and the Act to enable Joint Stock Banking Companies to be formed on the principle of limited liability, or any one or more of those Acts as the case may require, but does not include the Act 7 & 8 Victoria, Chapter 110.

General provision as to Interpretation

98.—(1) Where either a receiver is appointed on behalf of the holders of any debenture of a company secured by a floating charge, or possession is taken by or on behalf of those debenture holders of any property comprised in or subject to the charge, then, if the company is not at the time in course of being wound up, the debts which in every winding up are, under the provisions of Part VI relating to preferential payments to be paid in priority to all other debts, shall be paid out of any assets coming to the hands of the receiver or other person taking possession as aforesaid in priority to any claim for principal or interest in respect of the debentures.

Preferential payments when receiver is appointed under floating charge

(2) In the application of the said provisions section 285 of this Act shall be construed as if the provision for payment of accrued holiday remuneration becoming payable on the termination of employment before or by the effect of the winding up order or resolution, were a provision for payment of such remuneration becoming payable on the termination of employment before or by the effect of the appointment of the receiver or possession being taken as aforesaid.

(3) The periods of time mentioned in the said provisions of Part VI shall be reckoned from the date of the appointment of the receiver or of possession being taken as aforesaid, as the case may be.

(4) Where the date referred to in subsection (3) occurred before the operative date, subsections (1) and (3) shall have effect with the substitution for references to the said provisions of Part VI of references to the provisions which, by virtue of subsection (12) of the said section 285 are deemed to remain in force in the case therein mentioned, and subsection (2) of this section shall not apply.

(5) Any payments made under this section shall be recouped so far as may be out of the assets of the company available for payment of general creditors.

PART IV

REGISTRATION OF CHARGES

Registration of Charges with Registrar of Companies

Registration
of charges
created by
companies

99.—(1) Subject to the provisions of this Part, every charge created after the fixed date by a company, and being a charge to which this section applies, shall, so far as any security on the company's property or undertaking is conferred thereby, be void against the liquidator and any creditor of the company, unless the prescribed particulars of the charge, verified in the prescribed manner, are delivered to or received by the registrar of companies for registration in manner required by this Act within 21 days after the date of its creation, but without prejudice to any contract or obligation for repayment of the money thereby secured, and when a charge becomes void under this section, the money secured thereby shall immediately become payable.

(2) This section applies to the following charges:

(*a*) a charge for the purpose of securing any issue of debentures;

(*b*) a charge on uncalled share capital of the company;

(*c*) a charge created or evidenced by an instrument which, if executed by an individual, would require registration as a bill of sale;

(*d*) a charge on land, wherever situate, or any interest therein, but not including a charge for any rent or other periodical sum issuing out of land;

(*e*) a charge on book debts of the company;

(*f*) a floating charge on the undertaking or property of the company;

(*g*) a charge on calls made but not paid;

(*h*) a charge on a ship or aircraft or any share in a ship or aircraft;

(*i*) a charge on goodwill, on a patent or a licence under a patent, on a trade mark or on a copyright or a licence under a copyright.

(2A) The Minister may be regulations amend subsection (2) so as to add any description of charge to, or remove any description of charge from, the charges requiring registration under this section.

(2B) The power of the Minister under subsection (2A) shall include a power to amend by regulations the description of any charge referred to in subsection (2).

(2C) Every regulation made by the Minister under this section shall be laid before each House of the Oireachtas as soon as may be after it is made and, if a resolution annulling the regulation is passed by either House within the next 21 days on which that House has sat after the regulation is laid before it, the regulation shall be annulled accordingly, but without prejudice to the validity of anything previously done thereunder.

(3) In the case of a charge created out of the State comprising property situate outside the State, 21 days after the date on which the prescribed particulars could, in due course of post, and if despatched with due diligence, have been received in the State shall be substituted for 21 days after the date of the creation of the charge as the time within which the particulars are to be delivered to the registrar.

(4) Where a charge is created in the State but comprises property outside the State, the prescribed particulars may be sent for registration under this section, notwithstanding that further proceedings may be necessary to make the charge valid or effectual according to the law of the county in which the property is situate.

(5) Where a charge comprises property situate outside the State and registration in the country where the property is situate is necessary to make the charge valid or effectual according to the law of that country, a certificate in the prescribed form stating that the charge

was presented for registration in the country where the property is situate on the date on which it was so presented shall be delivered to the registrar of companies for registration.

(6) Where a negotiable instrument has been given to secure the payment of any book debts of a company, the deposit of the instrument for the purpose of securing an advance to the company shall not, for the purpose of this section, be treated as a charge on those book debts.

(7) The holding of debentures entitling the holder to a charge on land shall not, for the purposes of this section, be deemed to be an interest in land.

(8) Where a series of debentures containing, or giving by reference to any other instrument, any charge to the benefit of which the debenture holders of that series are entitled *pari passu* is created by a company, it shall, for the purposes of this section, be sufficient if there are delivered to or received by the registrar, within 21 days after the execution of the deed containing the charge, or, if there is no such deed, after the execution of any debentures of the series, the following particulars:

    (*a*) the total amount secured by the whole series; and

    (*b*) the dates of the resolutions authorising the issue of the series, and the date of the covering deed, if any, by which the security is created or defined; and

    (*c*) a general description of the property charged; and

    (*d*) the names of the trustees, if any, for the debenture holders;

so, however, that where more than one issue is made of debentures in the series, there shall be sent to the registrar for entry in the register particulars of the amount and date of each issue; but an omission to do this shall not affect the validity of the debentures issued.

(9) Where any commission, allowance or discount has been paid or made either directly or indirectly by a company to any person in consideration of his subscribing or agreeing to subscribe, whether absolutely or conditionally, for any debentures of the company, or procuring or agreeing to procure subscriptions, whether absolute or conditional, for any such debentures, the particulars required to be sent for registration under this section shall include particulars as to the amount and rate per cent. of the commission, discount or allowance so paid or made, but omission to do this shall not affect the validity of the debentures issued so, however, that the deposit of any debentures as security for any debt of the company shall not, for the purposes of this subsection, be treated as the issue of the debentures at a discount.

(10) In this Part—

    (*a*) "charge" includes mortgage;

    (*b*) "the fixed date" means, in relation to the charges specified in paragraphs (*a*) to (*f*), of subsection (2), the 1st July, 1908, and in relation to the charges specified in paragraphs (*g*) to (*i*), the operative date.

100.—(1) It shall be the duty of a company to send to the registrar of companies for registration within the time required by section 99 the particulars of every charge created by the company, and of the issues of debentures of a series requiring registration under section 99, together with any documents required by that section, but registration of any such charge may be effected on the application of any person interested therein. *Duty of company to register charges created by company*

(2) Where registration is effected by the application of some person other than the company, that person shall be entitled to recover from the company the amount of any fees properly paid by him to the registrar on the registration.

(3) If any company makes default in sending to the registrar for registration the particulars of any charge created by the company or of the issues of debentures of a series requiring registration under section 99 or any documents required by that section then, unless registration has been effected on the application of some other person, the company and every officer of the company who is in default shall be liable to a fine not exceeding £500.

(4) Proceedings in relation to an offence under this section may be brought and prosecuted by the registrar of companies.

Extension of time for registration of charges

106.—(1) The court, on being satisfied that the omission to register a charge within the time required by this Act or that the omission or mis-statement of any particular with respect to any such charge or in a memorandum of satisfaction was accidental, or due to inadvertence or to some other sufficient cause, or is not of a nature to prejudice the position of creditors or shareholders of the company, or that on other grounds it is just and equitable to grant relief, may, on the application of the company or any person interested, and on such terms and conditions as seem to the court just and expedient, order that the time for registration shall be extended, or, as the case may be, that the omission or mis-statement shall be rectified.

(2) The grant of relief by the court under this section shall, if the court so directs, not have the effect of relieving the company or its officers of any liability already incurred under section 100.

Notice to registrar of appointment of receiver, and of receiver ceasing to act

107.—(1) If any person obtains an order for the appointment of a receiver of the property of a company or appoints such a receiver under any powers contained in any instrument, he shall, within 7 days after the date of the order or of the appointment, publish in *Iris Oifigiúil* and in at least one daily newspaper circulating in the district where the registered office of the company is situated, and deliver to the registrar of companies, a notice in the form prescribed.

(2) When any person appointed receiver of the property of a company ceases to act as such receiver, he shall, on so ceasing, deliver to the registrar of companies a notice in the form prescribed.

(3) If any person makes default in complying with the requirements of this section, he shall be liable to a fine not exceeding £500.

PART VI
WINDING UP

(i) PRELIMINARY

Modes of Winding Up

Modes of winding-up

206.—(1) The winding up of a company may be—
(*a*) by the court; or
(*b*) voluntary.

(2) The provisions of this Act relating to winding up apply, unless the contrary appears, to the winding up of a company in either of those modes.

Contributories

Liability of contributories of past and present members

207.—(1) In the event of a company being wound up, every present and past member shall be liable to contribute to the assets of the company to an amount sufficient for payment of its debts and liabilities, and the costs, charges and expenses of the winding up, and for the adjustment of the rights of the contributories among themselves, subject to subsection (2) and the following qualifications:
(*a*) a past member shall not be liable to contribute if he has ceased to be a member for one year or more before the commencement of the winding up;
(*b*) a past member shall not be liable to contribute in respect of any debt or liability of the company contracted after he ceased to be a member;

(*c*) a past member shall not be liable to contribute unless it appears to the court that the existing members are unable to satisfy the contributions required to be made by them in pursuance of this Act;

(*d*) in the case of a company limited by shares, no contribution shall be required from any member exceeding the amount, if any, unpaid on the shares in respect of which he is liable as a present or past member;

(*e*) in the case of a company limited by guarantee, no contribution shall, subject to subsection (3), be required from any member exceeding the amount undertaken to be contributed by him to the assets of the company in the event of its being wound up;

(*f*) nothing in this Act shall invalidate any provision contained in any policy of insurance or other contract whereby the liability of individual members on the policy or contract is restricted, or whereby the funds of the company are alone made liable in respect of the policy or contract;

(*g*) a sum due to any member of the company, in his character of a member, by way of dividends, profits or otherwise, shall not be deemed to be a debt of the company, payable to that member in a case of competition between himself and any other creditor not a member of the company, but any such sum may be taken into account for the purpose of the final adjustment of the rights of the contributories among themselves.

(2) In the winding up of a limited company, any director, whether past or present, whose liability is, under this Act, unlimited, shall, in addition to his liability (if any) to contribute as an ordinary member, be liable to make a further contribution as if he were at the commencement of the winding up a member of an unlimited company, so, however, that—

(*a*) a past director shall not be liable to make such further contribution if he has ceased to hold office for a year or more before the commencement of the winding up;

(*b*) a past director shall not be liable to make such further contribution in respect of any debt or liability of the company contracted after he cased to hold office;

(*c*) subject to the articles of the company, a director shall not be liable to make such further contribution unless the court deems it necessary to require that contribution in order to satisfy the debts and liabilities of the company and the costs, charges and expenses of the winding up.

(3) In the winding up of a company limited by guarantee which has a share capital, every member of the company shall be liable, in addition to the amount undertaken to be contributed by him to the assets of the company in the event of its being wound up, to contribute to the extent of any sums unpaid on any shares held by him.

208.—The term "contributory" means every person liable to contribute to the assets of a company in the event of its being wound up, and for the purposes of all proceedings for determining, and all proceedings prior to the final determination of, the persons who are to be deemed contributories, includes any person alleged to be a contributory. Definition of "contributory"

209.—(1) The liability of a contributory shall create a debt accruing due from him at the time when his liability commenced, but payable at the times when calls are made for enforcing the liability. Liability of contributory

(2) An action to recover a debt created by this section shall not be brought after the expiration of 12 years from the date on which the cause of action accrued.

Contributories in case of death of member

210.—(1) If a contributory dies, either before or after he has been placed on the list of contributories, his personal representative shall be liable in due course of administration to contribute to the assets of the company in discharge of his liability and shall be contributories accordingly.

(2) If the personal representatives make default in paying any money ordered to be paid by them, proceedings may be taken for the administration of the estate of the deceased contributory or otherwise for compelling payment thereout of the money due.

Contributories in case of bankruptcy of member

211.—If a contributory becomes bankrupt, either before or after he has been placed on the list of contributories—

> (*a*) the Official Assignee shall represent him for all the purposes of the winding up, and shall be a contributory accordingly, and may be called on to admit to proof against the estate of the bankrupt or otherwise to allow to be paid out of his assets in due course of law any money due from the bankrupt in respect of his liability to contribute to the assets of the company; and
>
> (*b*) there may be proved against the estate of the bankrupt the estimated value of his liability to future calls as well as calls already made.

(ii) WINDING UP BY THE COURT

Jurisdiction

Jurisdiction to wind up companies

212.—The High Court shall have jurisdiction to wind up any company.

Cases in which Company may be wound up by the Court

Circumstances in which company may be wound up by the court

213.—A company may be wound up by the court if—

> (*a*) the company has by special resolution resolved that the company be wound up by the court;
>
> (*b*) default is made in delivering the statutory report to the registrar or in holding the statutory meeting;
>
> (*c*) the company does not commence its business within a year from its incorporation or suspends its business for a whole year;
>
> (*d*) the number of members is reduced, in the case of a private company, below two, or, in the case of any other company, below seven;
>
> (*e*) the company is unable to pay its debts;
>
> (*f*) the court is of opinion that it is just and equitable that the company should be wound up;
>
> (*g*) the court is satisfied that the company's affairs are being conducted, or the powers of the directors are being exercised, in a manner oppressive to any member or in disregard of his interests as a member and that, despite the existence of an alternative remedy, winding up would be justified in the general circumstances of the case so, however, that the court may dismiss a petition to wind up under this paragraph if it is of opinion that proceedings under section 205 would, in all the circumstances, be more appropriate.

Circumstances in which company deemed to be unable to pay its debts

214.—A company shall be deemed to be unable to pay its debts—

> (*a*) if a creditor, by assignment or otherwise, to whom the company is indebted in a sum exceeding £1,000 then due, has served on the company, by leaving it at the registered office of the company, a demand in writing requiring the

company to pay the sum so due, and the company has for 3 weeks thereafter neglected to pay the sum or to secure or compound for it to the reasonable satisfaction of the creditor; or

(*b*) if execution or other process issued on a judgment, decree or order of any court in favour of a creditor of the company is returned unsatisfied in whole or in part; or

(*c*) if it is proved to the satisfaction of the court that the company is unable to pay its debts, and in determining whether a company is unable to pay its debts, the court shall take into account the contingent and prospective liabilities of the company.

Petition for Winding Up and Effects thereof

215.—An application to the court for the winding up of a company shall be by petition presented, subject to the provisions of this section, either by the company or by any creditor or creditors (including any contingent or prospective creditor or creditors), contributory or contributories, or by all or any of those parties, together or separately, so, however, that— Provisions as to applications for winding-up

(*a*) a contributory shall not be entitled to present a winding up petition unless—

    (i) either the number of members is reduced, in the case of a private company, below two, or in the case of any other company, below seven; or

    (ii) the shares in respect of which he is a contributory, or some of them, either were originally allotted to him or have been held by him, and registered in his name, for at least 6 months during the 18 months before the commencement of the winding up, or have devolved on him through the death of a former holder; and

(*b*) a winding-up petition shall not, if the ground of the petition is default in delivering the statutory report to the registrar or in holding the statutory meeting, be presented by any person except a shareholder, nor before the expiration of 14 days after the last day on which the meeting ought to have been held; and

(*c*) the court shall not give a hearing to a winding-up petition presented by a contingent or prospective creditor until such security for costs has been given as the court thinks reasonable, and until a *prima facie* case for winding up has been established to the satisfaction of the court; and

(*d*) in a case falling within subsection (3) of section 170 a winding-up petition may be presented by the Minister;

(*e*) a petition for winding up on the grounds mentioned in paragraph (*g*) of section 213 may be presented by any person entitled to bring proceedings for an order under section 205.

216.—(1) On hearing a winding-up petition, the court may dimiss it, or adjourn the hearing conditionally or unconditionally, or make any interim order, or any other order that it thinks fit, but the court shall not refuse to make a winding-up order on the ground only that the assets of the company have been mortgaged to an amount equal to or in excess of those assets, or that the company has no assets. Powers of court on hearing petition

(2) Where the petition is presented on the ground of default in delivering the statutory report to the registrar or in holding the statutory meeting, the court may—

(*a*) instead of making a winding-up order, direct that the statutory report shall be delivered or that a meeting shall be held; and (*b*) order the costs to be paid by any persons who, in the opinion of the court, are responsible for the default.

Power to stay or restrain proceedings against company

217.—At any time after the presentation of a winding-up petition, and before a winding-up order has been made, the company or any creditor or contributory may—

> (*a*) where any action or proceeding against the company is pending in the High Court or on appeal in the Supreme Court apply to the court in which the action or proceedings is pending for a stay of proceedings therein; and
>
> (*b*) where any other action or proceeding is pending against the company, apply to the High Court to restrain further proceedings in the action or proceeding;

and the court to which application is so made may, as the case may be, stay or restrain the proceedings accordingly on such terms and for such period as it thinks fit.

Avoidance of dispositions of property and transfer of shares after commencement of winding-up

218.—In a winding-up by the court, any disposition of the property of the company, including things in action, and any transfer of shares or alteration in the status of the members of the company, made after the commencement of the winding-up, shall, unless the court otherwise orders, be void.

Avoidance of executions against property of company

219.—Where any company is being wound up by the court, any attachment, sequestration, distress or execution put in force against the property or effects of the company after the commencement of the winding-up shall be void to all intents.

Commencement of Winding-up

Commencement of winding-up by the court

220.—(1) Where, before the presentation of a petition for the winding-up of a company by the court, a resolution has been passed by the company for voluntary winding-up, the winding-up of the company shall be deemed to have commenced at the time of the passing of the resolution, and unless the court, on proof of fraud or mistake, thinks fit to direct otherwise, all proceedings taken in the voluntary winding-up shall be deemed to have been validly taken.

(2) In any other case, the winding-up of a company by the court shall be deemed to commence at the time of the presentation of the petition for the winding-up.

Consequences of Winding-up Order

Copy of order for winding-up to be forwarded to registrar

221.—(1) On the making of a winding-up order, an office copy or the order must forthwith be delivered by the company, or by such person as the court may direct, to the registrar of companies for registration.

(2) If a company makes default in complying with subsection (1), the company and every officer of the company who is in default shall be liable to a fine not exceeding £25 and if any other person makes default in complying with subsection (1) such person shall be liable to a fine not exceeding £125.

Actions against company stayed on winding-up order

222.—When a winding-up order has been made or a provisional liquidator has been appointed, no action or proceeding shall be proceeded with or commenced against the company except by leave of the court and subject to such terms as the court may impose.

Effect of winding-up order

223.—An order for winding-up a company shall operate in favour of all the creditors and of all the contributories of the company, as if made on the joint petition of a creditor and of a contributory.

224.—(1) Where the court has made a winding-up order or appointed a provisional liquidator, there shall, unless the court thinks fit to order otherwise and so orders, be made out and filed in the court a statement as to the affairs of the company in the prescribed form, verified by affidavit, and showing the particulars of its assets, debts and liabilities, the names, residences and occupations of its creditors, the securities held by them respectively, the dates when the securities were respectively given, and such further or other information as may be prescribed or as the court may require. Statement of company's affairs to be filed in court

(2) The statement shall be filed and verified by one or more of the persons who are at the relevant date the directors and by the person who is at that date the secretary of the company or by such of the persons hereinafter mentioned in this subsection as the court may require to file and verify the statement, that is, persons—

(*a*) who are of have been officers of the company;

(*b*) who have taken part in the formation of the company at any time within one year before the relevant date;

(*c*) who are in the employment of the company, or have been in the employment of the company within the said year, and are in the opinion of the court, capable of giving the information required;

(*d*) who are or have been within the said year officers of or in the employment of a company which is, or within the said year was, an officer of the company to which the statement relates.

(3) The statement shall be filed within 21 days from the relevant date or within such extended time as the court may for special reasons appoint.

(4) Any person making or concurring in making the statement and affidavit rquired by this section shall be allowed, and shall be paid out of the assets of the company, such costs and expenses incurred in and about the preparation and making of the statement and affidavit as the court may allow.

(5) If any person, without reasonable excuse, makes default in complying with the requirements of this section, he shall be liable to a fine not exceeding £500.

(6) Any person who states in writing that he is a creditor or contributory of the company shall be entitled by himself or by his agent at all reasonable times, on payment of the prescribed fee, to inspect the statement filed in pursuance of this section, and to a copy thereof or extract therefrom.

(7) Any person untruthfuly so stating himself to be a creditor or contributory shall be guilty of a contempt of court and shall, on the application of the liquidator, be punishable accordingly.

(8) In this section, "the relevant date" means, in a case where a provisional liquidator is appointed, the date of his appointment, and, in a case where no such appointment is made, the date of the winding-up order.

Liquidators

225.—For the purpose of conducting the proceedings in winding-up a company and performing such duties in reference thereto as the court may impose, the court may appoint a liquidator or liquidators. Appointment of liquidator

226.—(1) Subject to subsection (2), the court may appoint a liquidatory provisionally at any time after the presentation of a winding-up petition and before the first appointment of liquidators. Appointment and powers of provisional liquidator

(2) Where a liquidator is provisionally appointed by the court, the court may limit and restrict his powers by the order appointing him.

Publication
by liquidator
of his
appointment

227.—(1) In a winding-up by the court, the liquidator shall within 21 days after his appointment, publish in *Iris Oifigiúil* a notice of his appointment and deliver to the registrar of companies an office copy of the court order appointing him.

(2) If the liquidator fails to comply with subsection (1), he shall be liable to a fine not exceeding £250.

General
provisions as
to liquidators

228.—The following provisions relating to liquidators shall have effect on a winding-up order being made—

(*a*) the court may determine whether any and what security is to be given by a liquidator on his appointment;

(*b*) a liquidator shall be described by the style of "the official liquidator" of the particular company in respect of which he is appointed and not by his individual name;

(*c*) a liquidator appointed by the court may resign or, on cause shown, be removed by the court;

(*d*) a person appointed liquidator shall receive such salary or remuneration by way of percentage or otherwise as the court may direct, and if more such persons than one are appointed liquidators, their remuneration shall be distributed among them in such proportions as the court directs;

(*e*) a vacancy in the office of a liquidator appointed by the court shall be filled by the court;

(*f*) if more than one liquidator is appointed by the court, the court shall declare whether any act by this Act required or authorised to be done by the liquidator is to be done by all or any one or more of the persons appointed;

(*g*) subject to section 300, the acts of a liquidator shall be valid notwithstanding any defects that may afterwards be discovered in his appointment or qualification.

Custody of
company's
property

229.—(1) Where a winding-up order has been made or where a provisional liquidator has been appointed, the liquidator or the provisional liquidator, as the case may be, shall take into his custody or under his control all the property and things in action to which the company is or appears to be entitled.

(2) If and so long as there is no liquidator, all the property of the company shall be deemed to be in the custody of the court.

Vesting of
property of
company in
liquidator

230.—Where a company is being wound up by the court, the court may, on the application of the liquidator, by order direct that all or any part of the property of whatsoever description belonging to the company or held by trustees on its behalf shall vest in the liquidator by his official name, and thereupon the property to which the order relates shall vest accordingly, and the liquidator may, after giving such indemnity, if any, as the court may direct, bring or defend in his official name any action or other legal proceeding which relates to that property or which it is necessary to bring or defend for the purpose of effectually winding-up the company and recovering its property.

Powers of
liquidator

231.—(1) The liquidator in a winding-up by the court shall have power, with the sanction of the court or of the committee of inspection—

(*a*) to bring or defend any action or other legal proceeding in the name and on behalf of the company;

(*b*) to carry on the business of the company so far as may be necessary for the beneficial winding-up thereof;

(*c*) to appoint a solicitor to assist him in the performance of his duties;

(*d*) to pay any classes of creditors in full;

(*e*) to make any compromise or arrangement with creditors or persons claiming to be creditors, or having or alleging themselves to have any claim present or future, certain or contingent, ascertained or sounding only in damages against the company, or whereby the company may be rendered liable;

(*f*) to compromise all calls and liabilities to calls, debts and liabilities capable of resulting in debts, and all claims, present or future, certain or contingent, ascertained or sounding only in damages, subsisting or supposed to subsist between the company and a contributory or alleged contributory or other debtor or person apprehending liability to the company, and all questions in any way relating to or affecting the assets or winding-up of the company, on such terms as may be agreed, and take any security for the discharge of any such call, debt, liability or claim, and give a complete discharge in respect thereof.

(1A) (*a*) The liquidator of a company shall not sell by private contract a non-cash asset of the requisite value to a person who is, or who, within three years prior to the date of commencement of the winding-up, has been, an officer of the company unless the liquidator has given at least 14 days' notice of his intention to do so to all creditors of the company who are known to him or who have been intimated to him;

(*b*) In this subsection—

(i) 'non-cash asset' and 'requistive value' have the meanings assigned to them by *section 29* of the *Companies Act, 1990*, and

(ii) 'officer' includes a person connected, within the meaning of *section 26* of the *Companies Act, 1990*, with a director, and a shadow director.

(2) The liquidator in a winding-up by the court shall have power—

(*a*) to sell the real and personal property and things in action of the company by public auction or private contract, with power to transfer the whole thereof to any person or company or to sell the same in lots and for the purpose of selling the company's land or any part thereof to carry out such sales by fee farm grant, sub fee farm grant, lease, sub-lease or otherwise, and to sell any rent reserved on any such grant or any reversion expectant upon the determination of any such lease;

(*b*) to do all acts and to execute, in the name and on behalf of the company, all deeds, receipts and other documents, and for that purpose to use, when necessary, the company's seal;

(*c*) where any contributory has been adjudged bankrupt or has presented a petition for arrangement with his creditors in pursuance of the Bankruptcy Acts, to prove, rank and claim in the bankruptcy or arrangement for any balance against his estate, and to receive dividends in the bankruptcy or arrangement in respect of that balance, as a separate debt due from the bankrupt or arranging debtor, and rateably with the other separate creditors;

(*d*) to draw, accept, make and endorse any bill of exchange or promissory note in the name and on behalf of the company, with the same effect with respect to the liability of the company as if the bill or note had been drawn, accepted, made or endorsed by or on behalf of the company in the course of its business;

(*e*) to raise on the security of the assets of the company any money requisite;

(*f*) to take out in his official name letters of administration to any deceased contributory and to do in his official name any other act necessary for obtaining payment of any money due from a contributory or his estate which cannot be conveniently done in the name of the company, and in all such cases the money due shall, for the purpose of enabling the liquidator to take out the letters of administration or recover the money, be deemed to be due to the liquidator himself;

(*g*) to give security for costs in any proceedings commenced by the company or by him in the name of the company;

(*h*) to appoint an agent to do any business which the liquidator is unable to do himself;

(*i*) to do all such things as may be necessary for winding-up the affairs of the company and distributing its assets.

(3) The exercise by the liquidator in a winding-up by the court of the powers conferred by this section shall be subject to the control of the court, and any creditor or contributory may apply to the court in relation to any exercise or proposed exercise of any of those powers.

(4) The court may provide by any order that the liquidator may, where there is no committee of inspection, exercise any of the powers mentioned in paragraph (*a*) or paragraph (*b*) of subsection (1) without the sanction or intervention of the court.

Committes of Inspection

Meetings of creditors and contributories to determine whether committee of inspection should be appointed
232.—(1) When a winding-up order has been made by the court, the liquidator shall if the court by order so directs summon a meeting of the creditors of the company or separate meetings of the creditors and contributories of the company for the purpose of determining whether or not an application is to be made to the court for the appointment of a committee of inspection to act with the liquidator and who are to be the members of the committee if appointed.

(2) The court may make any appointment and order required to give effect to any such determination, and if there is a difference between the determinations of the meetings of the creditors and contributories in respect of the matters aforesaid, the court shall decide the difference and make such order thereon as the court may think fit.

Constitution and proceedings of committee of inspection
233.—(1) A committee of inspection appointed in pursuance of this Act shall consist of creditors and contributories of the company or persons holding general powers of attorney from creditors or contributories in such proportions as may be agreed on by the meetings of creditors and contributories or as, in case of difference, may be determined by the court.

(2) The committee shall meet at such times as they from time to time appoint, and the liquidator or any member of the committee may also call a meeting of the committee as and when he thinks necessary.

(3) The committee may act by a majority of their members present at a meeting but shall not act unless a majority of the committee are present.

(4) A member of the committee may resign by notice in writing signed by him and delivered to the liquidator.

(5) If a member of the committee becomes bankrupt or compounds or arranges with his creditors or is absent from 5 consecutive meetings of the committee without the leave of those members who, together with himself, represent the creditors or contributories, as the case may be, his office shall thereupon become vacant.

(6) A member of the committee may be removed by an ordinary resolution at a meeting of creditors, if he represents creditors, or of contributories, if he represents contributories, of which 7 days' notice has been given, stating the object of the meeting.

(7) Subject to subsection (8), on a vacancy occurring in the committee the liquidator shall forthwith summon a meeting of creditors or of contributories, as the case may require, to fill the vacancy, and the meeting may, by resolution, reappoint the same or appoint another person, qualified under subsection (1) to be a member of the committee, to fill the vacancy.

(8) If the liquidator, having regard to the position in the winding-up, is of opinion, that it is unnecessary for a vacancy occurring in the committee to be filled, he may apply to the court and the court may make an order that the vacancy shall not be filled or shall not be filled except in such circumstances as may be specified in the order.

(9) The continuing members of the committee, if not less than two, may act notwithstanding any vacancy in the committee.

General Powers of Court in case of Winding-Up by the Court

234.—(1) The court may at any time after an order for winding-up, on the applicaiton of the liquidator or any creditor or contributory and on proof to the satisfaction of the court that the order for winding-up ought to be annulled, make an order annulling the order for winding-up on such terms and conditions as the court thinks fit. Power to annul order for winding-up or to stay winding-up

(2) The court may at any time after an order for winding-up, on the application of the liquidator or any creditor or contributory, and on proof to the satisfaction of the court that all proceedings in relation to the winding-up ought to be styled, make an order staying the proceedings, either altogether or for a limited time, on such terms and conditions as the court thinks fit.

(3) On any application under this section the court may, before making an order, require the liquidator to furnish to the court a report relating to any facts or matters which are in his opinion relevant to the application.

(4) An office copy of every order made under this section shall forthwith be forwarded by the company, or by such person as the court may direct, to the registrar of companies for registration.

(5) If a company makes default in complying with subsection (4), the company and every officer of the company who is in default shall be liable to a fine not exceeding £25 and if any other person makes default in complying with subjection (4) such person shall be liable to a fine not exceeding £125.

235.—(1) Subject to subsection (2), as soon as may be after making a winding-up order, the court shall settle a list of contributories, with power to rectify the register of members, in all cases where rectification is required in pursuance of this Act, and shall cause the assets of the company to be collected and applied in discharge of its liabilities. Settlement of list of contributories and application of assets

(2) Where it appears to the court that it will not be necessary to make calls on or adjust the rights of contributories, the court may dispense with the settlement of a list of contributories.

(3) In settling the list of contributories, the court shall distinguish between persons who are contributories in their own right and persons who are contributories as being representatives of or liable for the debts of others.

236.—The court may, at any time after making a winding-up order, require any contributory for the time being on the list of contributories and any trustee, receiver, banker, agent or officer of the company to pay, deliver, convey, surrender or transfer forthwith, or within such time as the court directs, to the liquidator any money, property or books and papers in his hands to which the company is *prima facie* entitled. Delivery of property of company to liquidator

Payment of debts due by contributory to the company and extent to which set-off allowed

237.—(1) The court may, at any time after making a winding-up order, make an order on any contributory for the time being on the list of contributories, to pay in manner directed by the order, any money due from him or from the estate of the person whom he represents to the company, exclusive of any money payable by him or the estate by virtue and any call in pursuance of this Act.

(2) The court in making such an order may—

> (*a*) In the case of an unlimited company, allow to the contributory by way of set-off any money due to him or to the estate which he represents from the company on any independent dealing or contract with the company, but not any money due to him as a member of the company in respect of any dividend or profit; and

> (*b*) in the case of a limited company, make to any director whose liability is unlimited or to his estate a like allowance.

(3) In the case of any company, whether limited or unlimited, when all the creditors are paid in full, any money due on any amount whatever to a contributory from the company may be allowed to him by way of set-off against any subsequent call.

Power of court to make calls

238.—(1) The court may, at any time after making a winding-up order, and either before or after it has ascertained the sufficiency of the assets of the company, make calls on all or any of the contributories for the time being on the list of contributories to the extent of their liability, for payment of any money which the court considers necessary to satisfy the debts and liabilities of the company, and the costs, charges and expenses of winding-up, and for the adjustment of the rights of the contributories among themselves, and make an order for payment of any calls so made.

(2) In making a call, the court may take into consideration that some of the contributories may partly or wholly fail to pay the call.

Payment into bank of moneys due to company

239.—(1) The court may order any contributory, purchaser or other person from whom money is due to the company to pay the amount due into such bank as the court may appoint to the account of the liquidator instead of to the liquidator, and any such order may be enforced in like manner as if it had directed payment to the liquidator.

(2) All moneys and secuities paid or delivered into any such bank as aforesaid in the event of a winding-up by the court shall be subject in all respects to the orders of the court.

Order on contributory to be conclusive evidence

240.—(1) An order made by the court on a contributory shall, subject to any right of appeal, be conclusive evidence that the money, if any, thereby appearing to be due or ordered to be paid is due.

(2) All other relevant matters stated in the order shall be taken to be truly stated as against all persons and in all proceedings.

Power to exclude creditors not proving in time

241.—The court may fix a time or times within which creditors are to prove their debts or claims or to be excluded from the benefit of any distribution made before those debts are proved.

Adjustment of rights of contributories

242.—The court shall adjust the rights of the contributories among themselves and distribute any surplus among the persons entitled thereto.

Inspection of books by creditors and contributories

243.—(1) The court may, at any time after making a winding-up order, make such order for inspection of the books and papers of the company by creditors and contributories as the court thinks just, and any books and papers in the possession of the company may be inspected by creditors or contributories accordingly, but not further or otherwise.

(2) Nothing in this section shall be taken as excluding or restricting any statutory rights of a Minister of the Government or a person acting under the authority of a Minister of the Government.

244.—The court may, in the event of the assets being insufficient to satisfy the liabilities, make an order as to the payment out of the assets of the costs, charges and expenses incurred in the winding-up in such order of priority as the court thinks just.

244A.—Where the court has appointed a provisional liquidator or a company is being wound up by the court or by means of a creditors' winding-up, no person shall be entitled as against the liquidator or provisional liquidator to withhold possession of any deed, instrument, or other document belonging to the company, or the book of account, receipt, bills, invoices, or other papers of a like nature relating to the accounts or trade, dealings or business of the company, or to claim any lien thereon provided that—

    (*a*) where a mortgage, charge or pledge has been created by the deposit of any such document or paper with a person, the production of the document or paper to the liquidator or provisional liquidator by the person shall be without prejudice to the person's rights under the mortgage, charge or pledge (other than any right to possession of the document or paper),

    (*b*) where by virtue of this section a liquidator or provisional liquidator has possession of any document or papers of a receiver or that a receiver is entitled to examine, the liquidator or provisional liquidator shall, unless the court otherwise orders, made the document or papers available for inspection by the receiver at all reasonable times.

245.—(1) The court may, at any time after the appointment of a provisional liquidator or the making of a winding-up order, summon before it any officer of the company or person known or suspected to have in his possession any property of the company or supposed to be indebted to the company, or any person whom the court deems capable of giving information relating to the promotion, formation, trade, dealings, affairs or property of the company.

(2) The court may examine such person on oath concerning the matters aforesaid, either by word of mouth on or written interrogatories, and may reduce his answers to writing and require him to sign them.

(3) The court may require such person to produce any accounting records, instrument, or other document or paper relating to the company that are in his custody or power.

(4) The court may, before the examination takes place, require such person to place before it a statement, in such form as the court may direct, of any transactions between him and the company of a type or class which the court may specify.

(5) If, in the opinion of the court, it is just and equitable to do so, it may direct that the costs of the examination be paid by the person examined.

(6) A person who is examined under this section shall not be entitled to refuse to answer any question put to him on the ground that his answer might incriminate him but none of the answers of such person shall be admissible in evidence against him in any other proceedings, civil or criminal, except in the case of any criminal proceedings for perjury in respect of any such answer.

(7) If a person without reasonable excuse fails at any time to attend his examination under this section, he shall be guilty of contempt of court and liable to be punished accordingly.

(8) In a case where a person without reasonable excuse fails at any time to attend his examination under this section or there are reasonable grounds for believing that a person

has absconded, or is about to abscond, with a view to avoiding or delaying his examination under this section, the court may cause that person to be arrested and his books and documents and moveable personal property to be seized and him and them to be detained until such time as the court may order.

Order for payment or delivery of property against person examined under section 245 of Principal Act

245A.—If in the course of an examination under section 245 it appears to the court that any person being examined—

      (*a*) is indebted to the company, or

      (*b*) has in his possession or control any money, property or books and papers of the company,

the court may order such person—

      (i) to pay to the liquidator the amount of the debt or any part thereof, or

      (ii) to pay, deliver, convey, surrender or transfer to the liquidator such money, property or books and papers or any part thereof,

as the case may be, at such time and in such manner and on such terms as the court may direct.

Attendance of officers of company at meetings

246.—In the case of a winding-up by the court, the court shall have power to require the attendance of any officer of the company at any meeting of creditors or of contributories or of a committee of inspection for the purpose of giving information as to the trade, dealings, affairs or property of the company.

Power to arrest absconding contributory

247.—The court, at any time either before or after making a winding-up order, on proof of probable cause for believing that a contributory is about to quit the State or otherwise to abscond or to remove or conceal any of his property for the purpose of evading payment of calls or of avoiding examination about the affairs of the company, may cause the contributory to be arrested, and his books and papers and movable personal property to be seized and him and them to be detained until such time as the court may order.

Powers of court cumulative

248.—Any powers of this Act conferred on the court shall be in addition to and not in restriction of any existing powers of instituting proceedings against any contributory or debtor of the company or the estate of any contributory or debtor, for the recovery of any call or other sums.

Dissolution of company

249.—(1) When the affairs of a company have been completely wound up, the court, if the liquidator makes an application in that behalf, shall make an order that the company be dissolved from the date of the order, and the company shall be dissolved accordingly.

(2) An office copy of the order shall within 21 days from the date thereof be forwarded by the liquidator to the registrar of companies for registration.

(3) If the liquidator makes default in complying with the requirements of this section, he shall be liable to a fine not exceeding £250.

Enforcement of Orders made in Winding-Up by Courts outside the State

Enforcement of orders made in winding-up by courts outside the State

250.—(1) Any order made by a court of any country recognised for the purposes of this section and made for or in the course of winding-up a company may be enforced by the High Court in the same manner in all respects as if the order had been made by the High Court.

(2) When an application is made to the High Court under this section, an office copy of any order sought to be enforced shall be sufficient evidence of the order.

(3) In this section, "company" means a body corporate incorporated outside the State, and "recognised" means recognised by order made by the Minister.

(iii) VOLUNTARY WINDING UP

Resolutions for and Commencement of Voluntary Winding-Up

251.—(1) A company may be wound up voluntarily—

    (*a*) when the period, if any, fixed for the duration of the company by the articles expires, or the event, if any, occurs, on the occurrence of which the articles provide that the company is to be dissolved, and the company in general meeting has passed a resolution that the company be wound up voluntarily;

    (*b*) if the company resolves by special resolution that the company be would up voluntarily;

    (*c*) if the company in general meeting resolves that it cannot by reason of its liabilities continue its business, and that it be wound up voluntarily.

(2) In this Act, "a resolution for voluntary winding-up" means a resolution passed under any paragraph of subsection (1).

Circumstances in which company may be wound up voluntarily

252.—(1) When a company has passed a resolution for voluntary winding-up, it shall, within 14 days after the passing of the resolution, give notice of the resolution by advertisement in *Iris Oifigiúil.*

(2) If default is made in complying with this section, the company and every officer of the company who is in default shall be liable to a fine not exceeding £125 and for the purposes of this subsection, the liquidator of the company shall be deemed to be an officer of the company.

Publication of resolution to wind up voluntarily

253.—A voluntary winding-up shall be deemed to commence at the time of the passing of the resolution for voluntary winding-up.

Commencement of voluntary winding-up

Consequences of Voluntary Winding-Up

254.—In case of a voluntary winding-up, the company shall, from the commencement of the winding-up, cease to carry on its business, except so far as may be required for the beneficial winding-up thereof, so, however, that the corporate state and corporate powers of the company shall, notwithstanding anything to the contrary in its articles, continue until it is dissolved.

Effect of voluntary winding-up on business and status of company

255.—Any transfer of shares, not being a transfer made to or with the sanction of the liquidator, and any alteration in the status of the members of the company, made after the commencement of a voluntary winding-up, shall be void.

Avoidance of transfers of shares after commencement of voluntary winding-up

256—(1) Where it is proposed to wind up a company voluntarily, the directors of the company or, in the case of a company having more than two directors, the majority of the directors may, at a meeting of the directors, make a statutory declaration to the effect that they have made a full inquiry into the affairs of the company, and that having done so, they have formed the opinion that the company will be able to pay its debts in full within such period not exceeding 12 months from the commencement of the winding-up as may be specified in the declaration.

Statutory declaration of solvency in case of proposal to wind-up voluntarily

(2) A declaration made as aforesaid shall have no effect for the purposes of this Act unless—

    (*a*) it is made within the 28 days immediately preceding the date of the passing of the resolution for winding-up the company and delivered to the registrar of companies not later than the date of the delivery to the registrar, in accordance with the provision of section 143, a copy of the resolution for winding-up the company;

(*b*) it embodies a statement of the company's assets and liabilities as at the latest practicable date before the making of the declaration and in any event at a date not more than three months before the making of the declaration;

(*c*) a report made by an independent person in accordance with the provisions of this section is attached thereto;

(*d*) it embodies a statement by the independent person referred to in paragraph (*c*) that he has given and has not withdrawn his written consent to the issue of the declaration with the report attached thereto; and

(*e*) a copy of the declaration is attached to the notice issued by the company of the general meeting at which it is intended to propose a resolution for voluntary winding-up under paragraph (*a*) or (*b*) of section 251(1).

(3) The report referred to in paragraph (*c*) of subsection (2) shall be made by an independent person, that is to say, a person qualified at the time of the report to be appointed, or to continue to be, auditor of the company.

(4) The report shall state whether, in his opinion and to the best of his information and according to the explanations given to him—

(*a*) the opinion of the directors referred to in subsection (1), and

(*b*) the statement of the company's assets and liabilities embodied in the said declaration,

are reasonable.

(5) If within 28 days after the resolution for voluntary winding-up has been advertised under subsection (1) of section 252, a creditor applies to the court for an order under this subsection, and the court is satisfied that such creditor together with any creditors supporting him in his application represents one-fifth at least in number or value of the creditors of the company, and the court is of opinion that it is unlikely that the company will be able to pay its debts within the period specified in the declaration, the court may order that all the provisions of this Act relating to a credtiors' voluntary winding-up shall apply to the winding-up.

(6) If the court orders that all the provisions of this Act in relation to a creditors' voluntary winding-up shall apply to the winding-up, the person who held the office of liquidator immediately prior to the making of the order or, if no liquidator is acting, the company shall within 21 days after the making of the order, deliver an office copy of such order to the registrar of companies.

(7) If default is made in complying with subsection (6), any person who is in default shall be liable to a fine not exceeding £1,000.

(8) Where a statutory declaration is made under this section and it is subsequently proved to the satisfaction of the court that the company is unable to pay its debts, the court on the application of the liquidator or any creditor or contributory of the company may, if it thinks proper to do so, declare that any director who was a party to the declaration without having reasonable grounds for the opinion that the company would be able to pay its debts in full within the period specified in the declaration shall be personally responsible, without limitation of liability, for all or any of the debts or other liabilities of the company as the court may direct.

(9) Where a company's debts are not paid or provided for in full within the period stated in the declaration of solvency, it shall for the purposes of subsection (8) be presumed, until the contrary is shown, that the director did not have reasonable grounds for his opinion.

(10) Where the court makes a declaration under subsection (8), it may give such further directions as it thinks proper for the purpose of giving effect to that declaration.

(11) A winding up in the case of which a declaration has been made and delivered in accordance with this section is in this Act referred to as 'a members' voluntary winding-up' and a voluntary winding-up in the case of which a declaration has not been made and delivered as aforesaid or in the case of which an order is made under subsection (5) or in the case to which section 261(3) applies is in this Act referred to as 'a creditors' voluntary winding-up'.

Provisions applicable to a Members' Voluntary Winding-Up

257.—Sections 258 to 264 shall, subject to the last-mentioned section, apply to a members' voluntary winding-up.

258.—(1) The company in general meeting shall appoint one or more liquidators for the purpose of winding-up the affairs and distributing the assets of the company, and may fix the remuneration to be paid to him or them.

(2) On the appointment of a liquidator all the powers of the directors shall cease, except so far as the company in general meeting or the liquidator sanctions the continuance thereof.

259.—(1) If a vacancy occurs by death resignation or otherwise in the office of liquidator appointed by the company, the company in general meeting may fill the vacancy.

(2) For that purpose a general meeting may be convened by any contributory or, if there are more liquidators than one, by the continuing liquidators.

(3) The meeting shall be held in manner provided by this Act or by the articles or in such manner as may, on application by any contributory or by the continuing liquidators, be determined by the court.

260.—(1) Where a company is proposed to be, or is in course of being, wound up voluntarily, and the whole or part of its business or property is proposed to be transferred or sold to another company, whether a company within the meaning of this Act or not (in this section referred to as "the transferee company"), the liquidator of the first-mentioned company (in this section referred to as "the transferor company") may, with the sanction of a special resolution of that company, conferring either a general authority on the liquidator or an authority in respect of any particular arrangement, receive in compensation or part compensation for the transfer or sale, shares, policies of other like interests in the transferee company for distribution among the members of the transferor company, or may enter into any other arrangement whereby the members of the transferor company may, in lieu of receiving cash, shares, policies or other like interests, or in addition thereto, participate in the profits of or receive any other benefit from the transferee company.

(2) Any sale or arrangement in pursuance of this section shall be binding on the members of the transferror company.

(3) If the voting rights conferred by any shares in the company were not cast in favour of the special resolution and the holder of those shares expresses his dissent from the special resolution in writing addressed to the liquidator and left at the registered office of the company within 7 days after the passing of the special resolution, he may require the liquidator either to abstain from carrying the resolution into effect or to purchase that part of his interest which those shares represent at a price to be determined by agreement or by arbitration in manner provided by this section.

(4) If the liquidator elects to purchase the member's interest, the purchase money must be paid before the company is dissolved and, unless otherwise provided for, shall be deemed to be and shall be paid as part of the costs, charges and expenses of the winding-up.

[Margin notes:]

Provisions applicable to a members' voluntary winding-up

Power of company to appoint and fix remuneration of liquidators

Power to fill vacancy in office of liquidator

Power of liquidator to accept shares as consideration for sale of property to company

(5) A special resolution shall not be invalid for the purposes of this section by reason that it is passed before or concurrently with a resolution for voluntary winding-up or for appointing liquidators, but, if an order is made within a year for winding-up the company by the court, the special resolution shall not be valid unless sanctioned by the court.

(6) For the purposes of an arbitration under this section, the provisions of the Companies Clauses Consolidation Act, 1845, relating to the settlement of disputes by arbitration, shall be incorporated with this Act, and in the construction of those provisions this Act shall be deemed to be the special Act, and "the company" shall mean the transferor company, and any appointment by the said incorporated provisions directed to be made under the hand of the secretary or any two of the directors may be made under the hand of the liquidator, or, if there is more than one liquidator, then of any two or more of the liquidators.

Duty of liquidator to call creditors' meeting if he is of opinion that company is unable to pay its debts

261.—(1) If the liquidator is at any time of the opinion that the company will not be able to pay its debt in full within the period stated in the declaration under section 256 he shall—

    (*a*) summon a meeting of creditors for a day not later than the fourteenth day after the day on which he formed that opinion;

    (*b*) send notices of the creditors' meeting to the creditors by post not less than seven days before the day on which that meeting is to be held;

    (*c*) cause notice of the creditors' meeting to be advertised, at least ten days before the date of the meeting, once in *Iris Oifigiúil* and once at least in two daily newspapers circulating in the locality in which the company's principal place of business in the State was situated during the relevant period; and

    (*d*) during the period before the day on which the creditors' meeting is to be held, furnish creditors free of charge with such information concerning the affairs of the company as they may reasonably require;

and the notice of the creditors' meeting shall state the duty imposed by paragraph (*d*).

(2) The liquidator shall also—

    (*a*) make out a statement in the prescribed form as to the affairs of the company, including a statement of the company's assets and liabilities, a list of the outstanding creditors and the estimated amount of their claims;

    (*b*) lay that statement before the creditors' meeting; and

    (*c*) attend and preside at that meeting.

(3) As from the day on which the creditors' meeting is held under this section, the Companies Act shall have effect as if—

    (*a*) without prejudice to the powers of the court under section 256, the directors' declaration under that section had not been made; and

    (*b*) the creditors' meeting and the company meetings at which it was resolved that the company be wound up voluntarily were the meetings mentioned in section 266;

and accordingly, the winding-up shall become a creditors' voluntary winding-up and any appointment made or committee established by the creditors' meeting shall be deemed to have been made or established by the creditors' meeting so mentioned.

(4) The appointment of a liquidator at a meeting called under this section shall not, subject to subsection (5), affect the validity of any action previously taken by the liquidator appointed by the members of the company.

(5) Where the creditors appoint a liquidator at a meeting called under this section and there is a dispute as to any or all of the costs, charges or expenses incurred by, including the remuneration of, the liquidator appoitned by the members of the company, the liquidator appointed by the creditors, or any creditor, may apply to the court to determine the dispute and the court may, on such application, make such orders as it deems fit.

(6) Nothing in this section shall be deemed to take away any right in this Act of any person to present a petition to the court for the winding-up of a company.

(7) If the liquidator fails to comply with subsection (1) he shall be liable to a fine.

262.—(1) Subject to section 264, in the event of the winding-up continuing for more than one year, the liquidator shall summon a general meeting of the company at the end of the first year from the commencement of the winding-up, and of each succeeding year, or at the first convenient date within 3 months from the end of the year and shall lay before the meeting an account of his acts and dealings and of the conduct of the winding-up during the preceding year and shall within 7 days after such meeting send a copy of that account to the registrar. *Duty of liquidator to call general meeting at end of each year*

(2) If the liquidator fails to comply with this section, he shall be liable to a fine not exceeding £250.

263.—(1) Subject to section 264, as soon as the affairs of the company are fully wound up, the liquidator shall make up an account of the winding-up showing how the winding-up has been conducted and the property of the company has been disposed of, and thereupon shall call a general meeting of the company for the purpose of laying before it the account and giving any explanation thereof. *Final meeting and dissolution*

(2) The meeting shall be called by advertisement in 2 daily newspapers circulating in the district where the registered office of the company is situate, specifying the time, place and object thereof, and published 28 days at least before the meeting.

(3) Within one week after the meeting, the liquidator shall send to the registrar of companies a copy of the account, and shall make a return to him of the holding of the meeting and of its date, and if the copy is not sent or the return is not made in accordance with this subsection, the liquidator shall be liable to a fine not exceeding £500, so, however, that if a quorum is not present at the meeting, the liquidator shall, in lieu of the return hereinbefore mentioned, made a return that the meeting was duly summoned and that no quorum was present thereat, and upon such a return being made, the provisions of this subsection as to the making of the return shall be deemed to have been complied with.

(4) Subject to subsection (5), the registrar on receiving the account and either of the returns hereinbefore mentioned shall forthwith register them, and on the expiration of 3 months from the registration of the return the company shall be deemed to be dissolved.

(5) The court may, on the application of the liquidator or of any other person who appears to the court to be interested, make an order deferring the date at which the dissolution of the company is to take effect for such time as the court thinks fit.

(6) It shall be the duty of the person on whose application an order of the court under this section is made, within 14 days after the making of the order, to deliver to the registrar an office copy of the order for registration, and if that person fails so to do he shall be liable to a fine not exceeding £25.

(7) If the liquidator fails to call a general meeting of the company as required by this section, he shall be liable to a fine not exceeding £250.

264.—(1) Subject to section (2), where section 261 has effect, sections 272 and 273 shall apply to the winding-up to the exclusion of section 262 and 263, as if the winding-up were a creditors' voluntary winding-up and not a members' voluntary winding-up. *Alternative provisions as to annual and final meetings if liquidator is of opinion that company unable to pay its debts*

(2) The liquidator shall not be required to summon a meeting of creditors under section 272 at the end of the first year from the commencement of the winding-up, unless the meeting held under section 261 is held more than 3 months before the end of that year.

Provisions
applicable to
a creditors'
voluntary
winding-up

Meeting of
creditors

Provisions applicable to a Creditors' Voluntary Winding-Up

265.—Sections 266 to 273 shall apply in relation to a creditors' voluntary winding-up.

266.—(1) The company shall cause a meeting of the creditors of the company to be summoned for the day, or the day next following the day, on which there is to be held the meeting at which the resolution for voluntary winding-up is to be proposed, and shall cause the notices of the said meetings of creditors to be sent by post to the creditors at least 10 days before the date of the said meeting of the company.

(2) The company shall cause notice of the meeting of the creditors to be advertised once at least in 2 daily newspapers circulating in the district where the registered office or principal place of business of the company is situate at least ten days before the date of the meeting.

(3) The directors of the company shall—

(*a*) cause a full statement of the position of the company's affairs, together with a list of the creditors of the company and the estimated amount of their claims to be laid before the meeting of the creditors to be held as aforesaid; and

(*b*) appoint one of their number to preside at the said meeting.

(4) It shall be the duty of the director appointed to preside at the meeting of creditors to attend the meeting and preside threat.

(5) If the meeting of the company at which the resolution for voluntay winding-up is to be proposed is adjourned and the resolution is passed at an adjourned meeting, any resolution passed at the meeting of the creditors held in pursuance of subsection (1) shall have effect as if it had been passed immediately after the passing of the resolution for winding-up the company.

(6) If default is made—

(*a*) by the company in complying with subsections (1) and (2);

(*b*) by the directors of the company in complying with subsection (3);

(*c*) by any director of the company in complying with subsection (4);

the company, directors or director, as the case may be, shall be liable to a fine not exceeding £500, and in the case of default by the company, every officer of the company who is in default shall be liable to the like penalty.

Appointment
of liquidator

267.—(1) Subject to subsection (2), the creditors and the company at their respective meetings mentioned in section 266 may nominate a person to be liquidator for the purpose of winding-up the affairs and distributing the assets of the company, and if the creditors and the company nominate different persons, the person nominated by the creditors shall be liquidator, and if no person is nominated by the creditors, the person, if any, nominated by the company shall be liquidator.

(2) Where different persons are nominated as liquidator, any director, member or creditor of the company may, within 14 days after the date on which the nomination was made by the creditors, apply to the court for an order either directing that the person nominated as liquidator by the company shall be liquidator instead of or jointly with the person nominated by the creditors, or appointing some other person to be liquidator instead of the person appointed by the creditors.

Appointment
of committee
of inspection

268.—(1) Subject to subsection (2), the creditors at the meeting to be held in pursuance of section 266 or at any subsequent meeting may, if they think fit, appoint a committee of inspection consisting of not more than five persons, and, if such committee is appointed the company may, either at the meeting at which the resolution for voluntary winding-up is passed or at any time subsequently in general meeting, appoint three persons to act as members of the committee, provided that the number of members of the committee shall not at any time exceed eight.

(2) The creditors may, it they think fit, resolve that all or any of the persons so appointed by the company ought not to be members of the committee of inspection, and if the creditors so resolve, the persons mentioned in the resolution shall not, unless the court otherwise directs, be qualified to act as members of the committee, and on any application to the court under this subsection the court may, if it thinks fit, appoint other persons to act as such members in place of the persons mentioned in the resolution.

(3) Subject to subsections (1) and (2), and to rules of court, section 233 (except subsection (1)) shall apply to a committee of inspection appointed under this section as it applies to a committee of inspection in a winding-up by the court.

269.—(1) The committee of inspection, or if there is no such committee, the creditors, may fix the remuneration to be paid to the liquidator or liquidators. *Fixing of liquidators' remunderation and cesser of directors' powers*

(2) Within 28 days after the remuneration to be paid to the liquidator or liquidators has been fixed by the committee of inspection or by the creditors, any creditor or contributory who alleges that such remuneration is excessive may apply to the court to fix the remuneration to be paid to the liquidator or liquidators.

(3) On the appointment of a liquidator, all the powers of the directors shall cease, except so far as the committee of inspection or, if there is no such committee, the creditors, sanction the continuance thereof.

270.—If a vacancy occurs by death, resignation of otherwise in the office of a liquidator, other than a liquidator appointed by, or by the direction of, the court, the creditors may fill the vacancy. *Power to fill vacancy in office of liquidator*

271.—Section 260 shall apply in the case of a creditor's voluntary winding-up as in the case of a members' voluntary winding-up, with the modification that the powers of the liquidator under that section shall not be exercised except with the sanction either of the court or of the committee of inspection. *Application of section 260 to a creditors' voluntary winding-up*

272.—(1) In the event of the winding-up continuing for more than one year, the liquidator shall summon a general meeting of the company and a meeting of the creditors at the end of the first year after the commencement of the winding-up, and of each succeeding year, or at the first convenient date within 3 months from the end of the year, and shall lay before the meetings an account of his acts and dealings and of the conduct of the winding-up during the preceding year and shall within 7 days after the later of such meetings send a copy of that account to the registrar. *Duty of liquidator to call meetings of company and of creditors at end of each year*

(2) If the liquidator fails to comply with this section, he shall be liable to a fine not exceeding £250.

273.—(1) As soon as the affairs of the company are fully wound up, the liquidator shall make up an account of the winding-up, showing how the winding-up has been conducted and the property of the company has been disposed of, and thereupon shall call a general meeting of the company and a meeting of the creditors for the purpose of laying the account before the meetings and giving any explanation thereof. *Final meeting and dissolution*

(2) Each such meeting shall be called by advertisement in 23 daily newspapers circulating in the district where the registered office of the company is situate, specifying the time, place and object thereof, and published 28 days at least before the meeting.

(3) Within one week after the date of the meetings, or if the meetings are not held on the same date, after the date of the later meeting, the liquidator shall send to the registrar of companies a copy of the account, and shall make a return to him of the holding of the meetings

and their dates, and if the copy is not sent or the return is not made in accordance with this subsection, the liquidator shall be liable to a fine not exceeding £250, so, however, that if a quorum is not present at either such meeting, the liquidator shall, in lieu of the return hereinbefore mentioned, make a return that the meeting was duly summoned and that no quorum was present thereat, and upon such a return being made, the provisions of this subsection as to the making of the return shall, in respect of that meeting, be deemed to have been complied with.

(4) Subject to subsection (5), the registrar on receiving the account and, in respect of each such meeting, either of the returns hereinbefore mentioned, shall forthwith register them, and on the expiration of 3 months from the registration thereof the company shall be deemed to be dissolved.

(5) The court may, on the application of the liquidator or of any other person who appears to the court to be interested, make an order deferring the date at which the dissolution of the company is to take effect for such time as the court thinks fit.

(6) It shall be the duty of the person on whose application an order of the court under this section is made, within 14 days after the making of the order, to deliver to the registrar an office copy of the order for registration, and if that person fails so to do, he shall be liable to a fine not exceeding £250.

(7) If the liquidator fails to call a general meeting of the company or a meeting of the creditors as required by this section, he shall be liable to a fine not exceeding £250.

Provisions applicable to every Voluntary Winding-Up

Provisions applicable to every voluntary winding-up

274.—Sections 275 to 282 shall apply to every voluntary winding-up whether a members' or a creditors' winding-up.

Distribution of porperty of company

275.—(1) Subject to the provisions of this Act as to preferential payments, the property of a company on its winding-up—

    (*a*) shall, subject to subsection (2), be applied in satisfaction of its liabilities *pari passu*, and

    (*b*) shall, subject to such application, and unless the articles otherwise provide, be disturbed among the members according to their rights and interests in the company.

(2) Nothing in paragraph (*a*) of subsection (1) shall in any way affect any rights or obligations of the company or any other person arising as a result of any agreement entered into (whether before or after the commencement of *section 132* of the *Companies Act, 1990*) by any person under which any particular liability of the company to any general creditor is postponed in favour of or subordinated to the rights or claims of any other person to whom the company may be in any way liable.

(2) In subsection (2)—

"liability" includes a contingent liability; and

"person" includes a class of persons.

Power and duties of liquidator in voluntary winding-up

276.—(1) The liquidator may—

    (*a*) in the case of a members' voluntary winding-up, with the sanction of a special resolution of the company, and, in the case of a creditors' voluntary winding-up, with the sanction of the court or the committee of inspection or (if there is no such committee) a meeting of the creditors, exercise any of the powers given by paragraph (*d*), (*e*) and (*f*) of subsection (1) of section 231 to a liquidator in a winding-up by the court;

(*b*) without sanction, exercise any of the other powers by this Act given to the liquidator in a winding-up by the court;

(*c*) exercise the power of the court under this Act of settling a list of contributories and the list of contributories shall be *prima facie* evidence of the liabilty of the persons named therein to be contributories;

(*d*) exercise the power of the court of making calls;

(*e*) summon general meetings of the company for the purpose of obtaining the sanction of the company by resolution or for any other purpose he may think fit.

(2) The liquidator shall pay the debts of the company and shall adjust the rights of the contributories among themselves.

(3) When several liquidators are appointed, any power given by this Act may be exercised by such one or more of them as may be determined at the time of their appointment, or, in default of such determination, by any number not less than two.

276A.—(1) The appointment of a liquidator shall be of no effect unless the person nominated has, prior to his appointment, signified his written consent to the appointment.

(2) The chairman of any meeting at which a liquidator is appointed shall, within 7 days of the meeting, notify the liquidator in writing of his appointment, unless the liquidator or his duly authorised representative is present at the meeting where the appointment is made.

(3) A person who fails to comply with subsection (2) shall be liable to a fine not exceeding £1,000.

Consent to appointment as liquidator and notification of appointment

277.—(1) If from any cause whatever there is no liquidator acting, the court may appoint a liquidator.

(2) The court may, on cause shown, remove a liquidator and appoint another liquidator.

Power of court to appoint and remove liquidator in a voluntary winding-up

278.—(1) The liquidator shall, within 14 days after his appointment, deliver to the registrar of companies for registration a notice of his appointment.

(2) If the liquidator fails to comply with the requirements of this section, he shall be liable to a fine not exceeding £250.

Notice by liquidator of his appointment

279.—(1) Any arrangement entered into between a company about to be, or in the course of being, wound up and its creditors shall, subject to the right of appeal under this section, be binding on the company if sanctioned by a special resolution and on the creditors if acceded to by three-fourths in number and value of the creditors.

(2) Any creditor or contributory may, within 3 weeks from the completion of the arrangement, appeal to the court against it, and the court may thereupon, as it thinks just, amend, vary or confirm the arrangement.

Provisions as to arrangement binding creditors

280.—(1) The liquidator or any contributory or creditor may apply to the court to determine any question arising in the winding-up of a company, or to exercise in relation to the enforcing of calls or any other matter, all or any of the powers which the court might exercise if the company were being wound up by the court.

(2) The court, if satisfied that the determination of the question or the required exercise of power will be just and beneficial, may accede wholly or partially to the application on such terms and conditions as it thinks fit or may make such other order on the application as it thinks just.

(3) An office copy of an order made by virtue of this section annulling the resolution to wind up or staying the proceedings in the winding-up shall forthwith be forwarded by the

Power ot apply to court to have questions determined or powers exercised

company to the registrar of companies for registration.

(4) If the company fails to comply with subsection (3), the company and every officer of the company who is in default shall be liable to a fine not exceeding £125.

Cost of voluntary winding-up

281.—All costs, charges and expenses properly incurred in the winding-up, including the remuneration of the liquidator, shall be payable out of the assets of the company in priority to all other claims.

Savings for rights of creditors and contributories

282.—The winding-up of a company shall not bar the right of any creditor or contributory to have it wound up by the court, but in the case of an application by a contributory the court must be satisfied that the rights of the contributories will be prejudiced by a voluntary winding-up.

(iv) PROVISIONS APPLICABLE TO EVERY MODE OF WINDING UP

Proof of Ranking of Claims

Debts which may be proved

283.—(1) Subject to subsection (2), in every winding up (subject, in the case of insolvent companies, to the application in accordance with the provisions of this Act of the law of bankruptcy) all debts payable on a contingency, and all claims against the company, present or future, certain or contingent, ascertained or sounding only in damages, shall be admissible to proof against the company, a just estimate being made, so far as possible, of the value of such debts or claims which may be subject to any contingency or which sound only in damages, or for some other reason do not bear a certain value.

(2) Where a company is being wound up, dividends declared by the company more than 6 years preceding the commencement of the winding-up which have not been claimed within the said 6 years shall not be a claim admissible to proof against the company for the purposes of the winding-up, unless the articles of the company or the conditions of issue provide otherwise.

Application of bankruptcy rules in winding-up of insolvent companies

284.—(1) In the winding-up of an insolvent company the same rules shall prevail and be observed relating to the respective rights of secured and unsecured creditors and to debts provable and to the valuation of annuities and future and contingent liabilities as are in force for the time being under the law of bankruptcy relating to the estates of persons adjudged bankrupt, and all persons who in any such case would be entitled to prove for and receive dividends out of the assets of the company may come in under the winding-up and make such claims against the company as they respectively are entitled to by virtue of this section.

(2) Section 331 of the Irish Bankrupt and Insolvent Act, 1857, shall apply in the winding-up of an insolvent company and accordingly the reference in that section to the filing of the petition shall be read as a reference to the presentation of a petition for the winding-up of the company by the court or the passing of a resolution for voluntary winding-up, as the case may be, and where, before the presentation of a petition for the winding-up of the company by the court, a resolution has been passed by the company for voluntary winding-up, shall be read as a reference to the passing of the resolution.

(3) Subsection (2) shall not apply to a judgment mortgage created before the operative date.

Preferential payments in a inding-up

285.—(1) In this section "the relevant date" means—

(i) where the company is ordered to be wound up compulsorily, the date of the appointment (or first appointment) of a provisional liquidator or, if no such appointment was made, the date of the winding-up order, unless in either case the company had commenced to be wound up voluntarily before that date; and

    (ii) where subparagraph (i) does not apply, the date of the passing of the resolution for the winding-up of the company.

(2) In a winding-up there shall be paid in priority to all other debts—

    (*a*) the following rates and taxes—

        (i) all local rates due from the company at the relevant date and having become due and payable within 12 months next before that date;

        (ii) all assessed taxes, including income tax and corporation profits tax, assessed on the company up to the 5th day of April next before the relevant date and not exceeding in the whole one year's assessment;

        (iii) any amount due at the relevant date in respect of sums which an employer is liable under the Finance (No. 2) Act, 1959, and any regulations thereunder to deduct from emoluments to which Part II of that Act applies paid by him during the period of 12 months next before the relevant date reduced by any amount which he was under that Act and any regulation thereunder liable to repay during the said period, with the addition of interest payable under section 8 of that Act;

The amount referred to in [this] subsection shall be deemed to include any amount—

(i) which, apart from the provisions of Article 22 of the Regulations of 1988 (as amended by the Social Welfare (Collection of Contributions by the Collector-General) Regulations, 1989 (S.I. No. 72 of 1989)), or Article 22 of the Regulations of 1989, would otherwise have been an amount due at the relevant date in respect of sums which an employer is liable under Chapter 1 of Part II of the Principal Act or Chapter 1A (inserted by section 11 of the Act of 1988) of Part II of that Act, and any regulation thereunder (other than the said Article 22 of the Regulations of 1988 or Article 22 of the Regulation of 1989) to deduct from reckonable earnings or reckonable emoluments, to which the said Chapters 1 and 1A apply, paid by him during the period of 12 months next before the relevant date, and

(ii) with the addition of any interest payable under Article 23 of the Regulations of 1988 or Article 13 of the Regulations, 1989,

and

the relevant date shall, notwithstanding the provisions of subsection (1) of section 285 of the Companies Act, 1963, be deemed to be the date which is the ninth day after the end of the income tax month in which the relevant date (within the meaning of the said subsection (1)) occurred.

In this section—

"the Regulations of 1988" means the Social Welfare (Miscellaneous Provisions for Self-Employed Contributors) Regulations, 1988 (S.I. No. 62 of 1988);

"the Regulations of 1989" means the Social Welfare (Collection of Employment Contributions by the Collector-General) Regulations, 1989 (S.I. No. 298 of 1989).

    (*b*) all wages or salary (whether or not earned wholly or in part by way of commission) of any clerk or servant in respect of services rendered to the company during the 4 months next before the relevant date;

(*c*) all wages (whether payable for time or for piece work) of any workman or labourer in respect of services rendered to the company during the 4 months next before the relevant date;

(*d*) all accrued holiday remuneration becoming payable to any clerk, servant, workman or labourer (or in the case of his death to any other person in his right) on the termination of his employment before or by the effect of the winding-up order or resolution;

(*e*) unless the company is being wound up voluntarily merely for the purposes of reconstruction or of amalgamation with another company, all amounts due in respect of contributions payable during the 12 months next before the relevant date by the company as the employer of any person under the Insurance (Intermittent Unemployment) Act, 1942, or the Social Welfare Acts, 1952 to 1961;

The amount referred to in [this] subsection shall be deemed to include any amount—

(i) which, apart from the provisions of Regulation 31A (inserted by the Income Tax (Employments) Regulations, 1989 (S.I. No. 58 of 1989)) of the Income Tax (Employments) Regulations, 1960 (S.I. No. 28 of 1960), would otherwise have been an amount due at the relevant date in respect of sums which an employer is liable under Chater IV of Part V of the Income Tax Act, 1967, and any regulation thereunder (other than the said Regulation 31A) to deduct from emoluments, to which the said Chapter IV applies, paid by him during the period of 12 months next before the relevant date.

(ii) deducted by any amount which he was liable under the said Chapter IV and any regulation thereunder to repay during the said period, and

(iii) with the addition of any interest payable under section 129 of the Income Tax Act, 1967,

and

the relevant date shall, notwithstanding the provisions of subsection (1) of section 285, be deemed to be the date which is hte ninth day after the end of the income tax month in which the relevant date (within the meanig of the said subsection (1)) occurred.

(*f*) unless the company is being wound up voluntarily merely for the purposes of reconstructions or of amalgamation with another company, all amounts (including costs) due in respect of compensation or liability for compensation under the Workmen's Compensation Acts, 1934 to 1955 (being amounts which have accrued before the relevant date), to the extent that the company is not effectively indemnified by insurers against liability for such compensation;

(*g*) unless the company is being wound up voluntarily merely for the purposes of reconstruction or of amalgamation with another company, all amounts due from the compay in respect of damages and costs or liabilty for damages and costs, payable to a person employed by it in connection with an accident occurring before the relevant date and in the course of his employment with the company, to the extent that the company is not effectively indemnified by insurers against such damages and costs.

(*h*) all sums due to an employee pursuant to any scheme or arrangement for the provision of payments to the employee while he is absent from employment due to ill health;

(*i*) any payments due by the company pursuant to any scheme or arrangement for the provision of superannuation benefits to or in respect of employees of the company whether such payments are due in respect of the company's contribution to that scheme or under that arrangement or in respect of such contributions payable by the employees to the company under any such scheme or arrangement which have been deducted from the wages or salaries of employees.

(3) Subject to subsection (4), and notwithstanding anything in paragraphs (*b*) and (*c*) of subsection (2) the sum to which priority is to be given under those paragraphs respectively shall not, in the case of any one claimant, exceed £2,500.

(4) Where a claimant under paragraph (*c*) of subsection (2) is a farm labourer who has entered into a contract for payment of a portion of his wages in a lump sum at the end of the year of hiring, he shall have priority in respect of the whole of such sum, or such part thereof as the court may decide to be due under the contract, proportionate to the time of service up to the relevant date.

(5) Where any compensation under the Workmen's Compensation Acts, 1934 to 1955 is a weekly payment, the amount due in respect thereof shall, for the purposes of paragraph (*f*) of subsection (2) be taken to be the amount of the lump sum for which the weekly payment could be redeemed if the employer made an application for that purpose under the said Acts.

(6) Where any payment has been made—

(*a*) to any clerk, servant, workman or labourer in the employment of a company, on account of wages or salary; or

(*b*) to any such clerk, servant, workman or labourer or, in the case of his death, to any other person in his right, on account of accrued holiday remuneration; or

(*c*) to any such clerk, servant, workman or labourer while he is absent from employment due to ill health or pursuant to any scheme or arrangement for the provision of superannuation benefit to or in respect of him;

out of money advanced by some person for that purpose, the person by whom the money was advanced shall, in a winding-up, have a right of priority in respect of the money so advanced and paid up to the amount by which the sum, in respect of which the clerk, servant, workman or labourer or other person in his right, would have been entitled to priority in the winding up has been diminished by reason of the payment having been made.

(7) The foregoing debts shall—

(*a*) rank equally among themselves and be paid in full, unless the assets are insufficient to meet them, in which case they shall abate in equal proportions; and

(*b*) so far as the assets of the company available for payment of general creditors are insufficient to meet them, have priority over the claims of holders of debentures under any floating charge created by the company, and be paid accordingly out of any property comprised in or subject to that charge.

(8) Subject to the retention of such sums as may be necessary for the costs and expenses of the winding-up, the foregoing debts shall be discharged forthwith so far as the assets are sufficient to meet them, and in the case of debts to which priority is given by paragraph (*e*) of subsection (2), formal proof thereof shall not be required except in so far as is otherwise provided by rules of court.

(9) Subject to subsection (10) in the event of a landlord or other person distraining or having distrained on any goods or effects of the company within 3 months next before the relevant date, the debts of which priority is given by this section shall be a first charge on the goods or effects so distrained on, or the proceeds of the sale thereof.

(10) In respect of any money paid under any such charge as is referred to in subsection (9), the landlord or any other person shall have the same rights of priority as the person to whom the payment is made.

(11) Any remuneration inrespect of a period of holiday, absence from work through good cause shall be deemed to be wages in respect of services rendered to the company during that period.

(12) This section shall not apply in the case of a winding-up where the relevant date occurred before the operative date, and in such a case, the provisions relating to preferential payments which would have applied if this Act had not been passed shall be deemed to remain in full force.

(13) The Minister may by order made under this subsection vary the sum of money specified in subsection (3) of this section.

(14) The priority conferred by subsection (2) shall apply only to those debts which, within the period of six months after advertisement by the liquidator for claims in at least two daily newspapers circulating in the district where the registered office of the company is situated, either—

      (a) have been notified to him; or

      (b) have become known to him.

Effect of Winding-up on antecedent and other Transactions

Fruadulent preference

286.—(1) Subject to the provisions of this section, any conveyance, mortgage, delivery of goods, payment, execution or other act relating to property made or done by or against a company which is unable to pay its debts as they become due in favour of any creditor, or of any person on trust for any creditor, with a view to giving such creditor, or any surety or guarantor for the debt to such creditor, a preference over the other creditors, shall, if a winding-up of the company commences within 6 months of the making or doing the same and the company is at the time of the commencement of the winding-up unable to pay its debts (taking into account the contingent and prospective liabilities), be deemed a fraudulent preference of its creditors and be invalid accordingly.

(2) Any conveyance or assignment by a company of all its property to trustees for the benefit of all its creditors shall be void to all intents.

(3) A transaction to which subsection (1) applies in favour of a connected person which was made within two years before the commencement of the winding-up of the company shall, unless the contrary is shown, be deemed in the event of the company being wound up—

      (a) to have been made with a view to giving such person a preference over the other creditors, and

      (b) to be a fraudulent preference,

and be valid accordingly.

(4) Subsections (1) and (3) shall not affect the rights of any person making title in good faith and for valuable consideration through or under a creditor of the company.

(5) In this section, "a connected person" means a person who, at the time the transaction was made, was—

      (a) a director of the company;

      (b) a shadow director of the company;

      (c) a person connected within the meaning of *section 26(1)(a)* of the *Companies Act, 1990*, with a director;

      (d) a related company, within the meaning of *section 140* of the said Act, or

      (e) a trustee of, or surety or guarantor for the debt due to, any person described in paragraph (a), (b), (c) or (d).

288.—(1) Where a company is being wound up, a floating charge on the undertaking or property of the company created within 12 months before the commencement of the winding-up shall, unless it is proved that the company immediately after the creation of the charge was solvent, be invalid, except as to money actually advanced or paid, or the actual price or value of goods or services sold or supplied, to the company at the time of or subsequently to the creation of, and in consideration for, the charge, together with interest on that amount at the rate of 5 per cent per annum. Circumstances in which floating charge is invalid

(2) For the purposes of subsection (1) the value of any goods or services sold or supplied by way of consideration for a floating charge is the amount in money which at the time they were sold or supplied could reasonably have been expected to be obtained for the goods or services in the ordinary course of business and on the same terms (apart from the consideration) as those on which they were sold or supplied to the company.

(3) Where a floating charge on the undertaking or property of a company is created in favour of a connected person, subsection (1) shall apply to such a charge as if the period of 12 months mentioned in that subsection were a period of 2 years.

(4) In this section "a connected person" means a person who, at the time of the transaction was made, was—

> (*a*) a director of the company;
>
> (*b*) a shadow director of the company;
>
> (*c*) a person connected within the meaning of *section 26(1)(a)* of the *Companies Act, 1990*, with a director;
>
> (*d*) a related company, within the meaning of *section 140* of the said Act, or
>
> (*e*) a trustee of, or surety or guarantor for the debt due to, any person described in paragraph (*a*), (*b*), (*c*) or (*d*).

289.—(1) Subject to subsection (2), where— Other circmstances in which floating charge is invalud

> (*a*) a company is being wound up; and
>
> (*b*) the company was within 12 months before the commencement of the winding-up indebted to any officer of the company; and
>
> (*c*) such indebtedness was discharged whether wholly or partly by the company or by any other person; and
>
> (*d*) the company created a floating charge on any of its assets or property within 12 months before the commencement of the winding-up in favour of the officer to whom such company was indebted;

then (without prejudice to any rights or liabilities arising apart from this section) such charge shall be invalid to the extent of the repayment referred to in paragraph (*c*) unless it is proved that the company immediately after the creation of the charge was solvent.

(2) Subsection (1) shall not apply if the charge referred to in paragraph (*d*) was created before the operative date.

(3) In this section "officer" includes the spouse, child or nominee of an officer.

290.—(1) Subject to subsections (2) and (5), where any part of the property of a company which is being wound up consists of land of any tenure with onerous covenants, of shares or stock in companies, of unprofitable contracts, or of any other property which is unsaleable or not readily saleable by reason of its binding the possessor thereof to the performance of any onerous act or to the payment of any sum of money, the liquidator of the company, notwithstanding that he has endeavoured to sell or has taken possession of the property or exercised any act of ownership in relation therto, may, with the leave of the court and subject to the provisions of this section, by writing signed by him, at any time within 12 months after Disclaimer of onerous property in case of company being wound up the commencement of the winding-up or such extended period as may be allowed by the court, disclaim the property.

(2) Where any such property as aforesaid has not come to the knowledge of the liquidator within one month after the commencement of the winding-up, the power under this section of disclaiming the property may be exercised at any time within 12 months after he has become aware thereof or such extended period as may be allowed by the court.

(3) The disclaimer shall operate to determine, as from the date of disclaimer, the rights, interest and liabilities of the company, and the property of the company, in or in respect of the property disclaimed, but shall not, except so far as is necessary for the purpose of releasing the company and the property of the company from liability, affect the rights or liabilities of any other person.

(4) The court, before or on granting leave to disclaim, may require such notices to be given to persons interested and impose such terms as condition of granting leave, and make such other order in the matter as the court thinks just.

(5) The liquidator shall not be permitted to disclaim any property under this section in any case where an application in writing has been made to him by any persons interested in the property requiring him to decide whether he will or will not disclaim, and the liquidator, has not, within a period of 28 days after the receipt of the application or such further period as may be allowed by the court, given notice to the applicant that he intends to apply to the court for leave to disclaim.

(6) The court may, on the application of any person who is, as against the liquidator, entitled to the benefit or subject to the burden of a contract made by the company, make an order rescinding the contract on such terms as to payment by or to either party of damages for the non-performance of the contract, or otherwise as the court thinks just, and any damages payable under the order to any such person shall be deemed to be a debt proved and admitted in the winding-up.

(7) Subject to subsection (8), the court may, on an application by any person who either claims any interest in any disclaimed property or is under any liability not discharged by this Act in respect of any disclaimed property and on hearing any such persons as it thinks fit, make an order for the vesting of the property in or the delivery of the property to any person entitled thereto, or to whom it may seem just that the property should be delivered by way of compensation for such liability as aforesaid, or a trustee for him, and on such terms as the court may think just, and on any such vesting order being made, the property comprised therein shall vest accordingly in the person therein named in that behalf without any conveyance or assignment for the purpose.

(8) Where the property disclaimed is of a leasehold nature, the court shall not make a vesting order in favour of any person claiming under the company, whether as under-lessee or as mortgagee by demise, except upon the terms of making that person—

        (a) subject to the same liabilities and obligations as those to which the company was subject under the lease in respect of the property at the commencement of the winding-up; or

        (b) if the court thinks fit, subject only to the same liabilities and obligations as if the lease had been assigned to that person at that date;

and in either event (if the case so requires), as if the lease had comprised only the property comprised in the vesting order, and any mortgagee or under-lessee declining to accept a vesting order upon such terms shall be excluded from all interest in and security upon the property, and, if there is no person claiming under the company who is willing to accept an order upon such terms, the court shall have power to vest the estate and interest of the company in the property in any person liable either personally or in a representative character, and either alone or jointly with the company, to perform the lessee's covenants in the lease, freed and discharged from all estates, encumbrances and interests created therein by the company.

(9) Any person damaged by the operation of a disclaimer under this section shall be deemed to be a creditor of the company to the amount of the damages, and may accordingly prove the amount as a debt in the winding-up.

291.—(1) Subject to subsections (2) to (4), where a creditor has issued execution against the goods or lands of a company or has attached any debt to the company, and the company is subsequently wound up, he shall not be entitled to retain the benefit of the execution or attachment against the liquidator in the winding up of the company unless he has completed the execution or attachment before the commencement of the winding-up.

Restriction of rights of creditor as to execution or attachment in case of company being wound up

(2) Where any creditor has had notice of a meeting having been called at which a resolution for voluntary winding-up is to be proposed, the date on which the creditor so had notice shall, for the purposes of subsection (1), be substituted for the date of the commencement of the winding-up.

(3) A person who purchases in good faith under a sale by the sheriff of any goods of a company on which an execution has been levied shall in all cases acquire a good title to them against the liquidator.

(4) The rights conferred by subsection (1) on the liquidator may be set aside by the court in favour of the creditor to such extent and subject to such terms as the court thinks fit.

(5) For the purposes of this section, an execution against goods shall be taken to be completed by seizure and sale, and an attachment of a debt shall be deemed to be completed by receipt of the debt, and an execution against land shall be deemed to be completed by seizure and, in the case of an equitable interest, by the appointment of a receiver.

(6) Nothing in this section shall give any validity to any payment constituting a fraudulent preference.

(7) In this section, "goods" includes all chattels personal and "sheriff" includes any officer charged with the execution of a writ or other process.

292.—(1) Subject to subsection (3), where any goods of a company are taken in execution, and, before the sale thereof or the completion of the execution by the receipt or recovery of the full amount of the levy, notice is served on the sheriff that a provisional liquidator has been appointed or that a winding-up order has been made or that a resolution for voluntary winding-up has been passed, the sheriff shall, on being so required, deliver the goods and any money seized or received in part satisfaction of the execution to the liquidator, but the costs of the execution shall be a first charge on the goods or the money so delivered, and the liquidator may sell the goods or a sufficient part thereof for the purpose of satisfying the charge.

Duties of sheriff as to goods taken in execution

(2) Subject to subsection (3), where under an execution in respect of a judgment for a sum exceeding £20 the goods of a company are sold or money is paid in order to avoid sale, the sheriff shall deduct the costs of the execution from the proceeds of the sale of the money paid and retain the balance for 14 days, and if within that time notice is served on him of a petition for the the winding-up of the company having been presented or of a meeting having been called at which there is to be proposed a resolution for the voluntary winding-up of the company and an order is made or a resolution is passed, as the case may be, for the winding-up of the company, the sheriff shall pay the balance to the liquidator who shall be entitled to retain it as against the execution creditor.

(3) The rights conferred by this section on the liquidator may be set aside by the court in favour of the creditor to such extent and subject to such terms as the court thinks fit.

(4) In this section, "goods" includes all chattels personal and "sheriff" includes any officer charged with the execution of a writ or other process.

Offences antecedent to or in the course of Winding-Up

Offences by
officers of
companies in
liquidation

293.—(1) Subject to subsection (2), if any person, being a past or present officer of a company which at the time of the commission of the alleged offence is being wound up, whether by the court or voluntarily, or is subsequently ordered to be wound up by the court or subsequently passes a resolution for voluntary winding-up—

(a) does not to the best of his knowledge and belief fully and truly disclose to the liquidator when he requests such disclosure all the property, real and personal, of the company and how and to whom and for what consideration and when the company disposed of any part thereof, except such part as has been disposed of in the ordinary way of the business of the company; or

(b) does not deliver up to the liquidator, or as he directs, all such part of the real and personal property of the company as is in his custody or under his control, and which he is required by law to deliver up; or

(c) does not deliver up to the liquidator, or as he directs, all books and papers in his custody or under his control belonging to the company and which he is required by law to deliver up; and

(d) within 12 months next before the commencement of the winding-up or at any time thereafter conceals any part of the property of the company to the value of £10 or upwards, or conceals any debt due to or from the company; or

(e) within 12 months next before the commencement of the winding-up or at any time thereafter fraudulently removes any part of the property of the company to the value of £10 or upwards; or

(f) makes any material omission in any statement relating to the affairs of the company; or

(g) knowing or believing that a false debt has been proved by any person under the winding-up, fails for the period of a month to inform the liquidator thereof; or

(h) after the commencement of the winding-up prevents the production of any book or paper affecting or relating to the property or affairs of the company; or

(i) within 12 months next before the commencement of the winding-up or at any time thereafter conceals, destroys, mutilates or falsifies or is privy to the concealment, destruction, mutilation or falsification of any book or paper affecting or relating to the property or affairs of the company; or

(j) within 12 months next before the commencement of the winding-up or at any time thereafter makes or is privy to the making of any false entry in any book or paper affecting or relating to the property or affairs of the company; or

(k) within 12 months next before the commencement of the winding-up or at any time thereafter fraudulently parts with, alters of makes any omission in, or is privy to the fraudulent parting with, altering or making any omission in, any document affecting or relating to the property or affairs of the company; or

(l) after the commencement of the winding-up or at any meeting of the creditors of the company within 12 months next before the commencement of the winding-up attempts to account for any part of the property of the company by fictitious losses or expenses; or

(m) has within 12 months next before the commencement of the winding-up or at any time thereafter, by any false representation or other fraud, obtained any property for or on behalf of the company on credit which the company does not subsequently pay for; or (*n*) within 12 months next before the commencement of the winding-up or at any time thereafter, under the false pretence that the company is carrying on its business, obtains on credits for or on behalf of the company, any property which the company does not subsequently pay for; or

(*o*) within 12 months next before the commencement of the winding-up or at any time thereafter pawns, pledges or disposes of any property of the company which has been obtained on credit and has not been paid for, unless such pawning, pledging or disposing is in the ordinary way of business of the company; or

(*p*) is guilty of any false representation or other fraud for the purpose of obtaining the consent of the creditors of the company or any of them to an agreement with reference to the affairs of the company or to the winding-up;

he shall in the case of an offence mentioned in paragraph (*m*), (*n*) or (*o*), be liable, on conviction on indictment, to penal servitude for a term not exceeding 5 years or to imprisonment for a term not exceeding 2 years or to a fine not exceeding £5,000 or to both such penal servitude or imprisonment and such fine and, in the case of an offence mentioned in any other paragraph, be liable, on conviction on indictment, to imprisonment for a term not exceeding 2 years or to a fine not exceeding £2,500 or to both, or, in the case of any offence under this subsection, be liable, on summary conviction, to imprisonment for a term not exceeding 6 months or to a fine not exceeding £500 or to both.

(2) It shall be a good defence to a charge under any of paragraphs (*a*), (*b*), (*c*), (*d*), (*f*), (*n*) and (*o*) of subsection (1), if the accused proves that he had no intent to defraud and to a charge under any of paragraphs (*h*), (*i*) and (*j*) of subsection (1), if he proves that he had no intent to conceal the state of affairs of the company or to defeat the law.

(3) Where any person pawns, pledges or disposes of any property in circumstances which amount to an offence under paragraph (*o*) of subsection (1), every person who takes in pawn or pledge or otherwise receives the property knowing it to be pawned, pledged or disposed of in such circumstances as aforesaid shall also be guilty of an offence and shall be liable to be punished in the same way as if he had been guilty of an offence under the said paragraph (*o*).

(4) For the purposes of this section, "officer" shall include any person in accordance with whose directions or instructions the directors of a company have been accustomed to act.

294.—If any officer or contributory of any company being wound up, destoys, mutilates, alters or falsifies any books, papers or securities, or makes or is privy to the making of a false or fraudulent entry in any register, book of account or document belonging to the company with intent to defraud or to deceive any person, he shall be liable, on conviction on indictment, to imprisonment for a term not exceeding 2 years or to a fine not exceeding £2,500 or to both or, on summary conviction, to imprisonment for a term not exceeding 6 months or to a fine not exceeding £500 or to both. *Alteration or falsification of books*

295.—If any person, being at the time of the commission of the alleged offence an officer of a company which is subsequently ordered to be wound up by the court or subsequently passes a resolution for voluntary winding-up— *Frauds by officers of companies which have gone into liquidation*

(*a*) has by false pretence or by means of any other fraud induced any person to give credit to the company;

(*b*) with intent to defraud creditors of the company, has made or caused to be made any gift or transfer of or charge on, or has caused or connived at the levying of any execution against, the property of the company;

(*c*) with intent to defraud creditors of the company, has concealed or removed any part of the property of the company since or within 12 months before the date of any unsatisfied judgment or order for payment of money obtained against the company; he shall be liable, on conviction on indictment, to imprisonment for a term not exceeding 2 years or to a fine not exceeding £500 or to both or, on summary conviction, to imprisonment for a term not exceeding 6 months or to a fine not exceeding £500 or to both.

Liability where proper books of account not kept

296.—(1) If it is shown that proper books of account were not kept by a company throughout the period of 2 years immediately preceding the commencement of its winding-up, or the period between the incorporation of the company and the commencement of the winding-up, whichever is the shorter, every officer of the company who is in default shall, unless he shows that he acted honestly and that in the circumstances in which the business of the company was carried on the default was excusable, be liable, on conviction on indictment, to imprisonment for a term not exceeding 2 years or to a fine not exceeding £2,500 or to both or, on summary conviction, to imprisonment for a term not exceeding 6 months or to a fine not exceeding £500 or to both.

(2) For the purposes of this section, proper books of account shall be deemed not to have been kept in the case of any company if there have not been kept such books or accounts as are necessary to exhibit and explain the transactions and financial position of the trade or business of the company, including books containing entries from day to day in sufficient detail of all cash received and cash paid, and, where the trade or business has involved dealings in goods, statements of the annual stocktakings and (except in the case of goods sold by way of ordinary retail trade) of all goods sold and purchased, showing the goods and the buyers and sellers thereor in sufficient detail to enable those goods and those buyers and sellers to be identified.

Criminal liability of persons concerned for fraudulent of company

297.—(1) If any person is knowingly a party to the carrying on of the business of a company with intent to defraud creditors of the company or creditors of any other person or for any fraudulent purpose, that person shall be guilty of an offence.

(2) Any person who is convicted of an offence under this section shall be liable—

(*a*) on summary conviction to imprisonment for a term not exceeding 12 months or to a fine not exceeding £1,000 or to both, or

(*b*) on conviction on indictment, to imprisonment for a term not exceeding 7 years or to a fine not exceeding £50,000 or to both.

Civil liability of persons concerned for fraudulent or reckless trading of company

297A.—(1) If in the course of the winding-up of a company or in the course of proceedings under the Companies (Amendment) Act, 1990, it appears that—

(*a*) any person was, while an officer of the company, knowingly a party to the carrying on of any business of the company in a reckless manner; or

(*b*) any person was knowingly a party to the carrying on of any business of the company with intent to defraud creditors of the company, or creditors of any other person or for any fraudulent purpose;

the court, on the application of the receiver, examiner, liquidator or any creditor or contributory of the company, may, if it thinks it proper to do so, declare that such person shall be personally responsible, without any limitation of liability, for all or any part of the debts or other liabilities of the company as the court may direct.

(2) Without prejudice to the generality of subsection (1)(*a*), an officer of a company shall be deemed to have been knowingly a party to the carrying on of any business of the company in a reckless manner if—

(*a*) he was a party to the carrying on of such business and, having regard to the general knowledge, skill and experience that may reasonably be expected of a person in his position, he ought to have known that his actions or those of the company would cause loss to the creditors of the company, or any of them, or

(b) he was a party to the contracting of a debt of the company and did not honestly believe on reasonable grounds that the company would be able to pay the debt when it fell due for payment as well as all its other debts (taking into account the contingent and prospective liabilities).

(3) Notwithstanding anything contained in subsection (1) the court may grant a declaration on the grounds set out in paragraph (*a*) of that subsection only if—

(a) paragraph (*a*), (*b*) or (*c*) of section 214 applies to the company concerned, and

(b) an applicant for such a declaration, being a creditor or contributory of the company, or any person on whose behalf such application is made, suffered loss or damage as a consequence of any behaviour mentioned in subsection (1).

(4) In deciding whether it is proper to make an order on the ground set out in subsection (2)(*b*), the court shall have regard to whether the creditor in question was, at the time the debt was incurred aware of the company's financial state of affairs, and notwithstanding such awareness, nevertheless assented to the incurring of the debt.

(5) On the hearing of an application under this section, the applicant may himself give evidence or call witnesses.

(6) Where it appears to the court that any person in respect of whom a declaration has been sought under subsection (1)(*a*), has acted honestly and responsibly in relation to the conduct of the affairs of the company or any matter or matters on the ground of which such declaration is sought to be made, the court may, having regard to all the circumstances of the case, relieve him either wholly or in part, from personal liability on such terms as it may think fit.

(7) Where the court makes any such declaration, it may—

(a) give such further directions as it thinks proper for the purpose of giving effect to that declaration and in particular may make provision for making the liability of any such person under the declaration a charge on any debt or obligation due from the company to him, or on any mortgage or charge or any interest in any mortgage or charge on any assets of the company held by or vested in him or any company or person on his behalf, or any person claiming as assignee from or through the person liable or any company or person acting on his behalf, and may from time to time make such further order as may be necessary for the purpose of enforcing any charge imposed under this subsection;

(b) provide that sums recovered under this section shall be paid to such person or classes of persons, for such purposes, in such amounts or proportions at such time or times and in such respective priorities among themselves as such declaration may specify.

(8) Subsection (1)(*a*) shall not apply in relation to the carrying on of the business of a company during a period when the company is under the protection of the court.

(9) This section shall have effect notwithstanding that—

(a) the person in respect of whom the declaration has been sought under subsection (1) may be criminally liable in respect of the matters on the ground of which such declaration is to be made; or

(b) any matter or matters on the ground of which the declaration udner subsection (1) is to be made have occurred outside the State.

(10) For the purposes of this section—

"assignee" includes any person to whom or in whose favour, by the direction of the person liable, the debt, obligation, mortgage or charge was created, issued or transferred or the interest created, but does not include an assignee for valuable consideration (not including consideration by way of marriage) given in good faith and without notice of any of the matters on the ground of which the declaration is made;

"company" includes any body which may be wound up under the Companies Acts; and

"officer" includes any auditor, liquidator, receiver, or shadow director.

Power of court to assess damages against directors

298.—(1) Subsection (2) applies if in the course of winding-up a company it appears that any person who has taken part in the formation or promotion of the company, or any past or present officer, liquidator, receiver or examiner of the company, has misapplied or retained or become liable or accountable for any money or property of the company, or has been guilty of any misfeasance or other breach of duty or trust in relation to the company.

(2) The court may, on the application of the liquidator, or any creditor or contributory, examine into the conduct of the promoter, officer, liquidator, receiver or examiner, and compel him—

(*a*) to repay or restore the money or property or any part thereof respectively with interest at such rate as the court thinks just, or

(*b*) to contribute such sum to the assets of the company by way of compensation in respect of the misapplication, retainer, misfeasance or other breach of duty or trust as the court thinks just.

(3) This section has effect notwithstanding that the offence is one for which the offender may be criminally liable.

Prosecution of criminal offences committed by officers and members of company

299.—(1) If it appears to the court in the course of a winding-up by the court that any past or present officer, or any member, of the company has been guilty of an offence in relation to the company for which he is criminally liable, the court may either on the application of any person interested in the winding-up or of its own motion directs the liquidator to refer the matter to the Director of Public Prosecutions and in such a case the liquidator shall furnish to the Director of Public Prosecutions such information and give to him access to and facilties for inspecting and taking any copies of any documents, being information or documents in the possession or under the control of the liquidator and relating to the matter in question, as the Director of Public Prosecutions may require.

(2) If is appears to the liquidator in the course of a voluntary winding-up that any past or present officer, or any member, of the company has been guilty of any offence in relation to the company for which he is criminally liable, he shall forthwith report the matter to the Director of Public Prosecutions and shall furnish to the Director such information and give to him such access to and facilities for inspecting and taking copies of any documents, being information or documents in the possession or under the control of the liquidator and relating to the matter in question, as the Director may require.

(3) If it appears to the court in the course of a voluntary winding-up that any past or present officer, or any member, of the company has been guilty as aforesaid, and that no report relating to the matter has been made by the liquidator to the Director of Public Prosecutions under subsection (2), the court may, on the application of any person interested in the winding-up or of its own motion, direct the liquidator to make such a report, and on a report being made accordingly, this section shall have effect as though the report had been made in pursuance of subsection (2).

(4) If, where any matter is reported or referred to the Director of Public Prosecutions under this section, he considers that the case is one in which a prosecution ought to be

instituted and institutes proceedings accordingly, it shall be the duty of the liquidator and of every officer and agent of the company past and present (other than the defendant in the proceedings) to give all assistance in connection with the prosecution which he is reasonably able to give.

For the purpose of this subsection, "agent" in relation to a company shall be deemed to include any banker or solicitor of the company and any person employed by the company as auditor, whether that person is or is not an officer of the company.

(5) If any person fails or neglects to give assistance in the manner required by subsection (4), the court may, on the application of the Director of Public Prosecutions, direct that person to comply with the requirements of that subsection, and where any such application is made in relation to a liquidator the court may, unless it appears that the failure or neglect to comply was due to the liquidator not having in his hands sufficient assets of the company to enable him so to do, direct that the costs of the application shall be borne by the liquidator personally.

Supplementary Provisions as to Winding-up

300.—A body corporate shall not be qualified for appointment as liquidator of a company whether in a winding-up by the court or in a voluntary winding-up and— Disqualification for appointment as liquidator

    (*a*) any appointment made in contravention of this provision shall be void; and

    (*b*) any body corporate which acts as liquidator of a company shall be liable to a fine not exceeding £500.

300A.—(1) None of the following persons shall be qualified for appointment as liquidator of a company— Disqualification for appointment as liquidator

    (*a*) a person who is, or who has within 12 months of the commencement of the winding-up been, an officer or servant of the company;

    (*b*) except with the leave of the court, a parent, spouse, brother, sister or child of an officer of the company;

    (*c*) a person who is a partner or in the employment of an officer or servant of the company;

    (*d*) a person who is qualified by virtue of this subsection for appointment as liquidator of any other body corporate which is that company's subsidiary or holding company or a subsidiary of that company's holding company, or would be so disqualified if the body corporate were a company.

References in this subsection to an officer or servant of the company include references to an auditor.

(2) An application for leave under subsection (1)(*b*) shall be supported by such evidence as the court may require.

(3) If a liquidator becomes disqualified by virtue of this section he shall thereupon vacate his office and give notice in writing within 14 days to—

    (*a*) the court in a court winding-up;

    (*b*) the company in a members' voluntary winding-up;

    (*c*) the company and the creditors in a creditors' voluntary winding-up,

that he has vacated it by reason of such disqualification.

(4) Any person who acts as a liquidator when disqualified by this section from so doing or who fails to comply with subsection (3), if that subsection applies to him, shall be guilty of an offence and shall be liable—

    (*a*) on summary conviction, to a fine not exceeding £1,000 and, for continued contravention, a daily default fine not exceeding £50;

(*b*) on conviction on indictment, to a fine of £10,000 and, for contined contravention, a daily default fine not exceeding £250.

(5) This section shall not apply to a winding-up commenced before the commencement of *section 146* of the *Companies Act, 1990.*

Corrupt inducement affecting appointed as liquidator

301.—Any person who gives or agrees or offers to give to any member or creditor of a company any valuable consideration with a view to securing his own appointment or nomination or to securing or preventing the appointment or nomination of some person other than himself as the company's liquidator shall be liable to a fine not exceeding £500.

Disclosure of interest by creditors etc. at creditors' meetings

301A.—(1) Where, at a meeting of creditors, a resolution is proposed for the appointment of a liquidator, any creditor who has a connection with the proposed liquidator shall, before the resolution is put, make such connection known to the chairman of the meeting who shall disclose that fact to the meeting, together with details thereof.

(2) Subsection (1) shall not apply to any person at the meeting, being a representative of a creditor and entitled to vote on the resolution on his behalf.

(3) Where the chairman of a meeting of creditors has any such connection as is mentioned in subsection (1), he shall disclose that fact to the meeting, together with details thereof.

(4) For the purposes of this section, a person has a connection with a proposed liquidator if he is—

> (*a*) a parent, spouse, brother, sister or child of, or
>
> (*b*) employed by, or a partner of,

the proposed liquidator.

(5) A person who fails to comply with this section shall be liable to a fine not exceeding £1,000.

(6) In exercising its jurisdiction under section 267(2) or 272(2) (which relate to the appointment or removal of a liquidator) the court may have regard to any failure to comply with this section.

Enforcement of duty of liquidator to make returns

302.—(1) If any liquidator who has made any default in filing, delivering or making any return, account or other document, or in giving any notice which he is by law required to file, deliver, make or give, fails to make good the default within 14 days after the service on him of a notice requiring him to do so, the court may, on an application made to the court by any contributory or creditor of the company or by the registrar of companies, make an order directing the liquidator to make good the default within such time as may be specified in the order.

(2) Any such order may provide that all costs of and incidental to the application shall be borne by the liquidator.

(3) Nothing in this section shall be taken to prejudice the operation of any enactment imposing penalties on a liquidator in respect of any such default as aforesaid.

Notification that a company is in liquidation

303.—(1) Where a company is being wound up, whether by the court or voluntarily, every invoice, order for goods or business letter issued by or on behalf of the company or a liquidator of the company, or a receiver of the property of the company, being a document on or in which the name of the company appears, shall contain a statement that the company is being wound up.

(2) If default is made in complying with this section, the company and any of the following persons who knowingly and wilfully authorises or permits the default, namely, any officer of the company, any liquidator of the company and any receiver, shall be liable to a fine not exceeding £250.

304.—When a company is being wound up, all books and papers of the company and of the liquidators shall, as between the contributories of the company, be *prima facie* evidence of the truth of all matters purporting to be recorded therein.

305.—(1) When a company has been wound up and is about to be dissolved, the books and papers of the company and of the liquidator may be disposed of as follows—

　　(*a*) in the case of a winding-up by the court, in such way as the court directs;

　　(*b*) in the case of a members' voluntary winding-up, in such way as the company by special resolution directs, and in the case of a creditors' voluntary winding-up, in such was as the committee of inspection or, if there is no such committee, as the creditors of the company, may direct, so, however, that such books and papers shall be retained by the liquidator for a period of 3 years from the date of the dissolution of the company and, in the absence of any direction as to their disposal, he may then dispose of them as he thinks fit.

(2) If a liquidator fails to comply with the requirements of this section he shall be liable to a fine not exceeding £500.

306.—(1) If, where a company is being wound up, the winding-up is not concluded within 2 years after its commencement, the liquidator shall, at such intervals as may be prescribed, until the winding-up is concluded, send to the registrar of companies a statement in the prescribed form and containing the prescribed particulars about the proceedings in and position of the liquidation.

(2) If a liquidator fails to comply with this section, he shall be liable to a fine not exceeeding £500.

(3) An offence under this section may be prosecuted by the registrar of companies.

307.—(1) Where a company has been wound up voluntarily and is about to be dissolved, the liquidator shall lodge to an account to be known as The Companies Liquidation Account in the Bank of Ireland in such manner as may be prescribed by rules of court the whole unclaimed dividends admissible to proof and unapplied or undistributable balances.

(2) The Companies Liquidation Account shall be under the control of the court.

(3) Any application by a person claiming to be entitled to any dividend or payment out of a lodgment made in pursuance of subsection (1) and any payment out of such lodgment in satisfaction of such claim, shall be made in manner prescribed by rules of court.

(4) At the expiration of 7 years from the date of any lodgment made in pursuance of subsection (1), the amount of the lodgment remaining unclaimed shall be paid into the Exchequer, but where the court is satisfied that any person claiming is entitled to any dividend or payment out of the moneys paid into the Exchequer, it may order payment of the same and the Minister for Finance shall issue such sum as may be necessary to provide for that payment.

308.—Where a resolution is passed at an adjourned meeting of any creditors or contributories of a company, the resolution shall, for all purposes, be treated as having been passed on the date on which it was in fact passed and shall not be deemed to have been passed on any earlier date.

309.—(1) The court may, as to all matters relating to the winding-up of a company, have regard to the wishes of the creditors or contributories of the company, as proved to it by any sufficient evidence, and may, if it thinks fit, for the purpose of ascertaining those wishes, direct meetings of the creditors or contributories to be called, held and conducted in such manner as the court directs, and may appoint a person to act as chairman of any such meeting and report the result thereof to the court.

(2) In the case of creditors, regard shall be had to the value of each creditor's debt.

(3) In the case of contributories, regard shall be had to the number of votes conferred on each contributory by this Act or the articles.

Provisions as to Dissolution

Power of court to declare dissolution of company void

310.—(1) Where a company has been dissolved, the court may at any time within 2 years of the date of the dissolution, on an application being made for the purpose by the liquidator of the company or by any other person who appears to the court to be interested, make an order, upon such terms as the court thinks fit, declaring the dissolution to have been void, and thereupon such proceedings may be taken as might have been taken if the company had not been dissolved.

(2) It shall be the duty of the person on whose application the order was made, within 14 days after the making of the order, or such further time as the court may allow, to deliver to the registrar of companies for registration an office copy of the order, and if that person fails to do so, he shall be liable to a fine not exceeding £25.

Power of registrar to striked defunct company off register

311.—(1) Where the registrar of companies has reasonable cause to believe that a company is not carrying on business, he may send to the company by post a letter inquiring whether the company is carrying on business and stating that, if an answer is not received within one month from the date of that letter, a notice will be published in *Iris Oifigiúil* with a view to striking the name of the company off the register.

(2) If the registrar either receives an answer to the effect that the company is not carrying on business, or does not within one month after sending the second letter receive any answer, he may publish in *Iris Oifigiúil* and send to the company by registered post a notice that at the expiration of one month from the date of that notice, the name of the company mentioned therein will, unless cause is shown to the contrary, be struck of the register, and the company will be dissolved.

(3) If in any case where a company is being wound up the registrar has reasonable cause to believe either that no liquidator is acting, or that the affairs of the company are fully wound up, and the return required to be made by the liquidator have not been made for a period of 6 consecutive months, the registrar shall publish in *Iris Oifigiúil* and send to the company or the liquidator, if any, a like notice as is provided in subsection (2).

(5) The liability, if any, of every director, officer and member of the company shall continue and may be enforced as if the company had not been dissolved.

(6) Nothing in subsection (5) or (6) shall affect the power of the court to wind up a company the name of which has been struck off the register.

(7) If a company or any member or creditor thereof feels aggrieved by the company having been struck off the register, the court, on an application made (on notice to the registrar) by the company or member or creditor before the expiration of 20 years from the publication in *Iris Oifigiúil* of the notice aforesaid, may, if satisfied that the company was at the time of the striking off carrying on business or otherwise that it is just that the company be restored to the register, order that the name of the company be restored to the register, and upon an office copy of the order being delivered to the registrar for registration, the company shall be deemed to have continued in existence as if its name had not been struck off; and the court may by the order give such directions and make such provisions as seem just for placing the company and all other persons in the same position as nearly as may be as if the name of the company had not been struck off.

(8) A notice to be sent under this section to a liquidator may be addressed to the liquidator at his last known place of business, and a letter or notice to be sent under this section to a company may be addressed to the company at its regiseetered office, or, if no office has been registered, to the care of some officer of the company, or, if there is no officer of the company whose name and address are known to the registrar of companies, may be sent to each of the persons who subscribed the memorandum, addressed to him at the address mentioned in the memorandum.

Rules of Court

312.—Section 68 of the Court of Justice Act, 1936 (which confers power on a rule- making authority to make rules regulating the practice and procedures of the court in certain cases) shall extend to the making of rules in respect of the winding-up of companies whether by the court or voluntarily.

Rules of Court for winding-up

Disposal of documents filed with Registrar

313.—The registrar of companies shall, after the expiration of 20 years from the dissolution of a company, send all the documents filed in connection with such company to the Public Record Office.

Disposal of documents filed with registrar

PART VII

RECEIVERS

314.—A body corporate shall not be qualified for appointment as reciver of the property of a company, and any body corporate which acts as such a receiver shall be liable to a fine not exceeding £500.

Disqualification of body corporate for appointment as receiver

315.—(1) None of the following persons shall be qualified for appointment as receiver of the property of a company—

Disqualification of undischarged bankrupt from acting as receiver

> (*a*) an undischarged bankrupt;
> (*b*) a person who is, or who has within 12 months of the commencement of the receivership been, an officer or servant of the company;
> (*c*) a parent, spouse, brother, sister or child of an officer of the company;
> (*d*) a person who is a partner of or in the employment of an officer or servant of the company;
> (*e*) a person who is not qualified by virtue of this subsection for appointment as receiver of the property of any other body corporate which is that company's subsidiary or holding company or a subsidiary of that company's holding company, or would be so disqualified if the body corporate were a company.

References in this subsection to an officer or servant of the company include references to an auditor.

(2) If a receiver of the property of a company becomes disqualified by virtue of this section, he shall thereupon vacate his office and give notice in writing within 14 days to—

> (*a*) the company;
> (*b*) the registrar of companies;
> (*c*) (i) the debenture-holder, if the receiver was appointed by a debenture-holder, or
> (ii) the court, if the receiver was appointed by the court,

that he has vacated it by reason of such disqualification.

(3) Subsection (2) is without prejudice to section 107, 319(2) and 321.

(4) Nothing in this section shall require a receiver appointed before the commencement

of *section 170* of the *Companies Act, 1990*, to vacate the office to which he was so appointed.

(5) Any person who acts as a receiver when disqualified by this section from so doing or who fails to comply with subsection (2), if that subsection applies to him, shall be guilty of an offence and shall be liable—

> (*a*) on summary conviction, to a fine not exceeding £1,000 and, for continued contravention, to a daily default fine not exceeding £50;

> (*b*) on conviction or indictment, to a fine not exceeding £5,000 and, for continued contravention, to a daily default fine not exceeding £250.

Power of
receiver to
apply to the
court for
directions and
his liability on
contracts

316.—(1) Where a receiver of the property of a company is appointed under the powers contained in any instrument, any of the following persons may apply to the court for directions in relation to any matter in connection with the performance or otherwise by the receiver of his functions, that is to say—

> (*a*)   (i) the receiver;
>   (ii) an officer of the company;
>   (iii) a member of the company;
>   (iv) employees of the company comprising at least half in number of the persons employed in a full-time capacity by the company;
>   (v) a creditor of the company; and
> (*b*)   (i) a liquidator;
>   (ii) a contributory;

and on any such application, the court may give such directions, or make such order declaring the rights of persons before the court or otherwise, as the court thinks just.

(1A) An application to the court under subsection (1), except an application under paragraph (*a*)(i) of that subsection, shall be supported by such evidence that the applicant is being unfairly prejudiced by any actual or proposed action or omission of the receiver as the court may require.

(1B) For the purposes of subsection (1), "creditor" means one or more creditors to whom the company is indebted by more, in aggregate, than £10,000.

(2) A receiver of the property of a company shall be personally liable on any contract entered into by him in the performance of his functions (whether such contract is entered into by him in the name of such company or in his own name as receiver or otherwise) unless the contract provides that he is not to be personally liable on such contract, and he shall be entitled in respect of that liability to indemnity out of the asssets; but nothing in this subsection shall be taken as limiting any right to indemnity which he would have apart from this subsection, or as limiting his liability on contracts entered into without authority or as conferring any right to indemnity in respect of that liability.

(3) Where a receiver of the property of a company has been appointed or purported to be appointed and it is subsequently discovered that the charge or purported charge in respect of which he was so appointed or purported to be appointed was not effective as a charge on such property or on some part of such property, the court may, if it thinks fit, on the application of such receiver, order that he be relieved wholly or to such extent as the court shall think fit from personal liability in respect of anything done or omitted by him in relation to any property purporting to be comprised in the charge by virtue of which he was appointed or purported to be appointed which if such property had been effectively included in such charge or purported charge would have been properly done or omitted by him and he shall be relieved from personal liability accordingly, but in that event the person by whom such receiver was appointed or purported to be appointed shall be personally liable for anything for which, but for such order, such receiver would have been liable.

(4) This section shall apply whether the receiver was appointed before, on, or after the

operative date, but susbsection (2) shall not apply to contracts entered into before the operative date.

316A—(1) A receiver, in selling property of a company, shall exercise all reasonable care to obtain the best price reasonably obtainable for the property as at the time of sale.

(2) Notwithstanding the provisions of any instrument—

    (*a*) it shall not be a defence to any action or proceeding brought against a receiver in respect of a breach of his duty under subsection (1) that the receiver was acting as the agent of the company or under a power of attorney given by the company; and

    (*b*) notwithstanding anything in section 316(2), a receiver shall not be entitled to be compensated or indemnified by the company for any liability he may incur as a result of a breach of his duty under this section.

(3)   (*a*) A receiver shall not sell by private contract a non-cash asset of the requisite value to a person who is, or who, within three years prior to the date of appointment of the receiver, has been, an officer of the company unless he has given at least 14 days' notice of his intention to do so to all creditors of the company who are known to him or who have been intimated to him.

    (*b*) In this subsection—

        (i) "non-cash asset" and "requisite value" have the meanings assigned to them by *section 29* of the *Companies Act, 1990*, and

        (ii) "officer" includes a person connected, within the meaning of *section 26* of the *Companies Act, 1990*, with a director, and a shadow director.

Duty of receiver selling property to get best price reasonable obtainable

317.—(1) Where a receiver of the property of a company has been appointed, every invoice, order for goods or business letter issued by or on behalf of the company or the receiver or the liquidator of the company, being a document on or in which the name of the company appears, shall contain a statement that a receiver has been appointed.

(2) If default is made in complying with the requirements of this section, the company and any of the following persons who knowingly and wilfully authorises or permits the default, namely, any officer of the company, any liquidator of the company and any receiver, shall be liable to a fine of £100.

Notification that receiver appointed

318.—(1) The Court may, on an application made to it by the liquidator of a company or by any creditor or member of the company, by order fix the amount to be paid by way of remuneration to any person who, under the powers contained in any instrument, has been appointed as receiver of the property of the company notwithstanding that the remuneration of such receiver has been fixed by or under that instrument.

(2) Subject to subsection (3), the power of the court under subsection (1) shall, where no previous order has been made in relation thereto under that subsection—

    (*a*) extend to fixing the remuneration for any person before the making of the order or the application thereof; and

    (*b*) be exercisable notwithstanding that the receiver has died or ceased to act before the making of the order or the application thereof; and

    (*c*) where the receiver has been paid or has retained for his remuneration for any person before the making of the order any amount in excess of that fixed by the court for that period, extend to requiring him or his personal representatives to account for the excess or such part thereof as may be specified in the order.

Power of court to fix remuneration of receiver

(3) The power conferered by paragraph (*c*) of subsection (2) shall not be exercised in relation to any period before the making of the application for the order unless in the opinion of the court there are special circumstances making it proper for the power to be so exercised.

(4) The court may from time to time on an application made by the liquidator or by any creditor or member of the company or by the receiver, vary or amend an order made under subsection (1).

(5) This section shall apply whether the receiver was appointed before, on, or after the operative date and to periods before, as well as to periods after, the operative date.

Information to be given when receiver is appointed **319.**—(1) Where a receiver of the whole or substantially the whole of the property of a company (hereinafter in this section and in section 320 referred to as "the receiver") is appointed on behalf of the holders of any debentures of the company secured by a floating charge, then subject to the provisions of this section and section 320—

> (*a*) the receiver shall forthwith send notice to the company of his appointment; and
>
> (*b*) there shall, within 14 days after receipt of the notice, or such longer period as may be allowed by the court or by the receiver, be made out and submitted to the receiver in accordance with section 320 a statement in the prescribed form as to the affairs of the company; and
>
> (*c*) the receiver shall within 2 months after receipt of the said statement send to the registrar of companies, to the court, to the company, to any trustees for the debenture holders on whose behalf he was appointed and, so far as he is aware of their addresses, to all such debenture holders, a copy of the statement and of any comments he sees fit to make thereon.

(2) The receiver shall within one month after the expiration of the period of 6 months from the date of his appointment and of every subsequent period of 6 months, and within one month after he ceases to act as receiver of the property of the company, send to the registrar of companies an abstract in the prescribed form showing the assets of the company of which he has taken possession since his appointment, their estimated value, the proceeds of sale of any such assets since his appointment, his receipts and payments during that period of 6 months or, where he ceases to act as aforesaid, during that period from the end of the period to which the last preceding abstract releated up to the date of his so ceasing, and the aggregate amounts of his receipts and of his payments during all preceding periods since his appointment.

(3) Where a receiver is appointed under the powers contained in any instrument, this section shall have effect with the omission of the references to the court in subsection (1) and in any other case, references to the court shall be taken as referring to the court by which the receiver was appointed.

(4) Subsection (1) shall not apply in relation to the appointment of a receiver to act with an existing receiver or in place of a receiver dying or ceasing to act, except that, where that subsection applies to a receiver who dies or ceases to act before it has been fully complied with, the references in paragraphs (*b*) and (*c*) thereof to the receiver shall (subject to subsection (5)) include references to his successor and to any continuing receiver.

Nothing in this subsection shall be taken as limiting the meaning of "the receiver" where used in or in relation to subsection (2).

(5) This section and section 320, where the company is being wound up, shall apply notwithstanding that the receiver and the liquidator are the same person, but with any necessary modification arising from that fact.

(6) Nothing in subsection (2) shall be taken to prejudice the duty of the receiver to render proper accounts of his receipts and payments to the persons to whom, and at the times at which, he may be required to do so apart from that subsection.

(7) If the receiver makes default in complying with the requirements of this section, he shall be liable to a fine not exceeding £500.

320.—(1) The statement as to the affairs of a company required by section 319 to be submitted to the receiver (or his successor) shall show as at the date of the receiver's appointment particulars of the company's assets, debts and liabilities, the names and residences of its creditors, the security held by them respectively, the dates when the securities were respectively given and such further or other information as may be prescribed. Contents of statement to be submitted to receiver

(2) The said statement shall be submitted by, and be verified by affidavit of, one or more of the persons who are, at the date of the receiver's appointment, the directors and by the person who is at that date the secretary of the company, or by such of the persons hereafter in this subsection mentioned as the receiver (or his successor), may require to submit and verify the statement, that is, persons—

    (*a*) who are to have been officers of the company;

    (*b*) who have taken part in the formation of the company at any time within one year before the date of the receiver's appointment;

    (*c*) who are in the employment of the company or have been in the employment of the company within the said year, and are in the opinion of the receiver capable of giving the information required;

    (*d*) who are or have been within the said year officers of or in the employment of a company which is, or within the said year was, an officer of the company to which the statement relates.

(3) Any person making the statement and affidavit shall be allowed, and shall be paid by the receiver (or his successor) out of his receipts, such costs and expenses incurred in and about the preparation and making of the statement and affidavit as the receiver (or his successor) may consider reasonable, subject to an appeal to the court.

(4) Where the receiver is appointed under the powers contained in any instrument, this section shall have effect with the substitution for references to an affidavit of references to a statutory declaration; and in any other case references to the court shall be taken to refer to the court by which the receiver was appointed.

(5) If any person to whom subsection (2) applies makes default in complying with the requirements of this section, he shall, unless he can prove to the satisfaction of the court that it was not possible for him to comply with the requirements of the section, be liable—

    (*a*) on summary conviction, to imprisonment for a term not exceeding six months or to a fine not exceeding £1,000 or to both; or

    (*b*) on conviction on indictment, to imprisonment for a term not exceeding three years, or to a fine not exceeding £5,000 or to both.

320A.—Where, in contravention of section 319(1)(*b*) and section 320, a statement of affairs is not submitted to the receiver as required by those provisions, the court may, on the application of the receiver or any creditor of the company, and notwithstanding the provisions of section 320(5) (inserted by *section 173* of the *Companies Act, 1990*), make whatever order it thinks fit, including an order compelling compliance with section 319 and section 320. Consequences of contravention of section 319 or 320 of the Principal Act

321.—(1) Except where subsection (2) of section 319 applies, every receiver of the property of a company shall, within one month after the expiration of the period of 6 months from the date of his appointment and of every subsequent period of 6 months, and within one month after he ceases to act as receiver, deliver to the registrar of companies for registration an abstract in the prescribed form showing the assets of the company of which he has taken possession since his appointment, their estimated value, the proceeds of sale of Delivery to registrar of accounts of receivers any such assets since his appointment, his receipts and his payments during that period of 6 months or, where he cesaes to act as aforesaid, during the period from the end of the period to which the last preceding abstract related up to the date of his so ceasing, and the aggregate amounts of his receipts and of his payments during all the preceding periods since his appointment.

(2) Every receiver who makes default in complying with this section shall be liable to a fine not exceeding £500.

322.—(1) If any receiver of the property of a company—

    (*a*) having made default in filing, delivering or making any return, acount or other document, or in giving any notice, which a receiver is by law required to file, deliver, make or give, fails to make good the default within 14 days after the service on him of a notice requiring him to do so; or

    (*b*) having been appointed under the powers contained in any instrument, has, after being required at any time by the liquidator of the company to do so, failed to render proper accounts of his receipts and payments and to vouch the same and to pay over to the liquidator the amount properly payable to him;

the court may, on an application made for the purpose, make an order directing the receiver to make good the default within such time as may be specified in the order.

(2) In the case of any such default as is mentioned in paragraph (*a*) of subsection (1), an application for the purposes of this section may be made by any member or creditor of the company or by the registrar of companies, and in the case of any such default as is mentioned in paragraph (*b*) of that subsection, the application shall be made by the liquidator, and in either case the order may provide that all costs of and incidental to the application shall be borne by the receiver.

(3) Nothing in this section shall be taken to prejudice the operation of any enactments imposing penalties on receivers in respect of any such defaults as is mentioned in subsection (1).

Enforcement of duty of receiver to make returns

322A.—(1) The court may, on cause shown, remove a receiver and appoint another receiver.

(2) Notice of such proceedings shall be served on the receiver and on the person who appointed him not less than 7 days before the hearing of such proceedings and, in any such proceedings, the receiver and the person who appointed him may appear and be heard.

Removal of reciver

322B.—(1) On the application of the liquidator of a company that is being wound up (other than by means of a members' voluntary winding-up) and in respect of which a receiver has been appointed (whether before or after the commencement of the winding-up), the court may—

    (*a*) order that the receiver shall cease to act as such from a date specified by the court, and prohibit the appointment of any other receiver; or

    (*b*) order that the receiver shall, from a date by the court, act as such only in respect of certain assets specified by the court.

An order under this subsection may be made on such terms and conditions as the court thinks fit.

(2) The court may from time to time, on an application made either by the liquidator or by the receiver, rescind or amend an order made under subsection (1).

(3) A copy of an application made under this section shall be served on the receiver and on the person who appointed him not less than 7 days before the hearing of the application,

Court may determine or limit receivership on application of liquidator

and the receiver and any such party may appear before and be heard by the court in respect of the application.

(4) Except as provided in subsection (1), no order made under this section shall affect any security or charge over the undertaking or property of the company.

322C.—(1) A receiver of the property of a company appointed under the powers contained in any instrument may resign, provided he has given one month's notice thereto to— *Resignation of receiver*

(a) the holders of floating charges over all or any part of the property of the company;

(b) the company or its liquidator; and

(c) the holders of any fixed charge over all or any part of the property of the company.

(2) A receiver appointed by the court may resign only with the authority of the court and on such terms and conditions, if any, as may be laid down by the court.

(3) If any person makes default in complying with the requirements of this section, he shall be liable to a fine not exceeding £1,000.

323.—It is hereby declared that, unless the contrary intention appears— *Construction of references to receiver*

(a) any reference in this Act to a receiver of the property of a company includes a reference to a receiver and manager of the property of a company and to a manager of the property of a company and includes a reference to a receiver or to a receiver and manager or to a manager, of part only of that property, and to a receiver only of the income arising from that property or from part thereof; and

(b) any reference in this Act to the appointment of a receiver under powers contained in any instrument includes a reference to an appointment maded under powers which, by virtue of any enactment, are implied in and have effect as if contained in an instrument.

PART X

WINDING UP OF UNREGISTERED COMPANIES

344.—For the purposes of this Part, "unregistered company" shall include any trustee savings bank certified under the Trustee Savings Banks Acts, 1863 to 1958, any partnership, whether limited or not, any association and any company with the following exceptions— *Meaning of unregistered company*

(a) a company as defined by section 2;

(b) a partnership, assoociation or company which consists of less than eight members and is not formed outside the State.

345.—(1) Subject to the provisions of this Part, any unregistered company may be wound up under this Act, and all the provisions of this Act relating to winding-up shall apply to an unregistered company, with the exceptions and additions mentioned in this section. *Winding-up of unregistered companies*

(2) The principal place of business in the State of an unregistered company shall, for all the purposes of the winding-up, be deemed to be the registered office of the company.

(3) No unregistered company shall be wound up under this Act voluntarily.

(4) The circumstances in which an unregistered company may be wound up are as follows—

(*a*) if the company is dissolved, or has ceased to carry on business, or is carrying on business only for the purpose of winding-up its affairs.

(*b*) if the company is unable to pay its debts;

(*c*) if the court is of opinion that it is just and equitable that the company should be wound up.

(5) An unregistered company shall, for the purposes of this Act, be deemed to be unable to pay its debts—

(*a*) if a creditor, by assignment or otherwise, to whom the company is indebted in a sum exceeding £50 then due, has served on the company, by leaving at its principal place of business in the State, or by delivering to the secretary or some director or principal officer of the company, or by serving otherwise in such manner as the court may approve or direct, a demand in writing requiring the company to pay the sum so due, and the company has, for 3 weeks after the service of the demand, neglected to pay the sum or to secure or compound for it to the satisfaction of the creditor;

(*b*) if any action or other proceeding has been instituted against any member for any debt or demand due or claimed to be due, from the company or from him in his character of member, and notice in writing of the institution of the action or proceeding having been served on the company by leaving the same at its principal place of business in the State, or by delivering it to the secretary, or some director or principal officer of the company, or by otherwise serving the same in such manner as the court may approve or direct, the company has not within 10 days after service of the notice paid, secured or compounded for the debt or demand, or procured the action or proceeding to be stayed, or indemnified the defendant to his reasonable satisfaction against the action or proceeding, and against all costs, damages and expenses to be incurred by him by reason of the same;

(*c*) If in the State or in any country recognised by the Minister for the purposes of section 250, execution or other process issued on a judgment, decree or order obtained in any court in favour of a creditor against the company, or any member thereof as such, or any person authorised to be sued as nominal defendant on behalf of the company, is returned unsatisfied;

(*d*) if it is otherwise proved to the satisfaction of the court that the company is unable to pay its debts.

(6) A petition for winding-up a trustee savings bank may be presented by the Minister for Finance as well as by any person authorised under the other provisions of this Act to present a petition for winding-up a company.

(7) Where a company incorporated outside the State which has been carrying on business in the State ceases to carry on business in the State, it may be wound up as an unregistered company under this Part, notwithstanding that it has been dissolved or otherwise ceased to exist as a company under or by virtue of the laws of the country under which it was incorporated.

(8) Subject to such modifications as may be made by rules of court, the Bankruptcy Acts shall apply to limited partnerships as if limited partnerships were ordinary partnerships, and, upon all the partners of a limited partnership being adjudged bankrupt, the assets of the limited partnership shall vest in the Official Assignee.

Contributories
in winding-up
of
unregistered
company

346.—(1) In the event of an unregistered company being wound up, every person shall be deemed to be a contributory who is liable to pay or contribute to the payment of any debt or liability of the company, or to pay or contribute to the payment of any sum for the adjustment of the rights of the members among themselves, or to pay or contribute to the payment of the costs and expenses of winding-up the company, and every contributory shall be liable to contribute to the assets of the company all sums due from him in respect of any such liability as aforesaid.

(2) In the event of the death or bankruptcy of any contributory, the provisions of this Act relating to the personal representatives of deceased contributories and to the assignees of bankrupt contributories respectively shall apply.

347.—The provisions of this Act relating to staying and restraining actions and proceedings against a company at any time after the presentation of a petition for winding-up and before the making of a winding-up order shall, in the case of an unregistered company, where the application to stay or restrain is by a creditor, extend to actions and proceedings against any contributory of the company.

Power of court to stay or restrain proceedings

348.—Where an order has been made for winding-up an unregistered company, no action or proceeding shall be proceeded with or commenced against any contributory of the company in respect of any debt of the company, except by leave of the court, and subject to such terms as the court may impose.

Actions stayed on winding-up order

349.—The provisions of this Part relating to unregistered companies shall be in addition to and not in restriction of any provisions hereinbefore contained in this Act relating to winding-up companies by the court, and the court or liquidator may exercise any powers or do any act in the case of unregistered companies which might be exercised or done by it or him in winding-up companies formed and registered under this Act.

Provision of this Part to be cumulative

350.—Nothing in this Part shall affect the operation of any enactment which provides for any partnership, association or company being wound up, or being wound up as a company or as an unregistered company under the Companies (Consolidation) Act, 1908 or any enactment repealed by that Act.

Saving for enactments providing for winding-up under former Companies Act

Companies Act, 1990

Number 33 *of* 1990

Connected persons

26.—(1) For the purposes of this Part, a person is connected with a director of a company if, but only if, he is—

(a) that director's spouse, parent, brother, sister or child;

(b) a person acting in his capacity as the trustee of any trust, the principal beneficiaries of which are the director, his spouse or any of his children or any body corporate which he controls; or

(c) a partner of that director;

unless that person is also a director of the company.

(2) A body corporate shall also be deemed to be connected with a director of a company if it is controlled by that director.

(3) For the purposes of this seciton, a director of a company shall be deemed to control a body corporate if, but only if, alone or together with any persons refered to in *paragraph (a), (b)* or *(c)* of *subsection (1)*, interested in more than one-half of the equity share capital of that body or entitled to exercise or control the exercise of more that one-half of the voting power at any general meeting of that body.

(4) In *subsection (3)*—

(a) "equity share capital" has the same meaning as in section 155 of the Principal Act; and

(b) references to voting power exercised by a director shall include references to voting power exercised by another body corporate which that director controls.

(5) The provisionss of *section 54* shall have effect for the purposes of *subsection (3)* with the substitution of the words "more than half" for the words "one-third or more" in *subsection (5)* and *(6)* of that section.

Shadow directors

27.—(1) Subject to *subsection (2)*, a person in accordance with whose directions or instructions the directors of a company are accustomed to act (in this Act referred to as "shadow director") shall be treated for the purposes of this Part as a director of the compnay unless the directors are accustomed so to act by reason only that they do so on advice given by him in a professional capacity.

Creditors' voluntary winding-up

131.—(1) This section applies where, in the case of a creditors' voluntary winding-up, a liquidator has been nominated by the company.

(2) The powers conferred on the liquidator by section 276 of the Principal Act shall not be exercised, except with sanction of the court, during the period before the holding of the creditors' meeting under section 266 of that Act.

(3) *Subsection (2)* does not apply in relation to the power of the liquidator—

(a) to take into custody or under his control all the property to which the company is or appears to be entitled;

(b) to dispose of perishable goods and other goods the value of which is likely to diminish if they are not immediately disposed of;

(c) to do all such other things as may be necessary for the protection of the company's assets.

(4) The liquidator shall attend the creditors' meeting held under section 266 of the Principal Act and shall report to the meeting on any exercise by him of his powers (whether or not under this section or under section 276 or 280 of that Act).

(5) if default is made—

    (*a*) by the company in complying with subsection (1) or (2) of section 266 of the Principal Act, or

    (*b*) by the directors in complying with subsection (3) of the said section,

the liquidator shall, within 7 days of the relevant day, apply to the court for directions as to the manner in which that default is to be remedied.

(6) "The relevant day" means the day on which the liquidator was nominated by the company or the day on which he first became aware of the default, whichever is the later.

(7) If a liquidator without reasonable excuse fails to comply with this section, he shall be guilty of an offence.

139.—(1) Where, on the application of a liquidator, creditor or contributory of a company which is being wound up, it can be shown to the satisfaction of the court that— *[Power of the court to order the return of assets which have been improperly transfered.]*

    (*a*) any property of the company of any kind whatsoever was disposed of either by way of conveyance, transfer, mortgage, security, loan, or in any way whatsoever whether by act or omission, direct or indirect, and

    (*b*) the effect of such disposal was to perpetrate a fraud on the company, its creditors or members,

the court may, if it deems it just and equitable to do so, order any person who appears to have the use, control or possession of such property or the proceeds of the sale or development thereof to deliver it or pay a sum in respect of it to the liquidator on such terms or conditions as the court sees fit.

(2) *Subsection (1)* shall not apply to any conveyance, mortgage, delivery of goods payment, execution or other act relating to property made or done by or against a company to which section 286(1) of the Principal Act applies.

(3) In deciding whether it is just and equitable to make an order under this section, the court shall have regard to the rights of persons who have *bona fide* and for value acquired an interest in the property the subject of the application.

140.—(1) On the application of the liquidator or any creditor or contributory of any company that is being wound up, the court, if it is satisfied that it is just and equitable to do so, may order that any company that is or has been related to the company being wound up shall pay to the liquidator of that company an amount equivalent to the whole or part of all or any of the debts provable in that winding-up. Any order under this section may be made on such terms and condition as the court thinks fit. *[Company may be required to contribute to debts of related companies]*

(2) In deciding whether it is just and equitable to make an order under *subsection (1)* the court shall have regard to the following matters—

    (*a*) the extent to which the related company took part in the management of the company being wound up;

    (*b*) the conduct of the related company towards the creditors of the company being wound up;

    (*c*) the effect which such order would be likely to have on the creditors of the related company concerned.

(3) No order shall be made under *subsection (1)* unless the court is satisfied that the circumstances that gave rise to the winding-up of the company are attributable to the actions or omissions of the related company.

(4) Notwithstanding any other provision, it shall not be just and equitable to make an

order under *subsection (1)* if the only ground for making the order is—

      (*a*) the fact that a company is related to another company; or

      (*b*) that creditors of the company being wound up have relied on the fact that another company is or has been related to the first mentioned company.

(5) For the purposes of this Act, a company is related to another company if—

      (*a*) that other company is its holding company or subsidiary; or

      (*b*) more than half in nominal value of its equity share capital (as defined in section 155(5) of the Principal Act) is held by the other company and companies related to that other company (whether directly or indirectly, but other than in a fiduciary capacity); or

      (*c*) more than half in nominal value of the equity share capital (as defined in section 155(5) of the Principal Act) of each of them is held by members of the other (whether directly or indirectly, but other than in a fiduciary capacity); or

      (*d*) that other company or a company or companies related to that other company or that other company together with a company or companies related to it are entitled to exercise or control the exercise of more than one half of the voting power at any general meeting of the company; or

      (*d*) the businesses of the companies have been so carried on that the separate business of each company, or a substantial part thereof, is not readily identifiable; or

      (*e*) there is another company to which both companies are related;

and "related company" has a corresponding meaning.

(6) For the purposes of this section "company" includes any body which is liable to be wound up under the Companies Acts and "creditor" means one or more creditors to whom the company being wound up is indebted by more, in aggregate, than £10,000.

(7) Where an application for an order under *subsection (1)* seeks to require a licensed bank, within the meaning of *section 25*, to contribute to the debts of a related company, a copy of every such application shall be sent by the applicant to the Central Bank who shall be entitled to be heard by the court before an order is made.

Pooling of assets of related companies

141.—(1) Where two or more related companies are being wound up and the court, on the application of the liquidator of any of the companies, is satisfied that it is just and equitable to make an order under this section, the court may order that, subject to such terms and conditions as the court may impose and to the extent that the court orders, the companies shall be wound up together as if they were one company, and, subject to the provision of this section, the order shall have effect and all the provisions of this Part and Part VI of the Principal Act shall apply accordingly.

(2) In deciding the terms and conditions of an order under this section the court shall have particular regard to the interests of those persons who are members of some, but not all, of the companies.

(3) Where the court makes an order under *subsection (1)*—

      (*a*) the court may remove any liquidator of any of the companies, and appoint any person to act as liquidator of any one or more of the companies;

      (*b*) the court may give such directions as it thinks fit for the purpose of giving effect to the order;

      (*c*) nothing in this section or the order shall effect the rights of any secured creditor of any of the companies;

      (*d*) debts of a company that are to be paid in priority to all other debts of the company pursuant to section 285 of the Principal Act, shall to the extent that they are not paid out of the assets of that company, be subject to the claims of holders of debentures under any floating charge (as defined in that section) created by any of the other companies;

(*e*) unless the court otherwise orders, the claims of all unsecured creditors of the companies shall rank equally among themselves.

(4) In deciding whether it is just and equitable to make an order under *subsection (1)* the court shall have regard to the following matters—

(*a*) the extent to which any of the companies took part in the management of any of the other companies;

(*b*) the conduct of any of the companies towards the creditors of any of the other companies;

(*c*) the extent to which the circumstances that gave rise to the winding-up of any of the companies are attributable to the actions or omissions of any of the other companies;

(*d*) the extent to which the businesses of the companies have been intermingled.

(5) Notwithstanding any other provision, it shall not be just and equitable to make an order under *subsection (1)* if the only ground for making the order is—

(*a*) the fact that a company is related to another company, or

(*b*) that creditors of a company being wound up have relied on the fact that another company is or has been related to the first mentioned company.

(6) Notice of an application to the court for the purposes of this section shall be served on every company specified in the application, and on such other persons as the court may direct, not later than the end of the eighth day before the day the application is heard.

144.—(1) Where a receiver or liquidator of a company is obliged by the Companies Acts to make a periodic account, abstract, statement or return in relation to his activities as receiver or liquidator he shall incorporate in such account, abstract, statement or return a report as to whether, at the date of such account, abstract, statement or return any past or present director or other officer, or any member of the comapny is a person— *Duty of liquidators and receivers to include certain information in returns etc.*

(*a*) in respect of whom a declaration has been made under any provision of the Companies Acts that he should be personally liable for all or any part of the debts of a company,

(*b*) who is, or is deemed to be, subject to a disqualification order under *Part VII.*

(2) A receiver or liquidator who contravenes *subsection (1)* shall be guilty of an offence and liable to a fine.

145.—(1) Where a receiver or liquidator is in default in relation to the making or filing of a periodic account, abstract, statement or return in pursuance of any provision of the Companies Acts he shall be guilty of an offence and liable— *Penalty for default of receiver or liquidator in making certain accounts and returns*

(*a*) on summary conviction to a fine not exceeding £1,000 and, for continued contravention, to a daily default fine not exceeding £50;

(*b*) on conviction on indictment to a fine not exceeding £10,000 and, for continued contravention, to a daily default fine not exceeding £250.

(2) A person convicted of an offence under any of the following provisions, namely sections 262, 272, 306, 319(2) or 321 of the Principal Act, shall, in lieu of the penalty provided in any such section (as increased by section 15 of the Companies (Amendment) Act, 1982), be liable to the penalties specified in *subsection (1)*.

148.—(1) *Subsection (2)* applies if in the course of winding-up a company which is a subsidiary of another company, it appears that any director of the subsidiary's holding company has misapplied or retained or become liable or accountable for any money or *Extension of power of court to assess damages against directors* property of the subsidiary, or has been guilty of any misfeance or other breach of duty or trust in relation to the subsidiary.

(2) The court may, on the application of the liquidator, any creditor or contributory of the subsidiary, examine into the conduct of the director concerned and compel him—

> (*a*) to repay or restore the money or property or any part thereof respectively with interest at such rate as the court thinks just, or
>
> (*b*) to contribute such sum to the assets of the subsidiary by way of compensation in respect of the misapplication, retainer, misfeasance or other breach of duty or trust as the court thinks just.

PART VII

DISQUALIFICATIONS AND RESTRICTIONS: DIRECTORS AND OTHER OFFICERS

CHAPTER 1

Restriction on Director of Insolvent Companies

Application
of *Chapter 1*

149.—(1) This Chapter applies to any company if—

> (*a*) at the date of the commencement of its winding-up it is proved to the court; or
>
> (*b*) at any time the course of its winding-up the liquidator of the company certifies, or it is otherwise proved, to the court;

that it is unable to pay its debts (within the meaning of section 214 of the Principal Act).

(2) This Chapter applies to any person who was a director of a company to which this section applies at the date of, or within 12 months prior to, the commencement of its winding-up.

(3) This Chapter shall not apply to a company which commences to be wound up before the commencement of this section.

(4) In this Chapter "company" includes a company to which section 351 of the Principal Act applies.

(5) This Chapter applies to shadow directors as it applies to directors.

Restriction

150.—(1) The court shall, unless it is satisfied as to any of the matters specified in *subsection (2)*, declare that a person to whom this Chapter applies shall not, for a period of five years, be appointed or act in any way, whether directly or indirectly, as a director or secretary or be concerned or take part in the promotion or formation of any company unless it meets the requirements set out in *subsection (3)*; and, in subsequent provisions of this Part, the expression "a person to whom *section 150* applies" shall be construed as a reference to a person in respect of whom such a declaration has been made.

(2) The matters referred to in *subsection (1)* are—

> (*a*) that the person concerned has acted honestly and responsibly in relation to the conduct of the affairs of the company and that there is no other reason why it would be just and equitable that he should be subject to the restrictions imposed by this section, or
>
> (*b*) subject to *paragraph (a)*, that the person concerned was a director of the company solely by reason of his nomination as such by a financial institution in connection with the giving of credit facilities to the company by such institution, provided that the institution in question has not obtained from any director of the company a personal or individual guarantee of repayment to it of the loans or other forms of credit advanced to the company, or

(c) subject to *paragraph (a)*, that the person concerned was a director of the company solely by reason of his nomination as such by a venture capital company in connection with the purchase of, or subscription for, shares by it in the first-mentioned company.

(3) The requirements specified in *subsection (1)* are that—

    (a) the nominal value of the allotted share capital of the company shall—

        (i) in the case of a public limited company, be at least £100,000.

        (ii) in the case of any other company, be at least £20,000.

    (b) each allotted share to an aggregate amount not less than the amount refered to in *subparagraph (i)* of *(ii)* of *paragraph (a)*, as the case may be, shall be fully paid up, including the whole of any premium thereon, and

    (c) each such allotted share and the whole of any premium thereon shall be paid for in cash.

(4) Where a court makes a declaration under *subsection (1)* a prescribed officr of the court shall cause the registrar of companies to be furnished with prescribed particulars of the declaration in such form and manner as may be prescribed.

(5) In this section—

"financial institution" means—

    (a) a licensed bank, within the meaning of *section 25*, or

    (b) a company the ordinary business of which includes the making of loans or the giving of guarantees in connection with loans, and

"venture capital company" means a company prescribed by the Minister the principal ordinary business of which is the making of share investments.

151.—(1) Where it appears to the liquidator of a company to which this Chapter applies that the interests of any other company or its creditors may be placed in jeopardy by the relevant matters referred to in *subsection (2)* the liquidator shall inform the court of his opinion forthwith and the court may, on receipt of such report, make whatever order it sees fit. _{Duty of liquidator under this Chapter}

(2) The relevant matters are that a person to whom *section 150* applies is appointed or is acting in any way, whether directly or indirectly, as a director or is concerned or is taking part in the promotion or formation of any such other company as is referred to in *subsection (1)*.

(3) Any liquidator who contravenes *subsection (1)* shall be guilty of an offence and shall be liable—

    (a) on summary conviction, to a fine not exceeding £1,000 and, for continued contravention, to a daily default fine not exceeding £50, or

    (b) on conviction on indictment, to a fine not exceeding £10,000 and, for continued contravention, to a daily default fine not exceeding £250.

152.—(1) A person to whom *section 150* applies may, within not more than one year after a declaration has been made in respect of him under that section, apply to the court for relief, either in whole or in part, from the restrictions referred to in that section or from any order made in relation to him under *section 151* and the court may, if it deems it just and equitable to do so, grnat such relief on whatever terms and conditions it sees fit. _{Relief}

(2) Where it is intended to make an application for relief under *subsection (1)* the applicant shall give not less than 14 days' notice of his intention to the liquidator (if any) of the company the insolvency of which caused him to be subject to this Chapter.

(3) On receipt of a notice under *subsection (2)*, the liquidator shall forthwith notify such creditors and contributories of the company as have been notified to him or become known

to him, that he has received such notice.

(4) On the hearing of an application under this section the liquidator or any creditor or contributory of the company, the insolvency of which caused the applicant to be subject to this Chapter may appear and give evidence.

(5) Any liquidator who contravenes *subsection (3)* shall be guilty of an offence and liable to a fine.

Register of restricted persons

153.—(1) The registrar shall, subject to the provisions of this section, keep a register of the particulars which have been notified to him under *section 150*, and the following provisions of this section shall apply to the keeping of such a register.

(2) Where the court grants partial relief to a person under *secton 152* a prescribed officer of the court shall cause the registrar to be furnished with prescribed particulars of the relief, and the registrar shall, as soon as may be, enter the particulars on the register referred to in *section (1)*.

(3) Where the court grants full relief to a person under *section 152* a prescribed officer of the court shall cause the registrar to be so notified, and the registrar shall, as soon as may be, remove the particulars of any such person from the register referred to in *subsection (1)*.

(4) The registrar shall also remove from the register any particulars in relation to a person on the expiry of five years from the date of the declaration to which the original notification under *section 150* relates.

(5) Nothing in this section shall prevent the registrar from keeping the register required by this section as part of any other system of classification, whether pursuant to *section 247* or otherwise.

Application to this Chapter to receivers

154.—Where a reciver of the property of a company is appointed, the provisions of this Chapter shall, with the necessary modifications, apply as if the references therein to the liquidator and to winding-up were construed as references to the receiver and to receivership.

Restrictions on company to which *section 150(3)* applies

155.—(1) This section applies to any company in relation to which a person who is the subject of a declaration under *section 150* is appointed or acts in any way, whether directly or indirectly, as a director or secretary or is concerned in or takes part in the promotion or formation of that company.

(2) Subsections (2) to (11) of section 60 of the Principal Act shall not apply to any company to which this section applies.

(3) Sections 32 to 36 of the Companies (Amendment) Act, 1983, shall, with the necessary modifications, apply to any company to which this section applies as if the company were a public limited company so, however, that for the purposes of this subsection those sections shall apply as if—

> (*a*) in subsection (1) of section 32 the words "during the initial period" were deleted;
>
> (*b*) any other reference in any of those section to "initial period" were deleted; and
>
> (*c*) in subsection (2) of section 32 the words "relevant person" were defined to mean "any subscriber to the memorandum, any director or any person involved in the promotion or formation of the company".

(4) Without prejudice to *section 28, section 32* and *37* shall not apply to any company to which *subsection (1)* applies.

(5) From the date of a declaration under *section 150* a person in respect to whom the declaration was made shall not accept appointment to a position or act in any manner mentioned in *subsection (1)* of this section in relation to a company unless he has, within the 14 days immediately preceding such appointment or so acting, sent to the registered office of the company a notification that he is a person to whom *section 150* applies.

156.—(1) Where a company to which *section 155* applies allots a share which is not fully paid up as required by *section 150(3)(b)* the share shall be treated as if its nominal value together with the whole of any premium had been received, but the allottee shall be liable to pay the company in cash the full amount which should have been received in respect of the share under that subsection less the value of any consideration actually applied in payment up (to any extent) of the share and any premium on it, and interest at the appropriate rate on the amount payable under this subsection. Requirements as to shares allotted by a company to which *section 155* applies

(2) Where a company to which *section 155* applies allots a share which is not fully paid for in cash as required by *section 150(3)(c)* the allottee of the share shall be liable to pay the company in cash an amount equal to its nominal value, together with the whole of any premium, and shall be liable to pay interest at the appropriate rate on the amount payable under this subsection.

(3) *Subsection (1)* shall not apply in relation the allotment of a bonus share which is not fully paid up as required by *section 150(3)(b)* unless the allottee knew or ought to have known that the share was so allotted.

(4) *Subsection (1)* does not apply to shares allotted in pursuance of an employees' share scheme within the meaning of section 2 of the Companies (Amendment) Act, 1983.

(5) In this section, "appropriate rate" has the meaning assigned to it by section 2 of the Companies (Amendment) Act, 1983.

(6) Section 26(4) of the Companies (Amendment) Act, 1983, shll apply for the purposes of this section as it applies for the purposes of that section.

157.—(1) The court may, if it deems it just and equitable to do so, grant relief to a company to which *section 155* applies in respect of any act or omission which, by virtue of that section, contravened a provision of the Companies Acts or to any person adversely affected thereby, on whatever terms and conditions the court sees fit, including exemption from any such provision. Relief for a company in respect of prohibited transactions

(2) Relief shall not be granted to the company where the person referred to in *section 155(1)* complied with *subsection (5)* of that section.

158.—The Minister may, by order, vary the amounts mentioned in *section 150(3)(1)* and the order may— Power to vary amounts mentioned in *section 150(3)*

(a) require any company to which that section applies having an allotted share capital of which the nominal value is less than the amount specified in the order to increase the value to not less than that amount;

(b) make, in connection with any such requirement provision for any of the matters for which provision is made in the Companies Acts in relation to a company's registration, re-registration, change of name, winding-up or dissolution, payment for any share comprised in a company's capital and offers of shares in or debentures of a company to the public, including provision as to the consequences (whether in criminal law or otherwise) of a failure to comply with any requirement of the order, and

(c) contain such supplemental and transitional provisions as the Minister thinks appropriate, specify different amounts in relation to companies of different classes or descriptions and, in particular, provide for any provision of the order to come into operation on different days for different purposes.

CHAPTER 2

Disqualification Generally

Interpretation
of *Chapters 2*
and *3*

159.—In this Chapter and *Chapter 3*, except where the context otherwise requires—
"company" includes every company and every body, whether corporate or unincorporated, which may be wound up under Part X of the Principal Act and, without prejudice to the generality of the foregoing, includes a friendly society within the meaning of the Friendly Societies Acts, 1896 to 1977;

"the court" means the High Court except in relation to a disqualification order made by a court of its own motion under *section 160(2), paragraph (a), (b), (c), (d)* or *(f)* in which case it includes any court;

"default order" means an order made against any person uuder section 371 of the Principal Act by virtue of any contravention of or failure to comply with any relevant requirement (whether on its own part or on the part of any company);

"disqualification order" means—

> (*a*) an order under this Part that the person against whom the order is made shall not be appointed or act as an auditor, director or other officer, receiver, liquidator or examiner to be in any way, whether directly or indirectly, concerned or take part in the promotion, formation or management of any company, or any society registered under the Industrial and Provident Societies Acts, 1893 to 1978, or
>
> (*b*) an order under section 184 of the Principal Act;

"officer" in relation to any company, includes any director, shadow director or secretary of the company;

"relevant requirement" means any provision of the Companies Acts (including a provision repealed by this Act) which requires or required any return, account or other document to be filed with, delivered or sent to, or notice of any matter to be given to, the regiestrar of companies.

Disqualifi-
cation of
certain
persons from
acting as
directors or
auditors of or
managing
companies

160.—(1) Where a person is convicted on indictment of any indictable offence in relation to a company, or involving fraud or dishonesty, then during the period of five years from the date of conviction or such other period as the court, on the application of the prosecutor and having regard to all the circumstances of the case, may order—

> (*a*) he shall not be appointed or act as an auditor, director or other officer, receiver, liquidator or examiner or be in any way, whether directly or indirectly, concerned or take part in the promotion, formation or management of any company or any society registered under the Industrial and Provident Societies Acts, 1893 to 1978;
>
> (*b*) he shall be deemed, for the purposes of this Act, to be subject to a dis-qualification order for that period.

(2) Where the court is satisfied in any proceedings or as a result of an application under this section that—

> (*a*) a person has been guilty, while a promoter, officer, auditor, receiver, liquidator or examiner of a company, of any fraud in relation to the company, its members or creditors; or
>
> (*b*) a person has been guilty, while a promoter, officer, auditor, receiver, liquidator or examiner of a company, of any breach of his duty as such promoter, officer, auditor, receiver, liquidator or examiner; or
>
> (*c*) a declaration has been granted under section 297A of the Prinicipal Act (inserted by *section 138* of this Act) in respect of a person; or

(*d*) the conduct of any person as promoter, officer, auditor, receiver, liquidator or examiner of a company, makes him unfit to be concerned in the management of a company; or

(*e*) in consequence of a report of inspectors appointed by the court or the Minister under the Companies Acts, the conduct of any person makes him unfit to be concerned in the management of a company; or

(*f*) a person has been persistently in default in relation to the relevant requirements;

the court may, of its own motion, or as a result of the application, make a disqualification order against such a person for such period as it sees fit.

(3)　(*a*) For the purposes of *subsection (2)(f)* the fact that a person has been persistently in default in relation to the relevant requirements may (without prejudice to its proof in any other manner) be conclusively proved by showing that in the five years ending with the date of the application he has been adjudged guilty (whether or not on the same occasion) of three or more defaults in relation to those requirements.

(*b* A person shall be treated as being adjudged guilty of a default in relation to a relevant requirement for the purposes of ths subsection if he is convicted of any offence consisting of a contravention of a relevant requirement or a default order is made against him.

(4) An application under *paragraph (a), (b), (c)* or *(d)* of *subsection (2)* may be made by—

(*a*) the Director of Public Prosecutions; or

(*b*) any member, contributor, offier, receiver, liqduidator, examiner or creditor of any company in relation to which the person who is the subject of the application—

(i) has been or is acting or is proposing to or being proposed to act as officer, auditor, receiver, liquidator or examiner, or

(ii) has been or is concerned or taking part, or is proposing to be concerned or take part, in the promotion, formation or management of any company,

and where the application is made by a member, contributory, employee or creditor of the company, the court may require security for all or some of the costs of the application.

(5) An application under *paragraph (e)* of *subsection (2)* may be made by the Director of Public Prosecutions.

(6) An application under *paragraph (f)* of *subsection (2)* may be made by—

(*a*) the Director of Public Prosecutions; or

(*b*) the registrar of companies.

(7) Where it is intended to make an application under *subsection (2)* in respect of any person, the applicant shall give not less than ten days' notice of his intention to that person.

(8) Any person who is subject or deemed subject to a disqualification order by virtue of this Part may apply to the court for relief, either in whole or in part, from that disqualification and the court may, if it deems it just and equitable to do so, grant such relief on whatever terms and conditions it sees fit.

(9) A disqualification order may be made on grounds which are or include matters other than criminal convictions notwithstanding that the person in respect of whom the order is to be made may be criminally liable in respect of those matters.

(10) A reference in any other enactment to section 184 of the Principal Act shall be construed as including a reference to this section.

178.—The provisions of *section 139* shall, with the necessary modifications, apply to a company in receivership as if the references therein to the liquidator and to winding-up were construed as references to the receiver and to receivership.

Application
of section
299(2), (4)
and (5) of the
Principal Act
to receivers

179.—Section 299(2), (4) and (5) of the Principal Act shall apply, with the necessary modifications, to receivers as it applies to liquidators.

Companies (Amendment) Act 1990

(as amended)

Number 27 *of* 1990

1.—In this Act, unless the context otherwise requires— Definitions

"the Companies Act" means the Principal Act, and every enactment (including this Act) which is to be construed as one with that Act;

"examiner" means an examiner appointed under *section 2*;

"interested party", in relation to a company to which *section 2(1)* relates, means—

(*a*) a creditor of the company;

(*b*) a member of the company;

"the Minister" means the Minister for Industry and Commerce;

"the Principal Act" means the Companies Act, 1963.

2.—(1) Where it appears to the court that— Power of
court to
appoint
examiner

(*a*) a company is or is likely to be unable to pay its debts, and

(*b*) no resolution subsists for the winding-up of the company, and

(*c*) no order has been made for the winding-up of the company,

it may, on application by petition presented, appoint an examiner to the company for the purpose of examining the state of the company's affairs and performing such duties in relation to the company as may be imposed by or under this Act.

(2) Without prejudice to the general power of the court under *subsection (1)*, it may, in particular, make an order under this section if it considers that such order would be likely to facilitate the survival of the company, and the whole or in part of its undertaking, as a going concern.

(3) For the purpose of this section, a company is unable to pay its debts if—

(*a*) it is unable to pay its debts as they fall due;

(*b*) the value of its assets is less than the amount of its liabilities, taking into account its contingent and prospective liabilities, or

(*c*) section 214(*a*) and (*b*) of the Principal Act applies to the company.

(4) In deciding whether to make an order under this section the court may also have regard to whether the company has sought from its creditors significant extensions of time for the payment of its debts, from which it could reasonably be inferred that the company was likely to be unable to pay its debts.

3.—(1) Subject to *subsection (2)*, a petition under *section 2* may be presented by— Petition for
protection of
the court

(*a*) the company, or

(*b*) the directors of the company, or

(*c*) a creditor, or contingent or prospective creditor (including an employee) of the company, or

(*d*) members of the company holding at the date of the presentation of a petition under that section not less than one-tenth of such of the paid-up capital of the company as carries at that date the right of voting at general meetings of the company,

or by all or any of those parties, together or separately.

(2)   (*a*) Where the company referred to in *section 2* is an insurer, a petition under that section may be presented only by the Minister, and *subsection (1)* of this section shall not apply to the company,

(*b*) Where the company referred to in *section 2* is the holder of a licence under section 9 by the Central Bank Act 1971, or any other company supervised by the Central Bank under any enactment, a petition under *section 2* may be presented only by the Central Bank, and *subsection (1)* of this section shall not apply to the company.

(3) A petition presented under *section 2* shall—

(*a*) nominate a person to be appointed as examiner, and

(*b*) be supported by such evidence as the court may require for the purpose of showing that the petitioner has good reason for requiring the appointment of an examiner, and

(*c*) where the petition is presented by any person or persons referred to in *subsection (1)(a)* or *(b)*, include a statement of the assets and liabilities of the company (in so far as they are known to them) as they stand on a date not earlier than 7 days before the presentation of the petition.

(4) A petition presented under *section 2* shall be accompanied—

(*a*) by a consent signed by the person nominated to be examiner, and

(*b*) if proposals for a compromise or scheme of arrangement in relation to the company's affairs have been prepared for submission to interested parties for their approval, by a copy of the proposals.

(5) The court shall not give a hearing to a petition under *section 2* presented by a contingent or prospective creditor until such security for costs has been given as the court thinks reasonable, and until a *prima facie* case for the protection of the court has been established to the satisfaction of the court.

(6) The court shall not give a hearing to a petition under *section 2* if a receiver stands appointed to the company the subject of the petition and such receiver has stood so appointed for a continuous period of at least 3 days prior to the presentation of the petition.

(7) On hearing a petition under this section, the court may dismiss it, or adjourn the hearing conditionally or unconditionally, or make any interim order, or any other order it thinks fit.

(8) Without prejudice to the generality of *subsection (7)*, an interim order under that subsection may restrict the exercise of any powers of the directors or of the company (whether by reference to the consent of the court or otherwise).

(9)   (*a*) Where it appears to the court that the total liabilities of the company (taking into account its contingent and prospective liabilities) do not exceed £250,000, the court may, after making such interim or other orders as it thinks fit, order that the matter be remitted to the judge of the Circuit Court in whose circuit the company has its registered office or principal place of business.

(*b*) Where an order is made by the court under this subsection the Circuit Court shall have full jurisdiction to exercise all the powers of the court conferred by this Act in relation to the company and every reference to the court in this Act shall be construed accordingly.

(*c*) Where, in any proceedings under this Act which have been remitted to the Circuit Court by virtue of this subsection, it appears to the Circuit Court that the total liabilities of the company exceed £250,000, it shall make, after making such interim orders as it thinks fit, an order transferring the matter to the court.

4.—(1) Where the court appoints an examiner to a company, it may, at the same or any Related companies time thereafter, make an order—

> (*a*) appointing the examiner to be examiner for the purposes of this Act to a related company, or
>
> (*b*) conferring on the examiner, in relation to such company, all or any of the powers or duties conferred on him in relation to the first-mentioned company.

(2) In deciding whether to make an order under *subsection (1)*, the court shall have regard to whether the making of the order would be likely to facilitate the survival of the company, or of the related companies, or both, and the whole or any part of it or their undertaking, as a going concern.

(3) A related company to which an examiner is appointed shall be deemed to be under the protection of the court for the period beginning on the date of the making of an order under this section and continuing for the period during which the company to which it is related is under such protection.

(4) Where an examiner stands appointed for two or more related companies, he shall have the same powers and duties in relation to each company, taken separately, unless the court otherwise directs.

(5) For the purposes of this Act, a company is related to another company if—

> (*a*) that other company is its holding company or subsidiary; or
>
> (*b*) more than half in nominal value of its equity share capital (as defined in section 155(5) of the Principal Act) is held by the other company and companies related to that other company (whether directly or indirectly, but other than in a fiduciary capacity); or
>
> (*c*) that other company or a company or companies related to that other company or that other company together with a company or companies related to it are entitled to exercise or control the exercise of more than one half of the voting power at any general meeting of the company; or
>
> (*e*) the business of the companies have been so carried on that the separate business of each company, or a substantial part thereof, is not readily identifiable; or
>
> (*f*) there is another body corporate to which both companies are related;

and "related company" has a corresponding meaning.

(6) For the purposes of this section "company" includes any body which is liable to be wound up under the Companies Acts.

5.—(1) During the period beginning with the presentation of a petition for the appoint- Effect of petition to appoint examiner or creditors and others ment of an examiner to a company and (subject to *section 18(3)* or *(4)* ending on the expiry of three months from that date or on the withdrawal or refusal of the petition, whichever first happens, the company shall be deemed to be under the protection of the court.

(2) For so long as a company is under the protection of the court in a case under this Act, the following provisions shall have effect—

> (*a*) no proceedings for the winding-up of the company may be commenced or resolution for winding-up passed in relation to that company and any resolution so passed shall be of no effect;
>
> (*b*) no receiver over any part of the property or undertaking of the company shall be appointed, or if so appointed before the presentation of a petition under *section 2*, shall, subject to *section 6*, be able to act;
>
> (*c*) no attachment, sequestration, distress or execution shall be put into force against the property or affects of the company, except with the consent of the examiner;

(*d*) where any claim against the company is secured by a charge on the whole or any part of the property, effects or income of the company, no action may be taken to realise the whole or any part of such security, except with the consent of the examiner;

(*e*) no steps may be taken to repossess goods in the company's possession under any hire-purchase agreement (within the meaning of *section 11(8)*), except with the consent of the examiner;

(*f*) where, under any enactment, rule of law or otherwise, any person other than the company is liable to pay all or any part of the debts of the company—

    (i) no attachment, sequestration, distress or execution shall be put into force against the property or effects of such person in respect of the debts of the company, and

    (ii) no proceedings of any sort may be commenced against such person in respect of the debts of the company.

(*g*) no order for relief shall be made under section 205 of the Principal Act against the company in respect of complaints as to the conduct of the affairs of the company or the exercise of the powers of the directors prior to the presentation of the petition.

(*h*) no set-off between separate bank accounts of the company shall be effected, except with the consent of the examiner, and in this paragraph "bank account" includes an account with any person exempt by virtue of section 7(4) of the Central Bank Act 1971, from the requirement of holding a licence under section 9 of that Act.

(3) Subject to *subsection (2)*, no other proceedings in relation to the company may be commenced except by leave of the court and subject to such terms as the court may impose and the court may on the application of the examiner make such order as it thinks proper in relation to any existing proceedings including an order to stay such proceedings.

(4) Complaints concerning the conduct of the affairs of the company while it is under the protection of the court shall not constitute a basis for the making of an order for relief under section 205 of the Principal Act.

Effect on receiver or provisional liquidator of order appointing examiner

6.—(1) Where the court appoints an examiner to a company and a receiver stands appointed to the whole or any part of the property or undertaking of that company the court may make such order as it thinks fit including an order as to any will of the following matters—

(*a*) that the receiver shall cease to act as such from a date specified by the court,

(*b*) that the receiver shall, from a date specified by the court, act as such only in respect of certain assets specified by the court,

(*c*) directing the receiver to deliver all books, papers and other records, which relate to the property or undertaking of the company (or any part thereof) and are in his possession or control, to the examiner within a period to be specified by the court.

(*d*) directing the receiver to give the examiner full particulars of all his dealings with the property or undertaking of the company.

(2) Where the court appoints an examiner to a company and a provisional liquidator stands appointed to that company, the court may make such order as it thinks fit including an order as to any or all of the following matters—

(*a*) that the provisional liquidator be appointed as examiner of the company,

(*b*) appointing some other person as examiner of the company,

(*c*) that the provisional liquidator shall cease to act as such from the date specified by the court, (*d*) directing the provisional liquidator to deliver all books, papers and other records, which relate to the property or undertaking of the company, or any part thereof and are in his possession or control, to the examiner within a period to be specified by the court,

 (*e*) directing the provisional liquidator to give the examiner full particulars of all his dealings with the property or undertaking of the company.

(3) In deciding whether to make an order under *subsection (1)(a)* or *(b)*, or *subsection (2)(c)*, the court shall have regard to whether the making of the order would be likely to facilitate the survival of the company, and the whole or any part of its undertaking, as a going concern.

(4) Where the court makes an order under *subsection (1)* or *(2)*, it may, for the purpose of giving full effect to the order, include such conditions in the order and make such ancillary or other orders as it deems fit.

(5) Where a petition is presented under *section 2* in respect of a company at a date subsequent to the presentation of a petition for the winding-up of that company, but before a provisional liquidator has been appointed or an order made for its winding-up, both petitions shall be heard together.

7.—(1) Any provision of the Companies Acts relating to the rights and powers of an auditor of a company and the supplying of information to and co-operation with such auditor shall, with the necessary modifications, apply to an examiner. Powers of an examiner

(2) Notwithstanding any provision of the Companies Acts relating to notice of general meetings, an examiner shall have power to convene, set the agenda for, and preside at meetings of the board of directors and general meetings of the company to which he is appointed and to propose motions or resolutions and to give reports to such meeting.

(3) An examiner shall be entitled to reasonable notice of, to attend and be heard at, all meetings of the board of directors of a company and all general meetings of the company to which he is appointed.

(4) For the purpose of *subsection (3)* "reasonable notice" shall be deemed to include a description of the business to be transacted at any such meeting.

(5) Where an examiner becomes aware of any actual or proposed act, omission, course of conduct, decision or contract, by or on behalf of the company to which he has been appointed, its officers, employees, members or creditors or by any other person in relation to the income, assets or liabilities of that company which, in his opinion, is or is likely to be to the detriment of the company, or any interested party, he shall, subject to the rights of parties acquiring an interest in good faith and for value in such income, assets or liabilities, have full power to take whatever steps are necessary to halt, prevent or rectify the effects of such act, omission, course of conduct, decision or contract.

(6) The examiner shall apply to the court to determine any question arising in the course of his office, or for the exercise in relation to the company of all or any of the powers which the court may exercise under this Act, upon the application to it of any member, contributory, creditor or director of a company.

(7) The examiner shall, if so directed by the court, have power to ascertain and agree claims against the company to which he has been appointed.

8.—(1) It shall be the duty of all officers and agents of the company or a related company to produce to the examiner all books and documents of or relating to any such company which are in their custody or power, to attend before him when required so to do and otherwise to give to him all assistance in connection with his functions which they are reasonably able to give. Production of documents and evidence

(2) If the examiner considers that a person other than an officer or agent of any such company is or may be in possession of any information concerning his affairs, he may require that person to produce to him any books or documents in his custody or power relating to the company, to attend before him and otherwise to give him all assistance in connection with his functions which he is reasonably able to give; and it shall be the duty of that person to comply with the requirement.

(3) If the examiner has reasonable grounds for believing that a director of any such company maintains or has maintained a bank account of any description, whether alone or jointly with another person and whether in the State or elsewhere, into or out of which there has been paid—

>   (a) any money which has resulted from or been used in the financing of any transaction, arrangement or agreement particulars of which have not been disclosed in the accounts of any company for any financial year as required by law; or
>
>   (b) any money which has been in any way connected with any act or omission, or series of acts or omissions, which on the part of that director constituted misconduct (whether fraudulent or not) towards that company or its members;

the examiner may require the director to produce to him all documents in the director's possession, or under his control, relating to that bank account; and in this subsection "bank account" includes an account with any person exempt by virtue of section 7(4) of the Central Bank Act 1971, from the requirement of holding a licence under sectionm 9 of that Act and "director" includes any present or past director or any person connected, within the meaning of *section 26* of the *Companies Act 1990*, with such director, and any present or past shadow director.

(4) An examiner may examine on oath, either by word of mouth or on written interrogatories, the officers and agents of such company or other person as is mentioned in *subsection (1)* or *(2)* in relation to its affairs and may—

>   (a) administer an oath accordingly,
>
>   (b) reduce the answers of such person to writing and require him to sign them.

(5) If any officer or agent of such company or other person refuses to produce to the examiner any book or document which it is his duty under this section so to produce, refuses to attend before the examiner when required so to do or refuses to answer any question which is put to him by the examiner with respect to the affairs of the company, the examiner may certify the refusal under this hand to the court, and the court may thereupon enquire into the case and, after hearing any witnesses who may be produced against or on behalf of the alleged offender and any statement which may be offered in defence, punish the offender in like manner as if he had been guilty of contempt of court.

(5A) Without prejudice to its power under subsection (5), the court may, after a hearing under that subsection, make any order or direction it thinks fit, including a direction to the person concerned to attend or re-attend before the examiner or produce particular books or documents or answer particular questions put to him by the examiner, or a direction that the person concerned need not produce a particular book or document or answer a particular question put to him by the examiner.

(5B) *Section 23(1)* of the *Companies Act 1990* shall apply for the purposes of this section.

(6) In this section, any reference to officers or to agents shall include past, as well as present, officers or agents, as the case may be, and "agents", in relation to a company, shall include the bankers and solicitors of the company and any person employed by the company as auditors, whether those persons are or are not officers of the company.

9—(1) Where it appears to the court, on the application of the examiner, that, having regard to the matters referred to in *subsection (2)*, it is just and equitable to do so, it may make an order that all or any of the functions or powers which are vested in or exercisable by the directors (whether by virtue of the memorandum or articles of association of the company or by law or otherwise) shall be performable or exercisable only by the examiner. Further
powers of
court

(2) The matters to which the court is to have regard for the purpose of *subsection(1)* are—

    (*a*) that the affairs of the company are being conducted, or are likely to be conducted, in a manner which is calculated or likely to prejudice the interests of the company or of its employees or of its creditors as a whole, or

    (*b*) that it is expedient, for the purpose of preserving the assets of the company or of safeguarding the interests of the company or of its employees or of its creditors as a whole, that the carrying on of the business of the company by, or the exercise of the powers of, its directors or management should be curtailed or regulated in any particular respect, or

    (*c*) that the company, or its directors, have resolved that such an order should be sought, or

    (*d*) any other matter in relation to the company the court thinks relevant.

(3) Where the court makes an order under *subsection (1)*, it may, for the purpose of giving full effect to the order, include such conditions in the order and make such ancillary or other orders as it sees fit.

(4) Without prejudice to the generality of *subsection (1)* and *(3)*, an order under this section may provide that the examiner shall have all or any of the powers that he would have if he were a liquidator appointed by the court in respect of the company and, where such order so provides, the court shall have all the powers that it would have if it had made a winding-up order and appointed a liquidator in respect of the company concerned.

10.—(1) Any liabilities incurred by the company during the protection period which are referred to in *subsection (2)* shall be treated as expenses properly incurred, for the purpose of *section 29*, by the examiner. Incurring of
certain
liabilities by
examiner

(2) The liabilities referred to in *subsection (1)* are those certified by the examiner at the time they are incurred, to have been incurred in circumstances where, in the opinion of the examiner, the survival of the company as a going concern during the protection period would otherwise be seriously prejudiced.

(3) In this section "protection period" means the period, beginning with the appointment of an examiner, during which the company is under the protection of the court.

11.—(1) Where, on an application by the examiner, the court is satisfied that the disposal (with or without other assets) of any property of the company which is subject to a security which, as created, was a floating charge or the exercise of his powers in relation to such property would be likely to facilitate the survival of the whole or any part of the company as a going concern, the court may by order authorise the examiner to dispose of the property, or exercise his powers in relation to it, as the case may be, as if it were not subject to the security. Power to deal
with charged
property, etc.

(2) Where, on an application by the examiner, the court is satisfied that the disposal (with or without other assets) of—

    (*a*) any property of the company subject to a security other than a security to which *subsection (1)* applies, or

    (*b*) any goods in the possession of the company under a hire-purchase agreement,

would be likely to facilitate the survival of the whole or any part of the company as a going concern, the court may by order authorise the examiner to dispose of the property as if it where not subject to the security or to dispose of the goods as if all rights of the owner under the hire-purchase agreement were vested in the company.

(3) Where property is disposed of under *subsection (1)*, the holder of the security shall have the same priority in respect of any property of the company directly or indirectly representing the property disposed of as he would have had in respect of the property subject to the security.

(4) It shall be a condition of an order under *subsection (2)* that—

    (*a*) the net proceeds of the disposal, and

    (*b*) where those proceeds are less than such amount as may be determined by the court to be the net amount which would be realised on a sale of the property or goods in the open market by a willing vendor, such sums as may be required to make good the deficiency.

shall be applied towards discharging the sums secured by the security or payable under the hire-purchase agreement.

(5) Where a condition imposed in pursuance of *subsection (4)* relates to two or more securities, that condition requires the net proceeds of the disposal and, where *paragraph (b)* of that subsection applies, the sums mentioned in that paragraph to be applied towards discharging the sums secured by those securities in the order of their priorities.

(6) An office copy of an order under *subsection (1)* or *(2)* in relation to a security shall, within 7 days after the making of the order, be delivered by the examiner to the registrar of companies.

(7) If the examiner without reasonable excuse fails to comply with *subsection (6)*, he shall be liable to a fine not exceeding £1,000.

(8) References in this section to a hire purchase agreement include a conditional sale agreement, a retention of title agreement and an agreement for the bailment of goods which is capable of subsisting for more than 3 months.

Notification of appointment of examiner

12.—(1) Where a petition is presented under *section 3*, notice of the petition in the prescribed form shall, within 3 days after its presentation, be delivered by the petitioner to the registrar of companies.

(2)   (*a*) An examiner shall, within the time limits specified in *paragraph (b)*, cause to be published in *Iris Oifigiúil* and in at least two daily newspapers circulating in the district in which the registered office or principal place of business of the company is situate a notice of—

      (i) his appointment and the date thereof, and

      (ii) the date, if any, set for the hearing of the matters arising out of the report to be prepared by the examiner under *section 15*.

    (*b*) The time limits referred to in *paragraph (a)* are—

      (i) twenty-one days after his appointment in the case of *Iris Oifigiúil*, and

      (ii) three days after his appointment in the other case referred to in that paragraph.

(3) An examiner shall, within three days after his appointment, deliver to the registrar of companies a copy of the order appointing him.

(4) Where a company is, by virtue of *section 5*, deemed to be under the protection of the court, every invoice, order for goods or business letter issued by or on behalf of the company, being a document on or in which the name of the company appears, shall contain the statement "under the protection of the court".

(5) A person who fails to comply with the provisions of this section shall be guilty of an offence and shall be liable, on summary conviction, to a fine not exceeding £1,000 and, on conviction on indictment, to a fine not exceeding £10,000.

13.—(1) An examiner may resign, or on cause shown, be removed by the court. General provisions as to examiners

(2) If for any reason a vacancy occurs in the office of examiner, the court may be order fill the vacancy.

(3) An application for an order under *subsection (2)* may be made by—

(*a*) any committee of creditors established under *section 21*, or

(*b*) the company or any interested party.

(4) An examiner shall be described by the style of "the examiner" of the particular company in respect of which he is appointed and not by his individual name.

(5) The acts of an examiner shall be valid notwithstanding any defects that may afterwards be discovered in his appointment or qualification.

(6) An examiner shall be personally liable on any contract entered into by him in the performance of his functions (whether such contract is entered into by him in the name of the company or in his own name as examiner or otherwise) unless the contract provides that he is not to be personally liable on such contract, and he shall be entitled in respect of that liability to indemnity out of the assets; but nothing in this subsection shall be taken as limiting any right to indemnity which he would have apart from this subsection, or as limiting his liabily on contracts entered into without authority or as conferring any right to indemnity in respect of that liability.

(7) A company to which an examiner has been appointed or an interested party may apply to the court for the determination of any question arising out of the performance or otherwise by the examiner of his functions.

14.—(1) The directors of a company to which an examiner has been appointed shall, Information to be given when examiner appointed within 7 days of the appointment, cause to be made out, verified by affidavit and submitted to the examiner a statement in accordance with this section as to the affairs of the company.

(2) The statement shall, in so far as is reasonably possible to do so, show as at the date of the examiner's appointment particulars of the company's assets, debts and liabilities (including contingent and prospective liabilities), the names and addresses of its creditors, the securities held by them respectively, the dates when the securities were respectively given and such further information as may be prescribed or as the court may direct.

(3) A person to whom *subsection (1)* applies who makes default in complying with the requirements of this section shall be guilty of an offence and shall be liable, on summary conviction, to a fine not exceeding £1,000 and, on conviction on indictment, to a fine not exceeding £10,000.

15.—(1) It shall be the duty of an examiner to conduct an examination of the affairs of Examination of the affairs of company the company to which he is appointed and report to the court, within 21 days of his appointment or such longer period as the court may allow, the results of the examination in accordance with *section 16*.

(2) Notwithstanding any other provision of this Act the court may impose on the examiner such other duties as it deems appropriate.

(3) The examiner shall deliver a copy of his report under this section to the company on the same day as his delivery of such report to the court.

(4) The examiner shall supply a copy of his report under this section to any interested party on written application, provided that such supply may, if the court so directs, be subject to the omission of such parts of the report as the court thinks fit.

(5) The court may, in particular, give a direction under *subsection (4)* if it considers that the inclusion of certain information in the report to be supplied under that subsection would be likely to prejudice the survival of the company, or the whole or any part of its undertaking.

16.—The examiner's report under *section 15* shall comprise the following—

(*a*) the names and permanent addresses of the officers of the company and, in so far as the examiner can establish, any person in accordance with whose directions or instructions the directors of the company are accustomed to act,

(*b*) the names of any other bodies corporate of which the directors of the company are also directors,

(*c*) a statement as to the affairs of the company, showing, insofar as is reasonably possible to do so, particulars of the company's assets, debts and liabilities (including contingent and prospective liabilities) as at the latest practicable date, the names and addresses of its creditors, the securities held by them respectively and the dates when the securities were respectively given,

(*d*) whether in the opinion of the examiner any deficiency between the assets and the liabilities of the company has been satisfactorily accounted for or, if not, whether there is evidence of a substantial disappearance of property that is not adequately accounted for,

(*e*) a statement of opinion by the examiner as to whether the company, and the whole or in part of its undertaking, would be capable of surivival as a going concern and a statement of the conditions which he feels are essential to ensure such survival, whether as regards the internal managament and controls of the company or otherwise,

(*f*) his opinion as to whether the formulation, acceptance and confirmation of proposals for a compromise or scheme of arrangement would facilitate such survival,

(*g*) whether, in his opinion, an attempt to continue the whole or any part of the undertaking of the company would be likely to be more advantageous to the members as a whole and the creditors as a whole, then a winding-up of the company,

(*h*) recommendations as to the course he thinks should be taken in relation to the company including, if warranted, draft proposals for a compromise or scheme of arrangement,

(*i*) his opinion as to whether the facts disclosed would, warrant further inquiries with a view to proceedings under section 297 or 297A of the Principal Act, or both,

(*j*) such other matters as the examiner thinks relevant or the court directs, and

(*k*) his opinion as to whether his work would be assisted by a direction of the court extending the role or membership of any creditors' committee referred to in *section 21*.

17.—(1) Where, in a report made under *section 15*, the examiner expresses the opinion that—

(*a*) the whole or any part of the undertaking of the company to which he has been appointed would not be capable of survival as a going concern, or

(*b*) the formulation, acceptance, or confirmation of proposals for a compromise or scheme of arrangement wouuld not facilitate such survival, or

(*c*) an attempt to continue the whole or part of the undertaking of the company would not be likley to be more advantageous to the members as a whole, or the creditors as a whole, than a winding-up of the company, or

(*d*) there is evidence of a substantial disappearance of property that is not adequately accounted for, or of other serious irregularities in relation to the company's affairs.

the court shall, as soon as may be after the receipt of the examiner's report, hold a hearing to consider matters arising out of the report.

(2) The following parties shall be entitled to appear and be heard at a hearing under *subsection (1)*—

    (*a*) the examiner,

    (*b*) the company,

    (*c*) any interested party,

    (*d*) any person who is referred to in the report in relation to the matters mentioned in *subsection (1)(d)*.

(3) Following a hearing under this section, the court may make such order or orders as it deems fit.

(4) Without prejudice to the generality of *subsection (3)*, an order under that subsection may include any order for—

    (*a*) the discharge from the protection of the court of the whole or any part of the assets of the company,

    (*b*) the imposition of such terms and conditions as it sees fit for the continuance of the protection of the court,

    (*c*) the winding-up of the company,

    (*d*) the sale of the whole or any part of the undertaking of the company on such terms and conditions, including terms and conditions relating to the distribution of the proceeds of such sale, as the court sees fit, and, if necessary for that purpose, the appointment of a receiver,

    (*e*) the formulation by the examiner of proposals for a compromise or scheme of arrangement,

    (*f*) the summoning of the meetings mentioned in this Act for the purpose of considering proposals for a compromise or scheme of arrangement,

    (*g*) the calling, holding and conduct of a meeting of the board of directors, or a general meeting of the company, to consider such matters as the court shall direct,

(5) On the making of an order under this section, the examiner or such other person as the court may direct shall deliver an office copy of the order to the registrar of companies for registration.

(6) Where the court makes an order for the winding-up of a company under this Act, such a winding-up shall be deemed to have commenced on the date of the making of the order, unless the court otherwise orders.

18.—(1) Where, in the opinion of the examiner—   Further reports by examiner

    (*a*) the whole or any part of the undertaking of the company would be capable of surviving as a going concern, and

    (*b*) an attempt to continue the whole or any part of the undertaking of the company would be likely to be more advantageous to the members as a whole, and to the creditors as a whole, than a winding-up of the company, and

    (*c*) the formulation, acceptance and confirmation of proposals for a compromise or scheme of arrangement would facilitate such survival,

the examiner shall formulate proposals for a compromise or scheme of arrangement.

(2) Notwithstanding any provision of the Companies Acts relating to notice of general meetings (but subject to notice of not less than three days in any case) the examiner shall convene and preside at such meetings of members and creditors as he thinks proper, to

consider such proposals and report thereon to the court within 42 days of his appointment or such longer period as the court may allow, in accordance with *section 19*.

(3) Where, on the application of the examiner, the court is satisfied that the examiner would be unable to report to the court within a period of three months referred to in *section 5(1)* but that he would be able to make a report if that period were extended, the court may by order extend that period by not more than 30 days to enable him to do so.

(4) Where the examiner has submitted a report under this section to the court and, but for this subsection, the period mentioned in *section 5(1)* (and any extended period followed under *subsection (3)* of this section) would expire, the court may, of its own motion or on the application of the examiner, extend the period concerned by such period as the court considers necessary to enable it to take a decision under *section 24*.

(5) The examiner shall deliver a copy of his report under this section—

(*a* to the company on the same day as his delivery of such report to the court, and

(*b*) to any interested party on written application,

provided that such delivery under *paragraph (b)* may, if the court so directs, be subject to the omission on such parts of the report as the court thinks fit.

(6) The court may, in particular, give a direction under *subsection (5)(b)* if it considers that the inclusion of certain information in the report to be delivered under that paragraph would be likely to prejudice the survival of the company, or the whole or any part of its undertaking.

Examiner's
report under
section 18

19.—An examiner's report under section 18 shall include—

(*a*) the proposals placed before the required meetings,

(*b*) any modification of those proposals adopted at any of those meetings,

(*c*) the outcome of each of the required meetings,

(*d*) the recommendation of the committee of creditors, if any,

(*e*) a statement of the assets and liabilities (including contingent and prospective liabilities) of the company as at the date of his report,

(*f*) a list of the creditors of the company, the amount owing to each such creditor, the nature and value of any security held by any such creditor, and the priority status of any such creditor under section 285 of the Principal Act or any other statutory provision or rule of law,

(*g*) list of the officers of the company,

(*h*) his recommendation,

(*i*) such other matters as the examiner deems appropriate or the court directs.

Repudiation
of certain
contracts

20.—(1) Where proposals for a compromise or scheme of arrangement are to be formulated in relation to a company, the company may, subject to the approval of the court, affirm or repudiate any contract under which some element of performance other than payment remains to be rendered both by the company and the other contracting party or parties.

(2) Any person who suffers loss or damage as a result of such repudiation shall stand as an unsecured creditor for the amount of such loss or damage.

(3) In order to facilitate the formulation, consideration or confirmation of a compromise or scheme of arrangement, the court may hold a hearing and make an order determining the amount of any such loss or damage and the amount so determined shall be due by the company to the creditor as a judgement debt.

(4) Where the examiner is not a party to an application to the court for the purposes of *subsection (1)*, the company shall serve notice of such application on the examiner and the examiner may appear and be heard on the hearing of any such applicaiton.

(5) Where the court approves the affirmation or repudiation of a contract under this section, it may in giving such approval make such orders as it thinks fit for the purposes of giving full effect to its approval including orders as to notice to, or declaring the rights of, any party affected by such affirmation or repudiation.

21.—(1) An examiner may, and if so directed by the court shall, appoint a committee of creditors to assist him in the performance of his functions. Appointment of creditors' committee

(2) Save as otherwise directed by the court, a committee appointed under *subsection (1)* shall consist of not more than five members and shall include the holders of the three largest unsecured claims who are willing to serve.

(3) The examiner shall provide the committee with a copy of any proposals for a compromise or scheme of arrangement and the committee may express an opinion on the proposals on its own behalf or on behalf of the creditors or classes of creditors represented thereon.

(4) As soon as practicable after the appointment of a committee under *subsection (1)* the examiner shall meet with the committee to transact such business as may be necessary.

22.—(1) Proposals for a compromise or scheme of arrangement shall— Contents of proposals

    (*a*) specify each class of members and creditors of the company,

    (*b*) specify any class of members and creditors whose interests or claims will not be impaired by the proposals,

    (*c*) specify any class of members and creditors whose interests or claims will be impaired by the proposals,

    (*d*) provide equal treatment for each claim or interest of a particular class unless the holder of a particular claim or interest agrees to less favourable treatment,

    (*e*) provide for the implementation of the proposals,

    (*f*) if the examiner considers it necessary or desirable to do so to facilitate the survival of the company, and the whole or any part of its undertaking, as a going concern, specify whatever changes should be made in relation to the management or direction of the company,

    (*g*) if the examiner considers it necessary or desirable as aforesaid, specify any changes he considers should be made in the memorandum or articles of the company, whether as regards the management or direction of the company or otherwise,

    (*h*) include such other matters as the examiner deems appropriate.

(2) A statement of the assets and liabilities (including contingent and prospective liabilities) of the company as at the date of the proposals shall be attached to each copy of the proposals to be submitted to meetings of members and creditors under *section 23*.

(3) There shall also be attached to each such copy of the proposals a description of the estimated financial outcome of a winding-up of the company for each class of members and creditors.

(4) The court may direct that the proposals include whatever other provisions it deems fit.

(5) For the purposes of this section and *sections 24* and *25*, a creditor's claim against a company is impaired if he receives less in payment of his claim than the full amount due in respect of the claim at the date of presentation of the petition for the appointment of the examiner.

(6) For the purposes of this section and *sections 24* and *25*, the interest of a member of a company in a company is impaired if—

(*a*) the nominal value of his shareholding in the company is reduced,

(*b* where he is entitled to a fixed dividend in respect of his shareholding in the company, the amount of that dividend is reduced,

(*c*) he is deprived of all or any part of the rights accruing to him by virtue of his shareholding in the company.

(*d*) his percentage interest in the total issued share capital of the company is reduced, or

(*e*) he is deprived of his shareholding in the company.

Consideration by members and creditors of proposals

23.—(1) This section applies to a meeting of members or creditors or any class of members or creditors summoned to consider proposals for a compromise or scheme of arrangement.

(2) At a meeting to which this section applies a modification of the proposals may be put to the meeting but may only be accepted with the consent of the examiner.

(3) Proposals shall be deemed to have been accepted by a meeting of members or of a class of members if a majority of the votes validly cast at that meeting, whether in person or by proxy, are cast in favour of the resolution for the proposals.

(4) Proposals shall be deemed to have been accepted by a meeting of creditors or of a class of creditors when a majority in number representing a majority in value of the claims represented at that meeting have voted, either in person or by proxy, in favour of the resolution for the proposals.

(5)   (*a*) Where a State authority is a creditor of the company, such authority shall be entitled to accept proposals under this section notwithstanding—

(i) that any claim of such authority as a creditor would be impaired under the proposals, or

(ii) any other enactment.

(*b*) In this subsection, "State authority" means the State, a Minister of the Government, a local authority or the Revenue Commissioners.

(6) Section 144 of the Principal Act shall apply to any resolution to which *subsection (3)* or *(4)* relates which is passed at any adjourned meeting.

(7) Section 202, subsections (2) to (6), of the Principal Act shall, with the necessary modifications, apply to meetings held under this section.

(8) With every notice summoning a meeting to which this section applies which is sent to a creditor or member, there shall be sent also a statement explaining the effect of the compromise or scheme of arrangement and in particular stating any material interests of the directors of the company, whether as directors or as members or as creditors of the company or otherwise and the effect thereon of the compromise or arrangement, insofar as it is different from the effect on the like interest of other persons.

Confirmation of proposals

24.—(1) The report of the examiner under *section 18* shall be set down for consideration by the court as soon as may be after receipt of the report by the court.

(2) The following persons may appear and be heard at a hearing under *subsection (1)*—

(*a*) the company,

(*b*) the examiner,

(*c*) any creditor or member whose claim or interest would be impaired if the proposals were implemented.

(3) At a hearing under *subsection (1)* the court may, as it thinks proper, subject to the provisions of this section and *section 25*, confirm, confirm subject to modifications, or refuse to confirm the proposals.

(4) The court shall not confirm any proposals—

(*a*) unless at least one class of members and one class of creditors whose interests or claims would be impaired by implementation of the proposals have accepted the proposals, or

(*b*) if the sole or primary purpose of the proposals is the avoidance of payment of tax due, or

(*c*) unless the court is satisfied that—

(i) the proposals are fair and equitable in relation to any class of members or creditors that has not accepted the proposals and whose interests or claims would be impaired by implementation, and

(ii) the proposals are not unfairly prejudicial to the interests of any interested party.

(5) Where the court confirms proposals (with or without modification), the proposals shall be binding on all the members or class or classes of members, as the case may be, affected by the proposals and also on the company.

(6) Where the court confirms proposals (with or without modification), the proposals shall, notwithstanding any other enactment, be binding on all the creditors or the class or classes of creditors, as the case may be, affected by the proposals in respect of any claim or claims against the company and any person other than the company who, under any statute, enacment, rule of law or otherwise, is liable for all or any part of the debts of the company.

(7) Any alterations in, additions to or deletions from the memorandum and articles of the company which are specified in the proposals shall, after confirmation of the proposals by the court and notwithstanding any other provisions of the Companies Acts, take effect from a date fixed by the court.

(8) Where the court confirms proposals under this section it may make such orders for the implementation of its decision as it deems fit.

(9) A compromise or scheme of arrangement, proposals for which have been confirmed under this section shall come into effect from a date fixed by the court, which date shall be not later than 21 days from the date of their confirmation.

(10) On the confirmation of proposals a copy of any order made by the court under this section shall be delivered by the examiner, or by such person as the court may direct, to the registrar of companies for registration.

(11) Where—

(*a*) the court refuses to confirm proposals under this section, or

(*b*) the report of the examiner under *section 18* concludes that, following the required meetings of members and creditors of a company under this Act, it has not been possible to reach agreement on a compromise or scheme of arrangement,

the court may, if it considers it just and equitable to do so, make an order for the winding-up of the company, or any other order as it deems fit.

(12) Notwithstanding subsection (4), or any other provision of this Act, where the examiner forms the opinion that the company will be able to survive as a going concern, nothing in this Act shall prevent the examiner from including, in a report under section 15 or 18, proposals which will not involve the impairment of the interests of members or creditors of the company, nor the court from confirming any such proposals.

25.—(1) At a hearing under *section 24* in relation to proposals a member or creditor whose interest or claim would be impaired by the proposals may object in particular to their confirmation by the court on any of the following grounds—

Objection to confirmation by court of proposals

(*a*) that there was some material irregularity at or in relation to a meeting to which *section 23* applies, (*b*) that acceptance of the proposals by the meeting was obtained by improper means,

(*c*) that the proposals were put forward for an improper purpose,

(*d*) that the proposals unfairly prejudice the interests of the objector.

(2) Any person who voted to accept the proposals may not object to their confirmation by the court except on the grounds—

(*a*) that such acceptance was obtained by improper means, or

(*b*) that after voting to accept the proposals he became aware that the proposals were put forward for an improper purpose.

(3) Where the court upholds an objection under this section, the court may make such order as it deems fit, including an order that the decision of any meeting be set aside and an order that any meeting be reconvened.

Cessation of protection of company and termination of appointment of examiner

26.—(1) Subject to *section 5*, the protection deemed to be granted to a company under that section shall cease—

(*a*) on the coming into effect of a compromise or scheme of arrangment under this Act, or

(*b*) on such earlier date as the court may direct.

(2) Where a company ceases to be under the protection of the court, the appointment of the examiner shall terminate on the date of such cessation.

Revocation

27.—The company or any interested party may, within 180 days after the confirmation of the proposals by the court, apply to the court for revocation of that confirmation on the grounds that it was procured by fraud and the court, if satisfied that such was the case, may revoke that confirmation on such terms and conditions, particularly with regard to the protection of the rights of parties acquiring interests or property in good faith and for value in reliance on that confirmation, as it deems fit.

Disqualification of examiners

28.—(1) A person shall not be qualified to be appointed or act as an examiner of a company if he would not be qualified to act as its liquidator.

(2) A person who acts as examiner of a company while disqualified under this section shall be guilty of an offence, and shall be liable, on summary conviction, to a fine not exceeding £1,000 and, on conviction on indictment, to a fine not exceeding £10,000.

Costs and remuneration of examiners

29.—(1) The court may from time to time make such orders as it thinks proper for payment of the remuneration and costs of, and reasonable expenses properly incurred by, an examiner.

(2) Unless the court otherwise orders, the remuneration, costs and expenses of an examiner shall be paid and the examiner shall be entitled to be indemnified in respect thereof out of the revenue of the business of the company to which he has been appointed, or the proceeds of realisation of the assets (including investments).

(3) The remuneration, costs and expenses of an examiner which have been sanction by order of the court shall be paid in full and shall be paid before any other claim, secured or unsecured, under any compromise or scheme of arrangement or in any receivership or winding-up of the company to which he has been appointed.

(4) The functions of any examiner may be performed by him with the assistance of persons appointed or employed by him for that purpose provided that an examiner shall, insofar as is reasonably possible, make use of the services of the staff and facilies of the company to which he has been appointed to assist him in the performance of his functions.

(5) In considering any matter relating to the costs, expenses and remuneration of an examiner the court shall have particular regard to the proviso to *subsection (4)*.

30.—(1) An examiner or, where appropriate, such other person as the court may direct, Publicity shall, within 14 days after the delivery to the registrar of companies of every order made under *section 17* or *24*, cause to be published in *Iris Oifigiúil* notice of such delivery.

(2) Where a person fails to comply with this section, that person, and where that person is a company, the company and every officer of the company who is in default shall be guilty of an offence and shall be liable to a fine not exceeding £1,000.

31.—The whole or part of any proceedings under this Act may be heard otherwise than Hearing of proceedings otherwise than in public in public if the court, in the interests of justice, considers that the interests of the company concerned or of its creditors as a whole so require.

36.—(1) Any order made by a court of any country recognised for the purposes of this Enforcement of recon- struction orders made by courts outside the State section and made for or in the course of the reorganisation or reconstruction of a company may be enforced by the High Court in all respects as if the order had been made by the High Court.

(2) When an application is made to the High Court under this section, an office copy of any order sought to be enforced shall be sufficient evidence of the order.

(3) In this section, "company" means a body corporate incorporated outside the State, and "recognised" means recognised by order made by the Minister.

36A.—Proceedings in relation to an offence under section 11(6), 12 or 30 may be brought Proceedings by registrar and prosecuted by the registrar of companies.

Order 74
Winding-up of Companies

I *Preliminary*

1.—(1) In this Order unless the context or subject matter otherwise requires—

"the Act" means the Companies Act 1963;

"the company" means the company which is being wound up or in respect of which proceedings to have it wound up have been commenced;

"creditor" includes a company or corporation or a firm or partnership;

"debt proved" includes any debt which shall have been duly admitted without proof;

references to "Liquidator" shall, where appropriate, be construed at including "Official Liquidator".

(2) Words and expressions contained in this Order shall have the same meaning as in the Act.

(3) In this Order, a reference to a section or subsection is to that section or subsection in the Act unless it is indicated that reference to some other enactment is intended.

Application of this Order

2.—Rules which from their nature and subject matter are, or which by the headings above the group in which they are contained or by their terms are made applicable only to the proceedings in winding-up by the Court or only to such proceedings and to proceedings in a creditors' voluntary winding-up, shall not apply to the proceedings in a voluntary winding-up, or, as the case may be, in a members' voluntary winding-up.

Assignment of Judge

3.—All applications and proceedings (including petitions for winding-up) in relation to every winding-up under the Act shall be assigned to such Judge or Judges as the President of the High Court shall from time to time assign to hear such applications and proceedings but if such Judge or Judges shall be unable to dispose of such applications or proceedings, any other Judge of Judges of the High Court may dispose of any such application.

Use of forms

4.—The forms in Appendix M (annexed hereto) where applicable, and where they are not applicable, forms of the like character, with such variations as circumstances may require, shall be used, and the forms referred to in this Order are those in the said Appendix M. The directions contained in any form shall be observed in relation thereto. Where such forms are applicable, any costs occasioned by the use of any other or more prolix forms shall be borne by or disallowed to the party using the same, unless the Court shall otherwise direct.

II *Proceedings*

Title of proceedings

5.—(1) Every petition, summons, notice, affidavit and other proceedings in a winding-up matter shall with any necessary additions be entitled as in the Form No. 1 and where the company is in liquidation there shall be added after the name of the company the words "in liquidation".

(2) The first proceedings shall have a distinctive number assigned to it in the Central Office, and all proceedings subsequent to the first proceeding shall bear the same number as the first proceeding. Numbers and dates may be denoted by figures.

III *Service of documents in winding-up by the Court*

6.—Service of all notices, motions and other documents other than those of which personal service is required, may be effected through the Central Office or by sending them by pre-paid post to the last known address of the person to be served therewith; and the notice, motion or document shall be considered served at the time that the same ought to have been delivered in the ordinary course of post. When any such notices, motions or other documents are served by sending them by pre-paid post, a certificate of posting shall be obtained from the Post Office and shall be conclusive evidence of such service.

IV *Petition to wind-up a company*

7.—Every petition for the winding-up of a company by the Court shall be in one of the Forms Nos. 2, 3 or 4.

8.—The petition shall be presented at and shall be retained in the Central Office. A sealed copy thereof shall be taken out by the petitioner or his solicitor and shall be used as if it were an original.

9.—The petition and sealed copy shall be brought to the office of one of the Registrars who shall appoint the time and place at which the petition is to be heard. Notice of the time and place appointed for hearing the petition shall be written on the petition and the sealed copy thereof and the Registrar may at any time before the petition has been advertised, alter the time appointed and fix another time.

10.—(1) Every petition shall be advertised seven clear days before the hearing, once in *Iris Oifigiúil* and once at least in two Dublin morning newspapers or in such other newspapers as the Registrar when appointing the time and place at which the petition is to be heard shall direct. *Advertisement of petition*

(2) The advertisement, which shall be in the Form No. 5, shall state the day on which the petition was presented, the name and address of the petitioner, and the name and registered place of business of his solicitor, and shall contain a note at the foot thereof stating that any person who intends to appeat at the hearing of the petition, either to oppose or support, shall send notice of his intentions to the petitioner, or to his solicitors, within the time and in the manner prescribed by rule 15, and an advertisement of a petition for the winding-up of a company by the Court which does not contain such a note shall be deemed irregular.

11.—Every petition shall, unless presented by the company, be served on the company at the registered office of the company, and if there is no registered office, then at the principal or last known principal place of business of the company if any such can be found, by leaving a copy with any member, office or servant of the company there, or in case no such member, officer or servant can be found there, then by leaving a copy at such registered office of principal place of business, or by serving it on such member or members of the company as the Court may direct and when the company is being wound up voluntarily, every such petition shall also be served upon the liquidator appointed for the purpose of winding-up the affairs of the company. *Service of petition*

Verification
of petition

12.—Every petition for the winding-up of a company by the Court shall be verified by affidavit. Such affidavit which shall be in one of the Forms Nos. 6 or 7, shall be made by the petitioner, or by one of the petitioners if more than one, or in case the petition is presented by a corporation or company, by some director, secretary or other officer thereof, and shall be sworn after and filed within four days after the petition is presented, and such affidavit shall be sufficient *prima facie* evidence of the statements in the petition.

Copy of
petition

13.—Every contributory or creditor of the company shall be entitled to be furnished by the solicitor of the petitioner with a copy of the petition within twenty-four hours after making the request for such copy on paying for it at the rate specified in Order 117.

V *Provisional liquidator*

Appointment
of provisional
liquidator

14.—(1) After the presentation of a petition for the winding-up of a company, the Court, upon the application of a creditor, or of a contributory or of the company, and upon proof by affidavit of sufficient ground for the appointment of a provisional liquidator and without advertisement or notice to any person (unless the Court shall otherwise direct) may, upon such terms as in the opinion of the Court shall be just and necessary, make the appointment.

(2) The order appointing the provisional liquidator shall state the nature and a short description of the property of which the provisional liquidator is ordered to take possession, and the duties to be performed by the provisional liquidator.

(3) Subject to any order of the Court, if no order for the winding-up of the company is made upon the petition, or if an order for the winding-up of the company is rescinded or if all proceedings on the petition are stayed, the provisional liquidator shall be entitled to be paid out of the property of the company all the costs, charges and expenses properly incurred by him as provisional liquidator, including such sum as the Court may fix for his remuneration and may retain out of such property the amount of such costs, charges and expenses.

VI *Hearing of petitions and orders made thereon*

Hearing of
petition and
appearances
thereon

15.—Every person who intends to appear on the hearing of a petition shall serve on, or send by post to, the petitioner or his solicitor at the address stated in the advertisement of the petition, notice of his intention. The notice shall contain the address of such person, and shall be signed by him, or by his solicitor and shall be served, or if sent by post, shall be posted in such time as in the ordinary course of post to reach the address not later than five o'clock in the afternoon of the day previous to the day appointed for the hearing of the petition. The notice may be in the Form No. 8. A person who has failed to comply with this rule shall not, without the special leave of the Court, be allowed to appear on the hearing of the petition.

16.—The petitioner, or his solicitor, shall prepare a list in the Form No. 9 of the names and addresses of the persons who have given notice of their intention to appear on the hearing of a petition, and of their respective solicitors. On the day appointed for hearing the petition, a copy of the list (or if no notice of intention to appear has been given, a statement in notice to that effect) shall be handed by the petitioner, or his solicitor, to the Registrar prior to the hearing of the petition.

17.—Affidavits in opposition to a petition that the company may be wound up under the order of the Court shall be filed within seven days after the publication of the last of the advertisements required by rule 10, and notice of the filing of every affidavit in opposition to such a petition shall be given to the petitioner, or his solicitor, on the day on which the affidavit is filed.

18.—When a petitioner consents to withdraw his petition, or to allow it to be dismissed, or the hearing adjourned, or fails to appear in support of his petition when it is called in Court on the day originally fixed for the hearing thereof, or on any day to which the hearing has been adjourned, or if appearing, does not apply for an order in the terms of the prayer of his petition, the Court may, if, and upon such terms as it shall deem just, substitute as petitioner any person who would have a right to present a petition, and who desires to prosecute the petition.

19.—An order to wind up a company or for the appointment of a provisional liquidator shall contain at the foot thereof a notice stating that it will be the duty of the persons who are liable to make out or concur in making out the company's statement of affairs to attend before the Court at such time and place as the Court may appoint and to give to the Court all information which the Court may require. _{Winding up Order}

20.—Every order for the winding-up of a company by the Court which (subject to rule 19 hereof) may be in the Form No. 10, shall within twelve days after the date thereof, or within such extended time as may be allowed by the Court, be advertised in the Form No. 11 by the petitioner once in *Iris Oifigiúil*, and in each of the newspapers in which the petition was advertised, unless the court shall otherwise direct and shall be served upon such persons (if any) and in such manner as the Court may direct.

21.—A copy of every order for the winding-up of a company certified by the petitioner or his solicitor to be a true copy shall be left by him at the Examiner's Office within ten days after the same shall have been perfected, and in default thereof any other person interested in the winding-up may leave the same, similarly affected, and the Court may give the carriage and prosecution of the order to such person. Upon such order being left, a notice to proceed under the order shall be taken out and served upon all parties who appeared upon the hearing of the petition. Upon the return day of such notice to proceed, a time shall be fixed for the proof of debts and for the list of contributories to be brought in, and directions may be given as to the advertisements to be issued for all or any of such purposes, and generally as to the proceedings and parties to attend thereon. The proceedings under the order shall be continued by adjournment and when necessary, by further notice and any directions as aforesaid may be given, added to, or varied at any subsequent time as may be found necessary.

22.—A copy of every order for winding-up a company certified by the petitioner or his solicitor to be a true copy shall be served upon the company be pre-paid letter addressed to its registered office (if any) or if there is no registered office at its principal or last known principal place of business or upon such other person or persons or in such other manner as the Court may direct. This shall not apply when the company is the petitioner.

23.—For the purposes of section 292 notice that (1) a winding-up petition has been presented, or (2) a winding-up order has been made, or (3) a provisional liquidator has been appointed, or (4) a meeting has been called at which there is to be proposed a resolution for the voluntary winding-up of the company, or (5) a resolution has been passed for the voluntary winding-up of the company, shall be in writing and shall be addressed to the sheriff and may be served by being delivered by hand, or by registered post, at his office. _{Notice to the sheriff}

VII *Statement of affairs*

24.—(1) A person who under section 224 has been required by the Court to submit and verify a statement of affairs of a company shall make out such statement in duplicate one _{Preparation of statement of affairs}

copy of which shall be verified by affidavit. The verified statement of affairs shall be filed in the Central Office.

(2) The Court may from time to time require any such person as is mentioned in paragraphs (*a*), (*b*), (*c*) or (d) of subsection (2) of section 224 to attend before the Court on a date fixed by the Court for the purpose of requiring him to give such information in relation to the company as the Court may think fit and it shall be the duty of every such person to attend at the Court at such time and place and to give to the Court all information that the Court may require.

(3) When any person requires any extension of time for submitting the statement of affairs, he shall apply to the Court for such extension.

25.—A person who is required to make or concur in making any statement of affairs of a company, shall before incurring any costs or expenses in and about the preparation and making of the statement, apply to the Official Liquidator for his sanction and submit a statement of the estimated costs and expenses which it is intended to incur and if there shall be no Official Liquidator, shall apply to the Court; and, except by order of the Court, no person shall be allowed out of the assets of the company any costs or expenses which have not, before being incurred, being sanctioned by the Official Liquidator or the Court.

Dispensing with statements of affairs

26.—(1) Any application to dispense with the requirements of section 224 shall be supported by a report of the Official Liquidator showing the special circumstances which, in his opinion, render such a course desirable.

(2) When the Court has made an order dispensing with the requirements of the said section, it may give such consequential directions as it may see fit and, in particular, may give directions as to the sending of any notices which are by this Order required to be sent to any person mentioned in the statement of affairs.

27.—Every statement of affairs shall be in the Form No. 13.

28.—(1) Unless the Court shall otherwise order, the Official Liquidator shall, as soon as practicable, send to each creditor mentioned in the company's statement of affairs and to each person appearing from the company's books or otherwise to be a contributory of the company a summary of the company's statement of affairs including the causes of its failure and any observations thereon which the Official Liquidator may think fit to make.

(2) When prior to the winding-up order the company has commenced to be wound up voluntarily, the Official Liquidator may, if in his absolute discretion he thinks fit to do so, send to the persons aforesaid or any of them an account of such voluntary winding-up showing how such winding-up has been conducted and how the property of the company has been disposed of.

VIII *Appointment and duties of Official Liquidator*

29.—The Court may appoint a person to the office of Official Liquidator without previous advertisement or notice to any party or fix a time and place for the appointment of an Official Liquidator and may appoint or reject any person nominated at such time and place and appoint any person not so nominated.

30.—When the time and place are fixed for the appointment of an Official Liquidator, such time and place may be advertised in such manner as the Court shall direct so that the first or only advertisement shall be published within fourteen days and not less than seven days before the day so fixed.

31.—An Official Liquidator shall give security by entering into a bond which shall be in the Form No. 22 in Appendix G with two or more sufficient sureties in such sum as the Court may approve and the Court may accept as a sole surety any company carrying on business in Ireland and having power to enter into guarantees in lieu of two or more sufficient sureties if such company has deposited moneys in Court under the Insurance Acts 1909 to 1964. The Court may authorise an Official Liquidator to act as such without giving security for such time as the Court may fix.

32.—An Official Liquidator shall be appointed by order which may be in the Form No. 12, and unless he shall have given security, a time shall be fixed by such order within which he is to do so, and the order shall fix the times or periods at which the Official Liquidator is to leave his accounts of receipts and payments at the Examiner's Office and shall direct that all moneys to be received shall be paid into the Bank within seven days after the receipt thereof to the account of the Official Liquidator of the company, and an account shall be opened there accordingly, and an attested copy of the order shall be lodged at the Bank.

33.—When an Official Liquidator has given security pursuant to the direction in the order appointing him, the bond shall be filed in the Central Office and the proper officer in the Central Office shall indorse on the order appointing such Official Liquidator a certificate that the bond has been filed.

34.—An Official Liquidator shall on each occasion of passing his account and also when the Court may so require, satisfy the Court that his sureties are living and resident in Ireland and have not been adjudged bankrupt or become insolvent or that any company accepted as aforesaid is still in existence and is not in course of being wound up or dissolved and in default thereof he may be required to enter into fresh security within such time as shall be directed.

35.—Every appointment of an Official Liquidator shall be advertised in such manner as the Court shall direct immediately after he has given security.

36.—In case of the death, removal or resignation of an Official Liquidator, another shall be appointed in his place in the same manner as in the case of a first appointment and proceedings for that purpose may be taken by such party as may be authorised by the Court.

37.—An Official Liquidator shall with all convenient speed after he is appointed proceed to make up, continue, complete, check and rectify the books of accounts of the company in such manner as may be necessary or as the Court may direct.

38.—The Official Liquidator of a company, or any member of the committee of inspection of a company, or any other person employed in or in connection with the winding-up of the company shall not under any circumstances whatever accept from or arrange from any solicitor, auctioneer or other person connected with the company any gift, gratuity, remuneration, emolument, or pecuniary or other consideration or benefit whatever in addition to or apart from such remuneration as he may properly be entitled to under the provisions of the Act or this Order; nor shall any such person so employed as aforesaid give up or arrange to give up to any such solicitor, auctioneer or other person any portion of his proper remuneration.

39.—The Official Liquidator or any member of the committee of inspection of a company shall not, while acting as liquidator or member of such committee, except by leave of the Court, either directly or indirectly, by himself or any employer, partner, clerk, agent or servant, become purchaser of any part of the company's assets. Any such purchase made contrary to the provisions of this rule may be set aside by the Court on the application of any director or contributory in any winding-up.

Restriction on purchase of goods by Official Liquidator

40.—Where the Official Liquidator carries on the business of the company, he shall not, without the express sanction of the Court, purchase goods for the carrying on of such business from any person whose connection with him is of such a nature as would result in his obtaining any portion of the profit (if any) arising out of the transaction.

Costs of obtaining sanction of the Court

41.—In any case in which the sanction of the Court is obtained under rules 39 or 40, the cost of obtaining such sanction shall be borne by the person in whose interest such sanction is obtained and shall not be payable out of the company's assets.

42.—If an Official Liquidator is adjudicated a bankrupt, his office shall be vacated and he shall be deemed to have been removed as of the date of adjudication.

43.—Upon an Official Liquidator resigning, or being removed from his office, he shall deliver over to the new Official Liquidator all books kept by him and all other books, documents, papers, and documents in his possession relating to the office of Official Liquidator. An Official Liquidator shall not be released unless and until he has delivered over to the new Official Liquidator all the books, papers, documents and accounts which he is by this rule required to deliver on his resignation or removal as aforesaid.

Proceeds of sale of the company's assets

44.—Where property forming part of the company's assets is sold by an Official Liquidator through an auctioneer or other agent, the gross proceeds of the sale shall be paid over by such auctioneer or agent to the Official Liquidator and the charges and expenses connected with the sale shall afterwards be paid to such auctioneer or agent upon an order of the Court for the payment thereof. Every Official Liquidator by whom such auctioneer or agent is employed shall, unless the Court otherwise orders, be accountable for the proceeds of such sale.

45.—An Official Liquidator shall be described in all proceedings by the style of the Official Liquidator of the particular company in respect of which he is appointed.

Description and remuneration of Official Liquidator

46.—An Official Liquidator shall be allowed in his accounts or otherwise paid, such salary or remuneration as the Court may from to time direct and in fixing such salary or remuneration the Court shall have regard to any necessary employment of accountants, assistants or clerks by him. Such salary or remuneration may be fixed either at the time of his appointment or at any time thereafter. Every allowance of such salary or remuneration, unless made at the time of his appointment or upon passing an account, may be made upon application for that purpose by the Official Liquidator on notice to such persons (if any) and shall be supported by such evidence as the Court shall require. The Court may from time to time allow such sum (if any) as the Court shall think fit to the Official Liquidator on account of the salary or remuneration to be thereafter allowed. The Court may direct that an inquiry be held by the Examiner or the Master as to the salary or remuneration of the Official Liquidator and that the Examiner or the Master (as the case may be) do report thereon to the Court. The Master shall have the same powers as the Examiner in conducting any such enquiry.

47.—Where an Official Liquidator receives remuneration for his services as such, no payment shall be allowed in his accounts in respect of the performance by any other person of the ordinary duties which should have been performed by the Official Liquidator.

48.—The accounts of an Official Liquidator shall be left at the Examiner's Office or with the Master's Registrar (as the case may be) at the times directed by the order appointing him, and at such other times as may from time to time be required by the Court, and such accounts shall from time to time be passed and verified in such manner, and upon notice to such parties (if any) as the Court may direct.

IX *Proceedings by or against directors, promoters and officers when the company is being wound up by the Court*

49.—An application made to the Court under—
(*a*) section 184;
(*b*) subsections (1) or (2) of section 297;
(*c*) section 298 or
(*d*) subsection (2) of section 391,
shall be made by motion in which shall be stated the nature of the declaration or order for which application is made and the grounds of the application, and notice of such motion, together with a copy of every report and affidavit upon which it is intended to be grounded, shall be served personally on every person against whom an order is sought, not less than seven clear days before the day named therein for hearing the application. Where the application is made by the Official Liquidator, he may make a report to the Court stating any relevant facts and information which he shall verify by affidavit. Where an application is made by any other person it shall be supported by affidavit to be filed by him. The Court may give such directions as to the procedure for the hearing of the application and may direct that the date fixed for the hearing shall be advertised in such form as the Court may approve, and on the hearing the Court may allow any person interested to appear either by counsel or in person and to cross-examine any of the witnesses giving evidence or to give evidence.

X *General meetings of creditors and contributories in a winding-up by the Court and of creditors in a creditors' voluntary winding-up*

50.—When the Court directs a meeting of the creditors or separate meetings of the creditors and contributories of the company to be summoned under section 232, the Official Liquidator shall give notice in writing in the Forms Nos. 14 or 15 seven clear days before the day appointed for such meeting to every creditor or, as the case may be, to every creditor and every contributory, of the time and place appointed for such meeting or meetings and that the purpose of such meeting or meetings is to determine whether an application is to be made to the Court for the appointment of a committee of inspection to act with the Official Liquidator and who are to be the members of the committee if appointed. If the Court shall direct such notice may be given by advertisement. The Official Liquidator or, if he is unable to act, someone nominated by him, shall act as chairman of such meeting and such chairman shall make a report of the result of the meeting to the Court. Upon the result of the meetings of creditors and contributories being reported to the Court, if there is a difference between the determinations at the meetings of the creditors and contributories, the Court shall, on the application of the Official Liquidator, fix a time and place for considering the resolutions and determinations (if any) of the meetings, deciding differences and making such order as shall be necessary. In any other case the Court may upon the application of the Official

Committee of inspection

Liquidator forthwith make any appointment necessary for giving effect to any such resolutions or determinations.

51.—When a time and place have been fixed for the consideration of the resolutions and determinations of the meetings, such time and place shall be advertised by the Official Liquidator in such manner as the Court shall direct but so that the first or only advertisement shall be published not less than seven days before the time so fixed.

52.—Upon the consideration of the resolutions and determinations of the meetings, the Court shall hear the Official Liquidator and any creditor or contributory.

53.—Every appointment of a committee of inspection shall be advertised by the Official Liquidator in such manner as the Court directs immediately after the appointment has been made unless the Court shall otherwise order.

Liquidator's
meetings of
creditors and
contributories

54.—(1) In addition to the meetings of creditors or contributories held pursuant to section 232 or section 309 (each of which is hereinafter referred to as a "Court meeting of creditors" or a "Court meeting of contributories" as the case may be), the Official Liquidator in any winding-up by the Court may himself, from time to time, subject to the provisions of the Act and the control of the Court, summon, hold and conduct meetings of the creditors or contributories (each of which is hereinafter referred to as a "Liquidator's meetings of creditors" or a "Liquidator's meetings of contributories" as the case may be) for the purpose of ascertaining their wishes in all matters relating to the winding-up.

(2) In any creditor's voluntary winding-up the Liquidator may himself from to time summon, hold and conduct meetings of creditors for the purpose of ascertaining their wishes in all matters relating to the winding-up (each of such meetings and any meeting of creditors which a Liquidator or a company is by the Act required to convene in or immediately before such a voluntary winding-up and any meeting convened by a creditor in a voluntary winding-up under this Order is hereinafter called a "voluntary liquidation meeting").

55.—(1) When the Court directs a meeting of the creditors or contributories of the company to be summoned under section 309, the Official Liquidator shall give notice in writing in the Forms Nos. 16 or 17 seven clear days before the day appointed for such meeting, to every creditor or contributory, of the time and place appointed for such meeting and of the matter upon which the Court desires to ascertain the wishes of the creditors or contributories. If the Court so directs, such notice may be given by advertisement in which case the object of the meeting need not be stated.

(2) Where the Court appoints a chairman of such meeting, a memorandum of his appointment in the Form No. 18 shall be sufficient authority for the person so appointed to preside at such meeting and such chairman shall make a report of the result of the meeting in the Form No. 19.

56.—Except where and so far as the nature of the subject matter or the context may otherwise require, rules 58-83 (inclusive) shall apply to a Court meeting of creditors and to a Court meeting of contributories, to a Liquidator's meeting of creditors and to a Liquidator's meeting of contributories, and to a voluntary liquidation meeting, but so nevertheless that the said rules shall take effect as to a meeting held under section 232 subject and without prejudice to any express provision of the Act, and as to a Court meeting of creditors or Court meeting of contributories subject and without prejudice to any express directions of the Court.

57.—(1) The Liquidator shall summon all meetings of creditors and contributories by Summoning sending by post not less than seven days before the day appointed for the meeting to every of meetings person appearing by the company's books to be a creditor of the company notice of the meeting of creditors and to every person appearing by the company's books or otherwise to be a contributory of the company notice of the meeting of contributories.

(2) The notice to each creditor shall be sent to the address given in his proof, or if he has not proved, to the address given in the statement of affairs of the company, if any, or to such other address as may be known to the person summoning the meeting. The notice of each contributory shall be sent to the address mentioned in the company's books as the address of such contributory or to such other address as may be known to the Liquidator.

(3) In the case of meetings under section 270 any creditor may summon the meeting.

(4) This rule shall not apply to meetings under section 266 or section 273.

58.—An affidavit by the Liquidator or creditor, or the solicitor or clerk of either of such Proof of notice persons, or as the case may be, by some officer or clerk of the company or its solicitor that the notice of any meeting has been duly posted, shall be sufficient evidence of such notice having been fully sent to the person to whom the same was addressed.

59.—In the case of a company having its registered office in the County Borough of Place of Dublin or in the County Borough of Cork every meeting shall be held at such place in the meetings County Borough of Dublin or in the County Borough of Cork, as the case may be, as is in the opinion of the person convening the same most convenient for the majority of the creditors or contributories or both. In any other case every meeting shall be held at such place as is in the opinion of the person convening the same most convenient for the majority of the creditors or contributories or both. Different times or places may be named for the meetings of creditors and for the meetings of contributories.

60.—The costs of summoning a meeting of creditors or contributories at the instance of Costs of any person other than the Liquidator shall be paid by the person at whose instance it is calling summoned who shall before the meeting is summoned deposit with the Liquidator such sum meetings as may be required by the Liquidator as security for the payment of such costs. The costs of summoning such meeting of creditors or contributories, including all disbursements for printing, stationery, postage and the hire of room, shall be calculated at the following rate for each creditor or contributory to whom notice is required to be sent, namely, ten pence per creditor or contributory for the first twenty creditors or contributories, five pence per creditor or contributory for the next thirty creditors or contributories and three prence per creditor or contributory for any number of creditors or contributories after the first fifty. The said costs shall be repaid out of the assets of the company if the Court shall by order or if the creditors or contributories (as the case may be) shall by resolution so direct. This rule shall not apply to meetings under section 266 or section 270.

61.—Where a meeting is summoned by the Liquidator, he or, if he is unable to act, Chairman of someone nominated by him, shall be chairman of the meeting. At every other meeting of meeting creditors or contributories the chairman shall be such person as the meeting by resolution shall appoint. This rule shall not apply to meetings under section 266.

62.—At a meeting of creditors a resolution shall be deemed to be passed when a majority Ordinary in number and value of the creditors present personally or by proxy and voting on the resolution of resolution have voted in favour of the resolution, and at a meeting of contributories a creditors and resolution shall be deemed to be passed when a majority in number and value of the contributories

contributories present personally or by proxy and voting on the resolution have voted in favour of the resolution, the value of the contributories being determined according to the number of votes conferred on each contributory by the regulations of the company.

Copy of resolution to be filed

63.—The Liquidator shall file with the registrar of companies a copy cerfified by him of every resolution of a meeting of creditors or contributories.

Non-receipt of notice

64.—Where a meeting of creditors or contributories is summoned by notice the proceedings and resolutions of the meeting shall unless the Court otherwise orders be valid notwithstanding that some creditors or contributories may not have received the notice sent to them.

Adjournments

65.—The chairman may with the consent of the meeting adjourn it from time to time and from place to place but the adjourned meeting shall be held at the same place as the original meeting unless in the resolution for adjournment another place is specified or unless the Court otherwise orders.

Quorum

66.—(1) A meeting may not act for any purpose, except the election of a chairman and the adjournment of the meeting, unless there are present or represented thereat in the case of a creditors' meeting at least three creditors entitled to vote or all the creditors entitled to vote if the number entitled to vote shall not exceed three, or in the case of a meeting of contributories at least two contributories.

(2) If within fifteen minutes from the time appointed for the meeting a quorum of creditors or contributories, as the case may be, is not present or represented the meeting shall be adjourned to the same day in the following week at the same time and place or so such other day or time or place as the chairman may appoint, but so that the day appointed shall be not less than seven nor more than twenty-one days from the day from which the meeting was adjourned.

Creditors entitled to vote

67.—In the case of a meeting of creditors held pursuant to section 232 or of an adjournment thereof a person shall not be entitled to vote as a creditor unless he has duly lodged with the Liquidator not later than the time mentioned for that purpose in the notice convening the meeting or adjourned meeting, a proof of the debt which he claims to be due to him from the company. In the case of any other Court meeting of creditors or a Liquidator's meeting of creditors, a person shall not be entitled to vote as a creditor unless he has lodged with the Liquidator a proof of the debt which he claims to be due to him from the company and such proof has been admitted wholly or in part before the date on which the meeting is held; provided that the next four following rules shall not apply to a meeting of creditors held pursuant to section 232. This rule shall not apply to any creditors or class of creditors who by virtue of the Act or this Order are not required to prove their debts or to any voluntary liquidation meeting.

Cases in which creditors may not vote

68.—A creditor shall not vote in respect of any unliquidated or contingent debt or any debt the value of which is not ascertained, nor shall a creditor vote in respect of any debt on or secured by a current bill of exchange or promissory note held by him unless he is willing to treat the liability to him thereon of every person who is liable thereon antecedently to the company and against whom an adjudication order in bankruptcy has not been made, as a security in his hands and to estimate the value thereof, and for purposes of voting but not for the purposes of dividend, to deduct it from his proof.

69.—For the purpose of voting, a secured creditor shall, unless he surrenders his security, state in his proof or in a voluntary liquidation in such a statement as is hereinafter mentioned the particulars of his security, the date when it was given and the value at which he assesses it and shall be entitled to vote only in respect of the balance (if any) due to him after deducting the value of his security. If he votes in respect of his whole debt he shall be deemed to surrender his security unless the Court on application is satisfied that the omission to value the security has arisen from inadvertence. Votes of secured creditors

70.—The Liquidator may, within twenty-eight days after a proof or in a voluntary liquidation a statement estimating the value of security as aforesaid has been used in voting at a meeting, require the creditor to give up the security for the benefit of the creditors generally on payment of the value so estimated; provided that where a creditor has valued his security he may, at any time before being required to give it up, correct the valuation by a new proof and deduct the new value from his debt. Creditors required to give up security

71.—The chairman shall have power to admit or reject a proof for the purpose of voting, but his decision shall be subject to appeal to the Court. If he is in doubt whether a proof should be admitted or rejected he shall mark it as objected to and allow the creditor to vote subject to the vote being declared invalid in the event of the objection being sustained. Admission and rejection of proofs for purposes of voting

72.—For the purpose of voting at any voluntary liquidation meetings, a secured creditor shall, unless he surrender his security, lodge with the Liquidator before the meeting a statement giving the particulars of his security, the date when it was given and the value at which he assesses it. This rule shall not apply to a meeting of creditors held pursuant to section 266. Statement of security

73.—(1) The chairman shall cause minutes of the proceedings at the meeting to be drawn up and entered in a book kept for that purpose and the minues shall be signed by him or by the chairman of the next ensuing meeting. Minutes of meetings

(2) The chairman shall cause a list of creditors (or contributories) present at every meeting to be made and kept as in the Form No. 20, and such list shall be signed by him.

74.—A creditor or a contributory may vote either in person or by proxy. Where a person is authorised in manner provided by section 139 to represent a corporation at any meeting of creditors or contributories, such person shall produce to the Liquidator or other the chairman of the meeting a copy of the resolution so authorising him. Such copy shall either be under the seal of the corporation or be certified to be a true copy by the secretary or a director of the corporation. Proxies

75.—Every instrument of proxy shall be in either the Form No. 21 or the Form No. 22.

76.—A general and a special form of proxy shall be sent to each of the creditors or contributories with the notice summoning the meeting, and neither the name nor description of the Liquidator or any other person shall be printed or inserted in the body of any instrument of proxy before it is so sent.

77.—A creditor or a contributory may appoint any person a general proxy.

78.—A creditor or a contributory may appoint any person a special proxy to vote at any special meeting or adjourned thereof:

(*a*) for or against the appointment or continuance in office of any specified person as Liquidator or member of the committee of inspection, and;

(*b*) on all questions relating to any matter other than those above referred to and arising at the meeting or an adjournment thereof.

79.—Where it appears to the satisfaction of the Court that any solicitation has been used by or on behalf of a Liquidator in obtaining proxies or in procuring his appointment as Liquidator except by the direction of a meeting of creditors or contributories, the Court may order that no remuneration be allowed to the person by whom or on whose behalf the solicitation was exercised notwithstanding any resolution of the committee of inspection or of the creditors or contributories to the contrary.

80.—A creditor or a contributory in a winding-up may appoint the Liquidator or if there is no Liquidator the chairman of a meeting to act as his general or special proxy.

81.—No person appointed as either a general or a special proxy shall vote in favour of any resolution which would directly or indirectly place himself, his partner or employer in a position to receive any remuneration out of the assets of the company otherwise than as a creditor rateable with the other creditors of the company; provided that where any person holds special proxies to vote for an application to the Court in favour of the appointment of himself as Liquidator he may use the said proxies and vote accordingly.

82.—(1) Every instrument of proxy shall be lodged with the Official Liquidator in a winding-up by the Court, with the company at its registered office for a meeting under section 266, and with the Liquidator or if there is no Liquidator with the person named in the notice convening the meeting to receive the same in a voluntary winding-up, not later than four o'clock in the afternoon of the day before the meeting or adjourned meeting at which it is to be used.

(2) No person who is an infant shall be appointed a general or special proxy.

(3) Where a company is a creditor, any person who is duly authorised under the seal of such company to act generally on behalf of such company at meetings of creditors and contributories may fill in and sign the instrument of proxy on such company's behalf and appoint himself to be such company's proxy, and the instrument of proxy so filled in and signed by such person shall be received and dealt with as a proxy of such company.

83.—The instrument of proxy of a creditor, blind or incapable of writing, may be accepted if such creditor has attached his signature or mark thereto in the presence of a witness, who shall add to his signature his description and residence; provided that all insertions in the instrument of proxy are in the handwriting of the witness, and that such witness shall have certified at the foot of the instrument of proxy that all such insertions have been made by him at the request and in the presence of such creditor before he attached his signature or mark.

XI *Disclaimer*

84.—(1) Any application in a winding-up by the Court for leave to disclaim any part of the property of a company pursuant to section 290(1) shall be made *ex parte*, and in any other case by special summons. Such application shall be based on an affidavit showing who are the parties interested in the property and what their interests are. On the hearing of such application the Court shall give directions and in particular directions as to the notices to be given to the parties interested or any of them and as to advertisements to be published and may adjourn the application to enable any such party to attend.

(2) Where a Liquidator disclaims a leasehold interest he shall forthwith deliver the disclaimer to the registrar of companies. The disclaimer shall contain particulars of the interest disclaimed and a statement of the person to whom notice of the disclaimer has been given. Until the disclaimer is so delivered it shall be inoperative. A disclaimer shall be in the Form No. 23 and a notice of disclaimer in the Form No. 24.

(3) Where any person claims to be interested in any part of the property of a company which the Liquidator wishes to disclaim, he shall at the request of the Liquidator furnish a statement of the interest so claimed by him.

85.—(1) Any application under section 290(7) for an order for the vesting of any disclaimed property in, or the delivery of any such property to, any persons shall be grounded on the affidavit filed on the application for leave to disclaim such property.

(2) Where such an application as aforesaid relates to disclaimed property of a leasehold nature and it appears that there is any mortgagee by demise, chargeant or under-lessee of such property, the Court may direct that notice shall be given to such mortgagee, chargeant or under-lessee that, if he does not apply for such a vesting order within the time to be stated in the notice, he will be excluded from all interest in and security upon the property; and the Court may for the purposes aforesaid adjourn the original application. If at the expiration of the time so stated in the notice such mortgagee, chargeant or under-lessee fails himself to apply for a vesting order, the Court may make an order vesting the property in the original applicant and excluding such mortgagee, chargeant or under-lessee from all interest in or security upon the property.

XII *List of contributories in a winding-up by the Court*

86.—Unless the Court shall dispense with a settlement of a list of contributories, the Official Liquidator shall at such time as the Court shall direct make out and leave at the Examiner's Office a list of the contributories of the company and such list shall be verified by the affidavit of the Official Liquidator in the Form No. 25 and shall, so far as is practicable, state the address of and the number of shares or extent of interest to be attributed to each contributory and the amount called up, and the amount paid up in respect of such shares or interest and distinguish the several classes or contributories. The Official Liquidator shall, in relation to representative contributories or contributories liable for the debts of others, as far as practicable, observe the requirements of section 235(3).

87.—When the list of contributories has been left at the Examiner's Office, the Official Liquidator shall obtain an appointment from the Examiner to settle the same, and shall give notice in writing of such appointment in the Form No. 27 to every person included in such list, stating in what character, and for what number of shares, or extent of interest, such person is included in the list and that any application for the removal of the name of such person from the list or for a variation of the list should be made to the Examiner at the time appointed for the settlement of such list.

88.—The result of the settlement of the list of contributories shall be stated in a certificate by the Examiner. Certificates may be made from time to time for the purpose of stating the result of such statement down to any particular time, or is to any particular person, or stating any variation of the list.

89.—The Official Liquidator may from time to time vary or add to the list of contributories, but any such variation or addition shall be settled in manner aforesaid.

XIII *Collection and distribution of company's assets by Official Liquidator*

90.—The duties imposed on the Court by section 235(1) in a winding-up by the Court with regard to the collection of the assets of the Company and the application of the assets in discharge of the company's liabilities shall be discharged by the Official Liquidator. For the purpose of the discharge by the Official Liquidator of the duties imposed by section 235(1), the Official Liquidator shall for the purpose of acquiring or retaining possession of the property of the company be in the same position as if he were a receiver of the property appointed by the Court, and the Court may, on his application, enforce such acquisition or retention accordingly.

Power of
Liquidator to
require
delivery of
property

91.—Any contributory for the time being on the list of contributories, any trustee, receiver, banker or agent or officer of a company which is being wound up under an order of the Court shall, on notice from the Official Liquidator and within such time as he shall by notice in writing require, pay, delivery, convey, surrender or transfer to or into the hands of the Official Liquidator any money, property, books or papers which happen to be in his hands for the time being and to which the company is *prima facie* entitled.

XIV *Calls*

Calls by
Liquidator

92.—Every application of the Court to make any call on the contributories or any of them for any purpose authorised by the Act shall be made on motion on notice in the Form No. 28 stating the proposed amount of such call. Such motion which shall be grounded on an affidavit of the Official Liquidator in the Form No. 29 shall be served six clear days at the least before the hearing of the application on every contributory proposed to be included in such call, or if the Court shall so direct, notice of such intended call may be given by advertisement in the Form No. 30.

93.—When an order for a call has been made, a copy thereof shall be forthwith served upon each of the contributories included in such call together with a notice in the Form No. 31 from the Official Liquidator specifying the amounts or balance due from such contributory (having regard to the provisions of the Act) in respect of such call but such order need not be advertised unless for any special reason the Court shall so direct.

94.—At the time of making an order for a call the further proceedings relating thereto shall be adjourned to a time subsequent to the day appointed for the payment thereof, and afterwards from time to time, so long as may be necessary. At the time appointed by any such adjournment or upon a motion to enforce payment of a call duly served and upon proof of the service of the order and notice of the amount due and non-payment, an order may be made that such of the contributories who have made default or that such of them against whom it shall be thought proper to make such an order, do pay the sum which by such former order and notice they were respectively required to pay, or any less sum which may appear to be due from them respectively.

XV *Ascertainment of company's liabilities*

95.—For the purpose of ascertaining the debts and claims due from the company and of requiring the creditors to come in and prove their debts or claims, an advertisement in the Form No. 35 shall be published at such time as the Court shall direct, and such advertisement shall fix a time for the creditors to send their names and addresses and the particulars of their debts and claims, and the names and registered places of business of their solicitors (if any) to the Official Liquidator and appoint a day for adjudicating thereon.

96.—The creditors need not attend upon the adjudication nor prove their debts or claims unless they are required to do so by notice from the Official Liquidator but upon such notice being given they shall come in and prove their debts or claims within a time to be therein specified.

97.—The Official Liquidator shall investigate the debts and claims sent in to him, and ascertain in so far as he is able which of such debts or claims are legally due from the company, and he shall make out and leave at the Examiner's Office a list of all the debts and claims sent in to him, distinguishing which of the debts and claims, or parts of the debts and claims so claimed are in his opinion legally due and proper to be allowed without further evidence, and which of them in his opinion ought to be proved by the creditor, and he shall make and file prior to the time appointed for adjudication, an affidavit in the Form No. 36 setting out which of the debts and claims in his opinion are legally due and proper to be allowed without further evidence and stating his belief that such debts and claims are legally due and proper to be allowed.

98.—At the time appointed for adjudicating upon the debts and claims, or at any adjournment thereof, the Examiner may either allow the debts and claims upon the affidavit of the Official Liquidator or may require the same, or any of them, to be proved by the claimants, and adjourn the adjudication thereon to a time to be then fixed, and the Official Liquidator shall give notice in the Form No. 38 to the creditors whose debts and claims have been so allowed of such allowance. The Official Liquidator shall give notice in the Form No. 39 to the creditors whose debts or claims have not been allowed upon his affidavit, that they are required to come in and prove the same on or before a day to be therein named, being not less than seven days after such notice, and to attend at a time to be therein named being the time appointed by the advertisement or by adjournment (as the case may be) for adjudicating upon such debts or claims. If the creditor shall fail to comply with the requirements of this notice, his claim or the part thereof required to be proved shall be disallowed.

99.—The value of such debts and claims as are made admissible to proof by section 283 shall, as far as possible, be estimated according to the value thereof at the date of the order to wind-up the company.

100.—Such creditors as attend and prove their debts or claims pursuant to notice from the Official Liquidator shall be allowed their costs of proof in the same manner as in the case of debts proved in a cause.

101.—The result of an adjudication upon debts and claims shall be stated in a certificate to be made by the Examiner and certificates as to any of such debts and claims may be made from time to time. All such certificates shall show the debts or claims allowed and whether allowed as against any particular assets or in any other qualified or special manner.

XVI *Proof of debts*

102.—Save where the Official Liquidator or the Examiner shall require the same to be proved by affidavit, a debt may be proved in any winding-up by delivering or sending through the post particulars of the claim to the Official Liquidator. — Mode or proof

103.—An affidavit proving a debt may be in the Form No. 40 and may be made by the creditor or by some person authorised by him. If made by a person so authorised, it shall state his authority and means of knowledge. The affidavit shall contain or refer to a statement of account showing the particulars of the debt, and shall specify the vouchers (if any) by which the same can be substantiated and shall state whether the creditor is, or is not, a secured creditor. The creditor shall produce such vouchers if required to do so.

104.—A creditor shall bear the cost of proving his debt or claim unless he has been required to attend and prove the same by the Official Liquidator.

Discount

105—A creditor proving his debt shall deduct therefrom (*a*) any discount in excess of two and a half per cent. which he may have agreed for payment in cash on the net amount of his claim, and (*b*) all trade discounts.

Periodical payments

106.—When any rent or other payment falls due at stated times and the order or resolution to wind up is made at any time other than at one of those times, the persons entitled to the rent or repayment may prove for a proportionate part thereof up to the date of the winding-up order or resolution as if the rent or payment accrued due from day to day. Provided that where the Official Liquidator remains in occupation of premises demised to a company which is being wound up, nothing herein contained shall prejudice or affect the right of the landlord of such premises to claim payment of rent during the period of the company's or the Official Liquidator's occupation.

107.—On any debt or sum certain, payable at certain time or otherwise, whereon interest is not reserved or agreed for, and which is overdue at the date of the commencement of the winding-up, the creditor may prove for interest at a rate not exceeding six per cent. per annum to that date from the time when the debt or sum was payable, if the debt or sum is payable by virtue of a written instrument at a certain time, and if payable otherwise, then from the time when a demand in writing has been made, giving notice that interest will be claimed from the date of the demand until the time of payment.

Proof for debt at a future time

108.—A creditor may prove for a debt not payable at the date of the winding-up order or resolution, as if it were payable presently, and may receive dividends equally with the other creditors, deducting only thereout a rebate of interest at the rate of six per cent. per annum computed from the declaration of a dividend to the time when the debt would have become payable according to the terms on which it was contracted.

Proof under section 285

109.—Unless the Liquidator shall in any special case otherwise direct, formal proof of the debts mentioned in section 285(2)(*e*) shall not be required.

Workmen's wages

110.—In any case in which it appears that there are numerous claims for wages by workmen and others employed by the company, it shall be sufficient if one proof for all such claims is made either by a foreman or by a trades union official or by some other person on behalf of all such creditors. Such proof, which shall be in the Form No. 41, shall have annexed thereto as forming part thereof, a schedule setting forth the names of the workmen and others and the amounts severally due to them. Any proof made in compliance with this rule shall have the same effect as if separate proofs had been made by each of the said workmen and others.

Production of bills of exchange and promissory notes

111.—Where a creditor seeks to prove in respect of a bill of exchange, promissory note or other negotiable instrument or security on which the company is liable, such bill of exchange, note, instrument or security shall, subject to any special order of the Court made to the contrary, be produced to the Official Liquidator and be marked by him before the proof can be admitted either for voting or for any other purpose.

XVII *Dividends in a winding-up by the Court*

112.—The Official Liquidator shall not declare a dividend without the sanction of the Court. Upon the application of the Offical Liquidator for such sanction, the Court, if it grants the same, shall at the same time give such directions as may be thought expedient in regard to the amount of such dividend, and the time shall be declared. Dividends to creditors

113.—Upon the declaration of an interim or final dividend by the Official Liquidator he shall send notice thereof to each creditor whose proof has been admitted.

114.—The Court may upon the application of the Official Liquidator, or without any such application, postpone the declaration of a dividend already sanctioned to a later date.

115.—An application under rules 112 or 114 may be made to the Court *ex parte*.

116.—If a person to whom dividends are payable desires that they shall be paid to some other person, he may lodge with the Official Liquidator a document in the Form No. 42, which shall be a sufficient authority for payment of the dividend to the person therein named.

XVIII *Payment in of moneys and deposit of securities*

117.—If the Official Liquidator does not pay the moneys received by him into the Bank to the account of the Official Liquidator of the company in accordance with the order of the Court in that behalf, such Official Liquidator shall, unless the Court otherwise directs, be charged interest in his account at the rate of one half per cent. on the amount retained in his hands for every seven days during which the same shall have been so retained contrary to such order, and the Court may, for any such retention, disallow the salary or remuneration of the Official Liquidator or any part thereof.

118.—All bills, notes and other securities payable to the company or to the Official Liquidator shall as soon as they come to the hands of the Official Liquidator be deposited by him in the Bank for the purpose of being presented by the Bank for acceptance and payment or for payment only as the case may be.

119.—At the time of the service of any order for the payment into the Bank the Official Liquidator shall give to each of the parties served a notice in the Form No. 32 for the purpose of informing him how the payment is to be made; and, before the time fixed for such payment, the Official Liquidator shall furnish to the cashier of the Bank a certificate in the Form No. 33 to be signed by such cashier and delivered to the party paying in the money therein mentioned.

120.—For the purpose of enforcing any order for payment of money into the Bank, an affidavit of the Official Liquidator in the Form No. 34 shall be sufficient evidence of the non-payment thereof.

121.—All bills, notes and other securities delivered into the Bank shall be delivered out upon a request signed by the Official Liquidator and countersigned by the Examiner. Moneys placed to the account of the Official Liquidator shall be paid out on cheques or orders by the Official Liquidator and countersigned by the Examiner.

122.—All or any part of the money for the time being standing to the credit of the Official Liquidator in the Bank and not immediately required for the purpose of the winding-up may be invested in the joint names of the Examiner and the Official Liquidator. All such investments shall be made by the Bank upon a request in the Form No. 43 signed by the Official Liquidator and countersigned by the Examiner which request shall be a sufficient authority for debiting the account with the purchase money.

123.—All dividends and interest to accrue due upon any such investments shall from time to time be received by the Bank, under a power of attorney to be executed by the Examiner and the Official Liquidator, and be placed to the credit of the account of the Official Liquidator.

XIX *Sales of property*

124.—Any real or personal property belonging to the company may be sold with the approval of the Court in the manner provided by Order 51 or, if the Court shall so direct, by the Official Liquidator. The conditions or contract of sale shall be settled and approved by the Court unless the Court shall otherwise direct, and the Court may, on any sale by public auction, fix a reserve. Unless the court otherwise directs, all conditions and contracts of sale shall provide for the payment of any deposit into a joint deposit account bearing interest in the Bank in the names of the Official Liquidator and the Examiner and that the purchase money shall be paid by the purchaser into the Bank to the account of the Official Liquidator.

XX *Examination of witnesses*

125.—If a witness is examined in private, the transcript or notes of the examination shall not be filed or be open to the inspection of any person other than the Liquidator, unless and until the Court shall otherwise direct. The Court may from time to time give directions in regard to the custody and inspection of the transcripts and notes of examinations and the furnishing of copies or extracts therefrom.

XXI *Sanction of the Court*

126.—Every application by an Official Liquidator for the sanction of the Court to the taking or doing of any proceeding, act, matter, or thing which by the Act he is empowered to take or do with the sanction of the Court, shall be made to the court by motion on notice (where appropriate), or *ex parte* in pursuance of a motion paper setting forth shortly the nature of the application.

127.—Where the Court sanctions the drawing, accepting, making or endorsing of any bill of exchange or promissory note by an Official Liquidator, a memorandum to that effect shall be made and signed by the Examiner on such bill of exchange or promissory note.

XXII *Costs and expenses payable out of the assets of the company*

128.—(1) The assets of a company in a winding-up by the Court remaining after payment of the fees and expenses properly incurred in preserving, realising or getting in the assets, including where the company has previously commenced to be wound up voluntarily such remuneration, costs and expenses as the Court may allow to a Liquidator appointed in such voluntary winding-up, shall, subject to any order of the Court, be liable to the following payments which shall be made in the following order of priority, namely:

> *First*—The costs of the petition, including the costs of any person appearing on the petition whose costs are allowed by the Court.
>
> *Next*—The costs and expenses of any person who makes or concurs in making the company's statement of affairs.
>
> *Next*—The necessary disbursements of the Official Liquidator, other than expenses properly incurred in preserving, realising or getting in the assets hereinbefore provided for.
>
> *Next*—The costs payable to the solicitor for the Official Liquidator.
>
> *Next*—The remuneration of the Official Liquidator.
>
> *Next*—The out-of-pocket expenses necessarily incurred by the committee of inspection (if any).

(2) No payments in respect of bills of costs, charges or expenses of solicitors, accountants, auctioneers, brokers or other persons, other than payment for costs, charges or expenses fixed or allowed by the Court shall be allowed out of the assets of the company unless they have been duly fixed and allowed by the Examiner or the Taxing Master as the case may be.

XXIII *Statements by Liquidator to the registrar of companies*

129.—The winding-up of a company shall for the purposes of section 306 be deemed to be concluded: *Conclusion of winding-up*

> (*a*) in the case of a company wound up by order of the Court, on the date on which the order dissolving the company has been reported by the Official Liquidator to the registrar of companies;
>
> (*b*) in the case of a company wound up voluntarily, on the date of the dissolution of the company, unless on such date any funds or assets of the compay remain unclaimed or undistributed in the hands or under the control of the Liquidator or any person who has acted as Liquidator, in which case the winding-up shall not be deemed to be concluded until such funds or assets have either been distributed or paid into The Companies Liquidation Account in the Bank.

130.—The statements in relation to the proceedings in and the position of the liquidation of a company the winding-up of which is not concluded within two years after its commencement shall be sent to the registrar of companies as follows: *Times for sending Liquidator's statements, and regulations applicable thereto*

> (*a*) the first statement, commencing at the date when the Liquidator was first appointed and brought down to the end of two years from the commencement of the winding-up, shall be sent within thirty days from the expiration of such two years or within such extended period as the Court may allow, and subsequent statements shall be sent, in case of a winding-up by the Court, at intervals of one years or such other intervals as the Court may direct, and in case of a voluntary winding-up, at intervals of half a year, each statement being brought down to the end of the period for which it is sent. In cases in which the assets of the company have been fully realised and distributed before the expiration of any such period, a final statement shall be sent forthwith;
>
> (*b*) the statement shall be in the Form No. 44, shall be sent in duplicate, and shall be verified by an affidavit in the Form No. 45, which shall be sent with the statement to the registrar of companies.

XXIV *Payment of unclaimed dividends and unapplied or undistributable balances into The Companies Liquidation Account*

131.—(1) All moneys in hand or under the control of a Liquidator representing unclaimed dividends admissible to proof and unapplied or undistributable balances, which under section 307(1) the Liquidator is to pay into The Companies Liquidation Account, shall be ascertained on the date which is two months after the date of the meeting referred to in section 263, or in section 273 (as the case may be), and shall be paid into The Companies Liquidation Account within fourteen days from the said date.

(2) When a Liquidator desires to pay moneys into The Companies Liquidation Account, he shall make and file an affidavit entitled in the manner of the company in liquidation and in the matter of section 307, and setting forth:

(*a*) the name of the company of which he is Liquidator,

(*b*) his name and address,

(*c*) the dates on which the resolution for winding-up was passed and on which he was appointed Liquidator,

(*d*) the amount of the moneys to be lodged to the said account,

(*e*) the amount of the said moneys to be lodged which represents unclaimed dividends admissible to proof,

(*f*) the amount of the said moneys to be lodged which represents unapplied or undistributable balances,

(*g*) the names and last known address of the persons to whom the unclaimed dividends admissible to proof are payable and the amount payable to each such person,

(*h*) the names and last known addresses of the persons to whom the unapplied or undistributable balances are payable and the amount payable to each such person,

(*i*) the names and last known addresses of any persons (other than those mentioned in (*g*) and (*h*) hereof) who have claimed any interest in such unapplied or undistributable balances and the nature of such claim,

(*j*) his submission to answer all such inquiries relating to the moneys so to be lodged as the Court may make or direct.

Such affidavit shall have annexed thereto a schedule as prescribed by Order 77, rule 100. When the Liquidator has filed such an affidavit, he shall request the Accountant to issue a direction to the Bank to receive such moneys for the credit of The Companies Liquidation Account. Every application for such request shall be in the Form No. 7 in Appendix P.

(3) Moneys invested or deposited at interest by a Liquidator shall be deemed to be moneys under his control and when such moneys form part of the balance payable into The Companies Liquidation Account pursuant to sub-rule (1) the Liquidator shall realise the investment or withdraw the deposit and shall pay the proceeds into The Companies Liquidation Account.

(4) Every person who has acted as Liquidator, whether the liquidation has been concluded or not, shall furnish to the Minister for Industry and Commerce on request particulars in hand or under his control representing unclaimed dividends admissible to proof or unapplied or undistributable balances and such other particulars as the Minister may require for the purposes of ascertaining or getting in any money payable into The Companies Liquidation Account, and the Minister may require such particulars to be verified by affidavit.

(5) The Minister may at any time request any such person as is mentioned in sub-rule (4) to submit to him an account verified by affidavit of the sums received and paid by him as Liquidator of the company and may direct an audit of the account.

(6) If any person who has been requested to furnish particulars of any moneys in hand or under his control representing unclaimed dividends admissible to proof or unapplied or undistributable balances under sub-rule (4) or to submit an account under sub-rule (5) shall fail to furnish such particulars or to submit such account within twenty-one days after being requested to do so, the Minister may apply to the Court by special summons and the Court shall make such order as shall be necessary for the purpose of enforcing sub-rules (4) and (5) hereof.

(7) An application under section 307(3) shall be made by special summons in which the Liquidator who made the lodgment out of which payment is sought and the Minister for Industry and Commerce shall be named as defendants. If such Liquidator shall be dead or cannot be traced at the date of such special summons the Court may dispense with the necessity of naming the Liquidator as a defendant.

(8) An application by a Liquidator for payment out of The Companies Liquidation Account of any costs, expenses and disbursements of the voluntary winding-up, shall be made by special summons in which the Minister for Industry and Commerce shall be named as defendant.

(9) An application under section 307(4) for payment out of any moneys into the Exchequer shall be made by special summons in which the Minister for Finance shall be named as defendant.

XXV *File of proceedings*

132.—All orders, exhibits, admissions, memoranda, attested copies of affidavits, examinations, certificates and all other documents relating to the winding-up of the company shall be filed by the Official Liquidator, as far as may be, on one continuous file, and such file shall be kept by him, or otherwise as the Court may from time to time direct. Every contributory of the company and every creditor whose debt or claim has been allowed, shall (save as otherwise provided in this Order) be entitled at all reasonable times to inspect such file free of charge, and at his own expense to take copies or extracts from any of the documents included therein, or to be furnished with such copies or extracts at a rate not exceeding five pence per folio of seventy-two words, and such file shall be produced in Court, and otherwise, as on occasion may be required.

XXVI *Applications to stay or restrain proceedings*

133.—(1) An application under section 217 to stay proceedings in an action then pending against the company in the High Court or on appeal in the Supreme Court shall be made by motion in that action on notice to the plaintiff.

(2) An application under section 217 to restrain further proceedings in any other action or proceeding than those mentioned in sub-rule (1) shall be made by motion in the winding-up proceeding on notice to the plaintiff.

134.—An application to stay proceedings in an action or proceeding against a company in voluntary liquidation shall, if such action be pending in the High Court or on appeal in the Supreme Court, be made by motion in that action on notice to the plaintiff, and shall otherwise be made by special summons.

XXVII *Applications under sections 201, 245, 247 or 279*

135.—(1) An application by an Official Liquidator for an order under section 201 may be made by motion *ex parte*. On such application the Court may give such directions as it thinks proper in regard to the manner in which the meeting or meetings shall be summoned and in relation to the conduct thereof.

(2) When an order for the winding-up of a company has been made, applications under section 245 or 247 may be made by motion *ex parte*.

(3) When a petition for the winding-up of a company has been presented an application under section 247 may be made by motion *ex parte*.

(4) An appeal by a creditor or contributory under section 279(2) shall be brought by special summons.

XXVIII *Applications under sections 234, 236, 237, 243, 287(3), 299, 347 or 348*

136.—In a winding-up by the Court, an application under sections 234, 236, 237, 243, 287(3), 299, 347 or 348 may be made by motion on notice.

XXIX *Termination of winding-up by the Court*

137.—When the Official Liquidator has passed his final account, he shall apply to the Court for directions as to how the balance due thereon shall be applied; and when the application of such balance as so directed has been vouched to the Examiner, a certificate in the Form No. 46 shall be made up by the Examiner that the disposal of such balance in manner so directed has been vouched and that the affairs of the company have been completely wound up. In case the company has not already been dissolved, the Official Liquidator shall, immediately after such certificate has become binding, apply to the Court for an order that the company be dissolved from the date of such order.

XXX *Applications in voluntary winding-up*

138.—Every application or appeal to the Court in a voluntary winding-up may be made by special summons, save as otherwise provided in this Order.

XXXVI *Forms in voluntary winding-up*

139.—The declaration of solvency referred to in section 256 shall be in the Form No. 47.

140.—The statement of assets and liabilities referred to in section 261 shall be in the Form No. 48.

141.—The Liquidator's final account referred to in sections 263 and 273 shall be in the Form No. 49.

142.—The return of the final meeting in a members' voluntary winding-up shall be in the Form No. 50.

143.—The return of the final meetings in a creditors' voluntary winding-up shall be in the Form No. 51.

Order 75A
Proceedings under the Companies (Amendment) Act 1990

(S.I. Number 27 of 1990)

1.—In this Order, unless the context or subject matter otherwise requires—

(1) "The Act" means the Companies (Amendment) Act 1990 (No. 27 of 1990).

(2) Words and expressions contained in this Order shall have the same meaning as in the Act and where necessary the same meaning as in the Companies Acts 1963-1990.

(3) "The 1986 Rules" means the Rules of the Superior Courts SI No. 15 of 1986.

(4) "The Examiner" shall include the Interim Examiner.

2.—All applications and proceedings for or in relation to an appointment of an Examiner under the Act or concerning such examination shall be be assigned to such Judge as the President of the High Court shall from time to time assign to hear such applications and proceedings, but if such Judge or Judges shall be unable to dispose of such applications or proceedings, any other Judge or Judges of the High Court may dispose of any such application.

3.—An application under section 2 of the Act will be grounded on the petition and the affidavit of the party making such application and shall be heard and determined on affidavit unless the Court otherwise orders.

4.—(1) A petition for the appointment of an Examiner under the Act shall be presented at and shall be retained in the Central Office. A sealed copy thereof shall be taken out by the petitioner or by his solicitor and shall be used as if it were an original.

(2) The petition shall be brought to the office of one of the registrars who shall appoint the time and place at which the petition is to be heard.

(3) Every petition for the appointment of an Examiner shall be verified by affidavit. Such affidavit shall be made by the petitioner or by one of the petitioners if more than one, or in case the petition is presented by a corporation or company, by one of the directors, secretary or other officer thereof and shall be sworn before the presentation of the petition and filed with such petition and such affidavit shall be sufficient *prima facie* evidence of the statements in the petition. The form of the petition shall comply with section 3(3) of the Act and shall also, so far as applicable, comply with Form No. 2 in Appendix M of the 1986 rules.

(4) On the same day as the petition shall have been presented, the petitioner shall apply *ex parte* to the High Court for directions as to proceedings to be taken in relation thereto.

5.—(1) On the hearing of the *ex parte* application referred to in Rule 4(4) above or on any adjourned hearing or hearings thereof or on any subsequent application, the Court may make such order or orders as it thinks fit and may give such directions as it thinks fit and in particular may give directions as to the parties on whom the petition should be served, the mode of service, the time for such service, the date for the hearing of the petition (if different to that appointed by the Registrar) and whether the said petition should be advertised and if so, how the same should be advertised.

(2) On the hearing of such *ex parte* application, the Court may, if it thinks fit, treat the application as the hearing of the petition and may make such interim order or any other order it thinks fit including adjourning the hearing and may appoint any proposed Examiner on an interim basis until such adjourned hearing and an Examiner so appointed over any company or any related company shall be referred to as the Interim Examiner and shall have the same powers and duties in relation to such company until the date of the adjourned hearing as if he were an Examiner appointed other than on an interim basis.

(3) The Court may adjourn the hearing of the petition or any adjourned hearing until any party or parties which the Court considers should be notified have been notified of the presentation of the petition, whether by advertisement or otherwise, and may adjourn any hearing of the petition for any other reason that appears to the Court to be just and equitable.

(4) On the hearing of a petition or on the adjournment or the further hearing of such petition, the Court may, having heard the petitioner and any interested party or any person who has been notified of the petition and who appears thereto, as the case may be, appoint an Examiner, and may make such further or other order as it thinks fit.

6.—(1) An application for the appointment of an Examiner to be appointed an Examiner of a related company pursuant to section 4 of the Act if brought by the petitioner or by the Examiner shall be made *ex parte* to the Court provided that on the hearing of any such application, the Court may make such order or orders or give such directions as it thinks fit including directions as to whether, and if so, upon which parties notice of the application should be served, the mode of such service and time allowed for such service and whether the application should be advertised and if so, how the same should be advertised and may adjourn the hearing of such application to a date to be specified.

(2) The Court may, if it thinks fit, while adjourning such application, make such interim order as it sees fit including the appointment of the Examiner as the Examiner of the related company on an intrerim basis and may also confer on such Examiner in relation to such company all or any of the powers and duties conferred on him in relation to the first mentioned company on an interim basis until the adjourned hearing.

(3) An application for the appointment of an Examiner to be the Examiner of a related company shall, if brought by any person other than the petitioner or the Examiner of the first mentioned company, be brought by way of notice of motion served upon the Examiner and petitioner.

7.—In any case where an Interim Examiner has been appointed to any company or an Examiner has been appointed Interim Examiner of a related company of that company, and where upon the final hearing of the application or of the petition, as the case may be, no Examiner is appointed to that company or to that related company, as the case may be, or where a person other than the Interim Examiner is appointed as Examiner to the company or to the related company, such Interim Examiner shall prepare a written report for the Court in relation to the company or to the related company or both in such time as the Court shall direct. Such report or reports shall as far as possible in the circumstances deal with the matters specified in section 16(a) to (1) of the Act. Such Examiner shall keep and maintain a true record of all liabilities certified by him under section 10 of the Act and shall in his written report give a full account of all liabilities so certified to the Court and shall deal with such further or other matters as may be directed by the Court.

8.—(1) Any application by an Examiner of a company pursuant to section 5(3) of the Act in relation to any existing proceedings involving that company shall be brougth by motion on notice to all the parties to such proceedings including the company in relation to which the Examiner was appointed.

(2) Any application by any person under section 5(3) of the Act seeking the leave of the Court to commence proceedings in relation to the company shall be brought by way of motion on notice to the Examiner and to the company.

9.—(1) Any application by any Examiner pursuant to section 7(6) of the Act may be made *ex parte* to the Court and on hearing of any such application the Court may deal with the application and may make such order or orders in relation thereto as it thinks fit or may adjourn the application and give such directors as to proceedings to be taken upon it as it thinks fit.

(2) Any application, by any member, contributory, creditor or director of a company pursuant to section 7(6) of the Act shall be by way of motion on notice to the Examiner and to the company and the Court may make such order upon such application as if it had been brought by the Examiner.

(3) An application by the company or by an interested party pursuant to section 13(7) of the Act shall be made by motion on notice to the Examiner and to any other interested party or the company, as the case may be, and the Court may deal with any such application as if it were an application under section 7(6) of the Act and make such order as appears just and proper in the circumstances.

10.—Once an examiner has certified any refusal or refusals specified in section 8(5) of the Act, he shall thereupon apply *ex parte* to the Court for leave to produce the said Certificate in relation to such refusal and shall verify the facts in the Certificate by affidavit and thereupon the Court upon notice to the party concerned, may make such enquiries and give such directions in relation to the said refusals as it thinks fit and shall hear such evidence as may be produced in relation thereto and may make such order as seems just and proper in the circumstances.

11.—Any application to the Court by the Examiner pursuant to section 9 of the Act for the further vesting in him of all or any of the powers or functions vested in or exercisable by the directors of the company shall be made by notice of motion served upon the said directors, grounded on the affidavit of the Examiner specifying which, if not all, of the powers he seeks to have vested in him by Order of the Court and the Court may give such directions in relation to the hearing of the said application as it thinks fit.

12.—An application by the Examiner, pursuant to section 11 of the Act for the disposal of any property which is the subject of any security or of any goods which are in the possession of the company under a hire purchase agreement, shall be made by notice of motion grounded upon affidavit of the Examiner and served upon the holder of such security or the hire purchase company, as the case may be, or upon any other person who appears to have an interest in the property and the Court may upon the hearing of the application make such order under section 11 as appears just and proper and may give such directions concerning the proceeds of all such disposals as shall have been authorised by the Court.

13.—An Examiner wishing to resign pursuant to section 13 of the Act, shall do so by an application *ex parte* to the Court. On the hearing of the application the Court may, if it thinks fit, direct that notice of the application be served on the petitioner, the company, the directors of the company or any other interested party as may be appropriate. The application of the Examiner shall be grounded upon an affidavit sworn by him, specifying the reasons of the said proposed resignation, and the date of the said proposed resignation. Upon the application, the Court may make such order as appears just and proper in the circumstances.

(2) An application to the Court pursuant to section 13 of the Act to remove an Examiner shall be made by motion on notice to the Examiner, to the petitioner, to the company and its directors and to any other party as the Court may direct. Such application shall be grounded upon an affidavit of the moving party specifying the cause alleged to exist justifying the removal of the Examiner by the Court. On the hearing of the application, the Court may make such order as appears just in the circumstances and, if satisfied that cause has been shown for the removal of the Examiner by the Court shall order that he be removed forthwith or upon such date as the Court shall specify. The Court may either before or after ruling upon the application for the removal of the Examiner make such order for the production of any document of documents, or the preparation of such report or reports as it thinks fit.

(3) An application pursuant to section 13(2) of the Act to fill a vacancy in the office of an Examiner shall be made *ex parte* to the Court provided that the Court may, if it thinks fit, adjourn the application and make such order or give such directions as appear proper in the circumstances, including directions for service of notice of the making of an application upon such party as it thinks proper.

14.—When an Examiner has prepared a report of his examination of the company within the time prescribed or within such time as shall have been fixed by the Court, he shall effect delivery of his report under section 15 of the Act, by making an *ex parte* application to the Court for leave to deliver it. The report shall contain a part in which each of the matters specified in section 16 shall be dealt with in the order set out in the section. The Examiner shall verify by affidavit:

    (*a*) Whether the petitioner has complied with section 12(1) of the Act.

    (b) Whether he has complied with section 12(2) and (3) of the Act.

    (*c*) Whether and what portions of the report (if any) should be omitted from delivery under section 15.

He shall also draw to the attention of the Court any particular aspects of the report which are or may be relevant to the exercise by the Court of any other of its functions under the Act.

15.—On application for liberty to deliver a report under section 15 of the Act, and where it appears to the Court by reason of all or any of the matters specified in section 17(1) of the Act that a hearing is required to consider matters arising out of the report, the Court shall give such directions for the holding of a hearing to consider matters arising therefrom and shall make an order fixing the date of the hearing and an order directing the service of a notice of motion for the date of the hearing upon any party entitled to appear and be heard at such hearing, and upon such other party as the Court may direct and the Court may give directions as to the mode of service of such motion on any party or parties and may give directions as to whether, and if so, how the hearing for the consideration of the report should be advertised, and the Court may make such other order or orders as it deems fit.

16.—When an examiner has been given leave to deliver his report under section 15 and where the Examiner is formulating proposals pursuant to section 18 of the Act for a compromise or scheme of arrangement, any application for an extension of time for the delivery by the Examiner of his report thereon, shall be made *ex parte* to the Court within the time for the delivery of the report or as extended by the Court. Any party affected by the extension, may on notice of motion to the Examiner apply to the Court to set the said order aside upon grounds to be specified and verified in an affidavit and on such application, the Court may make such orders it thinks fit.

17.—When an Examiner has prepared a report pursuant to section 18 of the Act within the time prescribed or within such time as shall have been fixed by the Court, he shall effect delivery of his report by making an *ex parte* application to the Court to deliver it.

(2)   (*a*) The report shall contain a full account of each meeting convened by the Examiner and of the proposals put before each such meeting and shall contain as an appendix to the said report a copy of the said proposals which shall deal with each of the matters specified in section 22 of the Act in the order set out in that section.

(*b*) The Examiner shall in his application specify whether and if so, what portions of the report should be omitted from delivery under section 18(5) of the Act and he shall draw to the attention of the Court any particular aspects of the report which are or may be relevant to the exercise by the Court of any other of its functions under the Act.

(3) When the Examiner has been given leave to deliver his report pursuant to subrule 1 and where the Examiner has formulated proposals pursuant to section 18 of the Act for a compromise or scheme of arrangement and has reported to the Court thereon in the period prescribed or within such further period as may have been specified by the Court, the Eaxminer may apply to the Court *ex parte* for an extension of the period for protection pursuant to section 18(4) of the Act for such further period as may be necessary for the Court to enable it to make a decision in relation to the report of the Examiner on the proposals. Upon the making of the application, the Court may direct that the Examiner serve notice of the application on such party or parties as the Court thinks fit. The Court may adjourn the application to enable the service to take place, but may extend the period concerned until the adjourned date of the hearing or such other date as to the Court may seem fit, and the Court may further extend the period concerned in the event of any further adjournments of the said hearing.

18.—All meetings of members or classes of members or creditors or classes of creditors convened for the purposes of section 18 or section 23 of the Act shall be governed by the following rules:

(1) The Examiner shall summon all meetings of creditors and members by sending by post not less than 3 days before the day appointed for the meeting to every person appearing in the company's books to be a creditor of the company or a member of the company, notice of the meeting of creditors or members as the case may be.

(2) The notice to each creditor or member shall be sent to the address given in the report of the Examiner of the company, if any or to such other address as may be known to the Examiner.

(3) An affidavit by the Examiner or solicitor or by some other officer or clerk of the company or its solicitors that the notice of any meeting has been duly posted shall be suffiicent evidence of such notice having been duly sent to the person to whom the same was addressed. The Examiner may fix a meeting or meetings to be held at such place as in his opinion is most convenient for the majority of creditors or members, or both and different times and/or places may be named for the meetings of creditors and members.

(4) The Examiner shall preside at and be chairman of any meeting which he has convened and shall conduct the business of the meeting in an orderly manner so as to ensure the proper discussion of all proposals placed by him before the said meeting.

(5) Where a meeting of creditors or members is summoned by notice, the proceedings and resolutions of the meeting shall unless the Court otherwise orders be valid, notwithstanding that some creditors or members may not have received the notice sent to them.

(6) The Examiner may with the consent of the meeting adjourn from time to time and from place to place but the adjourned meeting shall be held at the same place as the original meeting unless in the resolution for adjournment another place is specified or unless the Court otherwise orders.

(7)   (*a*) A meeting may not act for any purpose except the adjournment of the meeting unless there are present or represented thereat in the case of a creditors meeting, at least 3 creditors ruled by the Examiner to be entitled to vote or in the case of a meeting of members, at least 2 members.

(*b*) If within 15 minutes from the time appointed by the meeting, a quorum of creditors or members as the case may be is not present or represented, the meeting shall be adjourned for the same day in the following week at the same time and place or to such other day or time or place as the Examiner may appoint but so that the day appointed shall be not less than 3, nor more than 21 days from the date from which the meeting was adjourned.

(8)   (*a*) The Examiner shall cause minutes of the proceedings of the meeting to be drawn up and entered in a book kept for that purpose and the minutes shall be signed by him.

(*b*) The Examiner shall cause a list of creditors or members present at every meeting to be kept and every such list shall be signed by him.

(9) A creditor or member may appear either in person or by proxy. Where a person is authorised in the manner provided by section 139 of the Companies Act 1963 to represent a corporation at any meeting of creditors or members, such person shall produce to the Examiner a copy of the resolution so authorising him. Such copies shall be under the seal of the corporation or be certified to be a true copy by the secretary or director of the corporation.

(10) Every instrument of proxy shall be, as far as possible, in either the Form No. 21 or Form No. 22 of Appendix M of the 1986 Rules.

(11) A general and a special form of proxy shall be sent to each of the creditors or members with a notice summoning the meeting and neither the name nor the description of the Examiner or any other person shall be printed or inserted in the body of any instrument of proxy before it is sent.

(12) A creditor or a member may appoint any person a special proxy to vote at any specified meeting or adjournment thereof on all questions arising at the meeting or an adjournment thereof.

(13) A creditor or member may appoint the Examiner to act as his general or special proxy.

(14)   (*a*) Every instrument of proxy shall be lodged with the Examiner no later than 4.00 in the afternoon of the day before the meeting or adjourned meeting at which it is to be used and the same shall be kept by the Examiner.

(*b*) No person who is an infant shall be appointed a general or special proxy.

(*c*) Where a company is a creditor, any person who is duly authorised under the seal of such company to act, generally on behalf of the company at meetings of creditors and members, may fill in and sign the instrument of proxy on such company's behalf and appoint himself to be such company's proxy and the instrument of proxy so filled in and signed by such person shall be received and dealt with as a proxy of such company.

(15) The Examiner shall have power to allow or disallow the vote of a person claiming to be a creditor or member, if he thinks fit, but his decision may be subject to appeal to the Court. If he is in doubt whether a vote should be allowed or disallowed, he shall allow it and record the vote as such subject to the vote being declared invalid in the event of an objection being taken and sustained by the Court.

19.—An application by the company pursuant to section 20 of the Act to repudiate any contract or any application arising out of such repudiation shall be made by motion on notice to the Examiner and on notice to the other contracting party or parties and on notice to any person referred to in section 20(2) of the Act.

20.—When on the consideration of a report under section 17 or under section 24, the Court considers that an order for the winding-up of the company should be made, the Court may order that the application for the winding-up of the company or of any related company be made by the Examiner or by such other person as the court may direct and the court may order that the provisions of Order 74 of the 1986 Rules, either in whole or in part, shall apply to the winding-up as ordered by the Court.

21.—(1) An application to the Court pursuant to section 27 of the Act for the revocation of confirmation of proposals confirmed by the Court, shall be made *ex parte* for directions as to the proceedings to be taken and the application shall be grounded upon an affidavit which shall specify the fraud alleged and shall supply full particulars thereof and shall specify the names and addresses of all parties who have or may have acquired interests or property in good faith and for value and in reliance on the confirmation of the proposals by the Court.

(2) Upon such application, the Court may make such order and give such directions for the hearing of the said application including directions for service of notice of the application upon all such parties as appear proper in the circumstances and may give such further directions as to the application, including particularly, whether and if so, how the same should be advertised and if it seems fit, directing the filing of any pleadings in the matter.

22.—An application by the Examiner pursuant to section 29 of the Act for payment to him of remuneration and costs and reasonable expenses properly incurred by him shall be made by application *ex parte* to the Court and upon an affidavit of the Examiner in which he shall set forth a full account of the work carried out by him to the date of the application and a full account of the costs and expenses incurred by him and shall vouch same and of the basis for the proposed remuneration which he is seeking to be paid. The Court may, where it thinks fit, order that notice of the application be given to all such persons as the Court may direct, and may give directions as to the service of the said notice and fix a date for the hearing of the application of the Examiner. The affidavit of the Examiner shall also specify what use, if any, he has made of the services of the staff and/or of the facilities of the company to which he has been appointed and the extent of such use.

23.—An application to the Court pursuant to section 33 of the Act shall be made by motion on notice to the person or persons concerned and the provisions of Order 74 Rule 49 of the 1986 Rules shall apply to such application as if the references therein to sections of the Companies Act 1963 was a reference to section 33 of the Act.

24.—An application by the Examiner to the Court pursuant to section 35 of the Act in respect of any property of a company alleged to have been improperly transferred to the use, control or possession of any person shall be made by motion on notice to such person and the provisions of Order 74 Rule 49 of the 1986 Rules shall apply to such applications as if the references therein to sections of the Companies Act 1963 was a reference to section 35 of the Act.

Index